THE THEORY AND POLICIES OF MUTUAL BENEFIT AND WIN-WIN STRATEGY

Research on Sustainable Development of China's Open Economy

Series on Innovation and Operations Management for Chinese Enterprises

Print ISSN: 2591-7188
Online ISSN: 2591-7196

Editor: Xiaobo Wu *(School of Management, Zhejiang University, China)*

Published:

Vol. 4: *The Theory and Policies of Mutual Benefit and Win-Win Strategy: Research on Sustainable Development of China's Open Economy*
by Lixin Yu and Wanling Chen

Vol. 3: *The Internationalization of Technological Innovation for Chinese Enterprises*
by Jin Chen

Vol. 2: *Basic Research and Industrial Innovation in China*
by Xielin Liu, Yubing He and Peng Cheng

Vol. 1: *Independent Innovation in China: Theory and Cases*
by Huibo Zhong and Jiasu Lei

Funded by Chinese Academy of Social Sciences
and
Research Center for International Trade and Economics
in Guangdong University of Foreign Studies

Published by

World Scientific Publishing Co. Pte. Ltd.
5 Toh Tuck Link, Singapore 596224
USA office: 27 Warren Street, Suite 401-402, Hackensack, NJ 07601
UK office: 57 Shelton Street, Covent Garden, London WC2H 9HE

and

Zhejiang University Press
No. 148, Tianmushan Road
Xixi Campus of Zhejiang University
Hangzhou 310028, China

Library of Congress Cataloging-in-Publication Data
Names: Yu, Lixin, 1953– author. | Chen, Wanling, 1964– author.
Title: The theory and policies of mutual benefit and win-win strategy : research on
   sustainable development of China's open economy / Yu Lixin and Chen Wanling.
Description: New Jersey : World Scientific, [2018] | Series: Series on innovation and operations
   management for Chinese enterprises ; 4 | Includes bibliographical references.
Identifiers: LCCN 2017055420 | ISBN 9789813235151
Subjects: LCSH: China--Foreign economic relations. | China--Commerce. | Mutualism--China. |
   Investments, Foreign--China. | Sustainable development--China.
Classification: LCC HF1604 .Y823 2018 | DDC 338.951/07--dc23
LC record available at https://lccn.loc.gov/2017055420

British Library Cataloguing-in-Publication Data
A catalogue record for this book is available from the British Library.

This edition is jointly published by World Scientific Publishing Co. Pte. Ltd. and Zhejiang University Press. This edition is distributed worldwide by World Scientific Publishing Co. Pte. Ltd., except China.

Copyright © 2020 by World Scientific Publishing Co. Pte. Ltd. and Zhejiang University Press

All rights reserved. This book, or parts thereof, may not be reproduced in any form or by any means, electronic or mechanical, including photocopying, recording or any information storage and retrieval system now known or to be invented, without written permission from the Publishers.

For photocopying of material in this volume, please pay a copying fee through the Copyright Clearance Center, Inc., 222 Rosewood Drive, Danvers, MA 01923, USA. In this case permission to photocopy is not required from the publisher.

For any available supplementary material, please visit
https://www.worldscientific.com/worldscibooks/10.1142/10854#t=suppl

Typeset by Zhejiang University Press

Printed in China

Series on Innovation and Operations Management for Chinese Enterprises – Vol. 4

THE THEORY AND POLICIES OF MUTUAL BENEFIT AND WIN-WIN STRATEGY

Research on Sustainable Development of China's Open Economy

Yu Lixin
Chinese Academy of Social Sciences, China

Chen Wanling
Guangdong University of Foreign Studies, China

About the Authors

Yu Lixin, a post-doctoral supervisor, is Research Fellow of the National Academy of Economic Strategies of the Chinese Academy of Social Sciences, Deputy Secretary-General of the Expert Committee for China Association of Trade in Services, and Member of China Society for World Trade Organization Studies. Yu's research has focused on theory and policy of international economy, trade in services, WTO rules, cross-border e-commerce and Internet finance. He has undertaken key projects from the National Planning Office of Philosophy and Social Science, the Chinese Academy of Social Sciences and ministries and commissions of the central government, as well as projects in cooperation with the World Bank. He has hosted or engaged in more than 50 research projects. Yu has published more than 340 research papers and reports and authored or co-authored 22 monographs. For his research achievements he has won more than 10 prizes from China Association of International Trade, the National Development and Reform Commission, the Chinese Academy of Social Sciences, etc.

Chen Wanling, PH.D., is a professor and doctoral supvisor of the School of International Trade & Economics in Guangdong University of Foreign Studies. Chen is Director of China Institute of International Trade, standing director of China Emerging Economy Research Association, Vice President and Secretary General of Guangdong Emerging Economies Research Council. His major research field is international trade theory and policy. Chen has presided 2 major projects in philosophy and social sciences of the Ministry of Education of China, 1 project funded by the National Social Science Fund, over 20 subjects of the Guangdong Provincial Humanities and Social Science Base and provincial (ministerial) or bureau-level projects, as well as local government entrustment and policy advisory subjects and a number of business-commissioned research projects. Chen has published nearly 100 papers, 3 monographs and 1 textbook. Chen has won 3 prizes of Philosophy and Social Sciences Excellent Achievement Award of Guangdong Province.

Contents

Introduction 1

1 Overview of the Theory of Mutual Benefit and Win-win Strategy 21

2 The Value Chain of the International Division of Labor and China's Trade Interests 51

3 Research on the Coordination of China's Policies of Foreign Trade and Foreign Capital 103

4 China's Import and Export Trade and Technical Measures to Trade 150

5 Technology Spillover of Foreign Direct Investment and Chinese Technological Progress 177

6 Coordination Between Introducing Foreign Investment and Implementing Anti-dumping Investigations 212

7 Sustainable Development of China's Foreign Trade with Resources and Environmental Restrictions 246

8 Research on the Competitiveness of China's Service Outsourcing Industry 287

9 Regional Economic Cooperation and Constructing China's Free Trade Area Strategy 344

10 Discussion on the Development of Regional Economic Integration Among China, Japan, and R. O. Korea 405

11 Strategic Planning of China's Direct Investment in Africa 456

12 Strategies for Promoting the Trade and Industrial Integration of Mechanical and Electrical Products of the Chinese Mainland and Chinese Taiwan 498

13 Research on China's Exchange Rate Regime, Opening of Capital Account, and the Effectiveness of Monetary Policy 530

14 The Internationalization of the RMB and the Choices of Paths and Strategies 562

References 594

Index 600

Postscript 603

Introduction

1 Foreword

China is one of the oldest civilized countries in the world. In the history of human kind, China has made numerous breakthroughs. A number of scholars at home and abroad believe that until 1820, China had always been one of the richest countries and our knowledge of world history confirms this view.

Copper smelting technology, the use of bronze and iron ware, the production of white potteries and painted potteries, and silk, all of these represented China's global leadership in production at that time. The Great Wall and the Terracotta Warriers and Horses of the First Qin Emperor's Mausoleum are also symbols of the Eastern civilization. In addition to enhancing technological development, some open-minded emperors also paid great attention to the development of economic and cultural communication with neighboring countries. For example, Emperor Wu of the Han Dynasty sent Zhang Qian to the West twice to establish the Silk Road that linked Chang'an (now Xi'an in Shaanxi Province) with the East of the Mediterranean through Xinjiang of China and Central Asia. Along this road, China's silk products were transported to the West. In the 660s, China established broad economic and cultural relations with many countries like Japan, Korea, India, Persia, etc. In the Yuan Dynasty, the Four Great Inventions, paper-making technology, printing, the compass, and gunpowder, had spread across the world and made great contributions to world civilization. In the Ming Dynasty, Zheng He led a large fleet to make seven voyages, passing through Southeast Asian countries, the Indian Ocean, the Persian Gulf, and the Maldives' islands, and reaching the farthest destinations, Somalia and Kenya on the Eastern coast of Africa. This had been the largest and the longest marine exploration in the world before the era of Columbus. In a sense, ancient China had attempted to open up and had achieved a certain degree of success. During the Qing Dynasty, although China secluded the country from the outside world, its feudal economy reached its peak, with the economic aggregate accounting for 32% of the world's total.

In over 100 years from the Opium War to the founding of the People's Republic of China, China's society had always been in wars and turmoil. After the establishment of the People's Republic of China, under the leadership of the CPC, the Chinese people has actively promoted production and construction, making great efforts to restore the national economy, and has achieved remarkable success. Especially since 1978, the reform and opening-up policy has focused on the process of modernization. Through reforming economic institutions and related modernization of social administrative institutions, China has embarked on the road of socialism with Chinese characteristics. Since the implementation of the reform and opening-up policy, China has undergone remarkable changes, successfully transforming from a highly centralized planned economy to a dynamic socialist market economy, and establishing the basic economic system of keeping public ownership as the mainstay with the development of varied forms of ownership.

To sum up, China's reform and opening-up over the past years has achieved great success and has generated valuable experience. While China has successfully blazed a trail to open up and develop, there are inevitably some serious and profound problems and conflicts. For many years, China's rapid economic growth and continuous foreign trade surplus have made China's external environment more and more complicated. The argument of China as a threat also brings a negative impact to China's international image in some countries and regions. In fact, while China provides good and inexpensive products to the world, it imports products with price fluctuations, which is conducive to reducing the global rate of inflation. In addition, China's economic growth brings opportunities to connect countries and regions. The importation of necessary products indirectly boosts the development of these countries and regions. Therefore, China's growth in economy and trade is not a threat to the world. Instead, it is clearly a contribution. Yet, as China rises and the external situation becomes more and more complicated, the argument of China as a threat is still an urgent problem that China needs to resolve using the opening-up strategy at the start of the new century. Implementing the mutual benefit and win-win opening-up strategy and promoting the idea of a harmonious world are the best ways to solve this problem.

2 The Basic Connotation of the Mutual Benefit and Win-win Strategy

Win-win is a concept derived from game theory, contrary to the zero-sum game. At the end, both parties can have the winning result in the game, or win-win, rather than a zero-sum result, in which one party wins and the other loses. As the integration of world's economy continues, different countries and different economies become increasingly interdependent. Winner-takes-all is less and less acceptable, while equality and mutual benefit are increasingly welcome. This win-win value of equality and mutual benefit is the basis for a harmonious world.

(1) Upgrading the strategy with a global view

At the beginning of reform and opening-up, China's strategic focus of opening-up was based on its own interests. As the opening-up broadened and intensified, China began to set its view beyond itself to reach the whole world, integrating its development with global economic development. In this process, China's strategy of opening-up has adjusted to the development of domestic and international economic situations. And China's opening-up has gained momentum. Against the new backdrop of the acceleration of economic globalization, opening-up becomes not only an important factor that decides its sound and fast economic development, but also the crucial part for China to participate in global cooperation and competition and sustainable development of globalization. The status of the mutual benefit and win-win opening-up strategy with global factors has been promoted as an important part of national development, which signifies that China, as an emerging economic power, in addition to seeking its own interests and development, is now taking its responsibility in the global economy into consideration. Considering its national interests, China formulates a whole set of long-term and systematic development strategies, such as intensifying domestic reforms, addressing international economic crisis and economic frictions, introducing foreign investments and technologies, and ensuring energy and financial security. This is also a key step in China's globalization strategy.

(2) Standing on a new starting point of a developing power

The mutual benefit and win-win opening-up strategy is grounded on China's objective understanding of its own comprehensive economic strength and international status. It is an improvement and also an adjustment to the opening-up strategy at the new starting point of China as a developing power. At the beginning of reform and opening-up, China was only a developing country with weak comprehensive economic strength and was seldom involved in the world economy. China's opening-up did not make a great difference to the outside world. The major content of the opening-up was how to introduce international resources, expand exports to generate more foreign currency revenue, and improve the international competitiveness of its own economy. World economic development was viewed as the external condition for China's economic development. China set the main goal in making full use of the external condition to develop China's economy without considering too much about international responsibility. Yet, after WTO accession, China has evolved from an under-developed economy with little influence on the world economy to one whose economy is big enough to decide the future economic landscape and the order of the global market. From the point of view of economic opening and world economy, opening-up at the new historic starting point requires China to review the world and address the international political and economic problems that it has encountered based on it being a significant world economic power. It also means that China should accurately understand its position from a global angle and promote world progress with China's development.

(3) Further improving quality and efficiency

The core of the mutual benefit and win-win opening-up strategy lies in mutual benefit, and win-win is the goal. To achieve mutual benefit, when formulating opening-up strategy and policy, a country should consider not only its own economic interests and the healthy growth of its domestic economy and industry, but also the influence of its development on world's economic system. When we say win-win, it means that China should view the realization of its own interests together with the promotion of common development as the basic principle to deal with economic relations and cooperation with the rest of the world. In the process of opening-up and dealing with economic relations, the implementation of the mutual benefit and win-win opening-up strategy requires that China should continue maintaining overall national interests as a priority. Meanwhile, it must also consider the interests of its trading partners and promote mutual development and benefit on an equal footing. The practice of the opening-up strategy over the past years has mainly led to success in scale and measure. As for quality and efficiency, the result is not good enough. At the new historic stage, to be committed to the mutual benefit and win-win opening-up strategy, the priority is to reformulate policy ideas of opening-up. China should always take national interests as a guide, make the improvement of citizens' livelihood as the standard of the efficiency of opening-up, and view the participation in international economic cooperation and competition, under the condition of globalization, as a new strength. China should change its pattern of economic growth to realize the transformation from the traditional expansion of quantity to a kind of opening-up that aims at quality and efficiency.

(4) Fostering a more conducive international environment

In the new century, the central government puts forward the mutual benefit and win-win opening-up strategy to drive the sound and fast development of an export-oriented economy and also sets it as a crucial layout of another developmental strategy to comprehensively construct socialism with Chinese characteristics. In the era of globalization, the opening-up strategy has gone beyond the purely economic domain, and is becoming an important part of China's overall strategic arrangement to cope with the increasingly fierce international competition and to construct a modernized socialist economic power. This contains two connotations: politics and economy. As for economy, the promotion of the mutual benefit and win-win opening-up strategy signifies that China's opening-up has realized a smooth transition from an adaptive to a strategic stage. The mutual benefit and win-win opening-up strategy is not only conducive to economic development, but also valuable in dealing with political relations among countries. In the new century, China has clearly shown its determination to be committed to peaceful development, which is clearly a sure way to achieve its national prosperity and its people's happiness. China is willing to try its best to actively contribute to the common development of different countries.

To sum up, mutual benefit and win-win strategy is an embodiment of the Scientific Outlook on Development and the guiding principle of China's foreign economic interactions. Mutual benefit and win-win is a mindset, and a proposal that can be put into practice. It has gone beyond the mere pursuit of interests. Its focus is, through economic cooperation with other countries and regions, to promote national development and reform to achieve the modernization of China.

3 Necessity of the Mutual Benefit and Win-win Strategy

International relations after World War II were grounded on peace and co-existence. At the turn of the century, people suddenly found that globalization had made the earth seem smaller, and resources scarcer. Yet at the same time, it had enlarged the gap between the North and South, and made international relations more complex. As a big country with a population of more than 1.3 billion, if China wants to rise in globalization, it must make the right decisions regarding international strategy. The CPC, under the guidance of the Deng Xiaoping Theory and the important lines of thought of the "Three Represents", starting from the overall development of the Party and nation in the new century, has put forward an important strategic idea of the Scientific Outlook on Development. Based on that outlook, the central government presented the goal of integrating domestic development and opening-up, and stated that China should continue opening-up and enhancing its capacity for the development. According to the outlook, the Eleventh Five-year Plan states that China should actively participate in international economic competition, and implement the mutual benefit and win-win opening-up strategy.

(1) The rational choice in economic globalization

After entering the 21st century, economic globalization exhibited new trends and enabled countries to obtain complementary advantages between each other by promoting rational flows of production factors. While promoting world economic sustainability, its negative influence on development is becoming increasingly manifest. First, economic globalization has worsened the imbalance of resource allocation and world development to some extent. It has given rise to a digital gap. With the new economy separated from the old one, the world's economy is undergoing a structural imbalance. Second, social progress is not going hand in hand with economic growth, and economic globalization is developing alongside the deterioration of the environment. Third, there are still irresolvable conflicts between economic globalization and the unsound rules of global economic governance. Fourth, globalization gives rise to more economic interdependence among countries, which means that any change in the international economy would cause countries to be bound together for better or for worse. Fifth, globalization also bears the potential risk of a global economic crisis. Therefore, with the new trends and features of globalization, it is necessary for China to make corresponding adjustments in the opening-up strategy. It means that according to the new development and challenges of globalization, China should specify new goals and targets of opening-up. This will lead to the transition of China's export-oriented economy, from gathering international factors to develop the national economy, to fully participating in world cooperation and competition to strive for a higher status of international division in global economic development and to gain greater interests of opening-up. By doing so, China can drive itself to change from an open developing large country to an open modernized economic power.

(2) The urgent need to be committed to the Scientific Outlook on Development and completing the goals of the 12th Five-year Plan

Entering the 21st century, based on the historic reality of China's economic and social development and an objective analysis of the international and domestic situations, China put forward the human-centered outlook, the Scientific Outlook on Development, which is comprehensive, coordinated, and sustainable. Over the past years of reform and opening-up, though China has rapidly developed its export-oriented economy and achieved great success, behind this success is the support of large resources and energy injection, the cost of ecological and environmental deterioration, and the typical extensive growth pattern with attention given only to quantity. As China continues its rapid growth and prices of international resources keep going up, this developmental pattern cannot be sustained. Reflecting upon and evaluating the conventional strategy, China should actively explore a new opening-up concept for higher efficiency and seek a new way of resolving the present problems for sustainable growth to realize scientific development. According to the CPC Central Committee's Suggestions on the Formulation of the 12th Five-year Plan for National Economic and Social Development adopted at the Fifth Plenary Session of the 17th CPC Central Committee, China must double its efforts in opening-up to reach the target. It should strive to implement the mutual benefit and win-win opening-up strategy, and make full use of international and domestic markets to acquire resources, technologies, and management expertise that are necessary to develop the national economy.

(3) A necessary guarantee for industrial upgrading in an export-oriented economy

After so many years of efforts, China has already primarily established a socialist market economic system and it has been improved. In this key period, choosing a reasonable growth pattern and keeping up the momentum for sustainable development are especially important. Over the past years of opening-up, China has fully utilized its comparative strengths in the international division of labor. Depending on large and good, but inexpensive exports, China soon became a big trading country. Yet, products for export consume too many resources. The companies' profits mainly depend on the quantity of products. Additionally, the processing pattern of many companies relies highly on raw materials and sales on the international market, thus boosting little development of the related industry on the domestic market. Besides, the limitations of a conventional export-oriented strategy appeared more prominent. As one of the countries with the fastest-growing economy, at the end of the transition period after its accession of the WTO, China is now fully involved in the global economic system. To seize strategic opportunities and create a good external environment for creating a well-off society in an all-round way, China should uphold the mutual benefit and win-win opening-up strategy and make full play in multilateral trade negotiations. It also needs to improve its influence on and participation in multilateral economic diplomacy, actively participate in the formulation and revision of the WTO rules, and take part in the policy review for WTO members. Moreover, the mutual benefit and win-win opening-up strategy requires China to establish close ties with its neighbors, understanding regional integration and FTA exclusiveness, following the developmental trends, using its strengths in foreign economic cooperation, optimizing resource allocation, and accelerating regional cooperation and FTA construction. By doing so, China can optimize and upgrade its industrial structure on the basis of regional cooperation and create a good external environment.

(4) An important manifestation of a responsible power

China's peaceful rise needs a new industrial pattern. It needs to look beyond the old one, which will inevitably bring about a scramble for resources and the cold war mindset that rejects peace, development and cooperation due to ideological differences. With regard to participation in international economic cooperation, China pays attention to combining its interests with those of the rest of the world instead of pursuing its own goals only and thereby threatening others' interests. It takes into consideration the whole world in establishing harmonious internationalism. The promotion of the strategy also demonstrates China's efforts in promoting the construction of a world political and economic order. China is the largest developing country in the world, and its developmental pattern is not only a matter of the rejuvenation of the Chinese nation, but also one that affects the development of the world economy. In an international society, China actively shoulders its international obligations, and does its best to make more contributions to the international community. During the 1997 Asian Financial Crisis, for the common interests of Asian countries, China stuck to a stable RMB exchange rate and provided aid to related countries as its capability allowed. This greatly contributed to the final victory over the crisis. By 2005, China had provided favorable tariffs to the least developed countries in Asia and Africa and exempted 38 countries' debts of over 13.7 billion yuan. The Chinese government is committed to the new developmental outlook with a focus on equality and actively promotes the mutual benefit and win-win opening-up strategy. It is willing to support developing countries and has taken steps to promote North-South cooperation and a balanced and orderly development of world economy.

4 The Essence of the Mutual Benefit and Win-win Strategy

To implement the mutual benefit and win-win opening-up strategy, China is committed to the basic national policy of opening-up and participating in international economic and technological cooperation and competition in broader areas and domains or at a higher level. This would better drive domestic development and reform and it would protect national economic security.

(1) Adjusting traditional foreign trade policies and implementing a sustainable trade strategy

As required in the Scientific Outlook on Development, China should create a balance among resources, the environment and the ecological system while maintaining a stable economic growth. The mutual benefit and win-win opening-up strategy requires a modified extensive growth pattern, transformation of the policy from export- to competitiveness-oriented, and the implementation of a sustainable trade strategy. First, while maintaining a steady growth, China should optimize its export structure and transform its manner of growth. Second, focusing on its self-owned brands, proprietary intellectual property rights and independent marketing, China should establish and improve policy support and an incentive mechanism, and guide companies to improve their comprehensive competitiveness. Third, China should implement the national strategy of indigenous innovation and support the exportation of indigenous high-tech and electromechanical products innovated by companies. Fourth, China should stop the processing trade of industries with high energy consumption and that are pollution-generating as well as those industries that are resource-extensive. By eliminating or reducing rebates and collecting tariffs, it will control the aforementioned exports. Fifth, by defining different industries for support, curb, or withdrawal, China should improve its guiding list, its product catalog, and enterprise grouping in the processing industry, and increase the access standard for the processing trade which would be guided toward a high value-added and technical industry. Sixth, China should establish and improve the system of environmental and economic accounting, accelerate the reform of market-oriented prices of resources and energy, and implement a system of collecting environmental charges and taxes based on the internalization of environmental costs. Seventh, China should promote the innovation of green technology and the development of marketable international ecological products, pay attention to the development of international environmental standards, and actively promote the ISO14000 environment management system to achieve the ecological development of foreign trade companies. Eighth, China should fully implement regulations such as the Labor Law to guarantee labor and accelerate the legislation for labor wages and social insurance to improve the labor contract and employee-insurance systems, export cost structure, and the income of laborers, especially migrant workers.

(2) Actively resolving technological barriers to trade (TBT) and establishing technical trade policies of importations and exportations

As a developing country, China is inevitably facing different problems brought by trade barriers when implementing its opening-up strategy and actively participating in international competition. Therefore, how to fully use technical trade policies within the WTO framework, how to establish a technical trade policy system that is in line with international standards and criteria as soon as possible, and how to protect the interests of domestic consumers and develop national industries are realistic and urgent problems that the Chinese government and enterprises should deal with. First, China should further improve and standardize the release and reporting system of technical regulations, streamline the numeration system of its technical standards, and create a smooth channel for companies to retrieve relevant information regarding the TBTs. Second, China should fully improve its overall technical standards according to the technical development of China's industries, and encourage competent export enterprises to adopt international standards and advanced foreign standards to meet the needs of international export markets. It should improve the technological level of its products and adjust its export structure. Third, China should collect information about the TBTs. In addition, it should set up a specialized department to carry out specific analyses, conduct policy studies, and strengthen the review of foreign TBTs. Fourth, China should give full scope of the service function of the government, and strengthen training to industries, organizations, and enterprises, which would enable them to form a bridge between companies and the government. Fifth, referring to the international standards, China should establish and improve its system of technical standards and regulations, improve the system of product certification, and establish mutual recognition with foreign certification authorities. Sixth, China should establish green trade barriers to forbid imports that do not align with environmental standards, adjust foreign investment policies, and prevent developed countries from using international investment to transfer industries with high energy consumption, those that are pollution-generating and resource-extensive, to China. Seventh, China should strengthen communication and cooperation and actively participate in formulating international standards.

(3) Deeply understanding developmental trends and characteristics in international trade and developing trade in services

To improve the development of its trade in services, China should seize the opportunity of being an important destination for international service industry transfer, improve its management system, formulate supporting policies, and create a good environment. First, China should expand its service exports like engineering contracts, design consultation, technology transferring, financial insurance, international transportation, education and training, information technology, and the culture of tourism, support enterprises to set up service operation institutions overseas, and provide support for international market expansion. Second, foreign investment should be encouraged in the development of software, cross-border outsourcing and logistic services, an export-oriented service industry should be developed, and the structure and competitiveness of the service industry should be improved by introducing foreign investment. Third, several outsourcing bases should be established for the service industry. China needs to formulate and implement measures to undertake outsourcing services, guide domestic enterprises to become involved in service outsourcing, and undertake international service industry transfer in an orderly way. Fourth, China should also enhance planning and guidance, steadily expand the opening-up of the service industry, establish and improve the legal system of trade in services in line with international rules, establish systems of trade in services statistics, standardization, policy coordination, and regulation, and study and formulate policies and measures in finance, taxation, insurance and foreign exchange that can encourage and strengthen service exportation to promote the development of the industry.

(4) Changing investment introduction concepts and improving the quality of utilizing foreign investment

First, it is necessary to promote foreign investors in the structural optimization and upgrading of the manufacturing industry. China should coordinate the structural upgrading of domestic industries with international manufacturing industry transfer, and guide investors to invest more in the high-tech industries and high-end manufacturing industry. Second, it is necessary to improve the opening-up of the service industry. China should attract foreign investors to modern logistics, legal consultancy, education and training, information services, engineering technologies and other services, forming a coordinated pattern with manufacturing. Third, China needs to optimize the regional distribution of foreign investment. Coastal areas in China's eastern region should continue to give scope to their strengths in capital, talents, technology, location-related and highly export-oriented capabilities to transform from quantity to quality investment. Fourth, it is necessary to diversify the way of using foreign investment. Since the 10th Five-year Plan, the major composition of foreign investment in China has been sole proprietorship. China should gradually change this trend, guide and supervise foreign investors in the transformation and reorganization of domestic enterprises, and cultivate acquisition and merger as a new growing point of attracting foreign investment while protecting domestically self-owned brands and industries. Fifth, China needs to use foreign loans reasonably and strengthen the risk control of foreign debts. Foreign preferential loans should keep supporting the development of the old industrial bases in China's central, western, and northeastern regions. During the process of infrastructure improvement, China should update its ecological environmental protection, resources conservation policy, education, hygiene and poverty alleviation in under-developed regions, and increase its support of project development for the basic medical services in rural areas. The sixth necessary measure is to improve laws and policies regarding the use of foreign investments. China should study the formulation of regulations for promoting foreign investment and strengthening the supervision of domestic enterprises' merger and acquisition by foreign investors.

(5) Actively conducting international economic cooperation and strengthening the development of regional economic integration

China should promote cross-border flows of production factors and improve the mechanisms and policies of allocation optimization. It should actively develop economic and technological cooperation with neighboring countries and others to realize mutual benefit and a win-win outcome. First, China needs to cultivate internationally competent subjects for foreign direct investment (FDI) and make enterprises become the subject of innovation of the FDI system. Second, China should diversify its investment subjects, encourage private enterprises to "go global" through providing a fair-play environment, and cultivate and develop China's cross-border companies. Third, there is a need to expand resource cooperation and development overseas on the basis of complementary advantages, equality and mutual benefit, encourage enterprises to participate in overseas infrastructure, and improve the level of engineering contracting and labor cooperation. The fourth measure is to strengthen the organization and management of overseas direct investment, improve the legal system that encourages and regulates overseas direct investment, and establish systems to manage FDI risks and regulate national assets overseas. The fifth is to steadily promote the facilitation of trade, investment, and transportation with overall planning, actively participate in international and regional mechanism for economic cooperation, strengthen dialogue, consultation, bilateral and multilateral economic cooperation between countries, and establish foreign trade areas (FTAs). The sixth is to give scope to the government's leading role in formulating a regional framework for economic cooperation, accelerate regional economic cooperation between China's mainland and Hong Kong, Macao, and Taiwan, and seek regional or sub-regional economic cooperation with neighboring countries. And finally, the seventh is to increase aid to other developing countries and further enhance cooperation in economy, technology, and energy resources with other developing countries.

5 The Guarantee for Implementing the Strategy

The mutual benefit and win-win opening-up strategy is the major global trend in foreign policies in the new era. Wanting to tally with economic globalization, China must be committed to the principle of mutual benefit and win-win, appropriately deal with trade frictions, and promote harmonious development with the rest of the world. Therefore, the Scientific Outlook on Development and other important theories guide China in the following ways to guarantee the implementation of the mutual benefit and win-win opening-up strategy and tackle the realistic problems in globalization.

(1) Changing the growth pattern of foreign trade and transforming the policy so that it can become competitiveness-oriented

It is astonishing that the growth pattern of China's foreign trade is still extensive with great pressure on resources and the ecological environment. The trade policy should be changed to become competitiveness-oriented while maintaining steady growth. The first measure is to improve companies' core competitiveness and increase the value-added of export products, and cultivate well-known brands by using technology to boost quality trade, and focus on supporting brand products with proprietary intellectual property rights, key enterprises with strong core competitiveness, high-tech export bases and industrial clusters. The second measure is to seize the opportunity of international industrial transfer to formulate a medium- and long-term development plan and promote the transformation and upgrading of the processing trade, further improve the technological level and extend the industrial chain of the processing trade to restructure industries, and change the pattern of participation in the international division of labor from depending on introducing foreign investment to both introducing and conducting foreign investment. China should give full play to and change the way of the governmental administrative function to focus on the healthy development of the processing trade. The third measure is to establish a new type of scientific evaluation system with comprehensive indicators for foreign trade, change the practice of focusing on quantity only to that focusing on efficiency and quality. This will be more conducive to measuring the effect of transformation. The fourth is to establish the scope of support from importations to the national economy. China has always adopted many restrictive policies, leading to an unreasonable structure of importations with 70% of the raw materials and intermediate goods and 20% of capital and equipment. While focusing on the growth of exportation, China should change the trade pattern to coordinate between importation and exportation, increase its support for a proactive import strategy, and formulate the catalog in which equipment and technologies are imported as a priority.

(2) Using foreign investment effectively and improving the quality of utilization

To introduce foreign investment, China should focus on improving the quality of introduced technologies to optimize the industrial structure. Guiding foreign investment to the right place helps adjust the industrial structure. The first measure to take is to step up the introduction of deep processing industries and technology-intensive projects such as electronics, machinery, instruments, industrial facilities, medicine, and construction materials. The second is to improve companies' international competitiveness, encourage foreign investors in the reorganization and transformation of conventional industries such as machinery, light industry, textiles, raw materials, and architecture and construction materials. The third is to attract foreign investment into the reorganization and transformation of state-owned enterprises (SOEs). This is an important path to further intensify the reform of SOEs. The fourth is to improve the investment environment and infrastructures in energy, transportation, and communications to encourage foreign investment in the construction of the infrastructure of cities in the central, western, and northeastern regions and the development of the continuous industry in the cities whose resources are coming to an end. Full use should be made of abundant human and other resources to guide labor-intensive foreign firms or ordinary processing industries to the central and western regions.

(3) Fully implementing the strategy of Going Global and improving the competitiveness of enterprises

To implement the strategy of Going Global, at the micro level, first, China should seek advantageous conditions in overseas investment to realize the dynamic development of enterprises. Second, enterprises should achieve large-scale and diversified operations to become industrial multinationals. Third, China should improve the infrastructure and increase investments in R&D to develop innovative enterprises. Enterprises can cooperate in processing the trade industry with foreign firms that have state-of-the-art technologies, high-value-added products, and R&D institutions, and based on assimilating advanced international technologies, they should seek innovative breakthroughs to cooperate, and compete with multinationals. Fourth, to fully use the idle money domestically and internationally for production and operation, enterprises need to expand financing channels using multiple approaches; for example, looking beyond the single way from bank loans to adopt bond or stock issue on the ever-improving domestic market and utilize a good reputation and reliable solvency to finance in the Euro-currency and other international markets. Fifth, conditional to its own situation, China could adopt multiple and appropriate ways, for example, using physical capital, to develop outbound FDI and make full use of the idle resources and surplus products on the domestic market to give scope to their due functions. Meanwhile, we need to notice cross-border mergers and acquisitions, realize a win-win situation and create a good international environment for overseas investment of firms. At the macroeconomic level, China should resolve economic disagreements and frictions in time by establishing a bilateral and multilateral dialogue mechanism and by appropriately dealing with interests among countries.

(4) Strengthening the relations with neighboring countries and regional cooperation

As international economic integration intensifies, regional economic ties are becoming closer. Neighboring economies share more common interests and opportunities for cooperation. China should establish closer economic ties with neighboring countries and regions, set up FTAs, including the Taiwan Strait Free Trade Zone, to expand trade in electromechanical products between the mainland and Taiwan area. First, governments should support the policy dialogue to strengthen the coordination of actions, promote information exchanges and the formulation of regional economic cooperation rules, and establish priorities and specific projects in economic and technological cooperation with other economies by determining capital sources and jointly formulating corresponding multilateral incentive measures to enable regional economic cooperation into a mechanism orbit as soon as possible. Second, companies should play the main micro role through cross-border operations. To strengthen international cooperation, they should establish and maintain relations with international, regional or transnational R&D centers through sharing of research topic and academic exchange activities. These R&D centers will become a company's consultants or think tank. Companies should have international, modern, and scientific decision-making policies, paying attention to the practicability of the ideas, enhance employee training, personnel cooperation, adjustment and exchanges both domestically and internationally, and establish connections with scientific research institutions, universities, and related institutions.

(5) Establishing and improving the national economic security system

To study China's national economic security with the concept of mutual benefit and win-win opening-up, it is better to understand security in globalization. Under globalization, the economic security of a country does not depend only on whether its internal economic structure is reasonable enough to fend off the impact from short-term fluctuations of the external economy, but also on whether its economy occupies an appropriate status in the global industrial chain, as a low status in the international division would let its economic structure be trapped in unfavorable situations. Agriculture with a low productivity, manufacturing with little core competitiveness, a shortage of energy and resources, service industries like finance far behind the international advanced level, are all China's weaknesses when China is fully participating in the international cooperation and competition after the transition period of China's accession to the WTO. China should study how to use the WTO rules, learn the experience and lessons from developed and some developing countries to avoid and cope with industrial risks and to safeguard industrial security, and then take effective troubleshooting approaches. China should establish and improve (1) a dynamic warning system of tracking, monitoring, and safety evaluation; (2) a long-term mechanism to appropriately protect domestic industries and the market; and (3) an adjusting system for importing and reserving strategic resources like energy and raw materials.

1

Overview of the Theory of Mutual Benefit and Win-win Strategy

Reform and opening-up are two important trends in China's economic development and social progress in the recent years. China's opening-up started from specific areas and then gradually spread over the whole country. In the new century, China's opening-up to the outside world reached a higher level. China's development cannot happen without the involvement of the world, and vice versa. In other words, China's opening-up has been deeply integrated into economic globalization. Hence, in the process of becoming an important country, China is at a critical juncture and needs to adjust its strategy of opening-up.

1.1 The History of China's Opening-up

Looking back at China's history in the past years, the features and developmental trend of an open economy can be seen clearly, which provides important lessons for opening-up in the future.

The opening-up process may be divided into three stages:

(1) Primary exploration (1978–1991): The Third Plenary Session of the 11th CPC Central Committee in 1978 implied that China had begun to open to the outside world from a state of being closed within its own boundaries. Then, China expanded its opening-up into various areas, by creating special economic zones (SEZs), economic and technical development zones (ETDZs), and bonded zones. Thus, the scenario of China's opening-up started from specific places and spread over the whole country.

(2) Expansion (1992—2000): The most important event is Deng Xiaoping's Talks in the South and the establishment of a specific goal of reform, that of creating a socialist market economic system. In the early spring of 1992, Deng Xiaoping made it clear in his speech that opening-up should be accelerated and expanded.

(3) Opening-up in an all-round way (since 2001): Having joined the WTO in January 2001, China emphasized that the domains and areas of opening-up should be comprehensive, with a goal of establishing an open market and an economic society. A comprehensive reform should be carried out on the economic, political, and social administration systems, using markets to allocate resources. In terms of the reform of the trade policy, China has followed international rules to achieve not only the free cross-border flow of goods, services, and factors, but also the integration of production, consumption, trade, and investment into the international economic community.

From the perspective of economics, opening-up is reciprocal. The aforementioned three stages can be labeled as surrendering partial benefit, mutual benefit, and win-win, respectively. The process of opening-up has improved from quantity to quality, enabling China to become internationally competitive and to be able to cooperate internationally at a higher level and in broader areas. Surrendering partial benefit means that within a period,

China used preferential policies and surrendered some of its benefit to others when it participated in international exchanges. Mutual benefit refers to the high efficiency of resource allocation due to the non-zero-sum game in economic activities. This is the economic basis on which parties involved are willing to conduct long-term trade. Win-win implies that dividends can be shared on a more equal footing to realize the coordinated development of both trading parties.

1.1.1 Primary Stage of Surrendering Partial Benefit (1978—1991)

In 1978, the Chinese government proposed the strategy of reform and opening-up with an emphasis on economic development, gradually developing an open economy at a low level. The opening-up policy at that time was predominantly to connect China with the world through the SEZs. By introducing the international systems of operating and managing the economy, China established pilot zones for economic reform and has gradually expanded its opening-up from the zones to coastal, riparian, and border areas. In 1979, the central government allowed Guangdong and Fujian to adopt flexible policies of foreign economic activities. In 1980, the four SEZs, Shenzhen, Zhuhai, Shantou, and Xiamen, were established. In 1984, China officially decided to open up 14 coastal cities including Dalian, Qinhuangdao, Tianjin, Yantai, Qingdao, Lianyungang, Nantong, Shanghai, Ningbo, Wenzhou, Fuzhou, Guangzhou, Zhanjiang, and Beihai, and established the ETDZs. In 1985, China gradually opened up the Yangtze River Delta, the Pearl River Delta, the Delta of Xiamen, Zhangzhou, and Quanzhou, the Liaodong Peninsula, and the Jiaodong Peninsula. In 1987, the Shatoujiao Bonded Area was established. The Hainan Province Special Economic Zone was established in 1988. In 1990, Shanghai Pudong was opened and set up as an ETDZ implementing SEZ policies. In 1991, China opened four northern ports such as Manzhouli, and approved Waigaoqiao in Shanghai, Futian in Shenzhen, and some other important coastal ports to set up bonded areas. At that stage, a gradual opening-up strategy was formed starting from the SEZs, coastal cities, and economic development zones (EDZs), to China's inland, and this is one of China's successful experiences of opening-up in the past years.

Due to the fact that China had a backward domestic economy and technology, the main purpose of opening-up at that time was to introduce much-needed foreign capital, and technology and management experience. Preferential policies in terms of taxation, interest, and land use were offered to foreign investors in order to realize the long-term strategic goal of opening-up. Hence, in essence, the opening-up at that stage meant surrendering partial benefit to foreign companies. "Surrendering benefit is like losing economic blood." As Deng Xiaoping said, "We should blaze a trail at a considerable cost," but this brought long-term and invaluable experience of development, and we have gradually proceeded to the stage of the all-round opening-up of mutual benefit.

1.1.2 All-round Opening-up of Mutual Benefit (1992–2000)

Deng Xiaoping's Talks in the South and the socialist market economy determined at the 14th National Congress of the CPC in 1992 symbolized that China had accelerated toward an intense opening-up, gradually developing into a comprehensive scenario of opening with wider domains and at a higher level. In 1992, China gradually opened up Wuhu, Jiujiang, Huangshi, Wuhan, Yueyang, and Chongqing, the cities along the Yangtze River with Shanghai Pudong as the leader, Harbin, Changchun, Hohhot, and Shijiazhuang, the capital cities in the coastal and border areas, Heihe, Suifenhe, Huichun, Manzhouli, Erenhot, Yining, Bole, Tacheng, Wanting, Ruili, Hekou, Pingxiang, Dongxing, and Dandong, the cities along the border, and 11 capital cities in China's inland including Taiyuan, Hefei, Nanchang, Zhengzhou, Changsha, Chengdu, Guiyang, Xi'an, Lanzhou, Xining, and Yinchuan. In the following two years, the State Council approved 18 ETDZs to be established in Wenzhou, Yingkou, Weihai, and Fuqingrong in 1992, in Dongshan, Harbin, Changchun, Shenyang, Hangzhou, Wuhu, Wuhan, Chongqing, Xiaoshan, Kunshan, Huizhou Daya Bay, and Guangzhou Nansha in 1993, and Beijing and Urumchi in 1994. In 2000, 15 export processing zones were established in Dalian, Tianjin, Beijing, Yantai, Weihai, Kunshan, Suzhou, Shanghai, Hangzhou, Xiamen, Shenzhen, Guangzhou, Wuhan, Chengdu, and Huichun. In the same year, following the implementation of the Western Development Strategy, areas of opening-up were further expanded to Western China, thus creating an open situation in the SEZs, the coastal cities and the EDZs, the economic zones along rivers, major cities in the inland, as well as in the areas along the railways, highways, or along the border. By then, the comprehensive scenario of opening-up had gradually come into shape.

At this stage, China gained tremendous benefit from opening-up with rapid economic growth. From 1992 to 2000, China's economic aggregate jumped from ¥2.66 trillion to ¥8.95 trillion; the total volume of its foreign trade rose from $165.53 billion to $474.3 billion; the actual utilization of foreign direct investment (FDI) grew from $11.01 billion to $40.72 billion, with the accumulated utilization of $323.31 billion; its foreign exchange reserves surged from $19.44 billion to $165.57 billion.

The rest of the world also gained enormously from China's opening-up, with foreign investors in the country receiving the most benefit. They made full use of China's inexpensive land, labor force, and other resources plus its preferential policies of tax reduction, leading to a higher return on investment (ROI) than in other places. Many foreign companies viewed China as a good platform for production and sales, and gained considerable profits from the process of investment, procurement, and production. In addition, trading partners also benefited greatly from the rapid development of China's economy and trade, not only improving the well-being of their consumers and easing domestic inflation by importing a large amount of inexpensive but high quality products, but also boosting the economy and employment due to China's fast rising appetite for imports.

Therefore, at this fully open stage, China brought great benefit to itself and to its partners. To provide a guarantee for improving the quality of opening-up, China gradually aligned itself with international rules and conducted important reforms of the systems of taxation, finance, trade, and foreign exchange to wipe out the obstacles that limited opening-up. With respect to import/export management, China canceled the import duties in 1992 and the mandatory plan in 1994. Since then, tariffs have been reduced a lot and now the overall tariffs are almost the same as the international standards, making China closer to the world market. At this stage, thanks to the division of labor and efficient resource allocation, both China and the rest of the world have gained from the rapid development of China's opening-up.

1.1.3 The New Type of Win-win Strategy (Since 2001)

After joining the WTO in 2001, China's opening-up went further, from a policy level only to the level of mechanism. As the opening-up proceeded to a new stage, new features arose: opening beyond specific areas to a more comprehensive level; the expansion in open domains and the transformation of opening-up models; the alignment of mechanisms with international rules. Adhering to the basic rules and commitment to the WTO, China has improved its market access in order to expand its open domains from conventional goods to trade in services, from limited levels to the whole market, from unilateral to bilateral opening-up to the other WTO members, and from policy deregulation in the pilot zones to predictable opening-up within the regulatory framework.

Since becoming a member of the WTO, China has made great achievements in opening-up and has become an important trade and economic power in the world. According to the statistics, in 2006, China overtook Japan to become the largest holder of a foreign exchange reserve with $1.07 trillion. In 2009, China surpassed Germany to become the largest exporter in the world, with a total value of $1.02 trillion. In 2010, China surpassed Japan to become the second largest economy, whose GDP reached $5.75 trillion. In 2012, China exceeded the United States to become the largest trader with a total volume of $3.87 trillion. These facts indicate that China's opening-up has evolved from the quantitative to qualitative aspects. China is no longer export-oriented, with emphasis on a growth in quantity, but it has begun to change to an open economy with a focus on both quantity and quality.

Since it entered the WTO, China has shared its dividends from opening-up with partners on an equal footing. A series of actions taken by China also imply that its opening-up strategy is evolving from mutual benefit to win-win.

First, in terms of import expansion, China cut tariffs substantially, canceled non-tariff measures on imports, and further opened up its trade in services. Tariffs were reduced from 15.3% before its membership in the WTO to 9.8% so far. Adhering to its commitment to the WTO, China has issued over 30 regulations to open up its trade in services covering finance, distribution, logistics, tourism, and architecture, laying down the basic pattern of service opening-up in an all-round way.

Second, China has fully developed its bilateral and multilateral economic and trade cooperation and accelerated the establishment of FTAs to share more opportunities with other countries and regions. By the end of 2009, 14 FTAs had been established or negotiated. Free trade agreements have been signed with ASEAN, Chile, Pakistan, Singapore, New Zealand, and Peru; negotiations are underway with the Southern African Customs Union, the Gulf Cooperation Council, Australia, Norway, Costa Rica, and Iceland. New mechanisms like the Sino-US Strategic Dialogue have also been established to settle trade conflicts.

Third, to reform the RMB exchange rate mechanism, on 21st July, 2005, China began implementing the managed floating system, based on the market supply/demand, referring to a basket of currencies. Additionally, China has undertaken a number of initiatives, including the adjustment of its foreign currency policy, the optimization of its foreign investment structure to improve the quality of its utilization, encouragement of overseas investment, improvement of the legal system, promotion of regional economic and cooperation development and active participation in a new round of multilateral trade negotiations within the WTO.

In the new situation, mutual benefit and win-win are the major trends for countries to conduct foreign economic cooperation. Only by implementing the opening-up strategy for mutual benefit and win-win can China seize opportunities in the new era of development and cope with new challenges. To fully improve its opening-up, China must keep developing this new type of strategy.

1.2 The Connotation and Significance of the Mutual Benefit and Win-win Strategy

At the Boao Forum of Asia 2008, former President Hu Jintao made a speech entitled "Continuing Reform and Opening-up and Advancing Win-win Cooperation". The speech clearly expressed that China has been and will always be committed to the mutual benefit and win-win opening-up strategy. This opened a new chapter of China's opening-up strategy.

1.2.1 Theoretical Connotation of the Mutual Benefit and Win-win Strategy

Generally speaking, this strategy means that countries obtain common development from economic exchanges. The core lies in mutual benefit, and the goal is to realize a win-win situation. Mutual benefit means that the opening-up policy should be conducive both to the healthy development of its own economy and to the benefit of its trading partners. Win-win means that policies issued by a country should tally with its interests and also promote the common development of others in the world. On the basis of mutual benefit established at the previous stage of the opening-up, adding win-win means that by intensifying reform, different parties are able to share dividends more equally and world economy can be developed in a coordinated way. This is a goal for opening-up and a guideline for foreign revenue distribution. The strategy of mutual benefit and win-win has the following features:

(1) A strategy on the basis of economic globalization

Over the past years of opening-up, China has gone through a transformation from domestic development to global cooperation by means of upgrading its strategic positioning and policy goal. During the early stage, China used the SEZs to attract foreign capital and technology. During the middle stage, it utilized export-oriented policies and then developed toward an open economy to coordinate the development with the rest of the world. This process showed that China's opening-up strategy has always been upgraded and improved in line with economic globalization.

With the rapid development of globalization, opening-up is not only an important way to participate in global cooperation and competition, but also a crucial factor that decides China's sustainable development. The mutual benefit and win-win opening-up strategy means that China's opening-up is based on globalization and guided by national interest. With a global view, the Chinese government formulated a set of systematic long-term developmental strategies with respect to national reform, introduction of capital and technology, solutions to international economic friction, and energy and finance security. This shows that the global strategy for China's economic development has bean basically formulated.

(2) The strategy of a great power for increased international responsibility

Since its opening-up, China's comprehensive economic strength and international status have improved, and it has gradually become a developing economic power and has transformed its opening-up strategy. Based on this, the strategy is in fact the innovation and adjustment of the previous development. During the early stage, due to its weak economic power, China opened up limited areas and did not participate very much in world economic activities. The opening-up was mainly to introduce capital and technology for urgent domestic needs, to expand exports for foreign exchange, and to improve its international competitiveness. The goal is to make full use of world economic development, which was viewed as an external factor for the development of its domestic economy, with little consideration of international responsibilities.

At the beginning of the 21st century, China has already become a large economy that can influence the world order of things. Yet, as an economic power, China must review the world and reposition its opening-up strategy. The mutual benefit and win-win opening-up strategy is to enhance regional cooperation by protecting bilateral and multilateral relations and trading systems, to establish good relations with resourceful neighboring regions, major markets, and trading partners while paying attention to others' benefit and settling trading frictions rationally, as well as shouldering responsibility that is in line with its national power. The first is through China's cooperation in FTAs, which provides a system guarantee for the development of economic relations with different countries and sharing opportunities with partners. The second is to actively shoulder a big country's responsibility in global and regional economic organizations, participating in the formulation and revision of international rules and promoting multilateral trading negotiations to maintain a free and open system. The examples include participating actively in the development of the WTO, the IMF, and other multilateral organizations, and enhancing dialogue and negotiation with organizations of other countries like the OECD. Therefore, whether considering national interests or global economic development, China must play a more active and important role in the regional and global economy.

(3) A mutual benefit strategy that takes care of the interests of both China and its partners

The mutual benefit and win-win opening-up strategy requires that the country should put its overall interests first, and at the same time balance the interests of its trading partners so as to promote common development and mutual benefit. Unlike the colonial foreign strategy of expansion and predation, this kind of opening-up is a just cause to get abundant support and also a new type of strategy, which takes care of others' benefits through balancing foreign competition against cooperation, domestic expansion against the use of overseas markets, domestic stability against international economic development, utilization of international public goods against their provision, national strength against the image in the world, and opening-up against independence. For developing countries, China should give before asking for a return, with more offers and less consideration of payback. The goal is to develop the domestic and the overseas markets in a coordinated way to achieve a balanced trade development. Domestic economic development serves as the basic guarantee for the mutual benefit and win-win opening-up strategy, and meanwhile an effective external environment is safeguarded for China's rapid and sustainable growth.

(4) A coordinated strategy balancing domestic reform and opening-up

Over the past years, domestic reform has provided the necessary system guarantee for the development of opening-up. The reform toward a socialist market system, in particular, paves the way for foreign economic development. Opening-up, in turn, promotes domestic reform especially after entering the WTO, since China carried out comprehensive reform both economically and politically. That opening-up and reform promote each other becomes a success. The mutual benefit and win-win opening-up strategy inherits the previous experience and further develops, emphasizing that future opening-up should connect and interact more with reform. Opening-up does not mean ignoring domestic reform and development. China should take opening-up as a good opportunity to create favorable conditions for domestic reform.

(5) A deep strategy with quality and efficiency as the core

History shows that China's early stage of opening-up was featured by increasing quantity. This is proven by China's stage of economic development. Although having achieved great economic success, China paid a great price. People's wealth and welfare suffered great losses; many difficulties of urgent needs emerged, such as the lack of the indigenous creativity of companies, the great pressure on resources and the environment, disorganized regional development, and the low quality of economic growth. In foreign trade, China's products are mostly at the low end. A large amount of exports with high consumption and pollution but low competitiveness kept worsening China's trade conditions and aggravating the vicious competition with neighboring developing countries. All these make it necessary for China to set improvement of the country and society's well-being as the standard to evaluate opening-up, to change the extensive way of growing economy from a conventional emphasis on quantity to quality and efficiency, and to innovatively utilize foreign investment and economic cooperation.

1.2.2 Significance for the Mutual Benefit and Win-win Strategy

Mutual benefit and win-win is the general strategy for China to follow in the new century. Against the backdrop of globalization, the strategy of opening-up covers not only the economic domain but political sphere as well. Opening-up has already become an important component for

China's participation in international cooperation and competition and also a developmental strategy for the construction of a modern socialist economic power.

(1) Creating the basic principles for China's opening-up in the new era

The mutual benefit and win-win opening-up strategy is the innovation of theory and ideas over the past years of opening-up. It is innovative in its guiding philosophy and in the basic principle for dealing with economic relations between China and the rest of the world. In fact, mutual benefit and win-win are the major trends of foreign policy around the world. To leap from a large country to a large global power, China must be committed to the mutual benefit and win-win opening-up strategy in the long run, and to the basic national policy of opening-up. To improve the economy, China should also develop the opening-up strategy in a broader area and at a higher level.

(2) Tallying with a certain path of economic globalization

China's opening-up goes hand in hand with economic globalization. During the early stage of opening-up, the global production factor flow showed resource complementarities among countries. Back then, the goal of opening-up was to use foreign resources to complement domestic shortage in supply, gradually upgrade the system and the philosophy, and eliminate the mechanism of barriers. Since the 1990s, multinational enterprises have become an important force driving economic integration. The development of international trade and finance enhances economic globalization. At that time, China's opening-up strategy was also adjusted from viewing globalization as an external condition to making full use of such an opportunity to develop China's export-oriented economy. At the beginning of the new century, globalization appeared with some new features. The free flow of production factors has realized complementary advantages among countries, but meanwhile has aggravated the imbalance of world resource allocation and economic development. This brings about the world economy's cyclical fluctuation and crisis. In fact, all countries are bound together for better or for worse. The opening-up strategy for mutual benefit and a win-win situation is the best choice for countries. This demonstrates that globalization has brought countries into an era featured by mutual benefit and a win-win situation. In this new context, China's opening-up must tally with globalization, actively adopt the mutual benefit and win-win strategy, and clarify the new rules that regulate the settlement of economic relations with others. As the white paper titled China's Peaceful Development, issued by the State Council in December 2005, pointed out, "China should tally with globalization and be committed to the strategy for mutual benefit and a win-win situation to appropriately settle trade frictions and promote common development."

(3) Helping improve China's image and responsibility as an economic and trade power

At the early stage of opening-up, China's economic scale was relatively small with limited participation in world economic activities. But with continuous opening-up and an expanded economic scale, China plays a more and more significant role in the world. China is an economic power, and thus its opening-up strategy is not only a national issue of development but also a significant strategic issue that is related to overall development of the global economy.

In the new century, China's economy and society are at a new historical point. The opening-up strategy is now facing different, new problems. An excessive trade surplus, the appreciation of the RMB, and inexpensive exports, in essence, lead to the loss of China's scarce resources and economic benefit. This is not only detrimental to sustainable development, but it also leads to economic or security problems. Hence, China's opening-up is in a dilemma. If it were at the primary stage, China could abandon the policy or make a substantive adjustment. But the fact is that it is at a stage at which China's development cannot go without the rest of the world and vice versa. Putting a halt to the process of opening-up would affect China's image, causing unbearable loss. China, as a large open country, cannot put an end to opening-up according to its own will, because it bears great responsibility for the development of the world economy. The wisest option is to open up in a more active and voluntary way, and shoulder more responsibilities in coordinating domestic and international situation. China should fully consider the influence of its development and open economy on the global economic system, and deal with uncoordinated problems with other countries. Using an opening-up policy and strategy to foster a harmonious and stable international environment could help China as well as the rest of the world to achieve mutually beneficial and win-win development.

(4) Making for a harmonious external environment

The mutual benefit and win-win opening-up strategy is also significant in dealing with international relations. In essence, the strategy is part of China's peaceful development. In terms of its economic meaning, the promotion of this strategy means that China's opening-up has already turned from being adaptive to strategic. That is, China uses the strategy that emphasizes cooperation and complementary strengths to deal with international economic relations. This strategy is conducive to eliminating other countries' worries that China "is a threat." While making full use of the world's resources, China emphasizes the developmental opportunities brought to its trading partners, and addresses international economic frictions with negotiations based on WTO rules instead of retaliation with trade sanctions. With this strategy, China's development is not to compromise others' interests and long-term benefit, but to focus on the sustainability of its opening-up. This is conducive to fostering a stable economic partnership and providing a good external environment for long-term and sustainable economic development.

(5) Conducive to coping with new challenges of globalization and maintaining national economic security

Economic globalization is a double-edged sword. It changed the original division of labor and the scenario of market exchange. On the one hand, it has benefited different countries. On the other hand, it has posed a strong impact on the existing structure of industry and even on national economic security. Likewise, it has brought China both opportunities and challenges for economic development. First, globalization of multinational enterprises increases risks in international resource allocation and also brings new challenges to China's economic security. Second, due to stronger mobility around the globe, there's a lack of experience and effective methods of control over the virtual economy and open capital accounts. Third, in terms of the industrial chain, the insufficient supply of resources and primary products and transportation risks are challenging China's future development. Thus, challenges faced by China's opening-up should be reviewed in a strategic global way, and this pushes China to adopt an innovative mutual benefit and win-win opening-up strategy. By adjusting policy and methods to attract foreign investment and increase foreign trade, China could gradually break the dominance of developed countries in the world's industrial systems, improve its status in the international division of labor, and safeguard national security in globalization.

1.3 Theoretical Exploration of the Mutual Benefit and Win-win Strategy

1.3.1 Theoretical Basis at a Micro Level

The mutual benefit and win-win strategy adopted to address new changes nationally and globally symbolizes a new stage in China's opening-up. Mutual benefit and a win-win situation are the purpose of the strategy. But how can this be achieved? Economics states that mutual benefit and a win-win situation are the result of interactions (exchanges or transactions) between countries, but not a zero-sum game. Its realization is theoretically grounded and leads to common benefit and development of the different parties. Therefore, this book uses the game theory in economics to analyze the strategy, which will help readers understand mutual benefit and win-win status better and provide ideas of how to realize the strategy.

In economics, the interaction between economic men (rational economic entities) is described as transactions. In one transaction, the economic man always chooses the best preference on his list as the rational basis of self-serving behavior. Personal choices always involve the choosing behaviors of others, and the agent may have different roles of choice due to the influence of the others in a group. Sometimes, the agent would be a proxy for the whole group, and sometimes be the true decision-maker for the group. The simplest choice of the economic man is the transaction between two persons, which is a cooperation agreement reached to eliminate external factors, uncertainties, and risk costs. Such an agreement is reached during the transaction process involving repeated negotiations. The following part will briefly state how economic men reach cooperation and agreement after negotiations, which can help elaborate how countries realize a balance that is a mutually beneficial and win-win situation.

Assume that Country A and Country B are rational economic men and have two choices in a transaction in opening-up: cooperation (reaching agreement) and betrayal. Each of them makes its own choice of which the other one has no idea. Now, a game model is formed and called the prisoner's dilemma, meaning that whatever the other side chooses, betrayal can always generate more efficiency or benefit than cooperation can do. Yet, when both parties choose betrayal, there will be less efficiency or revenue than when both parties choose cooperation (see Table 1.1).

In the game of the prisoner's dilemma:

(1) When Country A chooses cooperation, Country B has two choices: cooperation or betrayal. When Country B chooses cooperation, revenue for both countries is $R=3$, that is (3, 3); when Country B chooses betrayal, Country A, which doesn't know it beforehand, chooses the "stupid" cooperation, and it will suffer a loss, with its revenue, $S=0$, but Country B will then smartly gain a revenue, $T=5$, that is (5, 0).

Table 1.1 Prisoner's dilemma

Country B	Country A	
	Cooperation (A1)	Betrayal (A2)
Cooperation (B1)	$R=3, R=3$	$S=0, T=5$
Betrayal (B2)	$T=5, S=0$	$P=1, P=1$

Note: revenue of Behavior Chooser B is listed on the left.

R: revenue from cooperation of both parties. T: benefit from the "smart" choice of the betrayer. S: revenue from the "stupid" choice of the cooperator. P: revenue from betrayal of both parties.

1 Overview of the Theory of Mutual Benefit and Win-win Strategy

(2) When Country A chooses betrayal, the cooperative Country B will suffer a loss, $S=0$, A's revenue $T=5$, that is (0, 5). When B also chooses betrayal, both will suffer a loss, that is (1, 1).

Such a game is often played. When both A and B choose cooperation, both parties benefit, $R=3$. When the two are extremely selfish and want to gain everything from that betrayal but assuming that the other party will cooperate, they will fall into a dilemma, suffering a loss or gaining the minimum revenue only, $P=1$.

After the first round of the game, cooperator A may discover that its loss results from B's betrayal. Then in the second round, A may be very likely to choose betrayal in a retaliating manner, but now B turns to cooperation. Thus, revenues to A and B happen to get exchanged. In the third round, the two parties may both choose betrayal. In the fourth round, the situation may be one of the previous three. Every time A and B will make a choice according to the previous experience, and take the revenue from this new round of the game as part of the previous reward of the game, or take the new round of the game as the revenue weight of the previous game, marked as r ($0<r<1$). That is, revenue from every game will be taken as the discount factor of the reward of the previous game. Assume that in the first round, B gains T due to betrayal; then in the second round, B may be retaliated by A, and B's reward P will be reduced, namely, rP; in the third round, the B's revenue will be r^2P.

Assume that in a repeated game, B's total revenue will be U. When A uses the "retaliatory" strategy, B always betrays A, getting the revenue assumed to be U_B (Betrayal/Retaliation). In n times of the game ($n \geq 1$),

$$U_B(\text{Betrayal/Retaliation})=T+rP+r^2P+\ldots+r^nP$$

$$=T+rP\frac{1-r^n}{1-r} \quad (1\text{-}1)$$

Because $r<1$, $n\to\infty$, taking the extremum, we have:

$$U_B(\text{Betrayal/Retaliation})=T+\frac{rP}{1-r} \quad (1\text{-}2)$$

If B cooperates from the very start, both A and B can benefit:

$$U_{A,\ B}(\text{Cooperation/Cooperation}) = R + rR + r^2 R + \ldots + r^n R$$
$$= R\frac{1-r^{n+1}}{1-r} \quad (1\text{-}3)$$

Take the extremum:
$$U_{A,\ B}(\text{Cooperation/Cooperation}) = \frac{R}{1-r} \quad (1\text{-}4)$$

According to the prisoner's dilemma, we suppose: $T>R>P>S$. When A chooses to permanently retaliate B:
$$\frac{R}{1-r} \geq T + \frac{rR}{1-r} \quad (1\text{-}5)$$

Then we have:
$$r \geq \frac{T-R}{T-P} \quad (1\text{-}6)$$

When B alternately chooses cooperation and betrayal and A chooses retaliation, B's revenue will be:
$$U_B(\text{Alternation/Retaliation}) = T + rS + r^2 T + r^3 S + r^4 T + \ldots + r^{2n-1}S + r^{2n}T$$
$$= T(1 + r^2 + \ldots + r^{2n}) + S(r + r^3 + \ldots + r^{2n-1})$$
$$= T\frac{1-r^{2(n+1)}}{1-r^2} + rS\frac{1-r^{2n}}{1-r^2} \quad (1\text{-}7)$$

Take the extremum:
$$U_B(\text{Alternation/Retaliation}) = \frac{T}{1-r^2} + \frac{rS}{1-r^2}$$
$$= \frac{T+rS}{1-r^2} \quad (1\text{-}8)$$

A will certainly punish B for being capricious, that is:
$$\frac{R}{1-r} \geq \frac{T+rS}{1-r^2} \quad (1\text{-}9)$$

To simplify the formula, we get:
$$r \geq \frac{T-R}{R-S} \quad (1\text{-}10)$$

Capricious B may sometimes be forgiven by A. But if B always betrays A, it may be expelled by A from the transaction deal. So, in the condition that A retaliates, B has the following:
$$\frac{T+rS}{1-r^2} \geq T + \frac{rP}{1-r} \quad (1\text{-}11)$$

To simplify the formula, we get:
$$r \leq \frac{P-S}{T-P} \quad (1\text{-}12)$$

B's behavior incites A's retaliation. After many rounds of the game, they will discover:

$$\frac{R}{1-r} > \frac{T+rS}{1-r^2} > T+\frac{rP}{1-r} \quad (1\text{-}13)$$

S will gradually get cooperation with a reward: $\frac{R}{1-r}$

From A's perspective of treating the cooperative B capriciously, the retaliation factor or the discount factor, r, must be large enough:

When $r \geq \frac{T-R}{T-P}$, the permanent betrayer will turn to cooperation.

When $r \geq \frac{T-R}{R-S}$, the party with inconsistent attitudes will be forced to cooperate.

When $r \geq \frac{P-S}{T-P}$, with insufficient punishment, B may be capricious during cooperation.

In transactions, therefore, the two parties will work toward cooperation finally during the process of cooperation, betrayal, and punishment. Its conditions are as follows. 1) Neither of the parties gives up punishing uncooperative behaviors. When the punishment is severe enough or the factor r is too high for the two parties to conduct transactions, it will deter those countries with uncooperative attitudes or betrayal motivations. 2) Long-term transactions or game will push countries toward cooperation and finally reach a mutually beneficial and win-win situation. 3) Countries would establish just and appropriate international organizations or maintain a certain order. The cooperation and agreement of the two countries is often featured by externality by extending to a third country or even to more and then to a multilateral cooperation. International organizations and orders will gradually come into being, and the punishment against uncooperative behaviors will evolve into treaties, laws, or systems. Therefore, cooperation and international organizations will be formed to realize mutual benefit and a win-win situation.

Some research documents state that globalization provides a real foundation for the realization of mutual benefit and a win-win situation. The basic strategy of countries to realize mutual benefit and a win-win situation is still to return like for like. Countries voluntarily promote the realization of mutual benefit and a win-win situation. Using system innovation of international organizations, countries can expand cooperation benefits in the future and enable the establishment of cooperative relations. Additionally, to provide a good environment for sustainable cooperation, they should actively enhance exchanges in international politics, culture, and education, and uphold the responsible and risk-sharing attitude. Last, systems and mechanisms for communication should be established to improve information support for cooperation, which favors the formation of a mutually beneficial expectation and philosophy.

1.3.2 Evolution of China's Opening-up Philosophy and the Formation of the Mutual Benefit and Win-win Strategy

(1) Primary exploration

At the end of the 1970s, opening-up was still at its exploration and pilot stage. There were several features. First, in terms of the target of opening-up, one group was the Western developed countries, which was mainly for attracting foreign investment and technologies. Another group was the Soviet Union and East European countries, mainly for learning from others' strong points. The third group was developing countries, which would get aid from China to develop their economy. Basically, the philosophy in this period was to open up to all kinds of countries. Second, in terms of the range of opening-up, it started with the economy, and then extended to culture, education, technologies and so on. Third, in terms of the region and order, it started with the southeastern coastal areas, and gradually expanded to inland regions, and finally formed a multi-tiered and all-dimensional scenario of opening-up that covered the areas along the coast, rivers, borders, highways, and large inland cities. China adopted the strategy of experimenting in a small range of cities first and then promoting the experience to the rest of China. It set up the SEZs as the windows and bridges and then opened up the ETDZs. Fourth, in terms of the way to open up the economy, China first took the import substitution strategy by attracting foreign investment and facilities to produce products for daily use that are urgently needed on the domestic market. Then China changed the processing approach to exporting ordinary products to developed countries. Next, China began to export electro-mechanical products of higher technological levels to underdeveloped countries.

(2) Enriching the philosophy

Since the early 1990s, the basic thought in China has promoted the idea of further expanding and improving its opening-up to the rest of the world. First was the task of developing an open economy. China set this as a goal for opening-up, and put forward a policy of establishing a sound but more dynamic and open socialist economic system. Second, China joined WTO and put forward an opening-up strategy to combine "inviting-in" and "going global." By "going global", China actively participated in cooperation and competitions of international economy and technology. Third, China paid strategic significance of safeguarding its national economic security, avoiding and resolving the impact brought by international economic risks.

(3) Formation of the mutual benefit and win-win strategy

When China had comprehensively improved its opening-up, the white book titled China's Peaceful Development, was presented in December 2005, and the central government further clarified the implementation of the mutual benefit and win-win opening-up strategy. In October 2007, the central government put forward the idea of an open economic system that focused on both domestic and international markets, prompted win-win and mutually beneficial cooperation, and emphasized safety and effectiveness. There are several features of this strategy. First is coordination of opening-up and domestic development to promote development with opening-up, and to expand opening-up in continuous development. The second feature is to make improving an open economy the goal of mutual benefit and win-win opening-up. It requires that in opening-up, China should actively participate in and also cultivate new strengths for international economic and technological cooperation and competition. Third, China will emphasize a safe and effective open economic system, strengthen the monitoring and early warning of national economic security for reflecting and addressing crises, and use laws to protect China's overseas capital and security of personnel.

1.3.3 Theoretical Framework of the Economic Opening-up Strategy

The complete strategy for economic opening-up includes the basis, direction and targets, focuses, paths and policies and so on.

(1) The basis of the strategy refers to the domestic and international environment of a country (region), including comprehensive conditions such as the timing to implement supporting strategies, the environment, resources, economic strengths, and the political basis. All these should tally with conditions and trends in world economic development.

(2) The direction of the strategy relates to the contents of opening-up and mainly considers the international trade of goods and services, international investment, including FDI introduction and investment overseas, and economic cooperation.

(3) The targets of the strategy include the overall target and sub-targets. The overall target of the strategy refers to the level of opening-up in a relatively long period of time. It is the priority in the strategy system and determines other contents of the system. In actual opening-up, the targets are mainly expressed by trade dependency, the scale of foreign investment utilization, foreign currency reserve, market openness, market access, and other indicators of economic openness.

(4) Focuses of the strategy are crucial for the implementation of the targets whose realization is effectively guaranteed with more attention paid to the weak links. For instance, although indigenous innovation is the key to economic development, it is China's weakness as well.

(5) The paths and policies needed in order to realize the targets include reforms on opening-up policies and mechanisms, and protection for resources and the ecological environment.

1.4 Directions and Targets of the Mutual Benefit and Win-win Strategy

The mutual benefit and win-win strategy is the general guideline for China's opening-up in the future. Its overall targets are to safeguard and expand the national strategic benefit, to fight for and protect its own legitimate rights and interests, to appropriately deal with beneficial relations with partners, and to strengthen reciprocal cooperation and common development.

1.4.1 The Directions of the Mutual Benefit and Win-win Strategy

Over the past years of reform and opening-up, China has focused on "inviting-in" with less emphasis on "going global." To integrate China's economy into the international system and development of economic operations, the mutual benefit and win-win opening-up strategy basically requires the improvement of the quality of inviting-in, go global voluntarily, and realize a two-way free flow of factors. Opening-up will enable dividends of China's economic development to benefit neighboring and developing countries.

(1) Comprehensively improving the quality of the open economy

China's success over the past years is mainly manifested in the scale and volume of its foreign trade. But the quality and efficiency of its opening-up are not high. The strategy makes it necessary for China to broaden and intensify its opening-up to improve quality. Opening-up has undergone transition from a conventional emphasis on scale to an emphasis on quality and efficiency. First, use foreign investment to promote the optimization and upgrading of the domestic industrial structure. In the new era, China must seize the opportunity of international industrial transfer to effectively utilize foreign investment with an emphasis on improving the utilization quality, introducing advanced foreign technologies, management expertise, and skilled professionals, and promoting the optimization and upgrading of the domestic industrial structure. China should direct foreign investment more toward high-tech and modern service industries, high-end manufacturing, and also toward the old industrial basis in the central and western regions and the northeastern areas. China should implement national treatment to align foreign and domestic policies and create a fair-play market environment. Second, to combine inviting-in and going global, China should focus on introducing technologies, management expertise, and talents, urgently needed on the domestic market to promote industrial upgrading. Additionally, China should guide foreign investors into education, especially professional education and training. Inviting-in also includes introducing human capital and entrepreneurship, and cultivating a large group of Chinese entrepreneurs to enable a better and steadier way of going global. Third, to improve the innovation capabilities of its enterprises, China should pay attention to the absorption, assimilation, amalgamation of the technologies that have been introduced, and to innovation. China should direct and standardize foreign investors' participation in the transformation of the domestic enterprises. It should absorb foreign investment into state-owned enterprise (SOE) reform, improve the structure of corporate governance for modern system development, and push forward the strategic SOE reorganization. Besides, comprehensive indicators should also be focused, on technological levels, domestically supporting proportion, resources consumption, environmental protection, newly created jobs and others.

(2) Optimizing the export structure and promoting balanced trade development

China's long-term export surplus is due to the imbalance between domestic and overseas demands. Depending on the exports to boost economic growth leads to a series of problems like trade frictions, RMB appreciation, and inflation pressures. China should adjust the relations between domestic and overseas demands, actively promote balanced or neutral trade policies, and keep optimizing the export structure. First, China should actively expand its imports to help economic development. The government should issue tax policies that can encourage importing advanced technologies, key facilities and components, scarce domestic resources, and raw materials. Foreign currency reserve should be actively used to import strategic resources and conduct overseas investment, playing its own functions of retaining wealth and gaining benefits. China can make full use of its advantages of an import power, establish a long-term and steady supply-demand relationship with resource exporters, and gradually gain the dominance in importing resources. Second, China should optimize its export structure by guiding enterprises to transform from being quantity-oriented for foreign reserves to quality-oriented for efficiency improvement. It should double its efforts regarding economic, legal, and administrative means, strictly create standards of labor, safety, and the environment, and limit exporting resource commodities that cause high amount of pollution, consume a great amount of energy, but are low in terms of value addition. It should support exports of indigenous high-tech products, machinery and high-value-added labor-intensive products. It should actively explore non-conventional exports to diversify the market. By enhancing dynamic monitor of the prices and quantity of their exports, industry associations should establish a foreign trade promotion and regulation system that is quality- and efficiency-oriented. Third, to accelerate the transformation and upgrading of the processing of trade, China should improve the level of its industrial policies and depth of their processing capacity. By enhancing supporting capabilities, China will upgrade domestic industries. Fourth, China should double its efforts to reform the mechanism of the service industry. It should proactively expand the open areas, eliminate trade barriers, and promote the development of trade in services. Foreign investment should be encouraged in software development, cross-border outsourcing, and logistic services, and international service transfer should be undertaken in an orderly way.

(3) Actively implementing the strategy of "going global"

The strategy of "going global" has a great significance. It favors optimizing resource allocation, improves the international competitiveness of enterprises, and enables the host country to share the opportunities brought by China such as taxes, revenues in foreign currency, and job creation. This also provides a good chance for China to commit to mutual benefit and win-win opening-up. During this new historic stage, China should proactively implement the strategy of "going global," participate in international division of labor and competition at a higher level, and expand its room for development. First, China should further improve the policies and measures for enterprises to go global and provide good conditions to invest and operate overseas. With advantageous industries as a focus, China will guide companies to conduct overseas processing trade and promote production diversification. Second, China should expand its cooperation of resource development overseas. China will keep improving cooperation mechanisms with countries in Africa, Latin America, and with its neighbors, which have important strategic significance, and actively conduct bilateral and multilateral strategic cooperation regarding energy and resources. By doing so, China will reduce the risks from over dependency on resource import in a conventional way. When dealing with disputes on territories and resources of territorial seas, China should advocate the idea of setting aside disputes and developing in joint manner, and meanwhile should discuss feasible ways of joint resource development. Third, China should encourage overseas engineering contract and labor export. China should encourage companies to get involved in the construction of overseas infrastructures and develop labor cooperation on a regular basis. Fourth, China should intensify its reforms of overseas investors' property rights and distribution systems, and help to develop indigenous cross-border enterprises. Using the methods like cross-border merger and acquisition, buying of shares, overseas listing, and reorganization and alliance, China will establish a modern enterprise system that is in line with international common practices. Fifth, China should further enhance the service system for foreign investment. China should streamline its approval procedures for overseas investments, improve its registration system, and ease limitations. To practically safeguard the national economic security, China should improve the mechanism of overseas investment coordination, its guarantee system, and its risk and asset management.

(4) Actively conducting international economic cooperation and enhancing the construction of FTAs

In the situation of rapidly developing globalization, bilateral and multilateral economic cooperation and FTAs are already inclined toward politics and diplomacy, rapidly changing the world scenario regarding economy and politics. At the dawn of the transformation of the opening-up strategy, China should deal with economic relations on the basis of mutual benefit and a win-win situation, better participate in bilateral and multilateral economic activities, and expand regional economic cooperation. First, to avoid intensifying conflicts, China should appropriately deal with economic relations with major trading partners like Europe, the United States, Japan, and Russia, resolve disputes and disagreements on the basis of cooperation and a win-win situation, and flexibly use consultations, dialogues, and mechanisms of cooperation forums. Second, to realize mutual benefit and a win-win situation, China should actively develop economic and technological cooperation with the rest of the world, especially neighboring countries. China should give more aid to developing countries and become actively involved in making rules in multilateral trade and investments. Third, China should actively develop a new scenario of regional economic cooperation, and promote the establishment and development of FTAs. Theoretically, according to its developmental stage, regional economic integration can be divided into preferential trade arrangements, FTAs, customs unions, common markets, and complete economic integration. FTAs are more open than preferential trade arrangements, and have currently become an important way for countries to conduct strategic cooperation and competition. On the basis of equality and mutual benefit and by pursuing practical results in diversified ways of cooperation, China will focus on developing FTAs with neighboring regions, resource-abundant areas, major export markets, and strategic partners so as to construct a global network of economic cooperation.

(5) Accelerating the opening-up of China's inland areas to the outside world

The regional imbalance of opening-up affects the overall opening-up in China. Inland areas, including the border areas, are late-comers and have a slow pace of opening-up. In the domestic and international economic situation, the acceleration of opening-up is a must. Hence, to comprehensively improve its overall opening-up, China decided to further open coastal, inland, and border areas, and achieve the common promotion of internal and external opening-up. The strategic focus in coastal areas lies in quality, with a purpose of realizing the transformation from a processing center for international manufacturing to a center for research and development, logistics, and trade in services. Accelerating opening-up in China's inland necessitates speed. It requires these areas to keep upgrading conventional concepts and economic institutions in order to create an appropriate environment. It also needs to optimize an environment that will attract domestic and foreign investment into the upstream of processing the trade industry and also into rejuvenating the manufacturing industry. Improving the opening-up of the border areas focuses on ways and contents. It requires a change from a single pattern to diversified patterns, from low- to high-end opening-up, from unilateral to multilateral trade, from FTAs with a single country to a trade and economic cooperation area with several countries. Through this comprehensive opening-up, China could address the uncoordinated regional development through the free flow and allocation of production factors in a broader area such as the Yangtze River Delta and the Pearl River Delta.

1.4.2 The Targets of the Mutual Benefit and Win-win Strategy

In the new era, the strategy requires improving a safe and highly effective open economy that has good connections between domestic and international markets on the basis of mutual benefit and a win-win situation. This is the new goal for the open economy in the new era. Connection means that the expansion of opening-up goes hand in hand with the deepening of reform. Those outdated domestic economic institutions should be further eliminated to safeguard the expansion of opening-up and realize a highly effective open economy.

(1) Establishing a new institution for an open economy

Experience over the past years shows that further openness cannot move ahead without reform of domestic institutions. The mutual benefit and win-win strategy requires a new institution for an open economy. This needs to innovatively improve the domestic institutions and maintain China's unilateral, bilateral, and multilateral trade mechanism. First, China should innovatively utilize the management system of foreign investment. This involves managerial innovation of the related industries and requires taking approaches like national treatment before admission and a negative list to manage foreign investment. Second, for overseas investments, China should innovate the supervisory system, ease different restrictions, and actively eliminate barriers in terms of approval procedures, foreign currency management, financial services, and people moving across borders. Third, China should innovate its mechanism to promote technology diffusion, protect intellectual property rights, and monitor the free flow of human factors. Fourth, China should construct a management mechanism that emphasizes the function of society and alleviates the control of government, in which process and postmortem supervision should be enhanced. Fifth, China should improve its regulatory governance to supervise economic behavior, by improving the legal system and strengthening institutional regulations, while reducing policy control.

(2) Continuing to improve the open economic system

Opening-up is a system that involves rights as principal, open areas, and opening levels. It should be a complete and coordinated system. In terms of rights as principal, China should clarify enterprises and individuals as the dominant market position, and allow them to conduct legal economic activities. State-owned, private, and foreign enterprises or individuals—no matter what they are—should all be given national treatment. Meanwhile, industrial associations, chambers of commerce, and NGOs should play their own role in setting standards, regulating industries, and expanding international markets. In terms of open areas, China should implement the negative list, focusing on the opening-up of services in finance, education, culture, medical care, and easing restrictions on foreign investments in pensions, architecture design, accounting, audit, commercial logistics, and e-commerce. In terms of the levels, China should expand its opening-up in each industrial chain link and also in different service modes and branches. Access conditions and standards need to be reduced, and barriers to trade in services should be further eliminated.

(3) Establishing a new pattern for opening-up

An open economy is an economic system involving the two-way flow of products and factors. China is now fostering this new scenario of an open economy designed to promote the orderly free flow of factors, thus realizing highly efficient resource allocation and promoting in-depth integration of domestic and international markets. China should consolidate the leading position of its eastern coastal areas and national megalopolis, expand its opening-up to its inland areas, and allow the Yangtze River Delta, the Pearl River Delta and the Bohai Rim to play an important role as an open door. Establishing an international passageway should be promoted in China's inland, while collaboration and facilitation in customs clearance should be improved in inland, coastal, and border areas. To promote the opening-up of the rest of the world to China, a new mechanism for going global should be established. This not only requires the enhancement of the conventional market in developed countries, but it also needs expansion in emerging economies. China should enhance its cooperation with neighboring regions and form a new pattern of two-way opening-up. There should be further innovation in the opening-up policy to allow for facilitated flows of logistics, personnel exchanges and tourism in ports and cities along the border and economic cooperation areas. By implementing the Silk Road Economic Belt and the 21st Century Maritime Silk Road, China can enhance regional cooperation while taking care of bilateral and multilateral relations, and form a new pattern of opening-up that leads to international cooperation and competition.

2

The Value Chain of the International Division of Labor and China's Trade Interests

2.1 The Basic Theory and the Definition of "Virtuality" of International Trade Interests

2.1.1 The Concept of International Trade Interests

International trade interests refer to the increased benefits of a country from foreign trade, including both direct and indirect trade interests. The trade interest is achieved through international exchanges. The direct trade interest of a country includes two aspects: the export interest and the import interest, which are embodied in their savings of the labor productivity, the expansion of the scale of production, and the guidance in the growth of new industries and other aspects. The indirect trade interest refers to the promotion of economic growth and the improvement of a country's comprehensive national strength and people's welfare through the impact of foreign trade on technological progress, the adjustment of the industrial structure, and the role of market competition.

In reality, direct trade interest is more concerned with the micro level, such as enterprise labor productivity, product differentiation and so on. The indirect trade interest often involves macro-level economic development, such as sustained and healthy economic development. In free trade, it is possible to accumulate indirect trade interest only if it is obtained from direct trade interest. In the short term, direct trade and indirect trade interests often conflict. A country often achieves a long-term indirect trade interest by protecting infant industries, sacrificing immediate direct interests. Especially within global distribution of the industrial value chain, it resulted in the globalization of trade interest production and the nationalization of trade interest allocation. The comparative advantage of trade is a kind of potential interest, because the comparative advantage of a country is not necessarily to be enjoyed by its own citizens. For China, the foreign technology and brand may restrict the advantage of China's labor force. China, with the dominant factor of its labor force, participates in the international division of labor. However, a labor-intensive industry cannot become the leading industry to upgrade the scene in the industrial sector. There is a contradiction between direct and indirect trade interests.

In the case of the deepening of the international division of labor, if a country's production elements in international trade do not have control of the industrial chain, its actual distribution of interest in foreign trade will be less than the trade volume of the nominal trade interests. There will be the problem of "virtuality" of trade interests. Therefore, it is necessary to improve the control of the elements in the industrial chain, so that direct trade interests can be effectively converted into indirect trade interests, in order to promote China's economic growth and improve people's well-being.

2.1.2 The Definition of "Virtuality" of Trade Interests

The "virtuality" of trade interests refers to a kind of phenomenon that with the deepening of the international division of labor and the global distribution of the industrial value chain, a country's actual distribution of interest in foreign trade will be far less than the trade volume of the nominal trade interests; even the actual trade interest is not enough to compensate the value of the raw material and the expenses of environmental pollution control brought by manufacturing, which hinders indirect trade interests to be achieved. This phenomenon is mainly caused by different production processes in the product value chain, which is distributed to different countries. This new pattern of division of labor has caused the redistribution of trade interests in the global industrial value chain. If a country's elements of foreign trade in the international industrial value chain do not have the ability to control the industrial chain, then the value of the element in the product is in a smaller proportion and it will face the problem of "virtuality" of trade interests. Especially in the case of increasing international investment, transnational corporations allocate different production processes of products to the world's most appropriate area. They can avoid taxes and artificially reduce the profit margins of processing trade enterprises through internal transfer pricing. And also through outsourcing, they put production and processing with high input, pollution, and energy consumption in developing countries, resulting in the "virtuality" phenomenon of trade interests of developing countries.

In the international division of labor, China, with its rich elements of labor makes full use of the comparative advantage, while the input of the elements lacks the control of the industrial chain. A vast majority of goods in international trade is under the leadership of multinational corporations. The actual distribution of trade interests is necessarily less than the nominal trade interests of foreign trade. Therefore, China needs to gradually cultivate technology, brand, and other aspects of its competitive advantage in the process of foreign trade, and use all kinds of effective ways that comply with international conventions and rules to convert this comparative advantage from potential interests into practical interests so as to promote the harmonious development of trade and economy.

2.1.3 Review and Analysis of the Theories of International Trade Interests

(1) The classical theory of international trade interests

① Study on the trade interests from different perspectives

First, from the perspective of supply, study the theory of trade interests:

The first one is the mercantilist theory of trade interests. There are deviations from mercantilism in understanding the sources of trade interests. In the mercantilist theory, trade interests are the monetary form of increased wealth. Exploration of trade interests of mercantilism is confined to the field of circulation, but it does not go deep into the field of production.

Second is Adam Smith's theory of absolute advantage. Adam Smith believed trade interests come from the expansion of the division of labor. The degree of division of labor is restricted by the scope of the market. Foreign trade is a significant symbol of the expansion of the market; so the expansion of foreign trade must be able to promote the deepening of the division of labor and improve labor productivity, and it must be able to create more trade interests. Adam Smith studied trade interests from the perspective of the transition from circulation to production. He believed that if every country can specialize in products with absolute interests, and then exchange with each other, it is beneficial to all sides. Adam Smith put forward the vent for surplus model, which includes the initial thought that international trade has driven economic growth, the bud of indirect trade interests, which enlightened latter economists. The progress of Adam Smith's theory of international trade interests compared with the mercantilist theory of trade interests lies in the fact that he realized that the root of trade interests is the increase in labor productivity and the growth of material wealth. But Adam Smith did not explain the case in which if all of the productive sectors of a country compared with other countries are at a disadvantage, whether or not it is necessary for this country to participate in international trade.

The last one is David Ricardo's theory of comparative advantage. Ricardo further developed Adam Smith's theory of trade interests. Ricardo explained that international trade can also produce trade interests, in the case that all of the productive sectors of a country are at an advantage, or in the case that they are at a disadvantage compared with other countries. He developed Adam Smith's theory of absolute advantage into the theory of comparative advantage. The shortcomings of the theory of comparative advantage lie in the assumption that production specifications remain unchanged, and thus, labor productivity remains unchanged, and no matter what a country now exports and imports, it can only follow and repeat this pattern. To study international division of labor and international trade in such a static condition, that the countries participating in trade can obtain comparative interests is not in conformity with the facts. From a practical point of view, the status of a country in international division of labor can be changed, which leads to the basic changes of comparative interests and because of which the pattern of international trade will change.

Second, from the perspective of demand, study the theory of trade interests:

John Mill's equation of reciprocal demand (equation of international demand) provides an explanation for a country's interests in participating in the international trade from the perspective of demand. The equation of international demand he made is based on the assumption that any country in increasing demand of its output of goods will enable the country to get input goods at a lower price, even if the input items are from elsewhere. Otherwise, when other conditions assumed still remain, if the demand of the country for the commodities from any other economy increases, it means that a higher price will be paid for all foreign goods. Furthermore, he put forward the conclusion that the terms of trade depend on the intensity and elasticity of demand.

Third, from both the perspectives of demand and supply, study the theory of trade interests:

Marshall insisted that demand and supply are equally important in determining the terms of international trade and the structure of trade, and the benefits of foreign trade should be measured from the perspectives of the structure and strategy of trade. He pointed out that demand pushes forward the development of trade simply because it is built on the basis of the country's correct supply of goods to other countries with the starting point of its demand for foreign goods as well.

② Promotion from direct trade interests to indirect trade interests

Mill took the lead in clearly distinguishing the direct and indirect benefits of trade as the master of classical economics. And this distinction, that is, Mill's distinction greatly inspired the subsequent economists in their understanding of the benefits of trade from the point of view of indirect trade benefits, promoting the static interests of trade to the dynamic. But Mill's indirect interests are naturally caused by direct interests.

Friedrich List's discussion of the indirect interests of trade is more thorough than Mill's. He argued that the interests of trade in economic development are more significant than the direct returns.

(2) The neoclassical theory of international trade benefit

The neoclassical international trade theory still sticks to the assumption of the classical international trade theory that the market is totally competitive and no scale economy exists. Neoclassical economists use a new analysis tool—production possibility frontier (PPF) and its geometric curve to explain international trade motives in different situations of changing opportunity cost, namely, gaining international trade interests by pursuing opportunity cost. It expands international trade motives in the condition of constant opportunity cost that was affirmed by David Ricardo.

The Heckscher-Ohlin factor endowment theorem (H-O theory) indicates that in a nation, only products that are exported—intensive areas use their rich production factors to produce—and products that are imported—intensive areas use their scarce production factors to produce—are able to gain international trade benefits. This theory answers the questions related to the cost differences that exist when various countries produce the same kind of product. This theory is the further development of David Ricardo's comparative advantage theory. Wassily W. Leontief adopts the input-output method to study the American foreign trade commodity composition. His conclusion is widely divergent from this theory, namely, "Leontief's Paradox." Many economists interpret this phenomenon in many ways such as revising the H-O theory, extending production factors of single labor from Ricardo and double factors from the H-O theory for total factors, considering the product as the outcome of concurrent multiple factors, and putting forth the viewpoint that factor productivity decides comparative cost advantages and factor endowment advantages can substitute each other. The H-O theory neglects the influence of demand, technical differences, scale economy, and other factors.

The neoclassical trade benefit theory is the static analysis of the mutual advantages of trade. It mainly focuses on the increasing trade volume and on the amount of consumption in international exchange of micro commodities; that is, it is based on the view of value in use. Whether to pursue opportunity cost or utilize resource endowment, the effective allocation of international resources is achieved through trade among countries so as to increase the level of benefits with a global perspective. Some macro problems are mentioned, but the whole analysis is still limited to the commodity itself.

(3) The new trade benefit theory

Faced with a new international trade environment, the trade benefit theory continues to develop. The new trade theory absorbs reasonable factors of the traditional trade theory and inspects trade benefit due to scale economy, imperfect competition of the market, and other factors. The new trade theory develops static trade benefits into dynamic ones.

① Trade benefits arising from scale economy

The American economist Paul Krugman proposed the trade theory of scale economy in the 1970s. This theory, based on the scale economy and the imperfect competition of the world market in the production of enterprises, interprets trade within the same industry among rapidly growing industrial countries after World War II. It held that international trade benefits exist in scale economy, as well as resource endowment and technical gap. When two countries produce the same two kinds of products, the price is high and efficiency is low owing to small scale; if two countries divide the work and each produce one product, then the scale of the two kinds of products is expanded at the same time, production efficiency improves, and production costs reduces. This is the benefit of scale economy. Then each country exports part of its products to the other to realize the benefit of scale economy. This will bring greater benefits than no trade or each producing two kinds of products. Trade benefit refers to the benefit deriving from scale economy realized through international trade.

② Trade benefits arising from differentiated products

The trade theory of differentiated products stresses that the trade of the same or similar products among different countries, namely, intra-industry trade, can also bring trade benefits. These benefits come from more specific international divisions. On the basis of the international division of differentiated products, developing intra-industry trade may not only improve the scale of production and gain the benefit of a scale economy, but it may also satisfy consumers' diversified demand for the same product and demand for different levels of consumption for the same or similar products. The trade theory of differentiated products considers the satisfaction of consumers' needs as a kind of trade benefit. This is a kind of deep understanding of what trade benefits are and this theory also means that various countries have space to show their technology or creative advantages fully. They can make innovations in brand, quality, performance, packaging, advertisement, and after-sales services, thereby providing a condition for the expansion of trade benefits.

③ Trade benefits arising from strategic trade policies of nations

Many scholars like Grossman, James A. Brand, and Dixit, on the premise of scale economy and imperfect competition, use the industry organization theory and market structure theory as research tools and put forward the strategic trade policy theory. It advocates that the government should strengthen the competitive status of domestic merchants and expand the market share of domestic merchants in the international market through import protection tools such as tariffs, quota and so on, as well as export promotion policies of export subsidies and so on. This theory also stresses the importance of an external economy in international division based on specialization. It advocates that the government should properly support industries, which may produce a giant external economy. This theory upsets the optimality of the free trade policy on the condition of a scale economy and imperfect competition, it proves the reasonability of government intervention, it points out some strategic behavior that the government should change or maintain imperfectly competitive enterprises through some means of intervention, and that it makes international trade go forward in favor of the maximum benefit gained by one's own country, and thus describes the role of government in the realization of foreign trade benefits.

④ Trade benefits arising from technological advance

Technological advance has become an important factor of gaining indirect trade benefits, and related theories of technological advance and trade benefits produced by it are as follows: First, Krugman's theory of technology transfer. This theory points out that developing countries increase the types of commodities with comparative advantages and gain more comparative benefits by speeding up the introduction of technology. Second, Posner's theory of technological gap. It also points out that the enlargement of the technological gap is conducive to technology transfer among countries, and makes the technology exporter gain earnings from its exportatims of technology, and the technology importer improves labor efficiency and gains benefits through the utilization of technology. Third, the endogenetic growth model of technology proposed by Romer, Grossman, Helpman, Segerstrom, Krugman, and others. It holds that both learning by doing and R & D may endogenously produce technology and thus affect the trade model and produce trade benefits. Fourth, the product life cycle theory proposed by Vernon. It discusses that foreign trade may bring trade benefits for one nation from the view that foreign trade may adjust the life cycle of the product. Comparative advantages of one nation vary with the constant production of new products, and a trade benefit exists in dynamic comparative advantages. The enlightenment of these researches regarding the development of China's foreign trade is that benefits gained from international trade depend on the degree of technological advance of one's own country. Therefore, the main benefit of China is sharing limited resources and extremely uneven technology and human resources in the world for the result of technological innovation rather than gaining a wider market.

⑤ Trade benefit arising from competitive advantages of nations

The competitive advantage theory proposed by Michael Porter in 1991 is also incorporated into the new trade theory. The core of this theory is improving the competitiveness of one nation and enhancing the people's welfare by determining a competitive industry and innovating competitive advantages. More specifically, the competitive advantage theory of Michael Porter mainly includes the following factors. First, production factors. They include basic factors and promotion factors. Basic factors mean congenital factors of one nation; promotion factors are factors innovated through investment and development. Second, demand status. The domestic market finds fault with certain products in related industries and has a prospective demand, which is good for this nation to build an international competitive advantage over other nations. Third, related and supporting industries. The related industries of one nation should understand the activities and needs of the others and coordinate and cooperate. Fourth, strategy, structure, and competition of enterprises. In addition, Porter considers there are two additional factors, namely, opportunity and the government. The breakthrough and innovation of some technology, the oil crisis, wars, and the fluctuation of exchange rates are considered opportunities. The government can affect the basic factors of competitive advantages of its nation through a related system of economic management, a financial system, investments and so on. Porter's theory does not contradict to the comparative advantage theory. Comparative advantages are the basis and premise of competitive advantages. Only if one gives play to comparative advantages, will competitive advantages be formed.

The new trade benefit theory not only pays attention to trade benefits from the point of view of supply, but also analyzes trade benefits from the point of view of demand. The new trade benefit theory is the inheritance and development of the traditional trade theory. It develops international trade from "making up deficiencies" or by the exportation of residual products into objective requirements of economic development of many countries. It studies how one nation gains trade benefits by virtue of scale economy, technological advance, and product differences.

(4) Marx's trade profit theory

According to Marx's international value theory, trade benefit derives from the comparative differences between domestic value and international value. That is, $V_{d1}/V_{d2} < V_{w1}/V_{w2}$. Of them, V_{d1} and V_{d2} show the domestic value of commodities 1 and 2 respectively, and V_{w1} and V_{w2} show the international value of commodities 1 and 2 respectively. Take appropriate commodity units to enable $V_{w1}=V_{w2}$ and the exchange process of commodities is V_{d1}/V_{d2}. Because $V_{w1}/V_{w2}=1$, we get $V_{d1}<V_{d2}$. This formula shows that the national value of import commodity 2 is larger than that of export commodity 1. This is the value-added of the national value that international trade can bring about.

Marx not only studies trade benefits from the point of view of production, but also pays great attention to demand. He points out, "That the commodity value transfer from the body of commodity to value is the adventurous leap of commodity as mentioned elsewhere. If this leap is unsuccessful, it destroys the possessor of the commodity rather than the commodity. " Therefore, foreign trade is conducive to the realization of the commodity value. Thus, it plays an important role in balancing two major categories of society in various countries, thereby implying that importing resource raw material can relieve the restriction of the resource bottleneck of one nation and is conducive to the realization of the trade benefit of one nation.

(5) The international trade benefit theory of developing countries

Many developmental economists think the quantity, quality, and allocation of capital, technology, labor force, and other production factors play a decisive role in the economic development of a nation. Through international trade, the quantity of production factors may be increased, the quality of production factors may be improved, and resources are allocated reasonably. Therefore, international trade is good for solving the problem of undercapitalization and lag in technology in developing countries. However, those economists also contemplate whether or not poverty will increase in developing countries through the trade pattern of exporting labor-intensive and resource-intensive products. In this context, the developmental economists Prebish and Singer proposed the theory of terms of trade deterioration in 1950. This theory advocates that since the change of trade terms will be affected by demand elasticity of both parties for products, international division and trade advocated by the traditional trade theory will cause trade conditions that are unfavorable to developing countries. The specific reasons are as follows. On the one hand, developed countries utilize technological innovation to gain monopoly profits easily owing to abundant capital, powerful R & D, and comparatively less resource consumption. Therefore, foreign trade is more favorable to developed countries. On the other hand, the supply and demand elasticity of manufactured products is larger when compared to that of primary goods; developed countries that produce and export manufactured products can gain an increasing return effect by their increasing production and export scales and produce a scale economy by utilizing foreign investments more easily.

(6) Latest development of the trade benefit theory

With the development of the implementation of international divisions, the hysteretic trade benefit theory has not been able to interpret the distribution of trade benefits in different production links of products, namely, different links in the value chain. Especially when intra-product specialization appears, that is, when different working procedures or sections are distributed in different countries and economic entities, there is a redistribution of trade benefits.

The research on the industrial value chain in management science indicates that industrial chain profit appears as a "V" shape, called the "smile curve" (Figure 2.1). It analyzes the value-added of each section in the industrial chain with a smile curve. In the system of factor division in the situation of global distribution of the industrial value chain, it is possible for most enterprises to become a link in the multinational corporation industrial chain. According to the smile curve, profit from R & D and brand is the greatest, and processing and manufacturing links are located at the lowest end of the whole value chain. If a nation wants to gain more trade benefits, it should focus on processing and manufacturing links, but transfer to parts and equipment in the upstream of the industrial chain and sales and network in the downstream of the industrial chain. At present, multinational corporations usually outsource processing and manufacturing links to enterprises in developing countries, while most of the links require resources. In this situation, China will face a resource bottleneck, consistent with the sustainable development of China. China just gains a small profit from a cheap labor force and resources in the manufacturing link.

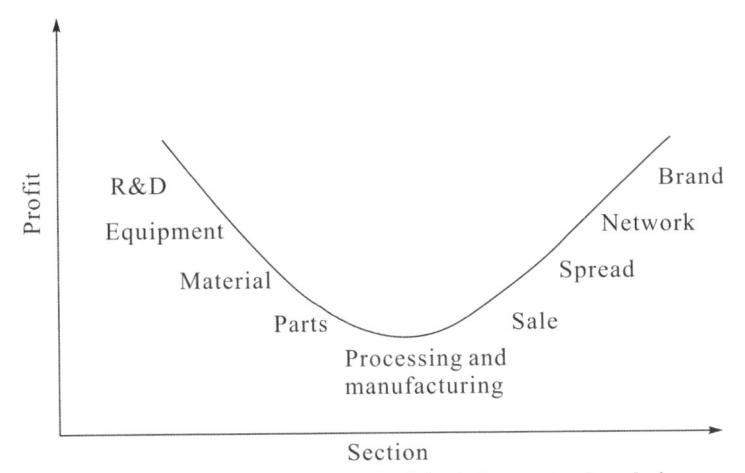

Figure 2.1 The "smile curve" of the industrial value chain

In the research on international trade, the influence of the phenomenon that different working procedures or sections are dispersed to different countries and economic entities on international trade benefits is also studied. Because the implementation period of this phenomenon is short, no complete and systematic theory about the distribution of trade benefits among countries in the same value chain has been formed.

Dixit and Grossman developed the production section model, expanded the model into a multi-stage production model, and utilized the model to consider the impact of structure change and policy change on the comparative advantage of one nation. Thus, the research on intra-product specialization affecting the trade benefits of one nation was started.

Later on, Krugman analyzed the influence of intra-product specialization on the trade benefits of different types of nations. He described intra-product specialization as "slicing up the value chain," and analyzed the impact of southern countries on northern countries under the system of intra-product specialization in a global perspective; meanwhile, he drew a conclusion that the rise of southern countries and their status in the global value chain will not endanger the economic benefit of northern countries. International division of production sections is a win-win process.

Deardorff analyzed the influence of intra-product specialization on national welfare specialization, trade modes, and factor prices. Deardorff used the Ricardian model and the H-O model to analyze small-size open economy of two nations, respectively. If production process separation does not change the price of commodities, the output value of both nations will increase; if production process separation changes the price of commodities, the welfare of one nation will deteriorate because the trade condition has become unfavorable; even if one nation benefits from production process separation, the possessors of some factors of this nation may probably be impaired; production process separation is the impetus for the equalization of factor prices.

There is less research on intra-product trade benefits by China's scholars. Tian Wen used an expansive Ricardian model to discuss the decision of the trade mode on the condition of intra-product specialization, utilized the longitudinal market relationship of the industry organization theory to discuss intra-product specialization and the distribution of trade benefits, and finally explained that developing countries need to conduct intra-product specialization based on comparative advantages. If they want to improve trade earnings further, they must constantly adjust their status in the specialization chain.

Cao Mingfu & Li Shumin established the three-country model of intra-product specialization. Through model analysis, they achieved the following. The source of benefit from global value chain specialization is first a "specialization benefit" and second a "trade benefit." All participants can gain a "specialization benefit" from global value chain specialization, but not all of them can gain a "trade benefit." The most developed country not only gains a "specialization benefit," but also occupies the "trade benefit" of other countries; backward countries can gain a "specialization benefit" from global value chain specialization, but their "trade benefit" may be negative. In addition, they discussed the profit and loss of the "cost benefit" of trading nations when international trade increased the "product benefit" of both parties in the trade. They thought the "cost benefit" of advanced countries given by international division and trade based on comparative advantages must be positive, and the "cost benefit" of backward countries must be negative. Their research has important theoretical value to the research on trade benefit change arising from intra-product specialization, but the model is too simple and hasn't been tested through empirical research.

2.2 Presentation of the Benefit "Virtuality" of China's Foreign Trade

The proportion of China's export trade volume in world cargo trade has leaped from the 32nd place in 1978 to the first place in 2009. However, factors that influence China's participation in the international division do not have the ability of controlling the industrial chain; the nominal trade benefit shown by trade volume has a certain "virtuality." That "virtuality" is expressed in the foreign trade commodity composition, foreign trade market structure, foreign trade mode, and foreign trade mainstay.

2.2.1 Presentation of Benefit "Virtuality" in the Commodity Composition of China's Foreign Trade

Foreign trade commodity composition refers to the proportion or status of various commodities in the foreign trade of a nation or a region during a certain period. Foreign trade commodity composition can reflect the level of economic and technological development, industrial structure, and resource situation of a nation or a region. Foreign trade commodities can be classified into primary products and manufactured products based on the processing degree of products. The proportion of primary product exportation in gross exports is declining year by year (see Table 2.1, Figure 2.2, and Figure

2.3). It declined from 50.30% in 1980 to 5.25% in 2009. The proportion of primary product importation in gross imports has remained at about 20% for many years, and has the tendency of increasing year by year. The proportion of manufactured product exportation in gross exports increased from 49.70% in 1980 to 94.75% in 2009. The proportion of manufactured product importation in gross imports was stable during that period at about 80%. Is this structure reasonable?

Table 2.1 Proportion of primary products and manufactured products of China

Year	Proportion of primary product exportation in gross exports	Proportion of primary product importation in gross imports	Proportion of manufactured product exportation in gross exports	Proportion of manufactured product importation in gross imports
1980	50.30%	34.77%	49.70%	65.23%
1985	50.56%	12.52%	49.44%	87.48%
1990	25.59%	18.47%	74.41%	81.53%
1995	14.44%	18.49%	85.56%	81.51%
2000	10.22%	20.76%	89.78%	79.24%
2001	15.24%	18.78%	90.10%	81.22%
2002	8.77%	16.69%	91.23%	83.31%
2003	7.94%	17.63%	92.06%	82.37%
2004	6.83%	20.89%	93.17%	79.11%
2005	6.44%	22.38%	93.56%	77.62%
2006	5.46%	23.64%	94.53%	76.30%
2007	5.05%	25.42%	94.95%	74.58%
2008	5.45%	32.00%	94.55%	68.00%
2009	5.25%	28.76%	94.75%	71.24%

Source: Data of 1980 to 2004 are from *China Statistical Yearbook (2005)*, and data of 2005, 2006, 2007, 2008, and 2009 are from the website of the Ministry of Commerce.

According to an input-output model, Shen Lisheng and Wu Zhenyu worked out the influence coefficient and driving force coefficient of various industries in China, and compared them with the influence of export products and the driving force of import products. They found the export product influence order is not totally consistent with the influence coefficient order, and the import product driving force order is not totally consistent with the driving force coefficient order. It indicates that the structure of export products and that of import products still have room for improvement toward a more reasonable structure. Meanwhile, this import and export structure also indicates that China is merely a large trade nation and that nominal trade benefits presented by the export and import trade volume are not totally reflected in the adjustment of the industrial structure. Whether primary products or manufactured products, the export proportion varies greatly, and the import proportion is stable. It indicates that the export structure of China adjusts rapidly with the international industrial transfer. China is only a "world factory"; China engages in the international industrial chain through processing and assembly for exportation. The deep processing of manufactured goods is insufficient, while China has a stable demand for primary products and manufactured products of foreign countries. China still needs to import advanced machines and equipment and many other high-value-added intermediate input products. China's factor input does not have a strong controlling force of the industrial chain, and trade benefits gained during the past years since reform and opening-up is limited.

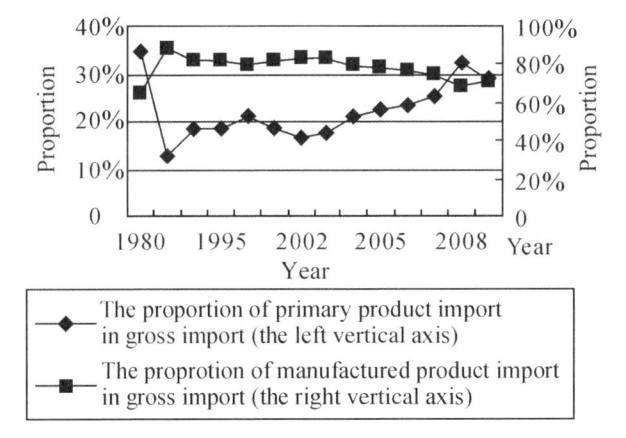

Figure 2.2 Change in the structure of import products

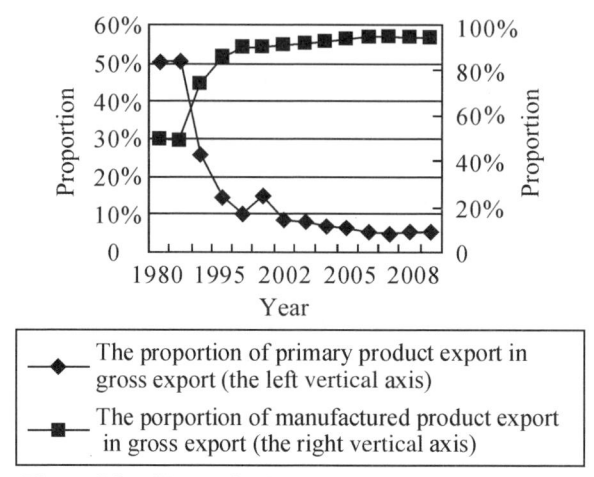

Figure 2.3 Change in the structure of export products

From the perspective of primary products segmentation, since 1990, the proportion of food and the main edible live animals in primary product exportation has been about 50%. Such products mainly depend on labor input rather than land or natural resource reserves. It indicates that the advantage of China is its labor force. The proportion of non-edible raw materials and mineral fuel, lubricating oil, and related raw materials is larger, accounting for more than 50% of the primary product imports. Especially since entering the new century, the proportion has remained at about 90%. It indicates that the resource reserves of China cannot meet the needs of its economic development. Economic development is restricted by a resource bottleneck, and China still needs to import a large quantity of resource products like raw materials and so on (see Table 2.2). The quantity of raw materials imported by China is large and this may cause an increase in the price of imported raw materials and a deterioration in trade conditions. China overpaid by $24.93 billion for imported petroleum, steel, iron ore, cotton, copper concentrate, potassium ore and aluminum oxide due to an increase in the international market price. And due to the fierce competition of labor-intensive product exports of China, especially on the present condition of a decreasing international demand, the price of such commodities has declined year by year, which even causes most small and medium-sized export businesses to go into insolvency in China, squeezes the trade benefits gained by China, and fails to realize the mutual benefit and win-win result in foreign trade.

Table 2.2 Proportion of imports and exports of China's various primary products in total imports and total exports

Year	Food and main edible live animals		Beverages and cigarettes		Non-edible raw materials		Mineral fuel, lubricating oil, and related raw materials		Animal and plant grease and wax	
	Exports	Imports	Exports	Imports	Exports	Imports	Exports	Imports	Exports	Imports
1980	32.8%	42.1%	0.9%	0.5%	18.8%	51.1%	47.0%	2.9%	0.7%	3.4%
1985	27.5%	29.4%	0.8%	3.9%	19.2%	61.2%	51.6%	3.3%	1.0%	2.3%
1990	41.6%	33.8%	2.2%	1.6%	22.3%	41.7%	33.0%	12.9%	1.0%	10.0%
1995	46.3%	25.1%	6.4%	1.6%	20.4%	41.6%	24.8%	21.0%	2.1%	10.7%
2000	48.2%	10.2%	2.9%	0.8%	17.5%	42.8%	30.9%	44.2%	0.5%	2.1%
2001	48.5%	10.9%	3.3%	0.9%	15.8%	48.4%	31.9%	38.2%	0.4%	1.7%
2002	51.2%	10.6%	3.4%	0.8%	15.4%	46.1%	29.6%	39.1%	0.3%	3.3%
2003	50.4%	8.2%	2.9%	0.7%	14.5%	46.9%	31.9%	40.1%	0.3%	4.1%
2004	46.5%	7.8%	3.0%	0.5%	14.4%	47.2%	35.7%	40.9%	0.4%	3.6%
2005	45.8%	6.4%	2.4%	0.5%	15.3%	47.5%	35.9%	43.3%	0.6%	2.3%
2006	48.6%	5.3%	2.2%	0.6%	14.8%	44.4%	33.6%	47.6%	0.7%	2.1%
2007	49.96%	4.73%	2.27%	0.58%	14.87%	48.53%	32.40%	43.14%	0.49%	3.02%
2008	42.09%	3.87%	1.97%	0.53%	14.57%	46.09%	40.64%	46.62%	0.74%	2.89%
2009	51.67%	5.13%	2.60%	0.53%	12.93%	48.69%	32.30%	42.86%	0.50%	2.64%

Source: Data of 1980 to 2005 are calculated as per the data of *China Statistic Yearbook (2006)* and data in 2006, 2007, 2008, and 2009 are calculated as per the data from the website of the Ministry of Commerce.

An analysis is made from the international competitiveness index of China's primary products: competitiveness index of commodity= (exportations minus importations)/(exportations plus importations). If the competitiveness index of commodity⩾0.5, it indicates that it has very strong competitiveness, if the competitiveness index>0 and

<0.5, it indicates that it has a strong comparative advantage, and if the competitiveness index≤0, then it has no competitive advantage. China's primary products, except food and live animals, coal, coke, and briquette products, have no competitive advantages (see Table 2.3). However, on the condition that Chinese resources are scarce, China still exports primary products like coal and so on. It indicates that the difference in price at home and abroad is huge. Those exports may be profitable for some enterprises. However, they may be unfavorable for the continuous development of the national economy. The input into coal mine safety production facilities in China is heavily insufficient, which causes a huge sum of safety debt. According to the calculation of the State Administration of Work Safety (SAWS), at least ¥68.9 billion input is needed to clear these accumulative safety debts. The death toll when China produces coal of one million ton is 3, while it is 0.03 in the United States, and 0.3 in Poland and South Africa. China's coal production accounts for 31% of the whole world, but the death toll in coal mines accounts for 79% of the whole world. Therefore, the direct trade benefit gained by China from primary product exportations will be offset owing to excessive social cost, which goes against the harmonious development of China's foreign trade.

Table 2.3 Competitiveness index of the primary products of China in 2009

Commodity composition	Primary products	Food and live animals	Beverages and cigarettes	Non-edible raw materials (except fuel)	Animal and plant grease and wax	Mineral fuel, lubricating oil, and related raw materials
Exports (USD billion)	63.099	32.603	1.641	8.156	0.316	20.383
Imports (USD billion)	289.202	14.824	1.954	140.822	7.639	123.963
Competitiveness index	−0.64	0.37	−0.09	−0.89	−0.92	−0.72

Source: Based on the related data from the Ministry of Commerce.

Subdivide manufactured products into labor-intensive products, including textiles and other light industrial products, rubber products, mining and metallurgical products, and miscellaneous products, and capital-intensive and technology-intensive products, including chemicals and related products, machinery and transportation equipment. The proportion of labor-intensive product exports and imports in manufactured product exportations and importations declined constantly, and the proportion of product exportations declined more rapidly than the proportion of product importations. The proportion of exportations declined from 75.90% in 1980 to 42.69% in 2009 and the proportion of importations declined from 35.96% in 1980 to 27.39% in 2009. The proportion of exportations and importations of capital-intensive and technology-intensive products tends to increase, and the proportion of capital-intensive and technology-intensive product exportations in manufactured products increased more rapidly than importations. The proportion of exportations increased from 21.80% in 1980 to 57.31% in 2009, and the proportion of importations increased from 61.48% in 1980 to 72.61% in 2009 (see Table 2.4).

Table 2.4 Proportion of labor-intensive products and capital intensive and technology-intensive products in imports and exports

Year	Proportion of labor-intensive products in exports	Proportion of capital intensive and technology-intensive products in exports	Proportion of labor-intensive products in imports	Proportion of capital intensive and technology-intensive products in imports
1980	75.90%	21.80%	35.96%	61.48%
1985	59.01%	15.75%	37.33%	56.02%
1990	54.67%	20.17%	25.31%	54.02%
1995	68.18%	31.82%	34.40%	64.96%
2000	57.58%	42.32%	30.59%	68.48%
2001	54.61%	45.15%	28.82%	70.33%
2002	51.88%	47.90%	27.77%	71.59%
2003	48.36%	51.40%	28.50%	71.12%
2004	46.50%	53.30%	27.96%	71.70%

(To be continued)

(Continued)

Year	Proportion of labor-intensive products in exports	Proportion of capital intensive and technology-intensive products in exports	Proportion of labor-intensive products in imports	Proportion of capital intensive and technology-intensive products in imports
2005	45.35%	54.43%	27.72%	71.89%
2006	45.07%	54.67%	26.18%	73.48%
2007	44.87%	55.13%	27.05%	72.95%
2008	44.28%	55.72%	27.16%	72.84%
2009	42.69%	57.31%	27.39%	72.61%

Source: Data of 1980 to 2008 are calculated as per the data of *China Statistical Yearbook (2009)* and data of 2009 are calculated as per the data from the website of the Ministry of Commerce.

Statistics show that capital-intensive products and technology-intensive products of China have experienced faster development since the beginning of the 1990s. This is the result of the industrial chain crossing borders and global operations of multinational companies incorporating Chinese production into the global production system. The proportion of capital-intensive and technology-intensive products in exports is not more than the import proportion in imports, and the products appear to be of a large quantity in exportations and importations. China still needs to import advanced machinery equipment and technology. In 2008, importations of electronic technology accounted for 47.1% of importations of high-tech products in China. The structure of the importations of China's manufactured products has a certain risk; the imported manufactured products are mainly technology, equipment, and energy, which are vital to national economic safety. China mainly participates in processing and assembly links in the production of capital-intensive and technology-intensive products. The input factors do not have the control force of the industrial chain, and the quantity of brands and patents is not great. In 2004, among the exportations of high-tech products, self-owned brands accounted for fewer than 10%. In high-tech industries such as communications, semi-conductors, biological medicine, computers and so on, the patents that foreign companies authorized accounted for 60% to 70%. All these restrict China from sharing more trade benefits.

By investigating the export competitiveness of China's manufactured products, we find that China is still inferior when it comes to some high-end capital-intensive and technology-intensive products and deep manufacturing (see Table 2.5). For example, in the area of finished chemical products, and specialized and scientific control instruments and devices, the export competitiveness index is still not high and is in an inferior status. Only some simple processing industries, such as those concerning clothes and shoes, are in an advantageous position. This indicates that China participates in international division with labor, resources and so on. It does not have the ability to control the industrial chain. China has low less value-added in the international industrial chain and gains benefits that are far fewer than the trade benefits as it may appear when seen by the trade volume.

Table 2.5 Competitiveness index of manufactured products of China in 2008

Commodity composition	Exports (USD billion)	Imports (USD billion)	Competitiveness index
Manufactured products	1350.698	770.311	0.27
Finished chemical products and related products	79.309	119.195	−0.20
Manufactured products classified by raw materials	261.743	107.159	0.42
Machinery and transportation equipment	673.325	441.918	0.21
Aircraft, spacecraft, and parts	1.640	10.056	−0.72
Miscellaneous products	334.606	97.619	0.55
Non-knitted or non-crocheted clothes and accessories	52.490	1.222	0.95
Unclassified commodities	1.715	4.420	−0.44

Source: Data from the Ministry of Commerce and *China Statistical Yearbook (2009)*.

Wang Yongqi constructed a measurement index of the trade structure reflecting the comparative advantages of a nation, namely, (capital goods exports/consumer goods exports)/(capital goods imports/consumer goods imports). When the index is less than 1, then the rate of capital goods exportations to consumer goods exportations is less than that of capital goods importations to consumer goods importations and the nation is a net importer. According to Mazumdar, the price of capital goods will decline, the reduction of investment costs caused by the price decline in capital goods will certainly enhance the earnings of trade benefit, and capital accumulation will take place. The index of China is less than 1; however, through Granger's causality test, we observe that the economic growth is the Granger reason for trade structure change, and trade structure promoting economic growth fails to get the support of empirical evidence. The results of the VAR forecast also show that the trade structure of China does not affect economic growth noticeably. Therefore, the contribution of China's foreign trade to economic growth is mainly reflected in trade volume rather than in structure. This certainly weakens the contribution of trade to economic growth.

2.2.2 Presentation of Benefit "Virtuality" in the Market Structure of China's Foreign Trade

China's economic structure and factor structure are strongly complementary with those of the United States, Japan, and the EU. Therefore, the export market of China's commodities mainly centers on these developed countries. In 2009, the trade volume of China with the United States, Japan, and the EU accounted for 45.23% of China's total trade. From Table 2.6, we can see that the total market share of China's exports to these countries appears stalled; getting rid of the influence of the financial crisis in 2009, that decline is mainly owing to the reduction in the Japanese market share. However, in 2008, the concentration of China's trade was enhanced; the absolute volume of China's exports to these countries has increased year by year. People have to worry about the stability of China's economic growth and national economic safety. Meanwhile, the situation of China's foreign trade also affects the effective running of Chinese macroeconomic policies, and goes against industrial upgrading through foreign trade, promotion of economic growth, and the realization of indirect trade benefits.

Table 2.6 Proportion of China's trade volume with the United States, Japan, and the EU in China's foreign trade

Year	US	Japan	EU	Total proportion
2002	15.65%	16.42%	13.98%	46.05%
2003	14.84%	15.69%	14.71%	45.24%
2004*	14.69%	14.54%	15.35%	44.58%
2005	14.88%	12.97%	15.28%	43.13%
2006	14.92%	11.78%	15.47%	42.17%
2007	13.90%	9.76%	16.49%	40.15%
2008	13.03%	10.96%	14.21%	38.20%
2009	13.51%	15.22%	16.49%	45.23%

*Data of EU of and after 2004 refer to data of 25 members.
Source: The website of the Ministry of Commerce.

According to statistics from the Ministry of Commerce, China's trade partners in 2009 mainly included the European Union, the United States, Japan, ASEAN, and R.O. Korea. Of them, the trade deficit of China with Japan was 33.027 billion USD, with R.O. Korea was 48.872 billion USD, and with ASEAN was 471 million USD; the trade surplus to the United States was 143.373 billion USD, and to the European Union was 108.526 billion USD. Compared with that in 2008, the trade surplus and deficit to other countries had no noticeable change, but trade deficit to ASEAN declined noticeably. This indicates that the trade surplus of China to the United States and the European Union was the outcome of the change in the flow of trade caused by roundabout production from the investment of Japan, R.O. Korea and ASEAN into China for industry transfer. From Table 2.7, we can see that the ratio of vertical specialization increased. In the increased 7 percentage points from 1992 to 2003, the increasing of ASEAN, Japan, and R.O. Korea accounts for 70%, while other countries and economies account for 30%. Therefore, China only gains a low processing profit and revenue, but it shows the constant increase in China's volume of import and export trade and makes trade benefits of China show certain "virtuality," which goes against the realization of indirect trade benefits in foreign trade.

The empirical results of the relationship of different countries' imports and China's economic growth calculated by Xu Guangyao shows that when the volume of trade between China and Japan increases by 100 million USD, the GDP of China will increase by 13 million USD correspondingly; when the volume of trade between China and France increases by 100 million USD, the GDP of China will increase by 140 million USD correspondingly. It shows that the importations from France have a greater impact on the increase in the GDP in China. This is because the main goods that China imports from Japan are home appliances, machinery, automobile parts and so on. Importations of these products mainly meet the production needs of enterprises in China invested by Japan. On the other hand, products imported from France are mainly products regarding spaceflights, nuclear power, and others with a high technological level. These products account for 45% of the total importations from France by China, and have a greater contribution in the economic development of China. China should import more from France, while the relationship between China and France and other EU countries is a trade surplus. Such trade situations make China import a limited anount of advanced products, restrict China on transforming its traditional industry through importing advanced equipment, and go against improving the factor structure of China in the industrial value chain or expanding its trade benefit.

Table 2.7 Ratio and changes of vertical specialization in total exports of China

Year	Total	Japan	R.O. Korea	Japan & R.O. Korea	US	ASEAN	ASEAN, Japan & R.O. Korea	Other economies
1992	0.1422	0.0229	0.0057	0.0287	0.0139	0.0072	0.0358	0.0925
1993	0.1436	0.0288	0.0096	0.0384	0.0136	0.0077	0.0461	0.0839
1994	0.1458	0.0306	0.0123	0.0429	0.0150	0.0089	0.0518	0.0790
1995	0.1483	0.0329	0.0145	0.0474	0.0155	0.0100	0.0574	0.0754
1996	0.1496	0.0317	0.0163	0.0480	0.0156	0.0109	0.0589	0.0751

(To be continued)

(Continued)

Year	Total	Japan	R.O. Korea	Japan & R.O. Korea	US	ASEAN	ASEAN, Japan & R.O. Korea	Other economies
1997	0.1519	0.0329	0.0184	0.0513	0.0152	0.0128	0.0641	0.0726
1998	0.1555	0.0317	0.0189	0.0506	0.0166	0.0144	0.0650	0.0739
1999	0.1521	0.0289	0.0167	0.0456	0.0155	0.0131	0.0587	0.0779
2000	0.2017	0.0379	0.0221	0.0600	0.0206	0.0207	0.0807	0.1003
2001	0.2047	0.0356	0.0209	0.0565	0.0224	0.0205	0.0770	0.1054
2002	0.2103	0.0363	0.0228	0.0591	0.0186	0.0221	0.0812	0.1105
2003	0.2182	0.0380	0.0265	0.0646	0.0166	0.0247	0.0893	0.1124

Source: Research Group of China Center for Economic Research, Peking University Vertical Specialization in China Export Trade and Sino-US Trade [J]. *World Economy*, 2006 (5).

From the market structure of imports and exports of high-tech products in China, we can see that a phenomenon of counter-comparative advantages exists. (This phenomenon means China doesn't import high-tech products from most developed countries like European and American countries, but that China exports high-tech products to these countries. This is inconsistent with the traditional comparative phenomenon on the surface, and actually reflects the roundabout production of ASEAN, R.O. Korea, and Japan in China and exporting to Europe and America.) High-tech products of China are mainly imported from the Asian area, and exported to European and American countries (Figure 2.4). The first four places from where high-tech products are imported to the Chinese mainland are ASEAN, Japan, R.O. Korea and the Taiwan area of China (see Table 2.8), and the total proportion accounts for more than 60% of China's importations of high-tech products, and ASEAN continues to be China's largest import source of high-tech products. In the first half of 2010, the amount of high-tech products imported from ASEAN by China reached 32.56 billion USD, accounting for 17% of the importations of China's high-tech products. The proportion of high-tech products China imports from Japan, the European Union, and the United States has been declining continuously (except from the EU in 2004 with a small range of rebound). It declined from 19.2%, 11.4%, and

13.5% in 2002 to 12.3%, 9%, and 7% in the first half of 2010, respectively. The proportion of high-tech products that China imported from ASEAN and R.O. Korea has been rising continuously. It increased from 15.5% and 8.8% in 2002 to 17.2% and 17.1% in the first half of 2010, respectively. The high-tech products that China has imported and exported are mainly electronics, computers, and communication products, and the technological levels are not very high compared with other high-tech products. Such counter-comparative advantages, inconsistent with traditional comparative advantages, reflect the restriction of European and American countries on high-tech product exports of China and also reflect the trade pattern according to which R.O. Korea, ASEAN, and other economies utilize cheap labor force and resource factor of China for roundabout production in China and export to the European and American market, but the volumes of exports do not accurately reflect the trade benefit gained by China.

	Japan	Taiwan, China	R.O. Korea
Import	10.68%	15.15%	14.87%

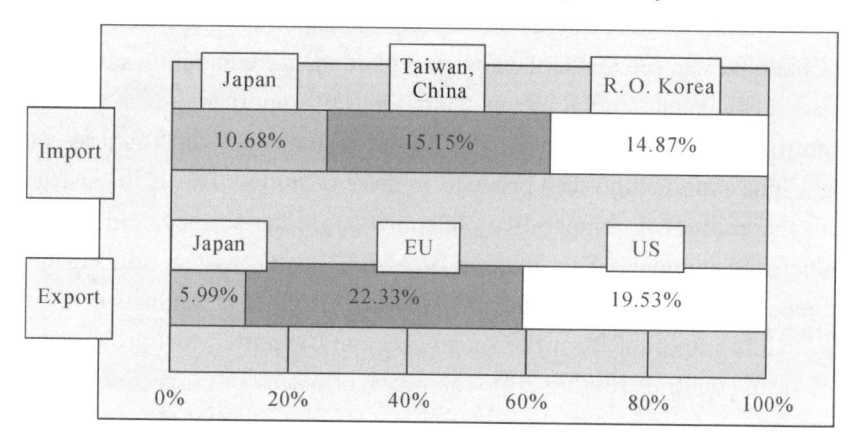

	Japan	EU	US
Export	5.99%	22.33%	19.53%

Figure 2.4 Economies importing and exporting high-tech products (in the first half of 2010)

Source: The website of the Ministry of Commerce.

Table 2.8 Countries and regions from which the Chinese mainland imports high-tech products (USD billion)

ASEAN	Japan	Taiwan, China	R.O. Korea	EU	US	Hong Kong, China
32.56	23.23	32.94	32.33	16.5	12.92	1.69

Source: The website of the Ministry of Commerce.

2.2.3 Presentation of Trade Benefit "Virtuality" in China's Foreign Trade Mode

Since 1993, among China's export trade modes, the ratio of processing trade is more than that of common trade, and it thus becomes the main trade mode. In 2009, the export volume of processing trade of China accounted for 49% of its total exportations and it increased by 1.6% from 2008. As is shown in Figure 2.5, the high-tech exports of China mainly adopts the trade mode of processing imported materials.

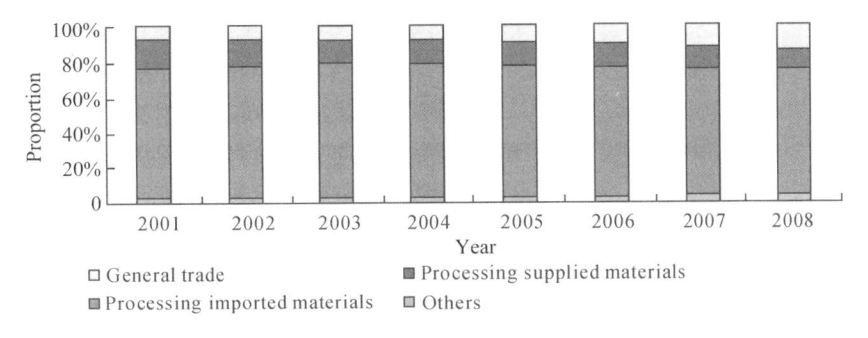

Figure 2.5 Proportion of various export trade modes of high-tech products
Source: The website of the Ministry of Science and Technology.

According to the "smile curve," the profit from manufacturing is less than that from R & D and marketing. While China is located in the processing link of the manufacturing industry, the profit China gains is far less. The export trade mode with processing trade as the primary factor indicates that China mainly depends on OEM production or on the trade pattern of low-end assembly and production has not changed. According to the 15th "Global Enterprise R & D Ranking List" issued by the Department of Trade and Industry of the United Kingdom in October 2005, the R & D strength of China is only 0.76%, far less than the 4.5% of the United States. And the technological altitude level of export products of China is far lower than 0.57, the world's level (see Table 2.9, Table 2.10).

Table 2.9 Total R & D of some countries and regions

Countries and regions	Number of companies	Total R & D input (billion pound)	Proportion in global R & D input	Growth rate of R & D input compared with last year	R & D strength
US	423	83.681	38%	7%	4.5%
Japan	207	48.542	22%	4%	4%
Germany	63	26.127	11.9%	1%	4.1%
France	45	13.302	6%	3%	2.6%
UK	167	10.571	4.8%	1%	2%
R. O. Korea	11	5.283	2.4%	40%	3.6%
Taiwan, China	22	1.355	0.6%	14%	2.3%
Chinese mainland	4	0.44393	0.2%	9.3%	0.76%
Hong Kong, China	2	0.06922	0.03%	9%	2.7%
India	1	0.04864	0.02%	68%	7.3%

Source: 15th "Global Enterprise R&D Ranking List" issued by the Department of Trade and Industry of the United Kingdom in October 2005.

Table 2.10 Technical altitude index of China and some other Countries

Countries	Export in 1995	Import in 1995	Export in 2003	Import in 2003
China	0.37	0.53	0.45	0.58
Japan	0.66	0.46	0.69	0.49
US	0.60	0.56	0.64	0.55
World	0.55	—	0.57	—

Source: Fan Gang, Guan Zhixiong & Yao Zhizhong. *International Trade Structure Analysis: Technological Distribution of Target Goods*, Apr. 2006, Working Paper Series.

Measure the trade benefit with the value-added rate of processing trade. The value-added rate of processing trade (export volume of processing trade/import volume of processing trade) can reflect the function of processing trade in the industrial structure upgrade to some extent. The bigger the value-added rate of the processing trade is, the longer the industrial chain of the processing trade in one country will be.

The higher the domestic supply rate of raw materials and spare parts is, the higher the technological level of processing trade will be. The value-added rate of the processing trade of China reached a small climax at the end of the 1990s and at the beginning of the new century; this was mainly because the Ministry of Foreign Trade and Economic Cooperation (MOFTEC) [1] issued the *Foreign Investment Industry Guidance Catalog* in 1995, which was the initial effect of encouraging, restricting, and forbidding the foreign investment policy of transforming the industrial policy of China from regional preference to a combination with industry. But the value-added rate of the processing trade of China in recent years has changed less, about 1.5 as is shown in Table 2.11. This fully indicates that the industrial chain of China is short, the value-added is not high, the rate of self-sufficiency of key technology is low, and related industries lack the support of auxiliary industries, thus restricting the industrial upgrade and trade benefits of China. However, the positive note is that since entering the new century, the value-added rate of the processing trade of China has increased, but whether China could achieve a mutual benefit and win-win result and fully enjoy the interest of foreign trade will only be tested by time.

A labor-intensive processing trade causes the structure of industrial exports to depart from the upgrade of the structure of the domestic manufacturing industry in China. It is harmful in terms of the gaining of indirect trade benefits by China. The test results of the growth model of the exportation of endogenous technical progress constructed by Bao Qun, Xu Helian, and Lai Mingyong show that neither the exportation of manufactured products nor the exportation of primary products exerts a contribution of an improvement of total factor productivity to the economy. The regression result of this model indicates that the proportion of manufactured product exports in the eastern coastal areas in the GDP is higher than that in the middle and western areas; this leads to the negative effect of the exportation of manufactured products on the economic growth in the eastern coastal

---

[1] The Ministry of Foreign Trade and Economic Cooperation was renamed the Ministry of Commerce in 2003.

areas to be larger than the latter. This is mainly because China's export products are mainly labor-intensive processing trade, and factors like the labor force provided in intra-product specialization do not have the ability to control the industrial chain, and the labor-intensive industry will not be the leading industry to drive industry upgrading. Therefore, the trade benefits China gained are far fewer than those expressed by trade volume and the effect of export division on economic growth is not obvious compared to the factor productivity advantage.

Table 2.11 Value-added ratio of the processing trade in China

Year	Total exports form the processing trade (USD billion)	Total imports form the processing trade (USD billion)	Value-added ratio of the processing trade
1991	32.43	25.03	1.3
1995	73.7	58.37	1.26
2000	137.66	92.56	1.49
2001	147.45	93.98	1.57
2002	179.94	122.22	1.47
2003	241.85	162.94	1.48
2004	327.99	221.74	1.48
2005	416.48	274.03	1.52
2006	510.37	321.49	1.59
2007	617.65	368.4	1.68
2008	675.183	378.404	1.78
2009	586.981	322.34	1.82

Source: Data of 1991 to 2005 are calculated as per some data from *China Foreign Economy and Trade Yearbook in 2005*, and data of 2006 to 2009 are calculated as per data from the Ministry of Commerce.

2.2.4 Presentation of Trade Benefit "Virtuality" in the Main Structure of China's Foreign Trade

With the expansion of China's opening-up and the acceleration of the reform of the domestic market, foreign direct investment (FDI) enterprises have increased continuously. The proportion of exclusively foreign-owned enterprises in different industries in China has expanded constantly, taking up the majority of the manufacturing, wholesale and retail, and real estate industries (see Table 2.12).

Table 2.12 Proportion of exclusively foreign-owned enterprises in various industries from 2004 to 2005

Items	Manufacturing		Wholesale and retail		Real estate	
	2004	January to April, 2005	2004	January to April, 2005	2004	January to April, 2005
Number of projects	70.3%	73.9%	83.4%	85.5%	54.5%	62.7%
Contracted foreign capital	79.9%	82.1%	73%	72.4%	64.9%	70.7%
Actual foreign capital	70%	78.2%	53.3%	65.5%	53.3%	49.5%

Source: Foreign capital statistics of the Ministry of Commerce.

The proportion of the exportations from foreign investment enterprises in the total amount of China's exportations increased from 27.51% in 1993 to 56% in 2009. The amount of importations by foreign investment enterprises accounts for 52% of the total imports of China. Owing to the slow transformation of the business mechanism and preferential policies of introducing capital, the original limited comparative advantages of state-owned foreign trade corporations in China are fading away. Capital and talents are being seriously lost; enterprises have the disadvantages of high cost and low efficiency, so that the proportion of state-owned foreign trade corporations declined from 72% in 1993 to 16% in 2009. The situation is the same in terms of importations, which declined from 60% in 1993 to 29% in 2009. Private enterprises have an upward trend, and the proportion of exports in 2009 reached 24%, but this was far behind that of foreign enterprises on capital and technology. Therefore, the mainstay of foreign trade of China transforms from state-owned enterprises to foreign investment enterprises. China's foreign trade is led by foreign merchants, and foreign investment enterprises have become the mainstay of China's foreign trade. The slow pace of investment abroad of state-owned and private enterprises in China restricts them from sharing trade benefits from other economies; thus, the trade benefits gained are more limited.

From the above analysis, we can see that the location of China in the international industrial chain by foreign merchants will produce a certain impact on the speed of upgrading of China's industrial chain. At present, foreign merchants consider China as a low-cost processing and assembly base. They mainly utilize a cheap labor force of China for assembly and production, but spare parts and core technology mainly depend on importations, which makes it difficult to improve the status of China in the international industrial chain. According to the general international standard, if the proportion of R & D expenses is less than 1% of the sales revenue of an enterprise, it is difficult for this enterprise to survive. In 2005, there were only 106 enterprises in the top 500 enterprises of China whose R & D expense proportion exceeded 2%. Thus, we can deduce that in the foreign-investment-dominant processing trade, the status of China in the international division is low, and the quality of factors provided is not high. These foreign investment enterprises not only utilize a cheap labor force and land resources of China to produce products for exportation, and incorporate Chinese enterprises into the global industrial chain, but also expand their sales in China, seize the domestic market share of China, and merge enterprises closely related with the economic safety of China.

Under the circumstances of constant flux of FDI, exclusively foreign-owned enterprises have an increasingly greater ability to control core industries of China and the technology spillover of China is comparatively limited. This is because the technology spillover effect of foreign capital is related not only to the original technological level and absorptive capacity of the host country, but also to the investment location of the host country by foreign merchants. The proportion of exclusively foreign-owned enterprises in China's high-tech product exportations is rising constantly (see Figure 2.6), and the trade benefits shared by them are also expanding. In 2004, the value-added of the national high-tech industry was ¥ 634.1 billion, the value-added of the high-tech industry of three kinds of investment enterprises accounted for 63% and that of state-owned enterprises only accounted for 21%. Chinese enterprises may lose the domestic market and lose the control of strategic departments and thus restrain China from gaining trade profit.

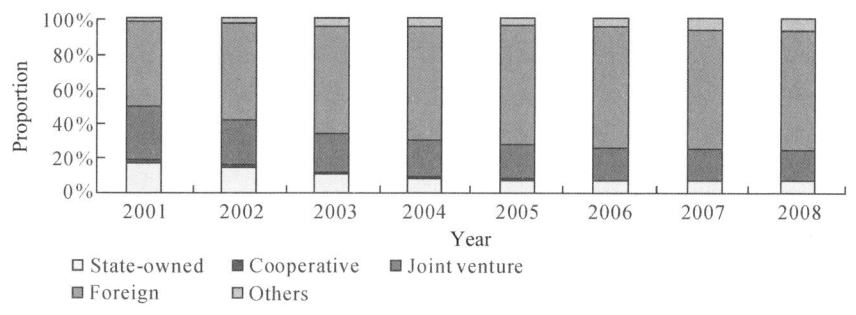

Figure 2.6 Types of export enterprises of high-tech products
Source: The website of the Ministry of Science and Technology.

2.3 Analysis of the Causes of China's Trade Benefit "Virtuality"

2.3.1 Macro-level: Implementation of the Trade Strategy and Adjustment of the Domestic Policies Related to Trade Are Insufficient

(1) The implementation of the trade strategy fails to achieve the effect of improving industrial chain factors

① The implementation of the market diversification strategy is not enough
The implementation of the diversification strategy in the Chinese market in 1990 broadens the international maneuvering room of China's foreign trade development greatly, and strengthens the anti-risk capability of China's foreign trade, but China's export market is still very concentrated. The exportation of low-cost products of China is mainly centered in developed countries. Such comparatively intensive exportation to developed countries makes China's exports rely excessively on developed countries. On the one hand, this will cause developed countries to pay close attention to the international competitiveness of China's export products and intensify China's trade friction with these countries; on the other hand, when a

large quantity of products of low technology are exported to developed countries by China (such as textiles, shoes, and toys), the competitiveness will be restricted in the face of perfect environmental protection legislation, technical standard, and advanced environmental protection technology. China has some similarity with developing countries regarding industrial structure. When some textile products are exported to developed countries from China, it must compete with labor-intensive products of other developing countries in order to occupy a share of the international market. Therefore, China not only faces anti-dumping and technical barriers to trade with developed countries, but also faces trade barriers from more developing countries, which increases the cost of the realization of trade benefits and squeezes the trade benefits of China.

② The awareness of big economy and trade strategy is insufficient

The big economy and trade strategy proposed by China in 1994 is an economy and trade development strategy based on import and export trade, mutual penetration and the harmonious development of commodities, capital, technology, and services, and joint participation of departments of foreign economy and trade, production, science and technology, and finance. The main purpose of this strategy is integrating domestic resources, breaking through the monopoly of the foreign trade area, encouraging various ownership enterprises to participate in international competition and cooperation, and realizing the diversification of operators of foreign economy and trade by strengthening the coordination and cooperation of departments, industries and enterprises. However, China's economic system is still in transition at present, the transformation of the government functions has not been implemented completely, the situation of export resultant force produced by integrating the domestic resources of each department has not been formed, the quality of export products is still inferior, the structure is unreasonable, value-added is low, and trade benefits are limited. The effect of implementing the big economy and trade strategy is mainly reflected in the diversification of operators of foreign economy and trade, while the cooperative work of government departments, industries and enterprises is not enough, the penetration of technology and service into foreign trade is not strong, thus restricting the extension of the industrial chain and making factors invested by China center on the low value-added links.

③ The strategy of "success through quality" and the strategy of promoting trade through science and technology are implemented slowly

China proposed the "success through quality" strategy early at the beginning of the 1990s and then proposed the strategy of promoting trade through science and technology in 1999. The purpose of these two strategies is to utilize high and new technology to transform traditional industries, optimize the composition of export commodities, improve the grade and value-added of export commodities, and strengthen international competitiveness by improving quality of export products and promoting international standards. For a long time, throughout the effect of the two strategies of China, the two strategies were implemented slowly. One reason for this is that the scientific base of China is weak, and R & D expenses are comparatively insufficient. R & D expenses of China are only 14% of those of the United States. And it is far behind Germany and Japan and other Asian and European countries. Consequently, Chinese industry lacks technological support and the impetus for upgrading. Another reason is that people only pay attention to whether export products are high-tech products, but ignore that the purpose of promoting high-tech product exportation is to increase the value added of products, which is the more fundamental task.

Therefore, on the condition that the industrial chain crosses borders, the strategy of promoting trade through science and technology should be endowed with a new connotation and impetus. On the basis of improving the capability for independent innovation and for constructing an innovative nation proposed by the CPC Central Committee, applying the processing trade mode with foreign investment playing the leading role in China at present, we should pay close attention to whether or not we are grasping the core technology and the key technology of products in processing, and we should implement the strategy of promoting trade through science and technology by increasing R & D input and relying on independent R & D and innovation to overcome technical difficulties.

(2) The adjustment of domestic policies related to trade is insufficient

Whether the policies of a country are harmonious with the development of foreign trade decides the effect of foreign trade of that country to some extent. If the domestic policies and trade-related policies are not adjusted fully, they will produce an adverse effect on China's trade benefit.

First, the imperfect adjustment of foreign investment policies of China restrains the enhancement of the control force of the industrial chain and the gaining of trade benefits. On the one hand, the policy of introducing capital is too general and lacks overall arrangement and regional coordination. During the process of adopting various preferential policies to attract foreign investment, it lacks a specific policy to ensure the overall coordination of the foreign investments of various provinces and cities. Each local government also lacks overall planning, and individual governments sell land at low prices to attract foreign investments in order to highlight achievement. They approve projects occupying much land, with low value-added and low technological level, and neglect the cultivation of a good environment and the combination with local industrial structure, which causes serious pollution to the Chinese environment, forms giant "external diseconomy," and puts China at the low end of the industrial chain. On the other hand, the regional policy of introducing capital lacks a related system of supporting policies and supporting measures. Introduction of foreign capital is a systematic project including capital, technology, information, intellectual property, logistics, and various services. Formulating a policy of introducing industrial capital without overall consideration of the import capital policy of introducing financial capital and commercial capital will certainly bring about a series of negative effects so that capital investment will not be able to improve technology and efficiency noticeably. China's current regional policy of introducing capital lacks the guidance of a diversified investment of upstream, midstream and downstream associated industries, fails to form complete systematic supporting policies of the industrial chain and the supply chain, and lacks the coordination of related industries. In addition, the target of introducing capital is indefinite. Advancement of the technological level is the key to realizing economic advancement, while the advancement of the ability for technological innovation is the key to the realization and consolidation of the advancement of the technological level, so the advancement of the ability for technological innovation has greater decisive significance. However, owing to a serious loss of intermediate technology, introducing capital plays a limited role in improving the control force of the industrial chain in China. Therefore, supporting domestic enterprise upgrading, including comprehensive competitive strength with technical strength, and cultivating effective competitors are important objectives of the utilization of foreign capital by China.

Second, the adjustment of exchange rates and foreign exchange management policies lags far behind, which restricts the enhancement of the industrial chain of China. China's exchange rate regime had no great change from 1994 to July 21, 2005. China's exchange rate reform falls behind the rapid development of foreign trade, which leads to a divergence between the actual price and nominal price of the currency. The import price is higher than the actual price, and the export price is lower than the actual price, which leads to a loss in the trade benefits in the process of buying what's expensive and selling what's cheap. Under the circumstances of an undervaluation of exchange rates, the import price is higher than the actual price, which causes an adverse effect on China importing resources and technical equipment from the international market at an abnormally high import price for China, while cheap resources not reflecting the market supply and demand become the object exploited by domestic enterprises, which causes a huge external diseconomy for China. On the other hand, undervaluation of the exchange rate will lower prices of the export products. In order to keep the competitive advantages of low prices, domestic enterprises often adopt the method of reducing the actual wage of domestic workers; they seldom strengthen international competitiveness by improving the technological level and labor productivity and absorbing the pressure of rising costs. The low price advantage of China's products is built on the basis of low cost of its labor force, which is harmful to Chinese enterprises adapting to the adjustment of exchange rates and digesting variations in exchange rates.

It creates a passive situation in international competition and restricts the extension of the industrial chain and the gaining of trade benefits. Because the domestic capital channel is not smooth, China uses US dollars gained from exportations to buy low-interest US government bond, but seldom uses US dollars to improve its industrial structure.

Third, the imperfect adjustment of domestic medical treatment and the public health and educational fee systems causes the imperfect policy of a Chinese labor guarantee and a social guarantee. People have a strong precautionary demand for currency, which causes a rise in China's savings rates. Domestic demand is affected by an insufficient desire to consume, and domestic demand appears to be immobile, although it has started, and small, although it has expanded. Healthy development of the domestic economy depends excessively on foreign trade, but trade benefits shared by China fail to transfer to the actual purchasing power, which is harmful to the improvement in the welfare of people's lives. And this deviates from the objective of indirect trade benefits. Meanwhile, the amount of these savings invested in the production department is comparatively limited owing to the unsound domestic capital market of China. It goes against the extension of the industrial chain of China and the improvement of the factor structure, and forms a certain constraint on the expansion of trade benefits.

2.3.2 Meso-level: Industry Associations Play a Limited Role in Improving the Control Force of the Industrial Chain

As intermediary organizations closely linked to the government and enterprises, industry associations become an important link of connecting production, learning, and research in the industrial chain and take a lubrication role in reducing trade friction. However, owing to historical reasons, industry associations in China develop slowly and some are set up by the government. They lack self-coordination, self-management, self-regulation, and self-service awareness and depend heavily on the government. They face the problem of miscellaneous staff, a lack of professional talents, a lack of standardization, and a low participation rate of enterprises. The imperfect function of industry associations doesn't enable them to integrate the upstream, midstream, and downstream associated products strongly, and they have a limited impact on improving the control force of the industrial chain. In actual operations, two kinds of industrial associations exist. That is, national industrial associations and local industrial associations formed after the transformation of competent departments of traditional industrial associations. Because Chinese law doesn't have a clear provision about the relation of these two kinds of industrial associations, when enterprises of individual regions face foreign tariff barriers and non-tariff barriers, the inconsistent paces of various industrial associations in China make the regional industrial associations weak when they investigate or cope with foreign trade barriers, and fail to negotiate as they wish. Some enterprises may have a free-riding thought, and thus make "a prisoner's dilemma". All in all, China's industrial associations have a limited lubrication function of improving the control force of the industrial chain and reducing trade friction. At present, the resultant force of promoting foreign trade from industrial associations, enterprises, and the government has not been formed; China's industrial associations haven't played their role well in promoting trade benefits gained through foreign trade.

2.3.3 Micro-level: Most Enterprises Are at the Low End of the Industrial Chain and Gain Limited Trade Benefits

Enterprises are the direct participants in production, so the places of enterprises in the international value chain decide how much trade benefit is gained. The scale of Chinese enterprises is small, Chinese enterprises lack the impetus of technological innovation and the linkage effect of trade enterprises and non-trade enterprises is not strong, all of which makes it difficult for the factors provided in the industrial chain to have a control force of the industrial chain and the trade benefits gained remain comparatively limited.

First, the small scale of the enterprises restricts the extension of the industrial chain. Compared with that of foreign enterprises, the scale of Chinese enterprises is small, and they lack the ability to integrate market resources and leads to national small and medium-sized enterprises standing everywhere. Repeat production and repeat construction are prominent, which causes low efficiency of resource allocation and a waste of resources; the enterprises fail to utilize big scale production to reduce costs and participate in market competition, which restrains scale economy benefits gained by China in international trade and further extension of the industrial chain; because the scale of Chinese enterprises is small, the strength of expanding abroad is limited, which restricts the Chinese enterprises in gaining trade benefits through foreign investment and integration with other countries' resources.

Second, the enterprises lack the impetus of technological innovation, which prevents the extension of the Chinese industrial chain toward high value-added. Enterprises should be the mainstay of technological innovation, but since the reform of the property system and the governance structure of state-owned enterprises are not in place, it is difficult to carry out technological innovation. Private enterprises have unsound technological innovation mechanisms and lack talents and capital, and the enterprises and the market expand far more rapidly than the innovation cycle, so the mentality of rushing for money makes the enterprises incapable of carrying out innovation, which prevents the extension of the Chinese industrial chain toward high value-added. At present, the R & D input of enterprises only accounts for 0.5% of turnover, and that of large enterprises accounts for about 0.7%, far behind the 4% to 5% of developed countries. 99% of Chinese enterprises have never applied for patents, and enterprises with patents are fewer than 0.03%. Because Chinese enterprises lack the impetus of technological innovation, China mainly relies on its cheap labor force to participate in production and share trade benefit. This also becomes the comparatively adverse basis of China in global trade benefit distribution and prevents the extension of the Chinese industrial chain toward a high value-added.

Third, the linkage effect of China's import and export trade enterprises with non-trade enterprises is not strong, which is bad for the adjustment and upgrading of the industrial structure. The linkage effect of upstream, midstream and downstream enterprises is not strong, and enterprises within the same department may produce plot separation owing to serving different multinational corporations. It leads to a not so smooth factor transmission of the production chain and the trade department's failure to drive the development of domestic non-trade departments, thus restricting the coordination and cooperation of factors for producing the same product in different links of the industrial chain, and affecting the adjustment and upgrading of the Chinese industrial structure.

Fourth, vicious competition of individual enterprises cuts down trade benefits mutually. At the beginning of reform and opening-up, China carried out the "export-oriented" foreign trade strategy, many enterprises in coastal areas greatly developed the exportation of labor-intensive products, and the value orientation of Chinese trade benefits had a certain "mercantilist" tendency. At present, on the condition that there is a surplus of domestic capacity in China and the international trade environment is changing rapidly, many Chinese enterprises lack long-term benefits and brand strategies. They increase exports through disorderly competition rather than independent innovation. They force prices down to gain orders. When facing foreign anti-dumping and technical trade barriers, they become very passive, and they seldom form strong negotiation powers. During the process of vicious competition, Chinese enterprises neglect that foreign enterprises occupy the Chinese market with technology, management advantage and low-price dumping methods, which causes the bankruptcy of Chinese enterprises and makes the market out of order. The enterprises are stuck in the lower end of the value-added of the industrial chain, which causes adverse effect on China's sharing of trade benefits in the global industrial chain.

2.4 Modes and Countermeasures of China's Sharing Foreign Trade Benefits

2.4.1 The Modes of China's Sharing Foreign Trade Benefits

First, from the view of longitudinal industrial growth, there are two aspects. The first aspect is that at the current stage, China should continue to give play to comparative advantages of the labor-intensive industry and improve the value-added step by step. In fact, China has a rich labor force. According to the supply and demand relationship of factors, China's cost of labor is indeed lower than that of other newly developing market-oriented countries. Therefore, China must give full play to our advantages regarding cost of labor. With regard to labor-intensive products, by extending the industrial chain, China can engage in the design and marketing links of labor-intensive products, change the input structure of factors with labor force as the principal factor, improve the value-added of export products, transform from OEM to ODM, and finally successfully move to OBM production, and make Chinese labor-intensive products achieve international competitiveness. The second aspect is that we should accumulate new comparative advantages by engaging in an assembly link of high-tech products. During the process of assembling products, we can improve the quality of our labor force step by step, and establish comparative advantages in some production link initially. Attract high-quality foreign capital in this industry through the processing trade and form industrial clusters. Improve supporting industries through the competition effect with local enterprises and produce a technology spillover and diffusing effect. Local enterprises will finally develop a capability for self-innovation and brand operations and realize the transformation of comparative advantages through "learning by doing."

Second, from the view of the area distribution of foreign trade, the multiple levels of each region's economic development in China, the imbalance of resource distribution and the diversification of the labor force and regional differences in external economic growth all make it so that China is unable to adopt comparative advantages of a single factor to guide international trade division. It must start from each region, consider the current stage of the comparative advantages of the various regions, and implement a gradual transfer strategy.

On the one hand, integrate domestic resources in a macro view, open markets domestically, and ensure that a place is given to the comparative advantages of the region as well as paying attention to upgrading and updating of the industrial structure. Implement the gradient transfer strategy that low and middle-end products or production links should be transferred to the middle and western areas to form a gradient transfer pattern of supporting industries that are transferring toward the middle and western areas. Improve the localization of spare parts and raw materials, realize industrial integration in regions, and make up for the industrial fault. During the process of undertaking labor-intensive projects with southern capital moving forward to the north, the middle and western areas should develop further extension of the special industrial chain of processing trade through the "spillover effect" of capital and technology and local enterprises' "learning effect," realize the optimization of the local industrial structure with intermediate input product localization as the link, and share more trade benefits; in the developed eastern coastal areas, encourage and support processing trade, extend and develop toward high and middle-end products or production links, transfer from the simple labor-intensive processing link to a deep processing link of the advanced manufacturing industry and the service industry, improve the capability for independent innovation constantly, and cultivate independent brands; in the old northeastern industrial bases like Changchun, where scientific research is good, the nation should make full use of favorable scientific research conditions, give proper supporting policies, and give play to the scientific research strength of these regions. On the other hand, coordinate trade benefit distribution of the regions through national tax revenue policies. This would not only solve the unemployment of China's labor force, but also make the comparatively backward regions absorb the labor-intensive industries step by step and coordinate industrial development in different regions, thereby realizing a mutual benefit and win-win result.

2.4.2 Measures and Suggestions for China to Share Foreign Trade Benefits

(1) Coordinate various policies aiming at improving the control force of the industrial chain at the macro-level

First, optimize the trade structure and the industrial structure by harmonizing various trade policies. The formulation of policies of foreign trade should be based on the principle of improving international competitiveness and the independent development ability of traditional manufacturing, to establish a system of technological innovation and an effective mechanism of innovation incentives, break through the original comparative advantages properly, and cultivate new advantages of a control force of the industrial chain. Besides, the formulation of policies of foreign trade should take exports and imports as the strategic orientation. At the same time of developing and exporting capital-intensive and technology-intensive electromechanical and high-tech products greatly, China should consider its economic safety of control force of the domestic industrial chain, actively open up an international import market, increase imports properly, and expand the importation of primary resource products and prime energy sources to make up for an insufficient domestic supply and ensure the sustainable development of the national economy. What's more, the formulation of policies of foreign trade should take reasonably and effectively protective trade promotion strategies as the basic orientation and provide tax preference and technical support for the industries encouraged to develop in order to realize the automatic adjustment of those industries. For reasonably protective industries, China should separate the "infant industry" protected by the policies of foreign trade from the backward inefficient protected industry to maintain the consistency and harmony of foreign trade and the orientation of an industrial structurial upgrading. At last, the formulation of policies of foreign trade should target on a smooth channel of international resource supply.

Second, coordinate trade relations with various countries to strive for good international developmental space to strengthen the control force of the industrial chain for China. During the process of foreign trade, whether it is carrying out foreign trade with developed countries or other developing countries, China must stick to sustainable development. China should actively carry out foreign cooperation, comply with regional economization tides, make efforts to promote the establishment of the Northeast Asia Free Trade Zone, seek for cooperation with various countries of ASEAN in the "10+3" frame, embed the development of China into the international developmental track, strengthen trade relations with newly developing markets with a comparatively stable trade environment and huge market potential, stress trade relations with Latin America, Eastern Europe, Central Asia, and Africa, and spread out the risks of the international market. In the aspect of crossing the trade barrier of developed countries and developing countries, China's export enterprises may transfer from export-oriented trade to equal stress on trade and investment in target market countries, strive to open factories directly in foreign countries, establish a batch of Chinese multinational corporations and enterprises, locate investment priority in regions of economic integration and major markets of product exportation, indirectly realize diversification of export markets, and share more trade benefits from abroad.

Third, tackle major scientific problems through macro-guidance of industry policies, guide, support, and encourage enterprises to conduct independent innovation and realize the endogeneity of trade growth. In view of the export trade volume, the composition of China's foreign trade commodities shows the tendency of constant optimization. However, each adjustment of the composition of China's export commodities goes with the transfer of the international industry. China's foreign trade relies on external demand to some extent and lacks endogeneity. The greater such external factors affect Chinese trade development, the more the uncertain factors. Therefore, China should speed up its investment in independent R & D and provide direct R & D subsidies and soft loans for enterprises in key industries and key technological areas, support enterprises to carry out R & D activities in major areas and increase endogeneity of trade growth.

Fourth, coordinate the policies of foreign capital, exchange rates, and internal demand and development of foreign trade, and provide a good environment for the adjustment of the industrial structure. At the outset, formulate laws and regulations to establish a fair mechanism for competition for domestic and foreign capital. Transfer the key point of macro-planning of introducing capital to cultivating a good macro-environment, provide service for various market subjects, establish and improve the system, policy and law environment suitable for a market economy, and adjust the goal of introducing capital into promoting the enhancement of Chinese technical strength. Then establish a system of exchange rates suitable for the current stage of China. At the same time of increasing flexibility of the exchange rate, assess the effect of the exchange rate reform at the right time, realize the linkage of domestic and foreign economy step by step during the adjustment of exchange rates, and enable the RMB to become a signal of guiding flow of domestic and foreign resources. At last, speed up the reform of domestic medical treatment and of the public health system and educational system, developing the policy of expanding internal demand, increase the flexibility of Chinese policies, and relieve the shock to domestic enterprises owing to the appreciation of the RMB.

(2) Set up powerful industry associations and promote the integration of the chain integration at the meso-level

First, industry associations should develop the integration of upstream, midstream, and downstream industrial chains by developing the functions of investigation, coordination, negotiation, and service, and provide timely, complete, and effective information to the enterprises. In the aspect of information collection, industry associations own the advantage of specialized division and the features of sufficient information, high pertinency, and low cost. It is able to know the prices, quality, and technical conditions of the enterprises' products and policy guidance of industrial development by the opportune intervention of the government, integrate the information and avoid the problems effectively such as dispersal and distortion of information, a lag in problem solving, and low pertinency regulation standards; thus, it can provide required information and suggestions for enterprises and the government to promote the integration of industrial chains. On the other hand, industrial associations should find vicious competitive behavior of foreign enterprises against China through prompt negotiations with domestic enterprises, collect important information of foreign enterprises' dumping at low prices and harmful pest residue jeopardizing the health of the Chinese people, and inspect the damage that

China may suffer due to the presence of foreign products. Meanwhile, establish the blacklist system for foreign enterprises with vicious dumping at low prices or establish a barrier and issue it on time, provide an effective guarantee for China's utilization of the WTO's mechanism for solving trade disputes and promoting the international realization of product value, and realize the trade benefits of China.

Second, rationalize the relationship between industrial associations and the government, mobilize the enthusiasm of the various parties, and make industrial associations develop the function of promoting the integration of the industrial chain. On the one hand, the government should strengthen its support and management of industrial associations. During the process of becoming a real civil organization, each level of government and the fiscal, tax, and price departments should encourage and support industrial associations to carry out paid information consultancy services, and make industrial associations get rid of their dependence on government. Industrial associations may strengthen their service function, solve capital problems by regulating self-running, collecting membership fees, and accepting domestic donations, put part of the money into improving their functions, establish information bases, achieve a virtuous circle, attract more enterprises for membership, and thus develop its information advantage on promoting the realization of enterprise values. On the other hand, industrial associations should strengthen the coordination and cooperation with each department of the government. During the process of improving themselves, industrial associations should coordinate with the government, cooperate with the industry and commerce department on the regulation of industrial development, prevent unfair competition, and avoid any lawsuit about anti-dumping, anti-subsidy, and special safeguard measures against China raised by foreign enterprises.

Third, improve the talent cultivation mechanism and cultivate professional talents required to fully promote the integration of industrial chains. The key to developing the function of industrial associations is the cultivation of people. Chinese industrial associations started late and industrial associations lack professional talents. Therefore, China should select a batch of young and middle-aged people from industrial associations for vocational training, and make them assume the burden of improving the function construction of industrial associations and blaze a trail of talent cultivation suitable for China's national condition. Meanwhile, establish reserve bases of experts and talents. When coping with measures regarding foreign anti-dumping and technical trade barriers, industrial associations may temporarily employ some renowned domestic experts to make up a panel of experts so as to propose targeted solutions. In addition, during the transformation of staff composition, avoid unsuitable staff, transform undertakers of such posts as chairmen and vice-chairmen, managing directors and directors from the retirees to entrepreneurs and industrial experts step by step, solve social insurance problems of the staff of industrial associations, and avoid the situation in which retirees control major leadership posts owing to incomplete stripping or interpersonal connections. Make efforts to cultivate professional talents required by industrial associations to provide a virtuous competitive environment for Chinese enterprises.

(3) Improve technological level and establish world-class enterprises with international competitiveness at the micro-level

First, expand the scale of enterprises in due time and gain scale economy. As a first step, enterprises should study the core competence of their own, make clear specific locations for themselves in the global industrial chain, and formulate specific strategies suitable for market development. And then, reconstruct existing technology, capital, equipment and staff, and gain advantages in the production and marketing of some products according to the goal of market positioning, form comparative advantages of value production surrounding special products and services. At last, with the increase in the market share of a certain product, develop supporting industries, exploit new products and new services, and establish a global industrial chain for multinational business.

Second, improve the technological level of the products and cultivate their own competitive advantages. As the brace of the national economy, middle-size and large-size state-owned enterprises should focus on major areas concerning the national economy and the people's livelihood; stress on the strengthening of independent innovation in technological area, assume the task of the development, research, and production of major national equipment, and cultivate an awareness and ability for the independent innovation of enterprises. Some competent private enterprises may also participate in it, jointly achieve the integration of Chinese enterprises in the industrial chain, and realize the trade benefits of export products. Other small-size and middle-size private enterprises may follow international industrial transfer by continuing to produce labor-intensive products, develop labor-intensive links with high-tech industries, accumulate capital, technology and so on step by step; realize the expansion of the industrial chain by producing featured products, or provide supporting equipment for core enterprises, and form a complete industrial network. Meanwhile, domestic enterprises may improve the technological level of their products and strengthen the international popularity and influence of enterprises through strategic cooperation with large multinational corporations on production business.

Third, cultivate an anti-risk awareness of domestic enterprises and identify a way to share trade benefits to rely on technological advancement. As a big exporting country, China faces a declivitous demand curve. The variation of export and import quantities may lead to the fluctuation of market prices. This "China factor" fails to turn into a "China advantage." The price of bulk commodities in China is based primarily on the international market. The appearance of a "deficiency of pricing power of international trade," especially the appreciation of the RMB, prevents enterprises from undertaking exports. China cannot manufacture products with a low-price competitive strategy any longer to gain meager trade benefits. Therefore, while cultivating superior future goods, enterprises should enhance the technological level of their products and upgrade the position in the global value chain constantly by transforming business modes and improving the efficiency of their resource utilization. In addition, enterprises must actively improve product value-added and resource output efficiency through the R & D of deep-processing technology of mineral resources to constantly strengthen the anti-risk awareness of enterprises, transfer the way to share trade benefits to rely on technological advances, and realize the sustainable development of foreign trade.

3

Research on the Coordination of China's Policies of Foreign Trade and Foreign Capital

3.1 Integration of the Theories of International Trade and International Direct Investment

Traditional international trade theories and international direct investment theories came into being at different times, their presupposition and research frames are different, and they developed on different tracks. Since World War II, especially since the 1970s, some phenomena about world economic development have appeared that cannot be interpreted by traditional international trade theories and international direct investment theories. Multinational corporations started to appear, and their effect on international trade and international direct investment is progressing constantly. Especially since the 1990s, international trade volumes related to multinational corporations have accounted for two-thirds of the world's total trade volume, and intra-corporation trade has accounted for one-third of the total trade volume. Meanwhile, affected by multinational corporations, international investment has lifted its status in the world economy rapidly with a higher developmental rate than that of international trade development. Multinational corporations play a more important role in intra-industrial trade growth. Trade volume of nations connected by multinational corporations has also grown greatly. Thus, international trade and international investment activities have begun to integrate. Hence, research on international trade and that on international direct investment are no longer separated but are developing in synergy. Economists have begun to explore interpreting new problems and new phenomena arising from international trade and international direct investment in the same frame.

Entering the 21st century, international trade and international direct investment activities have been closely related with the work and life of common people. Whether people enjoy various imported goods or products or people engage in business and service activities, it seems that they have a direct or indirect relationship with international trade and international direct investment. With the internationally frequent flow of capital, labor, technology, cargo, information and knowledge, the economy of various countries is integrated on day to day level. There is a difference in the form of international trade and international direct investment, but their boundary is getting vague. Their subjects tend to be uniform. The directions of the composition of the commodities within the international trade and the industrial adjustment of international direct investments are convergent, as are the fields of international trade and international direct investment. Both of them have the tendency to integrate.

3.1.1 The Basis for the Integration of Theories of International Trade and International Direct Investment

International trade theories and international direct investment theories are two mature branches of the development of international economics. Traditional international trade theories and international direct investment theories have different research frames and different theoretical bases.

Traditional international trade theories appeared in the 17th century, which considered a nation as a basic unit of analysis. In the frame of a neoclassical analysis, centered on the comparative advantage theory, and based on the condition of a completely competitive market, factors cannot flow freely among countries. The conclusion is that international trade is the only way to achieve optimal allocation of resources worldwide. Various countries can gain maximum returns from trade without direct investment. From Adam Smith's absolute cost theory to David Ricardo's comparative cost theory and then to Heckscher and Ohlin's factor endowment theory, the analysis logic and policy proposition of these theories are successive, and the basic premises are roughly the same. In the frame of the perfect free trade theory based on traditional international trade theories, the direct investment theory is unnecessary and cannot be established.

However, with the development of the world economy and continuous deepening of international divisions, a century after the appearance of international trade theories, economists who have studied the problem of direct investment have started to use different theoretical assumptions to establish the direct investment theory within a frame that is very different from that of trade theories. Early international direct investment also rejected international trade theories.

After World War II, with the development of the world economy, the traditional international trade theories could not interpret the constantly emerging new phenomena of international trade, such as increase in the trade volume among developed countries and the appearance of intra-industry trade and multinational corporations. Hence, many economists started to broaden their assumptions of traditional trade theories and establish new trade theories, such as the new factor theory, the new technology theory, and the scale economy theory that appeared after the 1960s. At the beginning of the 1970s, the new international trade theories absorbed part of the international trade theories when interpreting a multinational corporation's choice on exports and their direct investment mode. Whether enterprise behavior was involved in international trade theories, or a nation's factor was involved in international direct investment theories, both of them were aimed at being perfect interpretations of reality. After the 1980s, multinational corporations started to develop rapidly. Internationally integrative production and internal trade of corporations became an important force in promoting international investments and trade development. People came to know that trade and investment were different choices of the same enterprise for international business modes; so they connected trade and investment actively and sought a consistent interpretation.

Driven by world economic development, especially after multinational corporations appeared, international division became more detailed, and international production developed from an inter-industry division to an intra-industry division and from a product division to a factor division. The practical and theoretical basis on which international trade and international direct investment become integrated, get promoted, and develop mutually are becoming increasingly mature.

3.1.2 Development of the Integration of Theories of the International Trade and International Direct Investment

Research on the integration of international trade theories and international direct investment theories are carried out in two aspects: One is the theoretical interpretation of the integration phenomena of international trade and international direct investment; the other is the theoretical research on the relationship between international trade and international direct investment.

(1) The theoretical interpretation of the integration phenomena of international trade and international direct investment

① Relax assumptims and introduce new variables

R. Vernion from Harvard University incorporated international trade and international direct investment into the same analysis frame earlier. He proposed the theory of the product life cycle in 1966. This theory interprets an enterprise's choice on exports, license forms, and foreign direct investment by establishing a dynamic theory. Vernion divided the life cycle of products into three stages: a) the new product period; b) the mature product period; c) the product standardization period. Dynamic changes of the production technology of products transform the monopolistic advantage of an enterprise in a producing country; thus, an enterprise's economic behavior changes correspondingly. Vernion introduced the dynamic factor and the comparative advantage theory of international trade into the monopolistic advantage theory of international direct investment, so that it is possible to incorporate international trade and international direct investment theories into a uniform framework of theoretical analysis.

Australian scholar W. M. Corden abandoned the assumption that factors cannot flow between two countries in the factor endowment theory (H-O theory) raised by Swedish scholars Heckscher and Ohlin, based on traditional trade theories raised in 1974, as well as introducing the third factor—knowledge, and allowing international flow of capital, labor, and knowledge. It enables the extended international trade theory to interpret international direct investment phenomena to some extent.

The new factor trade theory and the new technological trade theory take natural resources and human capital as the production factors. The new factor trade theory is based on the assumption that natural resource endowment can also interpret the motivation of international direct investment besides interpreting the motivation of international trade, especially integrated international direct investment by early enterprises in order to gain a supply of raw materials. The new technological trade theory considers that human capital has a close relationship with international trade, technological license transfer, and international direct investment. International trade may be product exportation set up on a technology-intensive (human capital) basis; technological license transfer often derives from the advantage of human capital; and international direct investment includes the transfer of human capital among various countries. The new technological trade theory stresses that one nation gains monopolistic advantages owing to its technological advancement, which is connected to Hymer's monopolistic advantage theory. It breaks through the assumption of the neo-classical trade theory regarding the identical production factor among various countries. The core of theoretical analysis is that technological monopoly leads to imperfect competition on the market. This denies the basic premise of the classical trade theory. In addition, it adopts the dynamic analysis method connecting the analysis of a nation at the macro-level and the analysis of an enterprise at the micro-level. This is extremely similar to various interpretations of developing the monopolistic advantage theory by Johnson, Caves, Knickerbocker, and others.

② Establish a new theory of integration of trade and direct investment theories in the framework of a new theoretical analysis

Kojima elaborated the marginal industry investment theory systematically in the book *Foreign Direct Investment: A Japanese Model of Transnational Business Operations*. Kojima was of the opinion that the international division principle and the comparative cost principle are consistent, and international division can not only interpret foreign trade, but also interpret foreign direct investment. Therefore, a comprehensive theory of international trade and international direct investment can be established on the basis of the "comparative advantage (cost) principle." For trade, according to the established comparative cost, one country will gain trade benefits by implementing the specialization of the comparative advantage industry, and exporting those commodities, as well as shortening the comparative disadvantage industry and importing those commodities. For foreign direct investment, the country that makes investments starts investing from the marginal industry leading to a comparative disadvantage. In this way, the potential comparative advantage industry, which didn't emerge due to a lack of capital, technology, management skills and so on, may emerge in the other country owing to the adoption of advanced production functions. In this way, the comparative cost gap between two countries is enlarged to create a condition conducive to more trade benefits. The benefit of foreign direct investment arises from transplanting more advanced production functions in the hosting country. Trade is carried out as per a fixed comparative cost, and direct investment may create new comparative costs. Kojima's theory interpreted the "Japanese-style" foreign direct investment phenomenon perfectly at that time, but restricted by historical conditions prevalent at that time, it was only limited to countries with different factors; so it did not have the ability for a common interpretation. After the 1980s, the thought of an international division of labor in the enterprise and multinational corporations appeared. However, the attempt that Kojima integrated international trade and international direct investment theories in the same framework provided beneficial enlightenment for the following research.

(2) Theoretical research on the relationship between international trade and international direct investment

① The theoretical development of the relationship between international trade and international direct investment

A. Mundell's trade and investment substitution model

In 1957, Robert. A. Mundell did research on the mutual substitutional relationship between trade and investment on the basis of the standard international trade model of two countries, two kinds of products, and two factors. When factors of two countries cannot flow freely and there is no trade barrier, resource endowment differences must lead to trade until commodities and factors of the two countries are equal in price, namely, up to trade equilibrium. When tariff barriers, industry entry barriers, and other trade barriers exist between the two countries and capital can flow freely between two countries, as long as the marginal income of two countries from capital has a difference, international capital flow will certainly occur. That flow will result in a price equalization of products and capital, so that the result of international capital flow replaces international trade finally. Such investment is called "investment incurred by tariffs." Mundell's trade and investment substitution model shows that trade barriers will stimulate investment. The theory can interpret a correlation between trade and investment in international economic activities in part, but it fails to interpret the simultaneous growth of trade and investment between two countries.

B. Markuson and Svensson's complementary relationship model

Markuson and Svensson proposed that in the event of investment produced as a result of trade barrier, foreign direct investment mainly flows into the import substitution department of the hosting country, enabling foreign direct investment to produce products in the hosting country to make up for insufficient international trade. However, if foreign direct investment does not arise from trade barriers and when investment mainly flows into the export department of the host country, direct investment will lead to a further deepening of the international division and specialized production so as to expand international trade. At this time, foreign direct investment and trade form a new complementary relationship. Through research on various factors affecting commodity trade and factor flow, Markuson and Svensson thought whether international commodity trade and foreign direct investment show substitution or complementation depends on whether trade and non-trade factors are "cooperative" or "uncooperative." If trade and non-trade factors are cooperative, commodity trade and factor flow will be mutually promoted and a complementary relationship will be established.

C. The uncertainty model of a trade and investment relationship

Neary showed that the relationship between trade and factor flow is uncertain in the 3×2 specific factor model. He took America and Japan as the countries under study, labor, capital and land as analysis factors to expound the uncertainty relationship between trade and investment according to the comparative price difference between America and Japan on the assumption that labor and capital endowment in America and Japan are the same and land endowment is different. A. Patrie's research indicated that the motive for stimulating direct investment is different and so the relationship between trade and investment is also different. According to different motives of investment, Patrie divided international direct investment into three types: market-oriented, production-oriented and trade-promoted. Of them, market-oriented direct investment easily becomes a substitute of trade, and production-oriented and trade-promoted direct investment can increase international trade between the investing country and the invested country.

D. The compensation investment model

Bhagwati and Dinopoulos's compensation investment model mainly analyzes the relationship between trade and investment in view of political economics. Such a model is also analyzed in the general equilibrium international trade model of two standard countries, two kinds of standard commodities and two standard factors. The relationship between trade and investment does not merely depend on pure economic factors like factor price difference and real trade barrier. Under the circumstances of the trade protection threat, games of different interest groups may also produce substitution and complementation of trade and investment. This is compensation investment. Compensation investment describes a cross-time relationship between trade and investment in which the investment may not be an optimal choice in the view of profit maximization for a period of time by a vendor; it may even bring about loss, but investment will reduce or avoid the loss caused when the government of the hosting country assumes protection in the next period. Therefore, investment will realize a profit maximization of the second period in view of a complementary relationship of trade and investment. Such compensation is that the investment loss of the first period will be complemented by the anticipated earnings of the second period; so the purpose of compensation investment is to reduce the possibility that the host country might take trade protective measures to defuse tariff. Hence, it is also called tariff-defusing investment. This theory interprets well the Japanese direct investment in America on a large scale in the middle of the 1980s.

E. The economic integration model

Massimo Motta and George Noeman analyzed how oligopolistic enterprises make trade and investment choices in the situation that the world production system is controlled by oligopolistic enterprises, mutual penetration rates on the market are improved, and a regional economic integration organization is developed and improved rapidly. The theoretical assumption of the economic integration model is established based on three countries and three oligopolistic vendors, applies the analysis method of the game theory, and takes trade barriers within the integrated economic entity, trade barriers outside the integrated economic entity, and a market scale as the major factors of consideration for oligopolistic enterprises to make trade and investment decisions. In addition, they analyzed the impact of trade barriers, foreign trade policies, and government subsidies on welfare, and pointed out that reducing trade barriers within the integrated economic entity will bring more welfare than improving foreign trade policies (such as strengthening anti-dumping) or providing subsidies for investment enterprises.

In recent years, various international organizations also strengthen the research on the relationship between trade and investment in order to promote the development of trade and investment in various countries.

With further deepening of international divisions, the status of multinational corporations, as the carrier of trade and investment integration in the world economy, has improved constantly. More economists have started to take multinational corporations as their objects of analysis and have tried to establish a new trade and investment integration theory. However, so far, no significant and widely recognized theory has emerged. This is a new trend in the development of contemporary international trade and international direct investment theories. The trade and investment integration theory is not mature, but its impact on the real economy is worth stressing.

② Empirical test of the relationship between international trade and international direct investment

Since the 1970s, empirical research on trade and direct investment has made great progress. At the end of the 1970s, the American scholar C.F. Bergsten conducted an empirical analysis by connecting foreign direct investment and the actual exports of some industries. He was of the opinion that foreign direct investment and export trade are complimentary to each other as well as competitive (substitutional) to one another. Lipsey and Weiss studied the production and export behavior of subsidiaries established in developing countries by American multinational corporations according to the statistics of the 1970s. They also did further research in 1984 and found that such a positive correlation or at least an uncorrelated relationship exists widely in nearly 80% of industrial departments; that is, American foreign direct investment appears to have a positive impact on the international trade of the same industry. Hufbauer, et al. focused on studying the situation since the 1980s in America; they made a comparison between the total foreign direct investment and the total amount of exports in 1980, 1985, and 1990, and found that during the whole time span, the total amount of exports and total amount of foreign direct investment maintained a positive correlation. Gramham's research also certified this point. Meanwhile, many scholars came to similar conclusions through their empirical research of Japan, Germany, Sweden, and other countries. Lee Honggue did in-depth research on R.O. Korea's foreign direct investment of the electric appliance industry, and pointed out the motive for which R.O. Korea's electric appliance enterprises' foreign direct investment mainly shows maintaining and expanding the demand of exports, namely, improving the competitiveness of export products through foreign direct investment.

③ The results of the research on the relationship between international trade and international direct investment in China

So far, there is only a little theoretical research on international trade and international direct investment integration conducted by Chinese scholars. The reason is mainly that the development of multinational corporations in China has not been going on for long, and the research on the correlation of foreign trade, industrial structure, and trade protection between multinational corporations and China still remains a new field. The results of the research carried out by domestic scholars on integrating these theories is a synthesis of Western theories; Zhang Qing and Liu Xiaming utilized the existing theories to conduct empirical research on the relationship between China's trade and investment; some scholars raised the integrating standards of international trade theories and international direct investment theories under the comparative advantages; scholars from Nanjing University proposed a specific definition of trade and investment integration, and discussed problems generated in China's trade protection and opening-up strategy by trade and investment integration.

3.2 The Tendency of International Trade and Investment Integration and Its Development in China

Since the 1990s, the integrative development of international trade and international direct investment has been reflected not only in the rapid development of the quantity and the scale of international trade and international direct investment, but also in the carrier of both—multinational corporations develop fast and affect the development of the world economy. Today, multinational corporations have become the most important force in promoting economic globalization and trade and investment integration. Multinational corporation-oriented trade and investment integration is changing the traditional manner of carrying out international trade and international direct investment into a brand new form.

3.2.1 International Trends in the Integration of Trade and Investment

(1) International direct investment becomes an accelerator of the development of international trade

Since the 1990s, international direct investment has become one of the basic forms of international capital flow and one of the most active factors in the world economy. Its growth rate is not only far higher than the growth rate of the world output (GDP), but also higher than the growth rate of the international trade. It has become the strongest engine for the mobilization of the development of the world economy. The rapid development of international direct investment mobilizes the constant expansion of the scale of international trade and forms the tendency of international direct investment impacting international trade and the two growing simultaneously. For a long time, international trade and international direct investment have interacted with the economy and have taken the lead in the growth of the world economy. In recent years, world investment volume and trade volume are affected by the step-down developmental speed of developed countries, the inflow volume of global foreign direct investment in 2007 and 2008 decreased continuously and reached its lowest level in 2009, but inter-country investment and trade activities led by multinational corporations are likely to continue. The growth rate of international direct investment remains higher than that of international trade and the growth rate of international trade remains higher than the rate of economic growth. This trend is expected to continue.

(2) International direct investment results in the change of the composition of trade commodities

Intra-industry trade of manufactured products mainly arose from the international production level and vertical division and has become one of the most important symbols reflecting intra-industry trade quantity and structure; so we can say that international direct investment is an important factor in promoting the improvement of the composition of international trade commodities. The international division of multinational corporations enriches the content of international trade and makes more intermediate products become factors of international trade and international direct investment. Hence, it also promotes the composition of international trade commodities and international direct investment to evolve from primary products or roughly-processed products into manufactured products and highly-processed products. With technological advancement and the adjustment of the economic structure around the world, the composition of international trade commodities and the structure of international direct investment is entering a new period of adjustment. International demand for newly developed products like high-tech products and information products has increased day by day, and the proportion of these commodities in international trade and international direct investment has also increased. The change of the structure of international trade and international direct investment, innovation and the rapid growth of new trade and investment methods and the domination of trade and investment driven by multinational corporations will become a major impetus for promoting the continual growth of international trade and international direct investment at a faster speed.

(3) Technological innovation is the basis for developing international trade and international direct investment

The rapid development of international direct investment not only promotes the development of international cargo trade, but also mobilizes trade in services, especially technological trade. In the current world economic activities, the innovation and application of information technology strongly promotes changes in the world economic quantity and quality. The most significant factor influencing global economy is industrialization of information technology and its application in business fields. The cycle of "scientific and technological achievements–technological development–commercialization" is shortened constantly, so new discoveries, new inventions, and technological innovation will have an obvious impact on international trade and international direct investment. Brand new trade modes, such as e-commerce and electronic data interchange (EDI) will become major methods of international trade and international direct investment. This enables international trade and international direct investment to expand and spread out in space as well as gradually toward informatization and network in all aspects. Promoted by technological innovation, the positive participation of various countries makes the pace of integration of international trade and international direct investment more rapid as well as maintaining a closer relationship.

(4) International direct investment's influence on changes in the international trade modes is strengthened continuously

Large-scale penetration of multinational corporations around the world not only promotes the foreign trade development of host countries, but also opens up the international system of production integration characterized by the internal labor division witihin the corporations. International trade volume of various branches of multinational corporations is increasing dramatically, and this has become an important component of the current growth of international trade. Therefore, intra-corporation trade is a prominent manifestation of the mutual integration of international direct investment and international trade. In addition, business activities of multinational corporations involve nearly all fields of world economic production activities currently and control about 80% of the patents of new technology and new processes, 70% of international direct investment, nearly 70% of international trade, and 30% of international technology transfer. Such patterns will be enhanced further in a rather long period of time. With the intensified competition of multinational corporations, the investment and trade modes are also being changed constantly so that trade modes develop toward diversification and complication.

(5) The integration of international trade and international direct investment is being strengthened constantly

International trade and international direct investment tend to be uniform not only in the direction of the flow, but also in structural change. What's more, they show a joint developmental trend in content and scale. Corporation internalization of international trade behavior enables international trade and international direct investment to become different behaviors of the same subject. Therefore, only if multinational corporations rearrange their international production activities through integrated organization, and capitalize tangible and intangible assets in the whole system, can they fully utilize the ownership advantages and regional advantages of the host country to realize the maximization of profits and create more value. In a multinational corporation, any part of the value chain is arranged to the location where the overall interests of the corporation will be improved. In this way, the relationship between multinational intra-corporation trade and investment tends to be complicated, and trade mobility of the parent company and subsidiaries is increased and the importance is increased.

(6) The relevance of international trade and international direct investment policies is strengthened

The relevance of international trade and international direct investment decisions has become another important feature of the mutual integration tendency of international trade and international direct investment. Most international direct investment in the world will be affected by trade policies. The United Nations International Investment Center proposed a package of illustrative items of trade measures about investments (see Table 3.1).

Table 3.1 Illustrative items of trade measures about investments

Trade measures	Possible influence on international direct investment
Tariff and quantitative limitation of import	Attract foreign direct investment
Department management trade, including voluntary export restriction	Attract foreign direct investment
Regional free trade agreement	Promote international direct investment of member countries
Rules and policies of origin	Attract foreign direct investment in production of spare parts
Export processing zones	Attract export-oriented foreign direct investment
Export control (safety and diplomatic policy)	Attract foreign direct investment
Export subsidization	Increase export-oriented foreign direct investment
Non-spot trade agreements (cooperative production and buy-back)	Be determined by the nature of special agreement
Safety, health, environment, confidentiality and other national standards	Attract foreign direct investment

Source: World Investment Report of the United States in 1992, page 263.

Such items provide a general picture that various governments take various trade measures to affect international direct investment flow. In fact, most global direct investment flows are affected by one trade measure or another, but not all measures are effective. The impact of tariffs, department management trade, regional free trade agreements and export processing zones is greater than that of other measures. Different trade policies will attract different types of foreign direct investment. For example, tariffs and quantitative limitations will attract substitutes for imported goods and foreign direct investment, while export subsidization measures will increase export-oriented foreign direct investment. It may exert various impacts on the scale, the direction of the flow and the structure of international direct investment. For example, the export-oriented trade development policy of developing countries has become the effective policy model of attracting foreign direct investment.

(7) Dynamic interest becomes the goal of various countries' participation in trade and investment integration

In trade and investment integration, the rising of dynamic interest status has become the concern of various countries, especially of developing countries. In the context of world economic integration, the interaction of international direct investment and international trade changes traditional static trade and investment interest: ① Earnings from international direct investment will exceed trade earnings. International investment and international trade are promoted mutually, but for capital exporting countries, earnings from international investment cannot be reflected through the benefit of international trade. This is because international investment activities are a global resource integration that multinational corporations carry out with the help of capital. In order to utilize the factor advantages of a host country (such as a superior labor force), they may invest in this country by setting up factories, but spare parts and machinery equipment may come from other countries rather than from the home country. The products can be sold on spot or exported to other countries, and the export earnings will be recorded on the trade balance of the host country. ② Additional amounts of foreign exchange and trade volume of the country of origin will reflect in the international trade balance more directly than the volume of imports and exports. Promoted by global resource integration of multinational corporations, the export products of one country may not be produced by "domestic enterprises," but by a branch of a foreign country or even an importing country's multinational corporation; export products not only use imported raw materials and intermediate products, but most of them come from imports, and imports from the importing country of the final products. This is more prominent in processing trade. According to the traditional method of gathering statistics, the entire volume of exports of the processing trade is recorded as exports of the exporting country in the processing trade. This cannot reflect the real earnings gained by the exporting country completely and noticeably. If one uses the standard of the country of origin to calculate the value-added ratio and the additional amount of foreign exchange of export products of the exporting country, earnings from exports and foreign exchange earned from exports of one country will be measured correctly. ③ Dynamic interest of international trade is being stressed more and more by various countries. Enterprises engaged in production and exports in the market of one country include "domestic enterprises," foreign-owned enterprises and joint venture enterprises. Income from exports will not be solely enjoyed by the exporting country. Especially when multinational corporations carry out international business in developing countries, they will inevitably use the transfer price method to transfer profit, so direct trade benefits gained by developing countries will be at a large discount. However, the dynamic benefit of international trade is very prominent, such as increasing the employment and tax revenue of the host country, promoting industrial structural upgrading and the popularity of the idea of modern management and social modernization.

3.2.2 The Influence of Trade and Investment Integration on China's Economic Development

The influence of trade and investment integration on China's economy is mainly reflected in the following: With the constant increase in the quantity and scale of foreign direct investment flowing into China, especially after joining the WTO, many multinational corporations transfer their strategic focus onto China. Not only does foreign direct investment change China's foreign trade, but the development of foreign trade also changes foreign direct investment flowing into China. Both of them affect, interact with, and penetrate mutually in development, which plays an active role in promoting the rapid development of China's economy.

(1) Foreign direct investment exerts a great influence on China's foreign trade

Since joining the WTO, the scale of foreign direct investment flowing into China has been constantly expanding, the ways have become ever more diversified, and the level has been constantly enhanced. Moreover, the impact on China's economy is greater. In the aspect of foreign trade, foreign direct investment not only speeds up the growth of foreign trade, but also exerts significance on the mode, the structure, and the balance of China's foreign trade (see Table 3.2).

Table 3.2 The influence of foreign direct investment on the amount of China's imports and exports from 1999 to 2009

Year	National foreign trade (USD billion)			Foreign-invested enterprise				
	Amount of exports	Amount of imports	Balance	Amount of exports (USD billion)	Proportion in total exports	Amount of imports (USD billion)	Proportion in total imports	Balance of imports and exports (USD billion)
1999	194.93	165.70	29.23	88.63	45.1%	85.88	51.8%	2.75
2000	249.20	225.09	24.11	116.44	47.9%	117.27	52.1%	−0.83
2001	266.16	243.61	22.54	133.24	50.1%	125.86	51.7%	7.38
2002	325.57	295.21	30.35	169.94	52.2%	160.27	54.3%	9.67
2003	438.37	412.84	25.54	240.34	54.8%	231.91	56.2%	8.43
2004	593.36	561.38	31.98	338.61	57.1%	324.57	57.8%	14.04
2005	762.00	660.12	101.88	444.21	58.3%	387.51	58.7%	56.70
2006	969.08	791.61	177.47	563.83	58.2%	472.62	59.7%	91.21
2007	1218.02	955.82	262.20	695.52	57.1%	559.41	58.5%	136.11
2008	1428.55	1133.09	295.46	790.49	55.3%	619.43	54.7%	171.06
2009	1201.66	1005.60	196.06	672.20	55.9%	545.20	54.2%	127.00

Source: The data of 1999 to 2008 are from the website of the Ministry of Commerce, and the data of 2009 are from the statistical bulletin of the National Bureau of Statistics, http://www.stats.gov.cn/tjgb/ndtjgb/qgndtjgb/t20100225_402622945.htm.

The proportions of the amount of exports and imports of foreign-invested enterprises in the total amount of exports and imports rise constantly. Of them, the proportion of the amount of exports in the total amount of China's exports rose from 45.1% in 1999 to 57.1% in 2007, and the proportion of the amount of imports in the total amount of China's imports rose from 51.8% in 1999 to 58.5% in 2007; affected by the international financial crisis in 2008, the amount of imports and exports of foreign-invested enterprises decreased slightly, but still accounted for over 54% and 55% (see Table 3.2). The rapid growth of the amount of imports and exports of foreign-invested enterprises reflects its function in promoting the growth of China's foreign trade volume, and it has become dominant in developing China's foreign trade. In addition, the proportion of the amount of imports of foreign-invested enterprises in the total amount of China's imports is higher than that of exports, and imports grow faster than exports, which reflects that foreign-invested enterprises have strengthened the opening-up of the domestic market of China in recent years. The trend of the trade development of foreign-invested enterprises affects the developmental pattern of equilibrium growth of China's imports and exports and changes the unbalanced foreign trade pattern that the growth of China's exports is faster than that of its imports.

In view of the trade mode of foreign-invested enterprises, these enterprises mainly adopt processing trade, which makes processing trade the main mode of China's foreign trade. From 1999 to 2004, the processing trade was always above 55% of China's export trade mode; the proportion tended to decrease slightly from 2005 to 2007, but still accounted for over 50%; affected by the international financial crisis, the processing trade accounted for less than 50% from 2008 to 2009 for the first time in the past nine years, but appeared to have a slight rising tendency. From 2000 to 2004, general trade accounted for over 41% of export trade and appeared to have a slight decreasing trend from year to year. From 2005 to 2008, the proportion of general trade continued to rise and reached its largest proportion, 46.4%. The proportion of other trade modes was small (less than 5% before 2007), but tended to rise year by year (see Table 3.3).

Table 3.3 China's export trade modes from 1999 to 2009

Year	Total amount of exports (USD billion)	General trade		Processing trade		Others	
		Total amount (USD billion)	Proportion	Total amount (USD billion)	Proportion	Total amount (USD billion)	Proportion
1999	194.930	79.135	40.60%	110.882	56.90%	4.914	2.50%

(To be continued)

(Continued)

Year	Total amount of exports (USD billion)	General trade		Processing trade		Others	
		Total amount (USD billion)	Proportion	Total amount (USD billion)	Proportion	Total amount (USD billion)	Proportion
2000	249.200	105.181	42.20%	137.652	55.20%	6.370	2.60%
2001	266.155	111.881	42.00%	147.434	55.40%	6.783	2.50%
2002	325.569	136.187	41.80%	179.927	55.30%	9.482	2.90%
2003	438.370	182.034	41.50%	241.849	55.20%	14.488	3.30%
2004	593.370	243.640	41.10%	327.990	55.30%	21.740	3.70%
2005	762.000	315.090	41.35%	416.480	54.66%	30.430	3.99%
2006	969.080	416.320	42.96%	510.370	52.67%	42.380	4.37%
2007	1218.020	538.580	44.22%	617.650	50.71%	61.780	5.07%
2008	1428.550	662.862	46.40%	675.114	47.30%	92.717	6.30%
2009	1201.660	529.800	44.10%	587.000	48.80%	84.860	7.10%

Source: The data of 1999 to 2008 are from the website of the Ministry of Commerce of the People's Republic of China, and the data of 2009 are from the statistical bulletin of the National Bureau of Statistics, http://www.stats.gov.cn/tjgb/ndtjgb/qgndtjgb/t20100225_402622945.htm.

Therefore, China's export trade modes have a trend of diversified development that new trade modes like compensation trade and international subcontract are developing. In addition, the level of China's intra-industry trade driven by the processing trade is constantly improving. Moreover, most foreign-invested enterprises engaging in processing trade invest in manufacturing industries. It makes manufactured products become the leading part of the composition of the commodities in China's foreign trade. From the major composition of the commodities of China's exports and imports in recent years, we can see the increase in the volume of raw material imports of industrial products (such as iron ore and concentrate, unwrought copper and copper material, unwrought aluminum and aluminum material, steel material, etc.) and the increase in the volume of exports of industrial products (such as steel material, containers, video recorders, TVs, microcomputers, motorcycles, etc.) have a positive correlativity. The foreign direct investment mode changes the composition of the commodities of China's imports and exports. In recent years, with the constant upgrading of foreign-invested enterprises entering China, such as the international trade industry, the heavy chemical industry and other industries with high technological levels, the technological level of manufacturing vendors engaged in processed trade in China has improved constantly; the export competitiveness of manufactured products has also been improved. Finally, under the influence of trade and investment, the trade partners of one country are always closely related to their major investment partner countries. Regions investing in the Chinese mainland include Hong Kong and Taiwan of China, Japan, R.O. Korea, and the United States. They are also important trade partners of the Chinese mainland. Their total trade volume accounts for over 50% of the foreign trade of the Chinese mainland.

(2) The rapid development of foreign trade strengthens competitiveness and attract more foreign direct investment

First, the commodity export country can lay the foundation for direct investment outwardly by developing foreign trade to accumulate capital; correspondingly, the commodity import country may introduce knowledge, technology, culture, and ideas with such imported commodities as a carrier, leading to the change in the industrial structure and an improvement of productivity in it. Imports can meet and cultivate the demand of consumers for imported commodities, and when demand is expanded to some degree, it will require the commodities to realize local production and sales. Investment impetus and attraction exist together, which certainly causes a great increase in international direct investment. Therefore, international trade has the function of adjusting the industrial structure and geographical structure of direct investment.

Second, when the imported commodities become capital or production commodities, perfect infrastructure construction can strengthen this country's attractiveness for foreign capital.

Third, as the mainstream tendency of the current world economy, trade liberalization will promote the growth of international direct investment. It is good for broadening the information source and improving the quality of information transfer so as to ensure international direct investment's implementation in a wider range, on a larger scale and with fewer risks; trade liberalization means the loosening of policy measures like tariffs, non-tariffs, foreign exchange, import and export management, which is helpful in reducing the system cost of investment; in the loose environment of trade liberalization, enterprises can be liberated from non-productive rent-seeking activities, select production modes and locations completely according to economic principles, and supply the global market so as to improve their productive earnings and the economic efficiency of the world to a great extent.

The relation of trade growth to direct investment is fully reflected in China. Since joining the WTO, promoted by the rapid growth of foreign trade, the speed of economic growth in China has been maintained at a higher level. Especially, the eastern coastal area of China has become the main area of China's export processing foreign trade and has started attracting foreign capital. Long-term development of foreign-invested enterprises mobilizes economic prosperity in the Pearl River Delta and the Yangtze River Delta. The rapid development of local enterprises in such areas forms "accumulation areas" of the manufacturing industry, supporting the production of foreign-invested enterprises. Not only do such accumulation areas have a perfect infrastructure and perfect upstream and downstream industries associated with the export processing industry, but local governments also combine the actual developmental needs, and adjust and improve the local foreign trade policies, foreign capital policies and industrial policies to provide a good hardware and software environment for a new round of foreign direct investment. So far, the proportion of capital absorbed by the eastern provinces of China has exceeded 85%.

Entering the 21st century, China has started to further speed up the pace of reform and opening-up. Constantly open domestic markets, a rapidly developed economy, and increasingly perfect policies and laws make multinational corporations of various countries change their investment strategies gradually and intensify their investment in China. Driven by competitive pressure, multinational corporations speed up the adjustment of their investments in China, which speeds up the pace of China's economic globalization and trade and investment integration.

3.2.3 The Rapid Development of Multinational Corporations Accelerates the Integration of China's Trade and Investment

Since December 2001, when China joined the WTO, the strategies with which multinational corporations invest in China have changed greatly.

(1) Sole proprietorship and transnational mergers have become important ways of direct investment of multinational corporations

The form of investment in China by multinational corporations gradually breaks through the traditional "three forms of foreign-funded enterprises" and forms the pattern of diversified investment of sole proprietorship, joint venture, purchase, mergers, and industrial transfer. Moreover, the new sole proprietorship and transnational merger have become important ways of international direct investment. Of them, the foreign-owned way has become the main way that China utilizes foreign direct investment, and it rose year by year up to 2008. Affected by the world financial crisis in 2008 and the global decline in the scale of foreign capital in 2009, the quantity and amount of wholly foreign-owned enterprises investing in China declined. At present, the development of transnational mergers in China is slow. The Temporary Provision Rules for Foreign Investors to Merge & Acquire Domestic Enterprises came into force on April 11, 2003. The *Anti-monopoly Law of the People's Republic of China* came into force on August 1, 2008. Therefore, transnational mergers will certainly enter a rapid developmental period in the future years in China, and multinational corporations will also enter a period of substantial development. Multinational corporations have advanced technology, mature management modes, flexible operational mechanisms and effective market evaluation systems. Therefore, multinational corporations are permitted to purchase part of the stock rights of state-owned enterprises. It will change the pattern of the "sole majority shareholder" of state-owned enterprises and promote the change in the managerial mechanism of enterprises. Foreign mergers and acquisitions are good for state-owned enterprises to introduce capital and advanced technology and management, to cultivate top-end talents, and to accelerate the technological advancement of enterprises. With the help of brand advantages, market advantages and managerial mechanisms of multinational corporations, the core competitiveness of Chinese enterprises will also be improved. In addition, with the gradual loosening of the policies of the state-run stock rights of listed companies transferred to foreign capital, the entry of foreign capital into the capital market will result in the emergence of domestic enterprises with more diversified shareholder structures, a larger scale, and stronger competitiveness. Thus, it can change the whole level of management and operations of listed companies and improve asset competitiveness.

(2) International industrial transfer has undergone great changes

Since joining the WTO, multinational corporations have adjusted their strategic situations again, started to transfer technology-intensive and capital-intensive industries to China, such as micro-electronics, automobile making, home appliances, communication equipment, pharmacy, chemicals, etc., as well as strengthening investment in marketing, logistics and R&D and after-sale services in the manufacturing industry chain. It increases investment at both ends of the value chain and upstream industry projects like the heavy chemical industry and tertiary industry projects. The investment system is obviously enhanced. Such changes bring new opportunities for the adjustment of China's industrial structure. Since the 1990s, several industries with the fastest growth in China, such as electronics and communications equipment, instruments and culture, office supplies and the chemical fiber manufacturing industry, have had a rate of growth that is obviously linked with foreign investment. Meanwhile, the upgrading of the composition of China's export commodities and the enhancement of competitiveness are closely related with the investment of multinational corporations. From now on, multinational corporations will continue to direct their attention to manufacturing industries and use more advanced technology to produce advanced products to further improve the industrial structure of China's foreign trade.

(3) Localization and the systematic degree of the investment management of multinational corporations are greatly strengthened

First, set up or strengthen the headquarters in China. The regional headquarters is a node of multinational corporations in the global business network. It can coordinate the business activities of the various branches effectively, and provide uniform service for each institution. It can integrate the various kinds of resources present in the many different companies in China, and strengthen their competitiveness in a wholesome manner. Many multinational corporations turn original investment companies into regional headquarters, or develop a new headquarters in China, or transfer the Asia-Pacific regional headquarters to China, assuming the function of the Asia-Pacific regional headquarters. Especially, since the outburst of the world financial crisis in 2008, multinational corporations have further increased their investment in headquarters or operation centers in China, including some multinational corporations which are promoting the transfer of globalized business operation centers (namely globalization headquarters) to China. For example, SK Company invested 500 million USD in setting up China's headquarters in Beijing in 2008, which is also the globalization headquarters of this company; the new General Motors Corporation decided to make Shanghai its globalization operation center in 2009.

Second, integrate enterprises and operating structures in China. Enterprises in China of multinational corporations are enterprises outside the regional headquarters, and operating structures are branches and several operation centers in various regions. Because China's market has a great potential and there are big differences among regions and within the industry, it is difficult for multinational corporations to deploy resources for competition with only one Chinese headquarters. Multinational corporations usually set up several operational management centers in China to coordinate business in China. Such operational management centers are of two categories: One is operation centers of different businesses outside of China or Asia-Pacific regional headquarters; the other is branches in

China set up by business sectors of the parent company of multinational corporations, for example, R & D centers and purchasing centers. By initiating the integration of enterprises, operational management centers and Chinese headquarters, multinational corporations may increase their competitiveness to a great extent.

(4) R&D input of multinational corporations is strengthened noticeably

The adjustment of investment strategies, the updating of the way of investment and the expansion of investment fields of multinational corporations in China incorporate more Chinese enterprises into the trade and investment integration system and make Chinese enterprises a link in the global economic chains of multinational corporations. There are three kinds of ways to cooperate between Chinese enterprises and multinational corporations in general. ① The product-centered division cooperation mode. Multinational corporations mainly take charge of the final assembly of a product, or concentrate on matching products with difficult production technologies and prominent scale efficiencies. Chinese enterprises take charge of various intermediate products with low production technology requirements, small batches and a high degree of labor division on specialization. ② Multinational corporations work with supporting enterprises through the market method and establish China-based purchasing centers through competition. Chinese enterprises mainly take charge of each link of production in the product value chain. The scale is expanded further and forms the "world factory." ③ Entering industry division chains of multinational corporations, domestic enterprises can gradually enter the enterprise catalog of the purchasing centers of multinational corporations and utilize high-quality, superior products to gain stable production orders and finally enter the integrated production business system of multinational corporations. The intensification of the cooperation between domestic enterprises and multinational corporations on the one hand improves the self-competitiveness of the enterprises; on the other hand, it accelerates Chinese economic globalization and the process of trade-investment integration.

3.3 Potential Problems of China's Foreign Trade and Foreign Capital Policies Under Trade and Investment Integration

China's current policies of foreign trade and foreign capital are discordant with the process of trade and investment integration. There are two major problems: One is taking no consideration of the coordination of long-term and short-term interest when China participates in internationalization. Some policies are able to promote rapid economic growth but are bad for sustainability and rapid economic development. The other is that the policies of foreign trade are in conflict with those of foreign capital. The favorable range of the foreign capital policies is often not in conformity with the provision of the foreign trade policies. Therefore, in developing foreign trade and promoting foreign capital inflow, China must adopt the trade and investment integration theory, identify the new problems at the right time and solve them.

3.3.1 The Limitation of the Export-oriented Foreign Development Mode Is Increasingly Prominent

At the beginning of reform and opening-up, the gap of the level of industrial development, the technological level of production and capital between China and developed countries or newly developing industrialized countries was obvious. Therefore, in order to make full use of the rich Chinese labor force, China has formulated the export-oriented foreign trade development mode, to attract foreign investment enterprises with the purpose of ensuring a large quantity of exports and the main way of processing trade. Such an export-oriented foreign trade development mode established on the basis of comparative advantages stimulated foreign direct investment inflow, increased the scale of exports and strengthened export trade strategies in a certain period, which in turn promoted the development of the economy in China. Therefore, we can say that when China's foreign trade advantages are cheap labor force, low-technology and low cost products, the processing trade still has much room for development in China, and the export-oriented foreign trade development mode should become the main foreign trade mode of China.

(1) Export-oriented foreign-owned enterprises focus on the field of the low-technology and labor-intensive processing exports

There is a great gap between China's processing trade and that of Japan and R.O. Korea. The gap is mainly decided by economic and technological levels, the industrial structure, enterprise competitiveness and the economic system, and the specific manifestations are as follows: First, enterprise subjects and ways are different. For Japan and R.O. Korea, domestic enterprises gain order and import raw materials by means of trade, and utilize their domestic production capacity to process, assemble and export. China processes for export by attracting foreign capital and introducing foreign production capacity. It is a link of the production chain of multinational corporations. Second, industry subjects are different. The processing trade of developed countries focuses on technology-intensive and capital-intensive products, while China focuses on labor-intensive products, and even high-tech products also concentrate on low-end links where labor is comparatively intensive. Third, process depth and value added are different. Developed countries mainly focus on deep processing and high value-added product processing, and the industrial chain is long, while there is still a great gap between China and developed countries in the rate of trade growth, processing depth and matching capacity. Fourth, there is a big gap in product R & D and marketing ability. Multinational corporations in developed countries have great strength, and they have an excellent grasp of product R & D and marketing in their hands during the processing of production outsourcing, while most Chinese enterprises lack independent R & D, design and marketing abilities. Fifth, the degree of dependence on foreign capital and self-development abilities are different. Developed countries usually adopt leading domestic developmental modes, while China's processing trade depends on foreign merchants at present, and is basically dominated by foreign multinational corporations. It is fragile and may transfer outwardly with the change of external conditions. In addition, the independent development of Chinese enterprises is weak, and most of them adopt OEM without a self-owned brand.

(2) The development of China's foreign trade on quantity and quality is unbalanced

With the great support of export-oriented foreign trade development modes and related policies, the scale of China's exports has increased rapidly in recent years, but the composition and prices of export products fail to reflect the obvious improvement in China's trade conditions. On the contrary, affected by the rise of trade protectionism in developed countries and some developing countries, China suffers from increasing trade friction, which makes China's trade conditions tend to deteriorate.

With the improvement in industrialization and processing manufacturing abilities, the main problems that have existed in China's foreign trade are as follows: The dependence on foreign intermediate products and raw materials is more serious; reform of the foreign trade system leads to fierce export competition and an increasing quantity of export supply; processing trade accounts for over half of the amount of exports, which results in the rapid growth of domestic supply compared with the growth of foreign demand, and the growth of quantity is higher than the growth of amount; multinational corporations account for a bigger proportion of imports and exports. Of them, many internal purchases import at a higher price and export at a lower price. Thus, there is deterioration in China's price trade conditions.

(3) The effect of export-oriented foreign-invested enterprises on promoting China's export competitiveness is very limited

Viewed from the perspective of multinational corporations, the investment behavior in China conforms to long-term development strategies. They only focus on the static comparative advantages of China, rather than actively developing dynamic comparative advantages in China. Therefore, in view of the developmental patterns in China, the inflow of foreign capital and the enhancement of China's export competitiveness are not coordinated with each other. In other words, subsidiaries of multinational corporations will not develop labor force skills or introduce more complicated technology and integrate them into the economy of China by establishing relationship with domestic enterprises to improve the technological level and the capacity to explore the international market of China's domestic export enterprises. China's export-oriented foreign trade development mode can meet the demand of foreign-invested enterprises for China's cheap labor force and favorable policies, but it cannot effectively improve the export competitiveness of China or maintain China's long-term attraction to export-oriented foreign-invested enterprises.

Apart from rich capital and a comparatively higher technological level, labor-intensive, export-oriented and foreign-invested enterprises investing in China still own a mature channel of international market sales, business management level and brand. These are just what domestic enterprises of China need the most. Through years of reform and opening-up, domestic export enterprises have fallen behind foreign-invested enterprises in these aspects. They enter the international market with only price advantages. However, low price competition will certainly cause anti-dumping charges against China's export enterprises by other countries and regions. China has been the country that receives the most anti-dumping charges in the world. It clearly shows that China's export competitiveness needs to be enhanced.

In addition, following China, developing countries and regions near China have adopted the export-oriented foreign trade development mode to attract foreign capital, and therefore constitute a threat to China's static comparative advantages. The cheaper labor force and more favorable policies of importing capital of these countries and regions will offset China's labor force advantages. Therefore, only if China develops a new competitive advantage and attracts foreign capital with a higher technological level and more closely related with domestic economic development, can the country's export competitiveness grow. From the above analysis, we find that external competition and internal problems that China faces in developing foreign trade and foreign capital underline the urgency and importance of raising and improving China's current foreign trade development mode. Enhancing the export competitiveness of China's products, improving China's foreign trade conditions and increasing the trade benefits gained by China have become the main objectives of attracting foreign capital, and they represent the main standard of coordinating policies of trade and investment.

3.3.2 The Policy of Foreign Trade Conflicts with the Policy of Introducing Capital in Some Aspects After Joining the WTO

After joining the WTO, the Chinese government followed up on its promise to cancel tariffs and non-tariff barriers gradually and open the domestic market. With the increase in unfair trade charges, such as anti-dumping, anti-subsidy and quantity limits, China has sped up the research on and enactment of related laws such as the foreign trade anti-dumping law. An anti-dumping policy regrding imports is a necessary foreign trade protection method for a more open China. However, with the growth in China's implementation of import anti-dumping policies, this policy will exert a direct influence on foreign direct investment, and there may be a potential conflict with current favorable policies of attracting foreign capital and this may affect China's ability to attract foreign capital and the effect of its attracting foreign capital.

(1) Potential conflict of China's import anti-dumping policy and the policies of foreign capital after joining the WTO

Multinational corporations are the subjects of the host countries that attract foreign direct investment; they are also the main carriers of policies regarding the introduction of capital. In theory, the reason why anti-dumping measures contradict the policies of introducing capital is that the targeted interest of the governments of host countries is not in conformity with that of multinational corporations. Multinational corporations pursuing a monopoly of the global market do certainly have a conflict with the host countries' target of enhancing the global competitiveness of domestic enterprises. China also faces this problem in introducing capital. With the enhancement of opening-up, the difference in ultimate targets and interest between the host countries and multinational corporations certainly leads to a relationship between introducing capital and foreign trade. If multinational corporations want to occupy the Chinese market and realize profit maximization, they may use the trade mode of low price dumping during the earliest stage, but this will certainly threaten the survival and development of similar enterprises in China. In order to promote the economic development and enterprise competitiveness of China, it is impossible for China to prevent multinational corporations from occupying the Chinese market while striving for foreign capital.

(2) Manifestation of the potential conflict between China's import anti-dumping and policies of foreign capital at present

First, there are major conflicts between China's import anti-dumping objects and policies of introducing capital after joining the WTO. The important point of China's foreign capital policy adjustment is to transform from "quantity expanding" to "quality improving," from "general preference" to "differential preference" and "national treatment." The main purpose is treating foreign investment with different qualities of investment and different technological levels discriminatorily, hoping to attract large-size multinational corporations with abundant capital and advanced technology from economic entities such as America, Japan, and EU countries. However, actual practice of capital introduction proves that the source structure of foreign investment may change, but foreign capital investment industries encouraged by current foreign capital policies are usually those suffering from the heaviest anti-dumping sanctions, such as the chemical industry and the steel industry; products encouraged for investment in the Foreign Investment Industry Guidance Catalog usually are those suffering from the most frequent anti-dumping charge, such as chemicals of a high technological level like raw materials of synthetic rubber and synthetic fiber; multinational corporations with the above production capacity and the technological level of developed countries usually suffer the most from China's anti-dumping charge.

Second, a conflict exists between import anti-dumping and limiting investment projects' marketing behavior of multinational corporations. For investment projects of multinational corporations which are allowed and encouraged to enter according to the policies of foreign capital, China usually does not rigidly stipulate the early marketing behavior of multinational corporations. However, the loose policies in regard to foreign capital usually have a potential conflict with China's import anti-dumping policy. This is because, according to preferential foreign capital policies, when multinational corporations invest in large-size projects in China, they require China to allow a certain pre-sale volume. At that stage, multinational corporations usually adopt the method of penetration pricing to expand the market so as to realize the competitive strategy of occupying and maintaining a share of the market. But such a sale method and pricing method are just typical manifestations of dumping and will certainly become important objects of China's import anti-dumping policy.

Third, a conflict exists between anti-dumping of importations and no-limiting international transactions of multinational corporations. A no-limiting international transaction of multinational corporations is included in the policies of China encouraging foreign capital, but it has a conflict with anti-dumping measures for China to follow the WTO rules. Internal trade modes of multinational corporations include simple internal trade, longitudinal internal trade, lateral internal trade, and mixed internal trade. In addition, four modes appear successively with the external development of corporations as simple internal trade, longitudinal internal trade, lateral internal trade, and mixed internal trade. It's not difficult to find that the internal trade modes of multinational corporations have become a trade force exceeding country boundaries. Through transnational deployment of internal intermediate products with low costs, they produce the final products at low costs so as to realize the low price sale on a host country's market. Rules on the internal transaction of multinational corporations in current policies of foreign capital in China do not coordinate with China's foreign trade policies. With the speeding up of economic globalization, various forms of internal purchase of multinational corporations will continuously emerge, internal transactions of various multinational corporations will happen frequently, their trade scale will also expand increasingly, and all these will bring new challenges to China's anti-dumping measures in the future.

3.4 Targets and Measures of Coordinating China's Policies on Foreign Trade and Foreign Capital

3.4.1 Make Compliance with the WTO Rules, Maintenance of National Interest and the Creation of a Good Environment the Strategic Targets

As a member of the WTO, China must follow the WTO rules to adjust the policies of foreign trade and foreign capital in accordance with WTO requirements, such as reducing tariff and non-tariff levels, improving the transparency of policies and opening up of market and so on. Besides, China is a large country that is still developing, but the level of China's economic development is still not high. The actual developmental situation requires some policies to protect its interest. Therefore, it must recognize clearly that a large amount of foreign capital inflows to China; especially large-size multinational corporations enter China for pursuing the maximization of their self-interests, which certainly does not match with China's purpose of introducing capital. As a pursuer of different interests, the Chinese government must maintain its own interests and aim at improving its benefits by participating in international business. With the intensification of China's participation in global economic integration and regional economic integration, trade and investment liberalization will be realized gradually. Therefore, improvement in the soft and hard environment for investment will provide great convenience for China to carry on its international industrial transfer smoothly, and bring a huge contribution to the adjustment of China's industrial structure and enhancement of its trade and investment competitiveness.

3.4.2 New Thoughts of Coordinating Policies of Foreign Trade and Foreign Capital

(1) Draw lessons from integration of policies of trade and investment of multinational corporations

International trade and international direct investment are the forms of the realization of international production activities and international division.

Therefore, they have some common points. In the transformation of economic integration, many countries have clearly come to know that only if they open the doors to the outside world, can they gain more benefit in the new economic environment. So they adopt trade and investment liberalization policies. Developed countries have acquired more experience in policy formulation and coordination of international trade and international direct investment, and have gained many benefits in practice. However, trade and investment policies in many developing countries are formulated separately; in the internal trade and investment integration of multinational corporations, policies and actual situations usually become separated from each other and cannot achieve a predicted goal. Therefore, the government of China should learn from multinational corporations, which consider trade, investment, and related policies as a whole. If the formulation and implementation of related policies are harmonious, various policies will support each other and promote the growth of international trade and international direct investment and create the situation in which the whole function is larger than the sum total of local functions.

(2) Innovate investment and trade procedures

Based on the trend of international trade and international direct investment integration, complementarities of investment and trade are stronger, and the past trade-investment system and operational mode can no longer adapt to the changes of the times. So we must adopt the method of integrating both of them and innovating investment and trade procedures. On the one hand, we should shorten the time of trade, technological transfer and investment or jump into foreign direct investment, and M & A of multinational corporations makes the development by leaps and bounds more convenient and feasible. The developmental sequence of the international operation of enterprises can start from any place within the world production and sales system, and will not be limited to multinational corporations of the parent country, and overseas subsidiaries may also engage in transnational direct investment activities and trade activities. On the other hand, we should bring production enterprises closer to the international consumption market through various methods, organize production according to the requirement of the international market, promote the adjustment of the product structure, realize direct combination of production, circulation, investment and trade, reduce intermediate links, reduce transaction costs, and improve transaction efficiency to realize the integration and penetration of the localization of international enterprises and the internationalization of domestic enterprises.

(3) Give consideration to the gains and losses of different parties

China is developing international trade and international direct investment during the current stage, which has features different from developed countries and not completely the same as other developing countries. Such specialty mainly comes from the external and international environment that China has faced after joining the WTO. Of them, the connection among individual consumption, enterprise interests, industrial rise and decline and social welfare is far stronger than before. Such a feature requires that the policies of trade and investment consider the satisfaction of consumers, the enterprises' pursuit of profit, the adjustment of the industry's structure, and the realization of social welfare.

(4) Implement a balanced developmental strategy with the enhancement of international competitiveness as the guide

The international trade and international direct investment strategy that China is implementing during the current stage should be a balanced developmental strategy with the improvement of international competitiveness as the guide. The objective of such a strategy is improving and optimizing competitiveness of domestic trade products on the international market and the attraction of the domestic market to foreign investors all around. The experience of international trade and international direct investment in developed countries shows that if one nation wants to enter and occupy the international market in international trade, on one hand, it must strengthen the international competitiveness of high value-added industries, which requires the government to cultivate and adjust such international competitiveness; on the other hand, it requires the creation of a competitive domestic economic environment to attract more foreign direct investment. The core of this strategy is adjusting trade and investment policies according to the change in the international competitiveness of China, adopting a balanced developmental strategy of trade and investment, and realizing the virtuous circle of mutual promotion and coordinative development. Meanwhile, perfect trade and investment laws, regulations and corresponding supporting measures, pay attention to the complementary and creative function of the vertical division of multinational corporations to international trade, and combine introducing foreign direct investment with developing foreign trade. Encourage foreign direct investment in export industries and introduce foreign advanced technology, management experience, marketing skills and a sales channel, thus improving the international competitiveness of these industries and making it possible to attract foreign direct investment and China's developing foreign trade to combine organically.

(5) Affect international direct investment by further opening international trade

China can affect international direct investment by further opening up its international trade. The traditional international division theory proposed that in the free trade condition without market distortion, producing and exporting according to the comparative advantage will gain maximum benefits. When the internal advantage of multinational corporations leads to special national advantages of free trade, multinational corporations develop an equilibrium of the resource endowment difference of various countries through foreign direct investment. That is to say, they use the internal market to replace the incomplete external market, transfer the core asset of knowledge from the parent country to the host country through internal transactions, carry out internal transactions of multinational corporations and realize the equilibrium of vertical integration. In recent years, the rapid development of technological advances has resulted in an international scenario where the technological advantage has become the determinant compared to resource endowment, and thereby decides that the competitive advantage in international economic activities gets transferred from comparative costs to comparative technology and gives rise to the change in and extension of the connotation of competitive advantage.

(6) Adopt the optimal replacement policy of international economic resources to promote the development of economic trade and investment of the nation

The selection of the policies of international trade and international direct investment has different effects on the distribution of income, which may suffer lobbying and disturbances of other forms from various interest groups. Then, how should China select the trade and investment policies with its own characteristics? The optimal selection is determined according to the developmental trend of international trade and international direct investment and the specific conditions of economic development of China. It should adopt the optimal replacement policy of international economic resources according to the features of China's economic structure at the current stage, so as to promote the development of economic trade and investment of China. Specifically: ① Promote trade and investment liberalization actively, and establish a trade system with Chinese characteristics that connects with international practices. As a developing country, China should adjust the trade and investment policies dynamically and stage by stage, and promote trade and investment liberalization according to economic development, competitive capacity, and the reform process. At the current stage, it should make full use of various "exception clauses" of the WTO to expand its self-interest. In the middle of the 21st century, China will attain the level of a medium-developed country and assume more international obligation. ② Implement a "proper" protective policy of trade and investment. As an ideal objective based on global common interest, trade and investment liberalization will probably not be achieved completely in one country in a short span of time. It is impossible for China to sacrifice self-interest in pursuing trade and investment liberalization at a time when the country is going through an economic transition. Trade and investment protection is policies and measures that the government of one nation takes in order to make full use of its domestic and overseas resources.

3.4.3 Specific Measures to Reinforce the Coordination of the Policies of Foreign Trade and Foreign Capital

(1) Promote the level of the developmental mode of export-oriented foreign trade and carry out the developmental mode of competitive advantage-oriented foreign trade

① The key to promoting the level of the developmental mode of export-oriented foreign trade is to accelerate the upgrading and transition of the processing trade

The processing trade remains the main method of foreign trade of China at present and is expected to be the predominant method in the future as well. So the leading role of foreign-invested enterprises in the processing trade will not be changed, but strengthened further. At the same time, China has possessed the objective conditions for and strong subjective willingness to carry out the transition and upgrading of the processing trade. Therefore, when depending on the improvement of independence, China should properly guide and make full use of foreign enterprises to change the current situation. China's processing trade still focuses on industries that are labor-intensive and of a low technological level.

At present, the level of industrial agglomeration in the Pearl River Delta and the Yangtze River Delta has prominently improved. The level of marketization has also improved greatly; small and medium-sized enterprises and private enterprises have grown rapidly. Scientific research and technological levels are also being gradually enhanced and the transition and upgrading of the processing trade have shown realistic conditions in these areas.

Therefore, for the acceleration of the transition and upgrading of the processing trade, China must do the following: First, improve the technological overflow level of foreign enterprises, and strengthen the correlation of foreign enterprises and China's local enterprises. The technological overflow of foreign enterprises enables the production of China's processing trade to be transferred to the top end; original production is likely to be transferred to the local enterprises; it can speed up the flow and transfer of talents, production technology, management mode, and offshore marketing network to local enterprises so as to improve the level of the processing trade of local enterprises and provide the necessary conditions for local enterprises to become the subject of the processing trade. Second, strengthen the orientation role of the government. Sticking to combining external advantages with developing self advantages is the direction that the government must move along in the development of the processing trade. The government should start from a long-term strategy, purposefully reduce the processing trade with a low level, heavy pollution, large consumption and small earnings, and attract foreign enterprises in the processing trade with advanced technologies, a high value-added and a large investment scale. Third, rationalize the related policies. Related policies with the processing trade should be adjusted and improved properly with the change in external conditions, or else a systematic barrier will limit the transition and upgrading of the processing trade. To ensure the uniformity of processing trade policies, create a policy of an environment of fair competition for domestic and foreign enterprises engaging in the processing trade rather than excessive declination to foreign enterprises, because the transition and upgrading of the processing trade will lose its basis without relying on local enterprises. At the same time, much of the supporting production of foreign enterprises in the processing trade are completed by Chinese small and medium-sized enterprises. Therefore, actively support the development of Chinese small and medium-size enterprises; this will promote the attraction of a new round of foreign direct investment on a large scale and the improvement of the levels of the processing trade.

② The key to carrying out the developmental mode of competitive advantage-oriented foreign trade is to accelerate the development and application of technology and reasonable guidance of technology-intensive foreign capital

When developing countries introduce foreign direct investment under the export-oriented foreign trade strategy based on comparative advantages, it is possible and practical that the international competitiveness of labor-intensive products will decrease. This is mainly because the development goals of developing countries and multinational corporations are different. In view of trade benefits, whether multinational corporations invest in labor-intensive industries with the comparative advantage, or capital-intensive or technological-intensive industries in developing countries, the real purpose is gaining profit and strengthening its status in international competition. Therefore, only by relying on their own power, can developing countries realize the transition of the traditional trade developmental mode to the competitive advantage-oriented strategy, change the emphasis of development from industries lacking international competitiveness to industries with competitive advantages, increase their own technological R & D and level of application, and attract foreign direct investment according to the principle of emphasizing international competitiveness.

In the transition to the competitive advantage-oriented strategy, China should further introduce advanced technology and capital according to foreign capital-oriented policies. On the one hand, prompt traditional labor-intensive export industries with a low technological level and degree of efficiency to be transferred into modern labor-intensive export industries with more modern technologies and a higher degree of efficiency; on the other hand, prompt substitutive import industries with a low degree of efficiency and no competitiveness to develop into export industries that can compete with developed countries on the uniform market through advanced technology.

(2) The formulation of foreign trade policies should be coordinated with the foreign capital policies

The key to solving a potential conflict of foreign capital policies and anti-dumping measures lies in formulating a rational industrial developmental strategy, coordinating and adjusting the promotion of foreign capital policies and import anti-dumping to the adjustment and upgrading of China's industrial structure, and realizing sustainable and healthy economic development of China after it joined the WTO.

First, formulate the foreign economic strategies of coordinating industrial development with foreign capital policies, and import anti-dumping. Thus, formulate China's own strategy for industrial development, construct an industrial developmental framework, and make industrial classification policies, namely, key industries supported by the country, industries selected by the market, and backward industries. The government of China should establish four kinds of foreign capital policies according to the developmental goals of different industries: policies to encourage the importation of foreign capital, policies to allow the entry of foreign capital, policies to limit the entry of foreign capital, and policies to forbid the entry of foreign capital. Determine the industrial field and force to implement anti-dumping measures on importations while coordinating with the policies of foreign capital.

Second, on the basis of establishing the above foreign capital policies and anti-dumping implementation principle, formulate a policy combination to attain its goal of industrial development: For enterprises that should be supported by the country and will develop rapidly within 3 or 5 years with great potential, the country should try its best to give the largest policy declination as well as weakening the impact of the entry of foreign products and investment on related industries and products. The corresponding combination strategy of anti-dumping measures and introducing capital to be adopted is not only strengthening the anti-dumping survey, but also strengthening anti-elusion tactics, as well as discouraging industries and products from introducing capital, so as to realize the purpose of weakening the impact of foreign products on related Chinese industries in aspects of importations and investments. For industries which rely on market selection, and whose technological strength has no international competitiveness, the core of national foreign trade and foreign capital policy adjustment lies in building and providing a fairly competitive environment and making domestic enterprises compete fully under the framework of market rules. The combination strategy of anti-dumping measures and introducing capital measures corresponding to meeting the domestic demand by means of foreign direct investment is strengthening the anti-dumping survey, loosening anti-elusion tactics, motivating foreign enterprises to enter China from with-commodity to with-investment, and finally reaching the purpose of expanding capital import. For the backward industries, especially for the industries causing serious pollution to the environment, forbid the entry of foreign capital and relax the execution standard of anti-dumping of the foreign commodity.

Third, set up China's Investment Measure Committee, which should take charge of coordinating the WTO members and China with regard to laws, regulations, and policies of government-regulated foreign investments. With the mutual penetration of international trade and international direct investment, China's foreign capital policies can no longer be limited to the policy goals set at the beginning of reform and opening-up; they must be combined with new forms of trade dumping with transnational investments that have emerged in the field of international trade; China must amend and improve its current policies and laws regarding foreign capital, effectively combine them with foreign trade and bring out the best of each other. Meanwhile, the establishment of this committee not only reflects China's strict execution of the WTO rules, but is also good for adjusting and correcting policies and laws inconsistent with the WTO rules when China absorbs foreign investment. Import anti-dumping is a foreign trade method that must be adopted for a more open China after it joined the WTO, but this method is only limited to foreign trade areas, which can partly solve the problems brought on by the opening-up, but not the optimal choice because economic globalization makes the mutual penetration and influence of foreign capital and foreign trade deeper and wider, which in turn makes any party's policy act on the other party. In order to measure the implementation effect of a single policy, one must broaden their vision, surpass the self-evaluation system, and carry on an evaluation at a higher level and in a broader field.

Therefore, China's import anti-dumping should coordinate foreign capital with foreign trade to maintain its normal trade order and improve the quality of capital introduction.

(3) Adapt the situation of foreign investments of multinational corporations, take the further improvement of a soft environment for investment as the basis and key work of a new round of investment promotion, open new fields for investment, and accelerate the development of China's trade in services in the context of globalization

According to the trend and change in the choice of location for direct investment of multinational corporations in the 21st century, the following work should be done well to improve the construction of investment software: ① Take time to sort out related laws and regulations with foreign investment, unify the legislation of local capital and foreign capital, and further improve economic laws and regulations concerning foreign trade. ② Truly change the work style and promote a "close to merchants" service. ③ Continue to establish and improve intermediary services convenient for foreign investment enterprises such as asset evaluation, lawyers specially handling foreign-related matters, accounting audit, information consultancy, foreign merchant complaint, property management, warehouse logistics, and custom clearance companies. ④ Promote e-government construction actively and strengthen the construction of an information network of the government. ⑤ Government departments should coordinate further and support each other to form a joint force. ⑥ Intensify the cultivation and introduction of various talents further. In the opening-up aspect of the investment field, current large-scale investment focuses on finance, telecommunications, insurance and other service fields, petroleum, chemicals, building, medicine, automobiles, and other high-tech industries. Therefore, provinces and cities must combine the overall requirement of the WTO, further open their markets to foreign investors at the proper time. Investment invitations in banks, insurance, wholesale and retail businesses, building, communications, tourism and catering and recreation will make great achievements. Meanwhile, they need to speed up the structural adjustment of the service industry and the development of the weak and new service industries.

(4) Grasp the gradual global transfer of the industrial development of multinational corporations, adjust the strategy of capital introduction, and introduce the Top 100 multinational corporations, especially American, European and Japanese large-size multinational corporations to invest in key industries

At present, the tide of enterprise strategy adjustment, business reconstruction and institutional reform with multinational corporations as the subject has lifted worldwide. Facing a gradual global transfer of the industrial developmental strategy of multinational corporations, especially equipment manufacturing enterprises of developed countries that have gradually transferred to developing countries, provinces and cities of China should promptly adjust the strategy of capital introduction according to their own conditions, and improve the guidance in investment further. The high-tech industries, including the use of high and new technology and advanced adaptable technology to renovate and improve the traditional equipment manufacturing industry, remain the important industries of attracting capital in the next step. For those provinces with the equipment manufacturing industry as the leading industry (especially Northeastern Old Industrial Base), they should pay more attention to the use of the investment of multinational corporations. Meanwhile, attract the multinational corporations to invest in supporting industries, extend the main industrial chain, improve the technological level and international competitiveness of the Chinese equipment manufacturing industry and its supporting industries and make the Chinese equipment manufacturing industry bigger and stronger.

In the context of globalization, mutual integration and integrated development of international trade and international direct investment are rapid and have shown new contents and features. The relationship between international trade and international direct investment and their influence on economic development should be the object of key research on the economic development of China at present and in the future. Now, China is going through a very important transition period in developing foreign trade and applying foreign capital. Putting to good use the relationship between foreign trade and foreign capital and coordinating the content of the foreign trade with foreign capital policies will undoubtedly play an important guiding role in the development of the national competitiveness of China and the sustainable development of its competitive advantages.

Main reference websites:

The website of the World Trade Organization Official: www.wto.org

The website of the United Nations Conference on Trade and Development (UNCTAD): www.unctad.org

The website of the Ministry of Commerce of the People's Republic of China: www.mofcom.gov.cn

The website of the National Bureau of Statistics of the People's Republic of China: www.stats.gov.cn

The website of the Organization for Economic Co-operation and Development (OECD): www.sourceoecd.com

4

China's Import and Export Trade and Technical Measures to Trade

As a developing country, China, in implementing the opening-up strategy and participating in global competition, faces a big challenge, which is technical measures to trade. Not only are China's exports blocked by technical measures to trade, but the establishment of technical measures to trade in the country is also very old-fashioned. In 2009, the total amount of national imports and exports was USD 2207.27 billion; the amount of exports was USD 1201.67 billion and the amount of imports was USD 1005.6 billion. In view of the reality that plenty of foreign products flow into China, while China has not yet established strict technical measures to trade, many questions arise. How to comply with the gradual weakening of global tariff and trade barriers? How can we make full use of related provisions of technical measures to trade under the WTO framework? How can the system of technical measures to trade be established in conformity with international standards and specifications and how can its consumers' interests and national industrial development be protected? These are some of the questions to which the government and enterprises of China need to seek answers urgently.

4.1 Impact of Foreign Technical Barriers to Trade (TBT) on China's Exportations

4.1.1 Loss of China's Exports Suffering from Foreign TBT

(1) The influence of foreign TBT on China's export products

As is shown in the study by the Ministry of Commerce, 36.1% of the export enterprises were affected to some extent by foreign technical measures to trade in 2008, 34.6% in 2007, 31.4% in 2006, and 25.1% in 2005. About 15.13% of the export enterprises of China were affected by foreign TBT in 2005. Of the 22 types of export products, 18 types suffered USD 69.1 billion of direct loss owing to foreign TBT, accounting for 9.07% of the total amount of exports. In addition, the increased production cost of China's enterprises to cope with foreign TBT was USD 21.7 billion in 2005, accounting for 2.85% of the total amount of export trade; the loss of opportunity of export trade incurred by China's enterprises caused by foreign TBT reached USD 147 billion, accounting for 19.29% of the total amount of exports.

(2) The influence of foreign TBT on the structure of China's export products

According to a report about China's technical trade measures issued by the Ministry of Commerce and Administration of Quality Supervision, Inspection and Quarantine (AQSIQ), the impact of TBT on the structure of China's export products seems to have escalated gradually in recent years. The amount of loss regarding 6 types of export products suffering from foreign TBT are mechanical and electrical products (39%), agricultural products and food (34%), textiles (18%), chemicals (6%), ceramics (2%), and toys (1%).

In recent years, the most serious impact of foreign TBT on China's export products is that on agricultural products and food, mechanical and electrical products, and chemical, plastic and rubber products. Of late, the negative impact of foreign TBT is on the rise with regard to toys, ceramics, vehicles, ships and aircraft. 8 types of products suffering impacts of foreign TBT in 2008 were agricultural products and food, mechanical products, chemicals, mining and metal products, textiles and garments, plastic and rubber products, toys and furniture, vehicles, ships and aircraft, wood products and ceramics (see Figure 4.1).

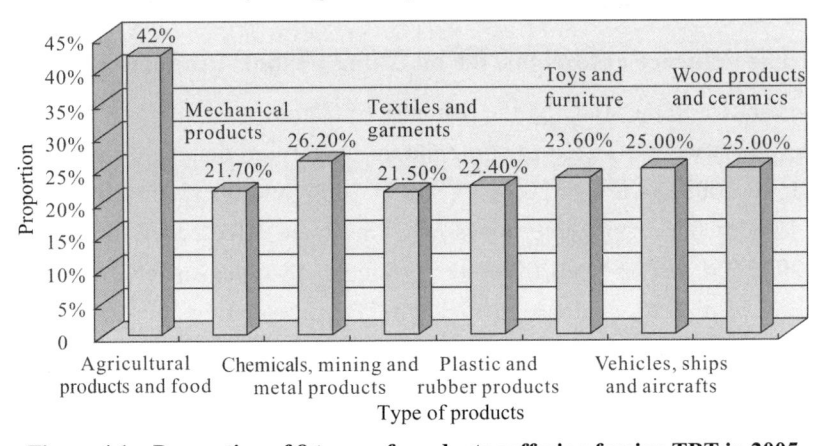

Figure 4.1 Proportion of 8 types of products suffering foreign TBT in 2005
Source: The figure is drawn according to the Annual Report of China's Technical Measures to Trade (2006) of AQSIQ.

In addition, according to the results of an industrial investigation, based on existing trends, the impact of foreign TBT has extended from labor-intensive products to high-tech products. Especially since the EU issued the Scrapped Electronic Appliance and Equipment Instructions and the Instructions on Prohibiting Usage of Some Hazardous Substances in Electronic Appliances and Equipment, China's mechanical and electrical high-tech product manufacturing enterprises have begun investing a large amount of capital in technological reform, which incidentally increases the export costs.

According to an investigation conducted by related departments, in 2006, China's foodstuff and native and livestock product industry was the industry that was affected most; about 35.98% of the export enterprises suffered from the impact to some extent with a direct loss of USD 4.3 billion, and mechanical and electrical products and the high-tech field was most seriously affected by the direct loss of USD 46.2 billion, which accounts for 60.95% of the total loss of that year.

(3) National condition of China's export trade affected by foreign TBT

According to the reports about the impact of foreign TBT on China in recent years published by the AQSIQ, China's export enterprises suffer from the TBT from the US, the EU, Japan, Canada, Australia, New Zealand, R. O. Korea and so on and the degree of damage is different owing to the category of the products (see Figure 4.2).

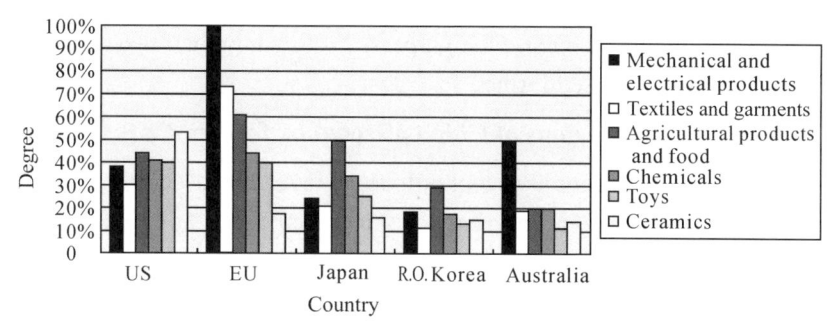

Figure 4.2 Degree of various Chinese products facing a negative impact due to the technical trade barrier of major countries in 2006
Source: Survey data from AQSIQ.

In 2006, China's sxport enterprises dealing in mechanical and electrical products encountered the most TBT in the EU, Australia and the US. 100% of the enterprises that export to the EU encountered TBT, and up to 73% of China's enterprises exporting textiles and garments encountered barriers in the EU. China's agricultural products and food industries generally encountered foreign TBT. The proportion of export enterprises that encountered TBT in the EU, Japan, and the US reached 61%, 50%, and 44% respectively. The proportion of China's enterprises exporting chemicals that encountered TBT in the EU, the US, and Japan reached 44%, 41%, and 34%. China's enterprises exporting toys encountered the most TBT from the EU and the US, and the proportion reached 40%. China's enterprises exporting ceramics encountered TBT from the US in an extremely remarkable manner, and the proportion reached 53%, and the proportion in the EU, Japan, Australia, and R.O. Korea was between 12% and 17%. From the analysis above, we can see that the TBT that China's export enterprises encounter are mostly from developed economic entities such as the EU, the US, Japan, Australia and so on, which accounts for 90% of the total. Of them, 40% of the enterprises are subjected by the EU, 27% are subjected by the US, and 25% are subjected by Japan. However, newly industrialized countries like R.O. Korea and some middle-income countries tend to adopt more concealed TBT measures in conformity with WTO rules to limit China's exportation of products, and these countries account for 8%. According to the investigation of related departments, the impact of the EU and the US on China decreased slightly in 2006, while the impact of Japan and R.O. Korea increased further.

(4) State of various regions of China affected by foreign TBT

Overall, China's science and technological level has a certain gap with developed countries. The current technical standards have not met the requirements of the technical specifications of the international market about advanced product manufacturing, which is the main reason that China's export enterprises are subjected frequently to foreign TBT. According to the investigation of related departments, the technical requirements that most export products of China are based on are national standards, industrial standards, enterprise standards, international standards, the importing country's technical requirements, the buyers' technical requirements and so on (see Figure 4.3). Of these export products, those depending on the buyers' technical requirements account for 27%; the others are those based on the importing country's technical requirements, accounting for 20%, and those depending on international standards, accounting for 12%. Products depending on the importing country's technical requirements, the buyers' technical requirements and international standards account for 59% in total. In addition, those depending on national standards, industrial standards, and enterprise standards only account for 40%. This indicates that in the production of export products, China's standards cannot meet the requirements of export production.

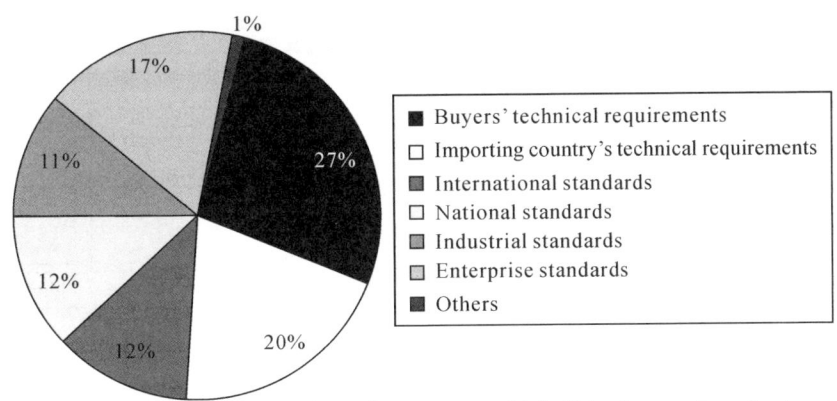

Figure 4.3 Types of technical requirements on which China's export products are based

- Buyers' technical requirements: 27%
- Importing country's technical requirements: 20%
- International standards: 12%
- National standards: 12%
- Industrial standards: 11%
- Enterprise standards: 17%
- Others: 1%

Source: AQSIQ.

Regional economic development in China is unbalanced. There exists a big gap among the eastern area, the middle area, and the western area in terms of the level of industrial and technological development. Thus, exports from these areas to other countries encounter TBT in different manners. According to the statistics of six types of products by AQSIQ, over 80% of the export enterprises in the middle and western areas, such as Ningxia, Xinjiang, Hunan, Yunnan, encounter TBT; however, 66% to 77% of the export enterprises in the eastern area, such as Tianjin, Beijing, Shanghai, Guangdong, Fujian, Zhejiang, Jiangsu, Shandong, encounter TBT. Only several provinces and cities, like Chongqing, Gansu, Jilin, Qinghai, encounter TBT in a relatively low proportion, which is between 37% and 50% (see Table 4.1).

Table 4.1 Situation of export enterprises subjected to technical barriers in different regions of the eastern, middle, and western areas of China in recent years

Region	Tianjin	Beijing	Shanghai	Fujian	Guangdong	Shandong	Jiangsu
Proportion of enterprises subjected to technical barriers	55%	63%	69%	72%	68%	72%	69%

(To be continued)

(Continued)

Region	Hainan	Zhejiang	Hebei	Liaoning	Jilin	Heilongjiang	Anhui
Proportion of enterprises subjected to technical barriers	79%	77%	71%	66%	41%	76%	76%
Region	Henan	Hubei	Hunan	Shanxi	Shaanxi	Ningxia	Qinghai
Proportion of enterprises subjected to technical barriers	66%	68%	88%	68%	73%	100%	50%
Region	Gansu	Xinjiang	Chongqing	Yunnan	Sichuan	Guizhou	Guangxi
Proportion of enterprises subjected to technical barriers	44%	80%	37%	85%	63%	73%	66%

Source: AQSIQ.

4.1.2 Analysis of the Problems of China's Export Products Subjected to Foreign TBT

(1) Export enterprises have no access to information of related rules of the WTO/TBT and lack effective resolutions

At present, China's standard numbering is relatively complicated, and the operations, modification, abolition, and combination of national standards cannot be obtained through a fully authorized channel, and even institutions that record industrial standards stated by a nation cannot handle all current information regarding standards owing to various reasons. Therefore, when a standard cites national standards or industrial standards, it may be inaccurate owing to negligence. In addition, foreign standards start to be formulated during the phase of product development, but China's standard formulation is relatively old-fashioned and the period taken to complete it is long. China's system of standardization lags behind international standards, and thus, it usually causes domestic qualified products to be withdrawn or destroyed by the importing country owing to the technology not being up to the standard. Moreover, a majority of China's enterprises have a limited scale of development, and a considerable gap exists between China and developed countries regarding technological levels, packaging and environmental awareness. The frequent appearance of various trade frictions and TBT crises makes a majority of China's export enterprises realize that improving their own levels of technology and management and strengthening the export products' competitiveness is the key to coping with foreign TBT, but the financial gap of technical reform and upgrading is still the "long-standing problem," making China's enterprises confused owing to the backwardness of gaining information on the foreign technical standards. Investigation by the Ministry of Commerce shows that the main difficulty that 50.7% of the enterprises think they need to cope with is "difficulty in technical reform and acquisition of international certification owing to a lack of capital." Another 43.7% of enterprises think that "information failure and ignorance of the changes in foreign specifications" is one of the main obstacles in coping with foreign TBT. Only 31.7% of the enterprises think there is "a big gap in the technological level and a failure to meet the technical requirements of foreign countries." All these fully reflect that currently China's export enterprises do not have a smooth channel to obtain information regarding WTO/TBT rules. They also lack a more effective platform for domestic TBT information and resource sharing.

(2) The technological level of the products is low and proprietary intellectual property rights are limited, which leads to low domestic standards, thereby failing to meet the needs of the international market

The quality of China's export products is low, and the technological level is not high. In view of the composition of its commodities, China's export products mainly focus on labor-intensive products like low-grade M&E, textiles, light industry and agricultural and sideline products. Because the production conditions are poor, and the technological level is out-dated, the quality of export products is not high and fails to have a persistent competitive advantage in international competition. The cost of China's labor-intensive products is low due to low salaries and the welfare level may improve when developed countries increase their exports, but they may still use various barriers to prevent the inflow of cheap labor-intensive products in the face of the pressure of domestic employment. Thus, the countries taking labor-intensive and natural resource-intensive products as their principal are always at a disadvantage. For example, the exportation of China's textile products has been limited by the United States to a large extent. Developed countries like the European countries, the United States, and Japan fully benefit from a technical advantage when they formulate technical regulations and standards. They input a large quantity of funds and manpower to develop new technology and new products as well as to formulate international standards, registering technological information and technological patents with a high technological level and proprietary intellectual property rights, so that they master the initiative of current international economic competition. Limited by the gap in the level of technological development, China's current standard is far from meeting the requirements of export production, and it ramains only at the international standard level of the 1980s. The first advantage of the technological standard implies the standard of the market; thus, it can be inferred that the agreement of standard information service departments and WTO/TBT affects not only the development of standards, but also the status of a nation's economy in global trade.

(3) Developed countries reinforce trade protection and enhance technical standards

As developed countries have intensified their trade protectionism based on strategic interests, China has become the second largest trading nation and its trading status has improved rapidly. In order to maintain and consolidate their dominant places in international trade competition, developed countries strengthen the implementation of TBT on China to achieve the purpose of limiting the increase in the amount of China's exported products and to protect their own domestic market and industries. In history, when the economy of one nation develops during a summit period, the protection of the economic trade of its own countries tends to increase. Since the beginning of this century, the economies of the United States and Japan have been running at an all-time high level and so the trade protectionism is inevitable. Many Chinese products cannot enter the international market owing to their failure in meeting the technical requirements of developed countries. Moreover, in the context of higher technology, safety, and sanitation and quarantine standards, some products that have entered the international market are forced to leave it.

(4) The strength to cope with TBT is not strong enough

A major reason why China's export products encounter foreign TBT is its incapability of coping with TBT. China's system of managing product quality is imperfect and inconsistent with international practice. The government of China has set up quality system certification and review institutions that are generally adopted by developed countries. It has set up China National Accreditation Board (CNAB), and China Import Commodity Inspection Bureau Laboratory Accreditation Committee (CIBLAC), successively, but the establishment of institutions is in its infancy. There are many loopholes that cannot contend with foreign TBT in production, processing, and circulation, and technical standards of various industries lack authority. Secondly, current technical regulations of various industries mostly focus on administrative laws and department regulations. The constraint efficiency is far lower than that of law, far from adapting to the increasing challenge of TBT. For a long time, the functional organization of each level of China's government was not used to abiding by the reflection of the highest will of the state, namely, laws and regulations to specify technical standards, regulations, and conformity assessment procedures of domestic products and execute them rigidly. The third is that each level of local government is seriously far behind modern times in terms of lab infrastructure construction to cope with foreign TBT and in their ability to test products; it also lacks a rapid and accurate inspection and quarantine apparatus. The main reason for this is the insufficient input that goes into infrastructure construction, the small scale of planned technical support, the lack of certified support of perfect test detection qualifications and a lack of an adequate level of technology and support of law enforcement.

The fourth, which is an important deficiency when social intermediaries cope with foreign TBT, is an enormous lack of the collection of related information, analysis and consultation services that serve export enterprises. Owing to the lack of sufficient, stable, and exact information sources, the WTO Agreement on Technical Barriers to Trade (TBT Agreement) requires each contracting party to set up information consultation points about technical standards and conformity assessment procedures to supply an answer to reasonable consultation from other contracting parties and gives priority to developing countries with regard to information notification and technical assistance.

4.2 Problem and Analysis of China's Technical Measures on Imports

4.2.1 China's Technical Measures on Imports

(1) The importance attached to technical measures on imports is relatively insufficient and technical standard strategy awareness is not strong

Because there is a certain gap between China and developed countries with regard to economic and technological development, China often suffers a terrible loss when encountering various technical standards, technical regulations and trade barriers regarding the environment, sanitation and animal and plant inspection and quarantine set up by foreign countries. Because of this, China is in the process of devising positive solutions to deal with this inadequacy. However, the assessment of damage to China caused by an amount of import products not complying with international standards is insufficient, and importance attached to technical measures and the sense of urgency are not enough. It fails to consider and plan at the level of national strategies, and lacks systematic research on technical standard strategies. As it is, a national technical measures system is completely absent in China at present.

The awareness of the importance of technical standards is not enough, and this results in China's seriously insufficient input to standardization, and the expense of technical standard formulation and modification cannot be guaranteed. It has been increased greatly in recent years, but compared to developed countries, the proportion is still low and it's difficult to solve the problem of a shortage of expenses. The American government allocated USD 700 million to a unit of American Institute of Science and Technology every year; while before 2000, the Ministry of Finance in China arranged for only 24 million yuan as a standard subsidiary. It was increased to more than 66 million yuan in 2001, but there is still a big gap with the actual need. Owing to such factors as concept, system, and policy, most Chinese enterprises don't pay much attention to the impact of technical standards on trade; the participation in standardization is uneven and they cannot play an important role and are in the margin of the standardization field. In addition, there is not much awareness of standardization among the Chinese people, the social basis of formulating technical standards is weak and standard specialty in higher education and basic education are not updated. All of them directly affect the overall level of China's standardization work.

(2) The national system of technical regulation is imperfect, and the formulation procedure and management need to be specified

China has formulated some technical regulations, but the system is extremely imperfect. Compared with foreign countries, this system is relatively old-fashioned. It is difficult for some regulations to adapt to technological and economic development. A complete and coordinated technical regulation system of various industries and areas has not been established in China yet. And some technical regulations are transformed from mandatory national standards and department documents under the planned economy, so they do not conform to the target, scope, and content stated by the WTO/TBT Agreement. An appreciable quantity of mandatory standards cannot meet international standards set by market economies. As is shown in sampling statistics of China's mandatory national standards, more than 40% of mandatory national standards have some contents that are not in conformity with the WTO/TBT.

Meanwhile, certain problems exist in the formulation procedure and management of China's technical regulations. The departments lack macro guidance, which results in the formulation work that cannot be coordinated and unified. Flexibility and openness are poor and transparency is not adequate. Poor flexibility is mainly reflected in the failure to adopt special procedures against emergency in safety, hygiene, and environmental protection or failure to adopt a rapid procedure in order to shorten the standard formulation cycle. It is also reflected in the failure to meet the need of fields with rapid technical development to adopt a formulation procedure of documents similar to standards (for example, a technical document for standardization). The poor openness is mainly reflected in the following factors: The first is that China has not formed a mechanism urging each party of the WTO to participate in the work effectively and finally reach some kind of coordination and unification; the second is that China has not widely absorbed the experience of countries with a market economy which take technical standards in formulating a technical regulation system, or that have broken away from the way of formulating technical regulations in a closed condition. Insufficient transparency means the project approval content of China's technical standards and the content of the standards cannot be known by those operating on the market as early as possible through effective channels of information transfer so as to establish an institutional notification system of technical regulation for enterprises to adjust production in time. Especially after entering the WTO, technical regulations related to trade should be known by each member of the WTO in time. China needs to improve itself in such aspects.

(3) The overall level of technical standards is not high, the conformity assessment procedure is unsound, and the environment, hygiene, and animal and plant inspection measures are imperfect

The formulation and application of technical standards need corresponding technical support. Because China's technical level is relatively old-fashioned and various problems exist in the organizational and managerial work of standardization, the overall level of China's technical standard is low, timeliness is poor, and standard formulation and technical research are seriously disjointed; some industries and products even fail to formulate specialized technical standards of their own industries. Especially in the high-tech field, the chain of scientific research and development is detached; because of this, the formulation of standards cannot meet the requirement of the rapid changes in market and technology. The system of modification is out-dated, which affects the effectiveness of Chinese industries seriously on the international market, especially in the high-tech industry. The survey shows that only fewer than half of the national standards can continue to be used in China; among international standards such as ISO and IEC adopted in China, 78.65% of them were standardized before 1994, and 736 ISO standards were invalid; 16.64% of the national standards need to be combined; 7.42% of national standards need to be abolished or decreased to industrial standards. More than 1/3 of them have problems and need to be revised; the proportion of the national standards widely used and used in a relatively large scope is 26.47% and 27.73% respectively. While international standards mainly formulated by China are fewer, the degree of China participating in international standardization work is low and at a passive acceptance state to international standards. In 2004, statistical data published by a foreign research institution showed that among 16,000 international standards in the world, 99.8% of them were formulated by foreign institutions—the United States is in the first place, and standards that China participated in were fewer than 2‰.

Meanwhile, China's manner of establishing and implementing other standards is rather out-dated. The procedures for the assessment of conformity and certification systems matching the technical standards are unsound. China's certification and accreditation system has obtained the international standard quality system certification (ISO9000), environment management system certification (ISO14000) and hygiene and food safety management system certification (HACCP), but it lacks relative regulations and standards, the work of certification organizations is irregular and TBT to protect the domestic market have not been established. In terms of green barriers, environmental awareness is weak, environmental standards are low, and requirements on environmental label and green package are not based on any concrete standards. Animal and plant inspection and quarantine systems also have problems. For example, quarantine approval is not rigid, quarantine personnel are insufficient and the technical level of quarantine needs improvement. It lacks a method for rapid detection, and the knowledge of imported plant diseases and their epidemics is not comprehensive.

The above problems have led China to fail to reach an ideal stage in establishing technical trade measures, and relatively weak import technical trade measures also bring certain damage to the management of China's importations.

4.2.2 The Analysis of Problems during the Establishment of Technical Measures on Imports

(1) The phenomenon that the threshold of China's technical measures on imports is low and imported products do not comply with international standards is a serious issue

According to statistics from related departments, the number of hazardous species that have entered China has exceeded 200, such as weeds, insects, hazardous animals, and diseases. Among the most hazardous species in the world, more than half of them have invaded China. They have invaded plenty of vegetation of China and caused huge economic losses. As the country with the largest amount of soybean importation, China imported 20.74 million tons of soybeans in 2003, which created a record in history and exceeded the domestic output for the first time; in addition, the importation of fish, plant oil, rapeseed, and chicken chopsuey has also increased dramatically. Large quantities of importations of these products without ensuring strict technical inspection bring a huge harmful impact on Chinese agriculture and lead to the entry of epidemic diseases and insect pests into China.

(2) China's environmental standard is low and the management of its imports is relatively disordered, which results in the entry of mass wastes and foreign pollution-intensified enterprises, thus destroying China's ecological environment

Prohibiting the inflow of foreign products that are not in conformity with environmental standards, waste material and hazardous material into China and preventing industries of high energy consumption and high pollution from getting relocated to China must be the important duty of the government of China. But driven by the desire to gain economic benefits and due to a lack of morality and legal concepts, China continues to import industrial refuse and hazardous waste. This not only violates the Basel International Convention and related provisions of China in controlling cross-border transfer and disposal of hazardous waste, but also results in the destruction of China's ecological environment. In recent years, Western countries have been responsible for releasing many environmental pollutants, hazardous articles, industrial and life refuse and obsolete goods inventory directly into China through export trade, such as scrapped old ships, automobiles, cables, appliances, obsolete military products, garments and tapes with plant diseases and insect pests and infective viruses.

In addition, some foreign merchants utilize the loophole of China's loose environmental standards and the not-so-strong environmental awareness to invest in and successively establish pollution-intensive enterprises with high pollution prevention costs or difficulty in governance or those forbidden to produce in foreign countries. They did so in order to evade strict pollution governance provisions and huge environmental taxes of their own countries and to gain high profits in rubber, plastic, chemicals, fibers, pesticides, process hides, printing and dyeing, papermaking and electroplate industries. At the beginning of the 1990s, foreign merchants built 75 enterprises producing foam plastics, fire extinguishing agents and cooling agents, and a majority of chemical components of these products are prohibited or limited by the International Convention on Protecting the Ozone Hole. According to the third general industrial investigation in 1995, we find that 16,998 pollution-intensive enterprises were invested in by foreign merchants; of them, 7,487 enterprises invested in serious pollution-intensive enterprises. A large number of pollution-inducing projects enter China, and this leads to a potential crisis for China's export under green barriers.

4.3 China's Measures to Cope with TBT

4.3.1 Strengthen Measures of China's Export Enterprises and Related Departments to Cope with TBT

(1) Aiming at unification, simplicity, and normalization, China should reform its domestic-related TBT information system, and provide a conducive information environment so that China's export enterprises can pass foreign TBT

① Improve and regulate the release and notification system of China's technical regulations

Generally speaking, there are two functions of technical regulations: One is to specify the production behavior of enterprises to guarantee the quality of products; and the second function is that they play the role of negotiating domestic and foreign industry technological development information, which has guideline values for enterprises in adapting to the international market better. Therefore, a set of specified release and notification systems of technical regulations is vital to industrial development and to the foreign trade of a nation. At present, the release and notification system of China's technical regulations is imperfect, which makes enterprises attach less importance to technical regulations or fail to acquire related accurate and appropriate information in time. Therefore, China shall comply with the definition of WTO/TBT strictly, formulate and promptly release related technical regulations of various industries abroad, increase the number of China's technical regulations, expand the coverage area, and force the production activities of enterprises to have laws to abide by to improve the overall quality of enterprises' technology and intensify the competitiveness of export enterprises. Especially in procedures related to hygiene, safety, environmental protection and conformity assessment and third-party certification, there is a big gap between China and developed countries.

② Simplify the numbering system of China's technical standards

Establish a unified and authorized institution for technical standard release and query, grasp information of all current standards, and enable the acquisition of complete information of implementation, modification, abolition, and combination of national standards. Renumber national, industrial, and enterprise standards, simplify the technical standard numbering system, and make it convenient for enterprises to query and observe.

③ Create a smooth channel for enterprises to acquire related information of TBT

Establish a unified real-time notification and warning platform of domestic and foreign technical standards, prevent enterprises from encountering foreign TBT owing to "information failure and ignorance of the changes in foreign specifications," and decrease institutional barriers owing to information failure. Establish a comprehensive national system of notification, consultation, discussion and warning of technical measures to trade, establish a notification and exchange system of production and import and export data of sensitive and important industrial and agricultural products and achieve information sharing and interaction. Achieve effective online notification, consultation, discussion, and warning and promote enterprises' capability of risk defense of and rapid reaction to technical measures to trade through rapid transmittance and sharing of information.

(2) Encourage enterprises' initiatives of independent research and development, change China's composition of export commodities further, and improve the technical level and value-added level of export products

① According to China's industrial and technical development status, improve the level of overall technical standards of China comprehensively

Trace the development of domestic and foreign industrial and technical standards, strengthen the differential research on domestic and foreign technical standards, and enable the formulation and revision of China's technical standards more rapidly and timely. Strengthen the formulation and revision of China's standards for important industries and advantageous export industries and improve the current technical standards comprehensively. Focus on adopting international standards to strengthen the national standards, and connect national standards with international standards gradually. Participate actively in international standardization activities, and in formulating international standards, and reflect China's reasonable requirements; especially try to include national standards of China's advantageous projects (such as traditional handiwork with Chinese features) and high-tech products into the international standard system. In addition, strengthen the enterprise standardization work, improve enterprises' standardization awareness and intensify the correlation of the standards and the market.

② Encourage powerful export enterprises to adopt international standards and advanced foreign standards to meet the needs of the international export market

The basis of the application of international standards and advanced foreign standards is the introduction of cost-effective technological innovations and an effective way of narrowing the gap in the level of quality between China and developed countries. Therefore, enterprises must pay great attention to these areas. For example, in order to achieve internationalization, Haier Group collected more than 2,400 standards, cooperated with standardization technical institutions, traced and researched related standards of international organizations and export countries, and established its own library of standards. Moreover, it compared the ISO/IIJC standards, the national standards of the United States, Europe, the Middle East, and Russia and its own enterprise standards and regarded them as the basis for product development, production, and inspection to enable itself to grasp the initiative in international competition and avoid trade barriers arising from inappropriate technical standards.

③ Improve the technological level of export products and change the composition of its export commodities

Strengthen intellectual property protection awareness and emphasize the application of patents, while the combination of technical standards and patents has become a trend in TBT of the manufacturing industry of developed countries. Therefore, China's export enterprises must strengthen research and development actively and improve the level of proprietary intellectual property rights to overcome foreign TBT. Only if it occupies a favorable place in technologies, can it occupy a favorable status in the international trade pattern. In addition, the government should continue to create a good environment and provide great support by means of formulating policies for enterprises' technological innovation and independent research and development, including strengthening intellectual property protection and giving tax preference to enterprises with technological innovation.

(3) Follow the TBT developmental trend of developed countries, strengthen the analysis of and research on important foreign regulations regarding standards, and provide measures and suggestions for domestic enterprises to cope with foreign TBT

① Collect data regarding foreign technical barriers actively, set up special institutions for analysis, and carry out policy research

At present, developed countries formulate technical standards more rigidly, so it is necessary to strengthen our research on the main methods of major trade partners implementing TBT and important regulations of some countries. Establish warning mechanisms and adopt active measures against the impact of trade partners' TBT on China's export trade. Study and learn from the experience of and lessons learned by foreign governments and enterprises on breaking TBT and provide measures and suggestions for enterprises. According to the special treatment meted out to developing countries in the TBT Agreement, try to speak up for China's exports in various occasions related to TBT.

② Against foreign TBT, strengthen review and discussion

Each functional department of the government should grasp, know, and strengthen the review process of foreign TBT and improve the review capability of each department through inter-departmental exchanges and learning as well as borrowing the experience of foreign reviews. Establish inter-departmental review mechanisms, set up a unified inter-ministerial expert reviews team to strengthen multi-department review, and improve the multi-department review procedure further. Carry out research on key technical measures, and mobilize and guide enterprises and industrial organizations to engage in review. Increase the manpower and financial support of review, focus on mobilizing multi-aspect powers, and make efforts to enhance the timeliness and effectiveness of review. Meanwhile, increase the strength of diplomatic negotiations, improve the proportion of China's review comments abroad, and decrease the impact of major trade partners' final measures issued on China's imported products to the minimum level.

(4) Give full play to the service function of the government and social intermediaries

① Give full play to the service function of government departments

The first step is to accelerate the construction of China's technical standards, laws, and regulations. The government of China always pays attention to the construction of the law system, but it is far behind when compared to Western countries in terms of the product quality management system and industrial and technical regulations. Therefore, it is necessary to speed up the construction of China's law system. The second step is to strengthen knowledge publicity, training, and popularity work of new trade barriers. Most enterprises do not have enough understanding of new trade barriers, so China needs to strengthen research and talent cultivation of new trade barriers, and make export enterprises pay more attention to new trade barriers and take measures to cope with them. The third step is to strengthen the infrastructure construction of technical detection labs. Expand the input of rapid and exact inspection and quarantine instruments and equipment and bring about a change to the situation that the ability and level of product inspection are generally weak. Meanwhile, cultivate a batch of high-quality inspection and detection personnel, improve test-detection qualification affirmation guarantees, and improve the technical level and technical guarantee ability of law enforcement.

② Social intermediaries provide information technology service

The first service provided is strengthening training to industrial organizations and enterprises. On the one hand, carry out the training of presonnels regarding the international rules of WTO/TBT-SPS and related international standards, guidance, suggestions, and developmental trends, help enterprises adapt to situation changes after China entered the WTO, and improve the capability of using international rules to protect their self-interest; on the other hand, carry out purposeful training, make industrial organizations and enterprises understand the relative laws, standards, and procedures of import countries and master the methods to cope with them, thus avoiding risk and reducing unnecessary loss at the time of exportation. Guide industrial organizations and enterprises in joining in notification reviews, diplomatic negotiations and so on to help them improve the ability to cope and lay the foundation for the future.

The second service provided is serving as a bridge between enterprises and the government, collecting and investigating TBT encountered by its own industry during exportation and carrying out research and analysis, providing related information services for members of its own industry, reflecting and raising opinions and suggestions on solving problems, representing enterprises to send their problems to foreign industrial organizations or government institutions, and helping enterprises solve problems if necessary. Therefore, a suggestion needs to be made that various related industrial organizations should arrange specialized leaders, departments, and full-time staff to take charge of such work and research and review the work of foreign TBT for consultation.

The third service is studying and utilizing technical regulations of TBT; studying specific requirements of formulation, approval, and implementation of conformity assessment procedures and the due rights enjoyed by member countries; studying the content of the formulations, approval, and implementation of good standard codes of conduct and due treatment of member countries; studying how to apply special and discriminated treatment to developing member countries on information assistance in TBT Agreement, and trying to gain more technical assistance and care; studying the content, procedures, and provisions about negotiation and dispute solution clauses in the TBT Agreement and maintaining the legitimate interests of enterprises.

4.3.2 Strengthen Construction of China's Import Technical Trade Protection System

(1) Build up a sense of standardization and promote the technical standardization strategy positively

① Strengthen unified coordinative management of the establishment of technical standards

China should establish an authorized institution to manage standardization work of related departments, industries, and products, specify formulation and amendment procedures of technical standards, and form a perfect and efficient system of technical standard decision-making. China states in a commitment about quality inspection after entering the WTO that "AQSIQ is responsible for all of China's policies and procedures related to the assessment of conformity, and other government departments and agencies must be authorized by AQSIQ before releasing their assessment of conformity policies and procedures." Therefore, we suggest that the State Council authorize AQSIQ to take charge of technical standard management, or that other departments draft and formulate technical regulations and conformity assessment procedures, release them in the form of decrees or rules and send notifications to the WTO members through the Ministry of Commerce in a timely manner.

② Increase investment in research and formulation of technical standards

In view of public economics, technical standard systems or technical measures to trade can be considered as a public product at the macro-economic level, and the nation should be one of the main producers or providers. At present, the fund that the government of China inputs to technical standards is relatively insufficient, so the government should increase its national financial support to technical standard work, increase its capital investment, incorporate technical standard construction into the national economic development planning system, and include technical standard costs in public financial expenditures to provide guarantees. Meanwhile, explore how to encourage and guide enterprises to increase capital investments in technological innovation and technical standard research and development and increase the sources of standardization expenses in various ways and at various levels. For example, comprehensively use economic policies of favorable credit and loan and tax deduction and exemption, and stimulation mechanisms of government direct subsidies, cooperation with enterprises on research, reward, and subsidies to encourage enterprises to increase development input and participate in the process of formulating standards.

(2) Establish and perfect China's TBT system

① Establish and perfect China's technical standard and regulation system with reference to international norms

On the one hand, adjust China's current technical regulation system. Reserve the technical standards suitable for the WTO rules and China's national condition, revise or abolish inapplicable technical standards not in conformity with the international trade development situation, improve some excessively low standards, and enhance the overall level of China's standards.

On the other hand, carry out in-depth research on international technical standards, draw lessons from the standardization strategy experience of developed countries, look for differences, and speed up the process of enlarging and perfecting the unestablished standards and regulations in China, perfect conformity assessment procedure, and speed up the improvement of animal and plant hygiene inspection and quarantine standards.

②Perfect China's product certification system and establish mutual recognition mechanisms with international authorized certification institutions

The first step is to promote the certification work of ISO14000 and ISO9000 series actively, expand the coverage area of certified products, increase support to some certification authorities, improve their strength, and try to build up a batch of world-famous authoritative certification bodies and signs; the second step is to issue related laws and regulations as soon as possible, strengthen the supervision and coordination of the National Certification and Accreditation Administration, regulate quality management systems and environmental management systems, and carry out the unified, specified, and effective implementation of certification work; the third step is to carry out international certification work actively, strengthen exchange and cooperation with foreign authoritative bodies, sign mutual recognition agreements of product certification, system certification, and lab accreditation, establish mutual recognition mechanisms and realize mutual certification. This can not only improve China's certification system and achieve international connection, but also save the expenses of repeated certification, as well as being good for China's enterprises to improve their own technological level, and succeed with improving quality and overcoming foreign TBT.

(3) Construct green trade barriers and prevent foreign products and industries not in conformity with environmental standards from transferring to China

① Construct green trade barriers and prohibit products not in conformity with environmental standards from entering China

The green trade barrier is also called the "environmental barrier." It is one of the most important and most concealed non-tariff barriers in international trade. Directed at the severe reality of the inflow of a large quantity of unaccepted products, pollutants, and even hazardous and toxic wastes to China, China should improve its environmental standards as soon as possible, perfect its environmental laws and regulations, construct a reasonable green barrier system, and prohibit such articles form continuing to transfer to China. Specific measures include the following: The first measure is to enhance green technical standards, perfect the environmental tariff system and the market access system, levy environmental value-added tax or forbid the importation of products that are not in conformity with China's standards; the second measure is to establish environmental sign and green package sign systems and promote the production and consumption of products with less environmental impact; the third is to perfect the green system of hygiene and quarantine and make rigid provisions of maximum limits of pesticide residue of foodstuffs, radioactive residue and heavy metal content; the fourth is to implement green production subsidies, include environmental and resource expenses in the cost of products and provide certain environmental subsidies for some enterprises.

② Adjust foreign capital policies and prevent developed countries from utilizing international investments to transfer "high-energy-consumption, high-pollution and resource-intensive" industries to China

In order to maintain sustainable economic development, China should speed up the process of changing foreign capital policies from "attracting foreign business and investment" to "attracting business but selecting investment," prevent developed countries from transferring "high-energy- consumption, high-pollution and resource-intensive" industries to China by using a new round of international industry transfer. The first step is to establish an efficient foreign-invested project approval system, emphasize environmental approval procedures, improve environmental standards and control project introduction according to the degree of pollution. Restrain investment projects that would pollute the environment seriously, have difficulty in pollution treatment, and consume a large quantity of resources and energy. Forbid the introduction of heavy-pollution technology, equipment, and production processes that have been obsolete on the international market. The second step is to strengthen the assessment and review of the environmental and ecological benefits of current foreign-owned enterprises, enhance the strength of law enforcement, and promote foreign-owned enterprises to adopt necessary measures to prevent environmental pollution. For example, for foreign-owned enterprises exceeding China's pollutant discharge standard, collect sewage charge according to the quantity and concentration of the pollutants that are discharged; for enterprises that cannot reach the governance goal on time, cancel the preferential policy; increase the amount of the penalty, urge enterprises to upgrade their equipment, and increase input to environmental governance facilities. The third step is to adopt preferential policies to encourage and guide foreign merchants to invest in ecological and environmental industries, introduce advanced technology and equipment for pollution prevention, clean production and cyclic utilization of waste.

(4) Strengthen exchanges and cooperation and participate in the formulation of international standards

International standards have become an important part of international trade rules and have been one of the main bases for solving trade disputes and conducting international arbitration. Therefore, occupying the commanding height of international standards and mastering the initiative of standard formulation is undoubtedly a shortcut for the enterprises of China to win a competitive advantage. Owing to historical reasons, the current international standards are mostly initiated and formulated by developed European and American countries or adapted directly from the standards of large enterprises in these countries, reflecting the economic benefit and technological level of European and American countries. With economic globalization, the competition in contending hegemony of international standards is fiercer. In order to enhance the international influence of Chinese standards, and get China to engage in the formulation process of international standards and related rules, the following measures may be taken: The first measure is to try to win the hosting, drafting, and formulation work of international standards relevant to China's interest, organize Chinese standardization experts to engage in it and aim at incorporating technical standards and industrial standards of competitive products in China into international standards; the second measure is to assume the work of the WTO and ISO secretariats, and participate in the review work that various standardization organizations carry out on other countries' standards; the third measure is to cast a substantial vote in consultative opinion of international standards, reflect the requirement of China's technical standards and enterprises fully and maintain the national interest of China; the fourth is to apply for patents for China's industries with comparative advantages and transform them into standards that can be followed; the fifth is to utilize the World Trade Organization platform to establish strategic alliances regarding standardization with main countries, gain the support of strategic partners, and enhance the right of speech.

5

Technology Spillover of Foreign Direct Investment and Chinese Technological Progress

The manner in which the mutual benefit and win-win opening-up strategy is reflected in China's foreign investment policy is becoming the main problem of the utilization of foreign capital in the new phase. We must, on the basis of strengthening and expanding the existing open results, further perfect the foreign capital policy, further enhance the quality and the level of the open economy and make use of foreign capital. The technology spillover effect of foreign direct investment and its positive role and impact on economic growth exists and cannot be denied. In fact, technology spillover is the main channel for foreign direct investment to drive forward Chinese industrial technological progress. However, "nationalism in technology" is an indisputable fact at any time, and will not change for quite a long period in the future. In the 21st century, the contention of world political and economic interests has gradually transformed from the perspective of capital to technology, and international competition, to a great extent, deals with the competition at the level of science and technology and depends on the ability of research and development. As it turns out at home and abroad, it is impossible to try to improve the level of a country's technology and to occupy a favorable position in international competition only through the introduction of foreign capital. For developing countries, it is important to take advantage of capital, but the key factors in determining the long-term sustainable and stable economic growth are technology, management, market and so on. In the new environment of expanding opening-up to the outside world, the following factors are of great significance both at the theoretical level and at the practical level of decision-making: How to understand the mechanism, the facilitation and the constraints of technology spillover of foreign direct investment in China, and what strategies can we adopt to bring the positive effects of technology spillover into full play? How to set up the pattern of technological progress that adapts to China's enterprises, to enhance the capacity of domestic enterprises, technology absorption and re-innovation, thereby raising the level of China's technology?

5.1 Basic Theories of Technology Spillover of Foreign Direct Investment

5.1.1 The Adjustment of China's Policy of Utilization of Foreign Capital in the New Stage

Over years of reform and opening-up, with China's rapid economic development, people's living standards have been improved significantly, and our international status has been rising. From 1978 to 2009, China's economy rose from USD 600 billion to USD 33 trillion; China's foreign trade volume increased from USD 20.64 billion to more than USD 2.2 trillion, the ranking of the total amount of trade rose from 29th to 2nd in the world. The enormous investment achievements have produced profound influence on China's economic and social development during this period. The degree of China's opening-up has continuously improved:

On the one hand, foreign investment plays a positive role in China's GDP growth, investment in fixed assets and employment; on the other hand, the dependence of China's economic growth on foreign capital has also continuously increased. However, too much emphasis on utilization of foreign capital has also brought about some negative effects, such as an unreasonable orientation in foreign investment, lower investment quality and the damage of fair market competition and so on.

On January 1, 2008, the new law on corporate income tax came into effect; domestic and foreign enterprises began to apply a unified corporate income tax rate, namely, "integrated income tax." Since then, China has gradually said goodbye to the era of "different tax" of enterprise income tax, and the preferential tax policies transformed from being region-oriented in the past to being industry-oriented. This started the new orientation toward the utilization of foreign capital policies in China. From the issuing of the new five-year plan of using foreign capital, to the releasing of new rules of foreign capital merger and acquisition, to the adoption of the enterprise income tax law, and to the releasing of a new version of the Catalogue of Industries for Guiding Foreign Investment, it is becoming increasingly clear that the goal of China's policies is to improve the quality and efficiency of the utilization of foreign capital.

5.1.2 Theoretical Overview of Technology Spillover of FDI

(1) The definition of technology spillover

From the perspective of economics, technology has some kind of external economic characteristic of "public goods," and its additional services do not raise costs. Thus, this phenomenon is called "market failure." Technology diffusion is a process of knowledge transfer and technology transfer, including unintended technology spillover. The technology spillover effect refers to what happens when technology comes into the host country along with the investment. Although foreign businessmen have carried out various control measures, technology spillover can still bring advanced technology to the host country, and promote the economic development of the host country indirectly. This kind of benefit that technology spillover brings to the host country is out of the control of technical subject, and it is an effect besides the returns of capital and technology investment. Kokko, in the book *Foreign Direct Investment, Host Country Characteristics and Spillovers*, investigates the local spillover of technology and production as a result of some multinational companies setting up subsidiaries in other countries. He argued that the technology spillover effect is a situation that when the multinational companies set up subsidiaries in the host country, local technology or productivity gets promoted; however, the subsidiaries of the multinational companies are unable to get complete revenue.

(2) The evolution of technology spillover theory

① The theoretical discussion and research achievements on technology spillover of foreign direct investment from foreign countries

The discussion of technology spillover can be traced back to the early 1960s. MacDougall, when he analyzed the general welfare effects of foreign direct investment in 1960, for the first time regarded the technology spillover as an important phenomenon of foreign direct investment.

The first research on the technology spillover effect was carried out in the field of international technology diffusion. Caves regarded the international technology diffusion as the starting point in 1974; then according to the different influences that technology diffusion had on local enterprises, he first comprehensively divided the exteriority of technology diffusion into three categories: (a) For an industry with strong industrial barriers, due to the forced entry of multinational companies, monopoly will be curbed, and the allocation of resources will be improved. (b) The pressure from increasing competition or the demonstration effect from multinational companies stimulates the local enterprises to use the existing resources more efficiently and promotes the local technical efficiency. (c) On account of competition, repeated imitation, or for other reasons, the entrance of multinational companies will speed up the transfer and diffusion of technology.

After Caves, the major contributors in this field were Findlay, Koizumi, and Kopecky. Findlay built a simple endogenous and dynamic model of advanced developed countries making direct investment and creating technology diffusion in the poor developing countries in 1978, which tested the effects of static characteristics such as technology gap and foreign capital share on the rate of technology diffusion. He also examined the indirect impacts of other variables such as the home country's speed of development, the foreign profit after tax, the host country's level of education and the marginal propensity to save and so forth, on technology spillover of foreign direct investment. Koizumi and Kopecky constructed the spillover model according to the traditional theory of international capital flow, made use of the local equilibrium theory to analyze the determining factor and effect of technology spillover, and thought that the levels of technology spillover were positively correlated with the share of foreign investment. Its innovation lies in the following fact: By introducing the technology spillover effect boldly to the traditional model of international capital flow, some of the conclusions of old models can be revised.

Lall inspected the association between the multinational companies and the host countries' enterprises from the perspective of foreign direct investment in 1980. He thought that multinational companies usually have the advantage of technology or information, and as the subsidiary companies connect with local suppliers or customers, the local firms may "free-ride" from multinational companies' advanced products, technology processes or market knowledge, so technology spillover occurs. Even though the subsidiary companies of multinational companies will charge the local enterprises or customers some fees, in most cases, they cannot grab all the benefits that the local enterprises gained from the improvement of their productivity.

Das put forward the competitive spillover model from the perspective of multinational companies in 1987. This model considered that technology spillover had become a potential cost to the multinational companies' subsidiaries because the local firms taking "a free ride" sooner or later will have enough ability to compete with multinational companies. Although there is the possibility of technology spillover, Das thought it was still profitable as long as multinational companies imported advanced technology. The progress of this model was to give full consideration to the multinational companies' subsidiaries admitting the existence of technology spillover, but in fact, it still ignored the decisions and actions of local enterprises.

In 1987, Wang and Blomstrom regarded technology spillover as the endogenous phenomenon of strategic competition between multinational companies' subsidiaries and the host country's enterprises. They built a fundamental model of a game between multinational companies' subsidiaries and the host country's enterprises. On the one hand, they assumed that the multinational companies' subsidiaries could realize the cost of technology diffusion; on the other hand, they assumed that the host country's enterprises could also realize the existence of spillover. Whether the multinational companies' subsidiaries or the host countries' enterprises, both may affect the level of spillovers through their investment decisions: The more the multinational companies invest in new technology, the more the spillover there will be; the more the host countries' enterprises invest in "learning," the stronger their ability to absorb the spillover will be. In fact, because the spillover promotes the technical progress of local enterprises and narrows down the technology gap with multinational companies' subsidiaries, the quasi-rent of multinational companies' subsidiaries is reduced; in order to maintain comparative advantage of their products' technology, multinational companies' subsidiaries are forced to introduce or develop new technologies, to restore their market share and profits. As a result, a new round of spillover occurs, which is called spillover positive feedback. By the same token, the learning behavior of the host countries' enterprises also shows this kind of effect.

Kokko, on the basis of his predecessors' research, systematically presented the occurrence of technology spillover in his book *Foreign Direct Investment, Host Country Characteristics and Spillovers* in 1992. He thought that the technology spillover happened based on two aspects: One was from demonstration, imitation and diffusion; the other was from competition. The former was an increasing function of the technical information difference, while the latter was mainly determined by the foreign companies and the market characteristics of local companies and their interaction. In fact, the technology spillover effect was not limited to these two aspects alone, such as the leading role of technology progress in related industries, and the guiding role of the technology spillover in the changes in the host countries' industrial structure. These were the results of the technology spillover effect, except that they were somewhat relatively indirect. Later, Kokko carried on a comprehensive elaboration of the technology spillover effect of foreign direct investment in 1994. He not only summarized the basic channels of spillover, namely, the forward and backward relationship, competition, demonstration, imitation, mobility and dissemination of one industry, but also verified the disequilibrium of the spillover effect in one industry or between industries by econometric methods. He thought that the foreign-invested enterprises were in a state of "enclave" operating, whose technology spillovers in host countries were generally very limited.

Considering the above theories, we can deduce the following: Findlay, Koizumi and Kopecky, Lall, and Das are of the opinion that spillovers are most likely to happen between countries with large technology gaps. It is the result of technical differences between the host countries' enterprises and the multinational companies' subsidiaries. The level of the spillover depends on the size of the technology gap and foreign capital share in the industry. It is difficult to avoid the cost of spillover for foreign companies, but if the host enterprises want to obtain such external benefits, that depends on the positive action of the host countries' enterprises. These conclusions are affected by various external variables, such as the speed of technological progress in advanced countries, the multinational companies' profit after tax, the host countries' propensity to save, and so on. But they did not consider the impact of the behavior of local enterprises and multinational companies' subsidiaries on the spillover, while Wang and Blomstrom were more comprehensive in seeing the impact of the local enterprises and multinational companies' subsidiaries' decision-making and behavior on the spillover. According to Kokko's classification, spillover effects summarized by Findlay, Koizumi and Kopecky, Lall, and Das have something to do with the technology gap, which belongs to the "demonstration—imitation—transmission" pattern; and the spillover summarized by Wang and Blomstrom depends on the market environment, the interaction of multinational companies' subsidiaries and local enterprises, which belongs to "competition."

② Chinese research progress on the technology spillover of foreign direct investment

The research on technology spillover in China was enhanced after the 1990s. Li Xiangyang suggestsd that the technology brought by foreign investment will not only act on one industry but also spread to other industries; Liu Xing and Gu Yuansheng quantified the effect of the use of foreign capital on technological progress in China. Li Ping made use of the existing model systematically to illustrate the principle, process and mechanism of technology diffusion. This further enriched and developed the technology diffusion exteriority theory in 1999; at the same time, he studied the empirical results of inter-industry technology spillover in China through a large number of regression analyses, and proved the technology diffusion at the levels of industries and enterprises and the existence of externalities. He Jie and Xu Luodan learned from Feder's measurement methods proposed in 1982, and established the regression equation, which was based on the production function. The results showed that with an increase of 1 percentage point in the technology level brought by foreign direct investment, China's domestic industrial enterprises' technology spillover effect (i.e., the increase in production) will be increased by 2.3 percentage points. Chen Guohong, making use of Granger's causality test, analyzed the causal relationship between China's industrial foreign direct investment and technology transfer, and considered that industrial foreign direct investment is the important reason for the technology transfer. Shen Kunrong and Geng Qiang pointed out that the provinces that introduced more foreign direct investment were the ones that maintained a faster economic growth rate and a higher level of economic development by obtaining a technology spillover effect greater than that of other provinces. The latest research achievement is an endogenous technological progress model of the expansion of intermediate products' categories constructed by Lai Mingyong et al. The results showed that in the open economy system, international technology spillover and diffusion have become an important external impetus to China's economic growth; at the same time, the demonstration effect, the competition effect, the industrial connection effect, and the personal training effect of foreign direct investment play an important role in the channels of technology diffusion.

The above findings confirmed the promoting effect of foreign investment on the technological progress in various aspects. There are also many scholars who worry about the effects of foreign investment in China. Li Lian analyzed and explained the policy of "exchanging market for technology" in 1994; Yu Guangsheng and Li Wei also rethought the policy; Wang Yungui, Tong Shuxing, and Chen Bingcai all expressed doubts about the effect of the policy, and pointed out that we cannot expect too much from the effect of technology transfer of foreign direct investment. Liu Ling pointed out in his writing that in Shanghai, a city with a strong industrial base in China, 80% of the enterprises with foreign investment belong to labor-intensive enterprises, and the technological level of these enterprises is generally low. Ni Yan also pointed out that the technologies multinational companies transfer to China are generally mature technologies, and that the transferred technology in the innovation stage and the developmental stage will be strictly controlled; after joint venture, most domestic enterprises cancel the original research and development institutions, and rely on large foreign multinational companies in technology, which reduce the ability of their own research and development and technology innovation. Bao Qun and Lai Mingyong stated that although foreign direct investment has promoted China's technological progress, the effect was achieved mainly by increasing the factor productivity of foreign capital enterprises themselves, and the technology spillover effect of the foreign capital enterprises on local enterprises was not obvious. Lin Yifu et al. supported the technology selection hypothesis by building a model of technology diffusion and economic growth, and considered that when a development strategy adopted by the government of a developing country deviates from the technology of the optimal selection, then it will affect the country's economic growth rate and the convergence to the developed countries' income level. Yu Junyan pointed out that due to external effects, foreign direct investment is likely to make the technology of the host country be locked in a low level trap. The results of the empirical analysis also showed that there is a weak negative correlation between foreign direct investment and the rate of China's technical improvement, indicating that foreign direct investment does not have any obvious promoting effect on technological progress on the basis of driving China's economic growth. In order to obtain more knowledge, technology and human capital, which are necessary for sustained economic growth, we must increase the self-consciousness of investments. There is more emphasis on the accumulation of the capability for independent innovation.

5.1.3 The Mechanism of the Technology Spillover from Foreign Direct Investment

(1) Demonstration and imitation

From the essential characteristics of technology, technological innovation can be copied effectively on condition that imitators have the opportunity to contact and communicate with technology owners or can acquire new technology through other channels. International trade and foreign direct investment just provide the chances for these opportunities; it enables the producers to get the product information and technical information from other countries.

Multinational companies in developed countries, with advanced technology, management experience and other advantages, after entering the host countries' market, break the original market equilibrium, intensify the local market competition, force local enterprises to imitate the multinational companies, encourage local enterprises to find and make use of more updated technology to improve the level of management, and more effectively make use of technology and resources to improve their market competitiveness. As multinational companies possess advanced technology and production processes, the technology transferred to the subsidiaries is generally more advanced than that of external transfer; so the subsidiaries of the multinational companies have stronger comparative advantages in technology compared with their competitors in the host countries, thereby gaining more market share and profits. This kind of technology demonstration enables enterprises in developing countries to use various methods, hiring staff having worked or trained in a multinational company to indirectly gain access to the production techniques and technology of the products, or doing product research and development through reverse engineering to improve their own level of production technology, and accumulate technical ability and practical experience through learning by doing, so as to further enhance the enterprises' capacity to absorb technology transfer and technology spillover.

(2) Industrial linkage

The so-called backward linkage refers to the connection between foreign companies and local suppliers. The host countries' enterprises provide raw materials, spare parts, and services required for production for the multinational companies' subsidiaries. Through backward linkage, on the one hand, the resources of the developing host countries realize efficient allocation, which strengthens the production capacity of upstream industries and improves production efficiency; on the other hand, in order to guarantee the quality and competitiveness of their products, the multinational companies' subsidiaries usually build productive facilities and provide technical assistance, information consulting services, and management training and other services for the suppliers, so as to promote the improvement of production capacity and operation and management ability of the developing host countries' enterprises.

The so-called forward linkage refers to the service of marketing of finished products, reprocessing of semi-finished products, components or raw materials and other services, which are provided by the host countries' enterprises for the multinational companies' subsidiaries. Through forward linkage, the quality of the enterprises' products and production efficiency of the developing host countries can be improved so as to make a positive impact on the level of technology of local distributors and downstream industries, and the transfer of related technology (such as maintenance and operation technology) to local enterprises and the development of the host countries' R & D industry can be accelerated. The higher level of quality, good reputation, and efficient market distribution technology of multinational companies could also become a source of technology spillover. Brash, in a study of the effect of General Motors Corporation on local suppliers in Australia, gave particular emphasis to the importance of strict quality monitoring from the multinational companies, and thought that the quality monitoring has special significance to the improvement of the suppliers' level of production.

(3) Human capital flow

The training of multinational companies provided for local employees is the foundation of the technology spillover of the host countries. All levels, from the simplest productive operators to regulators, from senior technicians to the top managers, almost all have opportunities to receive training. There are many ways to train. On-site guidance and expert seminars, and even sending candidates overseas to receive formal education are the different methods of training. When these employees flow from multinational companies' subsidiaries to local enterprises or set up their own businesses, the professional technology and management skills that they have learned when working in a multinational company will be outflows, so as to produce a spillover effect.

Kim, through empirical research, found that the majority of the 28 enterprises of CAD and CAM industries of R.O. Korea were the agencies of local sales and after-sales services of multinational companies at the beginning. Now most of them are active in the investment of R & D on their own. Based on the absorption of the multinational companies' technology, the host countries not only found national enterprises and replaced the imported products with their self-developed products, but also began to output new products to the rest of the world. Others confirmed that this kind of technology spillover effect is the most typical in computer and software industries; as long as there is employee flow, the spillover effect will occur. The most representative of this concept is the social network model in Silicon Valley. Shortly after its debut, a high-density chip became general knowledge in the international semiconductor industry. The reason for this is that Silicon Valley, whose gathering effect is huge, can obtain the decryption method of reverse engineering by just chatting for ten minutes with the key employees of innovation enterprises. In addition, many people are referred to as "the mole"; they work in many high-tech innovation companies at the same time, so the technology spillover is not surprising.

As a result of training, employees of multinational companies are able to accumulate human capital skills. With the loss of multinational companies' employees, part of their skills are absorbed by the local enterprises in the host countries. It is worth noting that most of the studies about management skills consider that management skills cannot be constrained by an enterprise as technical skills; they have stronger universality and vitality, and they should be fully utilized and exerted.

5.2 An Evaluation of the Technology Spillover of Foreign Direct Investment in China

In fact, on the condition of an open economy, foreign direct investment is one of the important sources of technological progress. A large quantity of international experience shows that multinational companies' direct investment has played an important role in international technology. On the basis of carding and path analysis of the above theories, this section explores and evaluates the positive and negative impacts of the technology spillover of foreign direct investment on China's technological progress.

5.2.1 Multinational Companies' Direct Investment Is an Important Approach to Obtaining International Advanced Technology

Enterprises with foreign investment are an important source of China's technology. According to available statistics, China signed 9773 technical contracts in 2007. The total amount of the contracts was about USD 25.42 billion, among which the technology costs were about USD 19.41 billion, accounting for 76.4% of the total amount of the contracts. The amount of technology imports was an all-time high. Out of this amount, the introduction of technology of foreign-invested enterprises was about USD 12.05 billion, with a year-on-year growth of 6.7%, accounting for 47.4% of the total amount of national technology importations. Throughout the year of 2007, the number of registered contracts for technology importations of foreign-invested enterprises reached 6176, accounting for 63.2% of the total number of contracts, and the contract amount was USD 12.05 billion, accounting for 47.4% of the annual contract value (see Table 5.1), and the technology introduction of foreign-invested enterprises was mainly conducted by multinational companies. The introduction of China's technology mainly involves machinery, electronics, energy, transportation, information, the chemical industry and other fields, and these areas are also the industries that multinational companies invest most in. Investment in high-tech industries is also mainly carried out by multinational companies. In several Chinese cities where high-tech industries are growing fastest, multinational companies are the main investors.

Table 5.1 Technology introduction according to the nature of enterprises in 2007

Nature of Enterprises	The number of contracts	Contract value (billion USD)	Technology fee (billion USD)	Percent of price	Year-on-year growth
State-owned enterprises	2158	11.24	5.66	44.2%	25.6%
Collectively owned enterprises	101	0.34	0.20	1.4%	46.2%
Foreign-funded enterprises	6176	12.05	11.86	47.4%	6.7%
Private enterprises	833	0.66	0.59	2.6%	46.4%
Others	505	1.13	1.10	4.4%	7.3%
Total	9773	25.42	19.41	100%	15.6%

Source: The website of the Department of Trade in Services and Commercial Services of the Ministry of Commerce.

Multinational companies are a product of modern management technology and organization innovation; its emergence and development cater to the needs of the development of modern science and technology, and it is convenient for the spread and transfer of science and technology throughout the world. For China, the multinational companies' direct investment not only brings the tangible resources such as capital, but more importantly, brings the intangible resources such as research and development, technology, organization and management skills and so on. Such a spillover effect in a broad sense has an important influence on China's technological progress.

5.2.2 The Analysis of the Positive Effects of the Technology Spillover of Foreign Direct Investment on China's Technology Progress

(1) The effect on the high and new technology industry in China

Foreign direct investment and technology are connected and they are difficult to separate. In recent years, in foreign direct investment, the investment in China's technology-intensive industry has grown rapidly; not only has it promoted the rapid development of related industries, but it has also allowed the technology of related industries to achieve certain development, especially the high and new technology industries. In 2008, due to the financial crisis, profound changes took place in the international economic situation, but on the whole, as an important part of the system of national innovation and the important base for the development of the high-tech industry, most of the economic indicators of China's 54 high-tech zones remained in stable growth. The total annual business revenue was 6.59857 trillion yuan, and the industrial value added reached 1.2507 trillion yuan, which increased by 20% and 17% respectively compared to those in 2007. According to the statistics of the country's 52632 enterprises in the high-tech zones, at the end of 2008, the number of employees was up by 7.165 million, the gross value of industrial output was 5.26847 trillion yuan, the industry sales output value was 5.03825 trillion yuan, the net profit was 330.42 billion yuan, the paid tax was 319.87 billion yuan, and the import and export value amounted to USD 330.85 billion, among which the import value was USD 129.33 billion, and the export value was USD 201.52 billion. Since 1992, the average annual growth rate of the five economic indicators (business revenue, gross industrial output value, profit, paid tax, and exports to earn foreign exchange) in the high-tech zones has respectively reached 42.4%, 42.28%, 36.09%, 43.49%, and 47.31%.

According to the type of enterprises, although the number of three kinds of foreign-invested enterprises in the high-tech industry accounted only for 36%, from some of the main economic indicators, it is clear that foreign-invested enterprises occupied a leading position in China's high-tech industry (see Table 5.2). By 2008, the proportion of the total output value of the foreign-invested enterprises in the total output value of China's high-tech industry had reached 70.3%, the proportion of employees had reached 60.2%, the value of exports had accounted for 89.9%, and taxation of profit had accounted for 54.6%. Although the value of these indicators in 2008 fell slightly compared to 2007, apparently the foreign-invested enterprises occupied a leading position in China's high-tech industries.

Table 5.2 Value added of high-tech industries according to the type of industries

Industries	State-owned and state-holding enterprises (billion yuan)	Three kinds of foreign-invested enterprises (billion yuan)
High-tech industry	150.3	728.6
Electronic and telecommunication equipment	59.4	413.8
Electronic computers and office equipment manufacturing industry	11.6	206
Medicine manufacturing industry	41.1	62.4
Medical equipment and instrumentation manufacturing industry	15	40.9
Aerospace plane manufacturing industry	23.3	5.4

Source: National Bureau of Statistics et al. *China Statistical Yearbook on High Technology Industry*.

As for the growth rate, it is clear that the growth rate of all industries of the high technology industrial sector in 2008 had different degrees of decline compared with that in 2007. The biggest drop was recorded in the medical equipment and instrumentation manufacturing industry. The growth rate dropped from 29.2% in 2007 to only 7.7% in 2008. The medicine manufacturing industry continued to maintain a relatively fast growth, although the growth rate in 2008 dropped by 3 percentage points compared to that in 2007. This was the only industry whose growth rate remained at more than 20%.

In terms of the exportation of high-tech products, foreign-invested enterprises showed a stronger export competitiveness than state-owned enterprises, especially the wholly foreign-owned enterprises. Their contribution to exportation was the largest; the Chinese and foreign joint ventures were the second; the cooperative enterprises were the smallest. And the technological level of foreign-invested enterprises was higher than that of state-owned enterprises. In its export structure, the proportion of high-tech products was large, which led to the optimization of structure and the improvement of the international competitiveness of Chinese export products. The inflow of foreign capital accelerated the development of China's high-tech industry; it promoted industrial development through a combination of capital, human, and technological progress and played an important role in the upgrading of the entire industrial technology development and technological structure in China.

(2) The linkage spillover effects on China's industries

The degree of amalgamation of the host countries' industries and foreign-invested enterprises is low, which is an issue to be faced in the long term. In the early days of China's utilization of foreign capital, foreign businessmen mainly regarded China as a base of low-cost processing and assembling. The components for manufacturing were mainly sourced through importation. The proportion of manufacturing and value added in China was very low. There are three reasons for this: One is that the multinational companies position China strategically at the base of processing and assembling; the second is that the technology level of domestic industries is relatively low, and the ability to provide qualified products for foreign investment enterprises is low; the third is that the entrance of matching enterprises of foreign-invested enterprises overseas into China is less, that is to say, the follow-up matching investment is less.

(3) The technology spillover effect of multinational companies' R&D in China

With the trend of a shortened product life cycle and increasing cost of technology development, multinational companies began to improve their long-term developmental strategy, change the concept of research and development based on their home countries, and transfer the base of research and development to the host countries. In recent years, research and development institutions in China set up by multinational companies increased rapidly. According to the Ministry of Commerce, at the end of 2005, the number of R & D institutions of multinational companies established in China was close to 700, and the total investment amount was more than USD 4 billion by 2008. R & D centers established by foreign investment in China had already surpassed 1,200; they were mainly located in Beijing, Shanghai, Shenzhen, Xi'an, Suzhou and other cities. Despite being influenced by the global financial crisis, the momentum of multinational companies setting up R & D centers in China has not diminished. R & D centers of multinational companies were mainly concentrated around technology-intensive industries, especially the electronics and communications equipment manufacturing industry. For instance, Motorola had set up 15 R & D centers in Beijing, Shanghai, Tianjin, Suzhou, Nanjing, Chengdu and other places; Microsoft and Nokia had also set up 5 R & D centers in China, which were mainly distributed in Beijing, Shanghai and other cities; China Technology Center, set up by General Electric in Shanghai, is the third largest global R & D center after those in the United States and India.

According to the function and the level of technology, R & D centers of multinational companies in China in general can be divided into three categories. The first is the basic development type. Their technological achievements are for the global market or for those engaged in basic research and these centers are generally global R & D centers. The second is the type of application development. Generally, these are regional R & D centers, which are mainly engaged in products' application development for the China market. The third is the type of technical support, mainly engaged in technology services of testing services and product maintenance, which is affiliated to the company's main business. At present, most R & D centers set up by multinational companies in China give priority to application development, but at the same time many R & D centers are engaged in basic research and development work in China. The importance of R & D centers increases significantly in multinational companies' global strategy.

For the protection of the core technology, R & D institutions established by multinational companies in China, in addition to the marked characteristics of sole proprietorship, are now actively seeking the opportunities to cooperate with China's universities and scientific research institutes. General Electric, Alcatel-Shanghai Bell, Motorola, and other multinational companies have launched close cooperation activities with scientific research institutions. For this kind of collaborative research and development institutions, the research topics are jointly decided by both parties; they not only carry out the developmental projects that the enterprises require, but are also involved in some of the basic research. The input and output effects of multinational companies are very good due to scientific project selection and standard R & D management. After the establishment of R & D institutions in China, multinational companies' management ideas, management principles, and implementation methods in the work of R & D will directly affect the managers of Chinese R & D institutions, providing useful experience for their decision-making and management, and intentional or unintentional competition in the process of contacting with the masters of multinational companies will certainly promote the level of management of the research and development institutions in China.

(4) The effect of human resources development and flow

Foreign investment in China must be combined with the development of human resources, which can make the technology, equipment, and management operate efficiently. Foreign investors must organize training on management ideas, management knowledge and technical ability for China's human resources. This strategy of talent localization, on the one hand, can resolve cultural conflicts, and promote effective cooperation, which is of great significance for the management of multinational companies in China, while on the other, it promotes an increase in the number of China's science and technology talents and the improvement of the level of the scientific research to a large extent. Studies have shown that almost all multinational companies that have larger investment projects in China set up training bases in China. The expenditure on human resource development in multinational companies far surpasses that in China's similar enterprises; the higher the technical level of investment projects in China is, the greater the investment in human resources will be. Global production networks and huge global information systems of multinational companies make the ability and efficiency of human resource development very high. And their employees in foreign-invested enterprises in China have the opportunity to receive training in corporate headquarters or other overseas subsidiaries, which will greatly inspire the Chinese employees' spirit of hard work. In addition, these domestic workers employed by the foreign-invested enterprises, once flowing into the domestic enterprises, or communicating with domestic companies, will spread the technology and knowledge of management learned in foreign-invested enterprises so as to realize technology spillover.

5.2.3 Analysis of Restrictive Factors of Technology Spillover of Foreign Direct Investment in China

Due to the for-profit nature of the foreign direct investment, the direct investment of multinational companies may not be able to have positive effects on long-term technical progress for China. From the current situation of foreign direct investment, China still has some limitations in acquiring the technology spillover effect. The following section will analyze the restrictive factors from two aspects, which are technology senders and receivers, and analyze the restrictive factors of the technology spillover effect respectively from the point of view of enterprises, government and market environment.

(1) Analysis of restrictive factors of technology senders

① The constraints of multinational companies' internal technical control

Glass and Saggi analyzed technology competition between foreign-invested enterprises and domestic enterprises based on the game theory model. Because the revenue of foreign-invested enterprises is a decreasing function of the technology spillover effect in the model, the optimal decision for foreign-invested enterprises must be to minimize the technology spillover to local businesses. Multinational companies always maintain their market share and competitive advantage by setting up a variety of technical barriers in order to get the monopoly profits in the host countries; besides, with all sorts of technology protection measures of the governments of home countries, they are always willing to squeeze the technology spillover effect to a minimum as much as possible.

② The restrictions of technology protectionism of the governments of multinational companies' home countries

Technology output as a tool of economic expansion in the developed countries, exploits and controls the developing countries by charging a high technology transfer fee and adding various unequal restrictive conditions. In this regard, all countries adopt technology protectionism, limit the exportation of cutting-edge technology strictly, carry out state intervention and the limitation of government policies and laws, and limit some advanced technology and equipment to be sold by multinational companies. The first impact of these restrictions is on the transfer of cutting-edge technology. The United States is the largest technology exporter. The government advertises by keeping a neutral attitude to most of the technology transfer, but in fact, the technology protectionism of the United States in the cutting-edge technology is more serious, especially for developing countries.

(2) Analysis of restrictive factors of technology receivers

① The limitation of China's domestic enterprises

    a. The overall technical foundation is weak

First, the overall technical level of the equipment in China's enterprises is lagging behind that of other countries. Adoption of new technology has the characteristics of increasing returns to scale. China's enterprises are generally established on a small scale, and they are out-dated in technology and equipment, and the enterprises that do matching production for multinational companies have a big gap with the requirements of the multinational companies in terms of quality and performance of products.

Second, the industrial technological level of domestic enterprises is low. In general, multinational companies only transfer applicable technology to the host countries. The level of technology transferred by multinational companies is equal to or slightly higher than the level of advanced domestic technology. After the reform and opening-up in China, with the fierce competition in the domestic market, technology intensity has somewhat increased under the strong impact of foreign trade and foreign investment, and textile, clothing, household appliances and other consumer industries have played a part in the international market. But in general, there is a large gap between China's industrial technological level and that of developed countries. The backward situation of the industrial technological level is the main factor that causes slow growth in the ability of China to supply intermediate products to foreign-invested enterprises; it has seriously affected the development of the domestic-funded supporting industries and has restricted technology transfer, diffusion and spillover of foreign capital.

Third, there is a lack of specialized technical personnel and management personnel with a strong professional ability. On the one hand, the basis of the domestic talent training is not enough to provide adequate scientific and technological personnel; on the other hand, in the talent competition with the foreign-invested investment enterprises, the limited technical personnel drain away to foreign-invested enterprises. Due to the lack of talents and the shortcomings of our management level, China's enterprises are often in a disadvantaged position. After the supply of certain technical expertise, foreign investors do not allow the enterprises to build technology development institutions by themselves; this almost deprives the ability of scientific research which is not strong at the beginning and restricts the effective assimilation and absorption of imported technology by China's enterprises, thus leading them to become highly dependent on the technology of multinational companies.

    b. The ability of technology assimilation and absorption for the innovation of domestic enterprises is weak

The ability of technology assimilation and absorption and imitation and innovation is crucial for the latecomers to exert the late-mover advantage and realize economic and technological catching-up. In addition to the subjective factors of multinational companies, the host countries' industrial technological level determines the initial level of technology transfer of multinational companies, and the ability of technology assimilation and absorption and the imitation and innovation of host countries' industries decides the effect of technology spillover. Studies have proved that the increase in technology spillover is associated with the absorptive capacity of local enterprises. If domestic absorptive capacity is insufficient, the connection between the multinational companies and the host countries' economy will clearly be weak; this kind of economic activity of multinational companies' subsidiaries in the "enclave" operation condition can only function as the assembly centers, and in that case, it is difficult to have a spillover effect on the local economy.

From the micro-view, assimilation and absorption ability refers to enterprises' technology, money, all kinds of material conditions, and management ability required for importing technology. From the macro-view, it should also include the introduction of matched national technology, resource environment, infrastructure conditions, and the corresponding financial and legal environment, social and cultural background and so on. At present, the assimilation and absorption and imitation and innovation ability of China's enterprises is far from the requirement of industrial development in reality and the target of industrial development in the future, and the enterprises lack a scientific and effective management mechanism of assimilation and absorption which is matched with the strategy of technology introduction. The insufficient input in research is the first barrier to assimilation and absorption and imitation and innovation.

c. The modern enterprise institution in China has not yet been fully established

Because the modern enterprise institution has not yet been fully established, property rights are not clear. The administration of China's technology introduction makes technology introduction a government role rather than an enterprise role to a great extent. As a result, technology introduction lacks comprehensive economic analysis, and the phenomena of blind introduction and redundant construction are serious. In addition, due to the unclear property rights institution within the enterprises, there have been no constraints of corresponding economic responsibility on the final decision makers of technology import and the major investors. As a result, the companies tend to focus on short-term interest return, rather than long-term development of the enterprises to actively absorb the advanced technology of the multinational companies to improve their level of technology management. At the same time, the investment in assimilation and absorption is very low after the introduction of technology, and there is a lack of incentive mechanism of prompting enterprises to care about new technology, learn new technology, introduce new technology, reform the old equipment and old technology, and promote scientific and technological achievements into real productivity, seriously affecting the technology spillover effect of foreign direct investment.

② The limitation of the external environment of China's enterprises

a. The technology market, commodity market, and the capital market have failed to effectively combine

First, the characteristics of China's market show that many industries have the phenomenon or tendency of monopoly of several multinational companies. With solid strength, scientific management, and brand advantage, foreign businessmen dominate the market, while many domestic enterprises do not have the competitiveness and lack necessary motivation on technological updating, which will inevitably affect the speed of technology diffusion and the spillover effect.

Second, the structure of China's market economy and the cultivation of the market show a divergence. The operations and development of the technology market is far away from the commodity market, which not only restricts the speed of industrialization and marketization of scientific and technological achievements, but also affects the transfer process of the commercialization of scientific and technological achievements.

Third, the imperfection of China's capital market also hinders the absorption and innovation of new technology by China's enterprises. In their cooperation with foreign enterprises, domestic enterprises need to introduce advanced equipment and related technology and to train a batch of technical management talents to meet the requirement. The funds of many domestic enterprises are insufficient and they need to get financial support from the external capital market, but the imperfection of external capital market makes it difficult for many enterprises to obtain financial support, which is not good for enterprises in realizing scale expansion in the process of technology absorption and innovation.

b. The government's encouragement and adjustment policies do not reach the goals

First, the incentive measures of the government toward high-tech industries failed to adjust in time. Although the Chinese government had formulated the preferential policies such as income tax, value-added tax, customs and business tax and other policies for foreign direct investment, strategic adjustment, especially the technical strategy for multinational companies, it did not formulate relevant preferential policies in time.

Second, the reform of the system of science and technology does not reach the goals. The enterprise is a micro subject of the development of an industry. Faced with market competition, enterprises have the most direct and strongest need for research and development; therefore, enterprises should be the main body of industrial technology introduction, absorption, and innovation. However, for a long time, China's basic scientific research institution has been dominated by government plans, scientific research institutions and tertiary institutions, and the management of projects lack orientation toward marketization and industrialization. In the case of undeveloped and non-standard risk financing, there is no reasonable allocation mechanism for the limited manpower and money, and the efficiency of input and output is very poor. In this context, the enterprises that hope to improve their level of technology to enter the system of global labor division of multinational companies, not only cannot obtain scientific and technological resources, but also cannot get technical assistance, and the foreign-invested enterprises cannot encounter strong competition on the domestic market. So, it lacks not only effective benefit incentives but also strong competition to promote technology transfer and technology spillover, whose pace will slow down correspondingly.

The imperfection of policy-making and implementation by the government seriously affects the technology transfer and spillover of foreign direct investment and hinders the technological progress and the upgrading of the industrial structure.

5.3 The Modes and Empirical Analysis of China's Technological Progress

5.3.1 Basis for the Selection of a "Foreign Capital-participated" Mode for Technological Progress

To choose a mode for technological progress not only depends on the stage of domestic economic development, but also depends on the change in technology. As for a majority of developing countries, it is obviously not realistic to try to repeat the technological progress mode of independent innovation. Just as Coe and Helpman's and Eaton and Kortum's empirical analysis of technology spillover of developed countries showed, developed countries cannot just rely on their own research and development forces to occupy the world technological frontier. In the case that the developing countries have a large initial technology gap with the developed countries, it is impractical to try to rely entirely on the domestic independent innovation system and the R & D ability to drive domestic technological progress; besides, the cost is huge and difficult to even estimate. Foreign direct investment has become an important channel through which developing countries are able to get technological learning and the opportunity to imitate, but for most of the developing countries with insufficient funds and an out-dated level of technology, it is difficult to succeed. It is common for many developing countries to seek another way — the "foreign capital-participated" mode to achieve technological progress. The noncompetitive characteristic of intellectual products provides opportunities for a country to imitate and learn other countries' advanced knowledge and technology at a lower cost. For developing countries, this mode is no doubt a sub-optimal choice to promote technological progress.

The analysis results show that multinational companies that regard global profit maximization as the decision-making objective have no intention of promoting the technological progress of the host countries' enterprises. Foreign companies will not consciously obey the host countries' governments' industrial guidance and macro-control, and they have no intention of promoting the technology spillover effect for the host countries' enterprises. The multinational companies even restrict their promoting effect through a variety of technology transfer restrictions. Foreign technology transfer only provides a possibility to absorb advanced technology; it is not a necessity. In the process of technical flow, to what extent local companies can effectively absorb the technology spillover and get the largest interest from the technology spillover depends on domestic enterprises' ability for the assimilation and absorption of technology transfer and technology spillover.

5.3.2 Analysis of Establishing the Mechanism of Assimilation and Absorption of China's Enterprises

(1) The defects of the mechanism of the assimilation and absorption of introduced technology

For a long period of time, the situation in China is "valuing introduction and underestimating absorption"; the implementation of cost on technology importation is very effective, but the input in assimilation and absorption is apparently insufficient. This leads to seriously bad assimilation and absorption, let alone possible innovation. In the process of technology import, China's enterprises often use the main capital and energy for the importation of hardware equipment and production lines, ignore the importation of technological patents and proprietary technology, and lack systematic integration and integrated innovation of imported technology.

The reasons for inadequate assimilation and absorption and possible innovation, include the input factors and the deep system, such as the imperfection of the related guidance policies, the tendency of paying attention to the amount of foreign capital while underestimating the quality, which is motivated by political achievement, the lack of competitive pressure because of the imperfection of market mechanisms and enterprise systems, and the lack of perfect research and development mechanisms and effective training systems and so on. Lack of information communication, coordination mechanisms, and the corresponding government guidance among enterprises led to repeated importations. In addition, the old ideas of "valuing hardware and underestimating software, valuing production technology and underestimating organizational technique" left by the planned economic system, were largely responsible for the failure to attract foreign investment and technology importation, which also led to the above results.

(2) The ideal mode of construction of the assimilation and absorption mechanism

Cohen and Levinthal, in the analysis of the role of enterprise development, put forward the concept of "absorptive capacity" for the first time. They thought the impact of enterprises' R & D investment on their technological progress is reflected in two aspects: On the one hand, research and development achievements directly promote technological progress; on the other hand, enterprises' R & D investment enhances the ability of absorption, learning, and imitation of foreign technology and makes the enterprises show greater abilities to absorb the diffusion of external technology. Thus, according to the situation of assimilation and absorption of China's enterprises, the idea of setting up the mechanism of assimilation and absorption is as follows: First, strengthen the investment of local enterprises' R & D, improve their technological level, and narrow the technology gap with foreign enterprises to encourage the foreign-invested enterprises to transfer more advanced technologies, and to promote the generation of the technological spillover effect of foreign-invested enterprises. Second, to reengineer the process of assimilation and absorption of technology introduction, enterprises can complete the linking of technology to the market by means of the process of technology introduction, innovation, and diffusion, and importation technology at the expense of leasing a market to the developed countries, while at the same time speeding up the assimilation, absorption, improvement, and innovation of foreign technology, to create a domestic market, even an international market.

In terms of the matching absorptive capacity, we need to increase the investment in human capital. The critical value of human capital is the bottleneck of the absorptive capacity, so the investment in education, especially in the popularization and improvement of elementary education, and the cultivation of science and technology talents is the key to enhancing the absorptive capacity of local enterprises. At the same time, the government should loosen the restriction of turnover to encourage all kinds of personnel to flow between foreign and domestic enterprises in order to form a technology spillover oriented by talent flow. In addition, the government should strengthen the construction of a matching system, perfect the market institution, such as improving the efficiency of the financial market, strengthen the protection of intellectual property rights, and actively guide the formation of industrial concentration areas, strengthening China's absorptive capacity of a technology spillover in many ways.

5.4 Countermeasures and Suggestions for Realizing Technological Progress in the Opening-up Strategy

The general guiding principle of attracting foreign direct investment at present and in the future in China should make expanding the technology spillover effect of foreign direct investment, promoting China's technological progress, and optimizing the industrial structure the goal. According to various factors that hinder the technology spillover of multinational companies, the following section puts forward the countermeasures and suggestions from three aspects: the government, the market, and the enterprise.

5.4.1 Government Level: Improve the Incentive Mechanism and Promote Technology Inflows of Multinational Companies

Identifying responsibilities. The government should give full play to its guidance and service functions in the process of technology introduction; after all, the enterprise is the main body of technological progress. The government should create conditions, as much as possible, to provide information consultation, policy guidance, legal protection and other services for enterprises, to give the rights of decision-making, investment and earnings of technology introduction to enterprises. Clarification of responsibility greatly enhances the autonomous right of the enterprises; it is not only beneficial for enterprises to import technology according to their needs, but also favorable to promote enterprises to assimilate and absorb technology.

Strategic positioning. A mistake committed while introducing technology in developing countries is that they hope to obtain advanced technology by carrying out large capital-intensive technology projects. In fact, subject to factor endowment, labor resources, and infrastructure conditions, such capital-intensive technology projects are not suitable for developing countries. Therefore, the Chinese government should fully understand the basic rule of technology transfer, clearly define the strategic positioning in the process of technology transfer, and import technologies that are most likely to exert domestic production potential and match the current level of domestic production and absorptive capacity.

Policy support. China should not only stay focused on the cost advantage of cheap labor, but also build up comprehensive systematic advantages, including an investment environment, industrial structure, and research and development ability, and work hard to tackle the national problems which go against the development of technological environment for enterprises in the field of politics, economy, law, education, science and technology and many other fields. First, for the introduction of technology, gradually achieve duty-free imports from hardware to software, encourage foreign investors to output technology or cooperative production rather than direct export by tax reduction or exemption. Second, earnestly implement the policies to encourage foreign investors to invest in high and new technology industries. For research and development projects, continue to offer various policy supports in tax, capital, infrastructure, talent employment and others to multinational companies. Third, encourage multinational companies to set up R & D centers. The government should further strengthen tax preference for foreign-funded R & D centers.

5.4.2 Market Level: Induce the Upgrading of Technology and the Technology Spillover of Multinational Companies

Although technology transfer has its own rules to follow, it is not to say that it is incapable of accessing foreign technology. The oligopolistic reaction theory provides an effective way; it is making use of competition among multinational companies to induce technology transfer. We must make full use of the Chinese market and its return on investment to attract multinational companies, to build a competitive atmosphere of technology transfer, and to induce multinational companies to transfer advanced technology. Let multinational companies accelerate the process of technology transfer and technology upgrading in competition with each other and improve the technology spillover effect in China.

Cultivate domestic competitors. Cultivating local enterprises that can compete with foreign-invested enterprises is an important aspect to maintain market competition. For more than ten years, promoted by fierce competition, the technological level and quality level of the products of a large number of enterprises in China have quickly been enhanced through the introduction of technology, and the scale of enterprises quickly expanded, winning a great reputation within the domestic and international markets, while the asset quality and technical level of these enterprises also stepped onto a new stage. But at present, various problems have caused some domestic enterprises to suffer a setback when competing with foreign-invested enterprises. To build an environment for equal competition, the following two aspects are needed: First, the equality of policy environment. Domestic companies can learn from the practices and experience of joint ventures during mutual cooperation, mergers, and acquisitions; the preferential policies for foreign enterprises can be given to strong domestic enterprises; the conditions for investment projects for the domestic and foreign investors should be open and non-discriminatory. Second, the equality of the system environment. In order to eliminate the institutional obstacles for the development of local enterprises, accelerate the transformation of domestic enterprises, making the enterprises become independent and self-financing legal entities and main bodies of market competition, and thus, the enterprises will have long-term unremitting intrinsic motivation for development. On the deep level of "motivation," the enterprises will have an equal status with foreign-invested enterprises, and will also seek joint ventures at any cost for immediate interests. Only by releasing the improper restrictions on property right restructuring of state-owned enterprises, and promoting the rational flow of resources in accordance with the market principles, can a country cultivate a batch of large enterprises and enterprise groups as soon as possible, and can these enterprises have the ability to exist and develop in competition with multinational companies.

Promote competition among foreign-invested enterprises. In some areas, because of the high technology and capital barriers, domestic enterprises may not be competitive in the short term. In this case, at least two multinational companies should be introduced to invest in a product area, thus to form competition among different enterprises. This is crucial experience for China in the introduction of investment from large multinational companies: In an industry, the behavior of enterprises is totally different between the monopoly of a foreign-invested enterprise and the competition of several foreign-invested enterprises.

Initiate competition with import products. Higher import tariffs and too many non-tariff measures have the same protective effect on both domestic enterprises and foreign-invested enterprises. If enterprises invested in by multinational companies lack competitors in China, and have no import commodities as potential competitors, the enterprises will tend to use technologies and products that have lost competitiveness on the international market. Therefore, in some industries monopolized by a handful of enterprises invested by multinational companies, reducing the import tariffs of similar products will place the products of foreign-invested enterprises and the imported goods in a competitive position, and will effectively change the behavior of the enterprises.

Accelerate the promulgation of implementing rules of anti-monopoly legislation. Some large multinational companies have the ability to form a power of monopoly on the Chinese market and obtain monopoly profits.

With the permission and encouragement of investing in China in the form of acquisition, the possibility of monopolizing by large multinational companies on a certain market in China is increasing. At present, it is mainly through administrative measures to manage relationships with large multinational companies. Under the rules of the WTO, administrative intervention is restricted, so it needs to accelerate the promulgation of implementing rules of anti-monopoly fair competition legislation, to regulate the investment behavior of multinational companies in China to make it more in line with the practice of market economy.

5.4.3 Enterprise Level: Make Innovation Breakthroughs to Cooperate and Compete with Multinational Companies

Strengthen the domestic enterprises' own technology accumulation. First, comprehensively promote the ability for assimilation and absorption; the ability to assimilate and absorb advanced technology is an important standard by which to measure the quality and efficiency of technology introduction. While perfecting facilities of the enterprises' research and development technology, the government should encourage and guide the enterprises to increase their investments in science and technology, and increase scientific research funds. At the same time, we should give scientific and effective organizational management to the assimilation and absorption of advanced technology. Second, seek innovative breakthroughs; the only way that enterprises can maintain their advantages is to try to learn faster than their competitors, leading the technology innovation trend in the industry. This requires the enterprises not only to have the ability to strengthen imitation, but also to widely search for and quickly grasp the deep experience of multinational companies, based on which they can catalyze the recipe of their own management and continuous improvement. Of course, at present and for a certain period in the future, the innovation of most enterprises in China may still be shown as "more profound imitative innovation"; that is to say, based on more detailed imitation of the relatively advanced technology and management operational modes of multinational companies, the enterprises combine their own targets and surrounding environment and the change of consumer demand to push current technology to take one more step forward.

Promote the connection of domestic enterprises and the foreign-invested enterprises. The economy of processing trade that puts both ends of the production process (the supply of raw materials and the marketing of products) on the world market goes against the local companies getting really useful technology and management experience from foreign companies. Strengthening the link between the domestic enterprises and multinational companies and improving the local suppliers' production capacity and technical ability are the major measures to expand the technology spillover effect. First, promote the technology upgrading of domestic enterprises. Technical ability has become one of the main criteria when multinational companies choose suppliers. It directly affects the suppliers as to what extent to make use of the opportunities provided by the association to carry out technology upgrading. More and more multinational companies require their suppliers to comply with the quality standards such as HACCP, VDA, ISO9000, QS90000 and so on. Choosing suppliers that have a certain technical ability has become part of the comprehensive plan of promoting outdated linkages of multinational companies' localization strategy. Second, strengthen the cooperation with multinational companies. Domestic enterprises should establish an elastic and flexible contact mechanism with foreign businessmen. Development of related industries mainly depends on the supply capacity of domestic enterprises. Domestic enterprises should participate in the production of parts and supporting services as much as possible, keep a long-term supply and marketing cooperative relationship with foreign businessmen, and become an indispensable link in the global industrial chain of multinational companies to promote technology introduction, assimilation and absorption, and expand the technology spillover effect.

Adopt flexible employment mechanisms. The flow of human resources is the most effective way of technology spillover; however, the technology spillover via this means in China is not noticeable. The main reason for this is that domestic enterprises (especially state-owned enterprises) pay only a little attention to advanced technicians and managers, and have not set up effective incentive mechanisms or provided broad developmental space for them. Domestic enterprises should learn from the reasonable practice of multinational companies in terms of absorption and training of human resources, strengthen vocational education and short-term training, and continually improve staff's professional capability and technical level. Attach great importance to the introduction of foreign intellectual resources, expand international communication and cooperation, and attract more students studying abroad to work in China. At the same time, further reform the personnel management system and guide the rational flow of talents.

Establish technology alliances. Establishing strategic alliances with foreign companies by setting up enterprise groups is another way to effectively promote technology spillover. In view of the weak capital and technical force of domestic enterprises, promoting mergers and reorganizations of enterprises and taking the road to collective development has become the inevitable trend for the development of capital- and technology-intensive industries. If the enterprise groups can establish technology exploring alliances with multinational companies, they will enhance their bargaining ability in the cooperation with multinational companies, and weaken the multinational companies' monopoly on technology so as to easily learn advanced foreign technology and management experience, and to achieve a high level of technology transfer. Additionally, in today's urgent need of technological progress, China's enterprises can also seek multinational companies that have common interests on the international market to form strategic technological alliances of equality and mutual benefit, to be fully in line with international standards from market to technology.

In conclusion, the essence of the mutual benefit and win-win opening-up strategy is to promote the upgrading of China's industrial structure, the improvement of the capability for independent innovation, the protection of the ecological environment, and the comprehensive and sustainable development of the economy and society through import trade, the utilization of foreign capital, and the opening up of markets.

6

Coordination Between Introducing Foreign Investment and Implementing Anti-dumping Investigations

Anti-dumping measures, the fundamental principles established by the General Agreement on Tariffs and Trade in 1947, are used for protecting domestic industries from the damage of dumping. Inheriting this trade rule, the WTO has established a complete set of mechanisms of operations, regulations, arbitration, and safeguard for each member to regulate their domestic market competition orders and maintain the interests of business parties by using reasonable and legitimate means. For China's future opening-up, it will be an important field that will throw light on how to use the powerful weapon given by the WTO to prevent multinational commodities from making significant push into the domestic market by using improper means and damaging the interests of China when China receives a large amount of foreign investment.

6.1 The Current Situation and Trend of Introducing Foreign Investments

From a global perspective, foreign investment in China has maintained a steady growth for many years. The statistics from UNCTAD "World Investment Report 2010" show that the global economic crisis has inflicted a severe impact on global investments. In 2007, the total foreign direct investment of countries around the world reached a record high of around USD 2.1 trillion, but due to the financial crisis, there was a 16% drop in the amount in 2008; then it increased by as high as 37% in 2009, and the annual total investment was just USD 1.1 trillion. After hitting the rock bottom in the second half of 2009, the total investment started to gradually recover. Although the sum of investments was continually declining, foreign investments flowed into developing countries and countries in transition and occupied an increasing share of global investment. Especially China, as a recipient of foreign direct investment, attracted a total investment of USD 29 billion in 2009, ranking only second to the United States. UNCTAD speculated that the amount of global foreign investments attracted by China would rise to the first position in the world in the next three years, and that the United States would drop to the fourth position.

Foreign direct investment in China has six forms, namely, Sino-foreign joint ventures, Sino-foreign cooperative enterprises, wholly foreign-owned enterprises, foreign-invested joint-stock enterprises, cooperative development enterprises, and others. In China's early stages of introducing foreign direct investments, Sino-foreign joint ventures were the main form of foreign capital. However, with the increasing standardization of the Chinese market economic system and the abolishment of various restrictive clauses after China joined the World Trade Organization, FDI in China showed a tendency of sole ownership. Since 1997, wholly foreign-owned enterprises, exceeding Sino-foreign joint ventures, have been the main form of utilization of foreign capital in China, and even in some joint ventures, foreign ownership occupied a large share in the ownership structure of companies (see Table 6.1).

Table 6.1 The ownership ratio of Sino-foreign joint ventures

Industry	Foreign ownership	Domestic ownership	Ownership shared by both
Machinery industry	21%	67%	12%
Chemical fiber industry	48.91%	49%	2.09%
Textile industry	52.03%	45.38%	2.59%
Household electrical appliance industry	75%	15%	10%
Color TV picture tube industry	93.3%	6.7%	0
Top 5 enterprises in the glass industry	60%	40%	0
Top 5 enterprises in the elevator industry	100%	0	0
15 major enterprises in the cleaning products industry	86.7%	13.3%	0
13 major enterprises in the pharmaceutical industry	92.3%	7.7%	0

Source: The National Bureau of Statistics of China.

Among these original Sino-foreign joint ventures, some foreign merchants transformed joint ventures into wholly-owned or foreign holding companies by increasing their capital after entering and operating in the Chinese market for several years. The main cases are as follows: In January 2001, China Schindler Elevator Co., Ltd announced the change of stock equity, forcing Chinese shareholders to drop out; in June 2000, American P & G Company terminated the joint venture relationship with Beijing Daily Chemical Plant. Many joint ventures were transformed into wholly foreign-owned companies. Foreign direct investment played an important role in Chinese economic development. By 2003, the production value made by branches of multinational companies in China had accounted for 23% of the total domestic value added, its taxation had shared 18% of the total tax revenue, and its value of export had accounted for 48%

of the total value of exports. Since its accession to the WTO, China has further increased its attractiveness to foreign investors. Some multinational companies from countries such as Japan, the United States, and the European Union countries have treated China as their prime destination for foreign investments, and have started to rearrange the distribution of their overseas production bases; they have even transferred some important R & D departments to China. Years of practice have indicated that the ceaseless expansion of the scale of foreign direct investment in China, including investment from multinational companies, makes the national policy of utilization of foreign capital infiltrate into different sectors of China's economic development. The policy effect has not only stimulated rapid economic growth but also impacted trade flow since China joined the WTO, which is mainly reflected in the use of the anti-dumping litigation of domestic companies of some industries to solve the frictions in trading with multinational companies.

6.1.1 Review of China' Foreign Capital Policies Before and After the Implementation of Anti-dumping Investigations

The development of China's utilization of foreign capital can be divided into five stages according to the implementation effect of the policies.

The first stage: The early stage of the utilization of foreign capital whose main characteristic was processing and compensation trades (1979–1986).

The second stage: The developmental stage of the utilization of foreign capital whose main characteristic was the processing trade (1987–1991).

The third stage: The stage of rapid growth of the utilization of foreign capital whose main characteristic was to attract investments form multinational companies (1992–1995).

The fourth stage: The stage of adjustment and improvement of the utilization of foreign capital whose main characteristic was to improve the quality of foreign investments (1996–2001).

The fifth stage: The stage of regulation, coordination, and development of the utilization of foreign capital whose main characteristic has been to coordinate China's foreign trade policies with foreign investment policies since China joined the WTO (2001–present).

6.1.2 Analysis of the Situation of Foreign Investment in China Before and After the Implementation of Anti-dumping Investigation

(1) The profile of foreign investments in China

Foreign direct investment in China started in 1979. By the end of 2009, the actual utilization of foreign direct investment had added up to USD 913.34 billion. From 1983 to 2009, the actual utilization of foreign direct investment increased with an average annual growth rate of 17.9%; since 2003, China has been the largest recipient country of foreign direct investment worldwide. Foreign direct investment has had a huge impact on China's economic development.

(2) Analysis of the developmental tendency of multinationals' direct investment in China

From a global perspective, multinational companies, as the main foreign direct investors, have grown quickly and have become a major force in promoting economic globalization around the world. The expanding scale of international production of multinational companies is driven by many factors, and the future developmental trend of its foreign investment is also affected by these factors, the most important of which are three points as follows.

First, it is the liberalization of policies. Opening up of markets allows for a variety of foreign direct investments and non-equity arrangements. Because the foreign direct investments of multinational companies play an important role in the economic development of the host countries, to attract more foreign direct investments has been the main target for countries in formulating their foreign policies. In 2001, there were 208 modifications in foreign direct investment laws in 71 countries, of which over 90% were to create a more favorable investment environment to attract inflows of foreign direct investments. In addition, there were 97 countries which signed 158 bilateral investment agreements in 2001. By 2009, the number of new double taxation agreements had reached 109. There are various regional and bilateral investment treaties that provide a reliable guarantee for the business interests of multinational corporations in the host countries.

Second, the rapid changes in technology have led to increased costs and risks; it is essential for enterprises to develop the world market to share such costs and risks. In addition, due to the decline in transportation and communication costs, which greatly reduces the cost of communication and liaison among companies, the production factor combinations can be easily achieved by multinational companies on a global scale, and optimal allocation of resources can be completed. According to the requirement of efficiency, the realization of integrated management in the global scope significantly promotes the efficiency-seeking foreign investment of the multinational companies.

Third, fierce competition is growing among multinational companies. Over the past 50 years, the continuous reduction of tariffs and improvement in the efficiency of production have increased the competition among countries; they encourage multinational companies to seek new ways to improve efficiency, gain international competitive advantages, and reduce costs by transferring certain specific production activities. This intensified competition has also led to a new form of international production, including new ownership and contractual arrangements.

The impact of these factors makes the situation of foreign direct investment of multinational companies present some uncertainty. However, from the increasing number of multinational parent companies and their overseas branches, the growing flows and stocks of foreign direct investments, the rising sales, the rapid growth of the GDP and increased export index, it can be justified that the pace of foreign direct investment of multinational companies would not be stagnant, but the different directions of the flow of foreign direct investments will show their preferences.

However, whether the growth trend of investment absorbed by China will continue or not is restricted by domestic and international factors. From a prudent analysis perspective of increased uncertainty, we cannot be blindly optimistic about the trend of foreign investments introduced by

China.

First, there is a substitution to some extent between China and the major developed countries in attracting foreign investments. In the 1990s, the growth rate of China's introduction of foreign investment and the growth rate of international direct investments showed a characteristic of a counter cyclical variation. That is, when global foreign direct investments were in a period of high growth, inflows of foreign capital to China would decrease; and when the global foreign direct investment fell, inflows of foreign capital to China would increase. This counter cyclical characteristic existed for two main reasons: One is the adjustment of the balance of international direct investments, that is, when the capital inflows of some industries in developed countries got saturated, the surplus capital would adjust and flow into China. The other reason is that China had a relatively stable and secure economic environment; that is, if the unstable factors appeared in the developed countries' economy, international capital would flow into China. It suggests that China's attraction for international capital is not completely independent and internal. In 2003, China surpassed the United States in attracting foreign direct investments. While it did not mean that China's attraction for international capital had surpassed that of the United States, it was mainly due to the "911" incident and the rational recovery of the new economy bubbles, and exposure of corporate accounting frauds in the United States. With the economic recovery and growth of the United States and other countries, as well as the new wave of international mergers and acquisitions that arose, the growth rate of foreign investments in China were likely to fluctuate.

Second, there is a certain gap between the growth rate of China's market demand and the multinational companies' expectations about the potential of China's market. Most multinationals' investments in China are market-seeking investments. But in recent years, due to the reform of housing, education, and health care systems in China, consumer income has mainly been used for housing and service consumption, and there has been a slow growth in consumer demand for manufactured goods while multinational companies have invested primarily in the manufacturing field, so the actual market demand has not been as high as expected. Additionally, the sluggish adjustment of China's economic structure, the increasing wealth gap, and the limited growth of most consumers' purchasing powers are also the main reasons for the low market demand. At the same time, because many multinational companies have been competing to invest in China, and a batch of competitive domestic enterprises have also come up, market competition has been more intensive. In addition, the urbanization process in China is slow, and various service facilities, especially integrated logistics, have lagged behind, so the costs of sales and service systems established by the multinational companies in China have increased. These factors are all likely to affect the further growth of multinationals' investments in China.

To add to this, the advantage of cheap labor is gradually disappearing, the preferential policies are no longer attractive compared to those of neighboring countries, and some small and medium-sized foreign-invested enterprises in Hong Kong, Macao, and Taiwan of China have begun to transfer their business to Vietnam and other Southeast Asian countries. Although China has an almost unlimited supply of cheap labor, due to the laggard reform of the household registration system and continuously rising costs of medical care, education and other services in the eastern coastal region, which hinder the inflow of labor from the Midwestern area, the labor cost in the eastern region is also increasing. In other words, the advantage of cheap labor is disappearing. In addition, the super national treatment given to foreign enterprises is still controversial in China, but in the surrounding areas such as ASEAN and Southeast Asia, the favorable degree given to foreign companies is higher than that in China. These changes have resulted in some small and medium-sized foreign-invested enterprises from Hong Kong, Macao, and Taiwan of China transferring their business to Southeast and South Asian countries like Vietnam. These small and medium-sized foreign companies cannot have much effect on technological progress and industrial upgrading, but their investment of aggressive exports helps increase employment, alleviate the huge employment pressure of China, and therefore, they are still the current targets of investments which China should actively strive for. Particularly, the adjustment of foreign policies must mainly focus on how such foreign investment from small and medium-sized companies can be introduced to the Midwestern region.

Finally, the institutional environment of attracting foreign direct investment is not perfect, and this restricts the further expansion of the scale of investment, especially the scale of attracting foreign capital from multinational companies. The first reason is that in a fierce competitive environment, multinational companies need to introduce the latest technology constantly, but the current patent protection system of China is not perfect, which will be a barrier for the introduction of advanced technology. The second reason is that the operational system of mergers and acquisitions has not yet been formed, the current system does not match with the mainstream of the foreign investments of multinational companies, and the "greenfield investment" increases the cost of investment of multinational companies. The third is that the human impact works greatly in investment selection, and the policies do not provide stability and clear predictability; this affects the investment expectations of multinational companies.

6.1.3 Basic Evaluation of the Influence of Implementing Anti-dumping Investigations on Foreign Direct Investments in China

According to the recent changes in China's foreign direct investment inflows in the past ten years or more, the implementation of anti-dumping investigations for imports in China has had little influence on the total flow of foreign direct investments. The result is a qualitative judgment basically based on experience due to the following three aspects.

First, the total number of cases about import anti-dumping investigations is limited; as of October 2010, there were a total of 64 anti-dumping investigation cases launched in China for imported products, and in the end, 52 cases had taken anti-dumping measures, 8 cases were terminated because applicants withdrew their appeals or domestic industries were not impaired, and 4 cases were still under investigation. The industries, products, and companies involved are too limited to affect the total flow of foreign direct investments in China.

Second, when foreign enterprises choose entry strategies, there are many factors to consider, such as circumventing the market barriers, reducing transportation costs, meeting the diversified demands of the market, adapting to a large market demand, taking advantage of local endowments and the governments' preferential policies, and maintaining competitive advantages over other competitors and so on. Therefore, circumventing some entry barriers, such as the anti-dumping measures, is just one of the factors to be considered for foreign companies.

Third, import anti-dumping policies only have a direct impact on the foreign-owned enterprises which initially took the way of commodity exportation into the Chinese market and later turned to the way of direct investment due to anti-dumping investigations. And anti-dumping measures will not have a direct impact on multinational companies that have adopted the mode of direct investment from the start, or have already established a long-term direct investment development plan in China.

Since 1992, the actual absorption of foreign direct investments in China has shown a sharp increase except in 1999, 2006, and 2009 (see Figure 6.1). This reflects the increased confidence of foreign investors in investing in China and the improvement in the Chinese investment environment. By the end of 2008, the top ten countries or regions that had the highest foreign investments in China (sorted according to the actual utilization of foreign capital) were Hong Kong of China, the Virgin Islands, Japan, America, Taiwan of China, R.O. Korea, Singapore, the Cayman Islands, the UK, and Germany. Their proportions of actual investments to the actual utilization of the national total foreign investments were 38.88%, 10.02%, 7.27%, 6.63%, 5.30%, 4.66%, 4.21%, 1.84%, 1.75%, and 1.68%. Among them, Hong Kong of China and the Virgin Islands were the main investors of foreign direct investment in the Chinese mainland. Together, they accounted for 48.90% of all foreign direct investments. The proportions of investment from the United States and Japan were not high, but they still maintained a steady growth. The contract amount and the actual amount of foreign direct investments from the EU were slightly lower than those in 2007. Although foreign direct investments that China attracts is growing continually, the structure of its sources reflects that the overall quality for using foreign capital is not high.

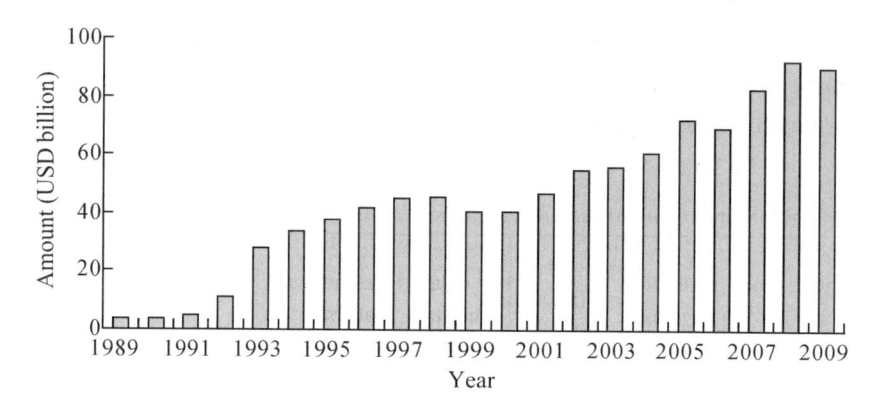

Figure 6.1 The amount of foreign direct investments actually used in China (1989–2009)
Source: The website of the Ministry of Commerce of China.

According to the fields into which foreign investments flow, the main area of foreign direct investment continues to be the manufacturing industry; the actual absorption of foreign capital in the manufacturing industry was USD 49.895 billion in 2008, and it increased by 22.1% from the previous year. Foreign investment in the manufacturing industry mainly concentrated in the following industries: ①communication equipment, computers, and other electronic equipment manufacturing; ②electrical machinery and equipment manufacturing; ③industrial chemicals and chemical products manufacturing; ④transportation equipment manufacturing; ⑤general equipment manufacturing; ⑥professional equipment manufacturing; ⑦textile, garment, shoes, and hats manufacturing; ⑧the non-metallic minerals industry.

Due to fierce global competition, many large multinational companies have begun to adjust their global production and business operation strategies both for seeking cheap production factors to improve their international competitiveness and developing a new market, and the trend of the transfer of foreign investments is more obvious, too. But at the same time, the policies of foreign investment and foreign trade of the Chinese government, to a certain extent, affect the strength and fields of foreign direct investment in China; analysis shows that if the import anti-dumping policies are implemented in the long term, the entry strategies of foreign companies of related industries and products will be influenced, and then the flows of foreign direct investments associated with these industries or products will also be influenced.

6.2 Mechanism of the Impact of Anti-dumping Investigations on Introducing Foreign Direct Investments in China

Since the reform and opening-up, attracting foreign investments has been an important national policy that the Chinese government has been actively advocating and promoting; however, the final aim of foreign investments from multinational companies is still to maximize their profits. In order to occupy the expanding market with great potential in China, multinational companies tend to exhibit behaviors which are contrary to the principle of fair competition, and then damage the interests of domestic enterprises, including dumping goods at low prices and circumventing anti-dumping measures. The circumvention of anti-dumping measures means taking certain means and methods to avoid the payment of anti-dumping duties to the host countries.

Since the mid-1980s, developed countries represented by European countries and the United States modified their anti-dumping laws to include circumvention of anti-dumping and anti-circumvention. The anti-circumvention measures expanded the applicable scope of the anti-dumping laws; the fields involved extend from the previous trade field to industrial investment, production, and other related fields. The objects involved range from finished products to related spare parts and raw materials. From the perspective of international practices, anti-circumvention measures have played the role of coordinator between the trade policy and the investment policy of one country. The implementation of the measures makes the early anti-dumping measures gradually intensify and constantly improve; at the same time, they regulate the quantitative and qualitative changes in transnational direct investment flows.

6.2.1 Coordinator of the Quantity of Foreign Direct Investments: Analysis of Anti-dumping Measures and Transnational Direct Investment Flows

Anti-dumping measures are not only the measures against dumping of foreign imports taken by the host countries in international trade, but also to some extent the measures that affect the direct investment projects of foreign countries and multinational companies in host countries. According to the different combinations of anti-dumping and anti-circumvention measures taken by the host countries, the influence on transnational direct investment flows will produce two effects.

The first case is the effect and mechanism resulting from the fact that the host countries only adopt anti-dumping measures, but not anti-circumvention measures. After the implementation of the anti-dumping measures taken by the host countries on certain products, the import enterprises will reduce the volume of imports. In order to maintain their market share in the host countries, the foreign manufacturers will take measures to circumvent the anti-dumping measures taken by the host countries by increasing the FDI to transfer the production places from the exporting countries to the host countries, and then the expansion of foreign direct investments will have a substitution effect on imports. In this case, anti-dumping measures taken by the host countries can stimulate the increase in foreign direct investments; the implementation of anti-dumping and foreign direct investments show a certain positive correlation, that is, to take anti-dumping measures is conducive to the expansion of the scale of foreign direct investments in host countries.

The second case is the effect and mechanism of the host countries to adopting both anti-dumping measures and anti-circumvention measures. After taking anti-dumping measures on foreign products, foreign companies will usually expand their local market share by investing in and building factories in the host countries, but the host countries will take anti-circumvention measures on imports at the same time, which will naturally restrict foreign direct investments in the host countries, resulting in setting up factories in the third country or selling products to the third country's market. In this situation, anti-dumping does not show any significant relationship with the flow of foreign direct investments. If the host countries take the measures of anti-dumping and anti-circumvention for foreign multinational companies well and for a long period, it may affect the market-seeking foreign direct investments. And in the long run, anti-dumping measures and foreign direct investments will show a certain negative correlation. Even though this situation has not yet appeared in China, the possibility exists.

From the practices of countries around the world, the two ways of anti-dumping measures taken by host countries listed above have different effects on the flows of foreign direct investments. This also confirms that the international anti-dumping activities have experienced two stages of development: The first stage, before the 1980s, is the stage of dumping and anti-dumping measures; the second stage, after the 1980s, is the stage of circumvention and anti-circumvention measures. After the host countries took anti-dumping measures on imports of certain products, and took anti-circumvention measures on foreign direct investors with evasion, the amount of imported products reduced while foreign direct investments did not increase but even decreased. In this way, anti-dumping and anti-circumvention measures effectively maintain the trade volume and the amount of foreign investments on the domestic market at a certain level, and make the anti-dumping measures become the coordinator of transnational direct investment flows.

6.2.2 The Coordinator of the Quality of Foreign Direct Investments: Analysis of Anti-dumping Measures and Transnational Direct Investment Structure

Based on the analysis of the influential factors of transnational direct investment flows in recent years, anti-dumping measures can play a role as a coordinator in the following aspects.

First, anti-dumping measures should be accorded with and integrated into China's overall opening-up strategy. The overall opening-up strategy is the most important factor that impacts transnational direct investment flows. Due to its special situation, China has taken the step-by-step developmental strategy from the beginning of its opening-up. It shows in the geographical distribution as a progressive opening-up, that is, areas (open areas) are after points (special administrative regions), and the inland is after coastal areas; in the industrial aspect, the service industry is after the manufacturing industry, and the manufacturing industry opens up to a large extent while the service industry opens up with more restrictions. It is obvious that this open mode is rational at the beginning, and this fact also proved its success. But under the current circumstances of opening-up, the strategic mode of promotion, after pilot projects, has been more and more difficult to adapt to the requirements of economic and social development, and it has caused great restrictions on attracting foreign direct investments. China has been a member of the WTO for over 10 years now. Anti-dumping is an important means for protecting domestic industries in the field of trade, and its implementation and utilization must be consistent with the overall requirements of the country's foreign strategy. In the repositioning of China's opening-up strategy, we must consider the leading role of anti-dumping in attracting foreign investments, and make anti-dumping play a regulatory role in its guiding reasonable flows of foreign investments.

Second, anti-dumping plays a positive role in the establishment of a market economic system and a competitive market environment. The restriction of the market economic system and the competitive market environment can affect the flows of transnational direct investments.

The current economy and legal systems on the Chinese market are not perfect. The legal basis, the legislative process and the operational mechanisms have not yet been fully transformed to those of a market economy; there are still a number of provisions that are contrary to the principles of a market economy in the relevant laws and regulations, and there are some problems in the process of implementation. Foreign investment in a market economic environment is still mainly managed by means of administration and approvals, which also create difficulties for the entry of foreign investments, its production, and its operations. In accordance with the commitments upon entering the WTO accession, China has cleaned up the relevant laws and regulations to conform with the basic WTO principles such as transparency and national treatment, but there is still a lot of work that needs to be done in investment-related services. Though anti-dumping is a means of protecting domestic industries in China's foreign trade field, the basis of its enforcement must also be improved as soon as possible and integrated with the international practices. At the same time, the limitation of a domestic market economic environment has an impact on the directions of the flows of foreign direct investments, and the outstanding problems are the lack of protection for intellectual property and problems in regional segmentation of the domestic market. The huge domestic market of China should be an important factor in attracting foreign investments, but the regional segmentation reduces the attractiveness for foreign investments, making it difficult to expand the scale of foreign investments, which is often positively proportional to the technological level of industries that are invested in. Lack of protection for intellectual property also greatly reduces the enthusiasm of foreign investment in high-tech projects, transferring advanced technology, and producing cutting-edge products. In order not to be copied, some foreign companies transfer their production departments to other countries and then export the products back to China; this will definitely affect the investment structure and the quality of the investments of foreign capital.

Third, anti-dumping measures help overcome the limitations of the industrial policies for foreign investments. An important means of government regulations on the economy is industrial policies. Combining the anti-dumping measures and industrial policies to encourage, support and restrict the flow of foreign investments is an important means to guide the structure of China's investments in the future. Since China proposed the establishment of the socialist market economic system, the role of industrial policies in macroeconomic management has become gradually familiar to people. However, in practice, the formulation and implementation of industrial policies is often with features of the planned economy, which has been embodied in the industrial policy of foreign direct investments. At the same time, in the formulation of industrial policies, anti-dumping has not been combined with protecting infant industries, ensuring economic security, encouraging industrial upgrading and technological progress and so on. In the future, it must be realized that anti-dumping plays an important role in the field of foreign investment, and that its coordination effect with the industrial policy should play a powerful role. In terms of coordination, it can be carried out in accordance with the following combinations: combining the implementation of anti-dumping and foreign policies of limiting foreign investments, restricting foreign investments in domestic industries that China needs to protect; combining the implementation of anti-dumping and industrial policies that ban foreign investments in China, prohibit foreign direct investments from entering industries that are related to China's national economy and political security, such as national defense, the military industry and other industries; combining the non-implementing of anti-dumping and normal foreign policies, giving full play to the mechanism of competition in the industries that foreign direct investments can normally enter, stimulating domestic industries to participate in domestic and international competition, improving the managerial level of the enterprises; combining the non-implementing of anti-dumping measures with the industrial policies of encouraging foreign investments, attracting foreign investments into the industries which need upgrading of technologies, introduction of foreign managerial experience and the expansion of the international market, to achieve industrial technological progress and export expansion. Give full play to anti-dumping after accession to the WTO in attracting foreign direct investments by coordination of anti-dumping implementation with national macro strategies, foreign investments, foreign trade policies and industrial policies, and make anti-dumping, to some extent, become the quality coordinator of foreign direct investments.

6.2.3 The Effect of China's Anti-dumping Measures on Foreign Direct Investments

How to evaluate the effect of foreign direct investments has been one of the debated topics in the economic circle, and even in different sectors of society, and the methods of its evaluation and indicators used are various. At present, the United Nations uses two quantitative indicators to measure the impact of foreign direct investments on the host countries: inward foreign direct investment performance index and inward foreign direct investment potential index. These two indicators are used to describe and evaluate the situation and prospects of countries to absorb foreign direct investments, and they are sorted by index to objectively reflect the ranking and status of an economy's potential performance in the world.

The implementation of anti-dumping measures in China has several effects on foreign investments.

First, the implementation of the anti-dumping measures leads to an increase in foreign capital flow. For large multinational producers, China's implementation of anti-dumping measures hinders the amount of their exports to China. So, in order to maintain their market share in China in the long-term, they will increase their direct investments to establish factories for manufacturing to achieve the purpose of occupation of market share. Therefore, the implementation of the anti-dumping measures will, to some extent, promote the increase in the inflow of foreign direct investments.

Second, the implementation of the anti-dumping measures will not promote an increase in foreign capital flow. Small and medium-sized foreign export enterprises will reduce their volume of exports after the implementation of anti-dumping measures, but they will not necessarily increase their foreign direct investments to China. For the small and medium-sized enterprises, the cost advantages of the products are the main advantages of competition, and under the condition that the capital scale is small, comprehensive competitive advantages are not obvious, and they are not familiar with the Chinese investment environment. They will not easily take market entry in the mode of direct investment, which has the greatest risk. In this situation, the implementation of anti-dumping will not lead to an increase in foreign capital flow.

Third, the implementation of the anti-dumping measures may lead to a reduction in foreign capital flow. For large multinationals with a global developmental strategy, in the case of implementing anti-dumping measures for their products but not taking anti-circumvention measures in China, they will gradually reduce direct investments and set up factories in a third country. They circumvent China's anti-dumping actions through the global reallocation of production resources and global sales. In this case, anti-dumping will reduce the amount of foreign direct investments in China. At present, this has not happened yet, but for the industries which own high profit margins, relatively low costs of production and a large market demand in China, if the anti-dumping measures have not been implemented properly, such possibilities would exist.

Fourth, China is a developing country and there are exceptional situations when it implements anti-dumping measures. European countries, the United States and other developed countries, with the implementation of anti-dumping and anti-circumvention measures, are against developing countries' products whose levels of technology and capital are mostly low, which are also the products with which the developed countries have difficulties in making structural adjustments. These cases especially happened in the conflicts of international trade in developed countries, such as general metal products, chemical products, machinery, electrical and sound equipment, plastics and rubber products, textiles, and so on. Anti-dumping and anti-circumvention measures will not have a significant impact on FDI flows in developed countries because the volume of foreign direct investments among developed countries occupies the dominant position in the absorption of foreign capital. Therefore, it is not enough to make a comprehensive judgment about the effect of foreign direct investments only according to amount invested.

China is comprehensively correcting and perfecting its foreign trade policies according to the World Trade Organization rules after its accession. With the constant improvement and reinforcement of China's anti-dumping and anti-circumvention measures, these measures will inevitably be more important to foreign direct investments in China. If the anti-dumping and anti-circumvention measures cannot be coordinated with policies of attracting foreign investments properly, it will produce a conflict between them, which will offset the effects of the two. On the contrary, if the anti-dumping and anti-circumvention measures can be handled well with the investment policies, it will make the two promote each other and complement each other. Anti-dumping measures are a regulator of China's investment policies; the guidelines of coordinating foreign investments and foreign trade policies should be based on the concept that the result of the policy implementation is supposed to not only meet the direction of the adjustment of the structure of investment in industries in China, but also meet the principle of fair competition between domestic enterprises and foreign enterprises as well as among foreign enterprises.

6.3 Conflict and Coordination Between Anti-dumping Investigations and Foreign Investment Policies

Anti-dumping investigation is primarily an institutional arrangement to maintain fair and free trade. It is against dumping and the purpose is to maintain fair competition within the market. Because there exist very close relations between trade and investment activities, and China treats attracting foreign investments as an important national policy, the anti-dumping investigation will inevitably involve some behaviors of multinational companies in China, which would have a conflict with the policies regarding the attraction of foreign investments. Then it becomes important to take the necessary and feasible measures to coordinate such a conflict.

6.3.1 Analysis of Potential Conflicts Between Anti-dumping Investigations and Foreign Investment Policies

(1) Analysis of the effects after foreign policies transform to those attracting multinational companies

① Analysis of the changes in fluctuations and structures of the sources in foreign investments brought about by a shifting focus on the policies regarding the attraction of foreign investments

In recent years, the focus of adjustment of Chinese foreign capital policies has been to achieve a transformation from quantitative expansion to improvement in the quality and transformation from the general preferential policy to the differential preferential policy and national treatment. The result of this policy change is that according to the different investment qualities and the different technological levels of foreign investment, the preferential policies that China offers also reflect those differences. Compared with enterprises from Hong Kong, Macao, and Taiwan of China, where the investment scale is small, the technological level is low and the international market competitiveness is weak, the mainland would prefer to actively introduce foreign-invested enterprises from the United States, Japan, and the European Union, which have strong competitiveness, abundant capital, and advanced technology on the international market. However, the Chinese mainland has adjusted its foreign investment policies in recent years, which has led to a change in the structure of the sources of foreign direct investments, and the investment growth of Europe and the United States in China has changed, too.

Investment patterns of the United States and the European Union in China have changed as China has adjusted its policies: From 2000 to 2002, the United States increased its foreign investments in China, especially topped by USD 5 billion in 2002 and created a historical record. But in the following few years, its actual investments in China fell, and reached their lowest point in 2007. In 2008, it once again increased its share but was still under USD 3 billion. During the same period from 2000 to 2002, the actual investments of the EU in China decreased year by year and picked up until 2003, and in the next few years, it rose gradually to more than USD 5 billion in 2005. During the next three years, except for a decrease in 2007, the actual amount of investments was maintained at about USD 5 billion (see Figures 6.2 and 6.3).

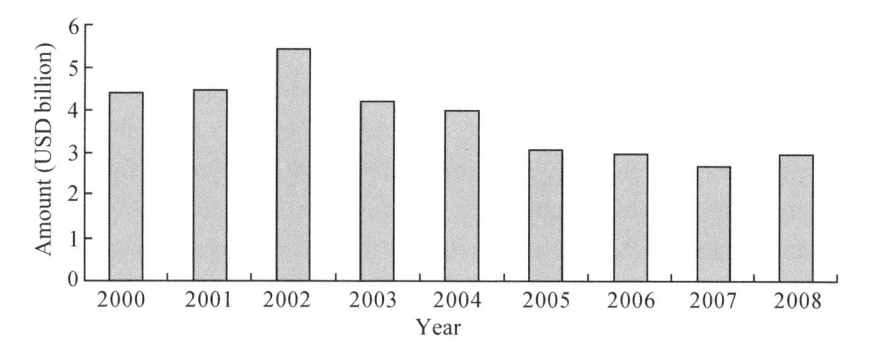

Figure 6.2 Actual investments of the US in China
Source: The Ministry of Commerce.

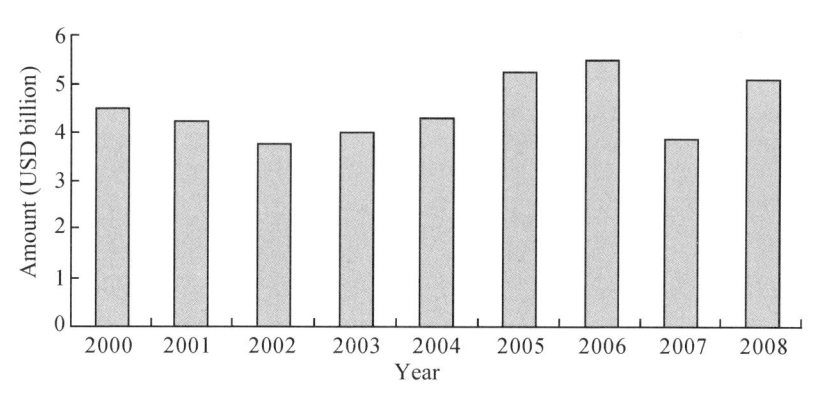

Figure 6.3 Actual investments of the EU in China
Source: The Ministry of Commerce.

② Multiple factors that influence the multinational companies' decisions regarding investments in China

It is worthwhile to pay attention to the fact that under the promotion of positive factors, such as accession to the WTO and sustained and rapid economic development, the absorption of foreign investments in recent years has shown a substantial and significant increase. The European Union's investments in China have remained at a relatively stable level, and the changes are less volatile, but the growth rate of the investments form the United States is negative in China and much lower than the average growth rate of China in attracting foreign investments. This suggests that numerous uncertain factors exist with regard to the investments of the United States in China. In other words, China has not formed a solid foundation to absorb the investments from the United States. There are a variety of factors that affect the multinational companies' investments in China, and foreign investment policy guidance is only one of them. It is hard to see factors that influence the increase or decrease in the scale of multinationals' investment. In fact, China has not formed a stable momentum of investment from the United States. Other non-policy factors (such as regional cooperation, the implementation of trade that measures the WTO allows) will have a significant impact on foreign investments in the future.

(2) Changes in multinational companies' investment behavior caused by the implementation of anti-dumping measures

① Changes in the investment behavior of multinational companies that were affected by the anti-dumping investigation

According to countries or regions of existing anti-dumping cases in China, the number of anti-dumping investigations that developed countries have undergone is the maximum; this was followed by the newly industrialized countries or regions, such as R.O. Korea and Singapore; others are developing countries whose level of development is similar to that of China, such as India, Malaysia, and others which also have increases in registration. Developed countries, in view of their long-term developmental interests, may increase their direct investments in China or transfer their investments to China's neighboring countries or regions to produce products and re-enter the Chinese market by exporting from the third country.

② Analysis of potential conflicts in the implementation of the anti-dumping measures and policies regarding the attraction of foreign capital

Anti-dumping practices in recent years show that, first, industries encouraged by existing foreign policies for foreign investment tend to be those that are worst affected by the anti-dumping sanctions, such as the chemical industry, the steel industry, and the newsprint manufacturing industry. Second, the products that are encouraged for investment in the Foreign Investment Industrial Guidance Catalogue, are often accused of dumping materials most frequently such as high-tech chemical synthetic rubber and synthetic fiber raw materials. Also, the countries that have the production capacity of those products are often subject to anti-dumping allegations (for example, Germany's BASF subsidiary companies in Japan, R.O. Korea, the United States and other countries have the most registrations of anti-dumping investigations in China).

On the basis of the theoretical analysis, a conflict exists between the implementation of the anti-dumping measures and the policies of attracting foreign capital, and it derives from the inconsistency between targets and interests of the host countries and the multinational companies. Multinational companies are always trying to strengthen their global competitiveness on the market and maximizing the profits. And the host countries are trying to promote domestic economic development, so as to improve the level of their welfare. The difference in the ultimate goals and interests has led to their different demands and strategies. Multinational companies which pursue monopoly interests of the global market may have conflicts with the host countries whose goals are to improve the global competitiveness of domestic enterprises. The conflicts encountered by both sides' goals and interests are listed in Table 6.2. However, the pursuits of goals and interests on both sides may achieve consistent results, otherwise it would be difficult to explain the explosive growth of the global FDI flows and stock in the past 20 years. The conflict of interests between the host countries and multinational companies is not exactly a zero-sum game, but the distribution of benefits often depends on the bargaining ability of both sides.

Table 6.2 Conflicts of goals and interests of the host countries and multinational companies

Host countries	Multinational companies
The goal is to promote domestic economic development and improve their welfare	The goal is to strengthen their global competitiveness to maximize profits
Hope to get high and new technology	Only allow their subsidiaries to use standardized mature technology
Expect foreign direct investment to promote exports	Be more interested in the local market
Hope to increase local procurement in order to strengthen the correlation effect	Retain the supply right of key components or equipment by the parent companies
Prefer foreign direct investment projects in joint ventures	Prefer sole proprietors
Encourage various channels of technology diffusion or spillover	Maintain their technological monopoly by strict intellectual property protection provisions
Hope subsidiary profits are used for reinvestment	Try to repatriate more profits to their home countries
Prefer investment projects for new plants	Prefer the occurrence of mergers and acquisitions
Hope to invest in the needed industries, such as manufacturing, infrastructure, etc.	Be interested in high-profit industries, such as finance, insurance, and other services

6.3.2 To Seek Places Where Policies to Solve the Conflicts of Anti-dumping and Attracting Investments Can Begin

(1) Policy orientation: Theoretical connotation of the benign interaction between trade and investment

① Constraint model of the internal trade of multinational companies

An in-depth study revealed that the phenomenon of multinational companies whose internal trade had dumped large quantities of goods in China in various forms has already existed. However, with the adjustment of China's foreign policies, as well as the rational use of the WTO anti-dumping rules, the conflict between anti-dumping measures and foreign policies has become increasingly serious. Against the background of the rapid development of economic globalization and regional economic integration, it is necessary to look for the equilibrium of the policy effect between the foreign trade policy (anti-dumping) and the foreign policy (attracting multinational companies' investments) and maintain the foreign economy's positive role in stimulating the development of the domestic economy. China also needs to combine these policies with its own national conditions to carry out more intensive research and exploration under the WTO multilateral trade rules. The constraint model of the internal trade of multinational companies discussed later provides a relatively clear reference platform for the parameters of policy revision for the studies to solve the conflicts between anti-dumping measures and foreign policy and to formulate new trade and foreign policies.

② The constraint of the comprehensive policy factors on the internal trade

Whether the integration of multilateral trading systems caused by the WTO, or the integration of economic and trade policies caused by regional economic organizations, policies are always formulated and implemented by specific countries. Besides, each country has its specific industry and market situations. Therefore, international business activities and the internal trade of multinational companies will be directly subject to the constraints of the specific environments of the home and host countries. The national environments that restrict the internal trade of multinational companies include three aspects: the policy environment, industrial environment, and the enterprise environment.

Policy environment. It includes: (a) Open strategy. The degree of openness of the country or the market will directly or indirectly limit multinational companies' internal trade. (b) Industrial policy. From the view of host countries, the industrial policy plays a guiding role for the policy of attracting foreign investments; therefore, it has a restrictive effect on the business and trade of the multinational companies. (c) Trade policy. Especially foreign trade policies, such as anti-dumping measures and technical measures to trade, directly affect multinational companies' importation and exportation. (d) Foreign investment policy. Although the WTO advocates the principle of national treatment, countries often take a certain degree of preferential treatment to foreign-invested enterprises in attracting foreign investment. This does not preclude that host countries' authorities take over comprehensive management, which includes the advisory services in advance, submit reviews, post-audit inspection, and disposal punishment to the import and export prices, and in particular, the transfer prices of internal trade of foreign companies. It is obvious that the continuous improvement of the policies will directly restrict the internal transactions of multinational companies.

Industrial environment. It includes the following: (a) Industries invested directly by foreign companies. If the local industrial products have strong competitiveness and can meet the primary demand of the local market, foreign companies will strive to increase exports and internal trade will be limited. (b) Upstream industries invested in by foreign companies. In the territory of host countries, the upstream industries of foreign companies will restrict their internal trade. If the products produced by the local upstream industries can effectively meet the demand of foreign companies, the vertical internal trade will be restricted. (c) Downstream industries invested in by foreign companies. When the local market profitability is relatively low, foreign companies will mainly focus on products for exportation. If the situation is just the opposite, internal trade will be greatly restricted. (d) Local infrastructure industry. The development of the local infrastructure industry also restricts the internal trade of the multinational companies.

Enterprise environment. The internal trade of multinational companies is also influenced by the internal environment of their foreign subsidiaries, which includes three dimensions: individualism, the interests of shareholders, and employees' participation.

③ Seeking anti-dumping and investment attraction policies through the game converges on the new equilibrium of interests

Overseas subsidiaries of multinational companies are not all wholly-owned enterprises; in fact, most of them are joint ventures or cooperative enterprises. Whether internal trade is conducive to the interest of one of the parties or not will restrict the development of internal trade. If one party of the cooperation is a local business, this constraint force will be greater. Although in most cases, the business modes of operating a joint venture have been determined during negotiations, in the real course of business, a fundamental change will occur with the status of the multinational company or the host country. If the multinational company with its advanced technology, quality products and solid strength, occupies a strong and powerful position in the initiative before the joint venture, then the host country with its unique advantages of geography and labor could change the passive position to a positive position after a joint venture and make renegotiation requirements on the relevant forms of cooperation and modes of operation.

(2) Basis of coordination between the policies of anti-dumping and those of the attraction of foreign investments: A reasonable constraint on the degree of multinational companies' internal trade

① The integration of international trade and investment dominated by multinational companies

Since the 1990s, the integration of trade and investment has developed rapidly and has become the most important force in promoting economic globalization. It has also had a profound effect on the international division of labor and international trade pattern. The so-called trade and investment integration, broadly speaking, refers to the international economic phenomenon that modern international trade is highly integrated with, interdependent with, symbiotic with and combined with foreign direct investment. This kind of integration not only shows the high consistency and synchronization of trade flows and investment flows, but also shows that international trade and international direct investment coexist complementarily and develop interactively. In a narrow sense, it refers to a phenomenon that in the international division of labor, which is dominated by multinational companies and characterized by the division of elements, multinational companies make increased amounts of international trade and international direct investments, embrace the value chain of multinational companies' international production, and show mutual dependence, joint action, and joint growth by their globalization of production and business, which are achieved by the allocation and utilization of the resources on a global scope.

International division of labor is the basis of international trade and international direct investment, and the integration of trade and investment is an important performance of the contemporary development of economic globalization; in essence, that integration is the result of the intensification of the international division of labor. To understand the development of trade and investment integration fundamentally, it is absolutely necessary to understand the concept of division of labor and grasp the new characteristics of the current international division of labor. Division of labor and specialization not only have a technical nature, but also have an institutional nature. The evolution of division of labor and specialization of a technical nature shows the "decomposition" process, which is manifested as two processes: One is that an increasing number of production links of the technical nature become independent from the roundabout production chain; the other is that more and more intermediate products are produced. The more detailed the division of labor is, the higher the degree of specialized production of intermediate products will be, and input factors of intermediate products are also more specialized. Thus, division of labor is more consistent with the characteristics of factors' division. At the same time, the more developed the division of labor is and the more frequent the exchange is, the higher the transaction cost will be, which makes the evolution of division of labor and specialization of an institutional nature not synchronous with the evolution of the technical nature, but synchronous with the process of common development between "decomposition" and "integration." The international division of labor is roundabout international production; development of the international division of labor also shows a separate development of a technical nature and of an institutional nature. Regarding the technical nature, with the decrease in barriers of factors' international flow, the roundabout product chain detours continuously into the international scope, the amount of intermediate products grows constantly, and investors actively look for appropriate manufacturing sites in the international sphere. Trade of intermediate products and investments for the production of intermediate products are growing, and the international division of labor increasingly shows characteristics of factors' division. Regarding the institutional nature, the development of contemporary multinational companies makes the production activities that are scattered at the international level become united by multinational companies. With the increase in the intermediate products, especially those that are difficult to price, production activities united by multinational companies increase, and multinational companies continue to grow stronger. This separation of international division of labor based on the technical nature and the institutional nature during development leads to the production of an increased number of intermediate products by multinational companies through international direct investment, and makes the trade of intermediate products become the internal trade of multinational companies.

② The internal trade of multinational companies makes trade and investment more complex

First of all, the internal trade of multinational companies leads to profound changes in the distribution of benefits. The development of economic globalization and the integration of trade and investment with the factor flows not only promote the improvement of the total interests of international trade division, but also make the international distribution of benefits more complex. In the integration of trade and investment, the trading countries are only the producers of the trading products, but they do not hold the ownership of all the trade interests, because factors, especially the capital required for the production of trading products, may come from countries outside the trading parties, and may even be from trade partners. Interests of trade and investment have been merged into a coherent whole and it is hard to tell which part of interest comes from trade that should be shared by the trading parties and which part is the interest of international direct investment that should be shared by the parties of investment. As the main driving force of trade and investment integration, multinational companies often make man-made interests flow between the trade interest and investment interest with internal transfer pricing and other methods for maximization of global interests. It makes the traditional benefit distribution mechanism quite weak, and also makes fair distribution of benefits more difficult.

The second is the profound change in trade protection problems against the background of the trade and investment integration of multinational companies. Although protective trade policies are "bad" compared to the free trade policies, governments take protective measures for their international trade almost at any time. Under the condition of integration of trade and investment, because of production internationalization and increasingly close economic connections among various countries and regions, great changes have taken place in the environment for the implementation of the protective trade policies, and the mindset of traditional trade protection is difficult to continue. It is mainly reflected in the following factors: (a) It is difficult to define the protected object. Under the circumstances of the integration of trade and investment, the "nationality" of enterprises and products is fuzzy. It has been difficult to define traditional "national industries" and "national products;" thus, there has been no possibility for implementing protection with the boundaries of national industries. (b) Protective measures tend to be ineffective. Under the conditions of factors' international flows, unilateral independent protection prevents the resource integration of multinational companies, which will meet opposition from enterprises and governments; thus, it is more difficult to implement protection with the boundaries of strategic industries. (c) Protection effect is weakened. The rapid development of the processing trade and increasingly standardized production of some technology and intermediate components make the intermediate products sometimes quite close to the final products, so multinational companies can use the processing trade to break the host countries' protection for the final products, which makes the effect of tariff and non-tariff protection weak.

③ Establishing the policy basis of an inclusive relationship between trade and investment

In the classic study of Western economics theory, the Mundell model isolates investment from trade, and holds the idea that investment can completely replace trade and that trade can also completely replace investment. However, in reality, due to the presence of factor flow barriers, investment and trade cannot replace each other completely, but only substitute each other to a certain degree. The Kiyoshi model takes the technical factors into study, and reaches the final conclusion that investment creates and expands trade. Comparatively, the Kiyoshi model is closer to the reality of the relationship between trade and investment, but of course, because there are a lot of barriers to trade, investment and trade in the complementary process cannot achieve complete equilibrium. If we take internal trade into the study, or from the perspective of the research object—internal trade, in reality, the relationship between investment and trade is mutual inclusion and promotion.

From the perspective of internal trade, the relationship between investment and trade is mutual inclusion; that is, investment includes trade, and trade also includes investment. In reality, the forms of foreign direct investment are not always in the way of capital investment; a majority of cases contain software and hardware technology transfer. In the joint ventures, a large amount of the investment of foreign investors are often injected into foreign investment projects as equity through hardware and software technology discount for the shares. Therefore, hardware and software technology, on the one hand, is in the form of capital; on the other hand, it is also the object of trade and the internal trade of multinational companies; that is, a multinational company's parent company or one of its subsidiaries sell related software and hardware technology to another subsidiary of the same multinational company. So this trading relationship is also an investment relationship. Therefore, it is named for the internal trade with investment. In reality, the scale of such investment is relatively large. This form accounts for about 50% of the foreign direct investments absorbed in China each year, and the mutual inclusion between investment and trade is relatively strong.

④ The policy basis for coordination of the interaction between trade and investment

Trade promotes investment. (a) The development of trade stimulates more investment. In the general sense, the sequence of development of investment and trade is as follows: Foreign trade is prior to foreign investment, and when the economy of a country or enterprise develops to a certain scale and possesses the corresponding strength, and on the condition that foreign trade is hindered in further development, foreign direct investment will be generated. From this perspective, the development of trade stimulates investment, and from the view of products that investment generates and products traded for buying and selling, investment replaces trade in part. (b) Trade decides the direction of investment. In a general sense, a country's comparative advantage stipulates the structure of products and areas in foreign trade. It also stipulates the structure of products and areas in foreign investment. In general, trade is the forerunner of investment, and the investment happens only when investors acquire a certain amount of experience in the trading of a certain product and in a certain area. From the perspective of internal trade, only when one region or product can be traded, will multinational companies invest in that area or invest to produce that product to form a link in the process of global integration management. (c) Trade supports the development of investment. It is not only because of the fact that not all inputs of the projects needed in investment can be gotten in local areas, and not all the products can be sold in local areas in a general sense, but more importantly, because direct investment depends on traded capital injection of advanced technology, equipment, and related items from the perspective of internal trade. Therefore, during the global integrated management of all investment projects, the internal trade of multinational companies plays an important role in promoting their foreign direct investment.

Investment promotes trade. In a general sense, it is obvious that investment promotes trade. International direct investment plays an important role in the development of international trade in the contemporary world: Foreign direct investment plays an indispensable role in the rapid development of China's foreign trade. From the perspective of an investor or home country, foreign direct investment greatly promotes foreign trade, and the promotion effect is mainly exhibited through internal trade. On the one hand, this is because foreign direct investment can drive the exportation of related technology and equipment; on the other hand, if the investor directly participates in the management of the multinational company's global integration, or in one of the links of the various areas of internal trade of the multinational company, profit-making trading will be produced in a great amount, and the promotion effect of foreign direct investment on foreign trade will be greater. Through the foreign direct investment of global integration management, investors expand both the export trade and the import trade, the intermediate product trade and the final product trade, and the trade in goods and services by the internal trade of multinational companies.

The theoretical analysis above undoubtedly lays a solid theoretical foundation and provides policy guidance for reevaluating the positive and negative effects brought about by the investment of multinational companies in China, handling contradictions between the anti-dumping and investment attraction policies in the new period, coordinating restrictions of the two in reality, and further standardizing the behavior of foreign direct investment and the implementation of anti-dumping measures.

7

Sustainable Development of China's Foreign Trade with Resources and Environmental Restrictions

With the development of economic globalization and international trade, countries around the world have paid more and more attention to the conflicts between international trade and the natural environment, which is inseparable from the defects of the traditional international trade theory. Mainstream economists think that there still exists a defect in the traditional international trade theory due to historical limitations, as it merely pursues short-term and narrow comparative economic benefits and ignores long-term and generalized environmental benefits, especially ecological and environmental benefits. Thus, the current international commodity prices do not reflect or fully reflect environmental costs; so it results in price distortion, and then leads the trade structure, and industry tends to become irrational, which goes against the mutual benefit and win-win result as well as the sustainable development of the global economy.

Reflecting on the development of foreign trade in China over the past years since the reform and opening-up, we find a misunderstanding that is not sustainable and some problems do exist. For a long time, the external environmental costs have protected Chinese manufacturers, maintained the competitiveness of export products, and promoted economic growth in the short run. However, in the long run, China sacrifices environmental interests and develops large-scale industry, which has high energy consumption, a low degree of efficiency, outdated technology, and unsustainable competitiveness or developmental ability. So China is destined to pay a painful price in the foreseeable future. To know the current problems in China and to promote sustainable development of China's foreign trade through the transformation of the manner of economic growth is of great significance to China's economic development, the world's economic growth, and the mutual benefit and win-win opening-up strategy.

7.1 Basic Theories of the Sustainable Development of Foreign Trade

7.1.1 The Origin and Meaning of the Concept of "Sustainable Development"

(1) The origin of the concept of "sustainable development"

"Sustainable development" is a new concept that attracted international attention in the latter half of the 20th century. It first appeared in the "World Conservation Strategy," which was formulated by the International Union for Conservation of the Nature and Natural Resources (IUCN) in 1980. This concept originally comes from the ecological background and refers to a strategy for the management of resources. In 1981, the IUCN made a further elaboration on the definition of "sustainable development" in an important work named "Conservation Natural," indicating that the goal of sustainable development was to "improve human beings' living quality, and keep developing within the limit of ecological carrying-capacity."

At the same time, other research institutions and international organizations also provided different explanations regarding the concept of "sustainable development" based on their own understanding. In 1987, the World Commission on Environment and Development (WCED) submitted the report "Our Common Future" to the United Nations, in which "sustainable development" was defined elaborately as follows: Sustainable development means meeting the demand of the present population without damaging the ability of later generation to satisfy their own needs. And through repeated consultations by countries around the world during the 15th Council of the UN Environment Program, which was held in May 1985, it reached a consensus and adopted the "Statement About Sustainable Development"; "sustainable development" was eventually defined as meeting the contemporary needs without compromising the capacity of the future generations to meet their own needs. Thus, "sustainable development" has a more uniform and widely accepted meaning.

On this basis, the UN held the Conference on Environment and Development in Rio de Janeiro, Brazil in 1992. The meeting adopted the "Rio Declaration," and the "Agenda 21" and determined sustainable development as the theme of the current human development initiatives and it marked the preliminary formation of the theory of sustainable development.

(2)The meaning of the concept of sustainable development

In general, the content of sustainable development includes three aspects: the sustainable development of ecology, the economy, and society. The sustainable development of foreign trade in this book is an important part of sustainable development. The sustainable development of the economy is not only limited to the growing economy, but also includes the entire content of the sustainable development. But in order to simplify the research, this book will rule out other factors; it only studies how to realize the sustainable development of China's foreign trade from the perspective of resources and the environment.

7.1.2 The Meaning of the Sustainable Development of Foreign Trade

Foreign trade is an important part of a country's national economy; the sustainable development of foreign trade is an important guarantee of sustainable economic development. The United Nations clearly put forward the concept of the sustainable development of trade in "Agenda 21," pointing out that it is a multilateral trading system which is open, fair, safe, non-discriminatory, and predictable; it is in accordance with the goals of sustainable development and enables the world production to get the best distribution according to comparative advantage. What's more, it is beneficial to all trading partners.

There are many different concepts of the sustainable development of foreign trade in China, and there is no unified expression up to now, but it can be mainly classified into three definitions: The first definition is using the authoritative definition of sustainable development. The sustainable development of foreign trade means that foreign trade builds up a mechanism of a virtuous cycle, improves China's export conditions, saves export resources, controls the pollution of the environment, and improves the quality of foreign trade personnel. It is not only a premise to ensure the current rapid growth of foreign trade but also a condition and basis to ensure the moderate growth of foreign trade for the next generation.

The second definition emphasizes the need to unify economic, social and ecological benefits and other benefits. The so-called sustainable development of foreign trade must take into account the dual goals of social and economic development and ecological protection. On the one hand, it should seek to maximize social and economic benefits, while limiting the ecological costs of foreign trade to a certain degree; on the other hand, improve the system of trade, perfect the mechanism of foreign trade operations, improve efficiency of trade, and mobilize and allocate foreign trade resources rationally and efficiently, so as to achieve the highly unified economic benefits, social benefits, and ecological benefits on the basis of following inherent laws of foreign trade development.

The third definition highlights environmental protection, resource conservation, and the efficient use of resources. The sustainable development of foreign trade is a process by which a country pushes forward the sustainable development of foreign trade through a series of trade policies to promote and improve the general ability of foreign economic activities, including economic benefits and ecological benefits on the basis of protecting its ecosystems and the sustainability of natural resources. Its essence is to increase foreign trade and economic interests in the context of protecting the environment and resources.

This book studies the sustainable development of China's foreign trade against the background of the increasing restrictions of resources and environmental conditions, and is more inclined to the combination of the three definitions. It has fitted the resource environmental factors into the framework of national foreign trade competitiveness, and measured the changes in China's comparative advantages in foreign trade and export competitiveness according to the resource environmental factors behind the movement of goods, and investigated the importance of the promotion of the sustainable development of foreign trade to improve the overall competitiveness of foreign trade.

7.2 The Unsustainable Development of China's Foreign Trade and Resources and the Environment

7.2.1 The Status of China's Foreign Trade Development and Resources and the Environment

At the beginning of reform and opening-up, the goal of China's foreign trade developmental policies was relatively concentrated. According to the actual national conditions that it had a shortage of foreign exchange funds, China developed an export-oriented foreign trade developmental strategy. Under the guidance of this strategy, the government developed a variety of preferential policies to encourage enterprises to increase exports, in order to earn foreign exchange to support state-building. Over the past years, China's foreign trade has achieved rapid development. In 1978, China's total import and export trade was only USD 20.64 billion. After 1994, the country's trade surplus continued to grow. By 2009, China's total import and export trade had reached USD 2.2 trillion, the export volume was USD 1.2 trillion, and it surpassed Germany to be the largest trading exporter. The rapid development of foreign trade makes China's foreign exchange reserves continue to increase. In 1978, China's foreign exchange reserves were only

USD 167 million, and were more than USD 200 billion in 2001, and then they have kept growing at a high speed. China's total foreign exchange reserve has remained highest in the world since 2007. As of the first half of 2010, China's total foreign exchange reserves had reached USD 2.45 trillion. However, China's resources and energy consumption and carbon dioxide emission are also very high, and the problem of energy and environment is very prominent. China's energy, mineral resources and one-time non-renewable resources have been in great shortage. According to the Division of Earth Sciences of the Chinese Academy of Sciences, up to 2020, it is expected that there will be only four or five of China's domestic resources in the 45 kinds of important strategic resources that can meet the domestic demand according to the current rate of consumption. There are two main problems with China's use of energy and resources: The first is the relative lack of the total resources and the second is the low efficiency of use.

Taking energy for example, since the reform and opening-up, China's pattern of coal and petroleum-based energy has not changed fundamentally. With the continuous expansion of the total population and total economy, energy and resource consumption is increasing. And with the improvement of people's living standards, energy consumption per capita is also growing. The bottleneck that restricts the development of China's economy is that China is not rich in energy reserves and its total energy reserves are dwindling. According to the conditions of China's domestic resources, petroleum production has been close to the upper limit of economic development, and it is difficult to increase its production. While the production of natural gas is currently limited, the per-capita quantity is far below the world average. Obviously, China's energy development will face pressure to meet the long-term huge energy needs.

The efficiency of energy use, which is also called energy intensity, refers to the energy consumption of per unit of economic quantity (or physical quantity, service quantity) output. The lower the energy intensity is, the higher the economic efficiency of energy use will be. At present, China extensively uses the assessment indicator of "comprehensive energy consumption of ten thousand yuan GDP" to assess the level of energy consumption at the levels of nation, region, and industry. The World Bank's "World Development Report 2002" pointed out that China's energy consumption per unit of GDP is 11.5 times that of Japan, 8.6 times that of Italy, 7.7 times that of France and Germany, 5.3 times that of England and 4.3 times that of the United States. These data suggest that the efficiency of China's use of resources is low and both economic growth and trade growth are extensive. In the past few decades, China's energy consumption of ten thousand yuan GDP has declined, and its energy efficiency has improved to some extent, but the growth speed tended to decline because of the saturation in the use of high-quality energy (such as electricity, petroleum). Although there is great potential for the improvement of energy efficiency in the future, the task is much more arduous than years before.

7.2.2 Analysis of the Unsustainable Problems in China's Foreign Trade and Resource Environment

(1) China's trade pattern has the feature of output of environmental value

Traditional international trade paid more attention to the amount of trade in products. The export-oriented policies that China had used for over three decades made "resource-intensive products with high energy consumption and pollution" occupy a large share of the export trade in China. The growth model of foreign trade is an extensive growth model, which is at the expense of resource consumption and environmental pollution. The more exports there are, the greater the consumption of domestic raw materials will be and the more serious the damage to the environment will be.

Changes in energy-intensive product exports are not completely consistent with the growth trend of the total amount of China's exports. Exports of aluminum and plate glass show an extraordinary trend in growth compared to the average growth rate of trade. However, the rate of growth of plastics and oil exports is substantially in line with the average level. It proves that China has exported its energy through these products in these years.

Taking China's bulk exports of textiles as an example, for every 100 meters of cotton, it consumes about 3.5 tons of water and 55 kg of coal, while there were 3.3 tons of waste water emissions and it produces 2 kg of COD and 0.6 kg of BOD. Thus, pressure on the environment, which is brought about by a large number of textile exports, can be expected. This means that the economic benefits obtained through a large number of exports are at the expense of the consumption of resources and the environment.

This trade pattern has the feature of "invisible output of environmental value;" in order to obtain economic benefits, it transfers environmental value into products to be consumed by consumers from other countries and China pays some environmental costs. Clearly, there are two key issues: First, whether the damage to the environment is reflected in the price of exported commodities. Second, is part of trade benefits that we get used for governance or compensation of the damaged environment? If the value of the environment in the process of trade has not been fully reflected, or the loss to the environment has not been fully compensated for, then such trade will result in serious environmental external diseconomy, which will further result in false profit of trade and will lead to more serious environmental damage.

This situation shows that the development of foreign trade at the expense of resources and the environment is partly offsetting the achievements of China's economic growth. It not only consumes a lot of contemporary human resources, but also damages the survival environment of our offspring. When China contributes to global economic growth, it actually bears the energy crisis and environmental pressure for developed countries.

(2) China's "output of environmental value" in trade leads to excessive trading

The actual amount of China's exports for many years has been excessively large compared to the due export volume with real environmental costs. It is also considered by academia as one of the reasons for China's trade surplus.

According to trade theory, only on the two basic premises of trade can both parties obtain benefits. First, the transaction is a voluntary act and not carried out by force. Buying or selling by force will make one suffer a loss.

Second, there is no external diseconomy. It means that both sides exchange their own value and don't make others' property a source of income for their own interests. Otherwise, there will be excessive trading. If one person can sell others' property and reap benefits for himself, then the person would tend to sell the property of others to benefit himself as much as possible, but not consider how much loss this act will cause to others; this may exceed the business interests for both sides after reaching a certain extent.

If we are to view the status of trade in China based on this principle, we will find that there still exist major problems. While the first premise that China's international trade is voluntary and not forced is satisfied, it is the second premise that is completely noncompliant. International trade does not denote the trade that happens among countries but only indicates the trade that happens among businesses. China's export enterprises have many large sewages, and they cause environmental externality that doesn't fully enter into the enterprise costs in the form of sewage charges; it is not reflected in the price of trade products either. It means that some companies exchange the public environmental values for their own interests, and these benefits are not used to compensate for the environmental damage that they have caused; this results in the output of a large number of implicit environmental values. So, in this case, China's total exports compared to those with the true environmental costs considered are much larger.

Because of these environmental costs that exist in the development of China's trade, the larger the trade surplus, the greater the environmental costs in the manner of trade development with "output of environmental value." In fact, China's serious environmental problems are not only attributed to production areas, but also to the trade processes. Historically, trade development with "output of environmental value" is objective to a certain degree. In the initial stage of trade development, it requires foreign exchanges to import advanced technology and products, and foreign exchanges to meet the huge consumer demand on the international market; therefore, encouraging exports has become an inevitable choice for the country. During the developmental stage, it is impossible to export mainly products with little resource consumption or little impact on the environment. It has to export mainly resource-based products (primary products) that have a relative export advantage or even export natural resources directly. But according to China's specific national conditions, even though we know it has a heavy environmental cost, we cannot avoid it.

Obviously, the trade development with "output of environmental value" cannot be used for long; transformation in line with the change in China's basic national conditions and the overall national situation must take place. Currently, two cases have determined that change must and can be achieved: First, China's environmental problems have become increasingly prominent; it is becoming increasingly harder to achieve exportation through the mass consumption of the environment, with harsh trading conditions requiring a change in the manner of the growth in trade. Second, China's foreign exchange reserves have reached USD 1 trillion, and this has made China own the world's largest foreign exchange reserves. China has gone through a period of foreign exchange shortages and can protect the environment and restore ecology with trade gains or in trade.

(3) Continued deterioration of trade terms is not conducive to the sustainable development of foreign trade

According to the Import and Export Price Index released by China Customs, the Ministry of Commerce prepared the Chinese Trade Index. From 1993 to 2000, if we make 1995 as the base period, we can see that China's overall trade index fell by 13%. In recent years, a worse phenomenon was observed with regard to China's terms of trade. This was not only due to the increase in the import and export demand, technological advances in the field of traditional industries, excessive competition among export companies, and low price dumping, but also due to the low pricing of production factors used in the production of export goods. For a long time, the prices of China's domestic factors have been lower than international prices, such as land, natural resources, energy, technology, human resources and so on. As of 2003, to calculate the electricity prices in 100 kwh, electricity prices in the cities were as follows: USD 21.69 in Paris, USD 21.9 in London, USD 17.73 in Tokyo, USD 13 in New York, while only USD 3 in Beijing.

The fact that the factors' prices are low is closely related to China's immature system of resource pricing. The reform of China's resource price is hysteretic, the degree of marketization is not high, and with the development of the economy, the growth of the population, and the improvement of living standards, China's resource prices, which were formed during a very long period of time, have exposed many problems gradually, and are unable to meet the needs of economic development. First, resource pricing is initiated by the government or under its guidance, so it does not truly reflect the market supply and demand and the scarcity of resources, resulting in low resource prices. Second, the price ratio among resource products is unreasonable. From the price ratio between electricity and alternative fuels, the price of electricity in megajoule of China is only about 70% that of fuel oil and natural gas, 67% that of liquefied petroleum gas, and 56% that of artificial gas, and the price of electricity is significantly lower. Third, the pricing mechanism cannot reflect market changes sensitively. The irrational resource pricing method leads to a serious distortion in resource market prices, which is manifested by the unreasonable price of natural resources, the low price of resource products and the over expansion of resource requirements. Fourth, China is losing its right to speak for international resource prices, resulting in a substantial increase in China's oil enterprises' production costs, thus leading to heavy losses in national finance. As of 2004, China's crude oil imports grew by 34.8%, but the amount paid increased by more than 70%.

Thus, on the one hand, China imports crude oil at high prices from the international market, subsidizes the import enterprises through national finance, offers the crude oil to domestic consumers and production enterprises at low prices, and then exports those products to foreign countries at low prices. In fact, it makes foreign consumers enjoy the Chinese government's subsidies to resources. Therefore, low pricing of production factors results in low prices of Chinese exports and worsens its terms of trade; it not only reduces the interests of China's foreign trade, but it is also bad for the sustainable development of China's foreign trade. On the other hand, the deterioration of trade terms is closely related to the structure of China's import and export commodities. At present, in China's export commodities, manufactured goods account for more than 80%, but labor- and resource-intensive products and semi-finished products still account for a large proportion. The situation in which the competitive advantage of export products is not strong has not been completely changed. And with the enhanced awareness of environmental protection and the rise of green trade barriers in the global scenario, many developed capitalist countries, like the United States, European Union countries, Japan and other countries, link imported products with the environment and establish a complete system of pollution-free manufactured goods and the entire process of agricultural production, processing, storage, transportation, and sales. It exerts a great influence on the competitive advantage of China's export products, since China's environmental protection industry and technology have just started, and are not conducive to improving trade terms. Take the textile and dye industry for example. Textile products form part of the traditional export products that occupy an important position in China's foreign trade. In recent years, the EU's requirements of chemical substances used in printing, dyeing and other processes of textile production are increasingly stringent. There are more than 100 kinds of dyes that are banned by the European Union while China uses them. If China continues to use these dyes, it will encounter technical barriers to trade; if imported materials are used, it will increase textile prices, thus affecting the competitiveness of the textile industry. However, in recent years, China's demand for foreign goods has increased rapidly, especially for mechanical and electrical products and high-tech products. The main top ten products that China imported in 2009 are as follows: mechanical and electrical products, high-tech products, integrated circuits, crude oil, agricultural products, iron ore and concentrates, LCD panels, plastics in primary forms, automatic data processors, and unwrought copper and steel. Of these, the top three are: machinery and electronic products, high-tech products, and integrated circuits.

The deterioration of the terms of trade may lead a country's trade to become "poor trade," resulting in the loss of national resources, encountering overseas anti-dumping, and making trade environment deteriorate, going against the sustainable development of trade. International economists believe that there are three necessary conditions for "poor trade": First, the growth of the country's trade must tend toward the export sector; second, foreign demand for the country's exports must be price-inelastic so that the expansion of export supply will lead to a large drop in prices; third, the country must be already engaged in a lot of trade, and thus, the decline in terms of trade will exert a significant influence on welfare, which would be enough to offset the benefit that it can obtain from serving more goods. For China, except that the second point does not fully apply to it, the other two can more or less reflect the truth of China's foreign trade. Therefore, it should take measures to prevent the deterioration of the terms of trade as soon as possible, and this can prevent the occurrence of "poor trade."

(4) China's extensive processing trade needs to change

Since the reform and opening-up, underestimated factor prices and vast government preferential policies have attracted a large number of foreign-invested investors to build factories in China. This trend makes the processing trade, dominated by foreign-invested enterprises, account for a large proportion of China's export trade. Data show that China ranked first among developing countries in attracting international capital for 18 consecutive years. In 2009, global transnational direct investment dropped by about 40%, while China's actual foreign investment attraction fell by only 2.6%, ranking second in the world. However, 84% of foreign enterprises investing in China use the processing trade, accounting for two-thirds of China's total processing trade. From 1993 to 2007, the proportion of value of processing trade exportations in the total value of China's exportations was always greater than 50%. Although it has decreased in recent years, it has been able to basically maintain about 50%. For example, in 2009, the proportion of export value of the processing trade in the total value of China's exports was still 48.85%.

At the beginning of the reform and opening-up, China reduced the access threshold of its processing trade in order to attract foreign investment. In the short term, the development of these industries is expected to make some contributions to China's economic growth. But in the long term, it is anticipated to further damage the fragile ecological environment in China, and further exacerbate the tense situation of China's energy, making China pay a high cost of environment and of resources. China developed its processing trade in order to give full play to its international comparative advantage of domestic natural resources and labor, and developed it vigorously by seizing the opportunity of developed countries' international industrial transfer. With the rapid expansion of the scale of its exports, the marginal cost of export production has shown a rising trend. The production of China's processing trade mainly relies on high input and high consumption of land, labor, capital and other scarce resources. According to calculation of international organizations, from 2000 to 2003, the value of the rate of growth of China's exports accounted for 33% of the global growth value, and the growth of fixed-asset investments accounted for 60% of the global value, and the growth of oil consumption accounted for 36% of the global value. Although part of intermediate inputs of China's processing trade are from abroad, there is still a need for China to provide matching materials, energy, and electricity. This makes the growth of China's exports pay a high cost in resources. At the same time, in order to develop its processing trade, China also paid a high environmental cost, causing serious environmental pollution.

As for the geographical distribution of foreign investments in China, the Pearl River Delta region is the earliest and densest area of foreign investment in China due to the relatively sound investment environment and the matching industrial base. The Pearl River Delta region was once at the forefront of China's reform and opening-up. From the late 1970s to the early 1980s, Guangdong created sustained rapid economic growth and represented a rapid industrialization miracle as the Pearl River Delta region's "vanguard" for 25 years. Thus, the Pearl River Delta region developed rapidly and became the main base for the "Made-in-China" products of the 20th century. Its development was primarily dependent on low-end manufacturing and the use of cheap labor. In fact, foreign traders earned money from the cheap labor force. A large number of businessmen from Taiwan, Hong Kong, and Macao of China invested "processing and compensation trades" in Guangdong, making Guangzhou the world's most important manufacturing base. But with the rapid growth of the economy over the years, many cities in the Pearl River Delta region have gradually been plagued by insufficient energy, resource constraints, environmental pressures, and rising labor costs, and the low-cost-based industry agglomeration and the weakening of the area's advantage regarding policies and geographical position made the Pearl River Delta region gradually lose its original advantages. This shows that the processing trade could not support the sustainable development of China's foreign trade and led to the deterioration of China's environmental capacity.

The processing trade enterprises of resource-intensive products with high energy consumption and heavy pollution are generally prohibited or restricted in developed countries. They mainly rely on China's preferential land, tax policy, and more relaxed environmental protection policies to reduce their operating costs. These products have low value-added, the industries lack inherent power to convert their production modes automatically. Therefore, China has to accelerate the upgrading of its industrial structure and the processing of the trade structure. After gradually implementing policies of restricting or prohibiting the production and exportation of industries with low skills, high energy consumption, heavy pollution, high resource consumption and low value-added, more efforts should be put toward the transformation of the processing trade. Independently innovating advanced manufacturing by enterprises that are funded by domestic sources, is the only economic base that can be relied on.

(5) Cross-border transfer of pollution makes China's environmental capacity severe

Environmental capacity refers to the capacity of certain spaces to accommodate waste material. It is an index representing a country's capacity for environmental self-purification, its carrying capacity, and its inclusive capacity. In a certain sense, the environmental capacity is also a resource. China's environmental provisions in terms of imports, foreign investments, and others are not perfect. Currently, the environmental requirement of imports and foreign-invested enterprises is low, and the entire standard of pollution-intensive enterprises and foreign products is relatively loose, which makes China's environmental capacity reduced to a grim situation. This situation can be mainly manifested in two aspects.

① Foreign countries transfer pollution-generating products and hazardous waste to China through exportations

Because of a smaller number of environmental regulations and standards in China, the low threshold of environmental protection could not achieve a green barrier. This has resulted in a large influx of low-standard foreign products. For example, many imported foods have been found to be of poor quality in several market sampling tests, such as the European dioxin levels in milk and wine. Imports of these inferior products not only inflict harm on the domestic market, but also endanger the health of consumers. Similarly, the quantity of some hazardous waste transferred to China that seriously pollutes the environment is mind-boggling and the speed at which this happens is exceptionally fast. Since 1993, China Customs, especially in Nanjing, Zhuhai, Xiamen, Shanghai, Haikou, and other cities have been seizing the import "foreign garbage" in the name of waste plastics processing. Only during the period of June to August of 1995, China Customs investigated a variety of "foreign garbage" 9 times, which reached 1,850 tons. China's coastal areas are the major land area for the importation and use of waste. The waste is mainly from the United States, Japan, and Hong Kong of China. The entrance of the hazardous waste, such as used ships, automobiles, cables, electrical and other industrial waste, and old clothes, old tapes and other garbage, has polluted the domestic environment seriously; particularly, some wasteful imported pests and diseases also had a serious impact on the health of people. In addition, some imported products have problems of large investment of resources, large consumption of energy, and cause serious pollution in using them. Some of these products, such as chemical raw materials, iron ore, crude oil, synthetic fibers, wool and so on, are of high pollution, high-energy consumption in use.

② Foreign countries transfer pollution-generating enterprises to China through foreign direct investment

First, the main body of the processing trade, foreign-invested enterprises, tend to transfer pollution-intensive industries to China. As we all know, China's environmental preference is low, environmental policies and standards are loose relatively, there is a low internalized degree of environmental costs required by policies, which means that firms will pay low environmental costs for their products, and their production costs in China are significantly lower than those in developed countries and newly industrialized countries which have higher environmental standards. Therefore, these foreign countries and foreign traders will tend to transfer industries with high-energy consumption, serious environmental pollution, and external negative effects to China when they invest in and export finance and technology to China. By doing so, these foreign traders can not only acquire cheap resources and labor but also benefit from the advantages of low environmental standards at the same time. Pollution-intensive enterprises were about 30% of the total foreign-invested enterprises in China in 1999. Serious pollution-intensive enterprises were 40% of all pollution-intensive enterprises. Additional data showed that funds invested in pollution-generating enterprises were a quarter of the total foreign direct investments in China. Second, foreign traders transferred foreign garbage to China through the processing trade. Some foreign firms transferred products with harmful technologies, processes, equipment, even waste and other "foreign garbage" that were obsolete or prohibited in their own countries, thereby polluting the environment in China to a great extent. What's more, some foreign traders sold seconds at best quality prices, affecting air, water and other ecological aspects of the environment of the importing countries and this indeed had serious consequences.

The situation corresponding to this pollution transfer is that the environmental protection industry is generally regarded as one of the high-tech industries in the world. Environmental protection technology and environmental protection industries in developed countries started early and developed to a higher level than those in China. As far as these developed countries are concerned, compared with the use of advanced environmental technology in their own countries, which increases costs, it is better to evade provisions of national environmental regulations, and transfer the pollution-generating industries to developing countries. In developing countries (including China), the environmental protection industry is still immature compared to other industries. The technical level of China's environmental protection industry is behind the developed countries by nearly 20 years. For example, in developed countries, more than 80% of the urban sewage has been incorporated into the public purification treatment equipment system, and the rate of sewage treatment is higher than 80%, while the rate of China's urban sewage treatment was only 20% in 2000. Therefore, developing countries should consider the consequences of this pollution-intensive industrial transfer, and must not provide an opportunity for developed countries to transfer pollution.

(6) The lagging construction of a green trade barrier system influences the sustainable development of trade

Foreign green trade barriers have exerted a serious influence on China's exports. According to the information provided by the State Environmental Protection Administration and the China Quality Inspection Association, Chinese exportation loses up to USD 200 billion each year due to a variety of green trade barriers, and direct economic losses caused by over-standard agricultural pesticides only reach over USD 70 billion. As the world's largest developing country, China is facing challenges from various forms of green trade barriers in developed countries to its export products. There are mainly six forms of green trade barriers in developed countries currently, namely, the green tariff system, green technology standards, green environmental labeling, the green quarantine system, the green packaging system, green subsidies, and anti-subsidies. Compared to the study of how to deal with foreign green trade barriers, China is seriously lagging behind with regard to the establishment of its own green trade barrier system.

At present, the problems in the construction of China's import and export technical barriers to trade, especially regarding the green trade barriers are as follows:

① On the export side. First, the export businesses have incomplete information on the WTO/TBT rules and lack effective means of solving various problems. Second, the low technological level of products and the lack of independent intellectual property rights have led to the low standards, which cannot meet the needs of the international market. Third, developed countries continue to strengthen trade protectionism and develop more stringent technical standards.

② On the import side. First, the emphasis on technical trade measures for imports is not enough, and the awareness of the technical standard strategy is not strong. We did not conduct a comprehensive examination of and planning for the technical trade measures for imports. Second, the national technical regulation system is imperfect and lacks standardization; it has many problems in the establishment and management of procedures. Third, the overall level of technical standards is not high, and the system of the assessment of conformity is not perfect. In the areas of environment, public health, animal and plant inspection and quarantine, there are almost no barriers. For example, the procedures for the assessment of conformity and the certification system are not perfect. In the aspect of green barriers, environmental consciousness is weak, environmental standards are low, and environmental labeling and green packaging requirements are almost in a defenseless state. Problems exist in animal and plant inspection; for example, quarantine approval is not strict, quarantine technicians are not adequate, quarantine technology needs to be improved, and the understanding of the plant diseases and epidemics from importations is not at all sufficient.

7.3 International Regulations and Experiences Relative to Sustainable Development of Trade

7.3.1 Trade-related International Laws, Rules and Conventions Aimed at Protecting the Environment

(1) Several provisions in the WTO agreements regarding issues concerned with the environment and trade

According to the WTO's concern for the environment and sustainable development, trade is not only free trade under the WTO framework, but also trade with sustainable development. The preamble to the Agreement Establishing the WTO explains the goal of the WTO like this: When dealing with trade and economic relations between the members of the parties, it should not only improve living standards, ensure full employment, ensure stable growth of real income and substantial effective demand, and expand the production and trade of goods and services, but also consider the optimal use of the world's resources and seek the best ways to protect and preserve the environment at the same time.

① The provisions in the "General Agreement on Tariffs and Trade," 1994

GATT allows a country to take any action to protect the environment, and there are almost no restrictions on a country in its attempt to protect the environment and to prevent damage to the environment from consumption of domestic and imported products. Typically, a country can apply the rules applicable to domestic products to imported products as well, and can also take the actions that they consider necessary to ensure that their production process does not harm the environment.

② The provisions regarding environmental issues involved in the Uruguay Round "Final Documents"

The preamble to the Agreement Establishing the WTO clearly identified sustainable development and environmental protection as one of the fundamental purposes and principles of the new multilateral trading system. The preface to the TBT Agreement provides that: As long as it is to protect human, animal or plant life and health and the environment, and as long as there is no intentional or unfair discrimination, it would not be regarded as a covert measure of restriction on international trade. The contracting parties can develop technical regulations. The Subsidies and Countervailing Measures Agreement provides that if you can help eliminate severe environmental pressures and adopt the most appropriate environmental means, you may be given environmental subsidies. If these non-actionable subsidies are in line with the criteria, the country will not be charged for constrained dispute action. Most of the contents of the Application of Sanitary and Plant Inspection Measures Agreement is closely related to ecological and environmental protection. It stipulates that the parties have the right to choose what is considered to be a reasonable way to protect people, animals, or plant life or health under its jurisdiction in the following aspects—the spread of disease carried or brought in by animals, and the lead-disease toxic content of additives, contaminants, toxins, food, beverages, and dietary products, as long as they do not intentionally or unfairly treat the same or similar overseas products. In the Agreement on Agriculture, what is related to environmental protection directly is the "domestic support section," which proposed the concept of "Green Box Policies," which refers to domestic support measures related to the environmental planning project, including government services and support for research and infrastructure construction related to environmental planning projects. And in order to reduce the hazards of modern agriculture on the environment, direct payments to agricultural producers in accordance with environmental planning do not find a place in the agreement's list of reductions. The General Agreement on Trade in Services (GATS) is related to environmental protection in Article VI (domestic regulations) and VII (recognition). Article XIV is a general exception clause similar to Article XX, where Section (b) allows members to adopt or strengthen "measures to protect human and animal life and health," as long as such measures "do not result in arbitrary or unjustifiable discrimination to members in the same case, or do not constitute a disguised restriction to international trade in services." The Agreement on Trade-related Aspects of Intellectual Property Rights (TRIPs) provides specialized environmental provisions. Article 27, Sections (2) and (3) provide that the situation in which countries can choose not to grant a patent due to environmental considerations and other reasons, the purpose for which is to encourage more research, innovation, and national technology transfer.

(2) Trade-related MEAs aimed at protecting the environment

Multilateral environmental agreement (MEA), or international environmental agreement, is a global treaty based on environmental issues. It is a product created after the international community widely recognized that no country can solve the global issues alone at the national level, and it is necessary to require close cooperation among countries in seeking new solutions collectively. Accordingly, consultations in order to form a multilateral environmental agreement have become increasingly an important part in most of the national environmental policies.

(3) Green barriers regime in international trade

The green trade barriers, or green barriers for short, are also named environmental trade barriers. It is a new term for non-tariff barriers; it means that in international trade, some countries, especially the developed countries and international organizations under their auspices, make laws or enact strict mandatory technical standards or set double standards, which are different from their own national environmental standards (in the name of environmental protection) with their advantages in the economy and technology, imposing controls on international trade activities which may cause environmental pollution and ecological damage, and restrict or prevent foreign goods from coming onto the domestic market with the corresponding initiatives. The forms of green barriers are summed up as follows: the green tariff system, green technology standards, green environmental labeling, the green quarantine system, the green packaging system, and green subsidies and countervailing duties.

Green trade barriers have their own significant features as follows.

a) The protective method is extensive. Its contents involve the entire process of production, processing, packaging, transportation, distribution, consumption and recycling of products related to the resources, environment and human health, and set a series of standards for some products in safety, health, pollution and so on.

b) The protective method is hidden. International organizations and other individuals only see the positive role of green barriers in environmental protection. But they ignore the obstacles that they have caused to international trade.

c) The implementation has a dual effect. On the one hand, the green trade barriers have positive significance, which is necessary for global sustainable development; on the other hand, they have been used by developed countries to some extent, and thus have become a tool for the implementation of their trade protectionism.

d) The result is discriminative. Since some measures of the green trade barriers have not completely been of a uniform standard in the international area, the developed countries often set up green technology standards in favor of their own interests, and even double standards, thereby greatly harming the interests of developing countries or backward industrial countries.

e) The technical regulations should be development-oriented. Green trade barriers are closely related to the technological advancements and the development of international trade, so their technical requirements should be developed with the development of science and technology persistently.

7.3.2 Experience of Developed Countries in Ensuring Sustainable Development of Trade

(1) Energy-related laws to ensure sustainable development of trade in Japan

Japan is one of the best countries to carry out energy-saving work and one of the most advanced countries in energy-saving technologies in the world. The reason why its energy-saving work can be carried out effectively and achieve great success is inseparable with its scientific and perfect energy-saving regulations.

In June 1974, the Ministry of International Trade and Industry (MITI) enacted "Project Sunshine," which was aimed at developing new energy sources and reducing the amount of oil used. In 1978, when the second energy crisis occurred, Japan developed the "Energy-saving Technology Development Program." In the summer of 1979, the government developed the "Long-term Energy Demand Forecasts," and proposed energy-saving goals. On August 1, 1979, Japan began to implement The Law Concerning the Rational Use of Energy (the Energy Act); its purpose was to seek the stable development of a citizen's life. On the one hand, it was to ensure the long-term development of Japan's foreign economic relations, and trade was not affected; on the other hand, the wisdom and ways of all citizens were centralized to make energy consumption effective and reasonable at every stage as much as possible. The law was a basic legal law enacted to achieve optimum energy use based on the characteristics of the industry, transportation, construction, people's lives, and other areas where energy was consumed. Surrounding this central task, Japan established a comprehensive energy policy system and energy-saving measures system, and funded measures to promote the use of energy-saving equipment, and so on. With the development of the Japanese economy and society, there occured a particularly serious impact of the growth of energy consumption and energy consumption on the environment, so MITI in March 1993 enacted the Amendment to the Energy Act, which was aimed at creating a stable and reasonable energy demand and supply structure in order to further improve the rational utilization of energy and adapt to the coordinated development of the economy, society, and the environment. The revised Energy Act with particular emphasis on the development and application of new energy and industrial technology and funding the promotion and application of new energy technologies, was advocated to establish a national new energy information network.

The Energy Act as a very successful law has a huge effect on energy conservation in Japan. The main reason for this is the fact that it is a good advocacy work of law. And it is not hollow. Under the guidance of a sound legal framework, it has a series of specific matching policies and measures to support; so it is operable.

(2) Emission trade system to ensure sustainable development of trade in America

The United States is the first country to practice emissions trading. From the 1970s, the US Environmental Protection Agency tried to use emissions trading for the management of air and water pollution. It gradually tried to establish the system for emissions trading policy, which involves compensation, storage, capacity surplus and so on as the center. In over 30 years of practice, this policy has achieved tremendous economic and social benefits.

Emissions trading is the most typical application of the Coase theorem in environmental issues. The emissions trading system is a system that issues emissions permits and allows emissions permit trading between pollution sources according to pollution control targets. Specific implementation steps of emissions trading generally are: First, the government departments determine environmental quality objectives in certain areas, and assess the environmental capacity and the maximum allowable pollutant emissions of the region according to environmental quality objectives. Second, the emissions will be allocated among pollution sources by the issue of emissions permits. Last, an emissions trading market will be established to make it tradeable and circulate in a more reasonable way. The main variables considered to set this system are as follows: systematic objectives and basic features, such as material basis for emissions permits, the contents of emissions permits, the conditions of emissions trading, the legal basis for emissions permits, and how to choose the participants; the initial allocation of emissions permits, such as free allocation criteria and how to choose the way for pricing and auction; a variety of flexible options, such as savings and credit of emissions permits; how to organize emissions trading, by using internal transactions or trading among enterprises by brokers, exchanges, or departments of environmental management; establishing effective emissions monitoring systems, such as a performance tracking system; encouraging sewage companies to comply with the provisions of environmental quality and standard measures, such as a penalty system; coordinating with other environmental policies. The essence of this trading activity can be summarized in three points: (a) Emissions trading is the performance of the commercialization of environmental resources; (b) emissions trading is a market-oriented form of a pollution permit system; (c) emissions trading is a measure of control of the environmental capacity.

In the emissions trading schemes that have been implemented or are being implemented by the United States, the emissions trading scheme of the EPA, the Acid Rain Program and Southern California's RECLAIM Program are more typical.

(3) Pollution-charging system to ensure sustainable development of trade in Europe

Pollution-charging is the state departments' penalty charges to production units and individuals that cause environmental pollution set according to the national laws, regulations and policies. There are two approaches to this. The first approach is the excessive charges. These charges are only for enterprises that exceed the national emissions standards. Specific emissions standards to determine the level of fees can be classified according to the duration of residual contaminants in the environment, the level of the accumulation of pollutants in the living body, the toxic extent of pollutants in the environment and the human body, and other factors; it can also determine the level of fees in accordance with multiples exceeding the number and concentration of pollutants discharged. The second approach is adopting the way that fees are charged for sewage regardless of its size. Pollution-charging for the same company can have different charging methods.

Pollution-charging, on the one hand, promotes enterprises to actively control pollution, strengthens the management of enterprises, and achieves the comprehensive utilization of resources and energy by applying some external pressure. On the other hand, it is commonly used to control pollution. Therefore, it has also opened up a funding channel for enterprises in controlling pollution. For example, the Netherlands and other European countries began to impose pollution charges on enterprises in the mid-1970s, and later gradually increased the fees of heavy metal emissions. The Dutch industrial waste of mercury, chromium and other toxic metals emissions in 1991 decreased by 83%~97% over the emissions in 1976. Of course, whether a pollution charge is imposed in accordance with the concentration or the total amount of pollution, it needs to measure each of the related indicators one by one; thus, the collection cost is quite high. In addition, although the charges are mandatory as a government's action, it has no law for protection basically and it is easy to make polluters generate resistance toward assumed quotas set by the government. Therefore, most industrialized countries with relatively sound tax systems seldom use the pollution-charging system.

(4) The levy of an environmental tax to ensure sustainable development of trade in Europe

Environmental tax means a tax on units and individuals that exploit, conserve, and use the environment according to the extent of the development, utilization, pollution, and damage with regard to the environment and resources to improve the environmental pollution costs and prompt polluters to reduce pollution. The main purpose of environmental taxes is to change market signals, reduce pollutant emissions in production and consumption, and encourage the production and marketing activity at the same time by pricing environmental resources.

The levy on climate change was imposed in 2001, and it is at the core of Britain's overall strategy on climate change. It is aimed at the industrial, commercial and public sectors, which are non-residential, and imposed on the suppliers who supply energy products for these sectors. Payable tax is based on the supply of energy products and the corresponding tax rate, with no threshold.

The sulfur dioxide tax is the main environmental tax in Western countries. It can be divided into direct and indirect environmental taxes according to the different objects of taxation. Direct environment tax is imposed on sulfur dioxide which is generated by burning fossil fuels (primarily coal). It is an environmental tax that is imposed on the emissions per unit. Indirect environmental tax is taxed on fossil fuels, which produce sulfur dioxide during combustion. It is an environmental tax that is imposed on the input goods. Some countries levy direct environmental taxes on goods of large emissions and impose indirect environmental taxes on goods of small emissions.

7.4 Exploring the Route of China Toward the Realization of Sustainable Development of Foreign Trade

To improve the competitiveness of China's foreign trade exports and make it continue to work as an engine in China's economic growth, changing the growth mode of foreign trade and achieving the sustainable development of foreign trade are not only the trends of world trade development, but also China's inevitable choice.

7.4.1 Create a Favorable Environment Conducive to the Development of China's Foreign Trade

(1) Insist on the implementation of the coordinated free trade policy

Fundamentally, free trade policy is conducive to sustainable development. Of course, free trade policy has some flaws. However, it is not free trade itself but the ignorance of the environmental costs in the production of goods that becomes the root reason for these defects. If the environmental costs in the production and exchange of goods are fully considered, which means if the environmental costs are internalized, the negative impact of free trade on sustainable development can be eliminated. Therefore, free trade policy should be treated as a standpoint for the policy of sustainable development. We cannot completely deny free trade policy just because it has some adverse effects, nor can we replace the protective policies.

Second, China must take appropriate measures to eliminate the negative impact of the free trade policy for sustainable development of trade. The fundamental measure is the implementation of environmental cost internalization, and this can be done predominantly in three ways: The first is by using coercion to make environmental standards. Environmental costs directly influence the environment and production costs so that manufacturers will actively invest in technology and equipment to control pollution and govern the environment in order to meet environmental standards, leading to the internalization of environmental costs. The second is to impose pollution taxes. The third is the definition of property rights. As long as the environmental property rights are clearly understood, the internalization of external costs can be achieved through resource negotiations and emissions trading between the parties. Therefore, from the experience of countries, environmental standards, collection of pollution taxes and emissions trading have become major ways of environmental cost internalization. Thus, the implementation of a coordinated free trade policy is the best choice for achieving the sustainable development of trade.

(2) Improve environmental regulations of trade and ensure the sustainable development of foreign trade

At present, China has enacted 6 environmental laws, 13 resource management acts and 395 environmental standards. The legal framework of sustainable development of trade has been generally completed, but there are still many problems which need to be solved. The problems are as follows: First, most of the Chinese environmental laws and regulations were established during the period of economic transition, and with the rapid development of China's economy and society, some of them have become outdated. Second, the laws and regulations are not systematic. Third, the policy does not match the regulatory instruments and there is not enough law enforcement.

Therefore, the Chinese government needs to improve trade-related policies and regulations. First, it should strengthen environmental protection legislation and law enforcement, and speed up making environmental trade regulations, which are connected with environmental laws. Second, we also need some means of regulating economic policies, such as the development of the environmental tax system and the system of fiscal credit stimulus. Next, strengthen the implementation of the assessment system of the environmental impact to ensure the sustainable development of China's foreign trade in production areas. Make a scientific evaluation of resources and environmental capacity regarding the planning of foreign economic development, analyze the requirements of environmental resources for the planning, in order to set up the environmental capacity of the entire region effectively, limit the total amount of emissions in the region, and propose appropriate measures during the implementation after the formulation of policies and regulations and prior to the implementation of the projects.

(3) Raise environmental awareness of the public

When improving the laws and regulations of the sustainable development of trade, government departments should strengthen the promotion of environmental protection, get people's support of the ideas of energy saving, and transform that support into conscious life habits.

a) As for the contents, it is not only to publicize the trade-related laws and regulations of China's sustainable development, but it is also necessary to publicize some important laws and regulations regarding the sustainable development of foreign countries, especially the international environmental conventions, protocols, and standards. These are the legal bases for the countries in exercising of green trade barriers with considerable complexity and variability, which has a huge influence on Chinese export enterprises, and should be publicized; in addition to promoting environmental awareness, we should publicize viable ways to protect the environment.

b) As for the objective, on the one hand, it should focus on the general public, making energy saving reflected in the people's daily life; on the other hand, it should also focus on some of the business managers and the persons responsible for publicity, because these people are important decision-makers who can affect corporate environmental investments and ensure clean production.

c) As for the ways, it should pay attention to diverse methods and media, for example, the education of children, the creation of energy day, Environment Day and so on by means of television, radio, online public service ads, and community posters, savings and environmental protection manuals. In short, this would not only benefit the whole community in the effective use of resources and environmental improvement, but also lay a good foundation for the healthy and sustainable development of China's economy and foreign trade by creating a three-dimensional system of a full range of publicity and raising people's awareness of environmental protection.

(4) Carry out international environmental cooperation actively and create a favorable external environment

First, intensify research on the relationships of restrictions imposed by international multilateral environmental conventions on trade and existing international multilateral trade rules, and strive for profit and avoid loss. On the one hand, implement some form of reasonable trade protection by using the exceptions of environmental protection; on the other hand, prevent foreign countries from abusing green trade barriers.

Second, actively participate in the formulation of the multilateral trading systems and multilateral environmental conventions. At present, there is a big gap between China's environmental management and developed countries' environmental management in trade; through full exchange of information and opinions with other countries, China can acquire the advanced experience and constantly improve China's system of environmental trade regulations and management. For China, actively participating in international forums on trade-environmental issues gives it a chance to fully express its interests and demands, restrain trade protectionism in the name of environmental protection and unreasonable practice in developed countries, and compensate for the lack of existing environmental provisions on the basis of multilateral negotiations, jointly develop fair and reasonable environmental protection terms with developed members to objectively assess the current situation and requirements of developing countries' sustainable development of trade. At the same time, China will be able to understand the new trend of environmental protection development in the world and the possible new impact on trade.

Third, use the WTO dispute settlement mechanism to resolve disputes on trade and environmental issues actively. Within a country's sovereignty, the environmental problems which are caused by market failures can be improved through government intervention and public participation. But in the international sphere, settling disputes between trade and environment should be made possible through consensus and multilateral environmental cooperation. Countries can make use of the mechanism for the settlement of disputes created by world organizations to find a fair and reasonable solution for trade and trade and environmental disputes with developed countries. At present, the WTO's procedures for the settlement of disputes and multilateral environmental treaties have many incompatibilities. In the future, China should take part in the modification and improvement of the procedures for the settlement of disputes in these areas, enhance its dialogue with other countries, and create a favorable international environment for the sustainable development of China's foreign trade.

7.4.2 Promote a Mode for the Growth of International Trade to Change from Environmental Output to Ecological Restoration

The ecological restoration mode for the growth of foreign trade is defined as a new mission and a new task for Chinese trade development to improve environment and restore ecology to build a new trading system consistent with the Scientific Outlook of Development. This system includes three aspects: 1) Control and reduce the proportion of products that consume the environment and resources in total exports, and so relieve the pressure on China. 2) Increase imported products which can replace China's products that consume the environment, and achieve "environmental inputs." 3) Earn economic benefits from the trade in green products, the trade in environmentally friendly technologies and other activities, which are conducive to protecting the environment by adjusting the structure of exportation. The priority is to reduce the exports that consume the environment, followed by the realization of environmental input, and finally green trade.

First, combine the objectives of China's foreign trade policy with environmental resources strategies, and further promote the adjustment of the product structure of foreign trade according to China's national conditions, in order to change the excessive growth of resource-intensive products with high energy consumption and pollution in China. In recent years, China has adopted a series of measures to adjust its export policy. In 2006, the Ministry of Finance and four other ministries issued the "Notice About Adjusting the Tax Rebate Rate of Some Commodities and Increasing the Prohibited Commodity Catalog of the Processing Trade," which was a measure for China to further suppress resource-intensive products with high energy consumption and pollution after an overall decrease in export tax rebates at the beginning of 2004. After the implementation of this measure, in the first three quarters of 2006, China's exports of crude oil, refined oil, coal, unwrought pierced aluminum were reduced by 21.8%, 21.1%, 11.9%, and 5.8% respectively. Second, to implement environmental input policy, China needs to develop and use international resources to meet the needs of China's development objectively according to China's special situation of having a large population and little land. China has contributed too many of its environmental benefits to the international market; now it is time to restore and repair the homeland. Third, China should further find greater profit margins from green food and trade in green services. For example, green food is a new product created by using new technologies and processes after improving environmental standards, and represents a new industry. In the past, China earned its trade interests mainly through traditional food exports. Now China can earn greater trade interests by fostering the green food industry. For example, China exported goods like crafts by cutting trees in the past, but now China can develop tourism by cultivating forests and attracting foreign tourists to China, which is a kind of trade with a low amount of environmental consumption.

The manner of achieving a growth in trade with the mission of ecological restoration negates the past way of achieving that growth, which achieves economic benefits by outputting environmental resources. This new mode of obtaining growth in trade does not merely emphasize the need for environmental protection, but particularly emphasizes obtaining greater trade benefits by upgrading the connotation of trade; so it is a win-win mode of growth in trade between trade and the environment.

7.4.3 Establish a System for Environmental Economic Accounting and Increase the Compensation for Resource Factors of Export Products

Over the years, the export prices of many resource-intensive products do not include the environmental costs. Exportation at low prices, not only leads the export trade to be fettered by anti-dumping and other trade barriers, but also does harm to the country's long-term developmental interests and causes a serious imbalance in the environment. Therefore, first, we must learn from foreign experience, establish a method of economical environmental analysis and a policy system for the Chinese situation, and strengthen the quantitative study of the impact of environmental change on the resources, human health, society, and the economy. Consumption of non-renewable resources, the growth and decline of renewable-updated resources, the destruction, restoration and improvement of the environment, should be included in the accounting system as social costs, and gradually achieve the commercialization of resources of the environment, the rationalization of prices, and the compensation of resource consumption and environmental destruction. By using economic levers such as taxes or fees and adjusting the price of resources, we can gradually recover environmental costs and constantly improve the taxation and fee policies about the development and utilization of resources.

Second, accelerate the reform of prices of market-oriented resources and energy. In the future price reform, we should gradually bring all kinds of environmental resources and energy into the market directly, adjust prices based on price patterns and on the supply and demand relationship, and make market prices accurately reflect the true value of environmental resources and energy, and finally establish an environmental resource and energy price system of the sustainable development of trade. Due to the fundamental role of energy and resources in the national economy and the extensive sectors related to prices, if we promote a market-oriented reform blindly, it is likely to lead to rising resource prices and cause cost-push inflation. That is the Chinese government's largest dilemma in the market-oriented reform. Therefore, the reform of prices of market-oriented resources and energy must be carried out step by step, which cannot be done overnight. In the short term, measures can be taken regarding the following three aspects of resources and energy and related products to promote the reform of prices of market-oriented resources and energy: 1) With regard to export enterprises, impose higher export resource tax on exported products. Taxation depends on the difference between the international and Chinese domestic market prices of resources and energy, and pollution control costs which make up for the environment. 2) As to productive or trading enterprises, gradually promote a reform of market-oriented resources and energy to make their prices rise steadily. 3) For the people's daily use, maintain the current price level or make adjustments to the change in the overall income levels of the people. In this way, it will promote the reform of prices of market-oriented resources and energy while China's trade losses can be reduced to a minimum, and will not suddenly have too much influence on the existing economic system. Conversely, it will be in favor of reducing the resistance to reform.

Third, try to make more reasonable price ratios of resources. Whether those ratios are reasonable or not affects the interests among different industries as well as different regions; it not only impacts the coordinated development of regional economy directly, but also affects the maximum efficiency of each resource. Therefore, to achieve sustainable economic development, we must rationalize the price ratios among China's current resource prices. We must pay attention to adjusting unreasonable price ratios among crude oil, natural gas and coal for power generation. In addition, establish and improve a relevant mechanism of industry price linkage and establish an interest adjustment mechanism between the upstream and downstream industries and regions. Reasonable price ratios of resources not only help to optimize and adjust the resource structure, but they are also conducive to China's resource industry's stable and healthy development and to establishing a stable foundation for the sustainable development of Chinese trade and economy.

Fourth, actively promote the reform of resource ownership and asset management and have clear and demarcated property rights. Market-oriented reforms should be efficient and must have a system with clear rights and responsibilities. Resources belong to the state, but in reality, many resource rights are blurred. State-owned enterprises and local governments, on behalf of the state, possess resources for a long time, and have a right to disposal and usufruct to a certain degree. Especially in recent years, local government officials, in order to pursue political achievements (GDP and fiscal revenue growth as key indicators of political achievements), have attracted investors with cheap resources, low prices, and low environmental costs, enlarging the distortions in resource prices. Therefore, it will be important to promote a resource ownership agency to be market-oriented, resource using rights and other "public authority" market-oriented reforms, establish a resource asset-based management system, a monitoring system, an operating system and other resource management frameworks, which would make the responsibilities and rights clearer. Eliminate the "government failure problems" caused by excessive nationalization and administration during the initial definition of natural resources and energy.

7.4.4 Promote the Upgrading and Transformation of the Processing Trade and Reduce the Consumption of Environmental Capacity

Regarding the situation in which the roughly processed export products with low value added still make up a large proportion of China's export structure, China can take the following measures.

First, adjust the developmental ideas of the processing trade and seize the opportunity of international value chain modularity, redefine China's position in the international division of labor, promote large and medium-sized enterprises to undertake the product processing work, which have abilities in development and design and links with high value-added like marketing, making Chinese enterprises become the ODM or OBM of multinational companies' rather than the OEM, and improving China's position in the international division of labor.

Second, improve the level of foreign technology spillover by strengthening the association of foreign-funded enterprises and domestic enterprises, improve the technological level and the value added of exported products, and promote the shift and upgrading of China's processing trade to high-end. Improving the technological level of export products is the key to the sustainable development of China's foreign trade. To form a real competitive advantage, it must combine Chinese labor resources with foreign advanced technology to improve the technological level of export products, change the situation of the high quantity and low quality of Chinese exports and thus enhance the competitiveness of Chinese exports.

Third, strengthen the political guidance and supervision of governments at all levels, resolutely put an end to introducing processing trade projects with a low technological level, serious pollution, high energy consumption and low income, put an end to transnational transfer of polluting industries, establish a government investment performance appraisal system with a rigorous assessment review, restrict correctively or relocate non-standard processing trade enterprises, increase the resources and environmental tax imposed on the foreign-funded enterprises, and guide the shift of China's processing trade industry from extensive to intensive actively.

Fourth, adjust the internal structure of the processing trade and promote the coordinated development of the processing trade. On the one hand, the government should formulate a long-term, rational industrial policy, adjusting the industrial structure of the processing trade, so that the processing industrial chain will spread farther and the quality and efficiency of the processing trade can be improved. By conducting an intense processing business of high-value-added products and deepening the processing level, extend the industrial chain of the processing trade and form a processing trade industrial cluster where the intra-industry and inter-industry can support each other. On the other hand, vigorously promote the development of the processing trade in the Midwest, adjust the regional structure of the processing trade and promote balanced economic and trade development.

Fifth, introduce foreign-founded companies with advanced technology, high-value-added products, and research institutions into the processing trade, give concessions and support in terms of policy to high-tech industries and high-value-added processing trade enterprises. This will create a good policy environment for the upgrading and development of these enterprises by providing personalized services, convenient customs clearance measures, and advanced and efficient processing trade management for businesses according to the size and industrial characteristics of the firm.

Sixth, seize the opportunities of economic integration, encourage processing trade to "go out," and actively cooperate with foreign enterprises in the processing trade. Using regional advantages, develop processing industries in Central Asia, South Asia and other export markets, and actively carry out economic and technical cooperation with neighboring countries, safeguard China's central and western regions' transport corridor in neighboring countries through economic ties, and actively promote the development of China's processing trade abroad.

7.4.5 Speed Up Industrial Restructuring and Develop the Environmental Protection Industry Vigorously

Corresponding to the export industrial restructuring, China should speed up the adjustment of its industrial structures and develop high-tech industries vigorously, particularly the environmental protection industry. The development of the environmental protection industry is not only conducive to environmental protection and the improvement of the efficiency of environmental funds, but it also has become a very dynamic industry on the export market because the environmental protection industry is the sector that provides public goods and services to protect the environment, use resources efficiently, prevent environmental pollution and resource destruction, and maintain and restore an ecological balance.

First, actively support China's environmental protection enterprises to enhance their technological innovation capability with (R & D) funding. The core of activating the development of the environmental protection industry is technological innovation. Only through technological innovation can we overcome the negative externalities caused by the economic activity and thus it will be easy to adapt to market demands for new products. The environmental protection industry belongs to the technology-driven industry, and is characteristic of high R & D investment and risk. Companies are reluctant and have no ability to bear risks caused by technology development. Therefore, they must establish a reasonable risk investment mechanism and create diversified financing channels. On the one hand, establish an open-end fund for green industry development by increasing government fiscal revenue, and raise funds by issuing corporate bonds, going public and many other channels. On the other hand, the financial sector should consider environmental factors as an important condition for bank credit, treat every loan with caution, refuse to give credit to the demand of high-pollution projects, and give great support to environmental protection projects on the credit funds. In addition, try to establish an "Environmental Protection Bank" in China, which can be created by the national registered capitals, or choose a policy bank from the country's four original policy banks to establish environmental credit funds to manage and supervise the total environmental protection investment and financing. Chinese companies can also take advantage of opportunities of environmental priorities, and actively apply for foreign investments in environmental protection, such as the Montreal Multilateral Fund.

Second, introduce advanced foreign environmental protection technology and equipment actively to enhance assimilation, absorption, and innovation. As for environmental protection technology, China started late and has lagged behind developed countries for decades. Thus, while researching and developing, China must also pay attention to introducing advanced foreign technology and equipment at the same time. Assimilation and absorption and further innovation on the basis of previous innovations need to bring China's environmental technology up to date with the developed countries as soon as possible. States should strongly encourage introducing environmental protection technology and equipment and provide convenient and preferential treatment on financial taxation and importation formalities.

Third, foster large-scale environmental groups and enhance the transnational operational capability of large companies. In a market economy, an important way for enterprises to reduce costs and enhance the competitiveness is to expand their scale of business and achieve economies of scale. Because the number of large enterprise groups in China's environment industry is very small, and a majority of enterprises have small scales, a low level of technology, and weak competitiveness, China should select some environmental protection companies which have a large size and strength, potential for development, better basic conditions, and a relatively high technological level, and give them priority support in capital, technology and policies. Meanwhile, restructure the environmental protection companies into corporations and straighten out the property rights of environmental protection enterprises. Encourage the environmental protection industry to use the asset link to implement trans-regional, cross-industry, cross-ownership unions and acquisitions. On this basis, innovate the enterprise system, accelerate the development of environmental protection products and technology, explore the international market, achieve economies of scale, and enhance the ability of transnational business and international competitiveness.

7.4.6 Establish and Improve China's System of Green Trade Barriers

The International Organization for Standardization promulgated a series of international environmental standards ISO14000 in 1996 formally, and the ISO14001 was recognized as the "green pass" in international trade officially. Chinese export products should fight through ISO14001 certification in order to obtain the permits of the international market and meet the certification requirements of its trading partners. Meanwhile, China should establish a complete standard system of green trading with ecological, social, and economic benefits as its focal point, and achieve a reasonable structure of imported goods.

a) Establish a system of green tariffs and market access. The establishment of a system of green tariffs and market access not only helps carry out strict checks on imported goods, prohibit toxic and hazardous wastes from being transferred to China, and shut out pollutant goods and equipment, but also plays a guiding role in introducing advanced products and technology. To prohibit the entry of toxic and hazardous wastes, China should impose an environmental surcharge on imported products.

b) Improve the green technology standards. China should transform the international standards of the ISO4000 environmental management system into national standards through the legislative process, and promote them nationwide. Meanwhile, China should refuse to import non-standard goods.

c) Improve the green hygiene quarantine system. Based on ecological and environmental protection, China should develop more stringent technical environmental standards to ensure that the Chinese people, animals, and plants are protected from the influence of pollutants, toxins, microorganisms, and additives, such as the provision of maximum residue levels of the pesticides in various commodities. The importation of non-standard products should be resolutely banned.

d) China should require imported goods to be labeled with a green environmental label by legislation. Given that China's domestic products are not currently implementing an environmental labeling system through legislation, it is necessary to develop management regulations of environmental labeling, standardize the management of domestic environmental labeling, and make it institutionalized as soon as possible. This is not only conducive to the exportation of Chinese products, but also conducive to the boycotting of foreign products without environmental labeling.

e) Establish a green packaging system. Green packaging means saving packaging materials, which are easy to recycle and to breakdown naturally, and which do not pollute the environment. China should first regulate domestic products through legislation to make them adopt green packaging.

Specifically, in the form of legislation, prohibit using certain packaging materials, such as mercury, lead, and other materials, develop regulations to force packaging materials to be recycled or re-used, establish a storage refund system, and adjust it through taxation. At the same time, through appropriate legislation, put an end to imported products that do not meet the Chinese green packaging requirements.

8

Research on the Competitiveness of China's Service Outsourcing Industry

With the acceleration of economic globalization and the reconstruction of the international industrial structure, trade in services has been significantly developed. Telecommunications, computer and information services, accounting, consulting, and other modern business services have been significantly developed, presenting a satisfactory momentum and gradually becoming the key areas of trade in services for the main countries that are engaged in worldwide trade in services. Meanwhile, with the strategic adjustment of transnational corporations and the rapid development of information technology, especially in the fields of computing, networking, and storage, service outsourcing is becoming a vital form of trade in services and an essential catalyst for the new wave of industrial transition worldwide. Under the influence of the global financial crisis, more transnational corporations are likely to outsource their non-essential businesses so as to increase their competitiveness with lower costs, which is expected to bring remarkable opportunities for China in such areas of business.

As service outsourcing plays a key role in trade in services, it is therefore expected to bring significant economic and social benefits to China. The structure of imports and exports and the structure of industries have become capable enough to upgrade to higher levels, which requires us not only to innovate the mode of our stock trading, but also to prioritize trade in services so as to increase the proportion of trade in services in the total volume of trade. Service outsourcing plays a unique role among various service trades. Having started service outsourcing, China, with a multitude of advantages, still needs to confront with more challenges. Hence, this chapter depicts the real situation of many cities and presents an analysis of whether service outsourcing in China has advantages in global competition or not. It also proposes favorable policies and measures with solid political and theoretical foundations based on the various factors governing the existing service outsourcing in China and the current situation as well as its defects.

8.1 Overview of the Theories of Service Outsourcing and Industrial Competitiveness

8.1.1 The Concept and Division of Service Outsourcing

(1) The concept of outsourcing and service outsourcing

The term "outsourcing" is the short form for "outside resource using"; it literally denotes the usage of outside resources. Outsourcing first appeared in the *Journal of Royal Society of Arts* in 1979, but its conception was originally proposed by two Americans—Gary Hamel and C. K. Prahalad in 1990. From their perspective, outsourcing essentially meant a sort of resource-integrated management mode, by which many important but not vital, businesses are distributed to more efficient contractors so as to make full use of internal resources in other more competitive and vital areas of the businesses. Rahul Sen and Shaidul Islam defined outsourcing as an economic activity which an enterprise strategically adopts in order to operate its business, which was once operated by local labor and resources by using those from outside. Loh and Venkatraman drew up a definition of outsourcing based on research on IT outsourcing: Outsourcing is the materials or human-resources and something related with both kinds of resources shouldered by the outside supplier, or the specific component of IT infrastrcture in customer structure. From this definition, it can be seen that outsourcing can be either the stock or service as long as it happens outside of the enterprise. Atkinson, with research on American IT service outsourcing, proposed that it means a process when a company signs a contract with others to operate a special business without any broad limitation. They also thought what people complained about outsourcing was actually the offshoring that was not welcomed by the in-house team. "When an American company sets its branch abroad, the employment opportunities will move to other countries, too. It includes two categories: stock and service."

In recent years, Chinese scholars have gradually been fixing their eyes on this economic phenomenon with the rapid development of offshore outsourcing in China. Zhang Jialin thought that outsourcing means that an enterprise realizes some of its businesses by separating tasks out to other contractors for cheaper labor costs, so as to reach the goal of reducing costs and improving enterprises' competitiveness. Zhan Xiaoning and Xing Houyuan deemed that service outsourcing meant an economic activity that the operator distributes the service process to other contractors in the form of business.

(2) Classification of service outsourcing

In general, service outsourcing can be classified in two ways: Firstly, based on regional division, it can be classified into onshore outsourcing and offshore outsourcing. The former is that enterprises distribute part of their business functions to other domestic enterprises, that is, the distributors and the contractors are located in the same country; the latter is that enterprises distribute part of their business functions to enterprises abroad, that is, the distributors and contractors are located in different countries. Secondly, according to business types, service outsourcing can be classified into business process outsourcing (BPO), information technology outsourcing (ITO), and knowledge process outsourcing (KPO) and so on. In 2006, the Ministry of Commerce of the People's Republic of China issued the Implementation of the Service Outsourcing "Thousand-Hundred-Ten" Project, which divided service outsourcing into ITO service and BPO service, including business transformation, business process and business process service outsourcing, management application service outsourcing, and basic technology outsourcing (IT, development and design of software, R&D of technology, basic technology platforms and management integration) and so on. (see Table 8.1)

Table 8.1 Classification of service outsourcing according to the business field

Service outsourcing		Content
ITO	Operations service	Processing and integration of bank data, credit card data, insurance data, tax data, law data, etc.
	Application service	Management information system service, information engineering and process design, remote maintenance, etc.
	Basic technology service	Software development and design, technology design, integration of basic technology and basic platforms, etc.
BPO	Internal management service	Logistics service, accounting service, finance center, HR service, wages and welfare service, data center and other internal management services, etc.
	Business operations service	Technology R & D service, sales and wholesales service, after-sales service, etc.
	Supply chain management service	Purchase, transport, overall warehouse plans service, third-party logistics service, etc.

Source: Implementation of the Service Outsourcing "Thousand-Hundred-Ten" Project of the Ministry of Commerce in 2006.

8.1.2 The Current Situation of Research on Industrial Competitiveness at Home and Abroad

(1) Theories of industrial competitiveness research

In the 1970s, a Harvard School scholar, Chelle proposed a "market structure—market conduct—market performance" three-stage model, that is, the structure-conduct-performance (SCP) model on the basis of Bain's "market structure—market performance." The SCP model, which originated from an analysis of industrial performance, induced industrial competitiveness into one problem and proposed two introductions of research on industrial competitiveness, that is, the industrial structure and the industrial conduct.

From the micro perspective, Michael Porter's diamond model, the theory of national competitive advantage, after analyzing complicated data and files, reckons that there are four factors that determine a nation's competitive advantage: essential productive factors, including natural and human resources, intellectual resources, capital resources, and infrastructure facilities; demand condition, which mainly refers to the feature of the domestic market demand; the situation of relevant and supporting industries, that is, whether these or relevant upper industries are internationally competitive or not; the enterprises' strategy, structure, and the rival's conduct. These four factors influence each other and constitute the diamond model. Meanwhile, there are two variables that influence a nation's competitive advantage: government and opportunity, of which the latter is uncontrollable, and the influence of the former can never be overestimated.

APEC divided competitiveness into macro competitiveness, micro competitiveness, and structural competitiveness. Macro competitiveness refers to legislative, educational, and technological competitiveness, while micro competitiveness means competitiveness related to whether an enterprise can get market share and profit or not, and structural competitiveness indicates outer competitiveness, the infrastructure facility of technology, the investment structure, and the mode of production.

Jin Bei devoted himself to research on international industrial competitiveness. From the perspective of basic theories, he researched the theoretical framework and logical structure of competitiveness and tried to use the analytic framework and tools related to economic subjects and managerial theory in competitiveness research.

Pei Changhong, who got an approximately similar analytic framework as Jin Bei, evaluated industrial competitiveness in two aspects: demonstrative index for analyzing results of international competitiveness and the analytic index to illustrate the reasons for the international competitiveness of an industry in a country.

(2) Research on the industrial competitiveness evaluation system

In 1996, the International Institute for Management Development, Lausanne (IMD) designed the industrial competitiveness evaluation system, which is comprised of 8 factors, 41 aspects, and 224 indices. In the next three years, it formed 8 competitiveness components through supplement, extension, and improvement: ① Domestic economic factors, including 7 competitive aspects. ② Degree of internationalization, including 8 competitive aspects. ③ Government influence, including 6 competitive aspects. ④ Financial environment, including 4 competitive aspects. ⑤ Infrastructure, including 4 competitive aspects. ⑥ Enterprise management, including 5 competitive aspects. ⑦ Scientific and technological development, including 5 competitive aspects. ⑧ National quality, including 7 competitive aspects. These 8 components comprise the index framework of international industrial competitiveness. But there are defects in such a framework, i.e. it fails to reflect the features of typical industrial structures.

The international competitiveness evaluation system raised by the World Economic Forum (WEF) in 1997 contained three aspects and three indices; the three aspects included the overall level of international competitiveness, real international competitiveness, and potential international competitiveness, while the three indices contained the international competitiveness index, the economic competitiveness index, and the market increasing competitiveness index. In 1998, the micro competitiveness index was introduced by the WEF, which was mainly comprised of business environment, and enterprise internal management, and the materialization of operational strategy. These indices, to some extent, compensated for the defects of the competitiveness evaluation index system raised by the IMD.

In 2002, the United Nations Industrial Development Organization (UNIDO) published the Industrial Development Report 2002—2003 in Vienna. It established an evaluation system to determine every country's industrial competitiveness, which selected four indices to measure the competitiveness in a country or region to produce and export manufactured products, which are per capita value-added of the manufacturing industry, the per capita of exported manufactured products, the proportion of high technology products in the value-added of the manufacturing industry, and the proportion of the high technology products in exported manufactured products.

8.1.3 Theoretical Research on the Competitiveness of the Service Outsourcing Industry

With regard to theoretical research on the competitiveness of the service outsourcing industry, Zhang Jitong advocated that service outsourcing makes it possible for enterprises to become temporary allies, which are similar to general industrial clusters in terms of the mechanism of their formation and industrial competitiveness while they also have some particular features. Hence, the purpose of the research is to figure out the advantages of the two industrial organizations by making a comparison between outsourcing and industrial assemblage competitiveness sources.

Zhao Ping thought that China presented a remarkable potential and competitive advantage for the service outsourcing industry, although China lagged behind India for several decades in this industry. China is well supported by a steady political environment, a rapid development of the domestic economy, the improvement of traffic infrastructure, varied and cheap labor of service outsourcing, favorable investing and financial environments, and other objective conditions. Meanwhile, she proposed several barriers for China's service outsourcing business and that we should learn from advanced experience of the Indian service industry, thereby shaping China's competitive advantage for service outsourcing by capitalizing on the domestic advantageous resources and overcoming the shortcomings of this industry.

The Research Group in the Institute of International Economy of the University of International Business and Economics of China has specifically illustrated the background of the global service outsourcing industry and summarized the respective features and main factors of the development of the global and China's service outsourcing industry. On the basis of this analysis of China's service outsourcing industry at the enterprise level, it drew a conclusion that the advantage of China's service outsourcing industry lies not only in costs, but also in interaction with customers, adequate industrial knowledge, process management and process reproducing capability, a strict pay-off method, and other more complex factors. Although there are various advantages to China's service outsourcing industry, its disadvantages cannot be neglected and put aside. In the meantime, it also proposed several approaches to China's service outsourcing industry such as introducing foreign investment, seeking foreign-funded partners, connecting with the government, establishing branches abroad and other service outsourcing modes. In addition, it estimated that the business process outsourcing will become a future trend and local service outsourcing companies, which invest in process outsourcing, will have a larger market.

Ren Licheng and Wang Kanliang built a model of service outsourcing industry competitiveness and industry value-added on the basis of ITO, BPO, labor intensiveness and capital intensiveness with a combination of the theories such as those on competitiveness, service outsourcing, value chain, and industrial upgrading. The model reflected the basic principle of the competitiveness of service outsourcing companies and industry value-added, and further analyzed the developmental features of ITO and BPO. It also discussed the influences that labor intensiveness and knowledge intensiveness had on different developmental stages, which also guided the upgrading of China's service outsourcing industry.

With Michael Porter's diamond model, Yang Qing and Du Yun demonstrated several factors affecting the competitiveness of China's service outsourcing industries regarding aspects of productive factors, demand conditions, company's strategies and relevant industry support, and enterprise structure. They proposed promoting the competitiveness of China's service outsourcing industry by fostering talents, exploring a diverse market, and implementing other relevant measures.

E Lili conducted a research on factors influencing the competitiveness of service outsourcing from the outsourcing party's perspective and summarized these factors into three aspects: external, catalyzing, and business environment. In the meantime, she analyzed the advantages and disadvantages of the competitiveness of China's service outsourcing industry and proposed several suggestions to promote the competitiveness of that industry.

Sun Xiaoqin adopted the factor analysis method to select the factors influencing service outsourcing and acquired an index system to evaluate the competitiveness of contracting places from a new perspective, which was used to evaluate the competitiveness of 17 contracting cities nation-wide. The results indicated that China's service outsourcing industry was in its primary stage, which required macroeconomic control and financial support from the government. The cost advantage alone cannot be a main attraction for transnational enterprises in selecting contracting places any more, but the internationalization and quality of enterprises have to be considered as well. According to the results of evaluation, some cities, such as Shanghai, Beijing, Guangzhou, and Hangzhou, had the strongest competitiveness of service outsourcing. Cities such as Tianjin, Chengdu, Suzhou, Shenzhen, and Wuxi were endowed with remarkable potential and others, such as Wuhan, Xi'an, Nanjing, Jinan, and Dalian, had an environmental advantage. Cities such as Hefei, Changzhou, and Daqing should strive to develop special industries. The essential way for China's service outsourcing to develop is to strengthen the internationalization of enterprises and improve their own quality.

8.2 Development and Competition of the International Service Outsourcing Industry

8.2.1 Developmental Trend and Features of the Competitiveness of the Service Outsourcing Industry Worldwide

With economic globalization and the further specification of international labor division ever since the 1990s, the economic interaction among countries has become more frequent and the competition among enterprises has become fiercer than ever before. Hence, as part of their interaction initiatives, enterprises have started taking advantage of the Internet and telecommunication facilities to seek contractors worldwide who could undertake the non-essential businesses in order to cut costs and improve efficiency. Service outsourcing, offshore outsourcing in particular, has become the key method for transnational enterprises to lay out a global market and improve their international competitiveness, thereby shaping the new trend of global economic development at the same time.

(1) The continuous expansion of the global service outsourcing market

With a shift of the direct investment orientation of transitional enterprises, service outsourcing has replaced manufacturing outsourcing and has become a new key area of investment and a new motivation for global economic increase. According to relevant data, the scale of the global service outsourcing market has expanded rapidly every year. The United Nations Conference on Trade and Development (UNCTAD) has estimated the scale of development of global service outsourcing in the book *The Global Investment Report in 2004—Transition to the Service Industry*. The results indicated that the global service outsourcing and software market would increase at a rate of 30%–40%. But according to data from Gartner, the volume of global service outsourcing trade was USD 304 billion in 2004, USD 334.4 billion in 2005, and USD 432.3 billion in 2009 (see Figure 8.1). From 2004 to 2009, the compound rate of increase in global service outsourcing reached an approximate rate of 8%. The global IPO business increased from USD 192.8 billion in 2004 to USD 244.2 billion in 2008, with a rate of increase of 26.7%. The global BPO business increased from USD 111.3 billion in 2004 to USD 157.5 billion in 2008, which indicated that the rate of increase surpassed 40%, for it was 41.5%. Although the new round of international financial crisis had an impact on the international economy, developed countries such as European countries, America and Japan and other regions that were affected by this crisis deliberately outsourced their non-essential businesses to enterprises in other countries with productive advantages so as to cut costs and improve their international competitiveness, which stimulated the development of the global service outsourcing industry to some extent. According to McKinsey's research report, more than 95% of the global Top 1000 enterprises have formulated service outsourcing strategies, and it is estimated that the total potential service outsourcing market will reach more than 600 billion dollars worldwide.

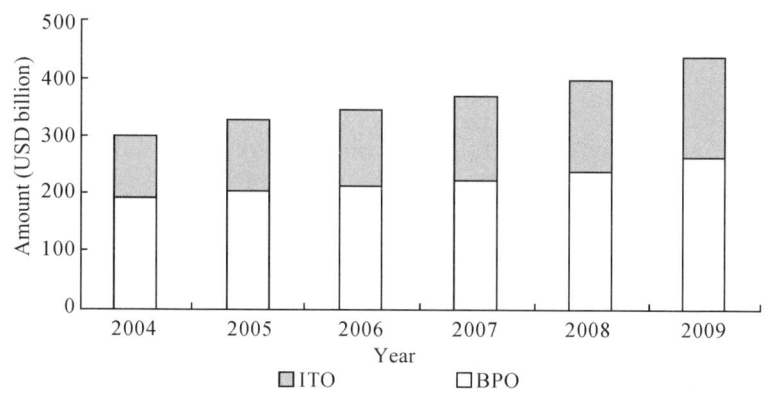

Figure 8.1 The scale of the global service outsourcing market 2004–2009
Source: Gartner.

(2) The optimization of the structure of the global outsourcing business

In the 1990s, IT and software industries were burgeoning, and the computer and network technologies matured gradually, because of which IT products and software service outsourcing have also developed correspondingly. At this stage, IT service outsourcing, namely, the business of ITO, has become the main form of international service outsourcing, and it has been growing constantly in subsequent years. But on the whole, the industrial level of international service outsourcing was relatively low, and the profit and value-added were also at a low level during this stage. With the development of economic globalization and regional integration, as well as the progress in the fields of science and technology, the business structure of international service outsourcing has been transformed to a higher level that features newer technology. Until now, the scope of the global service outsourcing business has been extended from traditional IT service outsourcing to a broader field, and the stage is characterized as follows: BPO maintains a higher growth rate compared with traditional ITO. According to the estimates of IDC, the compound annual growth rate of the global ITO market was 6.9% from 2004 to 2009, while the compound annual growth rate of the BPO market was 9.1%. The business structure of service outsourcing is developing to a higher level, and the requirements of knowledge and technology are also increasing. The business scope has been expanded to multiple fields representing modern and high-end services, including the finance, consulting, actuarial and insurance services.

(3) The law of the development of competitiveness within the global service outsourcing industry

According to the history of the service outsourcing market, the development of the industry can be roughly divided into three phases. The first phase is the origin of service outsourcing, which began primarily within the United States, and the business of service outsourcing was completed mainly in the United States. The nearshore and offshore outsourcing services appeared in the second phase, and some of the business of outsourcing began leaking out among developed countries. However, in recent years, with the maturity of the outsourcing model and the arrival of a new round of industrial transfer, many multinational companies have been outsourcing their non-core business tasks to developing countries where the cost of service is lower, which is the third phase of service outsourcing.

From the point of the main participants of international service outsourcing, the developed countries are the main outsourcing countries, while developing countries are also actively involved in this market and then become the main contracting countries in the international service outsourcing market. As the sponsor country of service outsourcing, the United States occupies 42% of the outsourcing market, and Western Europe accounts for 34%, Japan occupies 8% of the market, and the Asia-Pacific region excluding Japan accounts for 7%. In the contracting market, the first contracting group has initially been formed where the Asian countries such as India and Israel provide service to Europe and America, while Mexico and Canada mainly provide service to America, and Ireland, Spain, Poland, and Hungary mainly provide service to Western Europe; besides, China, Russia, the Philippines, and other Southeast Asian countries have become the second biggest contracting group. Developing countries have benefited a lot from the service outsourcing market. India has an absolute advantage in the international offshore market, and occupies 43% of it (see Figure 8.2). It is then followed by China. With its accelerated industrial restructuring and the increase in the developmental level of its service industry in recent years, China occupies an important place in the international service outsourcing market. The service outsourcing market of Asia, Latin America, and Eastern European countries, including the Philippines, is also developing, and the number of the countries and regions involved in service outsourcing is gradually increasing.

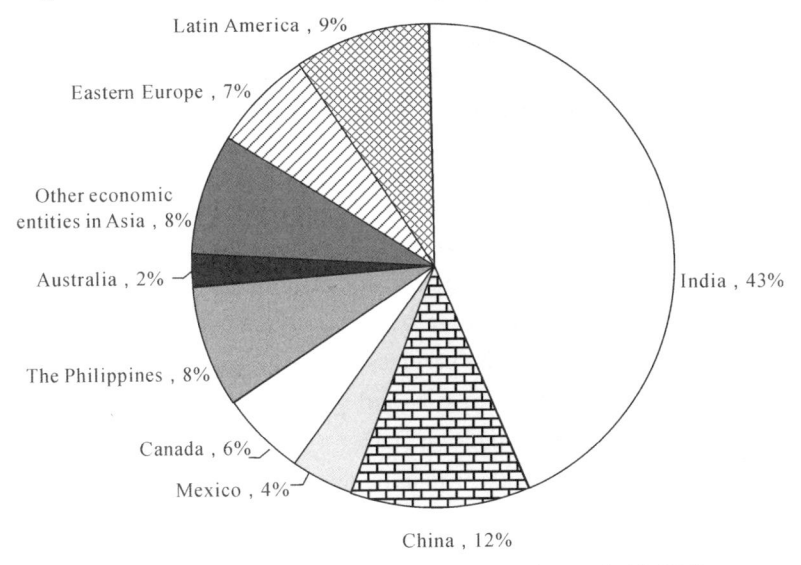

Figure 8.2 The International offshore outsourcing market in 2006

Source: Booz Auen Hamilton.

In short, the scale of the global service outsourcing market continues to expand, and the number of the countries, regions, and enterprises brought into the global outsourcing network is increasing. Offshore outsourcing has gradually become the main form of business. Cost reduction is a commercial factor which needs to be considered, and it is also the driving force of outsourcing. With the market competition intensifying, an increasing number of enterprises have realized that outsourcing can enhance the core competitiveness of enterprises to a great extent in addition to reducing costs considerably. Thus, outsourcing business including more technology and knowledge began to emerge, pushing service outsourcing to develop toward the high-end and modernization. In addition, with the adjustment of the international industrial structure, producer service has separated from the auxiliary section of the manufacturing industry to become a new industry. The separation of the servicing sector from the manufacturing industry provides a huge market for the development of the outsourcing industry. This also means that producer service will become the major catalyst for the development of the service outsourcing industry in the future.

8.2.2 Advanced Experience of the Major Service Providing Countries in Improving the Competitiveness of the Service Outsourcing Industry

(1) Development and competition mode of India's service outsourcing industry

As the most successful country to undertake the international service outsourcing business, India remains ahead of China by more than ten years. In general, the outsourcing industry in India has gone through three stages. The first stage existed from the early 1990s to 1998, when the main business was to provide office services for large financial and insurance enterprises. This was a kind of low-end service outsourcing, which took cheap labor as the main competitive element. The second stage started from 1999 and continued on to 2004, when the outsourcing business level and the technological level had risen to a greater degree, and the areas of business also had a great development. However, the business scale remained in the midstream and downstream of the industrial chain. The third stage goes from 2004 to the present, when the outsourcing companies of India began to change the priority of their business from ITO to BPO. A few multinational companies transferred the segment of the business with higher levels of knowledge and technology to India, and the business scale of service outsourcing has gradually transited to the upstream of the industrial chain.

The following experience can be concluded throughout the developing pattern of service outsourcing in India.

① Sound business choices and accurate market positioning

India has taken the software outsourcing business of the United States and Europe as the leading industry by virtue of its unique comparative advantage of language and culture, which both spots the target market and chooses the reasonable range of business, so it can play an important role in the international service outsourcing market. At the same time, India is also able to keep up with the times, and adjust its business level constantly with the changes in the fields of science and technology, and market, thereby maintaining its international market share in this way.

② Construction of institutional mechanisms which is conducive to the development of service outsourcing

The Indian government attaches great importance to the development of the service outsourcing industry, and creates an appropriate institutional environment which is conducive to the development of the service outsourcing industry at different levels by initiating reforms in the economic system and telecommunications industry, as well as by the construction of the legislation system for intellectual property. The economy of India is gradually moving toward liberalization, marketization, and globalization as a result of the economic system reforms brought about by successive governments. In addition, the Indian government has put emphasis on improving the construction of the supporting infrastructure of the service outsourcing industry, and has drawn up "The Policy of the Exportation of Computer Software, Software Development and Software Training" to provide strategic guidance for the industry.

③ The developing of high-quality human resources

The Indian government attaches great importance to the training of the personnel of the service outsourcing industry, and has therefore invested a lot of financial resources especially to higher education and technical training. Among developing countries, the quality of higher education in India stands on the top, and India is a great power when it comes to promoting higher education. The total number of scientific and technical personnel in India ranks third in the world, only after the United States and Russia, and the number of technical personnel with a high proficiency in English ranks second only to the United States. The outsourcing industry, especially the IT industry of India, is a concentration of talent due to the rapid development of education in the field of information technology, and it is precisely because of these personnel with low wage demands and high professional quality that India has been able to foster a large number of service outsourcing companies with international competitiveness.

④ The establishment of industrial associations and other intermediary organizations related to the development of the outsourcing industry

As a non-profit organization, the National Association of Software and Service Companies (NASSCOM) of India promotes the development of India's software outsourcing industry actively and effectively. The organization aims at promoting the development of the Indian software-driven IT industry by conducting forum activities. It plays a positive role especially in promoting the privatization and the opening-up of the telecommunications industry, and it is involved in promoting the government to enact anti-piracy laws, assisting the police in cracking piracy cases, and standardizing the business process of software outsourcing, as well as establishing a forum to improve the development of the outsourcing business.

(2) Development and competition mode of Ireland's service outsourcing industry

The development of the service outsourcing industry in Ireland can be generally divided into three stages. The first stage is the infancy state from 1970 to 1985, when Ireland explored the European market vigorously, and provided customers with professional services through the use of foreign software products. The second is the developmental stage from 1986 to 1995, when multinational corporations began to bring their advanced experience of management, training and so on into Ireland, and the local staff began to establish their own businesses, which gradually matured owing to the encouragement of the government. The high-speed developmental stage of the industry is from 1996 up to now, and the feature of the period is that the country's outsourcing companies have begun to develop products independently, and have shifted the emphasis on market development from onshore to offshore. With the diversification of investment capital flowing into the software industry, the number of the companies in Ireland engaged in software outsourcing increased from less than 400 in 1995 to more than 1,000 in 2003. Meanwhile, the BPO business in Ireland has also developed rapidly, and has formed strong international competitiveness.

The developing pattern in which the service outsourcing industry develops in Ireland has the following characteristics.

First, the guidance received from the government is clear, and it focuses on strengthening the management and coordination of the service outsourcing industry. The Irish government attaches great importance to scientific and technological innovation, and strengthens its capacity for scientific and technological innovation by making a developing plan for science and technology, setting up a special research fund, promoting the combination of production, teaching and research, improving the construction of an information network infrastructure, and establishing technology parks, etc. In addition, the government pays attention to the coordination among the relevant departments, and manages the software industry systematically.

Second, it has a sound government-supporting system. The Irish government has implemented a series of policies and measures in order to develop the service outsourcing industry. These measures included formulating the E-commerce Law in 1999 in order to develop Ireland into the electronics center of Europe, formulating strict and effective legal norms, and implementing tax breaks and subsidies to actively develop the service outsourcing industry.

Third, they pay attention to personnel training. Ireland has an excellent education system and training system, and public education investment constitutes a high proportion of public expenditure, which is higher than most European countries. Ireland's education system is unique in many ways. For instance, in the mid-1990s, the country started providing free higher education for all the students from the member states of the EU, as well as strengthening its own training and re-education, and widely popularizing the knowledge of electronic information and electronic business throughout the country. And the professional software training model is that trainees acquire the basic knowledge in the first two years; in the third year, they get hands-on practice in enterprises; in the final year, they complete an independent design. This method of training ensures that students are provided with both theoretical knowledge and practical skills, which to a great extent improves the students' professional ability.

Fourth, the innate language, geographical and cultural advantages play an important role, too. Irish people's native language is English, and Ireland is a member of the European Union. Labor mobility among the members of the European Union is more convenient, which has been the motivating factor for people to choose employment in Ireland. With this advantage, Ireland takes a number of preferential measures to attract a large number of high-quality talents who master two or more languages in the European Union, to engage in the service outsourcing business in Ireland. In addition, there are a large number of Irish immigrants in the United States, and Ireland has a very close relationship with the United States. To a certain extent, this makes a positive contribution to the trade flows between the two countries in the aspect of the service outsourcing business.

(3) Development and competition mode of Philippine service outsourcing industry

In the Philippines, the service outsourcing industry and the information software industry started in the 1980s, and in recent years, these industries have enjoyed rapid development. Now they have a good growth momentum and the Philippines has become a major international service outsourcing contracting country. The Philippine government has paid great attention to the development of the service outsourcing industry, has instituted a series of policies and measures for this industry, and has set up special funds to provide training for the local service outsourcing talents. According to the *Manila Bulletin*, the service outsourcing industry in the Philippines has become the world's second biggest, with only India ahead of it. And according to the latest edition of the *2009 Global Service Report*, although the Philippine population is only 1/10 of India's, it accounted for 15% of the global service outsourcing market. In 2009, the international financial crisis had a low impact on the service outsourcing industry in the Philippines, which grew by 19% in total to USD 7 billion, accounting for 5% of its GDP, and the number of service outsourcing employees reached 442,000. The service outsourcing industry is gradually becoming the main driver of economic growth in the Philippines.

According to the development of the service outsourcing industry in the Philippines, we can summarize it with the following characteristics.

First, the human resources of service outsourcing is large. The Philippines has a huge number of technical personnel, who have the skills to develop the service outsourcing industry. And a lot of university graduates join the workforce each year. Importantly, these workers generally have a high proficiency in English, have a strong ability for cultural understanding, but have a low expectation in terms of wages. Therefore, the Philippines has the advantage of developing service outsourcing at a low cost.

Second, the government intensively encourages policy-making regarding this sector. The Philippine government regards the service outsourcing industry as a priority industry. It has formulated the "Investment Priorities Plan," and formulated a series of preferential policies, including tax incentives, so as to promote the development of the service outsourcing industry. At the same time, it has established a service-outsourcing-enterprises-oriented "Applied Talents Training Fund" to strengthen the education and training of the personnel in the service outsourcing industry. In order to strengthen the construction of the service outsourcing legal environment, it has passed the *Data Security and Privacy Act*, and has built a relatively perfect intellectual property protection system, to create an effective legal system environment for the development of the service outsourcing industry.

Third, the service outsourcing industry has a sound management system. Because the government pays great attention to the development of the service outsourcing industry, it has set up an information technology and electronic commerce committee, with the president as its chairman. The prime responsibility of this committee is to supervise the implementation of developing strategies of information and e-commerce. At the same time, it has also set up an investment promotion bureau, specialized in the management of all aspects of the service outsourcing industry. In addition, they have also set up a business process outsourcing association to assist the government in promoting the development of the service outsourcing industry.

8.3 Development and Competition Trend of China's Service Outsourcing Industry

8.3.1 Developmental Status of China's Service Outsourcing Industry

China's service outsourcing industry started relatively late, and the general level of development needs to be greatly improved. However, with all the development seen in recent years, China has been able to seamlessly speed up the upgrading of the industrial structure, continuously strengthen the service industry foundation, and become an integral part of the international service outsourcing industry. The service outsourcing industry in China has made good progress and China has gradually become an important contracting country on the international service outsourcing market.

(1) The overall situation of China's service outsourcing industry

China's economy is in the acceleration stage of industrialization, so the foundation of the service industry is weak and the service outsourcing industry started relatively late. But in recent years, with the upgrading of the domestic economic structure and the acceleration of the industrial gradient shift, the level of the development of the service industry has made a significant breakthrough, with the fact that the service outsourcing industry developed from literally nothing. With the expansion of the scale of business, the total amount, and the business scope, China is gradually becoming an emerging global outsourcing center. In general,

China's service outsourcing started much later when compared with its manufacturing outsourcing, and later than countries such as India by ten years. Nevertheless, service outsourcing has developed quickly and achieved good success since the late 1980s to the present.

Statistics of the Ministry of Commerce of China show that in 2006, the total revenue of China's service outsourcing industry was USD 11.8 billion, including USD 7.56 billion from the IT service outsourcing industry and USD 4.27 billion from the BPO industry. Across the country, the revenue of offshore service outsourcing business undertaken by contracting enterprises accounted for about 12.2% of the whole industrial revenue, while most of the service outsourcing revenue came from domestic business. In 2009, China's service outsourcing exports continued to grow rapidly. There were 4,175 new service outsourcing enterprises, a total of 8,950 service outsourcing enterprises, and 1.547 million employees. There were 60,247 service outsourcing contracts, increasing by 142.6% year on year, and the total contract amount was USD 20.01 billion, increasing by 185.6% from the previous year. The contracts implemented amounted to USD 13.84 billion. As a whole, China's service outsourcing witnessed tremendous growth. With the help of markets at home and abroad, and domestic high-quality human resources, the service outsourcing industry in China looks promising.

(2) The present distribution of China's service outsourcing industry

In recent years, with a huge market scale, high-quality talent reserves, and low production costs, China has become the destination of numerous multinational companies' overseas activities, and a major player of outsourcing services from multinational companies. For now, China's undertaking business focuses on software service outsourcing of ITO and customer service of BPO.

China's IT service outsourcing market is mainly composed of software service outsourcing, hardware service outsourcing, IT training, and IT consulting. Among them, software service outsourcing covers a relatively high proportion, about 60%, and has a faster growth rate (see Table 8.2).

Table 8.2 Scale and growth rate of China's software outsourcing market

Year	Scale of software service outsourcing market (USD billion)	Growth rate
2006	1.43	—
2007	2.17	51.7%
2008	3.18	46.5%

Source: China Center for Information Industry Development (CCID).

The application system development service outsourcing occupies the highest proportion of total revenue, while the R&D of software products of a high technological level and high value-added only covers a small proportion, which should be prioritized for development in the future. In terms of market distribution, the main outsourcing countries of China's software service outsourcing are Japan and R.O. Korea, which have cultures that are similar to China's, followed by Europe and the United States. And in terms of contracting methods, most of the Chinese enterprises receive orders from secondary or tertiary subcontractors in Japan and R.O. Korea, which have low interest rates; for European and American markets, the multinational companies employ Chinese workers with high technical level in their offshore centers or subsidiary companies in China, which have higher interest rates than business with R.O. Korea and Japan.

For China's outsourcing enterprises, business process outsourcing has relatively weak competitiveness, and it is still in the early period of development. But in recent years, with the separation of the productive service industry from the manufacturing industry and the rapid development of the related business process outsourcing, the importance of business process outsourcing began to increase. The business process outsourcing industry in China has entered a period of rapid development, and prominent business process outsourcing companies from the United States, France, Britain, India and other countries have started to set up joint ventures or business process outsourcing centers in China. Business process outsourcing in China mainly includes businesses such as customer services, finance and accounting, human resources, procurement, and training. Among them, the customer service business occupies the largest proportion, which provides services such as customer analysis, customer care and order fulfillment. But on the whole, Chinese enterprises are not yet fully equipped to undertake offshore business process outsourcing, simply because the present laws and regulations are not clear, and language, culture, and contract risk are at a disadvantage. The development of China's business process outsourcing industry has a long way to go.

(3) Regional distribution of China's service outsourcing industry

With the increase in government's policy support and assistance to the service outsourcing industry, China has basically formed a regional distribution pattern on the basis of key demonstration cities. Among them, in North China, priority is given to Beijing; in East China, priority is given to Shanghai; in South China, priority is given to Shenzhen and Guangzhou; in Northeast China, priority is given to Dalian and Shenyang; in Central China, priority is given to Changsha; in Southwest China, priority is given to Chengdu; and in Northwest China, priority is given to Xi'an. With the development of the service outsourcing "Thousand-Hundred-Ten" project, this pattern of distribution was constantly improved and supplemented. In 2009, in order to promote the development of the service outsourcing industry, the General Office of the State Council promulgated the "Reply About Promoting the Development of the Service Outsourcing Industry" as a response to the Ministry of Commerce's policy suggestions about promoting the development of the service outsourcing industry and agreed to specify 20 cities, namely Beijing, Tianjin, Shanghai, Chongqing, Dalian, Shenzhen, Guangzhou, Wuhan, Nanjing, Harbin, Chengdu, Xi'an, Jinan, Hangzhou, Hefei, Nanchang, Changsha, Daqing, Suzhou, and Wuxi as the demonstration cities of service outsourcing, supported them in working hard to undertake the service outsourcing business, and gave them a series of preferential policies. It also made China's service outsourcing industry move from first-tier cities to second-tier cities, and eventually form the pattern of comprehensive development in the east, west and the center.

Of course, the developmental level and the developmental priorities of the 20 pilot cities have certain differences. In the first batch of China's service outsourcing bases, Dalian is the first city to be entitled. Its software and information service outsourcing industries are specially developed. Its outsourcing business with Japan is more advantageous. Xi'an focuses on developing itself into the "City of Service Outsourcing in West China," relying on the advantage of rich local human resources, and has formed the scale development of the service industry. Chengdu combines the information technology outsourcing and business process outsourcing with overall considerations, and has formed IT, finance, logistics, medicine and other key outsourcing business fields. Shenzhen relies on geographical advantages and takes advantage of Hong Kong and Macao. Shanghai tries to develop itself into the economical headquarters base and the R&D center, and has made great achievements in the information technology outsourcing business.

In the second batch of China's service outsourcing bases, Beijing adopts an outsourcing developmental model which focuses on information basis outsourcing with business process outsourcing as a supplement. Tianjin focuses on financial service outsourcing, biological medicine service outsourcing and embedded software and product design service outsourcing. Nanjing and Jinan focus on developing software outsourcing service. Wuhan relies on the abundant manufacturing potential to drive the development of the service outsourcing industry. Hangzhou focuses on product innovation, and improves its capacity through independent innovation and design to drive the development of the entire service outsourcing industry.

In the latest batch of 9 demonstration cities, Hefei focuses on data processing, software subcontracts, human resources management, finance and securities, and logistics as the key of its development of the service outsourcing industry. Changsha's animation and game industry has become a characteristic industry of service outsourcing, and Changsha is expected to become China's "Cartoon Outsourcing Base" in the future. Guangzhou, similar to Shenzhen, relies on Hong Kong and Macao, leveraging its geographical advantage to develop its service outsourcing industry. Harbin's outsourcing business focuses on providing the medical industry with leveraging research and developmental services. Daqing focuses on petroleum engineering technical service, software development and information processing services, and professional services. The service outsourcing industry in Suzhou relies on its Suzhou Software Park as the carrier, focuses on the development of software outsourcing, giving priority to embedded software. Wuxi relies on its strong manufacturing base to develop its service outsourcing industry. Chongqing's and Nanchang's service outsourcing industry are small, and are mainly composed of software outsourcing.

8.3.2 Competition Trend of China's Service Outsourcing Industry

The development of the service outsourcing industry in China mainly presents the following characteristics.

(1) China's service outsourcing industry grows fast, but the overall scale is small

Although service outsourcing industry in China started late, its development has been very rapid. Research shows that the global service outsourcing market is expected to grow at an average compound annual growth rate of 7% in the coming years, and China's service outsourcing market is expected to increase at an average compound annual growth rate of 19%, far higher than the global average. At the same time, the income from the service outsourcing industry will grow at an average compound annual growth rate of 22%. With the advent of the wave of the transferring of the international service outsourcing industry, the increasing demand for the domestic and offshore service outsourcing, and the government's promotion toward the 20 pilot cities, China's service outsourcing industry is expected to enter a period of rapid growth in the next few years. But at the same time, we should also notice that the overall scale of China's service outsourcing industry is small when compared to that of the world. And China still has a gap with other major international service contracting countries such as India, the Philippines, and Ireland. By 2007, India's service outsourcing revenue had increased by 10 times in 10 years. In the Philippines, outsourcing revenue reached USD 5 billion in 2007. According to the data released by an association of business processes, the Philippine service outsourcing industry's income rose by 19%, to USD 7.2 billion in 2009. In 2010, it reached a whopping USD 9 billion, with an increase of 25%. The European outsourcing market is largely monopolized by Ireland.

(2) Human resources are abundant, but the development of the service outsourcing industry is hindered by the lack of interdisciplinary talents

A large number of compound and high-level talents who master foreign languages and professional skills is the key to developing a modern high-end service industry or undertaking an international service outsourcing industry. After all, the service outsourcing industry is a knowledge-intensive industry. Only a country with the advantage of human resources will be likely to gain a foothold in the international service outsourcing market, and then get a substantial share of its profit. This has become the key factor for China in achieving transformation and developing its service outsourcing industry. However, a study shows that one of the bottlenecks in China's development of the service outsourcing industry is a lack of interdisciplinary talents. China has a large number of colleges and universities — just in 2010, more than 6 million university graduates found jobs — and therefore, it has an extremely rich talent pool. However, because China's personnel training mode, such as higher education and vocational education, has many defects and deficiencies, the talent market also has some unreasonable factors now, such as an unreasonable structure of human resources, a shortage of middle and senior technical personnel in service outsourcing. China does not have enough service outsourcing project managers with rich experience or middleware outsourcing talents like system architects. China lacks talents who are familiar with foreign languages, have a good cultural background, and know the international rules governing the outsourcing industry. It also lacks senior management personnel who can carve out a foreign market.

In addition, China's talent incentive mechanism is not perfect, especially with less attraction for the introduction of advanced talents.

(3) The service outsourcing level is low, the business scope is narrow, and priority is given to onshore outsourcing

The development of the service outsourcing industry is a gradual process. In general, the service outsourcing industry in China started late, and its foundation is weak. Therefore, the level of the service outsourcing business undertaking is low. Business basically focuses on the field of software and information service, which is narrow. Within the software and information service outsourcing industry, the business is mainly in the low-end of the industrial chain, which is largely labor-intensive work. It is to be noted that knowledge-intensive business in China is still in its infancy, and there is little business with high value-added and a high technological level. In the context of the current development of China's service outsourcing, most of the business belongs to the labor-intensive sector. Despite the fact that some powerful enterprises can also undertake the business of high knowledge content and a high technological level, they are not a majority on the whole. The level of China's service outsourcing remains to be further improved. At the same time, compared to the rapid development of the software and information outsourcing business, business process outsourcing has not yet formed a scale. In addition, most of China's service outsourcing business focuses on the domestic market, and the scale of offshore outsourcing business in the true sense has a big gap compared with other contracting countries around the world.

(4) The distribution of China's service outsourcing is even, but the development of its competitiveness is not balanced

China's service outsourcing industry is distributed across North China, Northeast China, Northwest China, South China, East China, Southwest China and Central China, and the service outsourcing central cities can influence surrounding areas or cities. At the same time, there are differences among various areas and central cities. Overall, it seems that cities where the service outsourcing industry develops relatively well are the first-tier cities of Beijing, Shanghai, Shenzhen and Guangzhou. But in recent years, with the rapid development of the software and information outsourcing industry, the cost of human resources in these cities is rising. It is hard to provide human resources which can meet the industry's developmental requirements, so the service outsourcing industry begins to shift to competitive second-tier cities. In these cities, the urban infrastructure is complete, human resources are abundant, and there is relatively stable liquidity. They are fully capable of undertaking the service outsourcing business. Second-tier cities' service outsourcing business is also increasing year by year, but there are still a certain number of gaps compared to the businesses in the first-tier cities. Take Shenzhen for example; in 2009, its software business income was more than 90 billion yuan, with an increase of 33% from 2008. Software exports accounted for more than USD 5.6 billion, an increase of 69% from 2008. Because these first-tier cities started early and the foundation is better, the service outsourcing business accounted for a large proportion in the whole nation. The momentum of growth is good in Xi'an, Wuhan, Changsha, Chengdu and other second-tier cities, but the gap between the first-tier and the second-tier cities in terms of scale and income still exists. While the regional distribution of China's service outsourcing industry is relatively balanced, the development of its competitiveness is not balanced from the perspectives of economic scale and industrial income and benefit.

8.4 SWOT Analysis of Competition Trend of China's Service Outsourcing Industry

According to the characteristics of the development of China's service outsourcing industry and the prospects for the future, this section uses the analysis framework of the SWOT model and summarizes many factors like the strength, the weakness, the opportunity, and the threat of the development of China's service outsourcing industry in order to capture the critical problems of that development and to put forward policy recommendations and an arrangement of the pattern of development that is conducive to the development of the industry.

8.4.1 Analysis of the Strengths

(1) A stable society and a good economic environment

Since 1978, China's reform and opening-up policy has been playing a role for more than 30 years. During this period, great changes have taken place in China. The achievements of China's economic development have been remarkable and the country's international standing has also increased substantially. Seen from GDP data, China's GDP maintained a growth rate of above 10% for 5 years, from 2003 to 2007, which achieved 10%, 10.1%, 11.3%, 12.7%, 14.2% respectively. In 2008, under the influence of the global financial crisis, the growth rate of China's GDP slowed down, which was 9.6%. According to IMF data, in 2008, the world's economic growth rate was 3.4%, with the advanced economies increasing by 1.0% and the emerging and developing economies increasing by 6.3%. In the advanced economies, the United States increased by 1.1% and the eurozone increased by 1.0%; however, Japan decreased by 0.3%. In the emerging and developing economies, Russia increased by 6.2%, India increased by 7.3%, and Brazil increased by 5.8%. In this depressed global environment, China's economic development is outstanding.

In 2008, it was primarily estimated that China's economic development had contributed to the world economic growth by more than 20%. In 2009, China's economy, stimulated by the package plan such as the 4 trillion investing plan and the ten industries revitalization plan, presented a V-shaped rebound and the growth rate of the GDP reached 8.7%. Moreover, in 2010, it reached 10.3%. In that year, China's GDP exceeded Japan and China became the world's second largest economy. The booming characteristics of China's economy has added to the world's confidence in China and has also provided good support for increasing the competitiveness of China's service industry. Meanwhile, China continues to practice reform and opening-up, improve systems and mechanisms beneficial to scientific development, and maintain social and political stability. In recent years, China has paid more attention to improving people's livelihood and the development of social programs has been constantly accelerated. Employment, social security, education and medical treatment are all the aspects that have achieved concrete improvement, thereby promoting social stability and harmony. A better social and political environment helps China to establish a good image and also provides a favorable atmosphere for the development of the service outsourcing industry.

(2) The government's strong support and promotion

The service outsourcing industry is one part of the modern service industry, and its status has been early recognized in the country, because of which policy support and great encouragement was provided by the government for the development of the service outsourcing industry. To speed up the development of software, strengthen the innovation capacity and international competitiveness of the information industry, in 2000, the State Council formulated the "Policies to Encourage the Development of the Software Industry and the Integrated Circuit Industry," making a number of preferential policies in aspects such as investment and financing, taxation, industrial technology, exportation, distribution of income, attracting and training talents, procurement and so on to promote the development of the basis for the service outsourcing industry. According to the "Approach of Recognizing Key Software Enterprises with a National Layout," these enterprises could pay the corporate income tax 10% less than regulation if they didn't enjoy tax exemption that year. In 2006, the Ministry of Commerce issued the "Notice on the Implementation of the Service Outsourcing 'Thousand-Hundred-Ten' Project" and planned to establish 10 service outsourcing cities of international competitiveness, encourage 100 of the world's well-known multinational companies to transfer their service outsourcing business to China, and cultivate 1,000 large and medium-sized service outsourcing enterprises with international qualifications. In 2007, "Several Opinions on Accelerating the Development of the Service Industry" of the State Council stressed the need to focus on improving the level of opening-up of the service industry, undertake international service outsourcing as the focus of expanding trade in services, give full play to China's strength in rich human resources, and actively undertake information management, data processing, accounting, technology research and development, industrial design and other international service outsourcing business.

In 2009, the State Council listed 20 cities such as Beijing, Shanghai and Tianjin as the demonstration cities of service outsourcing in its "Reply About Promoting the Development of the Service Outsourcing Industry." About the same time, local governments also introduced many policies to support the development of the service outsourcing industry. Suzhou, for example, provided regulations of preferential taxation, guidance on capital budgeting, capital support, carrier construction, talent introduction, training, special subsidies, intellectual property, certification, technical innovation, market development and so on, which has promoted the development of the service outsourcing industry of Suzhou Industrial Park. Dalian municipal government put forward the key areas of service outsourcing, and made rules in industrial park construction, talent introduction and training, and improvement of supporting infrastructure, in order to achieve a breakthrough in the development of Dalian's service outsourcing industry.

(3) Perfect the construction of infrastructure

With the rapid development of China's economy, the infrastructure has been occupying a large proportion of the investments. Modern infrastructure, such as communication facilities, transportation networks, and energy supply, is continuously being improved, which provides a good hardware basis for the development of the service outsourcing industry. Take communication facilities for example. According to China's Internet development statistics, by December 31, 2008, the scale of Chinese Internet users had reached 298 million, the penetration rate reached 22.6%, which was larger than the global average. The number of Chinese Internet users increases rapidly, among which broadband Internet users reached 270 million, accounting for 90.6% of all Internet users. China's Internet-based resource has maintained its rapid growth; in 2008, China's international export bandwidth reached 640, 287 Mbps, increasing by 73.6% from 2007, a growth that exceeded the growth of Internet users (see Figure 8.3). In 2010, Premier Wen Jiabao in the executive meeting of the State Council put forward recommendations to promote the integration of telecommunication networks, broadcasting and television network and the Internet, to enhance the interaction and the sharing of resources of the three networks, and to provide users with a variety of services such as voice, data, and radio and television. The integration has vital significance for promoting the development of information and cultural industries and enhancing the level of the national economy and of computing, which is also good for the development of the service outsourcing industry. In addition, the 3G network construction, fiber optic broadband network construction, the construction of the Internet of Things will have significant and far-reaching influence on the construction of the service outsourcing infrastructure.

The development of China's traffic network is fast, especially the construction of inter-city railways, which shortens the distance between cities. Civil aviation has also made rapid development in recent years; flights have been initiated between major cities in China; there are also direct flights to connect with the world's major cities. In addition, China has established many high-tech parks with a superior geographical position, a good lifestyle environment and complete infrastructure which provide a good investment environment for the development of the service outsourcing industry.

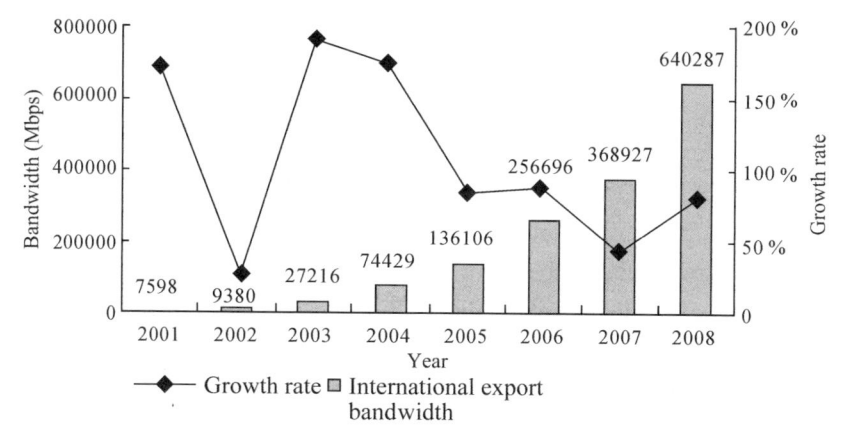

Figure 8.3 China's international export bandwidth from 2001 to 2008
Source: CNNIC.

(4) Rich human resources and lower wages

At present, China is going through a period of economic transition. With the acceleration of urbanization, a large number of the rural population have gone into cities, and after retraining, many workers have mastered the knowledge needed for the service outsourcing business. With the rapid development of China's higher education, every year there are a large number of graduates flooding into the talent market, which provides the development of the service outsourcing industry with abundant human resources. Since the reform and opening-up, China's secondary industry has enjoyed sophisticated development and China has been called the "world factory," which creates good conditions for the development of service outsourcing in China and helps enhance the confidence of foreign investors. The development of service outsourcing can also promote the development of the secondary sector, especially the promotion of technology and the improvement of employees' skills, which is conducive to the shift of China's secondary sector from labor-intensive to knowledge and technology-intensive, and the upgrading and optimization of the secondary sector can further provide a solid foundation for service outsourcing and promote the development of the service outsourcing industry. In the context of the current situation, China has abundant human resources, especially college graduates. Their employment situation is quite a serious problem. The service outsourcing industry can recruit such graduates to ease the pressure to a certain extent. Although the growth rate of the number of college graduates after 2003 has fallen, the absolute number of graduates increases year by year. According to statistics, in 2008, the number of college and graduate enrollments reached 5.7 million and 424,000 respectively. The number of undergraduate students of regular higher education reached 17.388 million, graduate students 1.105 million. The number of regular higher education students ranks first in the world, the ratio of higher education gross enrollment reached 22%, and China has entered the stage of popularization of higher education (Table 8.3).

Table 8.3 The number and growth rate of college graduates from 2001 to 2010

Year	Number	Growth rate
2001	1,104,100	9.48%
2002	1,418,200	28.45%
2003	2,122,000	49.63%
2004	2,800,000	31.95%
2005	3,380,000	20.71%
2006	4,130,000	22.19%

(To be continued)

(Continued)

Year	Number	Growth rate
2007	4,950,000	19.85%
2008	5,700,000	15.15%
2009	5,920,000	11.29%
2010	6,520,000	10.14%

Source: The website of the Ministry of Education.

In addition, McKinsey's research reported that China was one of the countries with the lowest labor costs in the world. Compared to India where the wages of service outsourcing labor is rising, China has a large labor cost advantage. Although the wages of software outsourcing and engineering technical personnel are on the rise in first-tier cities such as Beijing and Shanghai, second-tier cities such as Wuhan and Jinan have cheaper labor, and they are able to attract a large number of businesses with the advantage of lower costs.

(5) China has the advantage as the main contracting country of East Asian service outsourcing market

With the rapid development of international trade, China's domestic talents who are familiar with international trade rules, have flourished considerably, which has provided a good foundation for the development of the service outsourcing industry. Compared to Japan and R.O. Korea, China enjoys advantages due to its location. After years of economic cooperation with these two countries, China has established close economic ties with them. At the same time, because of historical reasons, the three countries have similar cultures, so China has advantages in undertaking service outsourcing business from Japan and R.O. Korea compared to India, Ireland and other countries.

In recent years, more and more Chinese people can speak Japanese and Korean, which offers China a natural advantage when taking service outsourcing businesses from Japan and R.O. Korea, and with the strengthening of the nearshore trend of international service outsourcing, China is sure to become the main contracting country of Japan and R.O. Korea. For example, multinational companies of Japan and R.O. Korea have set up many software R&D centers and customer service centers in Dalian, which is geographically close to them, and formed a preliminary trend of industrial concentration. As China, Japan and R.O. Korea further strengthen their economic ties in the future, the scale of China in undertaking service outsourcing from Japan and R.O. Korea will continue to expand.

8.4.2 Analysis of the Weaknesses

(1) The service outsourcing industry started late and the awareness is weak

A major portion of the Chinese economy is driven by the manufacturing sector. In contrast, the service industry is relatively backward, and its growth rate and contribution to the national economic growth is low. The service outsourcing industry started late, and although the developmental speed of this industry is fast, the overall size and income it generates are far less than other great powers on the international service outsourcing market. Enterprises engaged on the service outsourcing industry in China are small and medium-sized enterprises, which generally engage in the traditional industry with a low level, most of which are at the low end of the "smile curve." As of now, China can only undertake low-end business and it has not gained a clear advantage in the international service outsourcing market competition. Due to the lack of a perfect environment of intellectual property protection, most private entrepreneurs have a fuzzy understanding that outsourcing can lead to unwarranted disclosure of a company's business information, resulting in unnecessary loss to the company. This leads to a relative lack of awareness of service outsourcing at the entrepreneurs' level.

(2) The companies engaged in service outsourcing are small

At present, China's service outsourcing enterprises are of a small scale and companies generally hire about 50—100 employees. Their competitiveness is very weak and they don't have the ability to undertake major projects or develop skills for project research. At present, China's main outsourcing vendors are Neusoft and Sinocom, etc. The largest—Neusoft has more than 10,000 employees, and other companies generally have thousands of employees. Service outsourcing companies located in service outsourcing powers such as India are obviously larger than those in China. There is a lack of internationally competitive large enterprises to undertake service outsourcing. Companies in China are small, which don't have the ability to develop projects in a sustained manner, and thus it is difficult for big companies to compete with large enterprises on the international service outsourcing market.

(3) There is an absence of a reasonable talent structure, and a lack of mid-and high-end professional technical personnel

Although China has rich human resources, it can only basically meet the needs of the service outsourcing industry in the low-end market. The overall talent structure is a big problem in China. According to an on-the-spot investigation, one of the key obstacles in the development of the service outsourcing industry is the lack of professional technical personnel in the mid- and high-end market. Few can really conform to the requirements of the companies' development. Project management personnel, technical research and development personnel, database administrators, system developers, and senior designers are in short supply. On the one hand, because the structure of domestic education is unreasonable, the personnel structure is unreasonable and talents for the service outsourcing industry are in short supply. On the other hand, large multinational service outsourcing companies attract a large number of excellent talents at home and abroad with preferential treatment, leaving domestic enterprises with just second-rate or third-rate talents. Talent shortage will affect the development of China's service outsourcing enterprises, which is likely to affect the development of the entire service outsourcing industry.

(4) The level of language and communication skills need to improve

Compared with the main competitive countries such as India, Ireland, and the Philippines, the level of the Chinese people's skills in English listening, speaking, reading and writing is weak. Although in recent years, English is gaining popularity in China, and there is an increase in the number of people who know English, there is a decline in the level of skills in English of college students and working staff because many of them seldom use English to communicate and they lose exposure to English for a long period of time. Once they need to use English, they will find their mastery of English cannot meet the requirement of work, which becomes a big obstacle in their work.

In addition, there are significant differences in culture between China and European and American countries. Chinese employees sometimes cannot understand the thinking patterns of European and American customers or think in Western thinking patterns, which often leads to great misunderstanding. As a result, Western companies are reluctant to outsource information technology and business process business to Chinese enterprises. China is in a serious drawback regarding competition on the market because China has language and communication disadvantages compared to countries such as India.

(5) There are loopholes in the measures for the protection of intellectual property rights

Intellectual property is the first problem to solve in the development of the service outsourcing industry, but it is also a difficult problem of the legal system in China. Intellectual property rights have long restricted the development of China's service outsourcing industry, because the service outsourcing business contains trade secrets, patents, and copyrights, which have been the focus of outsourcing countries. If the legal environment of contracting countries is perfect enough, this problem can be satisfactorily resolved and the outsourcing countries will have confidence in the contracting countries, which will bring a steady stream of business to the contracting countries. From the present situation, China's intellectual property protection is not optimistic. Piracy, counterfeiting, and other intellectual property infringement phenomena emerge continuously. Although related management departments intensify supervision and punishment, because the relevant laws and regulations of the protection of intellectual property rights are not perfect, such phenomena still exist. The Chinese people's awareness of intellectual property rights protection is weak, the measures are imperfect, and protection is not enough, which affects the confidence of outsourcing countries and the expansion of the scale of offshore business of service outsourcing in China.

(6) There is a lack of international well-known brands and the global service outsourcing marketing experience is limited

China's information technology outsourcing and business process outsourcing companies haven't established internationally acclaimed well-known brands and haven't won recognition on the international market. An enterprise brand, as the intangible asset of enterprises, plays an extremely important role in the development of enterprises, because the brand is the combination of power, value, culture, and personality, and it bears a lot.

Chinese enterprises in international competition often lack brand shaping, because of which they are not able to win a place within the fierce market competition with the help of brand effect. In addition, China's service outsourcing enterprises do not understand the practice of the international market in depth or know the importance of self-publicity and promotion on the international market. It is hard for China's traditional commercial and operational mode to be in agreement with the usual practices on the international market, which to a certain extent has become the bottleneck that restricts the expansion of its service outsourcing enterprises.

8.4.3 Analysis of the Opportunities

(1) China has a huge growing domestic market and positive policies conducive to expanding domestic demand

Currently, due to the thought of "large and comprehensive, small and comprehensive" that rules the market scenes, most of the domestic outsourcing enterprises often do their business operations themselves. Most of them are not willing to outsource non-core services to professional service providers. But the situation has changed with the advent of the era of the service economy as well as the change in the mode of thinking of entrepreneurs; there is no doubt that the potential market for domestic service outsourcing will show its tremendous power. At the same time, in the context of the looming international financial crisis, the Chinese government introduced a series of policies to expand domestic demand, including an investment of 4 trillion yuan. China has focused on domestic economic development to drive economic growth by stimulating domestic demand. As a result, the huge domestic market and policy support have provided unprecedented opportunities for the development of the service outsourcing industry. With the support of the government, outsourcing bussiness from the government and large and medium enterprises will increase, which is very beneficial to China's service outsourcing industry when the global economy slows down.

(2) The post-crisis era provides an opportunity for China to develop the service outsourcing industry

Although the new round of international financial crisis makes the economies of most of the countries in the world slow down or even crash, the crisis has also made China recognize the importance of carrying out industrial structure adjustment and economic transformation, and of actively developing the service outsourcing industry. At the same time, there have been some changes in the international service outsourcing market. Since the U.S. subprime mortgage crisis in 2008, due to the decline in American domestic consumption, the rising labor costs in India, and the appreciation of the Indian rupee, India's service outsourcing industry got affected, the growth rate of its service outsourcing industry decreased, and the profits of its main enterprises also fell sharply. This gave China a good opportunity for development. In addition, India's third largest information technology outsourcing and business process outsourcing company got severely hit by the financial turmoil in 2009, which affected the confidence of the world's major outsourcing countries to invest in India. A large quantity of money which used to be invested in India's service outsourcing industry began to transfer to other countries, including China, which also provided opportunities for the development of China's service outsourcing industry.

(3) The Olympic Games and the World Expo rapidly promote China's international image, bringing enormous business opportunities

In 2008, the 29th Olympic Games were held in Beijing; and after that, China's status in the world has largely improved and China's influence and international appeal have been enhanced. All of these provided a favorable external environment for the development of the Chinese economy. The Olympic Games injected new momentum for the growth of

China's economy. This was an appropriate time for China to showcase to the world its infinite business opportunities and let the world get a further understanding of it, which has enhanced the confidence of multinational companies to invest in China. And in the future, there is expected to be a large number of international capital flowing into China which will surely promote the development of China's service outsourcing industry. The successful hosting of the 2010 Shanghai World Expo also launched many related new products and industries abroad, which would be conducive to the development of China's information technology outsourcing industry and business process outsourcing industry, and for the shaping of the brand.

8.4.4 Analysis of the Threats

(1) The subprime mortgage crisis slows the global economy

The international financial crisis, originating in the United States, slowed down the global economy. Although major countries have adopted a series of policies and measures, the world economy is still in the recovery period. The United States was one of the countries hit hardest by the crisis. Its economy slowed down, the unemployment rate increased, the domestic market started to shrink, and the purchasing power of consumers greatly diminished. The United States is one of the main international service outsourcing countries, whose domestic economic slowdown had a serious influence on the development of the international service outsourcing industry. For example, India's service outsourcing industry suffered significantly with a lower growth rate and reduced profits. Although the impact on China's outsourcing industry was limited, as an important market for China to develop its service outsourcing industry, the shrinkage of the European and American markets went against the development of China's service outsourcing industry. The economic slowdown in Europe and America led to the shrinking of foreign investment from these countries, which makes it not optimistic for the future of China's service outsourcing industry to introduce international capital. This has an enormous influence on its great development in the future.

(2) Exchange rate risks such as the appreciation of the RMB and the rise in labor costs

Since the RMB exchange rate reform, the appreciation of the RMB against the US dollar has continued. From 2005 to July 2008, the appreciation of the RMB reached 21%, while after July 2008, the exchange rate of the RMB against the US dollar kept around 6.83. By the end of 2009, the middle rate of the RMB against the US dollar was 6.827. The appreciation of the RMB against the US dollar was 0.15%. But since September 2009, the G7 countries, led by the United States, have put pressure on China for the appreciation of the RMB in turn; at the same time, China's interest rates were relatively high, and the appreciation of the RMB was expected. On the last trading day of 2010, the middle rate was 6.6227, which was a new high since the reform with the appreciation of 3.09%. The appreciation of the RMB will weaken the competitiveness of the service outsourcing business in China to a large extent: The continued appreciation of the RMB will lead to an increase in labor costs; it will also reduce dollar-denominated outsourcing income and directly affect the service outsourcing enterprises, preventing them from entering the stage of rapid development.

The international price of service that outsourcing enterprises in China provide will increase, following the appreciation of the RMB, and compared with similar foreign business, domestic business loses its price advantage, which is not conducive to China's service outsourcing industry on the international market. In addition, the average number of staff employed in the Chinese service outsourcing industry is rising, so the labor cost advantage is gradually weakening. Low cost is one of the driving forces of the service outsourcing industry, while the appreciation of the RMB and the increase in labor costs make the cost to undertake business increase, thus losing the price advantage and narrowing the room for profit. Thus, China's service outsourcing market would be squeezed by other countries with an advantage of prices.

(3) Emerging service outsourcing contracting countries compete with China

With the development of the international service outsourcing industry, and with more and more countries or regions involved, the competition among countries will become fiercer. For now, China is facing many powerful competitors on the international market. The competitiveness of China's service outsourcing industry is much weaker than that of India, especially in terms of the availability and quality of engineers, team cooperation, intellectual property and data privacy protection and there is a lot of room for improvement. In addition, the Philippines and Ireland have many advantages in undertaking service outsourcing business. With a rise in the service outsourcing industry in Latin America and central and eastern European countries, the international service outsourcing market will be redivided, and the service outsourcing industry in China will be faced with great challenges.

8.5 Measures to Improve the Competitiveness of China's Service Outsourcing Industry

8.5.1 Basic Judgment and the Main Factors of the Competitiveness of China's Service Outsourcing Industry

(1) Basic judgment of the competitiveness of China's service outsourcing industry

Overall, after years of development, China's service outsourcing industry has initially formed a scale and cultivated a batch of local service outsourcing enterprises of considerable market competitiveness, such as Neusoft, etc. But according to the domestic and international service outsourcing market and the development of the service outsourcing industry in some cities in China, the service outsourcing industry in China is still in its infancy. Although it has developed fast, its scale is not big, and the offshore service outsourcing is much smaller. From the perspective of business types, the traditional software and information technology outsourcing services occupy a dominant position and the development of business process outsourcing is lagging relatively far behind. From the perspective of the outsourcing market, Japan is China's main market, while China's service outsourcing enterprises undertake less business from the United States and European countries. And from the perspective of the form of service outsourcing enterprises, it has formed the common development pattern of foreign-funded enterprises, state-owned enterprises, and private enterprises.

With the development of the domestic service outsourcing industry, the number of local service outsourcing enterprises has become larger than that of foreign companies. But due to the technical level, management and brand marketing which obviously lag behind foreign enterprises, the major share of the domestic market is held by foreign enterprises. At the same time, there are some other problems, such as the lack of large-scale service outsourcing enterprises, a lack of high-end professional technical personnel, a lack of a brand effect, a lack of effective intermediary organizations of the service outsourcing industry, and a lack of an institutional environment for intellectual property protection. In the face of these problems, China should take them seriously and actively learn from the advanced experience of the foreign service outsourcing countries, and explore the development of the service outsourcing industry in China based on the actual situation of China's service outsourcing industry.

And the major cities where the service outsourcing industry is developed have various problems in addition to these common problems, including how to perform the market positioning, the implementation of dislocation competition. Cities should recognize the advantages and disadvantages of their own industry's development. They should then make full use of the advantages of resources, improve the areas where they have defects and formulate strategies suitable for the local development.

At the same time, it is important to be clear that the competitiveness of China's service outsourcing industry is mainly reflected in the core competitiveness of local enterprises. Whether the service outsourcing demonstration cities or other cities, in order to improve the comprehensive competitiveness of the region's service outsourcing industry, they should enhance the core competitiveness of the local service outsourcing industry through policy guidance and incentive mechanisms. This requires governments at all levels to improve the public service ability to create a good atmosphere for investment; they should promote China's service outsourcing industry through international exchanges, and strive to develop the diversified market; they also need to intensify the protection of intellectual property rights and data privacy to build a perfect legal environment for the service outsourcing industry; and they need to strengthen personnel training and the implementation of a series of introduction of high-end technical personnel. The most important way is to cultivate local service outsourcing enterprises, develop an international brand of enterprises, and enhance the overall competitiveness of China's service outsourcing industry through the agglomeration effect of the leading enterprises in the service outsourcing industry.

(2) Analysis of main factors of the competitiveness of China's service outsourcing industry

It can be concluded that the main factors influencing the competitiveness of China's service outsourcing industry are as follows: human resources, leading enterprises, and institutional environment. Human resources are the foundation for the development of service outsourcing, low labor costs are the driving force for the development of service outsourcing, and a reasonable structure of talent is the strong support for an increase in the competitiveness of the service outsourcing industry. The service outsourcing industry's leading enterprises are very significant, such as Neusoft, which is the main company in Dalian, in undertaking big international projects and subcontract them to small and medium-sized service outsourcing enterprises, which shows industrial concentration to a certain degree, and creates interactive development of the whole industrial chain. In order to improve the competitiveness of China's service outsourcing industry, it is necessary to create a group of large enterprises as a leader to lead a large number of small and medium-sized enterprises for supporting production to realize the benefits of a scale economy.

A good institutional environment attracts domestic and foreign enterprises to invest in the service outsourcing industry and engage in outsourcing business, and provides institutional support for the enhancement of competitiveness. So far, China has a large amount of relatively cheap labor, but there is a shortage of comprehensive talents for high-end service outsourcing business. Additionally, the lack of leading enterprises prevents service outsourcing demonstration cities from forming a scale economy with large enterprises as the leader and small and medium-sized enterprises for supporting production, and service outsourcing enterprises' overall competitiveness is not strong. The construction of the institutional environment for the development of service outsourcing competitiveness is not perfect and the system of intellectual property protection is not perfect enough, which needs to be further improved.

(3) Basic strategy to improve the competitiveness of the service outsourcing industry

Service outsourcers select their service outsourcing providers based on two main factors: service cost and service ability. Service cost refers to fees related to services provided by professional service outsourcing providers at the request of service outsourcers, including internal IT hardware maintenance, software development, or management functions. Service ability refers to the ability of service outsourcing providers to provide services. In order to attract the service outsourcing business or introduce high-quality service outsourcing enterprises to undertake business, the key lies in whether the contracting places meet the demand of the outsourcing parties and the service outsourcing enterprises. To establish long-term cooperation, the contracting party needs more information exchanges, closer coordination and cooperation relations with the outsourcing party to achieve a win-win situation through outsourcing services. Therefore, it requires the government departments in charge of the service outsourcing industry, and other research institutions of the major cities to investigate representative outsourcers and enterprises with strong ability to undertake business from the perspective of the foreign party, and create an investment environment that can meet the demand of the above enterprises. At the same time, in the introduction of outsourcing enterprises, pay attention to the introduction of related enterprises to extend the industrial chain to drive the development of the upstream and downstream links, so as to obtain greater benefits of regional labor division.

8.5.2 China's Policies and Measures to Promote the Development of Competitiveness of the Service Outsourcing Industry

(1) Deepen the understanding of service outsourcing, and attach great importance to the development of the service outsourcing industry at the srategic level

Emancipate the mind, change the ideas, and enhance the government's understanding and leadership skills regarding service outsourcing. The development of outsourced service should be considered at the strategic level of accelerating transformation of the mode of economic development and promoting strategic adjustment of the industrial structure. There needs to be full awareness of the importance and urgency of developing outsourcing service and accelerating the development of service outsourcing as an important task. First, guide the government's decision-makers and local economic leaders to recognize the importance of the development of the service outsourcing industry in promoting economic growth, promoting the upgrading of the industrial structure, and relieving employment pressure. Actively promote the successful experience of advanced regions in developing the service industry to create a developmental pattern of interactive development, complementary advantages, and dislocation competition.

Second, deepen the understanding of the features and laws of the development of service outsourcing of the leading cadres, entrepreneurs and people from all walks of society. Since the new century began, economic globalization has developed, social division of labor has become more detailed, market competition has become more intense, and some new characteristics and tendencies in the development of service outsourcing have appeared. Grasping the developmental trend of the service outsourcing industry is of great importance for China in developing service outsourcing in a sustainable, and healthy way. It is important to hold lectures, investigations, seminars, and training to deepen the people's understanding of service outsourcing and help them learn and master the features and laws of the development of service outsourcing.

Third, attach great importance to the progress of new forms of service outsourcing. This can be achieved by emancipating the mind, creating a loose developmental environment, and making effective supporting policies. Contend with new situations and problems in the development of service outsourcing seriously, help enterprises solve practical difficulties, guide enterprises to understand industrial developmental trends, and improve their market competitiveness.

Fourth, use the radio, television, newspapers, and networks to report service outsourcing developmental theories, international developmental trends, service industry developmental policies and experience of advanced provinces, cities, and regions. Establish and promote models of developing service outsourcing, and build a favorable environment to promote the development of service outsourcing.

(2) Carry on undertaking the transfer of the international service outsourcing industry and prolong the industrial chain to use foreign capital

Seize the opportunity of the international service outsourcing industry transfer after the financial crisis, give full play to the comparative advantage of China, strengthen the work of investment and capital introduction of the foreign high-end service industry, actively undertake the transfer of the international service outsourcing industry, and vigorously attract multinational regional headquarters, research centers, design centers, and procurement centers to locate their offices in China.

First, draw lessons from India and other countries in the development of the service outsourcing industry. Develop the business process outsourcing of information data processing, financial background services, human resources service, actively undertake R&D process outsourcing of software development and design, technical R&D, and engineering design, and cultivate service outsourcing industrial clusters. Speed up the construction of the "Public Support Platform for Software and Information Service Outsourcing," promote the interconnection, interaction and resource sharing among the bases and parks, improve the ability to provide public support services for small and medium-sized enterprises in the bases and parks, and foster a batch of service outsourcing enterprises with international qualifications. Support service outsourcing enterprises to strengthen marketing, participate in major domestic and foreign exhibitions, and expand the market. Perfect relevant supporting policies, provide convenience of Internet access and international line lease for the service outsourcing demonstration cities, improve the undertaking ability and service level of service outsourcing bases, and strengthen the incubation and radiation function of outsourcing bases. Optimize foreign trade channels, and create "green channels" for high-value-added products of software and service outsourcing.

Second, enhance the level of cooperation with foreign high-end service suppliers, promote technology introduction and management innovation of China's service outsourcing industry, and improve the quality of opening-up. Support domestic productive service enterprises to form strategic alliances with the well-known large enterprises and groups, and encourage international well-known software enterprises and domestic enterprises to establish research and development bases.

Third, actively participate in international economic cooperation and competition, and make full use of two resources and two markets at home and abroad. Perfect the promotion system for the development of China's service outsourcing industry, make policies of taxation and finance suitable for the development of the service outsourcing industry, cultivate new growth points like communications, finance, insurance, information services and consulting, develop the service outsourcing industry with Chinese characteristics, and constantly improve the proportion of offshore service outsourcing in China's service outsourcing business.

(3) Adjust and improve the service outsourcing tax policy, and strengthen the service outsourcing statistical system

At present, the service outsourcing enterprises of China have a relatively heavy tax burden, and there are some unreasonable phenomena. In the long run, in order to promote the development of service outsourcing, the government should reform the tax system and set up a tax system that adapts to and promotes the development of service outsourcing. First, make a comprehensive examination on the objects of taxation in all areas, formulate specific measures for the elimination of double taxation in the intermediary linkages of the outsourcing service, the research service, the business service, logistics, the human resource service, etc. and collect tax by difference, thereby reducing the tax burden on enterprises. For eligible service enterprises, the income tax should be taxed by the headquarters.

Second, identify IT service outsourcing enterprises of R&D, design and creation as high-tech enterprises so that they can enjoy the corresponding preferential policies of high-tech enterprises. Encourage service outsourcing enterprises to make technical innovation and use domestic equipment, and they should be promised with reduced income tax after the audit of tax authorities in accordance with the regulations.

Third, provide new service outsourcing enterprises with support policies in business registration and taxation.

Fourth, separate and develop the service outsourcing industry from industrial enterprises through tax policies. Give full play to the tax policy as a leverage and guide, make the enterprises fully understand the economic and social benefits of the development of the service industry, and encourage manufacturing companies to separate the productive service industry from the upstream and downstream links of production, creating a vast domestic market for the service outsourcing industry.

(4) Increase support of investment and financing for the service outsourcing industry

At present, the service outsourcing enterprises are small and medium-sized enterprises in China. Their overall size is small, and they generally face financing problems, which seriously restricts the development of the industry. In the future, we should intensify the investment and financing support for service outsourcing enterprises, actively promote institutional innovation, and help service outsourcing enterprises with great potential and good market prospect to solve the problem of financing. In 2009, major domestic commercial banks set up specialized institutions specifically for loans to small business. The China Banking Regulatory Commission will also try to allow enterprises to adopt proprietary technology, patents and copyright as their pledge to make up for the lack of guarantees and collateral, and help small and medium-sized enterprises obtain financing. This is very important for service enterprises, especially for small and micro service outsourcing enterprises to solve financing difficulties. First, make the fullest use of these advantages, promote the connection of financial institutions and service outsourcing projects, increase loans for service outsourcing enterprises, strengthen the financing ability of small and medium-sized service outsourcing enterprises, and overcome the bottleneck of lack of funds to create supporting conditions for the growth of the service outsourcing enterprises.

Actively coordinate with financial regulatory authorities and commercial banks, trust companies, and leasing companies, to explore financing businesses that take future cash flow income and intellectual property rights as guarantees to support the credit of potential and qualified service outsourcing enterprises and projects. Second, actively develop small and medium-sized financial institutions, form multi-level SME loan guarantee funds and guarantee agencies, and encourage financial institutions to support the development of small and medium-sized service outsourcing enterprises. Implement supporting policies of financing guarantee and interest subsidies for small and medium-sized enterprises, increase support for credit guarantee companies through capital injection, risk compensation and so on, and support commercial banks, security companies and other financial institutions for service outsourcing enterprises. Encourage venture capital firms to invest in the service outsourcing industry, and effectively expand the financing channels of service outsourcing. Increase investment in the service outsourcing industry infrastructures and improve the service outsourcing industry investment environment. Create a loose environment for the fair competition of economy with different types of ownership and attract private capital to invest in the service outsourcing industry. Third, support the service outsourcing enterprises to finance directly with the use of capital markets, increase the use of debt financing and equity financing tools, work actively to promote small and medium-sized enterprises to set bond issuance and collect developmental funds in many ways. Support the establishment of small loan companies to support the development of service outsourcing enterprises, expand sources of funding for small loan companies, improve the limit on small guaranteed loans, perfect the supervision system, and give its role into full play in the area of risk control.

(5) Enforce intellectual property rights protection, and improve the relevant laws and regulations

Only by protecting intellectual property rights, and creating a healthy and orderly environment of development can there be major development in the service outsourcing industry. This requires the government and related departments to have a unified understanding of intellectual property rights protection, strengthen coordination, and improve the mechanism of intellectual property rights protection and the efficiency of the implementation of intellectual property institutions. The following measures are to be taken: Fully implement the patent and intellectual property strategy, strengthen the innovation, protection, and use of intellectual property protection and cultivate a good credit environment and market economic order. Increase assistance for patent applications in key industries and fields, further the promotion and transaction of intellectual property rights, establish and perfect all kinds of intellectual property rights trading markets, and develop copyright trade. According to the features of creation, utilization, protection, and management of intellectual property rights, make supporting policies to improve the ability of the government, enterprises, and institutions to use the intellectual property institutions. Guide enterprises to strengthen their intellectual property management, from application for copyrights, trademarks, and patents to the control of commercial secrets, the control of information security, and intellectual property rights protection, and to improve the control of the intellectual property rights of enterprises. Actively establish international cooperation, eliminate overseas sources of counterfeiting and piracy, and protect superior domestic enterprises. At the same time, perfect relevant laws and regulations. The sensitivity to laws and regulations in the service industry, including the service outsourcing industry, is higher than in the manufacturing industry, so China should further improve relevant laws and regulations, complete the work on legislation and law revision, strengthen the transparency of laws, regulations and policies, and lay a solid legal foundation for the development of the service outsourcing industry. Attach great importance to the legislation of the following aspects: human resource services, credit management, and loans.

(6) Vigorously cultivate talents that meet the demands of the service outsourcing industry

China has abundant labor resources, but it is short of high-quality service outsourcing talents. Cultivate and introduce service outsourcing talents in various ways and build a strong supporting system. Broaden ways to cultivate talents, actively attract and hire foreign high-level service outsourcing talents, encourage students studying abroad to start a business in China, improve the talent incentive and guarantee system, and provide a good environment for the development of talents in the service outsourcing industry. According to the characteristics of different types of service outsourcing practitioners, many forms of vocational training are required to improve their vocational qualifications, professional ethics, service awareness, and competence. Guide the higher education institutions, vocational schools, and training institutions to establish majors of service outsourcing, strengthen personnel training, develop higher vocational education and high technical education of service outsourcing, and improve the service personnel training mechanism. Support higher education institutions, secondary vocational and technical schools, and enterprises in building training and practice bases.

In view of the much-needed human resources in the service outsourcing industry, it is necessary to make full use of the abundant educational resources in China, and focus on development and training. First, based on higher education institutions and scientific research institutions, provide field training for university graduates, and strengthen the ability to transform scientific research achievements. Second, improve the training of English, Japanese and other foreign languages for students, and vigorously develop inter-disciplinary talents with a high level of foreign languages, foreign cultural communication ability, and professional skills to meet the requirements of China's service outsourcing market. Third, learn from Ireland's manner of training service outsourcing talents, improve the students' ability of combining theory and practice, pay attention to students' practical operating ability, and provide practice bases as much as possible to make students familiar with the actual business in the shortest time and send more high-quality talents to the service outsourcing enterprises.

(7) Cultivate pilot cities and bring their demonstration effect into full play

In 2009, the State Council approved Beijing, Shanghai, Shenzhen, Dalian and 16 other cities as pilot cities of the service outsourcing industry in China, and implemented a series of preferential measures to promote the development of the service outsourcing industry. In order to make the 20 pilot cities develop well, the Ministry of Commerce developed a set of evaluation systems for evaluating service outsourcing demonstration cities to select the superior ones and eliminate the inferior ones.

Although these 20 pilot cities' economic strength and service foundation are not identical, in terms of the development of the service outsourcing industry, they do have common characteristics. In the process of cultivation, the pilot cities should, first, optimize the industrial structure, increase the competitiveness of the service industry, and enhance the basic strength of the service industry to support the further development of the service outsourcing industry. Many pilot cities have faced the problem of economic transformation and they have begun to treat the service industry as the focus of economic work in the future, develop productive service to optimize and consolidate the manufacturing base. It has created a large market for the service outsourcing industry by outsourcing some non-core businesses to professional companies, which has not only improved their work efficiency, but also helped develop new service outsourcing enterprises and promoted effective integration of resources. Second, the pilot cities should pay attention to reasonable positioning to realize dislocation competition at the same time. As the economic base and advantageous resources in the pilot cities are not identical, they should take account of their own conditions in advance, adjust suitable measures to local conditions, make clear positioning, and make plans to achieve the best operations possible. Third, strengthen communication and cooperation between cities, popularize advanced development experience and good modes of the service outsourcing industry, and bring their demonstration and leading roles into full play. Wuxi, with the introduction of a plan of high-end talents, has attracted an overseas elite to start business in Wuxi in two years. Other cities should learn from the good service outsourcing industry experience and innovate according to their own situation. Fourth, pilot cities should play the role of regional radiation, accelerate interactive activities as much as possible with the agglomeration and development of their service outsourcing industry, strengthen regional economic ties among regions, and establish economic zones with mutual-support and mutual-service.

(8) Expand the scale of service outsourcing and build service outsourcing brands

The service outsourcing enterprises are small in China. Small and medium-sized enterprises can hardly undertake large orders. In contrast, India has large-scale software companies which have a stronger ability to resist risks and can reduce business costs to the maximum extent through economies of scale. Thus, the service outsourcing enterprises in China should make efforts to become bigger and stronger, and some qualified enterprises should draw up a bigger developmental strategy in the long run. Fully integrate internal resources and the huge service outsourcing market at home and abroad to cultivate large enterprises.

First, strengthen the control of the governance structure of the enterprises, improve the comprehensive quality of the management authorities, and fully plan the future development of the enterprises. Second, continue to develop the traditional service outsourcing market and on the basis of maintaining the original competitiveness, extend the industrial chain continuously to achieve the optimal allocation of resources. Third, look into the international market, advance with the times, grasp the newest trend on the international service outsourcing market and focus on the emergence of new services; design new types of business actively to serve the world better. Fourth, build an effective incentive mechanism to attract a large number of high-quality service outsourcing talents, stimulate the enthusiasm of employees so that they will work and innovate, and pay attention to the workers' retraining to meet the needs of the service outsourcing market. In addition, as the other side of the smile curve, brand effect has occupied an impregnable position for enterprises in winning within the fierce market competition.

From the lessons of China's economic development, it can be seen that due to the lack of high-end brands in the manufacturing industry, China can only be a "big manufacturing country" rather than a "powerful manufacturing country." Therefore, enterprises should pay special attention to brand building and self-innovation on the development of service outsourcing, and produce products with independent intellectual property rights to form the core competitiveness on the international service outsourcing market. To create a famous brand, the first thing to do is to cooperate with multinational corporations and international investment institutions, draw lessons from the advanced experience of service outsourcing brand marketing, and rely on international agencies to build the brand strategy which is suitable for them. The second is to build China's service outsourcing forum, and gradually develop it to a national level to build a good platform for the marketing of the service outsourcing brand. The third is to follow the example of Canton Fair, invite foreign clients to China by means of conferences and exhibitions, and take such opportunities to strengthen links with major international outsourcing countries.

(9) Explore the international market actively and strengthen economic cooperation with neighboring countries and regions

Nowadays, the proportion of China's offshore service outsourcing in the world is low, and for the development of service outsourcing, it is not enough to rely only on the domestic market. Therefore, developing the international service outsourcing market in China is an urgent need. By strengthening international cooperation, there will be more service outsourcing business in China. In India, the service outsourcing business has developed rapidly in recent years; its government has promoted the development of service outsourcing enterprises with the help of intermediary agencies, and developed service outsourcing business internationally, such as improving business with the United States and European countries. China is supposed to draw lessons from the advanced experience of India, and create a good external environment for the development of service outsourcing enterprises with a certain degree of international competitiveness. Through coordination and communication with relevant departments, make an overall plan for the qualified enterprises and bring them into the world. Thus, the international image of China's service outsourcing industry would be established and intensified.

In addition, China should develop the liberalization of trade in services and strengthen its cooperation with neighboring countries and regions. The liberalization of trade in services could weaken the negative impact of trade barriers, and reduce the cost of trade in services, thereby improving the competitiveness of the service industry and enabling consumers to enjoy high-quality products with low prices. The intensification of global and regional liberalization of trade in services will promote China and its neighboring countries to cooperate in new areas. The regional service outsourcing business allows countries to benefit from it. Besides, with the deepening of international economic integration, regional economic and trade relationships have become increasingly close, and the common interests and cooperation opportunities between neighboring economies have also increased. China should establish close economic ties with surrounding countries and regions. For example, it is supposed to set up a free trade area for mechanical and electrical products to expand the cooperation between the mainland and Taiwan. The government should actively promote the establishment of ASEAN-China Free Trade Area, develop foreign economic cooperation, and optimize the allocation of resources.

(10) Support leading enterprises and truly realize the industrialization of service outsourcing

In the light of the development of the service outsourcing industry, most cities lack leading enterprises. If they could choose a few leading enterprises based on local conditions and meet the needs of the enterprises to a large extent, they would be sure to play an important role in the development of the service outsourcing industry. First, select a batch of local enterprises with good economies of scale, strong innovation ability, high-level management skills, obvious industrial advantages, and great market potential to support them; establish and perfect a mechanism to support key software and outsourcing enterprises, and give the enterprises support in policy, funding, developmental opportunities, etc. Second, pay attention to the "factory-like" trend of service outsourcing, promote and implement a strict standardized management system vigorously, and make service outsourcing industry industrialized as soon as possible. Pay attention to the cultivation of large leading enterprises to achieve economies of scale of the service outsourcing industry as soon as possible. Third, in order to make the service outsourcing industry industrialized, it is important to not only develop more large and integrated service outsourcing enterprises, such as Neusoft, but also standardize and industrialize the small-scale outsourcing companies, and finally industrialize the service outsourcing industry in the region or city. Finally, there should be large service providers specialized in outsourcing as well as independent comprehensive outsourcing enterprises, which together can bring service outsourcing into the international market in an orderly manner.

9

Regional Economic Cooperation and Constructing China's Free Trade Area Strategy

9.1 Evolution of the Theory of Regional Economic Cooperation

With the multilateral trading system coming into practice, the evolution and maturing of the theory of regional economic cooperation, and the increase in practical international experience, there has been active involvement in promoting economic cooperation with the neighboring countries and regions. Coordinated development between regional economic cooperation and the evolution of the free trade area is a strategic choice and a problem of intensifying opening-up that China has to face. Therefore, analyzing the theory of regional economic cooperation will offer a more philosophical guiding framework to promoting and enhancing international economic cooperation.

Generally speaking, the theory of regional economic cooperation can be divided into three categories: the traditional theory of regional economic cooperation based on the perfect competition model, the modified theory of regional economic cooperation based on the imperfect competition model, and other new theories related to regional economic cooperation since the 1990s.

9.1.1 The Starting Point of Theoretical Analysis: The Elicitation and Definition of the Concept

(1) The elicitation of the concept of region

There can be multiple definitions of "region," but the basic internal attribute of a region is determined. As Edgar Malone Hoover, a famous American regional economist said, all definitions consider "region" as a whole geographical category, so it can be analyzed by means of a holistic approach. As a whole geographical category, the standard attribute of a "region" is based on the general understanding of common regional interests. In other words, there are some common points and connections in a region, but also many differences among regions. Therefore, the concept of "region" is relative; it refers to either an economic zone constituted by several adjacent countries and areas or an economic zone in one country. In this book, every time we use the word "region" we imply the first concept, if not otherwise mentioned in particular.

(2) The definition of regional economic cooperation

After the end of the Cold War, regional economic cooperation began to show the trend of accelerated development. But only the European Union has been able to achieve regional economic integration so far. Economic cooperation is different from economic integration; they have both qualitative differences and quantitative differences. Economic cooperation means that nations try to eliminate the differences or some aspects of the economy, while regional economic integration means that nations try to eliminate all the differences that exist. From this perspective, economic cooperation is wider and easier to implement than economic integration. Therefore, using "regional economic integration" or "regional grouping" is not accurate and using "regional economic organization" or "regional economic cooperation" is more appropriate. In this book, we use "regional economic cooperation" as the context for several other issues discussed here.

There are many different definitions and explanations of regional economic cooperation in academia. But its special definition has reached a consensus: regional economic cooperation refers to the transnational regional economic organization which is built by two or more adjacent countries (areas) in order to achieve the economic aggregation effect and the complement effect, and promote free mobility and effective allocation of products and production factors.

Regional economic cooperation contains two levels of meaning: First, it refers to the elimination of trade barriers and discriminatory economic policies, which block the free mobility of production factors, and form the integration of an economic entity. Second, it means that the participating countries have to transfer part of their sovereignty to the subjective coordination of the supranational entity, which is established by signing an agreement. The former is considered functional regional economic cooperation, while the latter is called institutional regional economic cooperation.

(3) Connotation and extention of the forms of regional economic cooperation

Regional economic cooperation can be divided into six forms: preferential trade arrangements, free trade area, customs union, common market, economic union, and full economic and political integration, based on the level of unification of the tariff, the establishment of trade barriers, the mobility of production factors, the economic and political policies. The features of these forms are shown in Table 9.1.

Table 9.1 The features of regional economic cooperation

Features	Preferential trade arrangement	Free trade area	Customs union	Common market	Economic union	Full economic and political integration
Eliminating all customs	NO	YES	YES	YES	YES	YES
Establishing uniting barriers	NO	NO	YES	YES	YES	YES
Free factors mobility	NO	NO	NO	YES	YES	YES
Uniting economic policies	NO	NO	NO	NO	YES	YES
Uniting political policies	NO	NO	NO	NO	NO	YES

Source: Xue Rongjiu. *Economic competition and cooperation*. Beijing: China Economic Publishing House, 1997: 94.

1) Preferential trade arrangement: This is the most elementary and fundamental form of regional economic cooperation. In this form, members stipulate special customs on all or part of the products by forging a deal or using other methods.

2) Free trade area: Members eliminate internal tariffs and non-tariff barriers, but still have their own foreign trade economic policies.

3) Customs union: On the basis of the free trade area, members further establish unified external tariffs, in order to achieve accordance with the foreign trade policies.

4) Common market: Besides unified foreign trade policies, production factors (capital, labor, technology, etc.) can enjoy a free flow among members.

5) Economic union: This form uses coordinating mechanisms in nearly all of the parts of the national economy, such as fiscal policy, finance policy, trade policy, industrial policy, regional development policy, and social security policy, and tries to establish a supranational coordinating

mechanism based on transferred parts of sovereignty.

6) Full economic and political integration: This is the highest form of regional economic cooperation, and ultimately, it will form a regional "national economy system." The supranational management organization has plenty of supranational sovereignty, which means the organization has executive, legislative, and judicial powers in economic, political, and social areas recognized by all of the members of the region.

9.1.2 Perfect Competition Model—Concept and Limitation of Traditional Regional Economic Cooperation

The field of international economy has initiated two areas of regional economic cooperation analysis. One is analyzing the static effect of a customs union on trade, while the other one is analyzing the dynamic effect of a customs union on trade and economic growth. Although regional economic cooperation is more than a customs union, the general theory of economic effect of regional economic cooperation generalized from the research on a customs union is suitable for other forms of regional economic cooperation. Therefore, the customs union is considered the core element of the theory of regional economic cooperation.

The theory of traditional economic cooperation is a customs union theory, which considers perfect competition as the core hypothesis and is often called the complete competition model. Impacted by the institutional economic school (freedom inside, protection outside), this theory focuses on analyzing the change in trade flow and social welfare caused by eliminating internal tariffs and building unified tariffs externally.

The assumption of traditional regional economic cooperation is perfect competition, constant production costs, no transfer costs and that the world market price of a product is equal to the production cost of the country where the cost is the lowest. This theory considers the effects of "trade creation" and "trade diversion" as the foundation, analyzes the "production effect" and the "consumption effect," and initiates discussion about the terms of the trade effect. It contains some dynamic factors, but mainly focuses on static analysis.

(1) The impact of customs union on trade flow: The effect of trade creation and diversion

Jacob Viner devised the partial equilibrium framework to analyze customs unions in 1950. He thought the establishment of a customs union would cause trade creation and trade diversion.

The trade creation effect means that after the elimination of the internal tariffs in the customs union, some products that have a higher production cost in a member country will be replaced by the products with lower production costs in other member countries; this condition creates new trade. Trade creation has enhanced the scale effect and competition, promoted the development of the economy in the region, and led to the development of integral foreign trade.

The trade diversion effect means countries in the customs union use the same external protection tariffs, which results in cheap goods imported from non-member countries being replaced by more expensive goods produced by members.

Trade creation improves welfare, while trade diversion decreases welfare. A concrete analysis can be seen in Figures 9.1 and 9.2.

In Figure 9.1, S_a and D_a represent the supply and demand curves of country A respectively, while S_b and S_c represent the export supply curves of country B and country C. P_1P_3 is the import tariff of A (before the establishment of the customs union). At that time, a product that country A needs is provided at home, and the domestic equilibrium point is A, the price is P_1 and the supply and demand quantity is Q_1. After the establishment of the customs union, the products of B can be exported to A, but country C is still exclusive. In this condition, price becomes P_2 and the domestic demand increases from Q_1 to Q_2 (A provides Q_3, while imports Q_3Q_2 from B).

Trade creation has brought many benefits to A: First, because low-cost products from allied nations replace high-cost domestic product supplies partly (Q_3Q_1), country A has saved production costs (equal to the area of a) and the domestic producer surplus decrease, which is equal to the area of ABP_2P_1. Second, because of the expansion of the scale of consumption, the producer surplus increases, which is the area of ACP_2P_1. From the point of distribution, the loss of producer surplus transfers to the customer surplus, and the customs union has made the national welfare of A increase by the area of a + b.

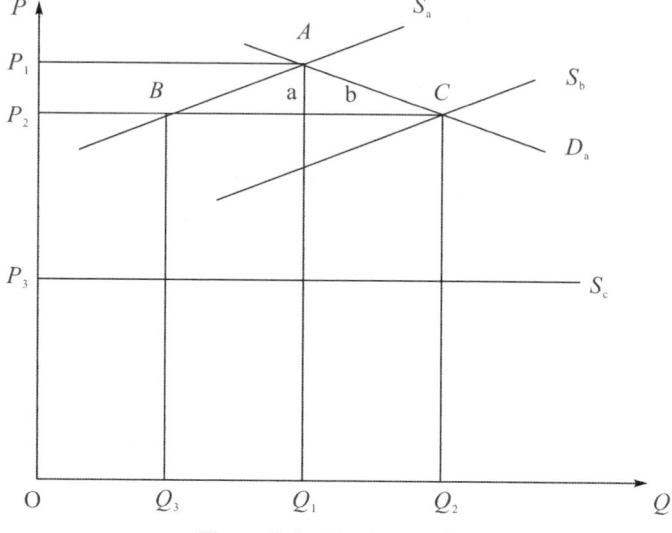

Figure 9.1 Trade creation

As can be seen in Figure 9.2 (neglect the supply of A), the domestic demand of A depends on the supply of B and C, and the import tariff of A is P_1P_3. When the whole demand of A relies on C, the domestic price of A is P_1, and the import is Q_1. When A and B establish a customs union, the domestic price of A is P_2 and import is Q_2.

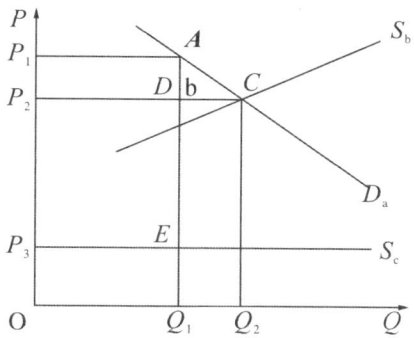

Figure 9.2 Trade division

Therefore, in order to maintain the original scale of imports, country

A has to increase the export products whose volume is equal to the area of P_2P_3ED, and the customer surplus is ACP_2P_1. Meanwhile, A has lost its tariff income (AEP_3P_1). From the view of the total national welfare, the customs union has helped country A improve its customer surplus (area b), but has lost its domestic resource (P_2P_3ED). So if $P_2P_3ED > b$, country A will experience a national net loss.

The trade creation effect is consistent with the free trade principle, while trade division is not. Therefore, the net effect of a customs union depends on the relativity of the trade creation effect and the trade division effect. As for the international economy, trade division is a kind of welfare loss, while creation denotes welfare increase. But for the countries in the union, trade division is welfare enhancement. Overall, for the members, a customs union is positive for their welfare and economic development.

(2) The impact of the customs union on world welfare: Production effect, consumption effect and terms of trade effect

Production effect is the decrease or increase in production costs led by the customs union. If the customs union prompts a country to import cheap products from other members to replace expensive domestic products, it is called positive production effect; otherwise, if the supply of a product transfers from a low-cost country to a high-cost one, it is called negative production effect. As the production cost remains unchanged, the positive and negative effects caused by the customs union are borne by the members.

Consumption effect is the impact that the tariff has on consumption, under the hypothesis that the consumption model remains unchanged in allied nations. An import tariff always restricts domestic customers' demand of imported products, while the reduction or elimination of the tariff will promote customers to buy more imported goods and decrease the demand of domestic low-quality and high-price products. Therefore, even when production efficiency does not improve, actual income will be enhanced because of the improvement of exchange and consumption. The related scholars' analysis has shown that the increased members' customer welfare caused by the elimination of internal tariffs is more than the negative effect of international welfare caused by its negative effect of production.

Terms of trade effect is a series of effects caused by the customs union that has influence on terms of trade in long or short terms. The establishment of the customs union will lead the terms of trade of net production to change. Under the condition of trade diversion, if the elasticity of the supply of export products of non-members is low and the supply is huge, the price will fall before the establishment of a new market, because the massive decline in import demand will lead to an excess supply. Therefore, non-member import countries will have better terms of trade. When an economic power joins the union, it will make the members import less from external nations, because of which the export product price of external nations will decrease and the terms of trade will become null and void.

It is generally recognized that the customs union cannot affect the international market price if the union is too small, for the elasticity of export demand and import supply can be considered infinitely great, and the formation of the customs union will not affect the terms of trade of all of the alliances; otherwise, a bigger economic union has larger elasticity of demand for external products, and the external region has less elasticity of demand for internal products. That means, the larger the union is, the easier it is to change the terms of trade. Arndt has made a detailed analysis of this situation; he has proved that if the number of member countries has reached critical mass, the customs union will improve the terms of trade of members based on a general equilibrium model, containing three or four countries. Kemp and Wan proved that after forming the customs union, the welfare of the countries outside of the alliance will not decrease, while the welfare of the members of the alliance will be improved.

9.1.3 Imperfect Competition Model—Modified Theory of Regional Economic Cooperation

The lack of an analysis of the dynamic effect is the biggest defect of the traditional theory of regional economic cooperation; therefore, emphasizing the analysis of the dynamic effect is a breakthrough for traditional theory creation. This is because the foundation of the analysis of the dynamic effect is that countries forming a customs union have imperfect competition, and this closely resembles actual life. Therefore, the question of assumption (perfect competition and constant returns to scale) of a traditional customs union becomes the most powerful impact for the traditional theory. Under this mentality, since the 1980s, the theory of regional economic cooperation has shifted from the traditional perfect competition model to the imperfect competition model; following is the brief introduction to the modified theory of regional economic cooperation.

(1) The effect of scale economies and the big market theory

The development of a new international trade theory is based on the assumption of economies of scale and imperfect competition. As one part of the international trade theory, the theory of regional economic cooperation has fully absorbed the key concept of the new international trade theory, and introduced economies of scale and imperfect competition. Furthermore, it introduces dynamic analysis in this theory, and analyzes the effect of scale economies, precompetitive effect and the effect of investment stimulation dynamically.

The effect of scale economies is the effect caused by members enlarging their scale of production after the establishment of the customs union. In the separate markets, factories' scale of production is restricted by the market. If the market is static or slowly extending, a single vendor has to grab the market from other competitors in order to explore the scale of production, and pay huge selling costs, which may make the vendor unprofitable. However, if the separate markets achieve unification, the expansion of the whole market will allow the vendor to increase the scale of production without competing with others and realize economies of scale smoothly. The establishment of the customs union will facilitate intense specialization and cooperation among members. Meanwhile, the extension of the market will lead to huge production, which in turn decreases production costs, research and development expenses, and will enhance the efficiency of the labor force and production equipment; finally, the enterprises of members gain benefits through scale production.

The big market theory is based on the scale effect; it mainly describes the nature and effect of the common market, and focuses on analyzing the situation of the economic and trade development of the European Community (EC). The theory holds the opinion that countries should combine all the separate markets formed by protectionism into a unified big market by using an institutional arrangement. And create a scale effect through the fierce competition of the big market, meanwhile creating more effective production combinations, and make all members benefit from this. Gasiorek et al. demonstrated the correlation between regional economic cooperation and production efficiency in 1992 by using the increasing returns model. After inspecting the effect of the establishment of the EC on the manufacturing industry, they found that regional economic cooperation had a great correlation with production efficiency. The benefit caused by the integration of the EC constituted 1% of its GDP.

(2) Other dynamic effects of the customs union: Precompetitive effect and investment stimulation effect

Precompetitive effect is the effect caused by companies entering competition, after fixing the countermand of tariffs among customs union members. Along with the establishment of the customs union and the abolishment of internal tariffs, vendors from different countries will have forced competition. First, the establishment of a unified market makes the number of competitors increase and intensifies the fierceness of competition; meanwhile, the abolition of tariffs makes the vendors, which have been protected before, to innovate, enhance their production and operation efficiency, and improve their competitiveness in order to survive. Because innovation and invention could strengthen big manufacturers' power of monopoly in the industry, which would help them achieve economies of scale along with the extension of the market, bigger vendors may use their own scale advantages and invest more money in analysis and exploration in order to expand their impact. From this point, the establishment of the customs union is a propellant for technology advancement and productivity improvement, and makes the internal market maintain strong market vitality and an innovation mechanism.

The effect of investment stimulation is the effect caused by the enhancement of investment after the establishment of the customs union. The establishment of the customs union will lead to specialized production and an increase in the scale of production. Meanwhile, there will also be an increase in the degree of competition among enterprises and an enhancement in the technical improvement and technical update. Moreover, the flow of capital, labor, and other production factors will further promote the allocation of production factors to be more reasonable and effective. These aforementioned factors will accelerate the progress of increasing and attracting investment among members. The establishment of the customs union will lead the capital in the region to be relocated in order to enhance the return on investments; meanwhile, external capital will flow into the region because of the high rate of return; therefore, regional cooperation has provided more possibility for stimulating internal investment and attracting external investment.

(3) Realistic thinking of the customs union theory: Summarize the conditions that form successful customs unions

Generally speaking, the customs union could be more useful in realizing the creation of trade, enhancing members' welfare, and getting better results under the following conditions. First, the higher the tariff barriers among the members, the more possible it is that the members will obtain the creation of trade after the establishment of the union; the lower the tariff barriers among the members and other countries, the less loss the trade division will bring. Second, the larger the scale of the customs union, the more low-cost producers; the nearer the geographic locations of members, the lower the transaction costs; and the fewer the barriers of the creation of trade among members, the larger the possibility of the creation of trade. Moreover, welfare will increase more noticeably if the economic and trade relations are intertwined before founding the establishment of the customs union. Finally, the greater the competition among the members before founding the customs union, the easier for the specialized division to develop further and the more likely that there will be the creation of trade. Therefore, countries that are members of the customs union have similar levels of economic development and are non-complementary countries.

9.2 The Current Situation of China's Regional Economic Cooperation

9.2.1 The Trend of Globalization and the Current Situation of Regional Economic Cooperation in China

After the Cold War, the world dedicated itself to developing the economy and strengthening national power. A new wave of carving out spheres of influence across Asia, Africa and Latin America had unwrapped once again, as the developed countries attempted to take up more of the market share. Economic cooperation organizations based on geo-proximity among those developing countries and free trade areas between those developing countries and relatively wealthier countries were created. Therefore, developing countries could catch up with the world's economic development at a quicker pace. Regional economic cooperation has a great and profound impact on the growth of world economy and international trade as well.

(1) General trend: The vigorous development of regional economic cooperation worldwide

Having emerged in the late 1950s, regional economic cooperation had gradually become an irresistible trend by the 1980s. According to a survey from Japan External Trade Organization (JETRO), 107 of the existing 194 regional trade agreements have now come into force, 1/3 of which were established during 1990 and 1994, and most countries have taken part in one or several economic cooperation organizations.

As the sizes of the regional economic cooperation organizations expand and the structures change, their impact on international trade and the world economy has become increasingly obvious. It gradually becomes a force to be reckoned with. After achieving regional economic cooperation, the economic advantage of the members can be further exploited, the layout of regional production can be more reasonable, the division of labor can also be further deepened, the cycle of new technology from development to production can be greatly shortened, and labor productivity can be improved greatly. It is estimated that after the unified market was established, the total benefit of the economy of the EU is that the GDP growth rate increased by 4.5–7 percentage points, the inflation rate declined by 4.5–6 percentage points, and 1,800,000–5,000,000 job opportunities were created additionally. In the mid-1990s, regional economic cooperation organizations of the EU, Asia-Pacific, and North America extended by a vast amount, covering up to 48.4% of world's population, 81.2% of the worldwide GDP, and 83.6% of the volume of global foreign trade.

Yet, the overall strength and business competitiveness of regional economic cooperation organizations have substantially improved. Hard-pressed export growth rate impacted by economic recession in certain areas may be found lower than the world average; nevertheless, a vast majority of member countries enrolled in major regional economic cooperation organizations have witnessed a higher speed of growth annually in their export business, especially during the 1980s and 1990s. The EU's export volume amounted to 37.80% of the world's total export volume in 1985, while this figure rose up to 51.01% in 2008; the export volume of the Asia-Pacific Economic Cooperation (APEC) increased to 44.90% in 2008, compared with 38.90% in 1985; and the figure for the North American Free Trade Area (NAFTA) rose from 17.40% in 1985 to 23.50% in 2008, followed by the growth of the ASEAN Free Trade Area (AFTA) from 3.90% to 6.08% during this period. The proportion of MERCUSOR dropped from 1.90% in 1985 to 1.32% as of 2008 (Table 9.2).

Table 9.2 The proportion of the export volume of the major regional economic cooperation organizations in world's total export volume (1985–2008)

Organization	1985	1990	1995	1998	2000	2008
APEC	38.90%	38.90%	46.30%	45.30%	45.20%	44.90%
EU	37.80%	44.10%	39.80%	35.50%	34.70%	51.01%
NAFTA	17.40%	16.20%	16.80%	18.40%	18.90%	23.50%
ASEAN	3.90%	4.30%	6.30%	6.10%	6.60%	6.08%
MERCUSOR	1.90%	1.40%	1.40%	1.50%	1.30%	1.32%

Note: Export volume as mentioned here refers to goods. Service export is excluded. Notwithstanding the current members of these regional economic cooperation organizations, figures shown here for the post-1980s are estimated and subjected to change due to historical inconsistency of membership.

Source: WTO official website; World Bank World Economic Development Index, 2000. Beijing: China Financial and Economic Publishing House, 2000: 329.

Meanwhile, the preference upon intra-regional trade business (trade within the area among member countries themselves) unfolded to be the typical trait of regional economic cooperation as explained in Table 9.3. From 1990 to 2008, this trend was witnessed by all the major regional economic cooperation organizations that trade within the regions considerably took up, or increased to a big portion of the export volume of those organizations. As it was for APEC, this portion took up about 70% in 1990. As for the EU, the rate of intra-regional exportation also kept increasing when it managed to get around the 1990s' economic depression and later when the European single market began to take its position. The rate of intra-regional trade of the EU stood at a relatively higher level against their total export volume. NAFTA, ASEAN, and MERCUSOR all suggested a rising trend of this proportion. The increasing range was 68%, from 8.90% in 1990 to 14.95% in 2008 (that was an accumulated rise of 6.05 percentage points) of MERCUSOR, which was the striking spike. ASEAN achieved an increase of 34.76% from 18.90% to 25.47% during this period (it rose by 6.57 percentage points), and the counterpart NAFTA witnessed a clear boom. From the 1990's initial 41.40% to 49.75%, which was a 20.2% increase as of the year of 2008.

Table 9.3　The ratio of intra-regional trade volume to its total export volume of the major regional economic cooperation organizations to its total export volume (1990–2008)

Organization	1990	1995	1998	2000	2008	Percentage points increased from 1990 to 2008
APEC	68.50%	72.00%	69.70%	72.60%	69.00%	0.50
EU	65.90%	62.40%	55.20%	61.80%	67.37%	1.47
NAFTA	41.40%	46.20%	51.70%	56.00%	49.75%	8.35
ASEAN	18.90%	24.30%	20.40%	23.70%	25.47%	6.57
MERCUSOR	8.90%	20.30%	25.10%	21.20%	14.95%	6.05

Note: Export Volume shown here refers to goods. Service export is excluded.
Source: WTO official website.

The overall strength and business competitiveness of these regional economic cooperation organizations were substantially enhanced by the fast development of these organizations. Tariff and non-tariff barriers of members in the areas have been cut down or even canceled, and this has made the internal trade proportion increase. As business thrives within the areas, this positive influence is very likely to spread across these areas, and as such, business transactions with non-member countries may grow. There is exclusiveness, however, when it comes to the international trade preferences among various nations within the regional economic cooperation organizations. And this exclusiveness against non-member countries constitutes a tough business deal when outsiders are involved. To cope with the trade barriers like tariffs and other similar barriers upon non-member countries, a growing number of "outsiders" opt to expand investment into these regions so that their market place can be preserved, and then if possible, expanded. And in order to enter the market, outside countries have to meet regional market requirements of technical specification of products, so that they will try to improve the international competitiveness of their products. In the process, international business would be raised to a new level.

(2) Global perspective: The current situation of regional economic cooperation of China

China, Japan, and R.O. Korea are a few of those countries that have powerful economic strength but joined the regional economic cooperation organizations rather late. According to the statistical survey (as shown in Table 9.4) conducted by the World Bank in 2009, 17 of the world GDP's top 20 sovereign states or regions are members of the regional free trade agreements or the customs unions. Three countries that are not involved in the institutional regional economic cooperation organizations are Japan, China, and R.O. Korea, whose GDPs rank second, third and fifteenth respectively, although these countries are member countries of APEC, which is an open, non-institutionalized organization and does not guarantee necessity for the members to conclude any free trade agreements.

It should be noted, however, that on the world GDP ranking list, various countries constituting major regional economic cooperation organizations are listed at the top. The United States, Canada, and Mexico from NAFTA are in first, tenth, and fourteenth positions respectively. Eight out of 28 EU core member states have made their way into the global GDP's top 20. Yet, to put the matter in perspective, the economic size and power of these countries mentioned somewhat benefit from their regional economic cooperation.

Table 9.4 World's GDP top 20 (countries/regions) and regional trade agreements they joined (2009)

Ranking	Nation	GDP (USD billion)	Share of world's total	Major regional trade agreements they joined
1	USA	14256.3	24.05%	NAFTA
2	Japan	5065.3	8.55%	–
3	China	4909.2	8.28%	–
4	Germany	3357.6	5.66%	EU
5	France	2679.8	4.52%	EU
6	UK	2186.1	3.69%	EU
7	Italy	2121.3	3.58%	EU
8	Brazil	1576.9	2.66%	MERCUSOR
9	Spain	1466.1	2.47%	EU
10	Canada	1339.4	2.26%	NAFTA
11	India	1232.9	2.08%	SAPTA
12	Russia	1228.2	2.07%	CIS
13	Australia	989.2	1.67%	CER
14	Mexico	875.9	1.48%	NAFTA
15	R.O. Korea	832.9	1.41%	–
16	Netherlands	794.2	1.34%	EU
17	Turkey	617.6	1.04%	EFTA
18	Indonesia	541.9	0.91%	EU
19	Switzerland	493.2	0.83%	EFTA
20	Belgium	471.1	0.79%	EU
Listed in Total		47035.1	79.35%	–
World's Total		59277.1	100.00%	–

Note: China-ASEAN Free Trade Agreement (CAFTA) was founded on January 1, 2010.

Source: Calculated according to data gathered by the World Bank, www.worldbank.com.

As a developing country, China should address the need for protecting its national interests and rights, improve its economic strength and participation in the formulation of global regulatory rules with the help of regional economic cooperation organizations, and be better off in the process of integration into the world economy. Disembarking from this regional economic integration "bullet train" would remove China from the benefit of regional cooperation and lead to its isolation from the rest of the world. Hence, there is a necessity for China, obliged by the tendency of world economic development as well as by the purpose of serving its own interest, to participate in and adhere to regional economic cooperation. As such, foreign trade will be exploited and economic growth will be achieved.

9.2.2 The Special Background: The Current Situation of Regional Economic Cooperation from the Perspective of China

From China's own perspective, the opening-up policy and the development of its economy have already brought China huge benefits while we are striving for regional economic cooperation and integration. So far China has joined the non-institutional regional economic organization APEC, promoted the process of "10+1" with ASEAN countries, and established the China-ASEAN Free Trade Area (CAFTA) in 2010. A number of economic cooperation and business collaborations with the adjacent regions and sub-regions are being conducted by China upon advantageous geographical proximity. Generally speaking, the framework of China's foreign regional economic cooperation deploys by means of involvement in well-recognized sub-regional economic cooperation and participation in higher-level functional regional economic cooperation organizations, and addresses a new regime of cooperation relations as the guidance, is breaking out of its shell.

(1) Regional economic cooperation between the mainland and Hong Kong, Macao, and Taiwan: From the lack of formal mechanisms to CEPA and ECFA

The large economic region, China, is truly a living example of regional economic inter-operation with no official trade agreements but an example of processing mass transactions and investments. According to the statistics of 1979–1990, intra-regional trade volume amounted up to 35% (from an initial 10%) in its total trade volume. Cheap labor forces and abundant resources available from the mainland, capital and technology as well as managerial experience from Taiwan, along with the trading and financing mediation roles functioned by Hong Kong are advantages that have laid a solid foundation for the fast economic development of China.

Since the 1980s, Hong Kong has gradually shifted its manufacturing industry northward to the South China region. Facilitated by this trend, the export of products, foreign investment in China, and the traditional Chinese enterprises' managerial systems have all witnessed a positive influence. Rapid growth in numerous aspects of trade was triggered by indirect business first and then by the unidirectional (one-way) non-governmental cooperation between the mainland and Taiwan. While this successful industrial transfer greatly supported the economic development of the mainland, it also perfectly solved the industrial upgrading problems in Taiwan.

The mainland is both geographically and culturally connected with Hong Kong, Macao, and Taiwan. Each side will substantially be the direct beneficiary of trade and business exchanges carried out in the area. This solid, processing-trade-centered "Greater South China" mode of trading effectively integrated China's commodity market as a whole; meanwhile, the internationalization of manufacturing production strengthened the economic relations among the regions. Direct investments from Hong Kong and Taiwan into the mainland made them increasingly dependent on the mainland.

On the basis of this cooperation, actions taken by the Chinese government in 2003 were the conclusion of the agreements Closer Economic Partnership Arrangement (CEPA Hong Kong) and Closer Economic Partnership Arrangement (CEPA Macao) with Hong Kong and Macao, respectively. Corresponding revisions and amendments were timely forwarded subject to the conditions of implementation of the agreements above. Committed to wiping out the tariff and non-tariff barriers of commodity trade within the region and realizing liberalization as well as promoting a better climate for trade in services and investment, the agreements would finally achieve joint development and mutual prosperity on both sides.

In June 2010, the chairman of the Cross-Strait Relation Association Chen Yunlin signed the Cross-strait Economic Cooperation Framework Agreement (ECFA) with the chairman of Taiwan's Straits Exchange Foundation (SEF), Jiang Bingkun. Hence, a great new chapter of economic and trade cooperation between the mainland and Taiwan began. The conclusions of ECFA help in building up business relations and promoting trades and transactions between the two sides.

(2) China and East Asia: Promoting regional economic cooperation in interaction

China has maintained good economic relations with East Asian countries. East Asia is the place that fuels China's take-off. It offers an opportunity to China to reposition itself and manage to be included in the international system of division of labor. China, in return, is also fostering a sound relationship with other countries in this region. The importance of East Asia to China can also be seen in terms of the foreign direct investment volume and foreign trade volume it harbors for China—over 50% of them are dedicated or related to East Asia. To some extent, East Asia is the standing ground for China, yet there is no such regional organization or institution that represents the interests of this area as a whole. Some areas remain uncovered by ASEAN, while the APEC coverage is far too large for organization and coordination to be efficiently carried out.

There has been a spectacular growth achieved by China-Japan, China-R.O. Korea, as well as China-ASEAN's economic and trade relations since the 1990s. Japan has raced up to be China's second biggest investor and one of the countries that has established economic and trade relations fastest with China. The China-Japan bilateral trade saw a 20% annual growth rate in the 1990s. R.O. Korea and other countries from the ASEAN are close neighbors of China and are becoming increasingly important business partners. Business relations between China and R.O. Korea started in the 1970s, and were taken seriously right after their establishment. Despite the homogeneity of the export goods between China and ASEAN, which later led to disproportionate export growth, the two were heading toward a more reasonable general tendency: to seek complementarity of trade and closer interdependency between the two sides. Particularly after the restructuring of China and ASEAN in 1994, trade volume ended up growing at an annual 20% booming speed.

Over the history of China-ASEAN cooperation, China has entered into a more comprehensive bilateral cooperation with other countries since the economic and trade commission was established in 1994. Besides the slump in the volume of trade that resulted from China's serious deflation in 1990 and the Asian financial crisis that happened in 1998, the average annual increase of China-ASEAN intra-regional trade has basically remained at 25%, especially in 1993, when the concept of market economy was vigorously promoted by the Chinese government (it increased by 71%) and then in 1997, when China's economic soft-landing was proved successful (it rose by 50% on a year-on-year basis). The value of trade between China and ASEAN has rocketed in recent years. According to the data, the bilateral trade value between China and ASEAN countries climbed upward at an annual growth rate of 26.7% from 2000 to 2008. At the end of this period, the value of foreign trade reached USD 231.12 billion; it realized a year-on-year growth rate of 13.9%. China is currently following Japan and the EU to become the third biggest economic and business partner of ASEAN. The launching of the China-ASEAN Free Trade Area (CAFTA) on Jan 1, 2010 has brought limitless opportunities of great development and immense prosperity for regional economic cooperation.

(3) China and APEC: Concrete practice of functional regional economic cooperation

Established in 1989, APEC is an open non-institutionalized forum-like regional economic cooperation organization. Up until now, APEC, which holds a pivotal position in the world economy, harbors 21 Pacific Rim members. This suggests a wide coverage of 45% of the world's population, 55% of the total world GDP, and 46% of the global trade volume. In 1991, China joined APEC, and Hong Kong of China, and Chinese Taipei joined

APEC as regional economies in the same year.

China's inner-APEC trade volume reached USD 1.43 trillion in 2009, constituting 64.7% of China's total trade across the world. Seven out of ten of China's biggest trade partners were from APEC. In 2009, 70% of China's incoming overseas capital in place was derived from the Asia-Pacific region, reaching USD 63.4 trillion.

After joining APEC, China has always been actively involved and has cooperated with APEC, showing its commitment and a great responsibility toward international affairs and national interactions. By this, China is undertaking an increasingly central position in the organization. By participating in activities of APEC, China managed to establish a mechanism for contact and a relationship of trust with other members, further proposed and advocated positive new ideas through the APEC platform, and created a favorable external environment for its own development. The APEC campaign is of crucial importance to the development and prosperity of China, which can be regarded as another channel, besides the WTO, that could bring China into the world economy.

(4) The current situation of China's sub-regional economic cooperation

The major sub-regional economic cooperation between China and its neighboring countries is currently divided into three parts: The first one is the Lancang-Mekong River basin economic cooperation in Southwest China, the second is the regional cooperation in Northwest China, and the third is the Northeastern regional development cooperation of the Tumen River areas.

① Sub-regional cooperation in the Lancang-Mekong River basin in Southwest China

Connecting Southwest China with Southeast Asia, the Lancang-Mekong River is an important international river that is helpful for China in launching economic and business cooperation with Southeast Asia and in accessing the South Asian market. Business development in this region will greatly favor the all-round development in the Greater Southwest Area and China. The international development and cooperation in the Lancang-Mekong River area concerns various industries, including transportation, energy, communications, tourism, investment and trade, human resource development, and environmental protection. The development of basic transportation infrastructure of the sea-land-air network, which is based on breakthrough in the middle and water-land connection strategies, is among the most important cooperation projects.

Recently, with more countries getting out of the shadow of financial crisis and incremental backward cash flow of financial aids, the international cooperation in the Lancang-Mekong River basin on the basis of adjustment and improvement is yet further in full swing. The project is committed to promoting multilateral cooperation, upgrading the "transport corridor" to an "economic corridor," namely, taking the extension along the traffic corridor as an initial point, integrating the infrastructure construction with production, investment, and trade into a whole process. This will speed up West China's economy, satisfying especially the need for investment in industries of all kinds such as transportation, energy, environment, tourism, and human resource development. This progression brings endless new opportunities for participation in international cooperation to the Southwest China region, or more generously, to West China.

② Sub-regional cooperation in Northwest China

The concept of five Central Asian countries regional cooperation (later known as Central Asia Regional Economic Cooperation, CAREC) was advocated by the Bank of Asia in 1996. The five central Asian countries currently contain member states including Turkmenistan, Kazakhstan, Kyrgyzstan, Uzbekistan, and Tajikistan. Endowed with exceptional geographical and cultural advantages, Northwest China's regional economy holds a great amount of similarity while maintaining its complementarity with the five neighboring countries. Since China itself, as a developing country, harbors an enormous demand for petroleum and gas resources and has come to be a pure oil-importing country since 1993, participation in the Central Asian energy development is of great strategic importance to China's national security and economic growth, while abundant crude oil and gas resources from Kazakhstan, Turkmenistan, and Uzbekistan can fuel this demand. On the basis of good cooperation with Central Asian countries, the West China region should embrace this particular opportunity, take the initiative to be devoted to this energy development rush of Central Asia, build up favorable conditions for its own energy and infrastructural and economic growth.

Currently, CAREC is still in its infancy, the cooperation mechanism is yet to be stable and systematic, the degree of market-economy development of Central Asian countries remains relatively low, the economic operational mechanism and macro-policy-making procedure need to be clarified, and the infrastructure conditions are weak. Nevertheless, countries from Central Asia are working together to improve the transportation system in the region, trying to facilitate the flow of goods and passengers. In the future, with the further opening-up of the Chinese border area, CAREC will be promoted further.

③ The Tumen River Area Development Plan (TRADP) in Northeast China

The prospect of economic cooperation in the Tumen River area is fairly vast on account of three major reasons as follows: First, countries in this region are of a highly complementary economic structure, which will not be changed in the short term. Second, Northeast Asia is one of those few blank areas on the world economic map that are yet to establish any institutional mechanisms for economic cooperation. With further advancement of economic globalization and regional economic cooperation, regional economic cooperation in Northeast Asia would be imperative. The Tumen River falls into one of the regional economic cooperation pilot projects, and this also suggests a piloted-development in Northeast Asia. Third, the political stability in Northeast Asia acts as another positive factor, along with the upstream economy of the countries nearby, all contributing to the development of the Tumen River area.

Briefly speaking, China's sub-regional economic cooperation at present has neither reached the lowest dimension compared with the actual regional economic cooperation nor matched economic sizes and coverage scale of the Special Economic Zone (SEZ). The Tumen River area, as both horizontal and vertical cooperation can be found, belongs to a mixed case; the regional economic cooperation between Xinjiang and Central Asia falls into the vertical one; and the Lancang-Mekong River basin operates as the horizontal type. But these areas in question are yet to be developed adequately to reach the level of "preferential trade arrangements"—the preparation phase is all too apparent. While a common goal of cooperation among members can be held, sub-regional cooperation is reckoned with a low-level preliminary schedule. Although the respective stakes and interests among members can be adjusted by the market, there exists no mandatory responsibilities internationally or there is no need for any regulatory obligations to be obliged.

We can conclude from the current situation of China's regional economic cooperation that a more active participation in multilateral trade is needed, although remarkable improvements have already been made in various aspects. This propels the process of integration, if a deeper external regional economic cooperation is sought or a breakthrough in the short term is pursued.

9.3 Motivation of Regional Economic Cooperation in China

After entering the 21st century, the several themes of foreign trade and economic development that China has to face are the extension of the space of China's foreign trade growth, the revolution caused by institutional change after entering into WTO, the implementation of the going-out strategy, and the strategy of large-scale development of the western region. All these seemingly independent problems can be combined through regional economic cooperation. Nowadays, noteworthy development of regional economic cooperation around the world has divided the world into several parts. Because the cost of regional transaction is falling, it will be hard for China to explore the world market further. Therefore, along with improving international competitiveness, establishing geopolitical regional economic cooperation and grabbing the surrounding markets are strategic overall programs. The multilateral trade regime represented by the WTO is a trend of global economic development. As for China, entering the WTO is a way to enter a multilateral trade regime and globalization, and regional economic cooperation can play the role of supplementing and transitioning during the globalization at present. The implementation of the going-out strategy, the strategy of large-scale development of the western region, and foreign regional economic cooperation should coexist and interact well.

9.3.1 Generalized Reasons for the Formation of Regional Economic Cooperation Organizations

The formation and development of regional economic cooperation organizations have shown that a region which has a good cooperation mechanism is an effective belt for increasing the economy. Its cooperation mechanism is not only good for the mobility of labor, material resources, capital and other production factors, but also good for the establishment of regional division mechanisms and the extension of the market. It will effectively take advantage of regional resource complementation and market complementation, accelerate the economic development of regional members, and enhance the foreign market competitiveness. Generally speaking, the reasons for the formation of regional economic cooperation are as follows.

(1) Non-equilibrium distribution of production factors in different countries (regions) is the key reason for regional economic cooperation

Regional economic cooperation derives from different regional divisions, and regional divisions are caused by the generally existing non-equilibrium in the region. This non-equilibrium is not only the difference in resources, but also other differences caused by many natural or non-natural factors. The non-equilibrium of production factors among countries and regions has determined that factors are mobile rather than static. Along with the economic development and the establishment of a unified big market, the relative free flow of factors (consider labor, capital, and technology as the main body) becomes a spontaneous internal demand. "Compared with a domestic and foreign market, a domestic market is limited, but the former is also limited compared with the international market." (Marx) The transnational flow of production factors is the objective basis for realizing regional economic cooperation and forming transnational economic cooperation. The aim of regional economic cooperation is to promote the flow of products and factors, eliminate the human factors that have stopped the effective economic operation, and create a suitable international economic structure by cooperating with others in order to ensure the maximum mobility of products and factors.

(2) Geographical advantages is the advantageous condition of regional economic cooperation

Geographical proximity to each other makes countries have better accessibility in areas of communications and transportation. In some conditions, geographical proximity is connected with similarity of economic levels. Therefore, countries will unite geographical neighbors that have the same political and economic needs to form regional economic cooperation organizations to adapt to the development of productivity and international competition, for economically developed countries need to compete, while economically developing countries need to survive. From the point that productivity development pushes the extension of the scale and scope of a market economy, the economic combination of countries starts from regions, extends to countries, and finally reaches the global level. Therefore, economic cooperation starts from regions in one country, then appears in transnational countries and regions, and finally extends to the world. In order to integrate into the world economy better, many countries will take advantage of a connection between a geological advantage and tradition, search for and establish a stable market scope, and have regional economic cooperation. This is one of the key reasons that regional economic cooperation developed well.

(3) Regional economic cooperation could realize economies of scale and improve economic benefits and international competitiveness

After the development of productivity reaches a certain level, any country will have the need to break the border. No matter what kind of competitive mode the regional economic cooperation adopts (open competitive mode or closed competitive mode), it will be helpful to eliminate the market barriers in the region, economize labor and capital, and divide and use resources more reasonably on a larger scope. Regional economic cooperation helps to decrease and eliminate the trade barriers among countries, and the trade among members could be expanded. Meanwhile, the elimination of trade barriers will provide convenience for companies to ally with each other. Regional economic cooperation has enhanced competitive mechanisms and has improved the energy of the entire economy and companies by investing and trading with each other. By eliminating the trade barriers, regional economic cooperation promotes factor allocation, makes the production division more suitable, and improves the overall economic operating efficiency and social welfare in the region. In the meantime, it has improved the overall strength of all the members, made them enjoy an advantageous position in international competition, and opened up competition.

(4) The defense strategy and clientele effect are the reasons for the formation of some regional organizations for economic cooperation

To establish regional economic organizations is one of the critical methods for developed countries to compete, contend, and divide the world into spheres of influence. In order to grab the world market, countries are establishing or hoping to establish regional economic organizations actively. However, in any considerable period of time, international competition and coordination are based on sovereignties. In the long run, the international economic relationship will transfer from competition among nations into rivalry among regional economic organizations, and from negotiation and coordination among nations into economic coordination among regional economic organizations. Moreover, because regional economic cooperation implies a different treatment internally and externally, there is exclusiveness. Although regional economic cooperation has improved external trade barriers relatively, but not absolutely, the development of regional economic cooperation does not mean the development of trade protection. But some of the previous organizations for regional economic cooperation have a large amount of domestic trade and intense internal competition, which makes the international market of external countries smaller, the international competition more intense and this has pushed some external countries to establish their own regional organizations. Therefore, some newly established organizations were somewhat forced into establishment. The establishment of the European Free Trade Association and the North

American Free Trade Area has reflected this reason to a great extent.

9.3.2　Factors Influencing Regional Economic Cooperation in China

In the modern context, in addition to general causes, there are some particular and specific reasons regarding regional economic cooperation in China. Regionalization is the reason why protectionism has been revived. The multilateral trading system will keep pace with regional economic cooperation in the long term, and regional economic cooperation is considered as the most effective method for exploring the foreign market. These factors constitute the historical background of China's regional economic cooperation. And the going-out strategy and the strategy of large-scale development of the Western region are the particular internal reasons for regional economic cooperation in China.

(1) External factors that affect China's regional economic cooperation

There are plenty of external factors that could affect China's regional economic cooperation. Among them, there are three key factors.

① Internal consistency and external exclusivity are obvious in global regional economic cooperation

Recently, economic competition among countries has focused on extending their own sphere of influence and establishing different organizations for regional economic cooperation at different levels. Along with the integrated development of these organizations (from junior to senior) and the constant extension of the scale of membership, trade protectionism has the tendency of revival.

The European Union continues to take in new members. The North American Free Trade Area has achieved investment and trade liberalization since 2005, and has eliminated tariff and non-tariff barriers among America, Canada and Mexico. Meanwhile, there is a great possibility that other South American countries, such as Brazil, Argentina, and Chile, will join the Greater North American Free Trade Area, and finally form an American Free Trade Area, which could compete with the European Union. After a period of adjusting and running, the Asia-Pacific Economic Cooperation will have a breakthrough in the 21st century and may establish a frame structure that could be accepted by all the members in trade and investment liberalization and improvement in economic and technology cooperation. The development of the main organizations for regional economic cooperation will make a huge impact on world economic and political patterns.

Well-developed regional economic cooperation enables the internal consistency to be fully reflected. Concrete reflection can be seen as follows: regional trade, the creation of trade divisions, a decrease in the price of tradable goods, the extension of the market scale, and the formation of economies of scale and an aggravation of companies' competition and enhancement of productivity. Furthermore, the function of the coordination of special policies of highly-developed organizations for regional economic cooperation will help members speed up the process of economic growth and recovery. The developmental process of the European Union (from a customs union, a unified big market to an economic alliance) has promoted the continuous prosperity of the EU to a larger degree, making the unemployment rate go down and the interactive transaction reach 61%. The North American Free Trade Area has achieved similar results. According to the statistics, along with the decrease in interacted tariffs, interacted trade increased from 33% in 1993 to 44% in 1996, and the employment opportunities in Canada and Mexico have increased noticeably.

It is worth noting here that regional economic cooperation will lead to exclusiveness toward external economic entities. For example, after the establishment of the North American Free Trade Area, Mexico has replaced China as the largest country from which America imports textiles; and because the European Community has formed a unified big market, 11% of the ASEAN trade opportunities have been edged off. In the 20th century, the competitors that China had to face under the international economic conditions were individual countries, but in the 21st century, they have all become organizations for regional economic cooperation. The development of the world economy is multi-polarized; therefore, countries need to obtain a greater competitive advantage. This cannot be realized by the power of a single country, and countries need to establish exclusive international organizations, based on which to explore international trade and grab the opportunities on foreign markets.

② The world multilateral trading system (WTO) has kept pace with regional economic cooperation

Since the 1990s, the WTO has enjoyed unprecedented enhancement, and regional economic cooperation has developed strongly. The coexistence of the two has shown their strong vitality, complementarity, and irreplaceability.

In nature, the WTO contains nearly all the international economic relationship rules (except the exchange rate regime), and it is a critical carrier of economic globalization. As for regional economic cooperation, it is a local practice in certain areas of economic globalization and world multilateral trading system and primary exploration. The two have the same fundamental direction of development, and they work towards the liberalization and integration of economic activities in their respective ways. The difference only boils down to the scope of their involvement. The former focuses more on a global economic fusion in a broader sense, while the latter pays more attention to the regional multilateral economic integration of specific regions.

Experience shows that it is unrealistic to realize institutional global economic integration through the world's multilateral negotiations. In this respect, not only have the WTO and the GATT (the predecessor of WTO) made unremitting efforts, but also the IMF, the World Bank, and the United Nations have made great efforts in financial order, economic development and other issues. Their efforts and setbacks make people realize that economic integration is an ever-developing process from part to entirety, small to large, and exclusive to open. Localized regional economic cooperation is a primary product. The success and extension of the practice are helpful factors in forming global economic integration.

Certainly, the establishment of regional economic organizations will improve the centripetal force of members and make regional economic cooperation reflect a certain degree of exclusiveness, but this is not to deny the contribution regional economic organizations have made. Therefore, as the representative of global free trade, the WTO has offered flexible regulations to regional economic cooperation when advocating the principle of free economy. The specifics are as follows: In the case of meeting certain criteria, allow organizations for regional economic cooperation to be established in the form of the customs union or free trade zone; allow the organizations for regional economic cooperation to deviate from the most-favored-nation treatment and provide special trade benefits to members; and only require organizations for regional economic cooperation not to form new trade barriers to external countries when promoting regional economic integration.

The world multilateral trading system is the specific reflection of economic globalization. It is not only useful for developed countries to search for new investment areas and trade markets, but also useful for developing countries to find investment partners and developmental opportunities. Along with the development of the world multilateral trading system, the space for regional economic cooperation will be explored constantly and cooperation will be intensified. Conversely, regional economic cooperation might realize regional economies of scale and international divisions, which could make capital, technology, labor, and natural resources be allocated and used reasonably. Regional international divisions will formulate conditions for global international divisions and regional trade liberalization will further enliven global international trade, and finally international economic globalization will be accelerated.

China should now accelerate in its integration with the world economy, transfer from a singly open economic exteriorization to an entirely open economic globalization, and move from a primary stage to an advanced stage of internationalization. In addition to continuing to explore bilateral trade relations, China should participate in organizations for multilateral trade and regional economic cooperation actively, in order to obtain more power from external agencies to push forward the entire reform and opening-up of China. Regional trade liberalization is the first stage of international trade liberalization, and will be the leading factor of trade liberalization in a long term. Therefore, it is critical for China to make use of several markets, multiple resources, and capital more effectively, explore foreign economic cooperation actively in different directions, channels, and forms, and at different levels and participate in regional and sub-regional organizations for economic cooperation more often.

③ Carrying on regional economic cooperation is the key to exploring the foreign market and trade opportunities in the future

China is now at the stage of economic take-off as a developing country, and its potential or real productivity is considerable. From the developmental progress of Japan, Singapore, R.O. Korea and other countries, we can see that it is not enough for China to count on the domestic market only. The overcapacity makes China explore the domestic market as well as the international market, while the latter is the critical part.

Recently, the world's economy has entered a slow growth stage, and traditional products on the international market have shown the condition of oversupply; meanwhile, regional trade protectionism has been strengthened. The unified big market of Europe, which considers the euro as the bond, will show its influence entirely in the following several years, and the American Free Trade Area will be set up in this period too. The effect of the trade division of these two regional economic cooperation organizations will counteract the advantage that the WTO has brought to China to a certain degree. From now on, China will have to face the forced competition of the international market and the restrictions the current regional economic cooperation organizations have set specially for China to export products, such as tariff barriers, non-tariff barriers, technology barriers, environmental barriers and so on. This will make China face more severe export conditions.

In the past 20-plus years, China has accumulated some market experience by exploring the European and American markets, which have become quite saturated recently. Therefore, in order to maintain the target of an export growth rate of 10%~15%, China needs to further explore the markets of developing countries. Because the real purchasing power of developing countries is limited, exploring the markets of developing countries is different from exploring those of developed countries, and it needs to depend on various methods, especially by investing. On the basis of the current situation, China should focus on surrounding countries and give key support and protection to investment in these countries. All in all, it is a critical method for exploring the foreign trade market by developing economic cooperation with surrounding countries.

(2) Internal factors that affect China's regional economic cooperation

The going-out strategy and the strategy of the large-scale development of the western region are the important strategies of China's foreign trade area and entire macro economy. Strengthening regional economic cooperation is good for pushing China into the global economic system, accelerating the progress of the entire opening-up process, and creating a better external environment for the going-out strategy and the strategy of the large-scale development of the western region, providing new developmental chances and facing the economic globalization tendency resiliently.

① The demand of the going-out strategy

Along with the constant improvement of China's economic level, the international division that China has taken part in has shown two tendencies: For developed countries, the division is transferring from vertical to horizontal, while for developing countries, it has shown an opposite tendency. Currently, the economic aggregate of China is in the second place in the world. The per capita GDP of the developed eastern region had exceeded 800 dollars in the 1990s, and now some places have reached 8,000—10,000 dollars and have the capability of going out. During the period of the Ninth Five-Year Plan, when China explicitly put forward border foreign economic opening-up strategy deployment, the going-out strategy began to take shape. Facing the historical opportunity that China had entered the WTO, employing the going-out strategy actively and using domestic and foreign resources and markets better are a strategic task for China.

Currently, the world economy has formed a structure of regionalization and conglomeration, and in order to improve productivity rapidly, it is necessary for China to join forces with the neighboring countries, establish regional organizations for economic cooperation that could eliminate trade barriers and promote the flow of production factors, and enjoy the regional trade benefits before integrating into the world's economy fully. In the 21st century, in order to realize the economic goal, China has to participate in regional economic cooperation actively, based on which it can occupy a larger economic share and acquire an international voice. For now, it is important for China to manage the investment in Southeast Asia, South Asia, Northeast Asia, and Central Asia well, and this matches the current level of economic development in China. Establishing huge multinational enterprises and expanding foreign direct investment outward could not only avoid trade barriers established by regional organizations but also obtain necessary domestic resources, ease the tension of domestic resources, reduce companies' production costs, and improve the international competitiveness of products. Therefore, China should encourage the enterprises that meet the requirements to undertake transnational operations, invest in foreign countries to build factories, develop material processing trade, extend product and technology output, and focus on supporting household appliances, light textiles and other foreign processing trade projects and resource development projects that have mature management experience and technology and could reflect the comparative advantages of China, in order to finally realize reversible circulation: attracting foreign investment—going out—attracting again—going out again.

② Relocating western development from the view of regional economic cooperation

If western development is restricted in the nation, West China can only be defined as remote border areas and economic corners. But if linking West China with the surrounding countries, the regional advantage of West China can be fully played through transnational regional cooperation and it is likely to form a large channel with a strategic significance. As China's strategy of economic development of the century, the strategy of large-scale development of the western region should not only connect with solving poverty and internal disparate developmental problems, but also link with regional economic cooperation, in order to explore the foreign market and have mutual complementarity in economy.

Putting western development in the condition of regional economic cooperation has strategic significance which is not only the exploration of the resources and market of West China, but that domestic and foreign investors could use West China as a springboard and get the opportunity to enter neighboring countries. The western region is close to Central Asia, the Middle East, Europe and other places, and has historic trade links with these places. The establishment of the New Eurasian Land Bridge has offered a great opportunity for regional economic cooperation. Through the land bridge, the western area could extend westward and trade with other countries, and it could extend to the east to enhance the economic link with central and eastern areas and reach out to the global market. The interconnection of the land bridge has obviously enhanced the regional advantage of the western area of China, making West China transform from a piece of hinterland, which is in the inland and far away from the eastern seaports to the forefront of economic opening-up that could lead to Europe, Western Asia and other surrounding countries.

The new land bridge runs through the central zone of Asia and Europe; its overall length is 10,900 km. The two sides of the land bridge connect the Atlantic and Pacific economic centers and have a prosperous economy, but its space capacity is small and it is short on resources. Apart from a few countries in the long and narrow central area, nearly all the countries and regions are considered as less developed, especially the Midwest of China, Central Asia, West Asia, the Middle East, and South Asia. Although the transportation in these regions is not convenient and the natural environment is bad, they have a large capacity of space, abundant resources, strong complementarity, and great prospects for cooperation in the future. Therefore, the western area should consider the area along the land bridge as the key part for development and big or middle cities along the bridge as the developmental core. And the area should take complete advantage of the land bridge, make sure west-east bidirectional development takes place, extend regional cooperation, and make the western area become the most active part of the China Land Bridge Economic Belt.

On the basis of the interconnection of the New Eurasian Land Bridge, the establishment of a modern Silk Road and railways and highways in Southwest China, the western area will change from being a piece of hinterland to an opening-up forefront, and further become a piece of open area along the border. From this point of view, changing the opening-up strategy of facing the Pacific Ocean into a westward opening-up strategy of facing inland provinces could turn the situation of a large number of stockpiled products around, which is caused by focusing only on releasing productivity but neglecting paying attention to a suitable market scale of development and productivity.

It can be said that the strategy of the large-scale development of the western region is a project that is opening to western, southern, and northern neighboring countries of China to a certain degree. The great initiative will promote Asian regional economic integration effectively, and drive the confidence-building cooperation and progress between China and neighboring countries. Western development and foreign regional economic cooperation could develop at the same time and promote each other.

We can consider establishing land bridges that start from Nyalam, Yatung, Ruili, and Mengla to Nepal, Myanmar, Bhutan, India, and other South Asian countries; moreover, breaking through the southwestern waterway, a main international artery of Ruili–Bhamo–Yangon of 1,393 km. Once the big railway, which is from Singapore, Malaysia, Myanmar, Thailand, and Laos to China's Yunnan, Sichuan, and Shaanxi, merges into the Lanxin Railway which goes all the way to Alataw Pass and enters Central Asia and Eastern Europe, is completed, the western area of China from south to north could connect 10 Southeast Asian countries, 7 South Asian countries, 5 Central Asian countries, and other Far East regions.

9.4 China's Strategic Goals and Modes for Becoming Involved in Regional Economic Cooperation

In the trend of global economic integration, it is impossible for any country to become independent completely. Against the background of the current rapid development of regional organizations for economic cooperation and the growth of multilateral trading mechanisms, China now faces the danger of being marginalized by regional organizations. For the long-term development of China's economy, China should speed up researching and exploring new ways of foreign regional economic cooperation, put forward the overall plan and the specific steps of its regional economic cooperation, and determine substantive steps to participate in regional economic cooperation.

9.4.1 China's Strategic Goals for Becoming Involved in Regional Economic Cooperation

Only by strengthening international economic cooperation can we have more right to speak out on international economy, and strengthen the great-power status of China. After the comprehensive analysis of various conditions, the authors think that the strategic goals of China's regional economic cooperation should be rooted in China, which would speed up the cooperation process between the mainland and Hong Kong, Macao, and Taiwan; it should be based on Asia, seeking to form regional or sub-regional organizations for economic cooperation with neighboring countries; it should break down the borders, cross the continents, and build a network of global cooperation.

Specifically, the entry into the WTO has cleared the obstacles that stand in China's way to obtaining nondiscriminatory treatment of normal trade. Taking this opportunity, first, China should create the conditions to make arrangements similar to free trade areas among the mainland, Hong Kong, Macao, and Taiwan, make them complement each other to pin down the ASEAN member countries and Japan, and increase the bargaining chips which can be used in trading with the European Union and the North American Free Trade Area; participate in and promote cooperation in East Asia, strengthen the "10+3" and the "10+1" dialogue mechanisms, and support the establishment of mechanisms for a bilateral currency swap within the framework of "10+3". According to the structural characteristic by which Chinese products have some technical advantages, China should also strive for signing free trade agreements with the surrounding countries, which are at a slightly lower level of development, but have the capacity to export raw materials and primary products. China should, with the help of APEC and ASEM, strive for the preferential conditions necessary for reaching mutually beneficial arrangements with the European Union and the North American Free Trade Area respectively, and try to obtain preferential arrangements for export processing with countries that have fewer quota restrictions to help China's products bypass the quota and anti-dumping restrictions.

(1) Root in China and accelerate economic cooperation of China as a whole

Due to the external pressure of international trade protectionism, the inner motive power for complementing each other and for obtaining shared interests, as well as geographical and blood relationships, China's reform, opening-up and other factors, constructing institutional regional economic cooperation between the mainland and Hong Kong, Macao, and Taiwan in time is not only the objective reflection of the increasingly close economic and trade relations between the mainland and Hong Kong, Macao and Taiwan, the constantly increasing dependence on each other, and the further expansion of the complementary cooperation area; it is also the inherent requirement for the economic development of China as a whole in the grim international economic environment and the trend of global economic cooperation and development.

The regional economic cooperation of China as a whole can realize the effective combination of the advantages of the mainland's manufacturing industry base, the internal market and the advantages of the information, technology and international sales network in Hong Kong, Macao, and Taiwan. The resource reconfiguration in the process of economic integration can highlight the comparative advantages of the products in the four places, and can produce strong trade creation and trade diversion effects, while reducing the over-dependence that Hong Kong, Macao, and Taiwan have on the United States, Europe, and Japan. Take Taiwan as an example—exports to the United States accounted for 48% of its total exports in 1984; in 1995, the figure fell to 23.6% and further dropped to 20.1% in 1998. The Chinese mainland replaced the United States and became the biggest export market for Hong Kong, Macao, and Taiwan.

At present, owing to some barriers between the mainland and Taiwan that have not yet been removed, both have not really reflected their respective comparative advantages in trade and are unable to realize the resource optimization effect completely. Trade creation has not played an effective role either. Therefore, China as a whole should continue to push forward regional economic cooperation within the frameworks of CEPA and ECFA in the future. Guided by the market mechanism and the export-oriented economy, China should give full consideration to its comparative advantages, improve the position and the competitiveness of China as a whole in the international system of the market division of labor, and lay the foundation for the smooth implementation of the "one country, two systems" policy and the peaceful reunification of China.

(2) Based on cooperation with Asia, seek to form regional or subregional organizations for economic cooperation with neighboring countries

Asia is the most economically dynamic continental zone and economic entity in the 21st century, and it is the most important and the most geographically advantageous region for China's foreign economic exchanges. As a result, it is very likely that Asia will become the center of China's regional economic cooperation.

Because Asian countries are different in their social systems, ideologies, and economic development, and because historical factors are complex, Asia is unlikely to form a unified regional organization for economic cooperation quickly like the European Union and the North American Free Trade Area. At present, there are only ASEAN, South Asian Association for Regional Cooperation (SAARC), and some sub-regional cooperation organizations.

However, with the increase in world competition and unremitting experimentation with regional cooperation modes, Asian countries will eventually venture down the road of collaboration. For the current circumstances, it is a realistic choice that some Asian countries with geographically, culturally, and economically convenient conditions take the lead in forming regional or subregional organizations for economic cooperation.

In the future, in the process of participation in and advocacy of forming Asian organizations for regional economic cooperation, China should play an active role and pay attention to the following aspects.

① Top priority—East Asian regional cooperation

East Asia is the world market around China, and it is an important and convenient channel for China's economy to integrate with the rest of the world. Actively advocating and participating in the regional economic cooperation of East Asia would help form a strategic counterweight to the United States and Europe, and it is conducive to China's development for China to construct the overall framework of regional economic cooperation. East Asian regional economic cooperation is the standpoint of China's international regional economic cooperation.

For now, though the East Asian countries have not established East Asian regional organizations for economic cooperation, the economic and trade development of the main countries and regions has been incorporated into the orbit of East Asian regional economic development. Recently, the economic and trade complementarity and dependency of East Asian countries have increased, trade exchanges between countries have become more frequent, mutual investment has increased, the regional economy has expanded, and vitality has been enhanced. East Asian countries are forming a structure of an inner loop, which considers emerging industrialized countries and regions as the center, and it is an important prerequisite for establishing regional organizations for economic cooperation in East Asia.

But great differences and diversity of economy, politics and culture among East Asian countries determine that East Asia regional cooperation has a long way to go, and has to choose the way and road of cooperation combined with their own characteristics, rather than copying the developmental modes of other regional organizations for economic cooperation. Unlike other regional organizations which start from trade cooperation and gradually expand the scope of cooperation, East Asian cooperation starts from the financial sector, of which East Asian countries have a consensus, and gradually establishes comprehensive cooperative relations of finance, trade, and investment. And the progress of regional financial and economic cooperation will be good for the region's countries in consolidating and expanding consensus, eliminating differences, and enhancing the countries' political determination and willingness to support and participate in regional economic cooperation. At the same time, it can also strengthen the ability to resist and guard against a financial crisis of East Asian countries, promote financial stability and economic development in the region, help the East Asian countries participate in global economic cooperation better, and promote the orderly development of globalization.

According to the current situation, with the help of the East Asia "10+3" (ASEAN plus China, Japan and R.O. Korea) framework, to establish an East Asian regional organization for economic cooperation is a feasible way for achieving regional economic cooperation in East Asia. The cooperation among East Asian countries should start from areas where the parties reach consensus easily, consolidate the basis of cooperation, and then expand it gradually. China can use the "10+1" or the "10+3" model to promote and integrate into regional economic cooperation in East Asia. Specifically, China should actively advocate building a regional organization for economic cooperation in East Asia, put forward a set of regional economic integration schemes first, and use it as a guide to lay the foundation of establishing a regional economic cooperation organization. At the same time, China has to deal with its relationship with the great powers, especially the relations between China and Japan, and make it clear that Japan will still be the dominant force in the East Asian economy for a long time in the future. In the near future, interdependence is the mainstay of the relations between the two countries.

② The most potential sub-regional economic cooperation—the Northeast Asian economic cooperation

Since the 1990s, the status of the Asia-Pacific region in the world political and economic pattern has increased constantly. Northeast Asia, as the most active sub-region in the Asia-Pacific region, has huge potential for development. Experts predict that it will become one of the fastest growing regions in the world in the next 15 years, and it is a hot spot that could form a regional organization for economic cooperation in the near future.

A. The huge potential of Northeast Asia for regional economic cooperation

Northeast Asia has an important strategic position; it can provide a channel to Europe for countries such as China, Japan, and R.O. Korea in economy. In terms of the global trade structure, the Northeast Asian region has two emerging markets with the highest potential and the great vitality in the world: China and Russia. And it has the rich natural resources of China,

Russia, and DPR Korea, the labor resources of China and DPR Korea, and the strong ability of foreign investment and the technology advantage of Japan, R.O. Korea, and Taiwan of China. The economic complementarity, transit trade, and related industrial potential power of the Northeast Asian region give it a broad developmental prospect. Realizing Northeast Asian regional economic cooperation, which is closely related to China, as soon as possible is an important problem that the economic cooperation and development of China needs to face.

Northeast Asian economic cooperation is sub-regional economic cooperation which is not in the form of cooperation among fully sovereign states but participation of a country's local regions in international cooperation. At the same time, because the parties within the Northeast Asian regional economic cooperation have different social systems, economic systems and levels of development, to find the ideal priorities for cooperation and more effective forms of cooperation, countries need a long period of run-in and mutual approval.

Because of the Russian political unrest, the Asian financial crisis, work of multilateral sub-regional economic cooperation, and other factors in the 1990s, Northeast Asian cooperation did not reach the expected goal, and the Northeast Asian economic circle has not formed. The Tumen River Economic Development Zone is the only multilateral cooperation project in Northeast Asia, led by the United Nations in 1991 while China, Russia, DPR Korea, R.O. Korea, and Japan participated in it, but the project developed slowly due to insufficient funds.

Northeast Asian regional economic cooperation will make substantive breakthroughs and become the hot topic of regional economic cooperation throughout the world in the 21st century. This is driven partly by the interval power of Northeast Asia. Most areas of Northeast Asia have rich resources, but economically lag behind and need to be further developed. These areas have actual demand and high enthusiasm for cooperative development and economic and technological cooperation. The strong complementarity of economic elements, the similarity of regional culture, the introduction of advantageous investments and foreign investment policies that have been introduced, and the establishment of cooperation and communication channels of sub-regional economic areas around the Sea of Japan, the Yellow Sea, the Bohai Sea and the Tumen River have created foundations to strengthen regional economic cooperation and economic integration in Northeast Asia.

On the other hand, the external conditions change. First of all, the fierce competition of European and American markets and the fragility of the Southeast Asian market highlight the attraction of the two biggest emerging markets—China and Russia, and this promotes the Northeast Asian regional cooperation effectively. Secondly, with China's and Russia's accession to the WTO, the market openness and economic and trade liberalization of the two countries will undoubtedly be improved to a great extent. This trend will minimize the friction and barriers in the aspect of the economic institutions of China, Russia, Japan, and R.O. Korea. Furthermore, the Northeast Asian countries will gradually get relieved of the current economic difficulties and the entire region's economic situation will be better. Economic upturn will make the Northeast Asian regional economic cooperation have ideal and effective priorities and forms of cooperation. Finally, political relations in Northeast Asia will develop in a positive direction; it will offer a more relaxed political environment for regional economic cooperation.

B. The key areas of Northeast Asian cooperation

Because Russia has resources but lacks the strength to exploit them independently, Japan and R.O. Korea are poor in resources but have a strong capital and technical strength, China has demands for energy and electric power resources, and cooperative development can reduce risks, cooperative development will become the important means for achieving regional economic cooperation in Northeast Asia. Recently, Northeast Asian cooperative development has mainly been concentrated on oil, natural gas, electricity, coal, forestry, and agriculture. The development will shift from bilateral to multilateral cooperation step by step. Technological cooperation has a huge potential in Northeast Asia; the parties have both internal demands in strengthening cooperation in science and technology, and favorable conditions for cooperation, which offers them strong complementarity and benefit-sharing. In the future, technological cooperation of Northeast Asia will mainly focus on the development of big projects, technology trade and setting up high-tech enterprises cooperatively.

China should fully prepare to promote Northeast Asian cooperation. On the basis of developing bilateral economic and trade relationships with Northeast Asian countries, China should further modify its economic and trade ties, broaden areas of cooperation, and accelerate the development of the Tumen River delta area to develop and promote the prosperity of the Northeast Asian economic circle. China should actively participate in dialogues with the main participants, explore the building of multi-level and multi-form economic cooperation institutions in Northeast Asia, and advocate gradually establishing a cooperation mechanism that conforms to international standards. As an advocate of a Northeast Asian regional cooperation organization, China should participate in the rule-making actively, make regional cooperation serve its own interests better, and strive to establish a just and reasonable new Northeast Asia economic order.

③ With the help of the western region's geopolitical and edge advantages, carry out regional economic cooperation with Central Asia, South Asia and other neighboring countries

With the increasing improvement in political relations among countries and the implementation of the strategy of large-scale development of the western region, the geographical advantages of the western region have been strengthened and the region has become the door through which China can open up westward and carry out regional economic cooperation. Although the economy of the countries to the west of China is less developed, the western region of China has natural Asian cultural ties and similar languages, customs, and habits with Central Asian and South Asian countries. Additionally, their resource pattern and economic infrastructure can complement each other well. In recent years, China's political relations with its neighboring countries and their political convergence on opening-up have provided convenience for China's border trade and regional economic cooperation with the surrounding countries.

China neighbors five Central Asian countries, Mongolia, and Pakistan in the northwest. The textile industry of China is relatively developed, and China has rich labor resources, which can make up for the disadvantage of Central Asian countries and Mongolia in these areas. Although the overall economic level is low in Central Asia and Mongolia, they have comparative advantages in wood, steel, cement, chemical fertilizers, heavy machinery and other industries. At the same time, the northwest region shares a border line of 3,306 kilometers and with Kazakhstan, Kyrgyzstan, and Tajikistan, including more than 10 ports that open to Central Asia and railways and highways linking the areas together. For China, Central Asia is the most convenient road leading to Europe, while China is the port for Central Asian countries into the Pacific Ocean and the international market, so that both sides can have economic and technological exchanges and cooperation on this basis.

Southwest China links the South Asian and Southeast Asian markets. Five provinces of Southwest China can have sub-regional economic cooperation with east and northeast India, Myanmar, and Bangladesh. Southwest China could have resource complementarity with South Asia, Southeast Asia—India, Myanmar, Nepal, Bhutan, Laos, Vietnam and other countries, for example, exchanging silkworm cocoons, silk, fine wines and traditional Chinese medicine in the southwest region for rubber, jade, oil, timber, coconut oil and precious metals from Southeast Asian countries. At the same time, Southwest China has advantages in electronics, aerospace, and machinery manufacturing, while Southeast Asian countries have more potential in the textile industry; the two sides can be complementary in these areas.

The western region's economic cooperation with neighboring countries can not only change the pattern of opening-up in coastal areas, expand areas of cooperation, and facilitate the implementation of a diversified opening-up strategy, but also promote economic and trade exchanges with the potential market of East Asia, Central Asia, and South Asia to create a number of regional markets full of vigor and vitality, make resources be allocated optimally on a larger scope, and create the huge market space for China's economic development.

Through cooperation with neighboring countries, we can expand the market space and the domain of commodity circulation, create the effect of economies of scale, and give full play to the advantage of the west as a channel and bridge; we can create investment demand and investment hot spots to attract foreign capital for the whole area; we can reduce the infrastructure investment costs, and give full play to the economic benefit produced by the energy, transportation, and communication networks; we can also promote the adjustment of the industrial structure by expanding the international division of labor and cross-border flow of production factors.

At present, there are many disadvantages in the region, such as different political and economic systems, patchy levels of development of science and technology, complex structure of the terrain, difficulty in infrastructure construction with high cost and low efficiency. However, in recent years, the region's economy, politics, security and international environment have been developing in a positive direction conducive to regional economic cooperation. Conditions of regional economic and trade cooperation have been mature. Nowadays, sub-regional economic cooperation between Northwest China and Central Asia and between Southwest China and the ASEAN countries has already started. It cannot be an underestimated economic growth pole for China to efficiently participate in the international division of labor and cooperation.

In regional economic cooperation with neighboring countries, China should pay attention to the following: ① The construction of channels is the top priority. Forming the modern transportation network can make the goods reach the best of their flow, and help achieve a win-win situation. ② Establish the sub-regional economic cooperation zone jointly to carry out small-scale international economic cooperation, and then, connect cities along the line through the construction of channels, gradually form a situation of regional propulsion from specific cities to the whole region, and eventually form an economic growth area with relative external independence and interior unity. ③ Set up new regional economic cooperation mechanisms, and strive for the capital, technology, and material support from international organizations with organizing and coordinating, and make regional economic cooperation run in an orderly manner.

(3) Cross national and continental borders and build a network of global cooperation

In the short term, the two trends—economic globalization and economic regionalization—will run in parallel. But in the long term, economic globalization is an irreversible trend. The gradual expansion of the existing international regional organizations and the further development of regional and intercontinental cooperation will pave the way for economic globalization. Therefore, regional economic cooperation, crossing national and continental borders will become the important direction for regional economic cooperation in the future.

At present, cooperation between the continents and the main regional economic organizations is being continuously strengthened. North America and Western Europe consider the Seven-power Summit as ties; East Asia and North America consider APEC as a bridge; Western Europe and East Asia consider ASEM as a channel. All these form the interwoven international economic relations among the three regions—East Asia, North America, and Western Europe. In addition, establishing a transatlantic free trade area is also an idea that is becoming more and more popular.

Therefore, from the view of global economic development, China should have a global strategic vision when setting foreign regional economic plans, and should pay attention to leveraging international organizations, formal meetings and existing regional organizations to build a global economic cooperation network for China while focusing on developing regional cooperation organizations with surrounding countries. It not only conforms to the developmental trend in today's regional economic cooperation, but also conforms to China's economic interests.

In the long term, the situation of world economy that the south is weak and the north is strong is likely to be aggravated further. Therefore, when choosing China's key objects of global regional economic cooperation, we have to place developed countries that have the advantages of capital, technology, management, talent and a leader status in the world economy in an important position. The United States, the European Union, and Japan not only meet the aforementioned conditions, but are also the most important trade partners of China at present and will continue to be so in the future. So it is important for China to handle its relationship with them well.

Sino-American economic cooperation has a great potential for the two sides have complementary comparative advantages and industrial products. Therefore, further developing economic cooperation meets the common interests of both sides. The bilateral trade volume was USD 385.34 billion in 2010, more than 150 times that of 1979. At the end of 2010, the total amount of American institutions investing in China was 59,000, and the actual investment was about USD 65.22 billion and all had achieved good benefits. Now the United States is the second largest export market for China and the main source of investment. Of course, because of the differences in social systems, values, and competitive strategies, friction, competition, and even conflicts are inevitable between these two countries. Considering expanding cooperation and reducing friction as the future direction of development, China could take advantage of APEC to strengthen the ties between China and the United States.

Strengthening the economic cooperation between China and Japan has far-reaching significance. The two have geographical advantages and strong economic complementarity and from the view of the current scale of trade, investment, and other economic and technical cooperation, the economic and trade relationship between China and Japan is one of the most important foreign economic relations for China. To strengthen the economic cooperation between China and Japan is beneficial to Japan's economic recovery and the sustained and rapid growth of Chinese economy, and it is also good for the prosperity of East Asia. In order to strengthen cooperation between China and Japan, China could make the best of Northeast Asia, the "10+3," APEC and other regional economic cooperation organizations.

The development of China-EU relations has a great potential. The EU is the third largest trading partner of China and the main source of foreign government loans; it is also the largest provider of advanced technology and equipment for China. Recently, the volume of trade between China and the EU has increased year by year; the two sides have carried out extensive cooperation in the areas of training, science and technology and developmental assistance. Overall, however, the economic link between China and Europe is still relatively weak; this does not reflect the economic status of the two, and it can't meet the needs of both sides in economic development either. The scale of the EU's foreign trade is much larger than that of the United States and Japan, but the size of China's volume of trade with the EU is always smaller than that with the United States and Japan. The two sides have great potential in trade in goods, trade in services, and economic and technological cooperation, and have a very wide scope. Strengthening the contact between them can not only bring economic benefits for both sides, but will also add substantially for establishing a partnership of equality and mutual benefit.

Therefore, both China and the EU have taken a more positive attitude. With the aid of ASEM held every two years (including the EU and ASEAN plus China, Japan, and R.O. Korea), China-EU relations are developing in depth and in breadth. Strengthening China-EU relations will help China promote multi-polarization in international relations, implement the strategy of market diversification, and broaden leeway of China in diplomacy.

9.4.2 Modes and Specific Measures

Different modes of regional economic cooperation are found at different times and in different areas for historical reasons and different economic levels according to their own conditions. Three main modes for the regional cooperation are horizontal/vertical cooperation, institutional/functional system and single-market/multi-regional cooperation, depending on the specific conditions of different countries.

With the current macro and micro factors taken into consideration, the overall strategy for China's regional economic cooperation should be guided as "vertical and horizontal alliance, development in many directions highlighting the key points, and giving priority to development." Three-dimensional cooperation (global cooperation, regional cooperation, and sub-regional cooperation) should be properly applied hand in hand. While actively organizing an open regional economic cooperation organization, there is an urge to transform the existing single-focused mode to a more sophisticated multi-focused mode.

(1) Development of cooperation at different levels: A balanced pattern of cooperation

Economic cooperation running in a world-scale is known as economic globalization; economic cooperation conducted in certain areas is reckoned as regional economic cooperation; the concept of sub-regional economic cooperation then derives as a kind of economic cooperation carried out in an even smaller geo-range. Generally, there is a positive connection between the scope of regional economic cooperation and the level of difference among its members; a wider scope leads to more differences and greater difficulties when it comes to interest coordination and thus, it is harder to increase the degree of regional economic cooperation, and vice versa.

Regional economic cooperation is operated at three different levels as global cooperation, regional cooperation, and sub-regional cooperation. China's strategy for the development of regional economic cooperation should absorb these three kinds of cooperation altogether, promoting the cooperation in three dimensions simultaneously (see Table 9.5).

Table 9.5 The development of China's regional economic cooperation at different levels

Type	Character	Organization
Global economic cooperation	Comprehensive	WTO, IMF, World Bank, intercontinental regional economic cooperation organizations
Regional economic cooperation	Intensive	ASEAN, APEC, etc.
Sub-regional economic cooperation	Realistic	The Tumen River and Mekong River cooperation projects

A. A special focus on comprehensive economic cooperation. This requires China to develop economic relations actively with various types of countries and regions to comply with the trend of globalization and meet the demand of China's economic development. To put the matter in perspective, China has already carried out a considerable amount of business cooperation (of all kinds) through bilateral/multilateral operations with quite a few international organizations. So far, China has joined the WTO, the World

Bank, the IMF, and other international and inter-regional cooperation organizations. Further cooperation will be unfolded in the future.

B. Significant attention to the regional cooperation priorities. From the geo-economic point of view and taking account of the actual situation, the key point of China's foreign regional economic cooperation is located in the Asia-Pacific region. This suggests that China should pay attention to the development of regional economic cooperation, especially in the Asia-Pacific region, and share more benefits from that cooperation in the future.

C. A close connection to reality. With active participation in and promotion of economic cooperation in the Asia-Pacific region, sub-regional economic cooperation can be proceeded simultaneously to the areas where regional cooperation is yet to be matured, but economic cooperation can be conducted on a small scale, such as the cooperation projects in the Mekong River area in Southwest China, and the area development cooperation in Tumen River area in Northeast China.

(2) Adapting to the new era: From a single-market mode to a multi-regional mode

Different cooperation modes for foreign regional economic cooperation distinguish themselves between one another in the specific conditions they are designed for. Since countries or regions are differentiated by natural resources, cultures, and social characteristics, as well as the existing economic base and political system, etc. they should go for the best-suited solutions in accordance with their own "outfit."

Besides the comprehensive economic cooperation, which is one of the most commonly used modes for regional economic cooperation, regional-focused cooperation, which should be based on geo-economic relations, also needs close attention. These region-focused relations can be either multi-regional or unitary. As mentioned earlier, the United States stands a good geographic advantage and wields strong economic power; hence, it could implement a multi-regional focused cooperation strategy. At present, China's geo-economic-centered region tends to be single over a rather long time span, but it does not provide a decisive judgment that China is incapable of developing multiple regionally focused economic cooperation in the coming years.

Geographical advantage, which plays a leading role when the level of productivity remains relatively low, will be impaired with the rapid increase in productivity, innovation of technology, and the alteration of the modes of transportation and communication. The development of the commodity market is bound to push the economy expansively outbound, trying to get rid of the boundary restrictions. Be that as it may, the development of the commodity market is expected as an irresistible tide that could further internationalize the world economy and globalize the life of mankind.

Such an international background provides great material facilitation for the development of China's multiple regionally focused economic cooperation. China in return, should promote its foreign economic cooperation by diversifying channels and setting up a multi-level, all-round layout. Efforts from the Chinese government at all levels, including financial aid and human resource development, should be made; governmental cooperation and civil collaboration can be started.

It needs to be clarified that a multi-region focused strategy does not mean that the importance of the individual areas is exactly the same, but suggests a prioritized order. Therefore, regional divisions are classified as the central zone, sub-central zone, and peripheral zone and different regions should adopt different policies. The mainland and Hong Kong, Macao and Taiwan are categorized as the central zone; any affordable methods focusing on the development and cooperation that could strengthen the institutional cooperation are worth trying. The sub-central zone primarily refers to the neighboring countries of China, the United States, and Europe; any other area in the world is also included. China needs to actively develop multilevel regional economic cooperation and dedicate itself to promoting that cooperation-in-prototype with all possible efforts. China should expand the right of speech, enhance its comprehensive strength, and attempt to become an advocate and leader when the timing is right. On the basis of existing cooperation of the China-ASEAN Free Trade Area (known as "10+3"), the Five Countries of Central Asia, the Lancang-Mekong River sub-regional economic cooperation, and the Tumen River sub-regional cooperation in Northeast Asia, China is expected to build up an economic cooperation network with geographical advantages; with the help of non-institutionalized organizations like APEC and ASEM, we will be able to promote intercontinental economic cooperation between China and the United States and the United Kingdom. The peripheral zone in terms of the specific area shows no obvious geographical advantages but have disadvantageous economic and trade relations. Nevertheless, China should be positively preparing to enlarge its potential economic and trade exchanges, conducting market research, and seizing the underlying business opportunities for the expansion of the global market to lay a good foundation for better participation in the global division of labor.

In general, China should regard its mainland, Hong Kong, Macao, and Taiwan as the central zone, marching eastward by promoting the progression of trade and investment liberalization of APEC, rooting the economic cooperation with the members from APEC, building up an effective cooperation framework in East Asia through the "10+1" process and the "10+3" process; fueling the cooperation with the Five Countries of Central Asia and the Northeast Asian area in the north, facilitating the transition from "preferential trade" and project development to a higher level; utilizing the advantage of the current ASEM to raise cooperation awareness westward; and seeking to establish closer economic and trade relations with members of the South Asian Regional Cooperation Agreement in the south with the help of the strategy of large-scale development in the western region and the geographical advantages, hence, casting a sound foundation for the future cooperation in the neighboring region (see Figure 9.3).

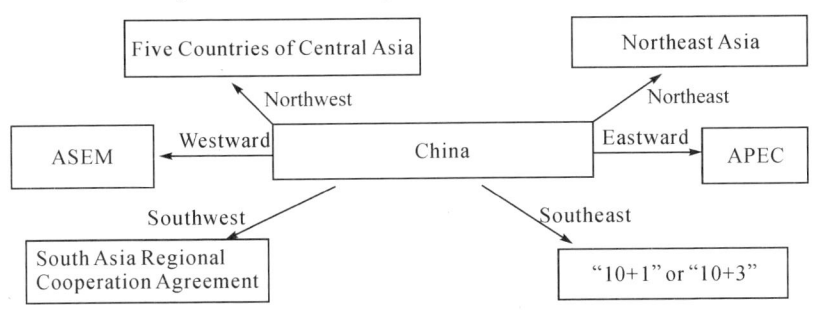

Figure 9.3 The idea of China's multiple regionally focused development

(3) Efforts made for an open regional economic cooperation organization and exploration upon the intersection of mutual benefit

A wider space for resource allocation results in the availability of more resources, higher efficiency of resource allocation, and more common interests among nations, while open and non-exclusive cooperation also complies with the world's political multi-polarization and the trend of economic globalization in addition to the common economic interests. So China should actively promote the formation of an open regional economic cooperation organization.

As is learned from the empirical practice of APEC and the WTO, the general idea of the formation of any regional economic cooperation organization comes as mutual market access, economic integration, hand-in-hand development, and mutual benefit. It comes as no surprise that an extended period of time and a detailed negotiation are needed for the members concerned before the final goals are achieved. The opening degree of the market in developed countries is indeed higher than that in developing countries, but this does not suggest complete opening. Therefore, China should take the initiative to develop a specific open process for the market in accordance with its own national conditions. A proper introduction of competition to the market can stimulate Chinese industries to thrive while protecting themselves from breaking down. It is necessary to build a reasonable relationship between "self-centered" awareness and a "win-win cooperation" in a global environment. Multi-stake holders from members of regional economic cooperation are responsible for bringing about coordination in the economic system and political set-up. They also need to be fully conscious of mutual interests, common responsibilities, and shared risks.

The basic principle to be followed in cooperation comes as "equality and mutual benefit, mutual opening up, driving for results, long-term cooperation and common development," while the fundamental standing ground for China is known as "mutual respect, consensus-based, step-by-step, steady development; mutual opening up and discrimination-avoided; extensive cooperation, mutual benefit; gap-narrowing, and common prosperity."

To insist on open regional economic cooperation, promotion should be made concerning the mutual opening-up of members in one regional economic cooperation organization and between members and other organizations or nations, and discriminatory practices in the process of international trading should be completely eliminated. Deliberate consideration should be taken as individual members may vary in economic development and specific circumstances. The basic principle as "voluntary participation, flexibility and consensus-based" should be set up and, a rational speed of economic and technical cooperation needs to be appropriately kept. Finally narrow the gap among the members and achieve common prosperity.

(4) Specific measures to promote regional economic cooperation with foreign countries

① A macro perspective: Piloting functions of government upon framework-setting in regional economic cooperation

At present, China's overall economic size is among the largest in the world, exposing a huge potential for development. It is one of the largest emerging markets and the important pillar of economic strength just after Japan in the Asia-Pacific region. Given China's economic power, it is well qualified to have its own right of speech and is fully capable of wielding more influence in the field of FTA's rule-making, the targeting of market liberalization and the selection of cooperative projects.

The promoting efforts from leading regional countries are indispensable to the establishment and the perfection of regional economic organizations. France and Germany are the main factors determining the movement of processes in the EU, as well as the United States in NAFTA formation; these countries are all living examples. Therefore, China may either consider joint development with other countries or opt for promoting regional economic cooperation by standing alone as a leading regional country. Japan and China, for instance, can collaborate with each other to promote regional economic cooperation in East Asia to achieve economic complementarity and mutual benefits.

To this end, China needs to strengthen bilateral/multilateral government contacts and further improve inter-governmental meetings and consultation mechanisms. The leading role in constructing the framework for regional economic cooperation of governments should be ensured. The improvement of the environment for foreign trade and cooperation will be the main task of great significance to the government of China.

The government should undertake the following tasks: Support policy dialogue, strengthen coordination of international actions, promote the exchange of information, contribute to the development of regional economic cooperation rules, prioritize the specific areas of economic and technological cooperation together with other countries, implement funding, and figure out the appropriate incentive mechanisms for multilateral cooperation so that the regional economic cooperation can take its position as soon as possible. We should urge advantage complementarity and joint investment and development, which refer to bilateral/multilateral cooperation that lays its foundation on the principle of "voluntary complementary exchanges, mutual benefits, and a shared market", and make sure that the production factors of members can enjoy a more reasonable and rational allocation and deployment. We should support industrial and commercial enterprises' participation in their cooperation on regional economic technical projects. There lies the necessity for the government to select and train managerial elites with strong strategic awareness, fluent in foreign languages and to get them involved in the business forums and policy dialogues, in order to safeguard and fight for the interests of China. Encourage economic and technical cooperation of middle and small-sized enterprises; advocate China-centered, large-scale project cooperation, and ensure that all participants and associates benefit. Motivate market-oriented reform, build up a favorable environment for foreign institutional regional economic cooperation, actively integrate China into the multilateral trading system, facilitate business investment, and propose more productive trading policies and systems of a regulatory framework to fuel the exchange of information and the sharing of benefits.

② A micro perspective: Central-role-playing of enterprises through transnational operations

The intrinsic power that motivates free trade areas and regional economic cooperation is market force, while businesses and enterprises serve as the major subjects driving the economic and technical cooperation and development.

Intergovernmental consultation and the common policy should act as the guidance for regional economic cooperation. The role of governments should be limited to making equal competition rules, which helps create a favorable environment for business and investment that should be applied to the market system. Also, the government should not determine the direction of development for the regional economy. Cultural prosperity and social progress in the region could be accomplished by individual businesses and enterprise entities that optimize the allocation of useful resources and act simultaneously as carriers for the foreign investments. Close connection and direct interaction with these companies are worth the attention from governments. As such, individual entities are the sources for economic growth. Local entities control, to a very real extent, the direction of economic development.

The promotion of regional economic cooperation is mainly driven by the transnational operation of enterprises. Therefore, the acceleration and promotion of transnational business turns out to be the basic point of strategic development for regional economic cooperation. Transnational business for Chinese enterprises is mostly conducted in two approaches as follows: In the first place, Chinese companies can set themselves as the parent companies and then take aggressive measures like outbound investment for expanding—this has been proved to be more successful for a wide range of Chinese companies, especially when the expanding efforts are made upon other emerging markets or countries with a similar background to that of China; based on this, a further expansion and infiltration can be imposed once the market opens. The second approach refers to an extension through the inducements of other countries' subsidiaries or branches in China, or by setting up joint ventures with overseas companies.

Transnational business can fasten the economic ties among different countries or regions, thus improving China's economic and trade environment, promising a wider market and thereby enhancing the international competitiveness of the enterprises involved. This also suggests a direct, yet more fierce, competition on the wider market. Therefore, companies and enterprises must be well prepared strategically in order to satisfy the requirements of regional economic cooperation and to comply with administrative standards set for international corporations, as well as the international standard systems' market needs and business practices, to appropriately organize their production and business activities.

③ A progressive approach to advancing regional economic cooperation
Generally speaking, regional economic cooperation is a step-by-step process, which can be observed both in time and space. Cooperation is restricted by various factors, as resources involved in regional economic cooperation flow among different geographic sites. Moreover, economic cooperation cannot be promoted simultaneously, as there exists a spectacular disparity in the level of development among different countries. This phenomenon results in an earlier establishment of regional economic cooperation organizations among countries with similar developing states and geographical locations. These kinds of cross-border regional organizations have unique advantages in promoting the economic interests of members, such as resource endowments, market alliances, geopolitical relations, political systems and values and cultures. In the best Chinese traditions, they are the perfect timing, the right place, and great efforts.

The overall advancement of regional economic cooperation is fairly hard to achieve in a short time on account of the complex surrounding situation of China. Efforts should be targeted at specific areas or countries to become infectious for others. The practice principle "start from easy ones, start from small ones and each step counts" should be followed and the measures taken must be both suitable for local conditions and for preparing for the future. The formation of regional cooperation forums and informal meetings in the first place can later be converted into a deeper form of cooperation if preferential trade agreements or free trade agreements for regional economic cooperation prove to be successful. Equality and institutionalization of cooperation forums and informal meetings promote mutual understanding among nations, thus avoiding unnecessary disputes. Focusing on issues of common interests does good to all the parties concerned. At the same time, the authorities-in-charge are required to be fully conscious of the dialectical unity trait between political collaboration and business cooperation. It requires us to build up reliable relations in regional economic cooperation from a strategic level if a more balanced global layout is wanted.

④ A longer shot upon interests: Incorporate international practice and abide by market rules

The total formation and smooth running of regional economic cooperation organizations rely on proper international practice and explicit market rules. Up until now from the 1990s, there are still extra miles for China to go in its adaptation to international conventions. Institutional obstacles keep growing as we try striding for more intense reform and comprehensive opening-up, while China needs a more stable market condition and a healthier external environment. Since China can benefit more from the current institutional environment, it's necessary for China to conduct institutional opening-up instead of policy opening-up. It's a favorable opportunity of joining the WTO to advance the institutional reform process; at the same time, the foreign trade system and the economic management system offer an invaluable chance to China to achieve full integration with the international rules and conventions. Hopefully, this timely shift would provide us with a great opportunity for the development of China's foreign regional economic cooperation.

During integration with international rules and conventions, China has to face certain external constraints and risks to accelerate this opening-up phase. We ought to be aware of the fact that economic turmoil will inevitably be triggered once these potential risks come into reality, and it can severely impact certain industries in China, making more companies face bankruptcy and more workers and employees in certain industries and departments become unemployed. Although China's economy is likely to be placed in a disadvantageous situation in the short term, we are confident that a more stable international market can be obtained in the near future. Additionally, integrating into the world economy would bring China more significance as well as more rights of speech when participating in the decision-making and the institution-building process of a globalized economic community, which in due course constitute a strong driving force of China's economic reform. Productive solutions come for China in the international division of labor as proper adjustment to business structure and more job creation to society. Hopefully, China will be guaranteed to be able to enjoy promising benefits in the years to come.

10

Discussion on the Development of Regional Economic Integration Among China, Japan, and R.O. Korea

10.1 Relative Theories and Influencing Mechanisms of the Regional Industrial Structure

For a long time, the theoretical and empirical studies of industrial structure and industrial structure adjustment, which rose after the war, are the focus of industrial economics and public policy-makers. Right from the time Western scholars C. Clark in 1940 and W. G. Hoffmann in 1931 made a great contribution to the formation and development of the modern theory of industrial structure, the theory of industrial structure got integrated into the theory of economic growth, the theory of international direct investment, the theory of international trade, the theory of international division of labor, and the competitive advantage theory, and got constantly enriched and developed. From the point of the trajectory of research and development of industrial structure, the research on industrial structure and international industrial structure adjustment, which influence each other, mainly consists of the following aspects: First, the European and American scholars researched the internal structure and the general evolutionary trend of industrial structure. Second, Japanese scholars researched the association between changes in a country's industrial structure and that of the neighboring countries or the world. Third, since the 1990s, in the context of economic globalization, regional integration and collectivization, there was research on the internationalism of the industrial structure. Because this book focuses on the mutual influences and mechanism of interaction of the adjustment of industrial structure of economies in a region, the rest of this chapter will sort out and explain the related theories.

10.1.1 The Evolution of the Theory of Industrial Structure and the View of the Mutual Influences of Industrial Structure Changes among Countries

Classical theory of industrial structure can be traced back to William Petty, the founder of British classical economics. By comparing the relationship between supply and demand and employees' income of different industries, Petty came to a conclusion that when compared with agriculture, industry had a higher income, but commercial income was higher than that of industry. He was the first person to notice some corelation and basic direction existing between economic growth and structural changes, and to reveal the trend that production factors transfer from low-productivity industries to high-productivity industries and the significance for economic development, laying the foundation for related research on economic development and industrial structure.

Another scientist who made an important contribution to the classical theory of industrial structure is A. G. B. Fisher. In his "material progress of the economic implications," he first proposed the three-sector theory . Since then the study of industrial structure has been divided roughly into three basic sectors.

The people who made pioneering contributions to the theory of modern industrial structure are the British economist, C. Clark and the German economist, W.G. Hoffman. In the 1940s, inspired by Petty and other economists, Clark researched the internal relations between the per capita income growth and the transfer tendency of the three sectors based on a number of countries' statistics, and believed that the employment structure would change with the growth of per capita income and the change of industrial structure. Clark also concluded from the comparison countries and regions at different levels of development at the same point, and considered that the countries and regions with high per capita income levels had a relatively small proportion of agricultural labor force, and the secondary and tertiary sectors had a relatively large proportion. Hoffman made pioneering research on the evolution and the stages of development of the industrial structure.

Clark and Hoffman led the research on modern theory of industrial structure, but its theoretical model was so simple that it was only a broad-brush description of the macroscopic changes in the industrial structure tendencies. Therefore, Simon Kuznets in 1966 and 1971, and Hollis Chenery in 1975 and 1986, further developed the theoretical model respectively. Starting from total economic growth, Kuznets investigated more than 50 countries' cross-sectional data and historical data and made a statistical regression and researched the states of the structural changes at different total growth points. Since then, in most cases, Chenery and others have always used the input-output analysis, the general equilibrium analysis and econometric models, and extended to analyze the samples of low-income developing countries. They finally formatted a structural change analysis with more uses. Overall, the studies of Kuznets, Chenery and others have greatly advanced the theory of industrial structure in terms of extension, intention, and methods, which gave the analytical methods and the conclusions of industrial structure more general significance.

Kuznets' research on changes in the industrial structure breaks through the limits of the country's economy for the first time, involving "international spread" of changes in the industrial structure. Kuznets studied three groups of factors that influenced industrial structure changes: domestic demand, foreign trade, and production technology along with variables. At the same time, in the analysis of the differences of the structural changes of developing countries and developed countries, he initially proposed the international spread of economic growth and structural change.

10.1.2 The Study of Regional Industrial Structure Linkage Represented by the Theory of the "Flying Geese Model"

After World War II, some Japanese scholars integrated the product life cycle theory and the comparative advantage theory into the field of industrial structure based on their national conditions, and gradually formed a series of theoretical hypotheses and models that described the industrial development orders within late-comer countries as well as the sophistication pathways and processes, namely the famous "flying geese model" theory.

The Japanese economist Akamatsu originally proposed and improved the basic "flying geese model." Through the empirical study on the production of domestic importation and the exportation of products of Japan's specific industry, Akamatsu pointed out that the conversion from import substitution to exportation was the motive power of Japan's economic development. The first "flying geese model" included the geese model development in three levels: First, the late-comer countries can use the experience of leading nations through trade relations, absorb their capital and technology to build modern industry, and achieve their industrial structure upgrading; second, countries can achieve the flying geese development of regional economy through the inter-national industrial transfer and delivery; and third, alternative rise and fall of the world economy is also a form of flying geese development.

In the 1970s, Kojima Kiyoshi and others further expanded and deepened the theoretical hypothesis, proposed that foreign direct investment should begin from the industries that had been or would be at a comparative disadvantage in a country, and used the "marginal industrial transfer" to summarize the dynamic changes of the comparative advantage of specific industries as well as interpret international industrial transfer and industrial structural changes, which are caused by industrial transfer. Specifically, Kojima's "flying geese model" is mainly related to the life cycle model of a newcomer country's specific industry, which describes the life cycle or process of creation, development, and tending to lead to its decline. It also explains internal changes of the domestic industrial structure and the rise and fall process of different industries. What is especially noteworthy is that the "flying geese model" is further expanded on the basis of the above model and used to study the objective process of the East Asian countries and regions, which in turn took off, and that is to say, with the dynamic changes in comparative advantages, by way of direct investment to achieve industrial transfer, the process of the East Asian newcomer countries catching up with the leading countries has the typical characteristics of the "flying geese model."

10.1.3 The Expansion of the Theory of Industrial Structure in View of International Investment Theories and International Trade Theories

The expansion of the theory of industrial structure in view of international investment theories and international trade theories mainly studies the international industrial transfer and upgrade due to the international flows of capital, technology and other production factors, and the most classic theories include Vernon's product life cycle theory and Dunning's eclectic theory of international production.

The American economist, Raymond Vernon proposed the product cycle model (PCM) in 1966. Then after the expansions and tests conducted by other economists, it gradually developed into one of the theories of trade and investment that have the most far-reaching impacts. The model considers international trade and investment as a whole from the perspective of a dynamic comparative advantage, and studies the industrial restructuring process of transnational enterprises.

The famous British multinational corporation professor John Harry Dunning proposed the eclectic theory of international production in 1977. The eclectic theory of international production considers that a business engaged in foreign direct investment must have three advantages, namely ownership advantages, internalization advantages and location advantages. Different combinations of the three advantages determine the types of foreign direct investment and international production.

10.1.4 Exploration of the Effect of Theory of Regional Economic Cooperation on Trade and the Industrial Structure within the Region

After the Cold War, regional economic cooperation tended to speed up development, and the wave of regional economic cooperation had a tremendous impact on the world's economic growth and the development of international trade, and the theoretical study of regional economic cooperation also became a hot academic concern.

The traditional theory of regional economic cooperation mainly focused on the static and dynamic effects of the customs union on trade and economic growth. In 1950, Jacob Viner first proposed the partial equilibrium analysis framework of the customs union, and he believed the establishment of a customs union would produce two effects: trade creation and trade diversion. The trade creation effect refers to an effect that after the cancellation of tariff barriers within the alliances, some of the domestic goods of a higher production cost are replaced by low-cost commodities of other member states, which results in new trade. Trade creation effect improves the economies of scale, enhances competition, promotes economic development within the region, and promotes the development of entire foreign trade. The trade diversion effect means that implementing unified protective customs tariffs causes the original importation of cheap goods from non-member countries to be replaced by the more expensive merchandise within the alliance members, and that trade transfers from the outside to the inside of a customs union. Traditional customs union theories are based on strict assumptions, emphasizing the analysis of static effects and impacts on the welfare, while ignoring the analysis of the effects on economic growth and industrial structure, which has significant limitations and shortcomings. However, it pays attention to the impact of regional economic cooperation on international trade regionalization. The forms of regional economic cooperation are not confined to customs unions, but from the study of the customs union, we can outline a general theory of the economic effects in regional economic cooperation, which can be applied to other forms of regional economic cooperation.

10.1.5 Research on the International Spread and Corelation and Interaction of the Industrial Structure in the New Era

Since the 1990s, waves of economic globalization and regional integration and collectivization have been irresistible, and the changes in industrial structure among countries have affected and interacted more closely with each other, particularly in the same region, the integration of the industrial structure and the allocation of resources between countries accelerate. Therefore, the academic study of contemporary industrial structure also gradually regards international industrial association as an important issue to explore. In this aspect, the overall evolutionary theory of international regional industrial structure of Wang Bin is representative.

Wang Bin's theory of international regional industrial structure, from a global perspective, uses the contemporary economic globalization and regionalization as an analytical basis; by investigating the transmission mechanism of the correlation and interaction of the industrial structure of economies in various international regions in the context of globalization, he compares evolutionary patterns and characteristics of different types of international regional industrial structures, analyzes the changes in contemporary international division of labor, which is associated with the internationalization of contemporary industrial structure, and the transformation of international contemporary industrial policy caused by the internationalization of contemporary industrial structure, and draws the conclusion that international regional industrial structural changes influence and restrict mutually, and finally evolve integrally. Thus, he constructs the general theoretical framework of internationalization of contemporary industrial structure, and proposes the analysis model of the overall evolution of international regional industrial structure.

After that, Tang Zhihong made a useful supplement on Wang Bin's theory, considering that in the context of economic globalization, the prominent feature of a state's industrial development is the opening of industrial structure, and the adjustment of industrial structure is subject to impacts of fluctuations of industrial development in the world. In long-term studies, we often study industrial structure from the perspective of a single country; however, economic globalization requires us to study the formation and evolution of the national industrial structure from the perspective of the global market. International trade, international capital flows, multinational companies and global economic organizations are the next main action mechanisms of the opening and interaction of a country's industrial structure in the context of economic globalization.

10.2 The Evolution and Interaction of the Industrial Structure of China, Japan, and R.O. Korea

10.2.1 The Industrial Structure Evolution of China, Japan, and R.O. Korea

(1) The economic development of China, Japan, and R.O. Korea

China, Japan, and R.O. Korea, which are located in the northeast of Asia are the major economies in East Asia; they are also important components of world economy. China is the world's largest developing country and the most populous country, and it also has the world's third largest land area; Japan is Asia's largest developed country whose economic output ranks second in the world. Compared with China and Japan, although R.O. Korea's economic output is small, its amazing economic growth rate and size in the past 30 years has attracted worldwide attention, and it is listed as one of Asia's newly industrialized countries (regions) —"The Four Dragons."

China's economic development has made great achievements after over 30 years of reform and opening-up, which is the world's most dynamic economy. From 1979 to 2009, China's gross domestic product (GDP) grew by about 16.74 times; the average annual growth rate reached 9.6% and the annual growth rate of per capita GDP was more than 8.4%. Now China's per capita GDP has reached USD 3,670. In the general law of economic development, this symbolizes that China's economy has entered "a new stage of development."

Japan's economy experienced 10 years of hard work to recover from the ruins after World War II to the pre-war level from 1945 to 1955. In the 1960s, Japan's economy soared at a speed of 10% and it entered the high-growth period. In the 1970s and 1980s, Japan's economy entered a stable period of growth, when the average economic growth rate was 5%. The economy grew by leaps and bounds and Japan quickly entered the ranks of advanced countries in the world, becoming the world's second largest economy just after the United States. In the late 1980s to the early 1990s, Japan experienced a "bubble economy," when its economy was overheating In the early 1990s, the "bubble economy" collapsed and sustained economic recession started. However, since 2003, Japan's GDP increased by 8% over the previous year, revealing a glimmer of economic recovery. Especially in recent years, Japan's foreign trade has also begun to show a trend of recovery, and it has had a significant increase in total imports and total exports as well. According to World Bank statistics, in 2009, Japan's nominal GDP reached USD 5,072.89 billion, and Japan has maintained its position as a world economic power.

Since the 1950s, R.O. Korea's economy began to recover from the brink of collapse, and in the 1960s, R.O. Korea successfully implemented a strategy of export-oriented economic development and began the implementation of its first five-year plan for economic development. In the 1970s, it entered the ranks of the newly industrialized countries (regions); in the 1980s, it started to become a country with strong competition on the international market, and in the beginning of the 1990s, it was determined to enter the ranks of developed countries. R.O. Korea's economic strength is strong, and steel, automobiles, shipbuilding, electronics and textiles are its pillar industries. In 2009, R.O. Korea's GDP reached USD 820 billion, an increase of 3.6 times that of 20 years ago, and an increase of 1.84 times that of 10 years ago, and the speed and the size of its economic development have attracted worldwide attention.

(2) The industrial structure of China, Japan, and R.O. Korea

Tables 10.1 and 10.2 show the proportion of the outputs of three sectors in the GDP and the proportion of employed population of China, Japan, and R.O. Korea. It can be seen that China, Japan, and R.O. Korea are at different stages of economic development, as well as the different distribution and upgrading and adjustment trend of the industrial structure of the three countries in different periods.

Table 10.1   The output structure of three sectors in China, Japan and R.O. Korea

Country	1980			
	Agriculture	Industry	Manufacturing	Services
Japan	4%	42%	29%	54%
R.O. Korea	14%	40%	28%	46%
China	30%	49%	41%	21%
Country	1998			
	Agriculture	Industry	Manufacturing	Services
Japan	2%	37%	24%	61%
R.O. Korea	5%	43%	31%	52%
China	18%	49%	37%	33%
Country	2008			
	Agriculture	Industry	Manufacturing	Services
Japan	6.3%	30.2%	20%	68.1%
R.O. Korea	7%	37.2%	23%	55.8%
China	6.5%	50.6%	40.1%	42.9%

Note: In this table, the classification of the three sectors is based on agriculture, industry, and services, and as in China, Japan, and R.O. Korea, the proportion of manufacturing output in GDP is representative, it is also listed.

Source: The data of 1980 and 1998 come from *World Development Indicators in 2000*, which was compiled by the World Bank, China Financial and Economic Publishing House, 2000, pp. 186–184. The data of 2008 were calculated by the data from the World Bank website.

10 Discussion on the Development of Regional Economic Integration

Table 10.2 The proportion of the employed population in three sectors in China, Japan and R.O. Korea in 2006

Country	The primary industry	The secondary industry	The tertiary industry
Japan	4.3%	28.0%	66.6%
R.O. Korea	7.7%	26.3%	65.9%
China	42.6%	25.2%	32.2%

Source: *China Statistical Yearbook 2009; The International Statistics Yearbook 2009; World Development Indicators in 2001*, Beijing: China Financial and Economic Publishing House, 2002.

According to the proportion of the output of the three sectors in the GDP of China, Japan, and R.O. Korea, we can see that in the developed country Japan and the newly industrialized country R.O. Korea, the industrial structure is almost the same; the phenomenon of tilting toward the tertiary sector is very significant. The proportion of the primary sector (agriculture) in the GDP is very low. It dropped to 4% in Japan in 1980, and further reduced to 2% in 1998. It dropped to 5% from 14% in the same period in R.O. Korea. In 1998, in R.O. Korea the proportion of the tertiary sector (services) in the GDP surpassed 50%. The output structure in R.O. Korea and Japan at the end of the 20th century already has had some similar characteristics, namely, the proportion is in the order of "the tertiary sector, the secondary sector, and the primary sector." The structure of China's output is obviously different from that of Japan and R.O. Korea, and the most prominent sector is industry, especially the high proportion of manufacturing in industrial structure. In China, the proportion of the secondary sector in the GDP is currently close to 50%, and the proportion of the tertiary sector and the primary sector is about 42% and 10% respectively. The significantly higher industrial structure shows that China is in the middle of the process of industrialization. Especially in recent years, along with a large quantity of the world's manufacturing transferred to China, the proportion of the output of China's secondary sector in the GDP also increased to a certain level. At the same time, the proportion of the employed population of China's primary sector is significantly higher and the proportion of the output of the tertiary sector is lower, which is an obvious feature. These facts show that China's first sector and tertiary sector lag behind. In general, it reflects that the level of China's industrialization has improved greatly, but compared with Japan and R.O. Korea, China is still a developing country, which is in the expansion phase of industrialization.

Overall, the output proportion of the three sectors and the proportion of the employed population in China, Japan, and R.O. Korea reflect that the industrial structures of the three countries are at different levels of development and have some complementary features.

10.2.2 The Interaction of the Industrial Structures of China, Japan, and R.O. Korea

(1) The industrial policy and the leading industries of China, Japan, and R.O. Korea in different periods

① The evolution of China's industrial policy and industrial structure at different stages of economic development

China's industrial restructuring began from the mid-1950s, which mainly resolved the "shortage" of the structure of industrial supply. Then China experienced the stages of industry-led development, the development of the processing industry, and the coordinated development of three sectors.

From 1953 to 1980, it was the stage of industry-led structure formation. China adopted policies tilting toward the secondary sector to achieve its aims. The proportion of the national income of the secondary sector had increased from 25.95% in 1953 to 53.93% in 1980. Within the secondary sector, the heavy industry had a momentum of rapid development, while the share of the processing industry rose fastest. During the years between 1981 and 1995, it was the stage of the development of the processing industry that was promoted by investment and pulled together by demand. During this period, the proportion of the output value of the primary sector dropped from 33.3% in 1982 to 20.5% in 1995, a decrease of 12.8 percentage points; the proportion of the output value of the secondary sector dropped from 46.4% in 1981 to 41.6% in 1990; the proportion of the output value of the tertiary sector increased from 21.8% in 1981 to 30.7% in 1995, which had an increase of 8.9 percentage points. Throughout the 1980s, it was the period for the primary, secondary, and tertiary sectors to develop in coordination with each other. It was during this period that the tertiary sectors had a relatively faster pace of development, and the evolution of industrial structure was basically "upgrading in adjustment." From 1996, it was the period of adjustment of the industrial structure when there was a relative surplus on the market. Viewing from the point of view of the continuous changes that occured from the "Ninth Five-Year" to the "Eleventh Five-Year", the proportion of value-added of the three sectors in the GDP changed differently: The proportion of the primary sector showed a steady downward trend; the secondary sector was basically stable; the tertiary sector had continued to rise. Industrial restructuring and conversion was promoted by investment basically.

② The evolution of Japan's industrial policy and leading industries at different stages of economic development

During the 20 years after World War II, Japan witnessed a sustained and rapid economic growth and its economic strength ranked second in the world. From the 1950s to the first half of the 1960s, Japan gave priority to restoring agriculture and light industry, developed its export-oriented textile industry, and actively fostered the heavy chemical industry for substitution. At this stage, Japan's leading industries comprised the labor-intensive light industry, which was export-oriented, and capital-intensive heavy chemical industry for import substitution. In the early 1960s, Japan's industrial policy shifted to achieve the structural adjustment of the heavy chemical industry, but also to pay attention to the development of some capital- and technology-intensive industries for import substitution. Correspondingly, Japan's leading export-oriented industries in this phase shifted to the capital-intensive heavy chemical industry, while the leading industry for import substitution shifted to the capital- and technology-intensive industries. Finally, the leading industry was the heavy industry, which had great elasticity of demand and high-value-added products, and stimulated the development of other industries. In 1970, the proportion of the heavy chemical industry in the Japanese manufacturing industry was 62.3%, and about 77% of the export products were heavy chemical products.

Since the 1970s, Japan experienced three periods of economic turbulence, which exerted a significant impact on the adjustment of its industrial structure. After the 1970s, the adjustment of its industrial structure can be roughly divided into three stages.

A. Transformation from capital-intensive to technology-intensive (1973 to mid-1980s)

Japan's rapid economic development is based on a large quantity of imported oil energy in the context of the development of the oil-rich Middle East. In 1973 and 1979, the two oil crises had a huge impact on Japan's economy, especially the heavy chemical industry, which was Japan's competitive industry for export trade, suffered severely. Japan's economy began to transform from capital-intensive to technology-intensive. In this phase, the industrial development of Japan was characterized by industries with cutting-edge technology as the core, low power, high efficiency, and high-tech as the orientation, which encountered a strong international competitiveness and promoted the sustainable development of the entire Japanese economy. The specific features are as follows: First, it reduced energy consumption to change the industrial structure and energy structure; second, it proposed "developing the nation via science and technology" and increased investments in technology. By increasing investments in research and development, design, and management, the government developed knowledge-intensive industries and drove the related industries, in order to promote the industrial structure from the heavy chemical industry to knowledge-intensive industries. As a result, the electronic information industry, which took the personal computer as the core, had a rapid development. In 1986, the output of Japan's electronic industry surpassed that of the automobile industry for the first time, and the electronic industry had become Japan's largest industry.

B. The development of knowledge-intensive industries and modern services (mid-1980s to 1997)

In the early days of the 1980s, with the sharp appreciation of the US dollar, the US economy was in the situation of the "three highs." To curb this situation, in 1985, the meeting of the finance ministers of five nations decided to force the appreciation of the yen significantly. Dramatic changes in the yen made the Japanese government carry out industrial restructuring again. The industrial restructuring goal was to gradually establish the leading role of the tertiary sector, which was represented by services, and knowledge-intensive industries. To this end, Japan's manufacturing sector accelerated its moving overseas, while simultaneously accelerating the development of the tertiary sector. Since the 1980s, Japan's leading industries could be summarized as electrical machinery (communications equipment), general machinery, transportation machinery (sedan), and chemistry. However, after entering the 1990s, output from these leading industries had some minor changes. The shrinking trend of growth as well as the appreciation of the yen made the leading industries lose their competitive advantages on the international market. In order to reverse this situation, the Japanese manufacturing industry started to outsource jobs overseas to cut cost. This led to a situation in which research and development stages were kept in Japan, while the production stage was shifted overseas. After the yen was appreciated, electricity, gas and other service industries developed; the growth rate of the tertiary sector in the 1990s was significantly higher than that of the primary and secondary sectors, and the proportion of the tertiary sector in the GDP increased.

C. Development of the information industry after the recession period (1998 to the present)

Japan's economy began to decline in 1996 and became a serious matter in 1998, and the domestic economy fell into a serious financial crisis. The Asian financial and economic crisis, which began in the second half of 1997 had a negative impact on Japan's economy and the yen, and weakened the competitiveness of Japan's foreign trade. Coupled with the launch of the euro in 1999, Japan's economy had received great shock, and a new round of adjustments in industrial policies was imperative. During this period, the Japanese government's task was to continue to accelerate the development and growth of the tertiary sector and knowledge-intensive industries on the basis of the previous stage and ultimately make the information industry the leading industry in the new period and a driving force of economic growth. The rapid development of Japan's information industry was mainly due to the government's macro-control, the adoption of industrial policies tilting toward it, coupled with a variety of economic instruments. Back in 1994, MITI and the Ministry of the Post Office put forward the plan for the construction of the nationwide information and communications infrastructure, namely, the information superhighway. In the late 1990s, Japan was more aware of the importance of the information industry and introduced a variety of policies and measures to accelerate its development. The government also adopted a series of preferential policies in finance, credit, taxation, prices, trade and others to enact the development of its information industry with strong economic fundamentals and great impetus.

③ The evolution of the industrial policy of the leading industries of R.O. Korea in different stages of economic development

Since the 1960s, R.O. Korea has undergone the adjustment of the industrial structure of importation substitution, of the export-oriented structural sophistication of the heavy chemical industry and the development of technology-intensive industries, which mainly relied on the government's support for the development of large enterprises.

During the first phase (1962–1971), based on the advantage of its labor resources, the government implemented a strategy of export-oriented development, and focused on the development of the light industry and other labor-intensive industries. R.O. Korea seized the favorable opportunity in the 1960s when the United States, Japan and other developed countries strove to develop capital-intensive industries and shifted the labor-intensive industries to developing countries, and developed the labor-intensive industries, which were mainly textile industries. It took advantage of abundant labor resources, low wages and higher quality of labor, and developed itself into an important contractor of labor-intensive industries, which made its economy grow quickly in a short time.

The second phase (1972–1981) was the developmental stage of the heavy chemical industry. In the 1970s, the industrial structure of R.O. Korea changed into the heavy chemical industry and continued to expand, and the heavy chemical industry achieved rapid development. At the beginning of the development of the heavy chemical industry in R.O. Korea, it was to achieve the substitution of the importation of capital and equipment, but with labor shortages and rising wages, which were caused by the rapid development of labor-intensive export-oriented industries, as well as the economic recession, the strengthening of trade protection in the late 1970s in major Western countries, and the price competition in developing countries, its exportation of the labor-intensive textile industry became limited. R.O. Korea was in a great urgency to change the export-oriented situation, which was based on labor-intensive industries. R.O. Korea seized the opportunity in which developed countries transferred their capital-intensive heavy chemical industries to emerging developing countries and started to upgrade from labor-intensive industries to capital-intensive industries. The heavy chemical industry, which was led by the government, reached its intended target in 1980, and the proportion of the heavy chemical industry in the manufacturing sector rose to over 50%.

The third phase (1982–1991) was when the adjustment of its industrial structure began to shift to technology-intensive industries. In the 1980s, its exports faced three major challenges: Trade protectionism was rising in developed countries, the competition between the newly industrialized countries and regions became more intense, and the gap between the developing countries in the labor-intensive products got narrower and narrower. Therefore, the government upgraded the technology of the traditional heavy chemical industry, and formed its main export industry. At the same time, the government supported the fine chemical industry, those of precision instruments, computers, electronic machinery, aerospace and other strategic industries, and regarded the information, new materials, bio-engineering and other emerging industries as industries to be developed positively in the future.

We reviewed adjustment of China's, Japan's, and R.O. Korea's industrial structure and the industrial policy of different stages as well as the leading industries formed thereby. We can see that the development of a country's industrial structure is influenced by various factors and constraints. In addition to objective factors, the government's conscious adjustment through industrial policy has played a considerable role in the development of the industrial structure. The evolution of the adjustment of the industrial structure and the leading industries also reflects the interaction and influence among the three countries.

(2) The interaction of the adjustment and upgrading of China's, Japan's, and R.O. Korea's industrial structure

After World War II, the East Asian economy experienced a phase of rapid growth. Viewing from the economic development in East Asia, from the postwar period to the early 1990s, the international community had witnessed four waves of industrial restructuring and transmission. Because the participating countries (regions) and the areas of economic interconnections were different, the overall scope was expanded naturally, and it presented a global evolution at different levels (see Figure 10.1). The evolution of the industrial structure in China, Japan, and R.O. Korea is also subject to the evolution of the mechanism of industrial division among various countries and regions of East Asia.

1950s	America → Japan (capital-intensive industries)

↓

1960s	America → Japan (technology-intensive industries) Japan, America, "the Four Asian Dragons" (labor-intensive industries and some capital-intensive industries)

↓

1970s	America ⟷ Japan (technology-intensive industries) Japan, America→ "the Four Asian Tigers" (labor-intensive industries) Japan, America, "the Four Asian Dragons" →"the Four ASEAN Tigers" (labor-intensive industries)

↓

The middle and late 1980s	America ⟷ Japan (creativity, knowledge-intensive industries) Japan, America→ "the Four Asian Dragons"(standardization capital and technology-intensive industries) Japan, America, "the Four Asian Dragons" →"the Four ASEAN Tigers" (labor-intensive, some low-capital and technology-intensive industries)

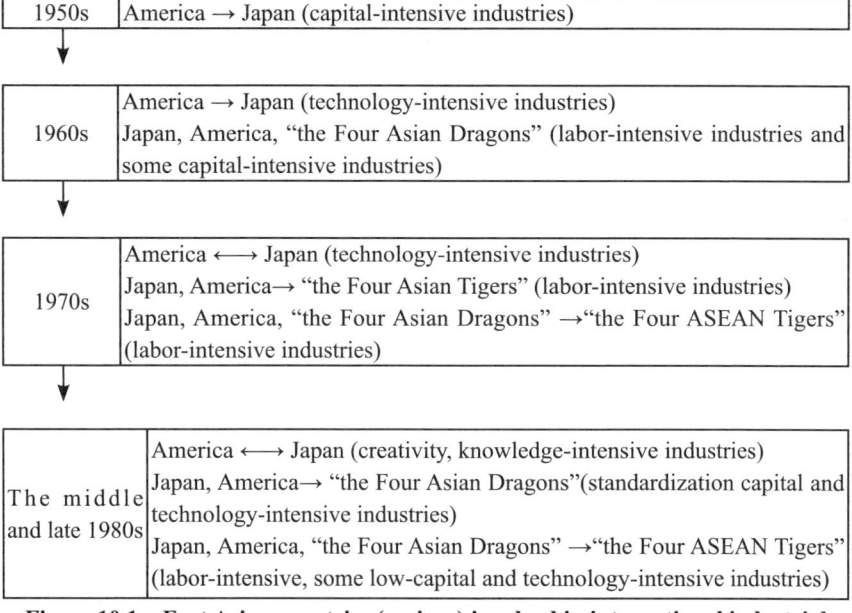

Figure 10.1 East Asian countries (regions) involved in international industrial adjustment and transmission waves in the postwar years

Source: Wang Bin. *The Internationalization of Contemporary Industrial Structure: Effects of Globalization.* Beijing: China Social Sciences Press, 2004: 71.

From 1950, as the country with the strongest modern industrial base in East Asia, Japan quickly accepted industrial transfer from the US, and actively supported steel, chemical and other capital-intensive industries. It first achieved industrialization and gradually carried out industrial upgrading. In the 1960s, R.O. Korea and other newly industrialized East Asian countries (regions) absorbed textile, clothing, food, groceries and other labor-intensive industries, which were transferred from Japan due to the Japanese industrial upgrading by taking advantage of the accumulation of industrial bases and the labor advantages of the 1950s. In addition, during this period, R.O. Korea also actively supported the development of the industries such as steel, chemical, civil machinery household appliances and other heavy industries for the substitution of importations. Since the 1980s, due to rapid economic development, the advantages of cheap labor in the Four Asian Tigers were weakened, while the Four ASEAN and the Chinese mainland, which had more comparative labor advantages, gradually took over the labor-intensive industrial transfer. China's eastern coastal areas at this stage began to join the adjustment of the East Asian industrial structure. Through industrial restructuring, the Four Asian Tigers vigorously undertook and introduced part of the capital-intensive industries from the United States, Japan and other developed countries, such as shipbuilding, steel and so on. After the 1980s, as the source of the East Asian industrial transfer, Japan developed and popularized the technology, knowledge and technology-intensive industries. At the same time, it further transferred the capital- and labor-intensive industries and part of low-value-added technology-intensive industries, which lost the comparative advantages to the Four Asian Tigers and ASEAN, the Chinese mainland and other countries (regions). Other East Asian countries (regions), according to their comparative advantages and their level of development, achieved a reasonable flow of international industrial capital within the region of East Asia. Thus, a flying geese picture in which Japan was the "leading goose" of East Asian economic development and industrial restructuring and upgrading was sketched out, and this led to the formation of a stepped industrial division system of technology-intensive and high-value-added industries → capital- and technology-intensive industries → labor-intensive industries.

Through industrial restructuring and the transfer to East Asia, we can see that Japan has always been the cradle of restructuring and transfer in East Asia, and acts as a protagonist in the process of restructuring and transfer; it plays an important role in the restructuring and the chain of changes of the East Asian countries (regions). It should also be noted that in the waves of international industrial restructuring and transfer in the postwar years, the functions and the roles of various countries and regions in this area are not isolated but interactive with and reciprocal to one another. In the process of adjustment of Japan, which is the source of ongoing industrial upgrading, it is necessary for a country (region) to absorb the industrial transfer of the adjustment in time; otherwise, it would be difficult to achieve a trouble-free upgrading. The emptiness of the international market caused by the industrial transfer of a leading country has become an important factor for the sophistication of a backward country's industrial structure. It is in such interaction that the industrial structure of these countries (regions), which are at different stages of development, is able to form an interdependent holistic evolution.

10.2.3 The Competitiveness and Convergence of the Industrial Structures of China, Japan, and R.O. Korea

China, Japan, and R.O. Korea have vast areas of land, abundant resources, and a large population; they also have similar languages, cultures and the resources needed for economic development, and they are themselves huge markets as well. They are highly economically complementary. Before the 1980s, the three countries essentially had a single vertical international division of labor, where Japan mainly supplied the technology and manufactured goods, while China and R.O. Korea provided raw materials and primary products. In the mid- and late 1980s, the accelerated pace of China's reform and opening-up and the rapid economic development of China along with the rise of a newly industrialized country, R.O. Korea, not only improved the level of the market in China and R.O. Korea, but also made the regional industrial division increasingly refined. It improved the overall standards and caused them to become linked more closely as well. Japan is a developed country, which has the capital, technology and other advantages, and R.O. Korea is an emerging industrialized country, which also has certain financial and technical advantages. When compared to Japan and R.O. Korea, China is a country with extensive resources, a rich labor force, and a large market. The economic structure makes them depend on each other strongly.

We can see from the above analysis that the development of the industrial structure of China, Japan, and R.O. Korea is mutually complementary and interrelated. At the same time, along with the economic development of China and R.O. Korea and the acceleration of industrial restructuring and upgrading, there was a certain degree of competition among the three countries. The analysis of the three countries' competitiveness from the perspective of revealed comparative advantage is as follows.

B. Balassa put forward the concept of revealed comparative advantage in 1965. It compares the proportion of exports of a commodity in total exports and the proportion of the trade of this commodity in the total volume of the world's trade. It can be formulated as: $RCAik=(X_{ik}/X_i)/(W_k/W)$, and RCA_{ik} stands for the comparative advantage index of the commodity k of country i, X_{ik} is the exports of k, X_i is the total exports of i, W_k represents the total world exports of k, W represents the total world exports of all commodities. If RCA_{ik} is greater than 1, it indicates that the country's exports of commodities are relatively concentrated, and the country has a comparative advantage in this commodity; if RCA_{ik} is less than 1, the situation is the opposite.

China, Japan, and R.O. Korea's comparative advantage index, which is calculated according to the 2009 WTO International Trade Statistics is shown in Table 10.3.

Table 10.3　China, Japan, and R.O. Korea's major industries' comparative advantage index

Item	2003			2006		
	China	Japan	R.O. Korea	China	Japan	R.O. Korea
Agricultural products	0.45	0.10	0.20	0.33	0.11	0.19
Aquatic products	1.49	0.24	0.63	1.32	0.31	0.40
Iron and steel	0.44	1.53	1.62	1.05	1.45	1.52
Chemical products	0.41	0.75	0.80	0.43	0.84	0.92
Electronic products	2.08	1.47	2.54	2.41	1.25	2.09
Automobile	0.08	2.19	1.20	0.17	2.50	1.54
Mechanical products	0.96	1.59	0.88	1.07	1.73	1.05
Textiles	2.61	0.58	2.37	2.64	0.56	1.63
Clothing	3.75	0.03	0.59	3.79	0.03	0.26

Source: Calculated according to the WTO International Trade Statistics 2009.

We can see from the results that there is a big difference among the comparative advantages in China, Japan, and R.O. Korea. China's comparative advantage is labor-intensive products. From 2003 to 2006, the comparative advantage index of labor-intensive products such as textiles and clothing was above 2.5, and cheap labor was a major source of China's export advantages. A study found that China's resource-intensive products experienced a rise in the initial period of reform and opening-up and have gradually declined since 1990, indicating that the primary products' exports such as agricultural products and minerals were not the most important sources of China's foreign trade income. Correspondingly, with the continuous development of China's manufacturing industry, manufacturing products became pillars of China's exports. However, from the data analysis, we can find that in recent years, comparative advantages of labor-intensive products in China have declined, while the comparative advantages of technology-intensive products have had a certain degree of growth. For instance, during the period of 2003–2006, the comparative advantage index of China's electronics industry remained above 2, and showed a certain degree of increase. It had certain comparative advantages theoretically. But in recent years, as can be seen from the constitution of Chinese exports, most of them have been assembled by using cheap labor, and have relied on the labor resources of high-tech products rather than high-tech innovation. In general, the element of comparative advantage is still labor.

Japan's comparative advantage is concentrated on technology-intensive products. According to the technological level, the comparative advantage of low and intermediate technology-intensive products, such as steel, ships, automobiles and machinery, is more significant, while the advantage of high-tech-intensive products is slightly weaker than the first two products, such as communications and aircraft manufacturing. This is because Japan's major research strengths lie in applied technology rather than research-related technology. Japan's comparative advantage of labor-intensive and resource-intensive products is small. For example, the change of the comparative advantage index of agricultural products is small, which remained at around 0.1, while the comparative advantage index of textiles, clothing and other labor-intensive products is declining. Analyzing from capital and technology, Japan's capital and technology have a large comparative advantage, which acts as the key driving force in promoting the economic development of the country.

Compared with China and Japan, on the whole, R.O. Korea's resource-intensive products do not have a comparative advantage, which fully shows that R.O. Korea has entered the intermediate period of industrialization. R.O. Korea's labor-intensive products were competitive products in history. Before 1990, the comparative advantage of labor-intensive products in R.O. Korea was even higher than that of China. However, with the rise in labor costs in R.O. Korea, the country's labor-intensive industries began to move out. R.O. Korea's foreign direct investment in the 1990s was concentrated on garments, textiles and other labor-intensive industries. R.O. Korea had certain comparative advantages in low-technology-intensive products such as iron and steel. In particular, R.O. Korea's industry with comparative advantage is the electronic communication industry, including mobile phones, LCD panels, and digital cameras. Telecommunication companies, which are represented by Samsung and LG have become the mainstays of R.O. Korea's telecommunications industry. Their advanced technology and the speed of manufacturing new products are praiseworthy for every nation. From the above analysis, by undertaking industrial transfer, R.O. Korea obtained power in the development of the flying geese pattern. By using their comparative advantages to achieve industrial upgrading, they could have a world-class level of industrial development in certain areas. Compared with China, R.O. Korea is at a higher level in the international division of labor. The industries of China and R.O. Korea are highly complementary, but compared with Japan, there is still a lack of capability for overall R&D, and the application of technology is also limited. We can definitely say that China, Japan, and R.O. Korea are in different positions in the international division of labor.

10.3 Analysis of the Mechanism of Adjustment, Upgrading, and Interaction of the Industrial Structures of China, Japan, and R.O. Korea

10.3.1 Promotion of Interaction of the Industrial Structure Due to Mutual Trade Development in the Region

(1) Impacts of the development of mutual trade on the interaction of industrial structure

International comparative advantage is based on the production factors of each country (region). When a country (region) intensively uses production factors, which are relatively abundant and thus cheaper than those in other countries, because of its comparatively low cost, on the one hand, it will guide the country to choose certain types of combinations of factors in the choice of industrial structure (such as labor-intensive or capital-intensive or other types); on the other hand, the specialized production in a low cost environment has a relatively favorable position in international trade, which is conducive to domestic industrial structural changes and adjustments in turn. There are generally two ways in international trade that international comparative advantage mechanisms promote change in the industrial structure of the country (region): First, developing countries mainly import one or a few products to develop the domestic market. When the industry is developed to a certain extent, the economies of scale can be fully reflected, and production costs decrease significantly. Then, using relatively low labor costs in developing countries to produce and export the products, comparative advantage can be obtained, and through the development of international markets, the industry can be developed further. Second, different from newly emerging countries (regions), the industrial structure of leading countries (regions) is on the basis of structural balance. Depending on the capacity for advanced production, the leading countries (regions) can always be in a good position in international trade so as to promote domestic industrial structural transformation and upgrading. In import and export trade, by developing new products at home, the leading countries can form the domestic market so as to promote the development of the industry. When the domestic market is saturated, it can explore the international market and implement exportation, and with the formation of foreign markets, related technology and capital can be further exported. When overseas production capacity is formed, it can transform this product to the domestic market at a lower price in order to promote the contraction of the domestic industry and force it to develop other new products. Such a cycle motivates the country (region) to transform and upgrade its industrial structure.

(2) Development of the mutual trade in the region deepens interdependence of industries among China, Japan, and R.O. Korea

After the 1980s, especially since the mid-1980s, an important change that took place in the development of foreign trade for China, Japan, and R.O. Korea was that mutual trade of the region was expanded and intra-regional trade dependence among the countries has increased rapidly. This promotes interdependence in the whole evolution of the various industrial structures within the region.

China, Japan, and R.O. Korea play important roles in world importation and exportation; about 15% of the world's total exports and 13% of the world's total imports are concentrated in these economies. Meanwhile, the three countries are also important trading partners with each other. Especially since the 1980s, intra-regional trade continues to develop among China, Japan, and R.O. Korea. In 2007, China overtook the United States and became Japan's largest trading partner; in 2009, China became the largest trading partner, largest export destination, and largest source of imports of R.O. Korea.

Figure 10.2 reflects the development of the mutual trade of China, Japan, and R.O. Korea since the mid-1990s. The rapid development of the economic and trade relations is related to the economic development of the three countries and the background of world economic regionalization on the one hand. On the other hand, the labor-intensive industries in Japan and R.O. Korea transfer to the Chinese mainland at a faster pace. As everyone knows, in the postwar years, which is a particular historical period, the United States, which is the most developed country in the Asia-Pacific region, established close political and economic relations with East Asia, so East Asian countries (regions), including Japan and R.O. Korea, had relied on the US market over a fairly long time after World War II. Since the reform and opening-up of China, the United States has become China's major export market with the enhancement of the export capacity of China. But with the Northeast Asian economic development, the trade surplus continued to accumulate, forming a huge trade deficit for the United States. In this context, the United States could not tolerate the economic expansion of Japan, followed by that of certain emerging countries of Asia. As a result, it regulated its trade deficit by forcing the Japanese yen to appreciate, canceling general preferential tariffs system for R.O. Korea, and creating trade barriers. As a result, since 1986, the growth rate of Japan and R.O. Korea's exportations to the United States slowed and the proportion of trade declined. Meanwhile, in addition to exploring international markets outside the United States, Japan and R.O. Korea also explored the market in the region actively, so that the mutual trade in this region expanded rapidly. It can be seen from Table 10.4

10 Discussion on the Development of Regional Economic Integration

that from 1985 to 2005, China, Japan, and R.O. Korea's value of trade increased from USD 66.39 billion to USD 219.68 billion; the proportion of intra-regional trade in the total volume of trade also increased significantly. At the same time, the proportion of trade with the United States in the overall value of trade showed an upward trend.

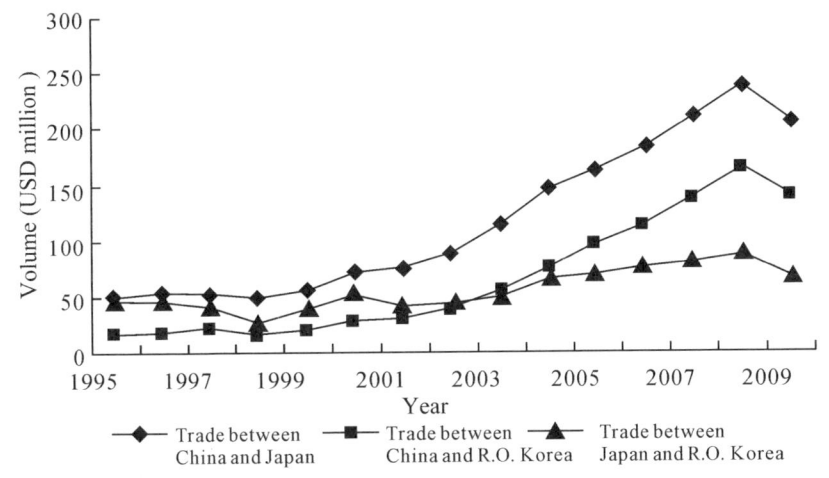

Figure 10.2 Trade among China, Japan, and R.O. Korea 1995—2009
Source: Based on *China Statistical Yearbook* over the years.

Table 10.4 Trade within China, Japan, and R.O. Korea, and their trade with the US

Item	1985		2005	
	Export	Import	Export	Import
Total trade of the three countries (USD billion)	234.81	204.06	1641.3	1436.1
Trade of the three countries with the United States (USD billion)	28.91	37.83	340.82	143.23
The proportion of the trade of the three countries to the United States	33.6%	18.5%	58.9%	31.7%
Trade within the region (USD billion)	31.62	34.77	101.64	118.04
The proportion of intra-regional trade	13.5%	17%	13.7%	21.1%

Source: *Direction of Trade*, KOTIS, 2000; *International Statistical Yearbook 2009*.

(3) Increase in the score of intra-regional trade propensity indicates that the institutional corelation of intra-regional markets is deepening

The intra-regional trade development and the increase in trade dependence could be seen as the inevitable result of the economic development of the three countries, especially China's economic growth. However, as can be seen from the study about factors that influence the trend in trade, the growth rate of intra-regional trade among China, Japan, and R.O. Korea is not proportional to the simultaneous increase in the economy, but shows a geographical preference, which has a greater impact than the economic growth rate. When the trade proportion in the region gradually increases, trade propensity will increase. As is shown in Table 10.5, China, Japan, and R.O. Korea's trade propensity score changed from 0.12 in 1988 to 0.20 in 1998, to 0.26 in 2008, thereby showing an upward trend. If including the transit trade with Hong Kong and Taiwan of China, the score of intra-regional trade propensity over the same period would increase from 0.25 to 0.45. Compared with other regions, after the 1990s, the score of trade propensity of China, Japan and R.O. Korea grows faster than that of the EU (0.34–0.49) and NAFTA (0.15–0.22). This shows that the trade dependence of China, Japan, and R.O. Korea on the market within the region increases more rapidly than other regions, so the institutional corelation of the market is growing rapidly as well.

Table 10.5 Changes of the score of the intra-regional trade propensity compared with other regions

Economies	1988	1993	1998	2008
China, Japan, and R.O. Korea	0.12	0.12	0.20	0.26
Japan, R.O. Korea, the Chinese mainland and Hong Kong and Taiwan of China	0.25	0.24	0.36	0.45
EU (15 countries)	0.34	0.35	0.42	0.49
NAFTA (3 countries)	0.15	0.18	0.23	0.22

Source: Data are calculated according to each year's data of the IMP, DOT, and IFS.

(4) The reflection of the adjustment of the industrial structure of the countries in trade structure changes

The regional trade development of China, Japan, and R.O. Korea is not only shown on the expansion of mutual trade and the enhancement of the score of trade propensity; more importantly, it is reflected in the changes in trade structure. As the international trade exchange is based on international comparative advantage, a country exports its own products that have a comparative advantage, and imports products whose price on the international market is lower than production costs and that can meet domestic production and consumption demand. Changes in the domestic industrial structure of China, Japan, and R.O. Korea affect each other through international trade, and are also reflected by changes in the commodity structure in international trade.

① The change in the structure of commodities in the mutual trade among China, Japan, and R.O. Korea

Table 10.6 lists the top 10 commodities in China-Japan trade in 2008 and 2009 as well as the proportion of trade of each commodity in the total amount of China-Japan trade. In 2008 and 2009, mechanical and electrical products ranked first. Compared to 2008, the export volume and the proportion of furniture, toys, and miscellaneous products increased in 2009, while the export volume of base metals and products declined slightly and the ranking of the exportations of minerals dropped significantly. Meanwhile, the rankings of food, beverages, and tobacco, and leatherware and bags rose rapidly. Compared to 2008, the ranking remained the same in Japan's exports to China in 2009, but there were still subtle differences, such as the ranking of textiles and raw materials, which changed with that of minerals, and the proportion of minerals, which were imported from Japan, declined from 4.0% in 2008 to 1.9% in 2009.

The structure of the commodities of trade between China and R.O. Korea (see Table 10.7) changed more significantly. In addition to a decline in the proportion of base metals and products and minerals, the proportion of almost all of the commodities increased in China's exportations to R.O. Korea; in R.O. Korea's exports to China in 2009, mechanical and electrical products, optical equipment, clocks and watches, and medical equipment and chemical products were still on the top, whereas rankings of minerals, leatherware and bags went down, but those of furniture, toys, and miscellaneous products rose at the same time.

Because the information about 2005 could not be found, Table 10.8

lists the changes in the structure of commodities of trade between Japan and R.O. Korea in 1995 and 2000. According to the statistics of the International Trade Association of R.O. Korea in 2000, in all categories of commodities, the commodity of the largest trade volume was mechanical equipment, accounting for 46.95% of the total bilateral trade, followed by metals and metalware, chemical industrial products, minerals, optical metrology instruments and so on. Compared with 1995, the biggest improvement in proportion in R.O. Korea's exports to Japan was in the exportation of mineral fuels and products, mechanical appliances, plastic products and so on in 2000; as for importations, the most significant change was the proportion of electrical and electric equipment, which increased considerably. However, only negligible changes were seen in the other categories.

Table 10.6 Structural changes in 10 major commodities in China-Japan trade

China's exports to Japan				China's imports from Japan			
2008		2009		2008		2009	
Mechanical and electrical products	37.2%	Mechanical and electrical products	37.6%	Mechanical and electrical products	42.8%	Mechanical and electrical products	41.1%
Textiles and raw materials	17.0%	Textiles and raw materials	20.0%	Base metals and products	13.3%	Base metals and products	13.2%
Base metals and products	6.8%	Furniture, toys and miscellaneous products	7.2%	Chemical products	8.4%	Chemical products	9.4%
Furniture, toys, and miscellaneous products	6.6%	Base metals and products	4.7%	Transportation equipment	7.4%	Transportation equipment	9.3%
Chemical products	5.3%	Chemical products	4.1%	Plastic and rubber	5.8%	Plastic and rubber	6.5%
Minerals	3.7%	Food, beverages, and tobacco	3.5%	Optical equipment, watches, and clocks, and medical equipment	5.6%	Optical equipment, watches, and clocks, and medical equipment	6.0%

(To be continued)

(Continued)

China's exports to Japan				China's imports from Japan			
2008		2009		2008		2009	
Optical equipment, watches and clocks, and medical equipment	3.3%	Shoes, boots, umbrellas and other light industrial products	3.2%	Minerals	4.0%	Textiles and raw materials	2.7%
Plastic and rubber	3.0%	Plastic and rubber	3.2%	Textiles and raw materials	2.7%	Minerals	1.9%
Food, beverages, and tobacco	2.9%	Optical equipment, watches, and clocks, and medical equipment	3.1%	Cellulose pulp and paper	1.3%	Cellulose pulp and paper	1.4%
Shoes, boots, umbrellas and other light industrial products	2.8%	Leatherware and bags	2.4%	Ceramics and glass	1.0%	Ceramics and glass	1.1%

Source: The Chinese Academy of International Trade and Economic Cooperation of the Ministry of Commerce.

Table 10.7 Structural changes in 10 major commodities in China-R.O. Korea trade

China's exports to R.O. Korea				China's imports from R.O. Korea			
2008		2009		2008		2009	
Mechanical and electrical products	35.9%	Mechanical and electrical products	44.1%	Mechanical and electrical products	38.9%	Mechanical and electrical products	39.2%
Base metals and metal products	26.6%	Base metals and metal products	15.5%	Optical equipment, watches and clocks, and medical equipment	13.5%	Optical equipment, watches and clocks, and medical equipment	17.2%

(To be continued)

(Continued)

China's exports to R.O. Korea				China's imports from R.O. Korea			
2008		2009		2008		2009	
Textiles and raw materials	6.7%	Textiles and raw materials	7.2%	Chemical products	12.3%	Chemical products	11.2%
Minerals	6.3%	Chemical products	6.8%	Minerals	9.9%	Plastic and rubber	9.0%
Chemical products	6.0%	Minerals	3.7%	Base metals and products	8.4%	Base metals and products	8.5%
Optical equipment, watches and clocks, and medical equipment	2.8%	Optical equipment, watches and clocks, and medical equipment	3.5%	Plastic and rubber	7.9%	Minerals	5.9%
Furniture, toys, and miscellaneous products	2.5%	Ceramics and glass	3.0%	Transportation equipment	3.8%	Transportation equipment	4.0%
Ceramics and glass	2.4%	Transportation equipment	2.9%	Textiles and raw materials	2.8%	Textiles and raw materials	2.6%
Transportation equipment	2.0%	Furniture, toys and miscellaneous products	2.9%	Cellulose pulp	0.5%	Cellulose pulp	0.5%
Plastic and rubber	1.8%	Plastic and rubber	2.1%	Leatherware and bags	0.4%	Furniture, toys, and miscellaneous products	0.4%

Source: The Chinese Academy of International Trade and Economic Cooperation of the Ministry of Commerce.

Table 10.8   Structural changes in 10 major commodities in Japan-R.O. Korea trade

China's exports to R.O. Korea				China's imports from R.O. Korea			
1995		2000		1995		2000	
Electrical and electric equipment	27.3%	Electrical and electric equipment	22.4%	Nuclear reactor mechanical apparatus	27.7%	Electrical and electric equipment	31.1%

(To be continued)

(Continued)

China's exports to R.O. Korea				China's imports from R.O. Korea			
1995		2000		1995		2000	
Iron and steel	9.4%	Fossil fuels and products	17.9%	Electrical and electric equipment	23.6%	Nuclear reactor mechanical apparatus	20.6%
Knitting and crocheted clothing	6.7%	Nuclear reactor mechanical apparatus	17.0%	Optical photographic equipment and parts	8.9%	Optical photographic equipment and parts	8.9%
Fossil fuels and products	5.4%	Iron and steel	5.6%	Iron and steel	6.6%	Iron and steel	8.3%
Fish and aquatic animals	5.3%	Fish and aquatic animals	4.0%	Organic chemicals	5.4%	Organic chemicals	4.8%
Nuclear reactor mechanical apparatus	5.2%	Knitting and crocheted clothing	3.4%	Plastic and products	3.2%	Plastic and products	3.6%
Other clothing	3.0%	Plastic and products	3.4%	Vehicles and spare parts	2.4%	Miscellaneous chemical products	2.5%
Iron and steel products	2.9%	Organic chemicals	1.9%	Fossil fuels and products	1.9%	Vehicles and spare parts	2.0%
Leather products	2.6%	Iron and steel products	1.9%	Miscellaneous chemical products	1.7%	Copper and products	1.3%
Plastic and products	2.2%	Optical photographic equipment and parts	1.2%	Iron and steel products	1.7%	Photographic and film products	1.3%

Source: KOITS data (2003).

② Analysis of the characteristics and reasons for the structure of the commodities in mutual trade among China, Japan, and R.O. Korea

As can be seen from the horizontal comparison of the structure of the commodities of trade among China, Japan, and R.O. Korea, the three countries' commodity trade has the following features: First, whether it is importations or exportations, electrical and electric equipment accounts for the largest proportion of all trade; second, the top 10 commodities in the mutual trade among the three countries are similar in types, which clearly shows the main content of the mutual trade; third, intra-industry trade has become the mainstream of the development of the trade among the three countries; fourth, the structure of China-Japan trade and that of China-R.O. Korea trade show signs of development from vertical trade to horizontal trade, while the structure of trade between Japan and R.O. Korea has clearer characteristics of horizontal trade. Vertical trade here means the advanced countries in the conventional sense export manufactured goods and key components to the backward countries, and import raw materials or fuels from these backward countries; horizontal trade refers to the trade between countries at a roughly similar level of development, including inter-industry trade and intra-industry trade at comparable levels.

These features exist, on the one hand, because the three countries are at different levels of economic development and have different endowments and advantages, as well as the differences in the varieties of the imported and exported goods, which are caused by the production and consumption demand in the domestic market. For example, from 1995 to 2005, China's increase in imported manufacturing equipment was largely due to its industrial restructuring and the expansion of construction investment, which was caused by the integration of social capital. On the other hand, the convergence of the three countries' main trade categories and the significant increase in the proportion of intra-industry trade are directly related to the expansion of mutual investment among the three countries. The adjustment of the structure of domestic industries of Japan and R.O. Korea requires the countries to transfer those industries that have lost the competitive advantage abroad, or set up those manufacturing processes which are at the low end of the industrial chain in China where the cost is relatively low. Overall, the three countries have a large overlap in the field of intra-industry trade, which is also a reflection of a more detailed international division. It should be noted that the rise of intra-industry trade indicates the promotion of a country's trade competitiveness. In this sense, China's trade competitiveness has been greatly improved. At the same time, it is worth noting that in contemporary international trade, the cost of industrial restructuring which is based on intra-industry trade is lower than that which is based on inter-industry trade, and the former also exerts a smaller impact on the domestic labor market. China can take advantage of favorable international conditions to implement the positive adjustment of the country's industrial structure and promote the development of China's foreign trade by expanding the scope of intra-industry and further exploring its depth.

The expansion of mutual trade and the increase in trade dependency within the region of China, Japan, and R.O. Korea not only reflect the increasingly close economic and trade ties between the countries in the region, but also show the deepening of interaction and interdependence in each country's evolution of industrial structure within the region. From the point of international trade, which is a link that connects the mutual effect of the industrial structure of each country, particularly from the content of the mutual trade, the trade in intermediate goods is increasing, and the structure of the trade is constantly changing. This means that the structural interaction conducted through trade relations is strengthening, and it also means that the impact of one country's industrial restructuring on other countries is increasing.

10.3.2 Analysis of the Role of Regional Direct Investment and Industrial Transfer in the Interaction of Industrial Structure

(1) The action mechanism of regional direct investment on the interaction of industrial structure

As another basic mechanism that links the interaction of the countries' industrial structure within the region, international direct investment has a compound conduction effect on the change in industrial structure, and it usually connects the visible and invisible effects. In practical operations, foreign direct investment uses the multinational companies as a carrier, directly uses other countries' comparative advantage on the basis of international division, and directly goes deep into other countries' industrial structure. Foreign direct investment could stimulate the exports of capital goods and of the investing country, which not only promotes the development of trade, but also deeply affects the economic growth and structural changes of the host country. In addition, foreign direct investment is also the carrier of international human capital flow and international technology transfer. It can promote the quality of labor and the level of management and production technology in the invested nation, thus indirectly promoting the economic growth and structural change of the host country. It is in this sense that direct investment makes the connection between countries' industrial structure closer and deepens interaction and influence.

(2) The development of mutual investment among China, Japan, and R.O. Korea deepens the interdependence and interaction of the industrial structure of the three countries

From the developmental status of mutual investment among China, Japan, and R.O. Korea, Japan's investments in China and R.O. Korea account for a considerable proportion of its foreign investments. Especially since the 1980s, the amount of investments has increased sharply. In the same period, R.O. Korea took advantage of the favorable opportunity when Japan expanded its foreign direct investment and accelerated transferring industries that had lost their comparative advantage abroad. On the one hand, it absorbed a large scale of investment from Japan and transferred the focus of attracting foreign investment from labor-intensive and capital-intensive industries to technology-intensive and knowledge-intensive industries; on the other hand, it transferred those labor-intensive industries that had lost their comparative advantage to Southeast Asian countries and the Chinese mainland, which had lower labor and raw material costs. And R.O. Korea had a rapid increase in foreign direct investment and had caught up with Japan. Therefore, the direct investment that used the multinational companies of Japan and R.O. Korea as carriers deepened the interdependence and interaction of the countries within the region in the evolution of industrial structure.

Japan's direct investment in China began in the 1980s, and since the 1990s, it has begun to reach a climax. Faced with this situation, the Japanese government adopted policies to encourage those sunset industries to invest in China, and the government offered a lot of support on formalities, insurance and so on to companies. As for investment in high-tech industries in China, the government neither encouraged it nor restricted it. This raised the Japanese firms' enthusiasm for direct investment in China; in 1997, Japan's direct investment in China reached a peak of USD 4.33 billion. After 1997, due to the impact of the Asian financial crisis, the Japanese government worried that its leading position in Asia would be challenged by China, so it began to restrict some high-tech industries' investment in China. Subsequently, Japanese companies' direct investment in China declined somewhat and declined to USD 2.9 billion in 2000, which accounted for 7.2% of China's utilization of foreign capital. After entering the 21st century, with the rapid growth of China's economy and the constant expansion of the consumption market, a new boom emerged in Japan's investment in China, and China's proportion in Japan's foreign direct investment increased rapidly, from 2.2% in 2000 to 8.7% in 2003. According to statistics from the Department of Foreign Investment Administration of China's Ministry of Commerce, in 2005, the Japanese firms' investment in China increased sharply. The amount of investment was up to USD 6.529 billion, an increase of 20% over 2004; this accounted for 10.82% of total foreign direct investment in China that year. This set a new record for Japan's investment in China after 8 years. In 2006, Japan's direct investment in China declined significantly, dropping by 29.6% compared with 2005. In general, after the large decline of the previous year, there should have been a rebound, but this phenomenon did not appear in the next year. In 2007, the number of Japan's investment projects in China was 1,974, a year-on-year decline of 23.8%; the actual amount received was USD 3.59 billion in place, a year-on-year decline of 22.0%. In 2008, there was a weak growth of 1.7%. Until 2009, Japan's total investment in China reached USD 4.117 billion, a year-on-year increase of 15%, which showed a good momentum of recovery.

Despite a late start, R.O. Korea's investment in China developed rapidly. In 1998, China became R.O. Korea's largest overseas investment destination. R.O. Korea's actual investment in China reached its peak in 2004, up to USD 6.248 billion. The amount of its investment exceeded that of Japan for the first time, and at that time, it was the largest Asian investor in China. In 2005 and 2006, R.O. Korea's investment in China fell slightly to 5.168 and USD 3.894 billion respectively and ranked 4th among countries and regions that had direct investments in China. It is worth noting that R.O. Korea's investment in China continued to decline in recent years, reducing from USD 7.06 billion in 2007 to USD 4.86 billion in 2008 and USD 2.62 billion in 2009, 31.2% and 46% lower than previous years respectively. Especially, the investment in manufacturing continued to decline. According to the R.O. Korean officials, the main reason was that the Chinese government increased investment restrictions, such as the new labor law stipulating that workers who have worked consecutively for more than 10 years or concluded labor contracts more than 3 times, should be offered lifetime employment by companies, and implementation of the total control of environmental pollution in environmental protection and so on.

(3) The fields of investment, the geographical distribution of the investment, and investment strategy present a feature of industrial integration

The international capital flow among China, Japan, and R.O. Korea shows characteristics of significant expansion, fully exploiting comparative advantages, as well as adjusting and integrating intra-regional industrial structure.

① The invested industries are largely concentrated in manufacturing, and the fields of investment present a strong complementarity

R.O. Korea's and Japan's investments in China are mainly concentrated in the manufacturing sector. The data of the State Council Development Research Center (DRC) of the State Council shows that the proportion of funds invested in the manufacturing sector by R.O. Korea and Japan reached 83.91% and 61.71% respectively in 2008. In comparison, the enterprises invested in by R.O. Korea are mainly labor-intensive, while the Japanese-owned companies have a high level of capital intensity. From the perspective of industries, Japan's investment in China is mainly concentrated on the manufacturing industries, which accounts for more than 70% of its total investment in China. Among China's foreign investments absorbed in the manufacturing sector, the Japanese-funded enterprises occupy 12.1% of the total amount. The distribution of Japan's investments in China reflects the trend that Japan's manufacturing industry is getting transferred to China at a faster pace. In recent years, the fields of Japan's direct investment in China are becoming more diverse. After joining the WTO, the domestic service sector of China has been opened up further. The Beijing Olympic Games and the Shanghai World Expo brought tremendous opportunities, which made the construction of urban infrastructures, such as residences and sewers, logistics, environmental protection, education, publishing, and retail become the new hot spots of investment for Japanese companies. With the rapid development of China's high-tech industries, Japanese companies' investment in China's high-tech areas, such as communications, electronics, and bio-pharmaceuticals is increasing.

The main areas of R.O. Korea's investments are toys, footwear, leather, textiles, clothing, electronic and electrical appliances assembly, petrochemicals and other manufacturing and food service industries. In the late 1990s, the investments of huge companies from R.O. Korea in China focused on the automobile, tire, cement, appliances, semiconductors (assembly), iron and steel and other manufacturing industries. In recent years, R.O. Korea's companies have paid more attention to the fields of IT industry, biotechnology, telecommunications, retail, financial services and so on. Overall, the invested industries tend to diversify.
② The geographical distribution of Japan's and R.O. Korea's investment in China reflects a certain degree of industrial agglomeration
The destination of Japan's investments in China has gradually shifted from the coastal areas in the 1990s to Midwest China. In the early 1990s, Japan's companies mainly invested in special economic zones in southern China, such as Shenzhen and Zhuhai, which are adjacent to Hong Kong, and gradually turned to the coastal cities in northeastern and northern

China. A majority of investments were in Jiangsu, followed by Liaoning, Shanghai, Guangdong, and Shandong. The proportion of investments in the coastal areas of China accounted for over 90%, and a major portion was concentrated in big cities. By the late 1990s, in order to narrow the gap between coastal and inland areas, China began to implement a new strategy for economic development in central and western regions, and correspondingly implemented the policy of encouraging foreign investment in the midwest of China. Therefore, Japan started to pay attention to the investment in the midwest of China. In March 1997, the Japanese Association for the Promotion of International Trade set up a committee for investment promotion in that part of China and actively promoted Japanese companies to invest in China's central and western regions.

R.O. Korea's direct investment in China is mainly concentrated in Northeast China, the Shandong Peninsula, and the Bohai Rim, because these areas are located close to R.O. Korea, and have well-developed traffic and convenient transportation. More importantly, many Chinese of Korean nationality live in these areas; they have a common language and similar customs with those of R.O. Korea, which are advantages for R.O. Korea in carrying out enterprise management. Therefore, R.O. Korea's investment which is concentrated on the Bohai Rim and in the northeastern region, accounts for nearly 84.3% of R.O. Korea's investment projects in China, and 68.5% of the amount of investment in China. Although in recent years, its capital has had a tendency to expand in Southern China, and most of it is injected into capital- and technology-intensive investment projects, the Northeast and Bohai Bay area are still the first choice for the investment of R.O. Korea's companies, among which Shandong and Liaoning provinces own the largest proportion of the companies funded by R.O. Korea in China.

In the 21st century, from constructing production bases to expanding the market, Japanese and R.O. Korea's companies have begun to adjust their investment objectives in China, and integrate various manufacturing resources that have already been established in China. The Japanese and R.O. Korean large well-known enterprises' investment in China has effectively promoted the development of interrelated industries in China, and is characterized by geographical concentration. The related industries of upstream, medium-stream and downstream developed through interaction, which deepened the regional industrial cooperation of Northeast Asia.

③ Transnational investment changes from the construction of assembly and processing bases to localization, making the domestic division of labor and production system extend abroad, eventually forming a transnational series of industrial chains

In the initial period of investment in China in the 1990s, the large Japanese and R.O. Korean enterprises mainly regarded China as an export processing base of assembly manufacturing to invest. They exported equipment and spare parts to China, invested in and built factories in China for assembly and processing, and then bought the products back to their own countries or exported to a third country. As a result, the enterprises in China became the parent companies' assembly plants and the processing plants of export products to other countries. But since China's accession to the WTO in 1999, the situation has changed and the capital operation mode has shown a shift toward localization, that is, businesses were set up in China through direct investment, intermediate goods and spare parts were purchased in China, and the products were mainly sold on the Chinese market. The localization of the production of part of the intermediate goods and spare parts carried out by foreign companies made the existing intra-firm trade, intra-industry trade, and the intra-firm related trade transfer to China fairly complete, and accelerated the integration of the production of multinational companies with the local economic development. From the point of the Japanese scholar, Seki Mitsuhiso, in the 1980s, the main purpose of Japan's investment in Asia was "to obtain cheap labor." After entering the 1990s, the characteristics of Japan's direct investments in Asian countries have changed in nature, that is, the companies providing supporting "raw materials and secondary processing sectors" to "the export processing base" began to directly invest in and set up factories in these countries. Now, a group of supporting processing bases with considerable characteristics and strength have been set up in Shenzhen, and other places, as well as in the

Yangtze River Delta around Shanghai and in other places. Forming a pyramid business relationship with the parent company, the serial companies and the subcontractors, the long-term stable transaction has been institutionalized within the enterprise system. This institutionalized long-term trading system could not only reduce the transaction costs, but also make it easy for the company to control the quality of production and the delivery time. Therefore, when the company invests in the overseas markets, which are full of uncertainties, in view of the stable transaction with the upstream and downstream manufacturers, the company would prefer joint investment with serial businesses, or the large enterprises would lead the related enterprises, especially the small and medium-sized enterprises to invest overseas and build an overseas division system, so that the domestic division of labor and systems of production could further extend overseas, and eventually form a serial industrial chain beyond national borders.

④ The constant improvement of the technical level of investment companies and investment projects and the upgrading of the investment structure make the industrial division show a trend that is changing from the traditional vertical integration to horizontal integration

Before the mid- to late 1990s, Japan's and R.O. Korea's investment in China followed the "theory of marginal industrial transfer," that is, the foreign direct investment would start sequentially from the country's industries that have been caught in comparative disadvantage. Japan and R.O. Korea's direct investment in China started with the labor-intensive industries, and the industrial division showed characteristics of vertical distribution. However, with the development of China's industrialization, the industrial structure continues to optimize and upgrade; the technical level is also rising constantly. Meanwhile, the market size in Asia, especially in East Asia has also been expanding; China's position within the market is getting increasingly important; Japan and R.O. Korea's investment in China is also shifting to expansion of both production and the market, and tends to improve the technological level of investment companies and projects, in exchange for the market. The trend of the industrial division developing to horizontal integration is getting more and more significant.

Currently, the gap in basic technology and special technical fields among China, Japan, and R.O. Korea is not great, but there still exists a great gap in the intermediate technologies that connects the two, such as production technology, assembly technology, and manufacturing technology of various standard modules. This difference provides room for the structural upgrading of Japan and R.O. Korea's investments in China. According to the survey of the Ministry of Economy, Trade and Industry (METI) of Japan, due to the technological advancement of Japanese companies, the labor productivity of Japanese companies is 6.5 times that of the productivity of Chinese enterprises, and because of the existence of the large technology gap, there is still large space for structural upgrading and potential for the Japanese companies' investments in China. With the upgrading of the technical level of Japanese and R.O. Korean companies' investments in China, their technical cooperation with China would be more profound in terms of both the level and the form of communication. The upgrading of the technical structure of the investing enterprises, the technical cooperation of China, Japan, and R.O. Korea would also promote the development of regional technology trade and trade in services.

As can be seen from the foregoing analysis, the direct investment within the region of China, Japan, and R.O. Korea promotes the adjustment of the division of labor within the region, making the industries within the region become integrated effectively. With the integration and upgrading of the industrial structure in the region, it is inevitably required for Northeast Asian countries to cooperate more closely in the area of trade and investment, and further open up the financial and capital markets, to form a tight economy.

10.4 The Strategy of China's Joining the New Industrial Structure Adjustment in Northeast Asia

10.4.1 The Different Choices of China, Japan, and R.O. Korea in the Upgrading of the Industrial Structure

The latest industrial restructuring of Japan began in the mid-1980s. This industrial structure adjustment, distinctly characterized by servitization and informatization is still in progress. The industrial structure's trend toward informatization and servitization not only shows a rise in the share of information industry and service industry in the GDP, but also shows a rise in the share of information and service as intermediate input in other industries. It has become an inevitable trend for the sectors of material production to put more information and services into production. In the 21st century, Japanese industrial restructuring is undergoing profound changes. According to the policies of the economy and industry in the 21st century issued by the Ministry of International Trade and Industry, the "self-sufficient" economic mode that had supported Japan's development for half a century cannot meet the demand of the new era. Japan should establish a "more open and interconnected mode," and place emphasis of the future sustainable industry on technological innovation, the information industry, services for an aging society, and the environmental protection industry.

Since the late 1980s, R.O. Korea's economy has slowly begun to get out of the previous period of industrialization. Combining with the new development of the world's economy and its own industrial structural evolution, the government began to shift its focus of industrial policy to the development of the knowledge- and technology-based "new generation of promising industries." Especially after the Asian financial crisis, Kim Dae-Jung government learned from the crisis, began to re-examine the industrial policy comprehensively and profoundly, and reformed "the sectors of finance, business and the labor market, as well as the public sector" substantially. In terms of adjustment of the enterprises' economic structure, the government regarded increasing the international competitiveness by means of improving the benefit of enterprises as a central part of the industrial policy, reformed the large corporations comprehensively, and made policies to promote the development of small and medium-sized enterprises. The government also reorganized the industrial structure by eliminating the debt guarantees between plutocrats and the chaebols, controlling the mega-volume loans of the chaebols, exchanging industry to establish the core enterprises and reducing the debt ratio. It has also devised implementation plans to develop high-tech industries, such as those of computers, semiconductors, fine chemical engineering and life science, and has selected cultivating and developing high-tech industries as the strategic measure for maintaining a steady economic growth.

From the direction of industrial restructuring and the trend of the adjustment of the industrial policy of Japan and R.O. Korea, we can see that in the 21st century, both Japan and R.O. Korea would take the high-tech industries, which are based on knowledge and technology, as the concentration of their upgrading of the industrial structure. At the same time, the governments continue to transfer abroad the industries that have lost their comparative advantage at home, so as to make room for upgrading and adjustment of the domestic industrial structure.

According to China's 12th Five-Year Plan for national economic and social development, in the overall context of a comprehensive expansion of opening-up, China would basically complete the full transition of the economic system and the economic structure in the mid-term stage of industrialization, to a more perfect market economic system and middle-late stages of industrialization. It can be concluded that in the context of the accelerating economic globalization, the basic trend of China's taking part in international division and cooperation in the future would be fully integrated into the world's economy in more fields, at a higher level and on a larger scale. Over the next decade or so, China is expected to continue to make full use of the opportunity of the accelerating transfer of international industrial structure in globalization, attract global manufacturing and its related resources of productive services with its unique advantages and favorable conditions, and rely on the important cities in the developed coastal areas and industrial belts to build the world's largest processing and manufacturing base and the "highland" with the rapid development of trade in services. The fast propulsion of economic globalization and the new changes of industrial transfer will create external conditions for this, and the various changes after China's economic development steps into a new stage will provide internal bases.

10.4.2 Suggestions for China to Be Involved in Northeast Asian Regional Economic Cooperation and to Improve Its Industrial Competition

(1) Based on the perspective of regional economy, include the interaction mechanism of industrial structure into the strategy for adjusting the industrial structure

The development of both economic globalization and regionalization will inevitably require all the countries in the world to participate in the international division and competition with more active and more open styles and patterns, thus accelerating economic globalization. Meanwhile, China's economic development is in a period in which there is a close relationship with international development, and the influence of the structural adjustment of regional countries is obvious. So the objective requirement for future industrial development should be breaking the boundary, expanding the perspectives and adjusting strategies from the domestic region to a new region including China, Japan, and R.O. Korea; and furthermore, they can reach a global scale so that an industrial system with strong competitiveness can be established in the context of globalization. Wang Bin said in 2004 that "after 30 years of an economical light-speed increase, what China is currently doing—the huge industrial structural adjustment, is an active adjustment when facing the adjustments of the global industrial structure under the conditions in which there are abundant commercial and technological revolutions, therefore this adjustment is kind of premeditated and predicted."

(2) Conform to the trend of knowledge-based economy, enhance the competitiveness of high-tech industries, and promote upgrading of the domestic industrial structure

Optimize the distribution and allocation of technological power and resources at the national level to support the high-tech industries. First of all, the government should allocate numerous financial and material resources to play its leading role in infrastructure, especially in the activities of basic research and development. Reduce the entry barriers that block the entrance of the emerging industries by the spillover effect of scientific research during the establishment and development of new industries. Second, China should implement the open technological mode to promote the socialization of science and technology and the industrialization of the results of scientific research. And by strengthening the connection of the chain of technological innovation and the industrial chain, establish close relations between research and production as well as an institutional and political environment which can facilitate the rational flow of talents. Finally, China ought to establish and improve the incentive mechanism of technological innovation and perfect the patent protection system to stimulate the enthusiasm of technological innovation.

When China gives priority to the development of high-tech and high-value-added industries, it should also rebuild the labor-intensive industries that have comparative advantages with technology and enhance the density of knowledge and technology to change their comparative advantages into real competitive advantages. The government should adjust the product structure of traditional industries to eliminate their outdated production capacity and reduce the redundant construction and excessive competition. In order to strengthen technological innovation in the traditional industries, the government should also set up a system of enterprise technological innovation, which regards enterprises as the main body. In key industries and technological fields, the government should play a guiding and leading role in expanding high-tech industries and penetrating them into traditional industries to promote the advanced development of the traditional technological system.

Strengthen cooperation and exchanges with other countries in the region and regard drawing talents and technology as a priority for the use of foreign capital. The validity of importing technology should be improved because the ultimate purpose is to make technological innovations which include making technological reconstruction adapt to Chinese conditions and improve the technological level and international competitiveness of China. Based on its own reality, China should selectively absorb foreign advanced technology and equipment, while at the same time ensuring that the identification and selection of industries with new advantages form a group of industrial sectors with a high technological level and strong competitiveness and connect with industrial structural upgrading in less time than developed countries. As a consequence, high-tech industries will become a powerful engine for promoting the new round of industrial structural adjustment.

(3) Make use of interactive mechanisms, such as international trade and international investment, to straighten out industrial undertaking with the focus on structural upgrading

① In terms of foreign trade, further expand trade within the region, and optimize the structure of import and export commodities

The adjustment of China's industrial structure should be based on its own comparative advantages, which should be fully played; in the adjustment of the structure of trade, competitive advantages have to be developed actively. Low labor cost is still the greatest comparative advantage of China at present and in the future, which also determines that the labor-intensive industries will still occupy an important position in China's export trade. A country, for the sake of efficiency, cost, especially structural upgrading, can't merely pursue occupying an industry fully as in the past, but should grab production links of high-tech and high value-added in a certain industrial chain worldwide according to its own comparative advantages and comprehensive strength, and leave the labor-intensive and low-value-added production links to other countries. As a result, a new system of international trade division of labor will be formed. In the new pattern of international trade, we need to view the "optimization" of the structure of export commodities from a new perspective. Improving Chinese competitive advantages in trade should focus on enhancing the competitive advantages of the leading industries. Therefore, we must combine the comparative advantages of certain products to plan for the long-term development of China's industries dynamically.

② In international direct investment, try to improve the level and depth of regional industrial cooperation, and straighten out industrial undertaking with the focus on the need for structural upgrading

International industrial transfer, which is mainly realized by international direct investment, is beneficial to developing countries in learning skills and product innovation skills, upgrading its manufacturing capacity gradually, and promoting the rapid growth of industries. The development of international investment of China, Japan and R.O. Korea is the direct reflection of the three countries' industrial structural adjustment and industrial transfer. At present, China is faced with the opportunity of a leap-forward development realized by further undertaking international industrial transfer. Seizing the opportunity and participating in the optimal allocation of resources on a larger scope and at a higher degree can not only accelerate the upgrading of traditional industries, but also promote the development of China's high-tech industries and technological innovation strongly. Therefore, first, comprehensive competitive advantages should be further cultivated to undertake international industrial transfer, which includes attaching great importance to the system construction, improving the protection of intellectual property rights, administrative, legal and other soft environment vigorously, and speeding up the reform of market orientation, especially enhancing the service consciousness of the government and strengthening services for market entities. Second, enhance the quality and level of utilization of foreign capital and guide the flow of foreign capital reasonably, which is good for the direction of the flow of foreign capital to be in line with industrial structural adjustment. Third, pay attention to combining participating in international division of labor with strengthening cooperation among domestic areas, study ways of narrowing gaps among domestic areas and solving the problem of unreasonable domestic regional structure from a broad perspective of international regional industrial integration, technology transfer and participation in the international division of labor, strengthen domestic regional economic cooperation, and realize industrial evolution and upgrading in a coordinated way from east to west.

③ Coordinate the "bringing in" and "going out" strategies, develop transnational operations, and realize the two-way transfer

From the perspective of industrial gradient transfer, if a country wants to achieve industrial upgrading, it must accept international industrial transfer and transfer some industries externally at the same time so as to realize industrial upgrading. Faced with the imbalance in industrial structure, overcapacity of processing industries, insufficient momentum of the growth of the high-tech industries and so on, transferring surplus production capacity and developing transnational operations is a good way. Therefore, whether from the point of a long run or that of the present, China must vigorously develop transnational operations and realize coordinated development between the input and output of industries. The implementation of the strategy of "going out" while implementing the strategy of "bringing in" must be hastened and enterprises with the right conditions to carry out transnational operations overseas must be actively promoted to prepare for the constant upgrading of the national medium- and long-term industrial structure.

(4) Based on Northeast Asia, China should actively participate in regional economic cooperation and promote regional economic integration

The function that has been widely accepted is that regional economic integration can promote the economic development of members. First of all, the conclusion of regional free trade agreements can abolish or reduce tariff and non-tariff barriers between member states, expand the market, and industrial division of labor can be formed according to countries' comparative advantages, which would improve the efficiency of the allocation of resources, reduce the low efficiency brought by monopolies, enhance the competitiveness of the relevant industries, and increase national welfare. Second, regional economic integration can promote the development of competitive industries and expand the investment between member countries and countries outside. Establishing free trade areas can strengthen the free flow of factors of production in the region, such as goods, labor, technology, capital and so on, and deepen members' economical dependence on each other. At the same time, regional international division of labor can make sales channels stable, promote the development of intra-regional trade, and intra-regional trade in member countries would have a significantly higher proportion in the total foreign trade. In the situation that global free trade is hard to implement, free trade areas can make it possible for the resources to be used and allocated reasonably on a smaller scope. Because factors of production among member states can flow more freely, companies in the region have the opportunities to achieve economies of scale. Companies achieving economies of scale can enhance the national income level and thus increase the market capacity, which directly leads to the expansion of the scale of trade of the regional integration of the member states. If China, Japan, and R.O. Korea build free trade areas, there will be a regional unified market with 1.5 billion consumers, more than USD 10 trillion in GDP, and USD 6.5 trillion in the total volume of trade, which consists of the most populous developing country and developed countries. Unfortunately, as can be seen from the history and current situation among Japan, R.O. Korea, and China, the main driving force has always been the market. Today, regional economic integration continues to develop with a tremendous growth and China, Japan, R.O. Korea, and the Asian region still lack a reasonable and comprehensive system of regional economic cooperation.

In the long run, actively participating in Northeast Asia regional economic cooperation, and coordinating economic relations with Japan and R.O. Korea can not only make China obtain more stable markets but also pave the way for coordinating development of the industrial structure among the three countries so as to implement structural adjustment more effectively and gain more interests in the international division of labor.

11

Strategic Planning of China's Direct Investment in Africa

China's foreign direct investment, which started in the early years of reform and opening-up, has reached a certain scale after more than 20 years. According to the "2009 Annual Statistical Bulletin of China's Foreign Direct Investment," which was jointly issued by the Ministry of Commerce, the National Bureau of Statistics and the State Administration of Foreign Exchange, China's net foreign direct investment was USD 56.53 billion in 2009, of which China's direct investment in Africa accounted for only 2.6%. By the end of 2009, China's foreign direct investment stock was USD 245.75 billion, of which investment stock in Asia and Latin America accounted for nearly 90% while that in Africa accounted for only 3.8%. China's direct investment in Africa has much room for growth.

According to an OECD report, the rate of return on Africa's foreign direct investment is the highest in the world, which was 29% on average in the 1990s and reached 40% in 2005. According to *The McKinsey Quarterly*'s latest report in 2010, the rate of return on Africa's foreign direct investment was 60% higher than that in Asian countries like China, India, and Vietnam. Africa has become one of the regions that have the highest rates of return in the world. In recent years, direct investment of Chinese enterprises in Africa has achieved high economic efficiency, and at the same time, the investment has also increased the local employment, and improved the local technology, level of management and quality of human capital, and it has promoted the economic development of African countries. At the opening ceremony of the African Development Bank Group Board's Annual Meeting in 2007, Chinese Premier Wen Jiabao said the following in his speech: To strengthen China-Africa cooperation, we should innovate cooperation ideas, improve the level of cooperation and achieve mutual benefits and a win-win situation. As an important part of China-Africa cooperation, China's direct investment in Africa must continue to achieve mutual benefits and win-win developmental goals. For this reason, China needs to develop a strategic plan for direct investment in Africa, in order to specify the current economic and social situation in Africa, and choose the countries, fields, patterns, and strategies scientifically to promote the long-term development of China's direct investment in Africa, and at the same time, help African countries achieve industrial developmental goals as well as shedding its status of poverty and backwardness.

11.1 The History and the Current Situation of China's Direct Investment in Africa

China's direct investment in Africa started at the initiation of the reform and opening-up, and developed relatively slowly in the first 20 years. In the 21st century, particularly due to the formation of the mechanism of the China-Africa Forum and the establishment of the "China-Africa new strategic partnership," China and Africa have further enhanced the willingness to expand investment cooperation, from the government to the private sector. Coupled with the significant results of African countries' economic reforms and the gradually increasing political stability, especially in today's situation, when the economic growth in developed countries is increasingly slow, the investment prospects in Africa have raised concern from China and even from the whole world. At present, China's direct investment in Africa is developing rapidly and has formed a win-win outcome.

11.1.1 The History of China's Direct Investment in Africa

Before the reform and opening-up, China's direct investment in Africa was limited only to the enterprises established for specific government projects. Since the early 1980s, with the aid of the reform and opening-up, the form of economic and trade cooperation between China and Africa has turned from pure commodity trade and the aid offered to African countries to mutually beneficial economic cooperation like project contracting, labor cooperation, consultation design, and joint ventures. During this period, China's direct investment in Africa was specifically for political purposes; it was also an important method that promoted the exportation of engineering equipment, raw materials, and other Chinese products to Africa. During this period, China's direct investment in Africa was in its initial stage, and the Chinese enterprises' investment in Africa was generally only on a small scale. From 1979 to the end of 1990, Chinese investment in Africa had a total of 102 projects. The total investment was USD 51.19 million; each project investment was about USD 500,000 on average, and the scale of investment was small. There were also some large and medium-sized projects, such as the Kinshasa wood-processing plants in Congo, of which the investment was more than USD 5 million.

In the early 1990s, China began to explore how to turn aid for Africa into bilateral joint venture cooperation between enterprises. Therefore, starting from the second half of 1995, the Chinese government has reformed the modes of foreign aid, changing the main body of cooperation between China and African countries from the government to enterprises, thus achieving diversification of foreign aid and funds and promoting direct cooperation between Chinese and African enterprises. China actively promoted the government discount preferential loans and joint venture cooperation ways of foreign aid projects, helped countries to set up production projects and closely link aid with direct investment, project contracting, labor cooperation, and exportation. Since 1995, the Chinese government has successively set up 11 "investment, development, and trade promotion centers" in African countries, and its purpose was to promote exchanges between Chinese and African enterprises, and provide information and services for bilateral investment and trade, which was mainly about bonded warehousing, trade negotiation, commodity display, legal, economic and trade advisory services and so on. From 1995 to the end of 1999, the Chinese government signed 39 framework agreements for discount preferential loans with 23 African countries, which helped enterprises with capital. Chinese companies could apply for the discount preferential loans as long as they had found the right programs in these African countries. During this period, Chinese enterprises set up 46 joint cooperation projects in Africa.

Since 2000, the Chinese government began to implement the "going out" opening-up strategy. From 2002 to 2006, the government continued to implement the strategy of "going out." The implementation of the "going out" opening-up strategy promoted the rapid development of Chinese enterprises' direct investments in Africa. In 2000, China set up 57 investment enterprises in Africa. The amount of China's investments was USD 216 million, which accounted for about 39.2% of the total amount of China's foreign investments in that year. In 2002, China set up 36 enterprises in Africa, the total agreement investment was USD 73 million, and China's investment was USD 63 million. After 2002, China's direct investments in Africa rapidly increased year by year. By the end of 2009, China had signed agreements to encourage and guarantee bilateral investments with 31 African countries, and signed an agreement on avoidance of double taxation with 10 countries.

11.1.2 The Current Situation of China's Direct Investment in Africa

(1) The Chinese investment in Africa grows rapily and the investment field is getting bigger

China's direct investment in Africa was USD 75 million in 2003; in 2004, it increased to USD 317 million, a rise by 3.2 times. This was due to the massive investment in Sudan's oil. China's direct investment in Africa grew by 23.7% in 2005, reaching USD 392 million, which included the large-scale investment concentrated in Sudan, Algeria, Nigeria, South Africa and other countries. In 2006, China's direct investment in Africa was USD 520 million, which had increased by 32.7% compared to that of 2005; the main investment destinations were Nigeria, Algeria, and Zambia. In 2008, the Industrial and Commercial Bank of China bought a 20% stake in South Africa's Standard Bank, which was the largest transnational merger of Chinese enterprises in Africa in that year, helping China's direct investment in Africa surge to USD 5.49 billion. In 2009, China's direct investment in Africa was USD 1.439 billion; it fell by 73.8% compared to the previous year. However, if the Industrial and Commercial Bank of China bought shares of South Africa's Standard Bank was excluded, China's non-financial investment in Africa had increased by 55.4% compared to 2008. By the end of 2009, China's direct investment in Africa was USD 9.33 billion, and the number of a variety of new enterprises was more than 1600. From the investment fields, between 1979 and 2000, the proportion of China's direct investment in Africa flowing to manufacturing, resources industry, services and agriculture were 46%, 28%, 18%, and 1% respectively. China's current number of investment cooperation projects in Africa is close to 8,000, involving agriculture and product development, textiles and clothing, home appliances, infrastructure, resources development and other traditional areas, as well as the deep extension into the fields of telecommunications, finance, medicine, automotive manufacturing, information, new energy development and utilization and other emerging fields.

(2) Private enterprises become an important subject for investment in Africa

The Secretary General of the China International Exchange Center, Wei Jianguo, said that there are three main types of Chinese enterprises that invest in Africa: The first type is large state-owned enterprises and large private companies, mainly to undertake large engineering projects. The second type is manufacturing enterprises transferring factories to Africa for the reasons of tax rates, labor costs, avoiding the non-tariff barriers such as quotas, and other factors. The third type is all sorts of traders. In the 1980s to the 1990s, most of China's enterprises that invested in Africa were large and medium-sized state-owned enterprises. However, in recent years, more and more private enterprises have invested in Africa. According to the statistics of The Export-Import Bank of China, most Chinese enterprises that invested in Africa were private enterprises. In 2006, a province with big private economy, Zhejiang Province, invested USD 56 million in Africa, and was considered the largest investment by a province in China. Other provinces have also actively promoted private enterprises to invest in Africa—Jiangsu Province held economic and trade fairs in Nigeria for seven years, and used the mode of Suzhou Industrial Park for reference to construct economic and trade cooperation zones in local areas. Shandong Province set up a special fund to encourage textile enterprises to invest in Africa.

(3) The scale of Chinese investment in Africa increases gradually

Since 2000, there are more and more large and medium-sized projects regarding Chinese investment in Africa, which account for more than tens of millions of dollars. These projects mainly include the following: the oil project of China Petroleum Engineering Construction Corporation in Sudan, the construction of the Chambishi Copper Mine in Zambia by China Nonferrous Metal Construction Co., LTD., the chrome development project in South Africa invested in by China's Steel Industry and Trade Group, the cement plant project in Cape Verde signed by China Building-Material Industrial Corporation for Foreign Econo-Technical Cooperation, the coastal railway and the north-south railway projects in Libya by China Civil Engineering Construction Corporation and so on. At present, the Zambia-China Economic and Trade Cooperation Zone, the Tianli Economic and Trade Cooperation Zone in Mauritius, the Nigeria Ogun Guangdong Free Trade Zone, the Suez Economic and Trade Cooperation Zone in Egypt, the Nigeria Lekki Free Trade Area and the East Industrial Park in Ethiopia, which were established by Chinese enterprises, are opening one after another, and part of the cooperation zones have begun to take shape. It is worth noting that from the time it was founded in June 2007 up to early

2010, the China-Africa Development Fund had successively invested in more than 30 projects in 40 African countries, and the cumulative amount was USD 800 million. This drove Chinese enterprises to invest more than USD 3 billion in Africa. Among them, the China-Africa Development Fund invested four projects in Ethiopia, and the total investment was USD 150 million, which was the highest in all African countries.

(4) China's investment projects in Africa achieve great benefits

Currently, many of the investment projects of Chinese companies in Africa have achieved remarkable economic and social benefits. In recent years, Africa has become the area where the mobile communications business has grown fastest in the world. China-Africa cooperation in the information communications industry has also become increasingly close. China's largest private telecommunications network technology maker Huawei Technologies Co., Ltd is a successful example of Chinese science and technology enterprises that invest in Africa. Huawei began to explore the African market in 1998, and the cumulative investment volume had reached USD 1.5 billion by early 2010. Its products and services had entered more than 40 countries in Africa, and Huawei became one of the top three communications equipment suppliers in the region. At present, the company has set up representative offices in over ten countries including South Africa, Nigeria, and Kenya, and has set up three teams of South Africa, East Africa, West Africa in Southern Africa, in order to improve the speed of response to the demand and services for customers. In addition, the Sudan Khartoum Refinery, the Great Friendship Farm, the Mauritius Tianli Spinning Mill, Hisense Co., Ltd in South Africa and the Mozambique Cinda Aquaculture Company, the Togo Tongmei Pharmaceutical Factory and other companies, wherein China has invested, are developing steadily in Africa. In addition to achieving substantial profits, these companies also play a significant role in local economic development.

11.2 Elements Promoting China's Direct Investment in Africa

Since entering the 21st century, economic globalization has increasingly become the most fundamental characteristic of world economic development. Keeping up with the development of the times, the Chinese government promptly put forward the implementation of the "going out" opening-up strategy, supporting Chinese enterprises in investing abroad, and Africa has become an increasingly important option for the Chinese enterprises' overseas investment. This is mainly because both sides push it with governments' macro policies; the African continent itself has resource advantages and market potential, the continent's economic situation and political situation are getting better, as well as the influences of other positive factors, such as the long friendly relations of cooperation between Africa and China.

11.2.1 The Chinese Government Encourages Enterprises to Expand Their Investments on the African Market

(1) The opening-up strategy of "going out" encourages Chinese enterprises to invest and establish business in Africa

China and Africa are strongly complementary in economic structure. For example, Chinese companies have mature technology in the textile, home appliances, agriculture, food processing and other industries, and products made in China have lower prices and a higher quality, thus possessing a competitive edge on the local market of Africa; African countries have energy, raw materials and other resources, which are in great demand in Chinese industrial development. The existing complementarity in reality is an important premise for China to make overseas investments in African countries. Investing in Africa, Chinese enterprises can not only enjoy local preferential policies, but also use the preferential policies provided by developed countries of Europe and America for African countries as well, which provides a new channel for China to export its products to developed European and American countries. Therefore, vigorously developing the African market is the realistic choice for Chinese enterprises to expand the international market and to alleviate the pressure of the domestic market. The African market is one of the key areas for China to implement the strategy of "going out" as well as to develop the overseas investment market. The Chinese government should promote the domestic enterprises which have competitive advantages to invest in African countries with the existing equipment and mature technology.

(2) The establishment of the Forum on China-Africa Cooperation and the China-Africa strategic partnership promotes China's investment in Africa to develop in depth and breadth

To strengthen the friendly cooperation between China and Africa in the new century and the new situation, cope with the challenges of economic globalization, and realize mutual development, the Chinese government organized and held the first ministerial conference of the Forum in China-Africa Cooperation in Beijing in October 2000, based on the common initiatives of China and African countries. It marked the establishment of the mechanism of the Forum on China-Africa Cooperation, which is held every three years. Now, the Forum on China-Africa Cooperation has become an important platform and effective mechanism by which China and Africa can carry out all-round cooperation.

During the first ministerial conference of the Forum on China-Africa Cooperation, both parties adopted two historical documents, the "Beijing Declaration of the Forum on China-Africa Cooperation" and the "Creed of Sino-African Cooperation in Economic and Social Development," and established the principle for China-Africa trade and economic cooperation "equality and mutual benefit, various forms, focusing on actual effect, common development."

In November 2006, the Beijing Summit of the Forum on China-Africa Cooperation, namely the third ministerial conference was held in Beijing. The meeting adopted the "Beijing Declaration of the Forum on China-Africa Cooperation" and the "Forum on China-Africa Cooperation Beijing Action Plan (2007–2009)." One of the most important results of the Beijing Summit is that Chinese and African leaders solemnly declared in the "Beijing Declaration" that China and Africa would establish and develop "a new type of strategic partnership—political equality and mutual trust, economic win-win cooperation and cultural exchanges."

In order to further strengthen China-Africa investment cooperation, during the Beijing Summit, the Chinese government decided to set up the China-Africa Development Fund, promote and support qualified Chinese enterprises to establish economic and trade cooperation zones as well as raise the level of investment in qualified African countries.

In November 2009, the fourth ministerial conference of the Forum on China-Africa Cooperation was held in Egypt, the aim of which was "deepening the China-Africa strategic partnership and seeking sustainable development," and the "Sharm El Sheikh Action Plan (2010–2012)" was adopted. The Chinese government proposed to expand the mutually beneficial and win-win cooperation with Africa and enhance the level of China-Africa practical cooperation. It included encouraging and facilitating trade and investment between China and African countries, promoting ways of cooperation to be diversified, strengthening cooperation in the major fields, such as poverty reduction, environmental protection, human resource training and capacity-building, and information and communications technologies, especially in infrastructure construction, agriculture, food security and other key areas.

With the convening of the ministerial conference of the Forum on China-Africa Cooperation and the Beijing Summit, and the establishment of the China-Africa new-type strategic partnership, the trade and economic cooperation between China and Africa has been raised to a new strategic height, which also promotes the rapid development of China-Africa trade and economic cooperation, and has made great achievements. At present, the mechanism for China-Africa trade and economic cooperation has become increasingly perfect, and has established a mutually beneficial, win-win and open situation of development . China-Africa investment cooperation is also developing in a more pragmatic direction, and the Chinese government also pays more attention to the win-win effect of investment. The Chinese government has declared that it will further simplify examination and approval procedures, strengthen the information service, promote more Chinese companies to enter Africa, and increase the chances of mutually beneficial cooperation. China will continue to work with African countries to sign investment protection agreements and agreements on avoidance of double taxation, creating a favorable environment for investment cooperation, as well as protecting the legitimate rights and interests of the investors. Currently, the Ministry of Commerce, the Ministry of Finance, the National Development and Reform Commission, the China Development Bank, the Export-Import Bank of China, insurance companies and other relevant units are busy formulating positive policies and supporting measures of investment in Africa, planning for China-Africa practical cooperation for a long period in the future, trying to innovate forms of cooperation, expanding the scale of investment, improving the levels of cooperation, providing high-quality services, and promoting the common development of China and African countries.

11.2.2 African Countries Encourage Foreign Direct Investment Inflows

(1) The reasons for African countries to attract foreign direct investment

① Foreign direct investment helps to compensate the shortage of construction funds in African countries

In order to realize the United Nations' "Millennium Development Goals," which include halving the population below poverty line before 2015, Africa needs development funds of USD 64 billion every year, which accounts for about 12% of the GDP of Africa. However, public investment and private investment in African countries are still faced with a shortage of funds, which limits rapid economic growth in Africa. The shortage of funds comes from the imbalance of exports and imports, inflows and foreign debt payments, as well as domestic savings and investments. Domestic capital shortage limits the public expenditure of the African governments in the construction of infrastructures, social security and service system, while such an increase in government spending will lead to the improvement of domestic demand and increase the enthusiasm of the private sector for participating in the domestic economy, so that it can maintain high levels of domestic economic growth. In order to make up for the lack of development funds, African countries need external funding support, including aid, loans, foreign direct investment and so on.

② The spillover effect of foreign direct investment of multinational companies helps achieve the extension of advanced technology and management experience to the host country

In recent years, there have been many research projects regarding the spillover effect on the host country of foreign direct investment by multinational companies. Blomstrom and Kokko made a detailed classification of the spillover effect of transnational corporations, and they think the spillover effect can be divided into the following forms: a. Competition-related spillovers, namely, the entrance of multinational companies increases the pressure of the competition among local enterprises, so that the local companies have to improve the technical level and the efficiency of their production to maintain their original market share. b. The spillover effect from the technology and management cooperation between multinational subsidiaries or branches and the local companies. c. Human capital spillovers. Multinational companies train their local staff in the host country, which improves their technical and managerial level. If these employees are hired by the local companies later, the technical and management level of local companies can be improved. d. Demonstration-type spillovers or imitation-type spillovers. The former refers to the demonstration effects of the multinational companies' operation and activities in the host country, and the latter regards the local companies learning or imitating the multinational companies' advanced technology and managerial knowledge actively.

③ Foreign direct investment is helpful to improving the competitiveness of the African export products

Over the past 30 years, the market share of African traditional export products around the world showed a downward trend. At present, most of the African export products are primary products of low value-added and some processed products at a low level, which generally have weak export competitiveness. In order to increase the competitiveness of the export products, African countries need the intervention of foreign capital in order to prolong the processing chain of traditional export products, improve the technological level of exports, expand the exportation of unconventional products, and achieve the diversification of the structure of their exports. By attracting foreign direct investment, African countries can open international markets better and increase product exportation. Generally speaking, multinational companies have the ability to increase the link between the host country and the international market, because many companies have a global link regarding the aspects of financial markets, consumer acceptance and traffic network, so the multinational companies can be used as a catalyst to promote export enterprises of the host country to expand exports. African companies can take advantage of the multinational companies to understand foreign markets, foreign customers, and foreign technology, export more products to the international market by using these domestic companies, and thus earn foreign exchange to make up for import spending and debt.

④ Foreign direct investment helps African countries to achieve poverty reduction

The present study shows that the most important way to overcome poverty is to increase employment, especially the formal sector of employment, while an important contribution of foreign direct investment to the social development of the host country is to create jobs, especially the employment of women. The increase of women's employment has a bigger contribution to poverty reduction, because women and children are the main groups affected by poverty. Much research on Southern African countries suggests that their lack of job opportunities is because of the shortage of domestic and foreign investment. So the African countries' governments expect to create new jobs and achieve the goal of reducing poverty by introducing foreign direct investment. In addition, foreign direct investment is helpful to promoting the African countries' economic growth and ultimately achieving the goal of reducing poverty by means of direct technology transfer, the effect of technology and management spillover, human capital formation, international trade integration, a competitive business environment, and promoting the development of enterprises.

(2) The policies and measures of African countries for attracting foreign direct investment

Being aware that attracting foreign investment may bring developmental opportunities to Africa, African governments have adopted various policies and measures to attract foreign direct investment, mainly including lowering the tax rate, exempting import duties, deducting the tax on foreign direct investment and reinvestment, offering guarantees on the loans and other fiscal and financial incentives, signing bilateral and multilateral investment treaties, establishing investment promotion agencies to be specialized in attracting foreign direct investment and so on. Countries such as Uganda, Mozambique, and Ghana attach great importance to promoting the process of domestic economic privatization and liberalization, in order to attract foreign direct investment inflows. At present, investment in South Africa does not need any special approval of the government, and the foreign investment is almost unlimited. At the same time, the South African government also enacts many incentive policies to promote foreign investment inflows. For example, South Africa introduced a foreign investment subsidy policy, which provides a subsidy of about 3 million yuan for enterprises investing in manufacturing, tourism and other industries. Countries such as Tanzania and the Democratic Republic of the Congo implement preferential tax policies, which could exempt the tax of the first five years for foreign investment projects of a certain amount. Cape Verde exempts tariffs, the consumption taxes and service taxes for the raw materials, finished products, semi-finished products and other raw materials needed for production in the first two years of foreign-invested enterprises.

(3) African countries expect more Chinese investment inflows

In recent years, because China's economy has achieved remarkable achievements, many African countries are eager to learn from China, which may be suitable for their domestic development, and expect that Chinese investment could bring vitality to Africa and change the situation of the long-term low level of industrialization. Goldman Sachs said in a report that China might overtake the United States in 2030 and be the world's greatest economic power. With the focus of the world economic growth increasingly transferring to Asia, "looking East" has become the strategic choice of some African countries' foreign policy. In 2007, during the annual meeting of the council of the African Development Bank Group in Shanghai, Donald Kaberuka, the president of the African Development Bank, suggested that Africa should expect Asian countries, including China, to help it achieve industrialization. Especially in the context of slow economic growth in developed countries due to the international financial crisis, the driving forces of China's factors in African countries' economic development have become more significant. Because of this, African countries are looking forward to more and more Chinese enterprises investing in Africa, to promote African countries' economic and social development.

11.2.3 African Macro Environment and Investment Prospects Get Better

In March 2010, the establishment of the African Union brought new opportunities for Africa to realize sustainable economic development, and it became the new starting point of African revitalization. Since the launch of the "New Partnership for Africa's Development," which is the economic and social developmental program of the African Union, due to the formulation of a correct developmental strategy, the implementation of prudent macroeconomic policies and the promotion of an economic structural adjustment, in recent years, the African economy has continued to develop, the continent's regional conflicts and wars have also gradually died down, and the political democratization process has also been accelerating. At present, the African countries are actively coping with the challenges of economic globalization, are accelerating the pace of economic reform and regional integration, and are trying to improve the investment environment, especially to improve the backwardness of infrastructures and the financial services industry. African countries are promoting economic integration by diminishing the developmental gap between countries and regions and strengthening regional coordination and cooperation. Economic integration can promote Africa to optimize its allocation of resources, manpower, money, and technology, speed up the economic development in Africa, and enhance its competitiveness on the international market.

11.2.4 China-Africa Long-term Friendly Cooperation Helps Chinese Enterprises Carry Out Their Investments

China and Africa are situated far away from each other, but the friendly exchanges between the two areas enjoy a history of over one thousand years. As early as the 9th and the 10th centuries, during the Tang and Song dynasties, there was trading between China and Africa. In the 15th century, Zheng He's fleet reached the east coast of Africa three times during the Ming Dynasty. Since the establishment of the PRC, the Chinese government has attached great importance to developing friendly cooperation with African countries. China firmly supported African countries in their fight against Western colonial rule and for national independence; and once African countries became independent, China strongly supported them in choosing their own political and economic systems and developmental paths. African countries also strongly supported the "One China" policy, and played a pivotal role in the process of China's return to the United Nations. Since the beginning of the 21st century, the political exchanges between China and Africa have become more frequent, and the establishment of "China-Africa new-type strategic partnerships" further consolidated and strengthened traditional China-Africa friendly relations.

The Chinese government's long-term selfless assistance to African countries also makes China-Africa friendship grow in intensity. Since the late 1950s, China has begun to lend aid to African countries, and the original recipients were independent diplomatic African countries such as Guinea, Mali, Ghana and so on. At the China-Africa Summit, China promised to make the scale of China's assistance to African countries in 2009 twice that of the amount in 2006; to support unity and the integration of African countries, China aided the construction of the African Union Conference Center financially; China also helped Africa build 30 hospitals and provide RMB 300 million to help Africa control malaria, which was used to provide artemisinin drugs and set up 30 anti-malaria centers. In 2009, although China's economy was impacted by the international financial crisis, the Chinese government still kept the promise, implementing various aid measures to Africa. By the end of 2009, China had signed bilateral aid agreements with 48 African countries, and the aid projects involved agriculture and fisheries, water conservation and electric power, transportation and telecommunications, culture, education, and health, food processing and industries in many other fields. In 2010, when it was the 60th year of the PRC promoting foreign aid, the Ministry of Commerce of China said that it would sign debt relief agreements with relevant countries in Africa in 2010, and exempt interest-free loan debt of heavily indebted poor countries and the least developed countries which had established diplomatic ties with China by the end of 2009. In short, China and African countries have a long-term friendly relationship with mutual trust, which is the solid foundation for Chinese enterprises to invest in Africa.

11.3 Constraints on China's Direct Investment in Africa

Although in recent years, the economic growth of the African continent has been in good conditions, and African countries attach great importance to attracting foreign investment and take various measures to attract foreign direct investment, the foreign direct investment inflows to Africa still lag far behind other developing countries. According to the World Investment Report released by UNCTAD, in 2006, the amount of foreign direct investment flowing into Africa was USD 35.54 billion, which increased by 17.4% compared with that in 2005; in 2007, the amount further increased to USD 52.98 billion, which rose by 49.1% compared with that in 2006. The proportion of foreign direct investment in the fixed assets in Africa increased from 18% in 2005 to 20% in 2006 and 21% in 2007. In 2008, foreign direct investment to Africa reached USD 72.18 billion, which increased by 36.2% over that in 2007. The main reasons for the increase in African foreign direct investment inflows were the increasing global demand for natural resources, the improvement of ROI prospects, and the improvement of the whole investment environment. For a long time, foreign direct investment in Africa has mainly flowed into the oil, gas, mining, and other primary sectors, but in recent years an increasing amount of foreign investment has also gradually flowed into the service industries, mainly in the finance, electric power, transportation, storage, and communications industries. In 2009, influenced by the international financial crisis, foreign direct investment inflow declined to USD 58.57 billion in Africa. Although it showed a significant downward trend compared with the inflow in 2008, it was still higher than the inflow in 2007. And because the total amount of foreign direct investment inflows in the world had a larger decline, the proportion of African foreign direct investment in the world's foreign direct investment inflows rose; it increased to 5.3%, which was the highest level since 1988.

Even so, the proportion of African foreign direct investment in the amount of world foreign direct investment is still far less than the average level of other developing regions, which also shows that the African countries still need more efforts to improve production capacity and economic diversification and create greater regional markets. There still exist many constraints on the foreign direct investment inflows to Africa; so before deciding to develop the African investment market, Chinese companies should fully understand the risks and challenges they may face when investing in Africa, and formulate corresponding strategies.

11.3.1 Constraints on Chinese Companies While Investing in Africa

(1) African countries' unstable macro economic, political, and security situations increase Chinese enterprises' investment risks

Although Africa maintains a rapid and stable momentum of economic growth, the economy of many African countries is weak, and is vulnerable to the impact of external changes. Due to the single economic structure of most African countries, and because exports are mostly primary products, there is a huge risk of being "unable to resist external shocks." Global economy downside risk will lead to a drop in the demand for African exports, and lead to a fall in export prices, which will directly affect the economic growth in Africa. Fluctuations in oil prices will generate certain economic fluctuations in oil importers and exporters. The increase in international oil prices will make African oil exporters relieve their financial pressure and the international balance of payments, while the falling oil prices will reduce the export revenues of African oil exporters, leading to the deterioration of the financial situation. The economic backbone in many African countries is agriculture; so unpredictable climate changes and disasters can also affect the development of the economy. The high inflation rate, excessive fiscal deficits, bad financing conditions and frequent monetary shocks in some African countries also make the macroeconomic condition become more unstable.

The imperfect market economic system, imperfect legal system, frequent changes of macro policies, and the lack of transparency in many African countries increase the foreign investors' trade costs and investment risks. In some African countries, prevalent bureaucracy, inefficient governments, serious corruption, and intense local protectionism in some places influence and hinder the investment and business operation activities of the foreign enterprises. In many African countries, the establishment procedure of foreign-invested enterprises is complex, the time and costs spent are huge, and there is a lack of a convenient investment environment. These constraints increase the risks of Chinese enterprises' investment in Africa.

In addition to the unstable macroeconomic situation, the political development in Africa is not balanced. For instance, many countries have tribal and religious conflicts, which are difficult to be eradicated in the short term; so the possibility of wars in Africa is higher than that in Asia and other developing countries. So the political instability will have negative influences on Chinese enterprises' investment in Africa. In some African countries, terrorist activities and criminal activities are very frequent, and this is not optimistic for the security situation of Chinese companies' investment in Africa.

(2) Poverty and narrow markets increase the market risks of Chinese enterprises' investments in Africa

Since the 1980s, sub-Saharan Africa has not only been the poorest region in the world, but it also has a slow pace in alleviating poverty. According to World Development Indicators in 2007 released by the World Bank, in sub-Saharan Africa, there were about 298 million people living below the poverty line in 2004 and the figure was 240 million in 1990. Most African countries are still far away from the "Millennium Development Goals" of the United Nations. It is estimated that in order to achieve this goal, an average annual growth rate of African countries must be kept at more than 7%. But according to the UN Economic Commission for Africa, between 1998 and 2006, only five countries' actual average annual growth rates of the GDP were more than 7%. In 2007, there were only 10 African countries whose economic growth rates reached or exceeded 7%. In 2009, under the impact of the international financial crisis, the growth rates of 29 African countries were at or below 3%, 17 countries were at 3% to 5%, and the economic growth rates of Ethiopia and the Republic of the Congo were more than 7%. It is thus clear that African countries still have a long way to go before truly achieving poverty alleviation.

Some research on the reasons why 81 companies of Britain, Switzerland, and Germany invested in the Southern African Development Community (SADC) has shown that investment of 84% of the enterprises stems from considering the capacity of the local market, 40% of the enterprises want to obtain the local raw materials, 21% derive from global strategic considerations, 19% consider privatization of local businesses, and 26% are for personal reasons. For China and India, the main cause of attracting foreign direct investment is the large capacity of the domestic market, while some African countries are unable to attract more foreign direct investment because of the limited capacity of the domestic market. In Africa, 31 countries have a total population of less than 10 million, and many countries have less than 5 million people. We can see that geographically narrow markets and large populations in poverty cause the low purchasing power, which makes Chinese enterprises face a high market risk when investing in Africa.

(3) Poor infrastructure increases the operational cost of Chinese enterprises' investment in Africa

Conditions of the infrastructure in African countries are generally inadequate. Due to underdeveloped transportation and communication facilities, the transportation costs and costs of important information access in Africa are very high. The transportation costs, whether in the continent of Africa or outside Africa, are very high, and the average transportation costs are even higher than the tariff costs, which results in greater restrictions on trade than the non-tariff barriers. High internal transportation costs also hinder the formation of the domestic market of the African countries. And energy, electricity, and water supplies in Africa lag behind, too. Africa's population accounts for 13.1% of the world's population, but energy consumption accounts for only 5.5% of the world's total energy consumption. Currently, only 34.3% of Africa's population have access to electricity. The Human Development Report in 2005 pointed out that in sub-Saharan Africa, local transportation, education, and healthcare facilities were in poor conditions, and 42% of the people did not have access to clean water.

(4) Underdevelopment of human capital restricts the Chinese enterprises' investment in technology-intensive industries in Africa

Africa's literacy is the lowest in the world. The quality of the African labor force is low, it lacks skilled technical workers, and the outflow of high-quality talent is a serious matter, which hinders the benign development of the African economy and reduces labor advantages of attracting foreign direct investment. In recent years, the research has shown that the conditions of the human capital play a crucial role in attracting foreign direct investment in the fields of manufacturing and services, and the backward situation of the human capital in Africa makes it attract less foreign direct investment in manufacturing and services. The standards of many multinational companies investing in the host country are to take advantage of the human capital advantages of the host country to establish export-oriented enterprises so that products can be exported directly. In this way, multinational companies will choose the necessary countries to make direct investment according to their global developmental strategies, and the selected countries will play different roles and complement each other. For example, China's largest foreign investment enterprises are mainly engaged in information and communication technology and products, which is mainly due to the technological superiority of the human capital of China. Sub-Saharan Africa's human capital is backward, and the foundation of the processing industry of manufactured products is weak, which restricts Chinese capital from being invested in production and processing fields of products at a high technological level.

(5) The Chinese government should strengthen strategic planning and the macro-control of enterprises investing in Africa

Currently, the Chinese enterprises investing in Africa develop independently and operate repeatedly. To seek short-term interests, many businesses use low-cost competition to expand their product market share in Africa, which affects the good reputation of Chinese products and Chinese companies in the minds of the African people. There are also some self-employed businessmen whose management practices are not standard, and some even undermine each other and sell fake and inferior products. This directly affects the reputation of Chinese products on the African market. With Chinese companies' investment in Africa becoming increasingly frequent and thorough, it is necessary for the government to strengthen the strategic planning of enterprises investing in Africa, further standardize enterprises' investment behavior, promote benign competition, and create and nurture a good image of the Chinese enterprises. In addition, the Chinese government still does not have enough and in-depth research for the feasibility of the invested fields and target market of enterprises' investment in Africa, and it also has to face the challenges of insufficient macroeconomic regulations and control of the investment industry guide and the scale of investments. Chinese enterprises in Africa also lack support and cooperation. Therefore, strengthening the government's effective management and regulation of enterprises, realizing a sustainable and healthy development of China's investment in Africa will be a long-term task.

11.3.2 Constraints on Foreign Direct Investment Inflows in African Countries

By summarizing several foreign companies' questionnaires to study the constraints on foreign direct investment into Africa can help us come to a conclusion, which is closer to reality. There are mainly four research projects: (a) World Business Environment (WBE), made by the World Bank in 1999/2000, is a survey that includes 413 foreign companies in 16 sub-Saharan African countries, and uses four levels to represent the constraints on foreign direct investment (1=no limit, 4=extreme limit). (b) The World Development Report (WDR), made by the World Bank in 1996/1997, is a survey that includes 540 foreign companies in 22 sub-Saharan African countries, and uses six levels to represent the constraints on foreign direct investment (1=no limit, 6=extreme limit). (c) World Investment Report (WIR), made by the UN Conference on Trade and Development in 1999/2000, is a survey that includes the world's top 100 multinational companies. (d) The survey of the Center for Research into Economics and Finance in Southern Africa (CREF-SA) includes 81 multinational companies of the Southern African Development Community. Summarizing the results of these surveys, we can see that corruption, weak infrastructure, crime, and unstable political and economic situations are the main constraints of sub-Saharan African countries in attracting foreign direct investment.

11.4 Strategic Planning of China's Direct Investment in Africa

Since investment in the continent faces risks and challenges in many aspects, such as politics, economy, security and so on, China should be more discreet in strategic planning of its investments in Africa. China needs to carefully choose the countries, fields, entry modes, and strategies regarding dealing with the investment risks and the international competition as well as measures that the government takes to encourage enterprises to invest in Africa.

11.4.1 Choose the Countries to Make Direct Investment in Africa Carefully

(1) Give preference to the top countries in economic development, business environment, and global competitiveness

① Africa's economic development engine

The concept of "SANE" was put forward at the annual meeting of the African Development Bank in 2007, which included four African countries—South Africa, Algeria, Nigeria, and Egypt, and it was called the African development engine.

South Africa is the most developed country and has the highest level of industrialization in Africa, with a population of 61 million and a big market capacity. South Africa's GDP in 2008 was USD 276.8274 billion, accounting for 18.0% of that of the African continent. With the expansion of construction and mining, as well as other factors, such as an increasing amount of investments of domestic companies, South Africa's real GDP growth rate was 3.7% in 2008 and the per capita GDP was USD 4,538. The legal system of South Africa has high transparency and stability, high efficiency. South Africa has perfect infrastructures and more mature financial markets. Egypt and Algeria are also in good condition with high levels of industrialization in Africa, with a population of 81.5 million and 34.4 million respectively and a big market capacity. In 2008, the total GDP of Egypt and Algeria accounted for 21.7% of that of the African continent, the real GDP growth rates were 7.2% and 2.4% respectively, and the per capital GDP were USD 2,023 and USD 4,887 respectively. Egypt's economic growth is mainly due to the domestic investment and the development of tourism, which are stimulated by the economic reform, while Algeria's economic growth is mainly due to the increasing public investment. In addition, the two countries' economic growth is also positively influenced by the increasing production of oil and gas and the rising oil prices. Nigeria is Africa's most populous country, with 151 million people and a big domestic market capacity, but its dependence on the oil industry is huge and domestic industrial diversity is poor.

② African countries with a better business environment

"Doing Business 2008" made by the World Bank stated that Mauritius ranked 27th in the world, which had the best business environment among the African countries, followed by South Africa (35th), Namibia (43rd), Botswana (51st), and Kenya (72nd). In *"Doing Business 2010"*, Mauritius rose to the 17th position, and South Africa, Namibia, Botswana, and Kenya, were in the 34th, 66th, 45th, and 95th positions respectively. Mauritius is the air-sea traffic crossroads, which connects Europe, Asia, Africa, and Oceania. So its strategic position is very important, and the domestic tourism industry and the financial industry are very developed; it is also an international business center. Botswana and Namibia are rich in mineral reserves. Kenya is a relatively developed country with a high level of industrialization in East Africa. It has a population of 38.8 million and a large domestic market capacity. In 2008, because of the political unrest caused by the domestic presidential election, Kenya's real GDP growth rate was only 1.7%, and the per capita GDP was USD 782. With the stability of the domestic political situation and the reduction of the negative impacts brought about by the international financial crisis, the economic growth rate was expected to reach 4.1% in 2010. Although Kenya encourages foreign direct investment, the costs brought by domestic corruption and terrorism are relatively large, and this limits large-scale foreign capital inflows.

③ African countries with strong global competitiveness

The global competitiveness index provides a comprehensive summary of the crucial factors of driving productivity and competitiveness, and divides them into nine pillars, namely, the system, infrastructure, macro economy, health and elementary education, higher education and training, market efficiency, technical preparation, enterprise maturity, and innovation. In the "Global Competitiveness Report 2006 to 2007" of the World Economic Forum, the African countries in the ranking of the global competitiveness index of 125 countries are Tunisia (30th), South Africa (45th), Mauritius (55th), Egypt (63rd), Morocco (69th), Algeria (78th), Botswana (81st), and Namibia (84th). The "Global Competitiveness Report 2010 to 2011" ranked 139 countries according to their global competitiveness index.

Namibia and Botswana rose to the 74th and 76th positions respectively, and Mauritius was still in the 55th place; the rest of the countries dropped to lower positions; Tunisia fell to the 32nd position, Morocco fell to the 75th place, Algeria to the 86th, South Africa fell to the 54th, and Egypt fell to the 81st position.

Overall, South Africa, Egypt, Algeria, Nigeria, Mauritius, Morocco, Tunisia, Botswana, Namibia, and Kenya are the 10 African countries with a better investment environment. In 2008, Nigeria, Egypt, South Africa, Algeria, Morocco, and Tunisia were among the top 10 countries in Africa of foreign direct investment inflows. The foreign direct investment of Namibia accounted for the biggest share of the GDP (8.12%), followed by Tunisia (6.77%), Egypt (5.76%), and Mauritius (4.11%).

There are some constraints on foreign investment inflows in these 10 countries. In the survey about the constraints that trouble business activities most, we can find that the top three constraints that trouble the investment in Algeria are poor access to capital, low efficiency of government agencies, and corruption; as for Egypt and Botswana, the constraints were poor access to capital, low efficiency of government agencies, and a lack of an educated workforce; Kenya had corruption, underdeveloped infrastructure, and poor access to capital; as for Mauritius, the constraints were low efficiency of government agencies, restrictive labor laws and regulations, and poor access to capital; as for Morocco, the factors were poor access to capital, high tax rates, and corruption; as for Namibia, the factors were the lack of an educated workforce, poor access to capital, and low efficiency of government agencies; as for South Africa, the factors were the lack of an educated workforce, restrictive labor laws and regulations, crime and theft; as for Tunisia, the factors were the poor access to capital, restrictive labor laws and regulations, and low efficiency of government agencies; for Nigeria, the factors were poor access to capital, underdeveloped infrastructure, and corruption. It also suggested that in order to invest in African countries, we need to take many factors into consideration, such as the local market investment advantages, disadvantages as well as the developmental trend of the economy, politics, and international relations before making the right investment decisions.

(2) Choose the corresponding African countries based on enterprises' motives of direct investment

First, if it is to pursue the market, we can choose the countries that have large domestic market capacity and a strong ability for market radiation to the neighboring countries, and are easy to enter the international market, such as South Africa, Tunisia, Morocco, Egypt, Nigeria, Ghana, Zambia and other countries. Ghana is known as "the portal of West Africa," which has a stable political environment and sustained economic development, so its investment environment is relatively good in the West African region. Zambia, located in Southern Africa, is the headquarters of the African regional group Common Market for Eastern and Southern Africa (COMESA), and it also has a strong radiation to the neighboring countries. The foreign direct investment inflows of Ghana amounted to 1.685 billion USD in 2009, which was the second largest recipient of foreign direct investment in the West African region after Nigeria. Foreign direct investment inflows of Zambia amounted to 959 million USD, which was the third largest recipient of foreign direct investment in the South African region after South Africa and Angola.

Second, if it is to pursue the factors, we can choose the countries that are rich in resources, such as Sudan, Angola, Nigeria, Cameroon, Gabon, Equatorial Guinea and other countries or choose the underdeveloped countries with low labor costs and low income levels. For example, Ethiopia, which is located in East Africa, has relatively rich untapped natural resources and raw materials, and it also has a large population and low labor prices. The modern industrial and commercial services are almost blank, and the government provides investors with a variety of preferential treatments and conveniences, which provides a broad developmental space for Chinese investors. Most West African countries are at a low level of industrialization, and many countries even have no industry or processing industries, let alone heavy industries. Their daily necessities, office supplies, industrial products, finished products, and semi-finished products all rely on importations. Most countries implement a free trade policy, so others can import as long as they pay the relevant taxes. In order to reduce costs, the Chinese enterprises can invest in West African countries, exporting the industrial semi-finished products, parts, components, and raw materials to West Africa to get deep processing and then sell the finished products to the local market or export them on the international market, which can bring them considerable economic benefits. Of course, since most West African countries are in the midst of a transition to economic liberalization and privatization, whose economic policies, investment policies, and market regulations are yet to be perfected, the Chinese enterprises' investment in Africa will encounter various difficulties, and even risks. Therefore, to develop the market in West African countries, investors should not only have a flexible management mind, but also an awareness of how to prevent risks.

Third, if investment is the strategy for global development, one can choose the African countries that enjoy a good economic developmental situation, a good business environment, and a high quality of human capital, and which should also encourage Chinese companies to invest there, such as Egypt, South Africa, Mauritius and so on.

(3) Try to stay away from sub-Saharan African economically fragile countries

According to the classification of sub-Saharan African countries in the "Regional Economic Outlook: Sub-Saharan Africa," which was published by the International Monetary Fund in April 2008, there were 14 economically fragile countries. These countries' political situations were unstable, and their macroeconomic systems were fragile; their economic growth was slow and they were easily affected by external shocks. For example, in 2007, the economic growth rate of Eritrea was only 2% due to domestic political instability and the over-control of the economy by the central government. The decline of vanilla export prices in Comoros and the falling tourism revenues led to an economic growth of only 2%. Zimbabwe's domestic political instability caused a negative economic growth of 2.5%. Cote d'Ivoire and Guinea had the slowest economic growth in West Africa, of which the economic growth rates were 2% and 1.5%

respectively in 2007. Cote d'Ivoire's political instability, underdeveloped infrastructure, and fragile economy affected the investments and production, especially in the cocoa and oil sectors. Besides the political instability, the backward agricultural production and infrastructure and the burden of higher oil prices in Guinea all led to reduced economic growth.

Because the macroeconomic and business environment in these countries are not ideal, Chinese enterprises should try to stay away from them, especially the landlocked countries, which are not resource-based, such as Burundi, Central Africa, and Zimbabwe, when investing in Africa.

11.4.2 Focus on the Preferential Areas for China's Direct Investment in Africa

In recent years, with the rapid development of China's economy, a large number of enterprises which have competitive advantages and economies of scale have emerged. These enterprises rely on existing equipment and mature technology to invest in African countries, which can not only enlarge the exports of Chinese products to these countries, but also avoid the tariff and non-tariff barriers and achieve multi-channel exportation. Specifically, when investing directly in Africa, Chinese companies should give priority to the fields with complementary advantages in order to achieve the goal of win-win development.

(1) Agriculture and resources

① Agriculture

First of all, Chinese enterprises can invest locally in Africa and engage in the processing of agricultural products. Africa is rich in agricultural products, such as cocoa, coffee, cashew nuts, cotton, sesame, peanuts, and other crops. But the agricultural product processing industry is very backward in many countries. For example, Cote d'Ivoire is rich in tropical cash crops such as cocoa and coffee, and its cocoa export ranks the first, coffee ranks the fourth, and cashew the fifth in the world. But due to the lack of capital, technology, and management experience, many promising areas, such as the deep processing of cocoa, soybean planting and processing, and palm oil, coconut, bamboo processing and papermaking all develop slowly. Chinese companies can take advantage of the rich agricultural resources to invest locally in Africa, engage in deep and fine processing of agricultural products, and supply the final products to Africa or to the international market.

Second, Chinese enterprises can establish agricultural technology centers in Africa to improve agricultural productivity. In Africa, the mechanization rate and fertilizer utilization rate in agricultural production are very low, and the agricultural product processing levels are also low. African countries need to improve their agricultural productivity, realize deep and fine processing of agricultural products, and develop new varieties to improve the competitiveness of their agricultural products on the international market. As an agricultural country, China has a relatively mature type of agriculture. Chinese companies can use domestic advanced agricultural technology for crop farming in Africa. By establishing agricultural technology centers in African countries, they can guide local farmers to use agricultural machinery, apply fertilizer reasonably, breed excellent varieties, use pesticides and so on.

Third, Chinese companies can invest to set up farms in Africa. In recent years, many African countries have begun to put the development of agriculture in an important position in the national economy, and they are really eager to introduce agricultural development experience and technology from China. In order to attract foreign investment in agriculture, many African countries have formulated preferential land lease systems and reduction or exemption policies of taxation on agricultural products and imported agricultural machinery, and so on. African land is very cheap. Take Zambia for example; the purchasing price (which can be used nearly a century after owning property) is only equivalent to the annual rent of China. In addition, the prices of main agricultural production goods, labor, and electricity are only half of those in China. Therefore, Chinese enterprises can build farms in African countries to develop the production of food crops and cash crops.

② Resource development

The continent has extremely rich energy, mineral resources, and agricultural forestry resources. Among them, the reserve of the oil energy, which is the strategic energy, is immense, accounting for about 12% of the world's total reserves. In the continent of Africa, we can explore all the minerals in the world, the reserves of platinum, chromium, manganese and other non-ferrous metals account for about 80% of the world's total reserves, and the reserves of gold, diamond, cobalt, vanadium and other minerals account for more than 50% of the world's total reserves. In China, many resources that are very important and concern the national economy and people's livelihood are scarce, and therefore, we need to import a large number of resources from African countries. Among them, oil imports form the biggest proportion. With the increase in China's oil importations, the exploitation of the international oil market will have a close relationship with China's future economic development and energy security.

China now imports a large amount of oil from Africa, while the cooperation with local regions on oil exploitation, oilfield services, and oilfield equipment supply have not been widely spread. In the future, Chinese enterprises should strengthen the cooperation with oil producers in a variety of forms; organically combine the commodity trade, direct investment, technology, and labor exportation with resources cooperation, in order to better meet the demand for oil. In addition, China has increased its importations of a lot of important resources, such as wood, iron, copper, and manganese, and these natural resource reserves and outputs are very rich in many countries in Africa. In the future, Chinese enterprises should strengthen investment cooperation with African countries in the field of resources to ensure the long-term development of China's national economy.

(2) Manufacturing

① The home appliance industry

The foundation of the home appliance industry in African countries is weak, the products cannot achieve self-sufficiency, and most of the equipment, parts, and raw materials need to be imported. In recent years, the demand for electrical appliances in African countries has been growing at an average annual rate of 5.5%, of which the demand for television has been growing at an annual rate of more than 16%. Now, in addition to a few countries, such as Egypt, South Africa, and Nigeria, the home appliance market of many African countries is almost vacant with a huge market space. However, since on the African market, the electrical appliances from R.O. Korea, Japan, the United States and other countries are given priority, and since Chinese home appliance enterprises in Africa have not taken shape, the promotion of Chinese home appliances brands remains to be further expanded.

At present, the Chinese home appliances enterprises' investment in Africa mainly includes Hisense's production base in South Africa, the home appliance industrial parks in Tunisia and Nigeria set up by Haier, and the factory co-founded by Jiangsu Shinco Electrical Appliance Co., Ltd. in Nigeria. Most domestic electrical appliances enterprises still remain in the phase of export trade, mainly exporting products directly to the African countries, which have not invested in factories directly in the local areas to promote the brands. Since the demand for home appliances in Africa has increased dramatically in recent years, the exports of Chinese home appliances to Africa are increasing at a rate of 15% per year. The Chinese home appliances enterprises are becoming more and more enthusiastic about making direct investments and establishing production bases in Africa, in order to increase their market share.

② The textile industry

The textile industry in African countries is generally underdeveloped, and most countries face the problem of backward production technology, outdated equipment, lack of skilled workers or high-quality raw materials, and so on, and they have to rely on a large number of textile importations to meet domestic consumption demands. Chinese enterprises can make use of their technology advantages in the textile-processing industry to cooperate with African countries. Cotton, the main raw material of the textile industry, is widely planted in Africa, but cotton processing methods of many cotton producers are very backward. To this end, China's textile enterprises can establish cotton-processing bases in cotton-producing coutries in Africa and then sell cotton cloth and clothes in the local areas or export them to neighboring countries, in order to obtain larger investment returns. Mali, in West Africa, produces high-quality cotton and Mali provides foreign investors with many preferential conditions. For example, for a new business enterprise, as long as it is an approved enterprise, when completing an approved plan in the process of founding, which requires imported machinery, equipment, tools, accessories, and building materials, taxes can be exempted in the first three years, and corporate taxes, industrial and commercial taxes, business taxes and so on can be exempted during the first eight years. These incentives are attractive to Chinese investors.

③ The car industry

Currently, there are many automobile giants from the developed countries competing on the African car market, such as Renault of France and Nissan of Japan, as well as some car companies from the emerging countries, such as Iran's Cordero. With the rapid development of China's automobile manufacturing industry, the Great Wall, Chery, Jiangling, Steyr, the Yellow River and other domestic cars are exported to the African market increasingly as well. At present, Chinese car companies not only export cars to Africa, but also invest in African countries in order to reduce transportation and customs costs. Chinese car companies have built several heavy car assembly plants in countries such as Tanzania and Uganda. China also built "Angola Automobile Industry Park" to manufacture Chinese cars in the capital city of Luanda. The park covers an area of approximately 40,000 square meters and mainly includes the passenger car joint workshop and the pick-up (cars) assembly workshop, of which the annual production capacity is 1,000 passenger cars and 30,000 SUVs and pick-ups. It can be clearly seen that Chinese enterprises have gradually realized that the African car market has tremendous potential, and so they are stepping up their efforts to invest in Africa.

(3) The service sector

① The financial services industry

Because of the greatly enhanced economic strength and a huge amount of China's foreign exchange reserves, China is an important funding source for the African countries, which lack funds and are eager to attract foreign direct investments. With the in-depth development of China-Africa investment cooperation, the financial sector, which was less involved once upon a time, is also beginning to involve itself in this venture. The People's Bank of China and the African Development Bank have set up a bilateral technical cooperation fund of 2 million USD. The China Development Bank Group has set up 18 groups in Africa and signed framework cooperation agreements with the East African Development Bank and the PTA Bank. Other domestic financial institutions will also set up branches or representative offices in Africa, providing credit support for African businesses and further aiding African countries to reduce their debt burden. On March 18, 2008, the Industrial and Commercial Bank of China Co., Ltd. and South Africa's Standard Bank Group Co., Ltd. held a meeting in Beijing to kick off their strategic cooperation, which declared that the two sides would carry out in-depth cooperation in the areas of trade financing, international settlement, investment funds, staple commodities, the global market, investment banks and so on. In December 2008, the China Development Bank signed an agreement with the Zambia Development Bank and formally established a developmental financial cooperative partnership. The Export-Import Bank of China has established stable cooperative relations with the African Export-Import Bank, and the two sides signed framework cooperation agreements, which aims to promote China-Africa economic and trade investment cooperation, and reached some credit agreements on the basis of this agreement. For example, in 2009, the two banks signed an agreement on credit limit to trade financing. The African Export-Import Bank used the funds, which came from the agreement on credit limits signed by the two sides, to finance the telecommunications projects of Mauritius customers in Zimbabwe and Burundi, to support their imports from China's ZTE Corporation.

② The telecommunications service industry

In recent years, great progress has been made in the telecommunications industry in many African countries, which generates enormous business opportunities. Compared with other regions, penetration of Africa's telecommunications services is still relatively low and its distribution is unbalanced. Take the mobile phone penetration for example; Tunisia is 84%, Algeria 88%, South Africa 92%, while Ethiopia is only 1%, and Zimbabwe and Malawi are 8% and 13% respectively. Africa's Internet penetration is only 5.4% at present, whereas the global average level is 21.9%; so Africa's telecommunications market has a great potential (May 31, 2009, *People's Daily*). Nowadays, mobile communications and Internet broadband industries have become new hot spots for investment following the traditional industry of natural resources. In 2009, telecommunications and services attracted the most foreign direct investments in Africa. According to the forecast of the World Bank, Africa's telecommunications industry will develop at a high speed in the next few years, and its investments are also expected to increase.

The African country which has the most developed and mature telecommunications market is South Africa. Egypt's telecommunications industry has also developed very fast. In addition, the telecommunications industry of Cameroon, Togo and Cote d'Ivoire of West Africa, Kenya and Uganda of East Africa, and Southern African countries like Botswana have also developed rapidly in recent years. The development of the African telecommunications industry provides opportunities for Chinese enterprises. Now there are two main Chinese enterprises conducting telecommunications business in Africa—Huawei Technologies Co., Ltd. and ZTE Corporation; the two companies have gained a foothold in Africa's telecommunications sector, and are gradually expanding the size of their market.

(4) The field of medicine

The foundation of the African medicine industry is weak. In addition to a few countries such as South Africa and Egypt, of which the foundations of the medicine industry are relatively better, other African countries rely on the importation of raw materials and packaging materials to produce drugs. Because the African continent has all kinds of diseases, there is a heavy demand for drugs. The production of drugs in many countries cannot meet domestic consumption needs and have to rely on importations to satisfy the domestic demand. The medical expense of Africa is about USD 6 billion every year, and 85% of it is for imported drugs; the main import sources are

European and American countries and India.

Although the potential of the African medical market is tremendous, China's investment and export quantity on the African market is negligible in addition to some artemisinin products and active pharmaceutical ingredients. Chinese drugs have the advantages of low prices and a high quality, which greatly satisfy the need of the African market and have strong competitiveness. Chinese enterprises should realize that the African market is a long-term market, so they should have the mindset of a long-term cooperation to develop that market.

11.4.3 The Strategies of Chinese Companies to Invest Directly in Africa

(1) Internal management of enterprises

First, China should obtain long-term competitive advantages of research and development. Facing the current increasingly fierce global competition, Chinese enterprises must seek their own competitive advantages to obtain long-term survival and development. The American management scientist Michael Porter once pointed out that in all the factors that change the rules of competition, technological change is one of the most significant. Enterprises' research and development activities and competitive strategies influence each other. On the one hand, when enterprises' competition strategies are determined, it would demand corresponding research and development; on the other hand, as important strategic resources, research and development activities are the basis for enterprises to develop competitive strategies. In accordance with this, the overall competitive strategies, which are dominated by enterprises' technological strategies will take shape. Thus, it can be seen that the level of enterprises' research and development is the fundamental source of gaining competitive advantages. Therefore, Chinese enterprises should increase their investments in product research and development to obtain long-term competitive advantages.

Second, China has to pay attention to the role of brands in the market competition. In general, the brand is the identification of the product; it refers to the product's trademark, especially the registered trademark. But when people talk about the product brand, it mostly refers to the quality, performance, and utilization of the product, as well as the market positioning, cultural connotation, and consumer's perception of the brand; the brand represents the product's image on the market. The competitiveness of the products and the enterprises are ultimately reflected in the brand's competitiveness. The brand possesses premium effect and scale effect, which are the direct sources of the brand strategy to produce benefits. The premium effect refers to the fact that the price of the particular product is higher than the general level, and the scale effect refers to the concept of obtaining economic benefits by the scale of operations and the expansion of market sales. Brand is an important weapon of multinational companies to realize their global strategy, which can be used to spread the influences of products, improve the market share on the international market, and enhance the international competitiveness of the enterprises. A brand can even directly represent the international market advantage of the products of a certain enterprise. Chinese companies should pay more attention to the effect of brand in international competition, actively take the strategy of brand competition, increase the investment to create famous brand products, and use the brand advantage as a significant means for market competition in the future.

Third, China has to actively carry out international marketing. Peter Drucker argues that the coverage of marketing is far beyond that of simple sales, so marketing should not be seen as a specific activity. He thinks that the real marketing should be a comprehensive cause through the efforts of the overall company, which is based on the customers' views. Northwestern University professor Schurz and other experts and scholars put forward the integrated marketing theory. Integrated marketing is an interaction process for the management of beneficial brand relationships, by leading people to learn together with the enterprise so as to keep the consistency of the brand communication strategy, in order to strengthen positive dialogue between the companies and customers and other interested parties, and promote the enterprise's mission of enhancing brand trust. At present, carrying out international marketing has become the only way for enterprises to expand their international market. In order to adapt to the objective requirement of the trend toward internationalization of domestic marketing, Chinese enterprises should consider the customers as the center of the marketing network, increase publicity, expand corporate recognition, and try to provide customers with a full range of services; attention has to be given to the collection of market information and the results of market research, determine the product's position on the market correctly, and take the right management countermeasures; new ways of marketing must be actively promoted; modern marketing means should be mastered; and great importance must be attached to the role of modern science and technology, the concept of management, and marketing on the international market.

(2) Enterprises' decision-making regarding external investments

First, full market research and on-the-spot investigation before the investment decision-making have to be conducted. There are 53 countries in Africa, which have many differences in their political, economic, social, and cultural development. Before investing in Africa, it is necessary for Chinese companies to comprehensively analyze and research various factors, such as the local political environment, the macroeconomic situation, the business environment, the foreign capital policy, market demand and potential, labor costs, purchasing power and resource advantages, carry out on-the-spot investigations and gain detailed understanding, truly understand the market environment and consumer demand, and choose countries and projects with a relatively high ROI and a relatively low level of risk.

Second, the China-Africa economic and trade cooperation zones have to be relied on to invest in and preferential policies have to be effectively used. The Chinese government supports competent Chinese enterprises in constructing trade and economic cooperation zones in the countries with qualified requirements to bring more Chinese companies to invest and establish factories in the host country, form a cluster effect, increase employment and tax revenue for the host country, expand exports, improve the level of technology, and promote economic development. At the same time, it also improves the Chinese enterprises' ability for internationalization and realizes mutual benefit and win-win results. The zones will be in line with the principle of "the enterprises as the main body, commercial operation as the basis, mutual benefit and win-win results as the purpose" to operate. The enterprises make decisions according to the market situation, the host country's investment environment, and investment attraction policies. At present, the projects of the economic and trade cooperation zones in Zambia, Mauritius, Nigeria, and Egypt, which are approved to be established by the Chinese government, have been initiated. If Chinese companies choose to invest in the China-Africa economic and trade cooperation zones, they can not only expand their scale of business with the help of the preferential policies provided by the governments, but also promote the economic development of Africa and achieve mutual benefits and win-win results.

Third, the fund support of the China-Africa Development Fund has to be used to develop the African market. The China-Africa Development Fund, which was approved by China's State Council, was established in June 2007, with a primary fund of USD 1 billion invested by the China Development Bank, and it finally increased to USD 5 billion. It is considered to be the world's largest fund that has been dedicated to African development. The China-Africa Development Fund hires professional teams for operation and management and guides and supports Chinese enterprises to expand their direct investment in Africa. China's Ministry of Commerce said that the China-Africa Development Fund will focus on supporting agriculture, manufacturing, infrastructure, resource development and other investment fields in Africa, as well as supporting Chinese enterprises in establishing industrial parks in Africa, and in other similar initiatives. Chinese enterprises can make full use of the fund support of the China-Africa Development Fund, and actively explore the investment market in Africa.

Fourth, with the aid of the preferential policies of developed countries in Africa, export-oriented processing enterprises need to be developed. At present, the developed countries have more trade preferential policies for Africa, such as the African Growth and Opportunity Act of the United States, which broadens access conditions to the textile clothing market in a majority of sub-Saharan African countries, with more than 7,000 kinds of products on the market enjoying preferential treatment of zero tariffs and no quota restrictions when entering the United States' market. The EU's

"Everything but Arms" policy stated that all goods exported from the least-developed African countries to the EU, except for arms, are free of tariffs and quotas. Chinese investors can take advantage of these preferential trade policies to develop export-oriented processing enterprises in Africa to better explore the market in developed countries.

11.4.4 The Chinese Government's Strategies of Encouraging Enterprises to Invest in Africa

First, the macro planning and management of enterprises' direct investments in Africa have to be strengthened. When Chinese enterprises "go out" to invest abroad, they need legal protection and support, but at present, China has not introduced relevant laws on overseas investment. Currently, we only have regulations made by the ministries and commissions, and internal policies of relevant government departments, which have low legal effects and have not risen to the height of law. This also makes the Chinese government lack a unified macro coordination and management structure, as well as unified planning and layout to organize enterprises' investments in Africa, and blind investment may unavoidably occur, as well as disorderly competition. Therefore, the Chinese government should formulate relevant laws as soon as possible, set up the foreign-related legal system which accords with the international convention, reduce unreasonable administrative intervention, establish unified enterprise management systems and industry standards to organize Chinese enterprises' investments in Africa, strengthen the regulation of investments by Chinese enterprises in Africa, and promote the smooth development of Chinese enterprises' investments in Africa.

Second, early warning mechanisms of the risk and insurance systems of enterprises' investments must be established in Africa. The risks faced by Chinese companies that invest in Africa are mainly divided into political risks, operational risks, and natural disaster risks. Natural disaster risks cannot be assessed. Political risks and operational risks, however, can be effectively prevented through the establishment of the overseas investment risk early warning mechanism. The overseas investment risk early warning system is a feedforward control system, which is to identify, predict, as well as put forward some measures to prevent or resolve those abnormal situations, the spacial scale and the time-space range as well as the extent of the harm from the risk. Through the establishment of an overseas investment risk early warning mechanism of risk identification—risk assessment—risk elimination, we can carry out the tracking and monitoring of the risks in enterprises' overseas investments, and take prompt measures to eliminate risks, so as to greatly reduce the risk for Chinese enterprises' overseas investments.

Third, the financial support for enterprises' investments in Africa has to be strengthened. At present, Chinese enterprises' investments in Africa still has relatively narrow financing channels. Because of system and regulatory regime, China still does not have a financing mechanism serving overseas investments, so that many enterprises have neither guaranty rights nor foreign funding rights; besides, they do not have their own financial companies. Without a strong financial policy support, the enterprises' overseas investments cannot develop smoothly; so financial support is an important factor in deciding the extent of investment in overseas markets, including the African market. To this end, the Chinese government should appropriately relax the financial control over enterprises and its foreign exchange control; and it should give necessary overseas rights of funding to those eligible multinational companies, allowing these companies to raise funds by issuing stocks and bonds on the international market. The government should also allow enterprises to establish financial companies in foreign countries, which could gradually strengthen enterprises' financial self-supporting function.

Fourth, the government's public service system for enterprises' investments should be established in Africa. First of all, special investment promotion agencies must be established to provide enterprises with information about the policy of overseas investments, and the agencies should also work in the formulation of foreign investment policy. Besides, the government should provide domestic enterprises with overseas information and advisory services to make decisions on overseas investments. A specialized system of overseas investment information consultation service must be developed, and an investment evaluation report must be generated. Foreign investment policies and regulations, as well as the latest information about their changes must be obtained from the embassies and business institutions, and then provided to investors. Then, the mediating role of the China-Africa Business Council should be actively played to perfect the intermediary service for enterprises' investment in Africa. Coordinate enterprises' investment behavior and avoid blind investments or disorderly competition.

12

Strategies for Promoting the Trade and Industrial Integration of Mechanical and Electrical Products of the Chinese Mainland and Chinese Taiwan

Nowadays, the global economic structure is adjusting quickly, the rapid flow of the production factors among the adjacent areas makes capital, technology, information, and labor resources break the geographical constraints to achieve optimal transregional allocation, and the interdependence of the regional economy is being expanded. Complementary regional economic cooperation is the inevitable choice for each economy to achieve further development and promote industrial competitiveness. At the same time, it is also the inevitable requirement of its industrial structural adjustment. The mainland and Taiwan are separate customs territories, which are established respectively; the rapid development of their mechanical and electrical industries presents a state of integration driven by ECFA's regional economic cooperation of trade and investment.

12.1 Current Trade Situation of Mechanical and Electrical Products in the Mainland and Taiwan

12.1.1 The Growth Rate of Trade of Mechanical and Electrical Products Between the Mainland and Taiwan Grows in Step with China's Exportation of Mechanical and Electrical Products

(1) The scale of trade of mechanical and electrical products between the mainland and Taiwan expands unceasingly

Since China's reform and opening-up, the economic exchanges and trade between the mainland and Taiwan and the investment of Taiwan-based businessmen in the mainland have developed for nearly 20 years. In this context, the acceleration of the increasing speed and expansion of the scale of the trade of mechanical and electrical products play a crucial role in promoting the exports of mechanical and electrical products from the mainland and driving the growth of overall export trade.

The mutual trading in mechanical and electrical products between the two sides includes electronics, machinery, and vehicles with about 25 categories of products. In 2000, the volume of trade of mechanical and electrical products between the two sides was only USD 14.274 billion, and the mainland imported products worth USD 11.911 billion from Taiwan and exported products worth USD 2.363 billion. In 2006, the volume of trade of mechanical and electrical products between the two sides reached USD 73.005 billion, which increased by 23% compared with that in 2005 (USD 59.419 billion). The mainland imported products worth USD 60.597 billion from Taiwan and exported products worth USD 12.408 billion in 2006, which increased by USD 11.026 billion and USD 2.56 billion respectively compared with the imports and exports in 2005. In 2007, the volume of trade of mechanical and electrical products between the two sides reached USD 83.47 billion, which accounted for 67% of the total volume of trade between the two sides, and the year-on-year growth was 14.3%. Among them, the mainland imported products worth USD 69.57 billion from Taiwan and exported products for a volume of USD 13.9 billion, and the deficit was USD 55.67 billion. However, under the influence of the international financial crisis in 2008 and due to a lack of a mechanism of institutional cooperation between the two sides, the volume of trade of mechanical and electrical products dropped to USD 59.984 billion, which decreased by 28.14% compared with that in 2007. However, the trade varieties of mechanical and electrical products were diversified. In all the categories of products, the top five types of mechanical and electrical products (according to the sum of money), which were exported to Taiwan by the mainland are electronic components, automatic data processing equipment and components and accessories, electrical equipment, communications equipment and parts, household appliances and consumer electronic products; the prominent five types of mechanical and electrical products Taiwan exported to the mainland are electronic components, automatic data processing equipment and components and accessories, electrical equipment, metal processing machines, communications equipment and parts. It turns out that the trade in mechanical and electrical products between the two sides mainly has centered on electronic components, automatic data processing equipment and spare parts, electrical equipment and so on. And it shows that the intra-industry trade of mechanical and electrical products is active, and the divisions of labor for specialized production and industrial integration have continuously expanded.

The reason the intra-industry trade of mechanical and electrical products between the two sides presents this characteristic is that behind the continuous expansion of the volume of trade of mechanical and electrical products between the two sides, the share of investments in the mechanical and electrical industry of Taiwan-based businessmen in the mainland increases year after year. This not only boosts the trade of mechanical and electrical products between the two sides, but also plays a positive role in promoting the mechanical and electrical products exported from the mainland to adapt to the international market demand for mechanical and electrical products.

(2) The growth of the trade in mechanical and electrical products between the two sides is positively related to the growth of total exportations

Analyzing the changes in China's exportations in the past 20 years, we found that the growth rate of the exportation of mechanical and electrical products and China's total export growth rate are inseparably interconnected, and the growth rate of the exportation of mechanical and electrical products remains slightly higher than China's total export growth rate. This suggests that the growth of the exportation of mechanical and electrical products has been a strong impetus for the growth of China's total exports. In 1995, the share of the exportation of mechanical and electrical products in China's total exports reached 29.5% from 6.1% in 1985, and became China's largest category of export products (see Figure 12.1). Since then, the share of the exportations of mechanical and electrical products in China's total exports remained at more than 30%, and in 2003, it was up to 51.9%, which occupied half of the total amount of exports. Although before 2000, there were no formally established trade statistics of mechanical and electrical products, in fact, during the 1980s and 1990s, they played an irreplaceable role in accelerating the upgrading of mechanical and electrical products and even the whole export growth in the entire mainland that Taiwan-based businessmen invested heavily in and for which they established factories in the regions of the Pearl River Delta and the Yangtze River Delta through companies registered in Hong Kong, and they used cheap labor in the mainland to implement the processing trade mode of "processing with supplied materials, processing with supplied samples, assembling with supplied parts, and compensatory trade" and "having stores in front and factories behind." According to the statistics of China's Ministry of Commerce, in 2000, the volume of trade of mechanical and electrical products was USD 14.274 billion, and since then, it has always maintained double-digit growth rates. Especially, the years 2002 and 2003 witnessed the most significant growth, and the growth rates of the volume of trade of mechanical and electrical products reached 57.9% and 41.8% respectively. Analyzing the growth trend of the volume of trade of mechanical and electrical products after 2000 objectively, we can see that except for the individual years, the growth rate of mechanical and electrical products' trade and the growth of mechanical and electrical products' exportations from the mainland kept the same pace (see Figure 12.1). The growth trend could verify that, since the beginning of the new century, with the mechanical and electrical products' trade between the two sides accelerating, the growth of China's mechanical and electrical products' exportations and the total exportations also speeded up synchronously. This positively related growth trend is obvious. At the same time, the share of China's exports of mechanical and electrical products in total exports continued to rise, too.

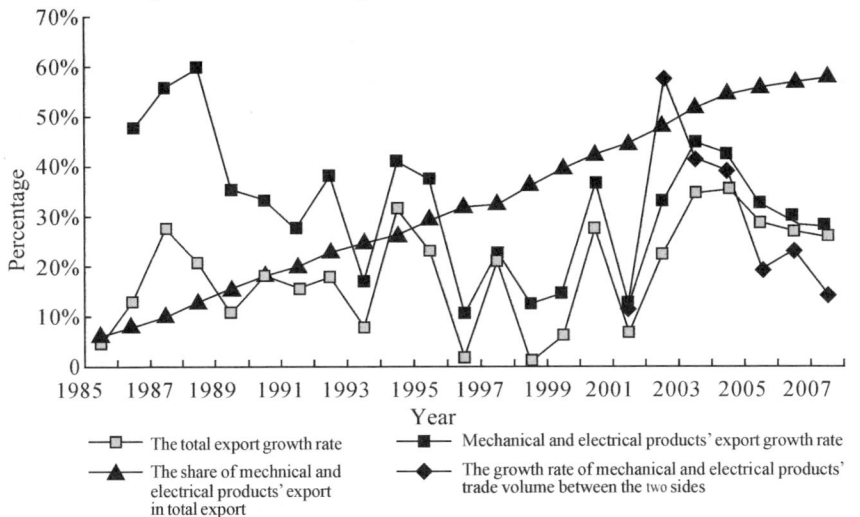

Figure 12.1 The growth of trade in mechanical and electrical products between the two sides and the total amount of exports of mechanical and electrical products

Source: *China Statistical Yearbook* over the years and statistics from the Ministry of Commerce of China.

12.1.2 Analysis of the Imbalance of Trade of Mechanical and Electrical Products and the Complementarity of the Industrial Structure Between the Two Sides

(1) The imbalance of trade of mechanical and electrical products between the two sides

Since the 1990s, the growth of trade between the mainland and Taiwan has speeded up noticeably. The overall volume of trade in commodities increased to USD 107.84 billion in 2006 compared with USD 4.04 billion in 1990, and the average annual growth rate was 21.1%. The total volume of trade between the two sides in 2006 increased by 18.2% compared with that in 2005. In 2008, the total volume of trade between the two sides was USD129.215 billion, increasing by 15.4% over that in 2007. Among them, the imports amounted to USD 103.34 billion, exports were USD 25.88 billion, and the deficit was USD 77.46 billion. In recent years, the trade of mechanical and electrical products between the mainland and Taiwan has maintained steady growth, and has become the main component of import and export trade between the two sides. In 2006, the total export-import volume of mechanical and electrical products between the two sides was more than USD 73 billion, and the year-on-year growth was 22.9%, accounting for 67.7% of the total amount of bilateral trade. In 2007, the total export-import volume of mechanical and electrical products between the two sides was USD 83.47 billion. However, in 2008, due to the international financial crisis, it declined. Table 12.1 reflects the growth of trade in mechanical and electrical products between the two sides in nine years. The mechanical and electrical industry is the leading industry of the bilateral trade, the development of the intra-industry trade of mechanical and electrical products has expanded more rapidly than the development of the inter-industry trade (Table 12.1).

Table 12.1 Trade of mechanical and electrical products between the two sides during the period 2000—2008

Year	Trade amount of mechanical and electrical products		Imports (the mainland from Taiwan)		Exports (the mainland to Taiwan)		Deficit (the mainland to Taiwan)	
	Amount (USD billion)	Growth rate	Amount (USD billion)	Growth rate	Amount (USD billion)	Growth rate	Amount (USD billion)	Growth rate
2000	14.274	—	11.911	—	2.363	—	9.548	—
2001	15.991	12.00%	13.404	12.50%	2.587	9.50%	10.818	13.30%
2002	25.255	57.90%	21.465	60.10%	3.790	46.50%	17.675	63.40%

(To be continued)

(Continued)

Year	Trade amount of mechanical and electrical products		Imports (the mainland from Taiwan)		Exports (the mainland to Taiwan)		Deficit (the mainland to Taiwan)	
	Amount (USD billion)	Growth rate	Amount (USD billion)	Growth rate	Amount (USD billion)	Growth rate	Amount (USD billion)	Growth rate
2003	35.806	41.80%	30.335	41.30%	5.471	44.40%	24.864	40.70%
2004	49.891	39.30%	42.168	39.00%	7.723	41.10%	34.445	38.50%
2005	59.419	19.10%	49.571	17.60%	9.848	27.50%	39.723	15.30%
2006	73.005	22.90%	60.597	22.20%	12.408	26.00%	48.189	21.30%
2007	83.470	14.20%	69.570	14.80%	13.900	12.00%	55.670	15.50%
2008	59.984	−28.14%	48.253	−30.64%	11.631	−16.32%	33.622	−39.60%

Source: According to statistics of the Ministry of Commerce and *China Trade and External Economic Statistical Yearbook 2009*.

From Table 12.1, we can also see that there has always been a serious deficit in the trade of mechanical and electrical products from the mainland to Taiwan. It corresponds to the developmental stage and the pattern of the division of labor in the mechanical and electrical industry; at the same time, it is also associated with the import restrictions of Taiwan's authorities on the mainland. Taiwan's authorities have taken the policy of "import tightly, export loosely" with regard to the mainland. They strictly control the manufactured products that the mainland exports to Taiwan, so that the trade of the mainland to Taiwan has always been in a deficit position. Especially in the trade of mechanical and electrical products, the imbalance between the two sides is growing. In 2000, the mainland imported mechanical and electrical products worth USD 11.911 billion from Taiwan, and exported products worth USD 2.363 billion, and the deficit was USD 9.548 billion; in 2006, the mainland imported mechanical and electrical products worth USD 60.597 billionfrom Taiwan, and exported USD 12.408 billion, and the deficit was USD 48.189 billion; in 2007, the deficit continued to expand to USD 55.67 billion; but in 2008, the trade deficit began to reduce. Overall, the scale of trade of mechanical and electrical products for nine years increased by 3.2 times, and the trade deficit also increased by 2.5 times correspondingly.

(2) Imbalance of the trade of mechanical and electrical products is contrary to the complementarity of industrial structure between the two sides

Further connecting to the present situation of the industrial structure of the two sides, in addition to the complementarity of resources, there is a wide relevance and complementarity in different industries of the two sides. According to the census data of the GDP of the National Bureau of Statistics in 2009, the proportion of the primary, secondary, and tertiary sectors in the GDP of the mainland was 10.3%, 46.3%, and 43.4% respectively. This is a typical structure of the developing countries which give priority to the secondary sector. Although the mainland has developed in the high and new technology industry, it is still based on labor-intensive manufacturing and processing industries. After the completion of the third stage of large-scale industrial structural upgrading in the 1980s, Taiwan has shown an evident tendency toward the same industrial structure as that of the post-industrial society. The proportion of Taiwan's primary, secondary, and tertiary sectors in the GDP was 2.1%, 32.4%, 65.5% respectively, and it presented a developmental trend that was mainly based on the services industry. Trade imbalance should not be the norm of the development of mechanical and electrical industries of the two sides, which is presented by the influence of the complementarity of the existing industrial structure on the trade of mechanical and electrical products. The status quo shows that in the field of the mechanical and electrical industry, there is a broad space for cooperation, and there are many industries whose potential of complementary advantages has not been tapped. The most prominent problem is that Taiwan's high-tech industries are mainly concentrated in the electronic information hardware industry. On the surface, it is a link of the supply chain of global electronic information products. However, actually, it has not gotten rid of the condition that the key technology and components are subject to the United States, Japan and so on. Taiwan is still on the edge of the core of the international industrial division, and many exports of technology and capital-intensive products to the mainland do not have independent intellectual property rights. Therefore, if Taiwan increases its importing of technology-intensive electronic information software products, which contain certain intellectual labor from the mainland, and does further research and develops electronic information hardware products to face the international market together with the mainland, the complementary advantages of the industrial structure of the two sides can be fully exploited, and it can also reverse the passive situation that the imbalance of the trade of mechanical and electrical products conflicts with the complementarity of the industrial structure.

12.2 Features of Integration and Investment of the Mechanical and Electrical Industries of the Two Sides

12.2.1 The Focus of the Integration of the Mechanical and Electrical Industries of the Two Sides is on the Division of Labor and Cooperation on the Electronic Information Manufacturing Industry

(1) The electronic information manufacturing industry leads in Taiwan-based businessmen's investments in the mainland

At the forefront in the field of the modern mechanical and electrical industry, electronic information technology has rapidly developed for over 30 years as the core technology of the fifth generation. Since China's electronic information technology industry started late, it is still in the passive and subordinate position in the international division of labor. Taiwan, as the key tie between the electronic information technology industry of the mainland and the countries with the core technology, performs functions that cannot be ignored in carrying out technology transfer and integrating the information technology industries of the two sides.

Since the mid-1980s, the Taiwan authorities have adopted a high-tech industrial policy, which centers on industrial upgrading, and it has played a positive role in promoting the development of the manufacturing industry and industrial upgrading, especially the ultra-high growth speed of its electronic information industry for the past 10 years. From 1986 to 2000, the average growth rate was as high as 26%, making it the mainstay of Taiwan's economy. But Taiwan's own market was narrow and at the same time, the cost of production was increasing, so a large number of businesses within Taiwan's electronic information industry and electrical appliances manufacturing industry as well as the high-tech manufacturing industry moved to the mainland. According to the statistics of Taiwan, among their investments in the industries in the mainland, the electronic information manufacturing industry accounted for 33.82% of the total amount, which presents the structural change that the proportion of a single sector was more than a third and ranked first. In addition, apart from the electronic information industry and electrical appliances manufacturing, the mechanical and electrical industry also covers machinery manufacturing, precision machinery manufacturing, and transportation tools manufacturing. The total proportion of these industries in Taiwan's investments in the mainland reached 46.32% (see Table 12.2).

Table 12.2 Taiwan's investments in the mainland (1991–August, 2004)

Industry	Number	Amount (USD billion)	Proportion
The electronic and electrical appliances manufacturing	5,885	13.092	33.82%
Machinery manufacturing	1,290	1.282	3.31%
Precision machinery manufacturing	2,961	2.050	5.30%
Transportation tools manufacturing	1,039	1.504	3.89%
Chemicals manufacturing	1,994	2.554	6.60%
Basic metal products manufacturing	2,799	3.365	8.69%
Non-metallic and mineral products manufacturing	1,422	1.998	5.16%
Food and beverage manufacturing	2,457	1.898	4.90%
Textile industry	1,176	1.397	3.61%
Agriculture, forestry, animal husbandry and fishery industry	532	0.207	0.53%
Service industry	1,778	1.326	3.43%
Plastic manufacturing	2,667	2.511	6.49%
Others	6,625	5.521	14.27%
Sum	32,625	38.705	100.00%

Source: According to statistical data of Taiwan's authority regarding investment.

(2) The characteristics of the integration of the division of labor and the investment development of the electronic information industry of the two sides

Since the beginning of Taiwan's investment in the mainland to the early 1990s, the investment of Taiwan-based businessmen in mechanical and electrical manufacturing mainly concentrated on the processing link, which is in downstream industries with lower value-added. This was due to the differences in the development of the electronic information industry between the two sides. The main equipment, raw materials, and even semi-finished products of Taiwan-funded enterprises were purchased directly from Taiwan. Because of this, Taiwan-funded enterprises, parent manufacturers and associated manufacturers maintained extremely close trade links. Taiwan's investment in the mainland and industries in Taiwan presented a vertical labor division. In the mid and late 1990s, the world's manufacturing industry began to set up production bases in the mainland because the mainland had maintained a high degree of economic growth over a long period of time. Taiwan also changed the ways that the main machinery and equipment, raw materials and semi-finished products were directly purchased from the Taiwan region in the past, and used the cheap labor and land of the mainland to process in a simple manner. They also began to transfer middle and high-end links in the production process to the mainland, and even the whole industrial chain was moved westward across the strait to the mainland. The division of labor and cooperation in the investment of Taiwan's computer industry in the mainland fully reflects the investment trends of Taiwan's mechanical and electrical industry in the mainland. From the longitudinal point of view, the characteristics of the developmental stages of labor division and cooperation in the electronic information industry of the two sides are as follows: The investments of Taiwan's computer industry in the mainland have experienced three stages. The first stage was that they transferred the tentative adjustment of the industrial structure to Fujian Province, with some lower-value-added IT hardware products transferred to Fujian for production. The second stage was the movement of higher-value-added IT hardware and software products to the Pearl River Delta. The third stage, presently occurring, is to transfer all mechanical and electrical products including the IT industry, which have negative growth in production and marketing in Taiwan to Jiangsu, Zhejiang, Shanghai, Shandong and other places. A majority of these industries are advantageous industries in Taiwan. For example, the mouses and keyboards produced in Taiwan account for more than 90% of the global market. In the LCD (liquid crystal display) industry, it accounts for 50% of the global market; and it accounts for 52% of the global market in the laptop industry. Besides, there are semiconductors, material manufacturing and so on. On the international market, Taiwan now accounts for a great proportion of the mouse production, and 90% of it has been transferred to the mainland, while 60% to 80% of the scanners, monitors, chassis and so on are produced in the mainland. According to reports in Taiwan, 86% of Taiwan-based businessmen have already established production bases on the mainland.

12.2.2 The Choice of Location for Taiwan's Investments to the Mainland is Mainly Determined by the Integration of the Advantageous Resources of the Mechanical and Electrical Industry

(1) The Pearl River Delta and the Yangtze River Delta are the first choice for investment and integration of the mechanical and electrical industry of Taiwan in the mainland

Taiwan-based businessmen began to invest in the mainland at the time of the implementation of the policy of family visits to the mainland in 1987. According to the Ministry of Commerce, by the end of 2009, 80,061 Taiwan-based projects had been approved, which actually used investments of 49.54 billion USD from Taiwan. Taiwan is the fifth largest source of funding of the mainland, ranking after Hong Kong of China, the British Virgin Islands, Japan, and the United States. Analyzing the investment area of Taiwan's mechanical and electrical enterprises in the mainland, it can be seen that the main area is mainly in the Pearl River Delta and the Yangtze River Delta. The reason why Taiwan values the above areas is that in addition to the convenient transportation, the deep and large economic hinterland, and potential market, most importantly, it can integrate the local advantageous resources, which are conducive to the development of the mechanical and electrical industry. For example, although the Pearl River Delta region has experienced high growth for 20 years in the process of the investment and integration of the mechanical and electrical industries of the two sides, it still has certain advantages. This is because, before directly opening "exchanges of mails, trade, air and shipping service," its advantage of traffic infrastructure being adjacent to Hong Kong and Macao could provide supporting services for the industrial chain of the mechanical and electrical industry, and there is still a certain attraction to the small and medium-sized mechanical and electrical businesses which center on export sales in Taiwan. Taiwan-based businessmen set up subsidiaries in Hong Kong, and receive orders from all over the world. Although the labor shortage in recent years could bring some trouble, the labor-intensive mechanical and electrical companies which are engaged in processing and assembling, are still reluctant to be far away from the Pearl River Delta, and only migrate to the north of Guangdong, the south of Jiangxi and Hunan, and other neighboring regions. The Yangtze River Delta, in the late 1990s, increasingly became a hot spot for the investment of Taiwan's mechanical and electrical industry in the mainland. This is because the region has rich scientific and technological resources, an unobstructed sales network, strong support for industrial cluster development, and relatively perfect transportation and logistics facilities of Shanghai and the surrounding urban agglomeration. Undoubtedly, it is the ideal area for Taiwan's mechanical and electrical enterprises, which attach great importance to the management of the supply chain. There are three industrial parks that have the most complete mechanical and electrical industrial chain in the Yangtze River Delta: Taiwan Precision Machinery Industrial Park of Zhangjiagang, Taiwan Machinery Industrial City of Xiaoshan, and Xishan Development Zone of Wuxi. Taiwan's high-tech industries have been continuously concentrated in the Yangtze River Delta, and have formed a comprehensive coordination system of the IT industry in Shanghai and Suzhou (including Kunshan and Wujiang).

(2) The IT industry in Guangdong shows that the mechanical and electrical industries of the two sides complement each other and interact healthily

Since the reform and opening-up, Taiwan-based businessmen's investments in the mainland have experienced the developmental course of starting from scratch and expanding from small to large. There have been three waves of investment booms. The first wave of traditional industries' investment in the mainland began in 1987, peaking in 1993. Around 1995, driven by the frequent communication between the two sides, an increasing number of Taiwan's capital-intensive and technology-intensive mechanical and electrical companies invested in the mainland. In 2000, there was another investment boom of high-tech industries, represented by the IT industry, in the mainland. What is worth noting is that with the expansion of Taiwan's electronic information industries' investment in the mainland, the IT industry in Guangdong presents the benign interaction with complementarity and closer industrial division and cooperation of the two sides. At present, driven by Taiwan's investment in the last 10 years, the industrial structure and product structure of the electronic information manufacturing industry in Guangdong have been greatly optimized and improved. In 2005, the output of investment, consumption, and the element categories in the electronic information products accounted for 47%, 26%, and 27% respectively in Guangdong. Currently, investment products have become the leading products of the electronic information product manufacturing industry in Guangdong. Along the east coast of the Pearl River from Guangzhou to Shenzhen, there has formed an information product manufacturing corridor, dominated by Taiwan's investments. A group of small and medium-sized cities aided by Taiwan's investments, including Dongguan and Huizhou, have formed the economy of the electronic information product manufacturing industry with a certain scale and international competitiveness. Thousands of manufacturing enterprises, tens of thousands of electronic information technology research and development institutions, electronic product distributors, and electronic information equipment suppliers have emerged in recent years. The enterprise alliance and industrial chain engaged in information product component manufacturing and information equipment supply and installation among enterprises have been formed. Since Taiwan's electronic information industry started earlier than the industry on the mainland, and many product categories undertake technology transferred from the United States and Japan's electronic information industry, the expansion of Taiwan's investments in the electronic information industry in Guangdong and the Pearl River Delta region is conducive to integrating local advantageous resources and improving the regional concentration of the local electronic information industry. Practice has proved that the IT industry of the Pearl River Delta region has developed from the start of small plants to the extension of the productive operations down to sales channels and customers, to manufacturers of ancillary products, and formed the electronic information industrial cluster that has a considerable scale, has industries linked closely, and has the upstream and downstream industries integrated. Almost all the small towns specializing in production have established relationships with universities and scientific research institutes in research and development, and technical training. Shenzhen and Dongguan have established university towns to provide intellectual support. Some big companies, such as Huizhou TCL, Shenzhen Huawei, and Konka, have established their own research and development bases in the United States, India, and other places rich in IT industry and scientific and research resources to form and encourage benign interaction and development.

12.3 Constraints on Expanding the Trade of Mechanical and Electrical Products and Industrial Integration of the Two Sides

12.3.1 A Lack of Trust Leads to the Limitation of Cooperation and Investment Between the Two Sides

(1) Although Taiwan currently lags behind in economic integration, it still strictly controls high-end mechanical and electrical projects to invest in the mainland

Taiwan is a typical export-oriented island economy, with foreign trade playing an irreplaceable role in economic development. In the past 20 years, the economic and trade relations between the two sides have developed rapidly, with great changes taking place in the regional structure of Taiwan's export trade. The trade center has moved from the United States and Europe to Asia and the Chinese mainland. In October 2001, for the first time the Chinese mainland replaced the United States as Chinese Taiwan's biggest export market. At the same time, the mainland became the main destination for Taiwan's investments. Statistical data regarding Taiwan's authority show that overseas investments in the mainland comprise 67.24%. Investments in manufacturing in the mainland comprise 77.7% of the total investments. Taiwan's economy, therefore, is increasingly dependent on the mainland. The mainland has become Taiwan's largest destination for interactive development. In the face of the trend of regional economic integration on a global scale, Taiwan should have a sensitive reaction, and take positive measures with surrounding economies for extensive cooperation. However, former Taiwan authorities ignored the objective reality that the intra-industry trade of the mechanical and electrical industry was developing rapidly, and placed artificial limits on IT industry projects of high-end technology spillover. Regardless of the actual need for the industrial integration of Taiwan with the mainland, they prevented the high-end series of mechanical and electrical industries' technology projects to invest in the mainland. In the transfer projects of the chip industry, for example, the former Taiwan authorities expressly prohibited 12-inch chip projects from being invested in the mainland, and stated that a certain number of 8-inch chips could be invested in the mainland only with the promise of not using them for military purposes as well as showing the "end user certificate," which is used as the basis of technology transfer to the mainland.

(2) Restrictions on the size of Taiwan's investment in the mainland have become the biggest obstacle to integration of the mechanical and electrical industries of the two sides

A few years ago, Taiwan's economic growth was quite weak, with its GDP and per capita GDP only equivalent to the level of the mid-1990s. Without a large trade surplus with the mainland, Taiwan's economic growth rate would have been negative. Limited by the insufficiency of its energy and raw materials, small market capacity, high labor costs and other factors, Taiwan's economic development required regional economic cooperation. The ongoing plan for a free trade area, which is directed by ASEAN and China, Japan, and R.O. Korea, increases the possibility of further weakening the economic competitiveness of Taiwan. If Taiwan is excluded from East Asia's regional economic cooperation and development of "10+1" or "10+3," it cannot enjoy the convenience of mutual tariff concessions, preferential conditions and investment and trade, and there is no doubt that the "marginalization" of Taiwan's economy will be more obvious. After 20 years of economic development across the Taiwan Straits, Taiwan's economy has developed closer economic ties with the mainland. Against the background of global economic integration, coordinating Taiwan's economy into the mainland's economic development can be the only way toward further development. In the late 20th century, however, Taiwan set a lot of obstacles for its businessmen who wanted to invest in the mainland, including the specified stipulation of investment quota of the mechanical and electrical industry, such as the condition that individual projects invested by Taiwan-based businessmen in the mainland must not exceed USD 50 million. For the capital- and technology-intensive mechanical and electrical industry, the quota is far less than the minimum amount of economies of scale. Later, due to political reasons, Taiwan changed its policy for money going into the mainland from notification to authorization, thus stopping the massive funds from flowing into the mainland. Taiwan's funds invested in the mainland are divided into two kinds: One is cash held privately and the other is the fund from registered companies in Taiwan. The former can output freely through a third place to the mainland, but the latter is surrounded by obstacles, and Taiwan implements control on the total amount of outflow of capital in the industry.

12.3.2 At First, the Exchanges of Mails, Trade, Air, and Shipping Services Were Blocked, Impeding the Development of Advantages of Integration of the Mechanical and Electrical Industry

(1) At first, the exchanges of mails, trade, air, and shipping services were blocked, affecting the further integration of the mechanical and electrical industries of the two sides

Before the issue of the "three exchanges" between the two sides was resolved, the two main reasons for Taiwan-based businessmen to invest in the mainland's mechanical and electrical industry might have been the following: First, they wanted to seek the production bases of high quality and low price on the mainland in order to lower prices of inputs and reduce the production costs; second, they took a fancy to the huge potential market of the mainland, through industry consolidation, expanding production capacity, and the sales market. Related studies found that, with an increase in Taiwan's investments in the mainland, the cooperation and division of labor in mechanical and electrical products manufacturing between the two sides also became increasingly intertwined. Taiwan-based businessmen's investments in the mainland has gradually developed from the early structure of vertical division (namely, transferring production of low-value-added products to the mainland, to maintain the competitiveness of the industry of Taiwan in the international supply chain), into the current structure: On the one hand, giving priority to developing the mainland's market opportunities as the growth strategy and on the other hand, gradually developing into the structure of a horizontal division of labor, to achieve complementarity and achieve a greater global market share and strategic objectives. Predictably, at present, the realization of the "three exchanges" will greatly promote the thorough development of economic cooperation between the two sides, especially for Taiwan's businessmen to make full use of high-quality resources and the market hinterland of the mainland in the layout of globalization.

(2) Before solving the issue of "three exchanges," it greatly impeded the development of advantages of integration of the mechanical and electrical industries of the two sides

At first, the "three exchanges" were blocked, seriously impeding the development of the advantages of the mechanical and electrical industries of the two sides. According to the analysis of the vendor's investment, at present, the division of the mechanical and electrical industries of the two sides formed a certain pattern, which is arranged according to different geographical advantages. Taiwan has the advantages of the system of complete global after-sale service and the ability for rigorous supply chain management, and the mainland has the advantages of cheap land and high-quality technical human resources team, so the essence of the integration and layout of the mechanical and electrical industries of the two sides is an important part of the global implementation of the strategic layout of Taiwan's manufacturers. Because the "three exchanges" did not have a breakthrough at first, a vast majority of Taiwan's manufacturers regarded the mainland as a manufacturing base, and took a fancy to the processing form which focused on reducing costs. But the mechanical and electrical industries of the two sides are limited to the development in the direction of a vertical integration of the supply chain, and management, planning, marketing, and product research and development activities are still based in Taiwan, so it is impossible to implement a profound division of labor of the two sides. Especially in the setting of regional branches, due to the need for a horizontal division of sales and providing customer service centers, most manufacturers set up branches in America and Europe, which also involve technical information collection and research and development functions. For the mainland, it has not completed replanning and redesign of the railway and highway transportation networks on the two sides. This suggests that the strong pressure of market demand to the early achievement of the "three exchanges" has not yet been formed, and objectively, it is not conducive to exploitation of the advantages of the integration of the mechanical and electrical industries of the two sides.

12.3.3 A Proper Mechanism for Institutional Cooperation Has Not Been Formed, Greatly Hindering the Expansion of the Scale of the Trade in Mechanical and Electrical Products Between the Two Sides

(1) Lack of a mechanism for institutional cooperation hinders the expansion of the trade in mechanical and electrical products between the two sides

At present, small and medium-sized enterprises (SMEs), which are the important base of Taiwan's economy, play a leading role in trade and investment in the mainland. Although small and medium-sized enterprises can react to the market flexibly, and business development has lasting toughness, thus playing a key role in exploiting the mainland's market of mechanical and electrical products, under the strong pressure of the world's famous multinational companies on the mainland, Taiwan's small and medium-sized enterprises must feel that their industrial scale is small, management of their supply chain is poor, and the labor costs are increasing. However, a few people in Taiwan are prejudiced, thinking that after the mainland's economy becomes powerful, the competition between the two sides would become increasingly obvious, and it would offset the economic complementarities. Under this misleading ideological trend, because of the lack of a mechanism for institutional cooperation, it virtually restricts the expansion of the trade in mechanical and electrical products between the two sides. In fact, to bring the strong enterprises of Taiwan to the forefront of investment and trade with the mainland as soon as possible will be the common aspiration of the mechanical and electrical industries of the two sides. Since China's reform and opening-up, the enhancement of the ability for importation substitution for the mainland is the result of the marketization of the economic system and the development of productivity, and the increased market share of its mechanical and electrical products in America, Europe and Japan is the inevitable outcome of technical progress and industrial upgrading of the mainland. It cannot be excluded that a majority of export products belong to Taiwan-funded enterprises in the business cooperation with the mainland. The ultimate result is that Taiwan can surely get the benefits from the growing market share of the mechanical and electrical products on the mainland, which can accelerate the transfer of Taiwan's traditional mechanical and electrical industry, and enhance the level of its high-tech mechanical and electrical products and the knowledge-intensive industry.

(2) The west bank of the strait blocks the handling of mechanical and electrical products, compromising the full potential of logistics due to the expansion of bilateral trade

The modern logistics industry is widely seen as "the third profit source," after resources and labor, in the world. As bilateral economic and trade cooperation is becoming more intense, the potential of the logistics market stands out increasingly on the two sides. Originally, by advantages of location, distance, time, and other aspects between Fujian and Taiwan, the best route of logistics between the two sides can be formed. However, today, Fujian, located on the west bank of the strait, has not given full play to the advantages of its important position of logistics. In the mid-1990s, Taiwan's proposal of construction of "an Asia-Pacific operating center" was to take advantage of preferential policies to attract cross-regional large-scale logistics enterprises to establish bases in Taiwan, and push logistics companies in Taiwan to become involved in international business. However, because exchanges of air and shipping between the two sides have not been accomplished, the plan failed. At present, the bilateral trade of mechanical and electrical products has reached USD 70 billion. The share of transfer of the island's laptop industry increased to 46% of the total, and 43% of that belonged to the mainland; transfer of the desktop computer industry was as high as 94%, and the proportion of investment in the mainland accounted for 52%; the transfer of the LCD screen industry reached 72%, and production on the mainland accounted for 69.4%. Large-scale trade of the mechanical and electrical products inevitably brings about demand for logistics. The demand for logistics on the two sides will become greater and greater. However, as the most important logistics portal for connecting the mainland and Taiwan, Fujian Province has not been given full play to the role of handling mechanical and electrical products. This not only undermines the role of Fujian Province, which is the bridgehead of economic and trade exchanges with Taiwan, but also greatly weakens the scale of growth of the trade in the mechanical and electrical products between the two sides.

12.3.4 Technology and Talent Advantages of the Two Sides Have Not Been Fully Utilized in the Integration of the Mechanical and Electrical Industries

(1) Taiwan's advantageous products with practical technology can make up for the lack of competitiveness of the mainland's mechanical and electrical industry

Until now, the traditional dominance of the mainland's mechanical and electrical industry is still labor- and resource-intensive of which there are few product series, and the product structure is unreasonable. Many products still have low technology standards, at a low grade, energy-intensive and low-value-added, unable to cater to the change in the international market demand for medium- and high-grade goods. The export structure of mechanical and electrical products still gives priority to the low-value-added labor-intensive products, and export growth is mainly promoted by price competitive advantages, which relies on cheap labor and raw materials. A large number of export products are distributed on the low price market and the market capacity and development space are small. The current problems influencing the improvement of the export competitiveness of mechanical and electrical products from the mainland are that many mechanical and electrical manufacturing enterprises and industries do not have the ability of changing comparative advantages into competitive advantages, and still rely on traditional means of price competition in the international competition. And their ability for the technological innovation of mechanical and electrical manufacturing enterprises is weak; the non-price competition means are weak. They are unable to adapt to the quick changes in the demand of the international market in the knowledge economy era.

(2) The mainland's reserve of talents in basic research and scientific research can provide support for the mechanical and electrical products of the two sides in developing into high-technology and high-value-added products

Though Taiwan's high-value-added mechanical and electrical industry has developed more rapidly, its export products are mainly manufactured on contract. Although some production of mechanical and electrical products has attained an advanced level, the core technology is still based in the United States, Japan and other developed countries. Therefore, from the perspective of the attributes of the industry, the science and technology-value-added of Taiwan's mechanical and electrical industry is still at a low stage of development in the supply chain. Lack of original technology is an important reason for the low value-added of the manufacturing products; there has always been the problem of "focusing on applied research but neglecting basic research" in Taiwan's mechanical and electrical industry, so that the level of scientific innovation lags far behind developed regions. Scientific research is the basis of the development of science and technology, and only the development of science and technology can drive the industry to upgrade toward high value-added. Through industrial agglomeration, Taiwan has created good contract manufacturing, and has fully utilized the advantages of the investment-oriented economy, thereby creating the economic boom in Taiwan. But the most difficult phase is transferring the technology from efficiency-oriented to innovation-oriented. At present, Taiwan's mechanical and electrical industry is facing a bottleneck. Taiwan's educational development cannot meet the needs of the development of the industry, and there are not enough high-tech industry-related engineers and technical personnel to meet the requirements of the industry. The autonomous innovation of science and technology is not enough, they have not developed their own key technology, and the technological base of high-tech industries are subject to patents from outside. It is difficult to resolve the shortage of basic research and talent if Taiwan only relies on its own strength.

In comparison, the mainland has strong scientific research strength.

Through the accumulation of years of scientific research, some areas of high-tech and advanced science have reached quite a high level. However, because the system of managing scientific research had defects in the past, there are still some barriers in the industrialization of scientific and technological achievements. There are some problems in the mainland's mechanical and electrical industry, such as paying less attention to science and technology, a rigid research and development mechanism, lacking the ability of commercialization and marketization of scientific research and so on. The development of the mechanical and electrical industries on the two sides, especially the separation of scientific research and market development, causes such a phenomenon: In the mainland, a large number of scientific research achievements and patents are being abandoned. In some cases, because of a lack of the professional senior management personnel with development experience of commercialization and marketization, it is difficult to transform the scientific research achievements into actual products. In Taiwan, they spend a large sum of money in buying technology every year. From the fee structure of research and development activities in the past 5 years on the two sides, the mainland mainly focuses on basic research and applied research, and Taiwan mainly focuses on applied research and technology development. In the basic research of science and technology, the mainland is relatively strong; and with regard to the development of commodities, Taiwan is relatively strong. So, the complementarity of technical elements is very strong. However, constrained by the lack of a mechanism for institutionalized cooperation in the integration of the mechanical and electrical industries, the mainland's talent advantage and basic research advantage cannot closely connect with Taiwan's product development and marketing advantage; so it cannot form a powerful industrial integration effect, and bilateral cooperation is also greatly undermined.

12.4 Strategy Promoting Trade in Mechanical and Electrical Products and Industrial Integration Between the Two Sides

12.4.1 Build Logistics Demonstration Areas to Expand the Trade in Mechanical and Electrical Products Between the Two Sides

(1) Establish the overall strategic principle of "taking the easiest first" for the integration of the mechanical and electrical industries between the two sides

Based on the objective reality that the structure of the current foreign trade of mechanical and electrical products in Taiwan has greatly changed, namely, the trend in trading of "departure from the United States for Asia," the mainland's preferential trade policy to Taiwan should be adjusted. With the overall strategic principle of "taking the easiest first," the mainland should grasp the strategic opportunities that the mechanical and electrical industry in Taiwan speeds up transferring to the mainland, actively plan to set up regional cooperation demonstration zones that have different functions, a clear division of responsibilities, and that are conducive to the integration of the mechanical and electrical industries of the two sides. Strive for building an industrial belt that is conducive to industrial integration from the north to the south between the two areas within 3–5 years. Develop the situation that complies with the world developmental trend and promotes regional cooperation. Using the measures for a mutually beneficial and win-win policy to resolve all factors hindering the expansion of trade in mechanical and electrical products. The recent aim of regional cooperation of trade expansion and industrial integration between the two sides should be positioned at taking some kinds of the institutional arrangements of the "preferential tariff zones" that are different from free trade areas.

(2) Build an economic cooperation hub port between Fujian and Taiwan, taking logistics as the forerunner, so as to expand the scale of trade in mechanical and electrical products

From the overall realistic economic strength of four major economic regions of China, the Strait Economic Zone between Fujian and Taiwan, whether it is for the economic aggregate, or for the per capita economic indicators, is at the top. So, this area should be considered a key area for policy-making to promote scale of trade in mechanical and electrical products and speed up industrial integration.

According to the region's geographical advantages, building the modern logistics industry and promoting the expansion of trade in mechanical and electrical products should be taken as the main leading goal. Here are some specific ideas: First, plans should be made at the earliest. Fuzhou, Quanzhou, Xiamen, Wenzhou, and Shantou on the west bank should be connected with Keelung, Kaohsiung and other important ports, and folk force should be used to formulate the modern logistics plan of the Strait Economic Zone, which would be beneficial to the expansion of trade in mechanical and electrical products. Second, action should be taken for making Taiwan's leading logistics enterprises participate in the construction of a cooperation hub port of the Strait Economic Zone. After basically completing industrialization in the 1980s, Taiwan has actively promoted the modernization of logistics, and accumulated much valuable experience in promoting the development of the modern logistics industry with preferential policies. The mainland could come up with the favorable terms that make Taiwan a base of operations in the Asia-Pacific region, take reciprocal preferential tariff rates, facilitate the cross-strait logistics business to extend to ports of each other, and form a large logistics market including warehouses, orders, procurement, and distribution. Third, the logistics hub should be taken as the platform and conditions created to lay a solid basis of logistics for the later integration of the mechanical and electrical industries of the Pearl River Delta and the Yangtze River Delta economic zones. The mechanical and electrical manufacturers, by signing contracts with logistics service providers, can deliver the goods transportation, inventory management, sorting, picking, barcode labels, and returns, repair and replacement, Internet order fulfillment, computer distribution, and other sales channels to logistics partners completely. This is absolutely beneficial to an increase in the profits of value-added links on both ends of the production and processing chain of mechanical and electrical products of the two sides. Fourth, speed up the construction of China's eastern coastal high-speed rail transportation network, construct high-speed railway lines between Fuzhou and Xiamen, and extend northward to Wenzhou, Ningbo, and Shanghai, southward to Shantou and Shenzhen, and westward to Ganzhou and Chenzhou. Take the high-speed rail network as the foundation of the logistics hub port; thoroughly break through the traffic bottleneck between the Pearl River Delta and the Yangtze River Delta. Expand trade in mechanical and electrical products to better exploit the key role that the Strait Economic Zone plays in the national economic growth.

12.4.2 Build a Cooperation Area of Integration of the Mechanical and Electrical Industries with the Main Products Having a Clear Division

(1) Create the core area of integration of the mechanical and electrical industry in the Yangtze River Delta that centers on the precision machinery and new information products

Based on the areas of Taiwan's investment in the mechanical and electrical industry in the mainland, with the transfer of regional economic development and the scientific development center, Taiwan's investment in the Yangtze River Delta region has been increasing in recent years. This is mainly due to the region's broad economic hinterland, complete supporting facilities, close inland transportation network with Shanghai and the surrounding urban areas and low costs, which comply with the demand for industrial integration of Taiwan-based businessmen who give consideration to both the domestic and foreign market. According to the current developmental situation, Taiwan-based businessmen have the intention to transfer the information industry, with the precision machinery and semiconductor products as the dominant areas into the Yangtze River Delta. The mainland should be aimed at the investment trend, and select the best areas that suit the development of the precision machinery and information development industry in the Yangtze River Delta, which can be used as the exclusive economic zone of integration of the mechanical and electrical industries between the two sides. The first is to make some preferential policies related to land for research and development, intellectual support, taxation, and financial services. On the basis of having absorbed investments in IC design, packaging, testing, and other professional areas, use the advantages of local intelligence to attract complete information industrial chains at a higher level of knowledge and technology, such as the IC chip manufacturing, memory IC, micro components, logic IC, and analog IC, to root in the Yangtze River Delta. The second is to coordinate the division of labor and cooperation of the information industry in the cities surrounding the Yangtze River Delta and to improve the abilities of industrial integration and supporting. Taiwan's investment in the mainland drives the finishing parts exportations, and drives the industrial design and the semi-finished products to sell to the mainland. The third is to speed up the construction of the cross-sea bridge outside of Hangzhou Bay, and accelerate the construction of the railway artery from Shanghai to Ningbo and then to Fuzhou, shorten the distance between the Yangtze River Delta and the Strait Economic Zone, and improve the conditions of the transportation infrastructures and the collaboration on industrial integration. After Taiwan-based parent companies' integration of the upstream and downstream industries and the value chain extension, eventually, products can be exported back to Taiwan or abroad. In this process, the Yangtze River Delta will be integrated into the core area, which regards the cross-strait emerging microelectronics technology as the leading technology; the precision machinery and information industry in the area will have a clear division, and intra-industry trade will be closely connected.

(2) Improve the key area of integration of the mechanical and electrical industry in the Pearl River Delta, which takes home appliances and communication electronic products as the leading products

Since the 1990s, the investment of Taiwan's electronic industry in the mainland is mainly concentrated in the Pearl River Delta, including Shenzhen, Dongguan, Foshan, Shunde, Panyu, Guangzhou and other cities. After more than 10 years of development, there has been many important processing and export bases of electronic components (such as the board, keyboard, mouse, computer chassis, power supply, etc.). At present, the production value of the three electronic products of Guangdong: investment, consumption, and components, occupies an important position in the whole country. The production of digital SPC switches for the investment in communications equipment was 3,528 lines, ranking the first in the nation. The consumption of color TVs produced were 15,949,100 sets, also the first in the nation. Nationwide, the production of large-scale integrated circuits, chip capacitor resistors, and the magnetic material of components ranked among the top. But in recent years, due to the narrow regional market, the limited ability for industrial support, rising labor costs and other factors, development of Taiwan's investment in the Pearl River Delta region is slow. For this reason, China should take corresponding countermeasures, aiming at the prominent contradictions of the Pearl River Delta and Taiwan's mechanical and electrical industry in the process of integration, to promote the rapid development of electronic products in the Pearl River Delta and their development in an integrated manner. The first is to speed up the construction of the railway linking Shenzhen with Xiamen, realize the connection of a traffic thoroughfare between the west bank, Fujian and the Pearl River Delta, and reduce logistic costs of electronic products, which benefits the expansion of intra-industry trade between the two sides. The second is to encourage the subsidiaries in Hong Kong to radiate their present practical operational advantages of contacting clients, undertaking orders, and financial operations to the Pan Pearl River Delta, including North Guangdong, Southern Hunan, Southeast Guangxi and other regions, and overcome the plight of a labor shortage, and the atrophy of the labor-intensive electronics industry. The third is to strengthen the industrial ties of the Pearl River Delta. Under the coexistence of the traditional vertical and horizontal division of labor, by integrating and competing to form the electronic component and hardware production bases in South China, which center around the Pearl River Delta, in order to lay the foundation for the future formation of a functional division of labor on the hardware and software of home electronic products.

12.4.3 Structural Adjustment to Improve the Competitiveness of the Mechanical and Electrical Products of the Two Sides

(1) The policy of structural adjustment, which is oriented toward improving the competitiveness, will lead to the complementarity of the mechanical and electrical industries of the two sides

The economic and trade development between the two sides shows that in the condition of economic globalization, which is increasingly competitive, if the mechanical and electrical industries of the two sides remain together, they will boom; if not, they will be burned up together. Especially, in the current era when high-tech is rapidly developing, a large number of Taiwan-based investors flock to the mainland and restructure and adjust the mechanical and electrical products, technology, and supply chain. This is the result of market benefits and objective economic laws, which cannot be transferred by the subjective will of a handful of people. Therefore, the implementation of a policy of structural adjustment oriented toward improving the competitiveness of the mechanical and electrical industry, can not only cause complementarity of the mechanical and electrical industries of the two sides, but also gain unprecedented public approval. Here are some suggestions on policy measures: The first is to set up the oriented objective of policy guidance on the strategy of competition and cooperation of the mechanical and electrical industries of the two sides, and it is mainly for the mechanical and electrical enterprises to improve their own competitiveness in order to explore the joint market or reduce the cost, carrying out cooperation in some areas such as research and development, and in other areas, such as marketing, carrying out competition. The second is to encourage Taiwan's investors to invest in industrial bases in groups, to change the traditional pattern that Taiwan's investors invest in the mainland separately. The investment that several related industries make in groups is beneficial to the formation of a related industrial chain of a certain industry in the mainland. The third is to change the traditional capital model of only introducing capital from the manufacturing industry, to introduce financial capital and services capital to meet the actual demand of structural upgrading of the mechanical and electrical industries of the two sides. The fourth is to take the model of the division of labor and cooperation in the field of hardware and software of the electronic information industry, to speed up the structural upgrading of the information technology industry of the two sides. The core technology of the information industry is chip manufacturing and processing technology. Because the development of China's software industry is less than 20 years old, although it has made great progress, compared to that in the United States, Japan and other developed countries, there is still a big gap.

(2) Clarify the policy goals of technical exchanges and cooperation and promote the structural upgrading of the mechanical and electrical industries of the two sides

The integration of the resources of the two sides is conducive to structural upgrading of the existing mechanical and electrical industries on the mainland and in Taiwan, but the key lies in policy goals of efficient technology exchanges and cooperation. Therefore, based on the reality that current technology and intelligence advantages fail to get optimal allocation in the integration of the mechanical and electrical industries of the two sides, we propose the following policies and measures: The first is to adjust the object and scale of the technology to be introduced to adapt to local conditions, in order to promote the improvement of the strength of the technology for the mechanical and electrical industry on the mainland. Second, flexibly use appropriate technology communication, in order to meet the practical need of structure upgrading of the mechanical and electrical industry of the mainland. Third, in order to speed up the implementation of accumulating technology innovation ability and to ensure that the introduction of Taiwan's technology can be assimilated and absorbed, we can adopt the measures to establish the cooperation and exchange platform of research and development at different levels, give full play to the government's guidance regarding policies, encourage the enterprises, universities, and research institutes of the two sides to participate together, and emphatically promote innovation of common technology in the research and development of the mechanical and electrical industries of the two sides. The fourth is to improve the supporting measures of technology importation and technology interaction, including social rewards, technology support and preferential economic policies to further enhance support.

12.4.4 Seize the Favorable Opportunity of the Signing of the ECFA, Promote the Development of Cooperation Between the Two Sides in the Mechanical and Electrical Industries

Driven by the Economic Cooperation Framework Agreement (ECFA), economic cooperation between the two sides is entering a new stage. According to the regulations of the ECFA, the two sides, from January 1, 2011, have fully implemented the "Early Harvest Plan" of trade in goods and services. In terms of trade in goods, the mainland will reduce taxation on Taiwan's small and medium-sized enterprises, the traditional industrial products and 18 agricultural products. Tax reduction regarding the mechanical and electrical products will enhance the competitiveness of the industry of Taiwan on the mainland. In terms of trade in services, the professional design, hospital services, civil aircraft maintenance, banking, securities, and insurance are six service branches that have been recently opened up, which is beneficial to using soft power services to promote the mechanical and electrical industrial production in Taiwan, and provide more space for the distributors on the mainland's market and provide better services for Taiwan-based businessmen.

In addition, the signing of the agreement on investment guarantee is conducive to the integration of the mechanical and electrical industries. It is beneficial to mechanical and electrical companies in Taiwan. At the same time, it is also advantageous to the upgrading and transformation of the mechanical and electrical industry, and mechanical and electrical enterprises of the mainland. The fact that Taiwan-funded banks set up branches on the mainland can be beneficial to asset integration, and can provide the supporting services for the integration of the mechanical and electrical industries.

13

Research on China's Exchange Rate Regime, Opening of Capital Account, and the Effectiveness of Monetary Policy

13.1 Theories of Exchange Rate Regime, the Opening of the Capital Account, and the Effectiveness of the Monetary Policy

13.1.1 Overview of the Exchange Rate Regime and the Opening of the Capital Account

(1) Classification of exchange rate regimes

Exchange rate regime, also known as exchange rate arrangement, refers to a series of arrangements and regulations which the monetary authority of a nation makes for the basic ways of changing the national exchange rate; it refers to political choices which a country makes for achieving sustainable economic growth and increasing people's welfare under the conditions of economic opening up.

Until now, relatively huge disputes still remain in the standard of classifying exchange rate systems on the global scale. The main classification methods, taxonomies, are de jure taxonomy and classification based on the truth (represented by LYS taxonomy); both have been formulated by the International Monetary Fund. The former is mainly classified according to the exchange rate regimes claimed by members, while the latter is classified by measuring the actual expressions of each member's exchange rate and using statistical clustering.

(2) Meaning of the opening of the capital account

The capital account, also known as the capital project, is included by the international balance of payments. Based on the classification of the *Balance of Payments Manual* developed by the International Monetary Fund before 1993, a balance of payments account can be divided into the current account and the capital account. In 1993, the capital account was changed into the capital and financial account by the International Monetary Fund in the *Balance of Payments Manual* (the fifth edition), including the following parts:

Capital account: Capital circulation and the acquisition and abandonment of non-financial or non-productive assets.

Financial account:

(1) Direct investment is investment in an enterprise which is not included by the investor's operating system.

(2) Investment in securities refers to investment in stocks, bonds, money market instruments, derivative securities and so on.

(3) Other investments. This is a remaining system, including all capital transactions that are out of direct investments, investments in securities, or changes in reserve assets.

(4) Reserve assets are used to compensate the international balance of payment deficit or to intervene in the exchange rate by one authority, which can control the deficit scale or deal with foreign assets for other purposes.

During the decades after World War II, the expression—capital account—was widely acknowledged. After 1993, in addition to accurately utilizing capital and financial accounts on some formal occasions, people would prefer to use a capital account to substitute a capital and financial account and the two expressions would not be contradictory on most occasions.

There are various definitions and understandings about the opening of the capital account at home and abroad. For example, do not control or tax on, or carry out appropriate subsidies for international capital transactions (Peter J. Quirk, a specialist of IMF is of this view). Deregulating the controls of capital flows in the capital account can be divided into two aspects. The first is to regulate the controls of cross-border capital transactions; the second is to cancel regulations of foreign exchanges related to capital transactions, including the transfer of cross-border funds and currency exchange. Or deregulate diverse controls of currency exchange, foreign payments and transactions on capital account transactions, mainly to accomplish free capital flows. Do not regulate cross-border capital transactions directly or take relative measures that would influence the transaction costs.

However, there is not an acknowledged and clear definition. We think we can define the opening of the capital account in four aspects.

First, the opening of the capital account mainly refers to the release or cancelation of regulations on subaccounts in capital and financial accounts, including the release or cancelation of the regulations on the transfer of cross-border capital, direct investments, investments in securities and other investments. In this way, opening the capital account is no less than reducing or canceling the regulations on cross-border securities investment on capital transactions. As for Chinese situations, the capital account has been relaxing regulations since the 1980s when China started to carry out the policy of introducing foreign investments. As such, opening the capital account, nowadays, amounts to relaxing or canceling regulations on subaccounts of capital accounts which are still not open. Foreign exchange control is mainly reflected in two aspects: The first is to regulate currency exchange and the second is to regulate cross-border capital transactions.

Second, the opening of capital account is not completely equal to freedom of exchange of capital account. With the opening of the capital account, requirements of free exchange of cross-border capital transactions, which are included by capital account, would gradually increase. Convertibility means using or exchanging foreign exchange freely according to the given exchange rate. If holders of one certain currency can freely exchange their currency to an international main currency according to the market exchange rate (whether it is flexible or stationary), that currency can be completely regarded as a fully convertible currency.

Convertible regulations are different from transacting regulations. Convertible regulations are used to regulate exchange transactions in international current accounts and capital accounts and it does not mean regulating current accounts or capital accounts themselves. Additionally, the two types differ in methods and objects.

Opening of the capital account mainly attends to canceling regulations on capital transactions, but not to asking for exchanging freedom of exchange in the capital account. Convertibility of capital account always means cancelling the regulating measures in currency exchange. Moreover, convertibility of the capital account depends on your own will, which does not only take the responsibility of actual payments and transacting requirements of international capital transactions, but would also be responsible for unattainable payments and transacting requirements without international capital transactions. In a nutshell, if there are only legal demands, they should be ensured to be exchanged.

In practice, the opening of the capital account is always related to its convertibility. They are difficult to be distinguished one from the other. Many capital transactions themselves are foreign exchanges. For example, forward exchanging transactions of currency and foreign currency to be delivered at the maturity date is a complete exchange process. With the opening of the capital account, development of cross-border capital transactions would improve the demands for the convertibility of capital accounts, but during the process of canceling regulating and controlling measures, the opening of the capital account and capital account convertibility are related but different; they can work together and they can work one after another.

Third, the opening of capital account is not equal to complete freedom of capital flow. Complete freedom of capital flow is just an ideal condition; the opening of the capital account does not mean complete freedom of capital flow and it does not exclude the management of capital transactions. Countries vary in the degree. Many countries would carry out different capital controls for the sake of all kinds of requirements, such as national security. The monetary authority of a nation can carry out regulations on some subaccounts in capital accounts under the circumstances of releasing or canceling regulations on main subaccounts. Therefore, the monetary authority can maintain its regulations on some subaccounts in the opening of the capital account.

Fourth, the process of opening of the capital account is not a one-way process. Under the circumstances of relaxing or canceling regulations on some subaccounts, the monetary authority of a nation can also carry out regulations on the capital subaccounts on which the regulations have been canceled, when all kinds of conditions change at home and abroad. It means that the general trend of capital account is opening, but policies of some subaccounts can be changed according to concrete situations. In some way, opening of capital account can be referred to as the improvement of the degree of opening and that changes can be maintained. In conclusion, the understanding of opening of capital account cannot be defined in clear terms.

13.1.2 The Meaning of the Effectiveness of Monetary Policy

The principle of effectiveness of monetary policy is drawn from currency theory in Western economics and financial economics. Effectiveness of monetary policy has three meanings.

The first meaning is based on a qualitative sense; it is similar to the meaning of money neutrality. Money neutrality means whether the monetary system can systematically influence factual economic variables, such as outputs, prices, employment and so on. If it can, then it indicates that the currency is not neutral and the monetary policy is effective; if not, then it indicates a lack of effectiveness of the monetary policy. Therefore, the meaning of effectiveness of monetary policy can be substituted by the principle of money neutrality. Money neutrality is a discourse of a basic proposition in the Western quantity theory of money that the quantity of money only influences the level of prices in economy but does not influence factual output. The vast majority of contemporary Western economists think that short-term monetary policy is not neutral, which has been supported by many experimental data. But it is debatable among economists on whether long-term monetary policy is neutral.

The second meaning is based on the quantitative sense. On the basis of acknowledging the effectiveness of the monetary policy, it discusses how much effect the monetary policy has on the economic variables quantitatively. In this regard, what the contemporary Western economists accept generally is that the smoother the IS curve (which reflects the market equilibrium of the commodity) is and the deeper the LM curve (which reflects the market equilibrium of money) is, the greater the effect of the monetary policy is.

The third meaning is to study the time when the monetary policy influences economic operations, which means the time lag of the monetary policy. The time lag of the monetary policy refers to a period that starts from the formulation of the policy to getting partial or whole effects. Time lag can be divided into internal time lag and external time lag. Internal time lag represents the period that starts from formulating to taking steps by the monetary authority, whose length depends on prediction, efficiency and motives of the monetary authority. External time lag, also known as influential time lag, refers to the period that starts from taking measures to having effects on political aims and it is really decided by objective economic and financial conditions. Western economic theory shows that the length of the time lag of the monetary policy is often longer than half a year.

13.2 China's Exchange Rate Regime and the Current Situation of the Opening of Capital Account

13.2.1 The New Stage of the Reform of the RMB Exchange Rate Regime

On July 21, 2005, the People's Bank of China issued the "Announcement about Improving the Reform of the Formation of the RMB Exchange Rate Regime." Its main content is as follows:

(1) Since July 21, 2005, China has begun to implement a system based on the supply and demand of the market, referring to a basket of currencies, which consists of the managed floating exchange rate regime. The RMB exchange rate was no longer pegged to the dollar, but it formed a more flexible RMB exchange rate regime.

(2) The People's Bank of China publishes inter-bank foreign exchange market's closing prices of tradable currencies such as the dollar to the RMB exchange rate every working day after the market is closed, which would be the middle prices of the next day.

(3) At 19:00 on July 21, 2005, the dollar against the RMB market price was adjusted to 8.11 yuan, which would be the middle price in transactions between authorized banks at the inter-bank foreign exchange market on the next day, and the authorized banks for dealing in foreign exchange can adjust their posted rate to the customers beginning at that time.

(4) At present, the daily dollar against the RMB at the inter-bank foreign exchange market is still 0.3% around the middle price announced by the People's Bank of China. The transaction prices of other currencies against the RMB change within a certain range around the middle prices announced by the People's Bank of China.

(5) The People's Bank of China will adjust the space of the floating exchange rate according to the growth of the market and the economic and financial situation. At the same time, according to the economic and financial situation both at home and abroad, and on the basis of market supply and demand, the People's Bank of China will refer to a basket of currencies

exchange rate changes, to manage and regulate the RMB exchange rates, in order to maintain the normal floating of the RMB exchange rates and keep the RMB exchange rates basically stable at a reasonable and balanced level, to maintain a basic equilibrium in the balance of payments, and to maintain the stability of the macro economy and financial markets.

On January 3, 2006, China once again adjusted the way to form the middle price. The China Foreign Exchange Trading Center would address an inquiry to all the inter-bank foreign exchange markets before opening quotations every day, and regard all the offers as samples. It would remove the maximum and minimum and get the weighted average to get the middle price of the RMB against the dollar for that day. The weight would then be decided by the China Foreign Exchange Trade Center according to the transactions on the inter-bank foreign exchange market and the offers. On the basis of the price, the authorized banks for dealing in foreign exchange decide their buying and selling rates in accordance with the relevant provisions of the floating range. Further, the perfection of the middle price of the RMB exchange rate reflects the market's increasingly important role in determining the RMB exchange rate.

13.2.2 Main Evaluation of Current Exchange Rate Reform

(1) Return to the real managed floating exchange rate system

In 1994, China's foreign exchange control system established a managed floating exchange rate system, which was on the basis of market supply and demand. In order to block the spread and contagion of the 1997 Asian financial crisis, the Chinese government promised no depreciation of the RMB, and greatly narrowed the exchange rate volatility. From 1998 to the eve of the reform, the benchmark of the RMB against the dollar remained at 8.2760 to 8.2800, and it resulted in a widespread debate. Practice has proved that a managed float is suitable for China's national conditions, and should be insisted on for a long time to come. The reform reiterated the return to a managed float, but it is not a simple regression. It emphasizes the role of market supply and demand in determining the exchange rate, playing the basic role of the market mechanism in the allocation of resources, and found a reasonable and balanced level of RMB exchange rate through the market mechanism, which determines the market orientation of reform.

(2) Introduce the reference to a basket of currencies

In order to keep the RMB exchange rate basically stable after the RMB was no longer pegged to the dollar, the Chinese government put forward the reference to a basket of currencies. Compared with being pegged to the dollar, the introduction of reference to a basket of currencies not only increased the flexibility of the mechanism for the formation of the exchange rate, but also changed the currency policy target, that is, it changed from the stabilizing bilateral exchange rate of the RMB against the dollar to stabilizing the multilateral nominal effective exchange rate.

(3) Adjust the level of the RMB exchange rate within a narrow range all at once

Since 2002, the RMB has faced pressure from appreciation due to both economic fundamental factors and anthropic factors from the international community. In general, the economic fundamentals are the foundation, and international factors magnify the effect. As a result, the benchmark rate of the RMB against the dollar was adjusted from 8.2765 to 8.11 all at once, with an appreciation of about 2%. The amplitude had a certain gap with market expectations and requirements of the international community; it only partially released the pressure from the appreciation of the RMB and became one of the focuses of controversy after revaluation. In spite of this, the cautious approach ensured the subsequent RMB exchange rate, which was beneficial to further advancing reform and enhancing confidence in the market. And it had something in common with the unification of the RMB exchange rates in 1994. In the next 3 years, the RMB experienced a gradual appreciation and so far, the exchange rate of the RMB against the dollar has appreciated by 22%. But at the same time, China's foreign exchange reserves rose from USD 800 billion at the end of 2005 to USD 2.6 trillion at the end of 2009.

13.2.3 The Actual Effect of the Control of China's Capital Accounts over Hot Money

Although the foreign exchange control of China is very strict nominally, in practice, the control of the capital account of China is "strict nominally, easy actually"; from the inflows of a huge sum of hot money, we can see the actual effect of the control of China's capital accounts.

Hot money, also called floating capital or short-term speculative capital, also called "idle capital," refers to the floating capital that has no special use in the world. The short-term speculative capital flows rapidly in the international financial market, which calls for the highest reward and minimal risks. The short-term speculative capital flows are mainly to escape political risks, to pursue benefits brought by the change of exchange rate, the change of prices of important commodities or the change of prices of international securities, and hot money floating is the speculative action of pursuing the benefit of the change of exchange rate. Its biggest characteristics are short-term, interest arbitrage and speculation. On the market of foreign exchange, this kind of speculative capital always exchanges from currency of a tendency toward devaluation to currency of a tendency toward appreciation, which increases the instability of the market of foreign exchange. Hot money is not fixed. Some of the long-term capital under certain circumstances may transfer to short-term capital, too. The key to the transferring from short-term capital to hot money lies in whether the economic and financial environment will lead to capital progressing from investing to speculation and from speculation to escaping. At present, in fact, the relatively stable exchange rate system and the RMB of China still have room to appreciate and this financial environment provides opportunities for arbitration.

From 2006, hot money flow in China can be roughly divided into three stages. The first stage, from January 2006 to September 2008, presented a net inflow; the second stage, from October 2008 to February 2009, presented a net outflow. During the half year since February 2009 when there was an outbreak of the financial crisis, China had faced a continued large-scale net outflow. The third stage, from March 2009 until now, presents a net inflow. With the recovery of the European and American economies, hot money flow reverses and begins to change from the developed countries to emerging economies. China is faced with a gradual and sustained expansion of a net inflow of hot money.

As for the scale of hot money, economists suppose that the maximum figure is USD 150 billion and this figure seems to continue to increase.

At present within the territory of China, there is a large quantity of hot money. So we can find that the actual effect of the control of China's capital accounts is pretty loose.

13.3 The Influence of China's Exchange Rate Regime and Capital Account Management on the Effectiveness of Its Monetary Policy

13.3.1 2003—2007 Monetary Policy

From 2003 to 2007, on the issues of the excessive growth of money and credit, haphazard investment in some industries and regions, and a sharp rise in low-level expansion, the People's Bank of China pursued a tight and prudent monetary policy. The specific measures are as follows.

(1) Advance the marketability of interest rates steadily

Since January 1, 2004, the People's Bank of China has expanded the floating ranges of the lending rates of financial institutions. On the basis of the benchmark interest rate, the upper limit of the floating range of the loan rates in commercial banks and urban credit cooperatives has expanded to 1.7 times the benchmark interest rate; the upper limit of rural credit cooperatives has doubled. The lower limit of the floating range of the loan rates in financial institutions has remained at 90% of the benchmark interest rate. Financial institutions can autonomously decide the loan rates in accordance with market principles in the prescribed range. Since March 2005, the interbank deposit rate of financial institutions has increased. According to the sustained rise in the interest rates within the international financial market, the upper limit of the deposit rate in domestic commercial banks of US dollars and HK dollars increased 5 times in 2005 alone, among which the one-year deposit rate of US dollars had cumulatively increased by 2.125 percentage points to 3% and HK dollars by 1.8125 percentage points to 2.625%. The RMB deposit and loan calculation and settlement rules have been modified and improved; financial institutions have been permitted to determine the calculation and settlement rules of all kinds of deposits, except current deposits and regular lump sum deposits. In 2006, to curb excessive investments and guide reasonable growth of investments and monetary and credit, the People's Bank of China raised the benchmark deposit and loan interest rates in financial institutions twice. The first move was to raise the benchmark loan interest rate from April 28, among which the one-year benchmark loan interest rate in financial institutions was raised by 0.27 percentage points, from 5.58% to 5.85%. The second was to raise the benchmark deposit and loan interest rates from August 19, among which the one-year benchmark deposit interest rate in financial institutions was raised by 0.27 percentage points, from 2.25% to 2.52%; the one-year benchmark loan interest rate was raised by 0.27 percentage points, from 5.85% to 6.12%. In 2006, the construction of a Chinese benchmark interest rate system of the money market started. Shanghai's interbank offered rate started trials from October to December 2006 and the official run started on January 4, 2007, trying to provide a pricing benchmark of products within one year for the financial market. On August 19, 2006, the government expanded the lower limit of commercial housing loans to individuals to 85% from 90% of the legal loan interest rate, thus expanding the price range of housing loans.

(2) Strengthen the ability to regulate the basic currency by open market operations

First, the open market operations trading day was changed from every Tuesday to every Tuesday and Thursday since February 25th, 2003, thus enhancing the open market operations. Second, under the condition of lacking securities tools, in April 2003, the People's Bank of China creatively started open market operations of the central bank's circulation of bills. In addition, approved by the Fifth Session of the Standing Committee of the Eighth National People's Congress, the central finance's loans and overdrafts from the People's Bank of China before the Law of the People's Bank of China was issued in 1995 were changed into national debts, which are standard and available for open market operations. In 2005, to coordinate the reform on the mechanism for the formation of the exchange rate, a series of policies were introduced, thus adjusting the open market operations appropriately, and the money market rate was guided down moderately. From September to December, in view of the fact that the new mechanism for the formation of the RMB exchange rate ran smoothly and the interest margin between China and America expanded further after the FED continuously raised the interest rates, the People's Bank of China enhanced the open market operations duly, controlling the money supply growth rate, and promoting the money market interest rates in a reasonable way. In 2006, under the condition that the pressure of excess liquidity caused by the international balance of payments surplus continued to exist, the People's Bank of China increased the hedge on the open market. The central bank bill issued that year was 3.65 trillion RMB, which was 860 billion RMB higher than that of the same period in the previous year. At the end of the year, the central bank held a bill balance of 3.03 trillion RMB.

13.3.2 Constraints of China's Exchange Rate Regime and the Opening of Capital Account on the Effectiveness of Its Monetary Policy

In the current exchange rate regime and capital account management, China's monetary policy is predominantly constrained as follows.

(1) Rapid increase in foreign exchange reserves leads to difficulty in implementation of the monetary policy

Under the present exchange rate regime in China, foreign exchange reserves come from the balance of payments. The increase or decrease is the result and difference of the balance of payments. Change of foreign exchange reserves is an important point of monetary policy and exchange rate policy. The increase and decrease of reserves have become the important channel which influences the monetary base on issuing money and the monetary squeeze. More importantly, foreign exchange reserves of endogenous growth increased the difficulty in making the monetary policy. When the central bank regulates the money supply, it must pay special attention to forecasting the change of foreign exchange reserves, and monthly forecasting as far as possible, to prevent fluctuations in foreign exchange reserves from causing instability to the issuing of a monetary base. Fluctuations in foreign exchange reserves give the RMB exchange rate depreciation or appreciation pressure. Objectively, it also increases the difficulty in the implementation of the monetary policy.

Since 2003, China's foreign exchange reserves have grown sustainably. By the end of 2006, China's foreign exchange reserves had swelled to more than USD 1 billion, becoming the largest in the world; by 2009, it had swelled to more than USD 2 billion. China's foreign exchange reserves were up to USD 2.45 billion in June 2010. The RMB was faced with great pressure of appreciation, which was opposite to the current tight monetary policy. Under the current exchange rate regime, owning a great amount of foreign exchange reserves, the People's Bank of China was assuming a great risk in the exchange rate. A majority of foreign exchange reserves of China are US dollar assets. Actually, it has been acknowledged that the foreign exchange asset is mainly used to buy US dollar assets according to the usage of foreign exchange assets in recent years. Increased attention should be paid to the maintenance and appreciation of foreign exchange reserves in the context of US dollars' continuous depreciation and unsustainable exchange rates of major countries. The risk of the exchange rate of foreign exchange reserves also increases the difficulty in the implementation of the monetary policy. Controlling the money supply, the People's Bank of China should not only focus on the proportion between US dollar assets and other assets in the usage of foreign exchange reserves, but also keep an eye on the exchange rate between the US dollar and other currencies in order to avoid an unsustainable money supply due to the undulating exchange rate between the US dollar and other major currencies (such as the euro).

Owning great amount of foreign exchange reserves, the People's Bank of China has paid a considerable price for it. On the one hand, the main usage of foreign exchange reserves is buying American government bonds; at the same time, the preferential policy to absorb foreign investment increases the cost of using offside funds. It is obvious that there are huge losses of the efficiency of capital usage. China's financial burden is equal to the product of the gross amount of reserves and the difference between the financing cost of outside capital and the income of capital reserves. On the other hand, administration cost of the great amount of foreign exchange reserves is increasing while the marginal utility of stabilizing the exchange rate is decreasing. Since China has entered the WTO, opened the financial market, and relaxed the control over capital items, it might have to pay a heavy price to maintain the current rate regime. Since March 2003, foreign governments have brought great pressure on the Chinese government to urge an RMB appreciation. The expectation of an RMB appreciation is continuously on the rise. For instance, a research report by JPMorgan Chase & Co. in December 2004 showed that the exchange rate between the RMB and the US dollar would appreciate by 7% by 2005. Although since July 2005, the RMB has appreciated by a certain extent, the range of appreciation is far from the foreign and domestic expectation. So the RMB is still assuming great appreciation pressure. If China wants to maintain a steady exchange rate, the scale of foreign exchange reserves will be larger and the costs will be higher.

(2) The improvement of the endogenous growth of money supply decreases the independence of monetary policy

In 1996, the People's Bank of China formally considered money supply as an intermediate target. The central bank hopes to control the money supply to achieve the desired effect. The funds that are outstanding on foreign exchange account for a large proportion in the base money supply, which shows that the influence of funds outstanding for foreign exchange on the base money supply is very big, and the adjustment of the monetary policy of the money supply is largely affected by the funds outstanding for foreign exchange. In China, the imbalance of the exchange rate market is inevitable and it occurs often, the central bank has to be involved in buying and selling. The process, in fact, is the supply and recycling of monetary base. But at present, China's stable exchange rate strengthens the endogenous growth of the money supply and reduces the initiative of the central bank to control the money supply. With the constant improvement of the degree of opening up to the outside world, the money supply further relies on the national economic operations. The higher the degree of opening to the outside world, the greater the proportion of the money supply related to foreign economic activities, and the stronger the endogenous growth, the weaker the initiative of the central bank to control the money supply and the poorer the effectiveness of the monetary policy to keep a control over the money supply. The imbalance of international payments would lead to a change in the money supply. The money supply received official intervention which aims at maintaining a stable exchange rate. Therefore, the current exchange rate regime greatly limits the capability of the implementation of the monetary policy in China, and weakens the independence of the monetary policy.

The central bank can perform an offset monetary policy when using the monetary policy to maintain a stable exchange rate, but as the effect of sterilized intervention is greatly related to the scale of open market operations, the bearing capacity of the fiscal deficit, the degree of capital control, and the asset adjustment of the microscopic economic subjects, combined with the recurrent and uncertain imbalance of China's foreign exchange market, it is very difficult to make a sterilized intervention for the central bank. In addition, China's bond market is not big; also, it cannot achieve a large-scale sterilized intervention. Of course, the mechanisms of the commodity market and the monetary market are still not perfect. There are many obstacles, and the government cannot take market measures to regulate the economy.

(3) The dual goals of the monetary policy increase the difficulty in achieving policy objectives

The Law of the People's Bank of China has set a single goal of monetary policy, namely, to "keep the stability of the currency value and thereby promote economic growth." But under the current exchange rate regime, the monetary policy actually has dual goals to maintain the stability of the currency value at home and abroad, which is to maintain price stability at home and to keep the exchange rate relatively stable abroad. Price is the embodiment of the currency value at home; any price change will bring the change of the real exchange rate, which influences the operations of the external economy and the internal economy. To fix the rate artificially is ultimately only to fix the nominal exchange rate, but what influences economic operations is some real variables, rather than nominal variables. For example, when the central bank tries to adopt an expansionary monetary policy to stimulate consumption and economic growth, keep the rising prices and the nominal exchange rate unchanged to make the domestic currency's real exchange rate appreciate relatively and make its exports less competitive; the amount of the exports declines, the amount of the imports increases, and as a result, there is an oversupply of the domestic commodity market and prices tend to fall again. At the same time, it's impossible for the foreign inflation rate to come down to zero; in this case, if the nominal exchange rate remains unchanged, the change in the foreign inflation rate will inevitably change the real exchange rate of the local currency, which will cause a domestic price fluctuation, eventually leading the domestic price to change with foreign prices, which can destroy the domestic equilibrium.

(4) The mechanism for the transmission of interest rates becomes weak

The interest rates are an important tool of the monetary policy in China and they are also the mechanism of the main channel of transmission of the monetary policy affecting the economy; the change of the central bank's monetary policy is often characterized by changes in interest rates in the first place. At present, the degree of marketization of interest rates is low; bank deposits and loan rates are basically set directly by the central bank. According to the needs of the monetary policy, the central bank directly adjusts interest rates to influence the amount of the money lent of financial institutions and corporate deposits, thus influencing the enterprises' scale of investments and economic aggregate. Under relatively stable exchange rates, the ability for interest rates to affect the economy is greatly reduced. For example, when the central bank attempts to lower the interest rates to relax the monetary market, in order to expand business investments and household consumption, the arbitrage capital will do its best to exchange the RMB into foreign exchange funds and flow abroad, leading to an increase in the demand for foreign exchange and fluctuations in exchange rates. In order to maintain the stability of the exchange rates, the central bank usually sells US dollars for RMB, which slows down the credit expansion effect of lowering the interest rates. Though the RMB is not convertible under the current capital account, as a result of the current situation of China's capital control, which is "strict nominally, easy actually", short-term funds at home and abroad often arbitrage through a variety of violations and even illegal means. Since March 2003, the expectation of an RMB appreciation has become intense, a lot of arbitrage has flown into China, and foreign exchange reserves have increased dramatically, and in order to maintain the stability of the exchange rates, the central bank has to buy foreign currency, which has resulted in the extremely fast growth of the RMB's money supply, and weakens the central bank's credit crunch to a certain extent.

(5) Relaxing control over capital account poses a more serious challenge to the implementation of the monetary policy

At present, China is gradually relaxing control over capital accounts, and control over capital accounts is strict nominally, easy actually; many of the so-called controls are actually auditing the authenticity. After joining the WTO, foreign banks began to enjoy the "national treatment" in business, capital flow barriers have been further reduced, and the scale and frequency of cross-border capital flows, which are abnormally sensitive to interest rates and exchange rates, increased. With the improvement of the liberalization of capital flows, the relationship between interest rates and exchange rates generated from the mechanism of interest rate parity has become increasingly close; it will eventually make the scope of exchange rate policy, which is independent of the monetary policy, more and more limited. The actual level of capital controls differs from what the law requires. The study shows that the degree of actual capital controls is lower than the degree of law.

Under the condition that the international capital liquidity becomes stronger, because the imbalance of the exchange rate is inevitable and occurs frequently, we can't form the equilibrium rate of exchange, and the central bank's intervention in the foreign exchange transactions is necessarily frequent. Therefore, with the continuous decrease in capital flow barriers, China's monetary policy will face a greater challenge.

(6) Change in the supply channels of the monetary base leads to changes in the distribution pattern of social funds

After receiving the foreign exchange, foreign enterprises can obtain RMB funds instantly through exchange settlement. From the perspective of money creation and money supply, foreign exchange settlement of all businesses and individuals results in a foreign exchange surplus. Banks sell the foreign exchange to the central bank and the central bank's monetary base (funds outstanding for foreign exchange) goes to the deposit reserve account of commercial banks in the central bank, causing deposit reserves to increase in commercial banks and the expansion of the money supply multiplied. As there are innate differences in the capital, technology, and management between domestic-oriented companies and companies involving foreign investments, it is not practical to make the capital flow free among these companies. The capital utilization is different between companies with sufficient funds and companies with a lack of funds even though the levels of costs and benefits are the same, which leads to the unreasonable social capital allocation objectively. On the premise that the monetary policy maintains the domestic price level, export enterprises have relatively abundant capital, and funds allocated to domestic-oriented companies have to be reduced.

13.4 The Reform of the Regime of China's Foreign Exchange Rate and the Opening of the Capital Account to Promote the Effectiveness of the Monetary Policy

At present, China has relaxed the fixed exchange rate and free capital flow to improve the effectiveness of the monetary policy. But, according to the analysis of the effectiveness of the monetary policy from 1998 to 2007, we can see that it is difficult for our monetary policy to take effect in the context of the opening of capital accounts and exchange rate regime. Therefore, in order to ensure the independence and effectiveness of the monetary policy, it is inevitable to introduce a reform in the current exchange rate regime and opening of capital accounts.

13.4.1 Further Reform to Improve the Managed Floating Exchange Rate System

In July 2005, China implemented a reform concerning the mechanism for the formation of the exchange rate, which focused on three principles "independent, controllable, and progress step by step." It is a key point in the reform of our exchange rate regime, which is the starting point for transferring the managed exchange rate system into a free floating exchange rate system. However, the market is not mature enough so that China could not implement the fully floating exchange rate system in case the unstable RMB exchange rate system disrupts the economy. The current reform can start to deal with the problems of our exchange rate regime, and perfect the managed floating exchange rate system and then gradually move toward the fully floating exchange rate system.

It is a chronic procedure to develop a real managed floating exchange rate system. Because there are inherent problems in the mechanism for the formation of the exchange rate formation and external factors that restrain that mechanism from further reforming and operating, including misunderstanding and operational environment, advice about further reform is provided.

(1) Further release the pressure of RMB appreciation

As for the causes of the expected appreciation, economic fundamentals is the foundation, including stable and rapid growth of the Chinese economy, continuing the double balance of payments surplus, the rapid expansion of the size of foreign exchange reserves and so on, and the international pressure magnifies the appreciation pressure. The constant expected appreciation has affected the normal operations of the market and the economy, increasing international economic friction, putting us in a disadvantaged situation in international trade negotiations with trading partners and competitors. It is necessary to take active and prudent measures to solve it. Exchange rate reform should not only insist on the principle of autonomy and not change because of external pressure, but also prevent no change or slow change caused by external pressure, which may make us lose the opportunity for reform. At present, it is necessary to further improve the construction of the infrastructure of the foreign exchange market, be clear with the objectives of the exchange rate policy, enhance the effectiveness of the central bank's intervention in the foreign exchange market, and achieve the adjustment of the exchange rate to balance through the market mechanism on this basis, which can solve the problems of the pressure from appreciation fundamentally.

(2) Expand the space for elasticity of the exchange rate of the RMB against the US dollar

The elasticity of exchange under the existing framework doesn't restrict each other, but there are potential conflicts. The daily amplitude of fluctuation of the non-US dollar interbank exchange rate is ± 3%, that is, ten times the US dollar. If the proportion of the US dollar in the currency package is less than 50%, then once non-US dollar currencies against the US dollar appreciate over 0.6% in the currency package, the exchange rate of the RMB against the US dollar may deviate from the level determined by the currency package, causing distortion of the mechanism for the formation of the exchange rate and the market. To resolve potential conflicts, it is necessary to coordinate the relationship between the relevant exchange rate arrangements, select the appropriate time, and improve the daily amplitude of the fluctuation of the US dollar.

(3) Deepen the mechanism for the formation of the benchmark exchange rate

Making a centralized enquiry to determine the benchmark price is normal practice in financial markets such as the gold market, but against the special background of China's foreign exchange market, introduction of this method may cause the exchange rate to deviate from the level of equilibrium. At present, the People's Bank of China is the main or only buyer of the US dollar on the interbank markets; the market maker banks are almost invariably sellers, so these banks will overvalue the US dollar as they are driven by profit. Assuming that the equilibrium exchange rate is at 6.8 and the market exchange rate is at 7, the People's Bank of China will accept the offer passively so that they don't have to worry if they can't sell.

Thus, the offer must be 7 instead of 6.8, resulting in the undervaluation of the system of RMB when there is an expected appreciation. Expectation is hard to be reflected in the real exchange rate. On the contrary, when there is an expected depreciation, the RMB will be overestimated. To solve this problem, we can constrain the offers of market makers. The China Foreign Exchange Trade System can, according to the inquiry, independently sell and buy a certain amount of foreign exchange, which restricts the market makers' behavior. In the long run, passive acceptance of offers should be gradually reduced.

(4) Adjust the methods for intervention in the foreign exchange market

The People's Bank of China's passive acceptance of offers has resulted in the daily and lasting interventions in the foreign exchange market. Problems brought by such acceptance are also apparent, especially for the marketization issue decided by the exchange rate. The People's Bank of China needs to reduce the passive market intervention and transfer to the more flexible and market-oriented means, such as the adjustment in the monetary policy and verbal intervention. During this transitional period, it is necessary for the People's Bank of China to act flexibly and use a combination of means of exchange to reach the target of intervention; we can consider limiting the maximum amount of foreign currency that the People's Bank of China can buy, such as no more than USD 10 billion every month, letting the market digest part of the total amount of US dollars by making additional purchases and appreciation. This adjustment makes it necessary for us to relax restrictions on banks' foreign exchange positions in the meantime. The first thing is to enhance the exchange settlement positions of the banks designated by the exchange, transfer to the proportion management when conditions become mature, link the positions' scale of the banks' local and foreign currency to their capital or property. It is also a kind of disguised intervention by arranging the exchange rate regime, such as giving foreign exchange transaction centers the right to determine the weight when setting the benchmark rate. However, this practice is suspected to manipulate the exchange rate, which needs to fade out gradually, to put the bank in the leading position in forming the exchange rate.

(5) Raise the transparency of information when setting the exchange rates

Opaque and asymmetrical information is an important factor causing the misunderstanding and disturbance on the market. The departments concerned are supposed to strengthen propagation, make the market further understand and accept the new exchange rate regime, and more importantly, increase the transparency of the information. After the new regime has been used for some time, we can publish some basic rule-driven information about the basket of currencies, including the exchange target that we are operating at, the ways of intervention in the foreign exchange market, the rules about constituting the basket of currencies and its adjustments. To the market, we can increase the information about trades through the foreign exchange, including publishing the progress made by the intervention in the market, to get every participant in the market to require complete information as much as possible, and make their own trade decisions on the basis of this information.

(6) Push forward the related reform measures steadily

Accelerate the process of the marketization of interest rates, and dredge the transmission system of interest rates–exchange rates. The marketization of interest rates is the premise for the policies of exchange rates and interest rates benefiting from being associated together. If the interest rate is not completely open and the exchange rate is rigid, the inflows of foreign capital will increase the burden of the rise of the currency's supply and inflation, which cannot be remitted by the change in interest rates. For now, the marketization of interest rates in China isn't very good; only a small portion of interest rates are determined by the market, thus making the inelastic rate of growth in investment, consumption, and imports and exports, and the rate's function in adjusting the economy is limited and the transmission between the interest rate and exchange rate is blocked. The marketization of interest rates is imperative. To meet the requirements and process of the reform of the economic system, China's reform in interest rates is advancing gradually, operating under the principle of "loaning before saving, fixing the great sum before floating the petty sum, and taking the foreign currency before the domestic currency."

Reform the system of exchange settlement and sales. The current system of exchange settlement and sales not only makes the risks concentrate on the central bank, but also increases the cost of enterprises and hinders the development of the exchange market. The enterprises play a leading role in the market economy, while the forcible system of exchange settlement and sales makes part of enterprises' profit transfer to foreign exchange banks, which is unfair and unnecessary. Reform of the system of exchange settlement and sales, extension of the autonomous right of the enterprises to use exchange, and transition from the voluntary exchange settlement system and sales to eventually canceling the system of exchange settlement and sales, are feasible in the reform of the exchange rate. Based on the prevailing situations in China, the enterprises that run the foreign trade business can open special foreign exchange accounts in the foreign exchange banks and deposit and withdraw foreign currency freely. Under the circumstances of no large-scale drawing of money, the central bank does not need to ask; meanwhile, the enterprises can also take technological operations on foreign exchange to avoid foreign exchange risks.

13.4.2 Gradually Open the Capital Account

The opening of the capital account is an important condition for improving and giving full play to the effect of the monetary policy. China has gradually loosened control over the capital account, but it is far from reaching the standard of opening the capital account. It requires China, while fully recognizing that opening the capital account will bring risks, to go step by step and gradually open the capital account.

(1) The risks of opening the capital account

Opening the capital account is a double-edged sword. It can bring both benefits and risks to a country. It may bring adverse selection and increase ethical risks.

Existence of adverse selection is because the creditor doesn't fully recognize the characteristics of the debtor so that he or she cannot evaluate the latter's credit standing and his or her responsibility correctly. This information asymmetry results in investment flowing into the low-quality enterprises eventually, because they provide a higher ROI. Because of the features of international capital which emphasize seeking high profit, the speculative flow of capital is likely to appear after the opening of the capital account: A large quantity of capital flows to some high-risk enterprises and projects to gain more compensation, thus resulting in excessive investment in these industries and projects, contributing to the whole nation's economical risk. Also, currently, many of China's financial organizations are experiencing bad management conditions and have low efficiency, and they lack competitiveness compared with their counterparts abroad. Once the capital account opens, in order to avoid the bad influence brought by bankruptcy on society, China will provide the government guarantee to attract more capital to flow to these financial organizations; this will certainly trigger moral risks and enlarge investigation risks.

(2) Principles of opening the capital account

① Based on the reality of China, select the appropriate way to open the capital account

In order to keep the security of the national sovereignty and economy, the country that wants to open its capital account has to choose a suitable developmental model or approach for itself. However, in the practice of opening the capital account in the recent decades, which started from the 1970s or the 1980s, there is no unified standard mode for countries. Modes of opening of the capital account can be roughly classified into four types: the "Step by Step" type, which is represented by the United States, Japan, and R.O. Korea; the "Comprehensive and Radical" type, which is represented by Australia and New Zealand; the "Sequential and Alternating" type, which is represented by developing countries such as Chile; and the "Driven by Breakthrough" type, which is represented by European countries such as Germany and the United Kingdom. Practical experience shows that there is no prevailing mode to follow for the opening of the capital account, and countries have to find a suitable developmental mode or approach based on their own reality.

Opening of capital account smoothly and safely needs a certain number of preconditions. These preconditions involve not only the macroeconomic and microeconomic levels, but also the international economic and financial environment, which mainly include a favorable macroeconomic environment, a stable and open domestic financial system, the balance of current accounts, an exchange rate that shows equilibrium and sufficient flexibility of the exchange rate, prudential and effective macro financial supervision and regulation ability, good legal structures, transparent information disclosure, relatively abundant foreign exchange reserves, a dynamic microeconomic foundation, effective international cooperation on financial regulation, reform of the crisis rescue mechanism and so on.

Obviously, China has not fully met the above conditions. There are many contradictions of the macroeconomy of China, such as imperfect micro mechanism, fragile financial system, weak financial regulation, and severe international environment. There is still a great distance to go to achieve the required preconditions for capital account. Therefore, gradually opening the capital account step by step becomes an inevitable choice.

② Use the experience of and learn lessons from other countries

According to the experience and lessons in opening the capital account of other countries, most countries in the world are cautious about opening the capital account. Most emerging industrialized countries and regions achieved the opening of the capital account after the 1990s. Historical experience shows that financial liberalization, which is characterized by the opening of the capital account, is an important reason for the financial crises or financial difficulties of many countries. A prominent feature of the Asian financial crisis is the crisis of the capital account. Different from the traditional current account crisis, the Asian financial crisis was characterized by the sudden reversal of capital flows and large capital outflows, which resulted in political instability and domestic social and political shocks. It impressed us deeply that some emerging industrialized countries and regions or developing countries implemented the opening of the capital account so simply that they didn't have the ability to guard against economic and financial crises, which were caused by international capital flows.

(3) Gradually open the capital account in a proper sequence

Opening the capital account will undertake fair risks, and in order to avoid these financial risks, we must do it gradually and in a proper sequence.

① Reasonably decide and flexibly adjust the opening sequence of the capital account

According to international experience and the actual situation of our nation, the opening of the capital accounts should be done in a certain sequence, following gradual and prudent procedures: First, lift the restrictions on long-term capital accounts. That is, the liberalization of long-term capital transactions should be given priority over the liberalization of security investments or short-term capital transactions. Second, the liberalization of security investments should come before the liberalization of short-term capital transactions, especially before that of short-term speculative transactions. Third, the opening of transactions related to physical assets (such as direct investments, trade financing) should take precedence over those unrelated to physical assets (such as security investments, credit financing). Fourth, the opening of short-term capital inflows should be given priority over that of short-term capital outflows. Last, the liberalization of overseas transactions of Chinese residents should be given preference over the liberalization of non-residents' participation in China's market.

It should be noted that the sequence of China's capital account opening is just a principle, and must not be modeled or fixed; instead, it should be flexibly adjusted according to the actual economic developmental situation of China and the changes in the international financial environment.

② Gradually realize the main contents of opening

The capital account transactions that are still under control in China embody themselves mainly in three aspects, whose contents are exactly the difficult and important points of opening capital account as well as the main contents of the gradual realization of opening capital account. First, the overseas direct investment fields. Further lift the restrictions from domestic institutions on overseas direct investments, and support the enterprises in "going out." Second, the equity investment fragments. Explore new methods of utilizing foreign capitals and gradually relax the restrictions on domestic investments of qualified overseas institutions. Third, the debt securities investment fragments. Broaden the ways of domestic foreign exchange funds, and allow qualified domestic institutions to invest in the overseas stock market; relax financing limitations of overseas institutions and enterprises on the domestic capital market, optimize the structure of the domestic capital market, and allow qualified overseas institutions to issue bonds in RMB and Chinese depository receipts in China; we can study and use for reference the international experience, and open up the domestic stock market phase by phase and step by step. Constantly summarize experience and lessons, and promote the orderly opening-up of the stock market under the premise of controllable risks.

③ Actively promote supporting reforms

Capital account opening is not only a matter of reforming the foreign exchange management system, but also one that requires mutual support from other reforms. It has to follow a proper sequence, which mainly includes the following points.

A flexible mechanism for the formation of the RMB exchange rate. In an open economy, if we want to maintain the autonomy of monetary policies under the condition of open capital control, we must adopt the floating exchange rate system. As for China, its special economic structure and economic system have determined that monetary policies still have great significance as a macro control means after the capital account is opened, so the realistic choice is also the implementation of the floating exchange rate system. At present, although the exchange rate system of China is a floating one under control, the space for automatic changes in the rate is rather small, and yet the changes are in a certain sense decided by the government. After the capital account is opened, the floating range of exchange rate fluctuations must be increased. In the short run, we can appropriately extend the flexibility of exchange rates; and in the medium and long term, we need to perfect the mechanism for the formation of the exchange rate market, and enhance the part that the market plays in exchange rate formation on the premise of not negating control and management.

The market-oriented mechanism for the formation of the interest rate.

After the capital account is opened, the interest rate will be an important means for regulating the outflows and inflows of capital. Corresponding to the range of exchange rate fluctuations, the range of interest rate fluctuations should also be expanded to realize the interest rate marketization. It is easy to lead to capital flights when the domestic interest rate is not as high as the international interest rate after the capital account is opened if the interest rate is rigid and can't reflect the real supply and demand of fund as well as floating with it. However, when the domestic interest rate is higher than the international interest rate, there's a great possibility of causing interest arbitrage. Both the circumstances can increase the risks of the opening of the capital account. China has made great progress in recent years in the reform of the interest rate, but has not achieved it yet. The marketization of the interest rate should be carried out smoothly according to the rough order of "foreign currency before domestic currency, loans before deposits, rural areas before urban areas, large before petty, and long-term before short-term." Of course, the deregulation of interest rates does not mean the government will loosen its regulation and control of macro finance, but means that the government will provide highly efficient market supervision—the government should regulate nominal money supply effectively to maintain the market price and promote economic growth.

④ Improve the financial supervision system

A complete financial supervision system is the presupposition for the opening of the capital account. Under the circumstances that if the financial supervision system is not complete, excessive capital inflows cannot be monitored and screened, banks will be encouraged to step into departments and industries with high risks such as real estate, the stock market and so on. The prices of the assets of these departments will expand so rapidly that a bubble economy would appear and it would end with large non-performing loans and drive the country into a terrible crisis. According to the Basel Agreement, measures of financial supervision should, at least, include strict market access systems, limits of lending ratios from banks to departments or industries, review and supervision over credit programs and financial standing of banks, restraining all kinds of irregularities and so on. At the same time, it should also strengthen supervision over the securities market that includes completing all kinds of transaction regulations, standards and procedures for being on the market, improving systems of information disclosure, developing accounting, evaluation, auditing, law and other intermediaries actively and obliging them to service fairly and so on.

13.4.3 Make Legitimate Arrangements to Ensure the Order of the Reform of Exchange Rate Regime and Opening of Capital Account

There are always disputes about arrangements for the order of the improvement of the managed floating exchange rate system, and the opening of the capital account so as to promote the reform of the exchange rate regime. We firmly believe that we should not only argue about the order of the two but make decisions on the basis of the fact of China's exchange rate regime and the opening of the capital account.

According to the 11th Five-Year Plan, "promote market-oriented interest rate reform steadily, improve the managed floating exchange rate system, and gradually realize the convertibility of the RMB under the capital account." It indicates that the two exist side by side and play a part together.

Improving the mechanism for the formation of the exchange rate is not only to get rid of the situation of pegging to the dollar and increase the flexibility of the RMB exchange rate, but at the same time, we should also gradually exploit the function of the market, which plays a fundamental role in the formation of the exchange rate. However, at present, the RMB is not fully convertible; China still has some restrictions on foreign exchange income and expenditure, and market supply and demand, which are reflected by the foreign exchange market, does not tally with the facts. This means the market price reflected is not reasonable either. Specifically, the RMB has now just realized current account convertibility. It has no restrictions on foreign payments and transfers of some current accounts such as the importation of trade in goods and services, but also relaxed restrictions on enterprises keeping foreign exchange earnings from current accounts, but there are still more restrictions on capital account transactions.

In mature markets, the domestic currency capital account is fully open. With the implementation of the free-floating exchange rate system, central banks generally do not often intervene in the foreign exchange market on a large scale. As a result, the balance between the capital account and the current account has become the two sides of a coin: when the current account is in surplus, the capital account is in deficit; when the current account is in deficit, the capital account is in surplus; the total balance of international payments has remained basically balanced. Therefore, the free flow of capital and exchange rate fluctuations adjust the balance of international payments from the quantity and price respectively, to promote international payments to maintain a basic balance.

At present, China has adopted a prudent and progressive asymmetric capital account opening policy and the RMB capital account convertibility has been partially achieved. This strategy helps to reduce capital outflows when there is a shortage in foreign exchange, while it also limits the impact of the risk of short-term capital flows, and has achieved positive results. However, because capital controls have long been "loose for inflows and strict for outflows," China has continued to maintain a large balance of payments surplus and a substantial increase in foreign exchange reserves in recent years. This makes a lot of foreign exchange in the form of official foreign exchange reserves over-centralized and reduces the effectiveness of the monetary policy. It also increases the difficulty in the operation and management of reserves; at the same time, reasonable demand for foreign exchange in the private sector, such as diversification and risk-averse, is difficult to be met, and the pressure of RMB appreciation has been exaggerated.

Therefore, in order to improve the mechanism for the formation of the RMB exchange rate and play the market's decisive role in the exchange rate formation, we should relax restrictions on cross-border capital transactions selectively and step by step, and gradually achieve capital account convertibility.

In summary, currently in China, when it comes to promoting the reform of the exchange rate regime, improving the managed floating exchange rate and the opening of the capital account, we should not mechanically decide which is first or last, but should make them coordinate with one another, and steadily promote them, depending on the domestic and foreign economic, financial, and political situations. In the process of improving the managed floating exchange rate system, we should select the necessary capital accounts and systematically release them while continuing to reduce capital controls, simultaneously promoting the formation of a real managed floating exchange rate system.

14

The Internationalization of the RMB and the Choices of Paths and Strategies

14.1 An Overview about the Internationalization of the RMB

14.1.1 Introduction

Since the reform and opening-up for more than 30 years, with China's rapidly developing economy and the rising status of the RMB, the internationalization of the RMB has received increasing attention in the areas of industries and academia. Domestic scholars have extensively discussed whether the RMB should be internationalized and how to promote the process. Although most of them believed that the internationalization of the RMB is an inevitable result of economic development, its conditions, paths, and strategies remain a debate, which requires scientific and comprehensive research.

After the collapse of the Bretton Woods System, the status of the USD was hit again. The rise of the EUR and the increase in China's economy led the trend of the international monetary system (multi-polarization) to be more obvious. Against the background of the shake up of the USD and the development of the Chinese economy, the RMB, as China's legal tender, must own the remarkable international situation and be responsible for it. This will draw the attention of the whole world.

The State Administration of Foreign Exchange announced in August 2010 that "China will promote the capital account reform in some important parts"; this is expected to provide a start to accelerating the opening of the capital account and will have a deep influence on the internationalization of the RMB. Besides, the opening of the capital account provides relatively complete external conditions, and at the same time, the construction of the offshore market, the offshore forward exchange rate market, and the offshore financial product market becomes the important reference for the internationalization of the RMB. Only by combining these three markets can we accelerate the path of the internationalization of the RMB.

In conclusion, it is very important to make a study on how to reach internationalization smoothly under the current circumstances, avoid risks in a suitable way, and finally reach the achievement of getting maximum benefit of RMB internationalization.

14.1.2 Literature Review of the Internationalization of the RMB

In the 1960s, international researchers began systematic research, although they could not arrive at a final definition of currency internationalization. Cohen is the first person to hold the view that the function of international money was an extension of domestic ones. Hartmann further defined that different functions of international money were respectively classified into the international monetary payment, the unit of account and a store of value. Tavlas argued that those definitions were too broad. He thought that money would be internationalized when it plays a role as international monetary payment, the unit of account and a store of value in international transactions. Mundell affirmed that when the scope of currency circulation is beyond the statutory circulation area or when the multiples of the currency are imitated by other regions, the currency becomes internationalized.

In the 1980s, many domestic scholars began to focus on the problem of the internationalization of the RMB . They started from the Chinese developing economic power, and analyzed the RMB's potential benefits and realistic conditions. Zhao Haikuan estimated that the RMB could become one of the international currencies, or at least, partly play the role of a world currency. Aiming at the situation of the RMB becoming a world currency, the Chinese government should take a positive attitude and take measures to speed up this process.

Zhong Wei pointed out valuable suggestions on the internationalization of the RMB. He suggested a combination of RMB capital account convertibility and the process of the internationalization of the RMB. Wu Nianlu brought out the difference between convertibility and internationalization and analyzed the benefits and risks of currency internationalization. He supposed that to create good surroundings, research should be conducted to realize RMB capital account convertibility in the environment of reforming the international monetary system. Li Xiao, Li Junjiu, and Ding Yibing were of the opinion that the internationalization of the RMB should be reached by "institutional RMB regionalization" in the system of regional monetary cooperation in East Asia. Also, faced with the choice of paths, the "Asianization" of the RMB should combine market self-process and the government's institutional coordination, and combine monetary integration in the sub-region and the overall coordination of the pan-region. Liu Qun researched the possibility of the internationalization of the RMB and its meaning from the perspective of China's economic strength. He found that if the RMB achieved internationalization, it would benefit China in making good use of international resources. With continuing growth of China's economic strength, the RMB is bound to go forward to attain the status of a world currency. Wang Yuanlong held the view that an important premise for the internationalization of the RMB was capital account convertibility. This means peripheral internationalization, regional internationalization, and global, internationalization, and the currency function become a strategy in which the RMB turns to international settlement, investment, and storage currency. Li Daokui and Liu Linlin thought that the internationalization of the RMB would bring benefits more than harm, and presented a dual-track approach to reaching the goal of the internationalization of the RMB. The first track means realizing capital account convertibility step by step, synchronizing with China's financial reform. The second track means shaping the RMB foreign exchange trading market, especially in Hong Kong.

14.2 The Present Situation and Problems of the Internationalization of the RMB

14.2.1 The Process of the Development of the Internationalization of the Current RMB

Since the 1960s, China has been getting more and more adjusted to the trends of the world, and has also gradually begun to reform the foreign exchange control. On December 1, 1996, China reached the goal of RMB convertibility under the current account. In 1997, the Southeast Asian financial crisis led China to become more cautious in exchange management. Although exchange structural reform had been started in 2005, China didn't give a certain answer to the question of when the RMB capital account would be opened.

The main function of the RMB abroad is to establish itself as a medium of exchange and a valuation method in frontier trade, not a reserve of other countries.

With regard to the calculation and amount of RMB foreign circulation, Zheng Xiaozhou thought that since the opening of Union Pay in Hong Kong, RMB trading in Hong Kong has grown sharply. From 2004 to 2006, the transaction of Union Pay in Hong Kong grew from 2.845 billion yuan to 12.36 billion yuan, and the RMB has become an important medium of exchange. Zhong Wei thought that the RMB's flow in Indonesia by tourism is 0.4 billion yuan. In Singapore, in diverse ways, the cross-border flow is 5 billion yuan every year, while in Vietnam, the flow in border trade is 5 to 6 billion yuan every year, and in Hong Kong, the flow by tourism and back flow is 18.8 billion yuan every year. Lu Hao pointed out that the RMB has been widely used in northern Laos and some areas in Myanmar and Thailand. In Russia, the circulation of the RMB was relatively limited; the RMB was mainly used by the Chinese and Russians who carried out trading business, and it was also widely used by people who speculate in foreign currency.

Thus, we can see that the RMB was used only in the border areas. However, even if it is not an officially reserved hard currency, the RMB is still capable of playing a role as an international currency in a region. This will bring real economic benefits for the domestic growth of China.

14.2.2 Existing Problems and External Difficulties of the Internationalization of the RMB

(1) Inconspicuous economic core competitiveness leads to the limitation of the internationalization of the RMB

According to the internationalization of other currencies, the initial stage of the USD and the GBP was based on domestic core competitive advantages. The United Kingdom was based on excellent techniques in textiles and steel industry, while the base industries in the United States were the steel, automobile, and chemical industries. At present, although China has had a breakthrough in economic aggregate and has become the most active emerging economy around the world, the per capita level of economic development has no competitiveness and it lacks the core advantages that emerging strategic industries possess. These limit the path and the base of economic competitiveness of the internationalization of the RMB.

In manufacturing, the value-added per capital in China is USD 14,000, equivalent to only 18% of that of the United States and 13% of that of Japan, showing a huge gap compared with the manufacturing sectors in developed countries. The added value per capita of China's high technology industry differs slightly from that of manufacturing, but the two indicators in the developed countries are obviously different. This also suggests that the technological level of China's high-tech industry is low.

In China's high-tech exports, computer and communications occupy an absolutely dominant position, followed by electronics. Over the years, these two have always maintained a favorable balance, while other high-tech products contribute to the trade deficit. This shows development imbalances and structural defects in China's high-tech imports and exports.

(2) China's financial market is still not perfect, which greatly restricts the process of the internationalization of the RMB

The lower level of marketization of China's financial system cannot provide the support of a good domestic environment for the internationalization of the RMB, and also fails to form market-oriented interest rates. Especially in the open financial environment, this reduces the feasibility and effectiveness of the monetary policy that the monetary authority uses in open market operations to control capital flows. Due to these reasons, the process of the internationalization of the RMB would be slow to a great extent.

The commercial banks are still the core of China's financial system and especially the state-owned commercial banks occupy absolute dominance. The market is dominated by the traditional model of credit financing, using direct financing tools such as stocks and bonds, and with a low level of marketization.

At present, commercial and policy banks are the main force in China's credit market, of which non-banking financial institutions and foreign banks occupy a small proportion. Depending entirely on the commercial banking system, especially on monopolistic state-owned banks, leads to a fragile financial system, failure to cope with the complex situation, and finally to the late opening of China's financial markets.

At the same time, the stock market is not well developed, because of which financing inability is intensified. Under the influence of frequently issued policies, the volatility in the stock market revealed regulatory loopholes and institutional drawbacks, largely reflecting the immature development and unreasonable hierarchical structure. The low-developing stock market failed to replace commercial banks in becoming important financing channels for the national economic development. Additionally, there is a great gap between share offerings and the scales of investment in fixed assets, resulting in the weak contribution of the stock market to China's economic development.

With respect to the issue of bords, national debts and policy bank debts always maintain a dominant position. The development of other forms of security markets is low. Although the corporate bond market has existed for a long time, its size is small. In 2009, the sum of national debts, central bank bills, and policy bank debts occupied 82.3% of the bond balance, while in the United States, the sum of national, municipal, and federal agency bonds accounted for only 38% of the total. The three kinds of bonds monopolized China's market, while truly market-oriented commercial bank bonds, corporate bonds and short-term financing bonds have developed slowly.

(3) The status of the USD is still unshakable, which has affected the process of the internationalization of the RMB

Since the outbreak of the financial crisis in the United States, the international monetary system, with the USD as the center, has been questioned again, which has raised international calls to put forward the reform of the system. Although also affected by the financial crisis, China has continued to maintain rapid growth and has actively participated in international cooperation, contributing to the global economic recovery and leading to the increased international status of the RMB. Admittedly, however, the United States is still the world's leading power, and it is not so easy to bring about any change in the dominance of the USD in the monetary system in a short period of time.

First of all, the role of the USD as an "anchor currency" has been further strengthened. In 2006, the number of countries pegging to the USD exchange rate increased to 28. Since the reform of the exchange rate regime in 2005, the RMB has continued to appreciate. But after the outbreak of the US financial crisis, the RMB exchange rate against the USD remained relatively stable. Second, the USD is still the main currency for transaction settlements on the international trade market, and its status as an international reserve currency remains stable. Since the world's most important resource, oil, is priced in USD, the United

States can export inflation to the world through currency depreciation to maintain its economic development. Although the rise of the EUR and the decline of the USD as an official foreign exchange reserve in some countries is observed, the status of the USD as an international reserve currency is still unshakable (Figure 14.1). This is because the USD reserves remain attractive for many emerging markets, especially for the developing countries. Finally, the stable status of the USD in the existing international monetary system will greatly affect the advancement of the internationalization of the RMB, which poses challenges to the choice of paths for the internationalization of the RMB. The paths for the internationalization of the RMB cannot simply copy the traditional model in other countries, and must be selected according to the contemporary international monetary pattern and practical circumstances in China.

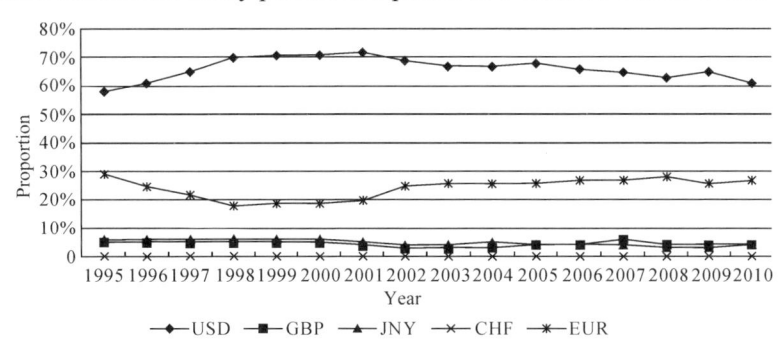

Figure 14.1 The proportion of the world's major currencies in international foreign reserves

Source: Currency Composition of the Official Foreign Exchange Reserves (COFER), IMF.

14.3 Cost-benefit Analysis of the Internationalization of the RMB

14.3.1 The Cost of the Internationalization of the RMB

(1) The internationalization of the RMB may lead to foreign exchange asset devaluation

Exchange rate fluctuations will bring a lot of risks to foreign exchange assets. The appreciation of the RMB and the expected appreciation has attracted international speculative capital, and this has become an important reason for hot money flows into China. The appreciation of the RMB has fully indicated that the reform of the internationalization of the RMB will be accelerated. The faster the RMB appreciates, the higher people are expected to increase it further, and the greater size and faster speed the hot money inflows would have. Continuous hot money inflows increase the money supply and fuel inflation. It is difficult to achieve the anticipated goal of macro-economic regulation. The appreciation of the RMB seems to enter such a cycle: persistent surplus in balance of international payments, increased expectation of RMB appreciation, the massive influx of international capital, an increase in money supply and inflation pressure, forcing the RMB to rise further; hence, appreciation seems to move in cycles. It is specifically needed to note that, with the acceleration of the internationalization of the RMB, once the weak USD becomes strong and the RMB appreciation reaches the peak, this would possibly cause a reversal of the pattern of international capital flow and bring huge risks to the Chinese economy.

From the start of the reform and opening-up to the early 1990s, China's foreign exchange reserves were always fairly low. But, since 1996, when the RMB current account was opened, China has become the world's biggest country in foreign exchange reserves of which the USD accounts for about 70%. If the RMB wants to realize internationalization, first, its exchange rate should change according to market supply and demand. China's huge trade surplus and America's deficit make the exchange rate of the RMB against the USD change.

(2) The internationalization of the RMB may place China in a "Triffin Dilemma"

The original meaning of the Triffin Dilemma is that the United States, which provides international settlement and reserve currency, needs a long-term trade deficit, while the USD, as the core of the international monetary system, must maintain the stability of the currency value, which requires the United States to maintain a long-term trade surplus. These two requirements contradict each other and become a paradox.

After the internationalization of the RMB, China would provide international reserve assets to other countries through the weakening of the position in balance of international payments. If a country needs to increase its international reserve assets, it must keep the surplus in balance of international payments. If the USD and other reserve assets can't meet the needs of the country, which is also willing to hold more RMB, China must provide RMB assets through a deficit in the balance of international payments. A deficit in the balance of international payments affects China's economic development and the stability of the RMB. This will make the country not willing to hold more RMB assets. On the contrary, if China has a surplus in balance of international payments, even though the RMB has the higher value, credit, and strong stability, this cannot meet the needs of international solvency during the development of the world's economy.

(3) RMB internationalization may increase the difficulty in financial regulation

Mondale's ternary paradox points out that among exchange rate stability, free capital flows and monetary policy independence, only two goals can be achieved. At present, China can control monetary policy independently and maintain exchange rate stability, but capital cannot flow freely. In order to realize the internationalization of the RMB, free capital flow is an essential premise. Then, for the independent monetary policy and stable exchange rate, one of them must be sacrificed.

The internationalization of the RMB will produce spillovers of our monetary policy to other countries. At this point, the exchange rate of the RMB is not only decided by China's policy, but by the international market. Due to the unbalanced economic development of countries and regions, the impact of the monetary policy on them is different. Therefore, the monetary policy will receive various pressures. Where maintaining the stability of economic growth, how to use the appropriate monetary policy to face and balance these pressures will bring enormous challenges to China's future.

(4) The internationalization of the RMB may enlarge the risks to the RMB exchange rate

On July 21, 2005, the People's Bank of China announced the reform of the RMB exchange rate. The RMB no longer pegs the USD only but refers to a basket of currencies, thus forming an exchange rate system of certain elasticity. In October 2008, the financial crisis spread to the world. All countries took rescue measures actively, and the exchange rate of the RMB against the USD began to stabilize even with a slight decline. After 2009, the Chinese economy stabilized and recovered, keeping the exchange rate of the RMB against the USD at about 6.8. Since April 2010, the United States has put pressures on the RMB appreciation. Since then, the RMB appreciated against the USD (Figure 14.2). On the other hand, because the main component of the RMB currency basket is still the USD and since the exchange rate reform, the exchange rate of the USD against the EUR has fluctuated, the RMB against the EUR has also presented a substantial fluctuation (Figure 14.3).

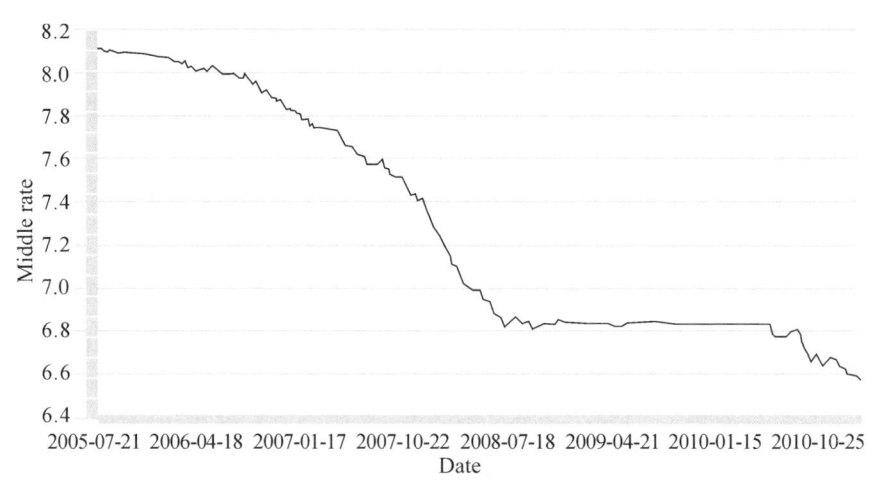

Figure 14.2 The middle rate of the exchange rate of the RMB against the USD, July 2005—October 2010

Source: http://www.pbc.gov.cn.

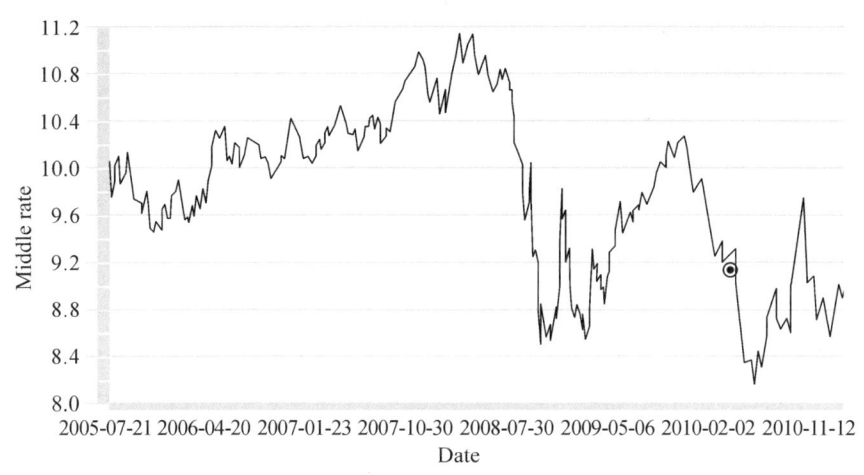

Figure 14.3 The middle rate of the exchange rate of the RMB against the EUR, July 2005—November 2010

Source: http://www.pbc.gov.cn.

When the RMB becomes an international currency, it will inevitably require convertibility of the capital account and a free flow on the market. The RMB exchange rate will respond more to market demands, and will be hit at any time in the international arena. This will possibly increase the loss of capital which uses the RMB in valuation, settlement, and reserve, accompanied by a rise in the transaction, accounting, and economic risks. When the RMB works as an international currency, the risk will become more intense compared with that where it is unconvertible and under control.

14.3.2 The Benefit of the Internationalization of the RMB

(1) Gain seigniorage revenues

When getting the reserve currency status, a certain amount of RMB must be held by other countries for international trade, debt repayment, and other demands. In order to obtain RMB reserves, these countries need to export goods or financial assets to China. If using the RMB to buy goods, China could substitute imports for similar domestic resources in investment. This not only saves the domestic resources, but also obtains benefits. Buying financial assets to provide international reserves could directly yield the corresponding returns. Generally, other countries, in order to hold RMB reserves need to pay the corresponding cost, which constitutes the RMB international seigniorage revenues.

(2) Promote the development of international trade and overseas investment

The RMB, as an international currency, is widely used in international terms, payment, and settlement. Realizing international monetary payments makes the RMB a scarce resource. When the RMB becomes an international currency, China can directly use the RMB in valuation, payment, and settlement in the economic and trade exchanges with other countries. This is conducive to expanding China's foreign economic exchanges and will bring China's import and export traders, investors, and consumers a lot of convenience. This makes them engaged in the international economic transactions because they can use local currency more and be less disturbed by foreign exchange risks. After the internationalization of RMB, domestic investors can go overseas and their investment ability will be greatly enhanced. This will also reduce the risks from exchange rate changes in implementing the strategy of "going out." Investment income is further guaranteed. It is conducive to expanding China's foreign direct investment, promoting the level of China's enterprises' internationalization, and participating in international competition at a higher level.

(3) Optimize the structure of China's foreign exchange reserves

The principle for the management of China's foreign exchange reserves is "safe, flexible, and retain the value." Only on the premise of safety, can value be retained. But reserve asset is a payment tool and should be realized at any time, so it should also be flexible. Due to the influence of the financial crisis, the security and value of China's USD-denominated foreign exchange reserve assets are greatly threatened. After the RMB realizes internationalization, China's foreign trade can be conducted without using the foreign exchange reserves, and there is no need to hold a lot of foreign exchange reserves to adjust the balance of the economy at home and abroad.

At the same time, China will have deficit financing ability that where there is balance of payments deficit, China can carry out financing by issuing RMB rather than through a large domestic economic adjustment.

(4) Promote China's international status

Monetary internationalization means the improvement of the status of a currency in the international monetary system and in the world's economy. It is beneficial to increasing the voice of a country in international affairs and improving its ability to deal with international affairs. It also makes China own right of issuance and regulation of an international currency to influence the change of the international economic situation. At the same time, China's economic operations and policy changes will also affect other countries, which changes the situation in which the USD has had long dominance, to strengthen China's economic and political status and is conducive to China's sustained economic growth and improvement of its comprehensive competitiveness.

Above all, although monetary internationalization also has some risks, through the analysis of the above, the benefits of the internationalization of the RMB are significantly greater than the cost. Therefore, actively promoting the internationalization of the RMB has positive significance.

14.4 The Real Conditions of the Internationalization of the RMB

14.4.1 Improvement of China's Overall Economic Strength and Domestic Currency's Position Are Necessary Requirements for the Internationalization of the RMB

Experience suggests that in the history of currency internationalization, to become an international currency is based on its strong economic strength and perfect financial market. The improvement of China's overall economic strength is a necessary condition for the internationalization of the RMB. Since the reform and opening-up, China's economy has maintained a good momentum of sustained and rapid growth, suggesting that the internationalization of the RMB has a very solid economic foundation. The foundation will continue to strengthen, which will effectively promote the RMB to become a dominant international currency.

In 2010, China's GDP was 39.798 trillion yuan, at an annual growth rate of 10.3%, which exceeded Japan to become the world's second economic power. In 2010, the national import and export value was USD 2.97276 trillion. The strong momentum of foreign trade once again became the important stimulant for economic growth in China. With regard to absorption of foreign investment over the years, China has been able to reach the third position in the world, attracting USD 50 billion–60 billion yearly, the top among all developing countries, and has ranked among the leading countries in the world. In 2010, the amount of actual use of foreign capital was USD 105.735 billion, a rise of 17.44%. The international status of the RMB, with China's powerful economic strength and stable political environment, rose enormously. This led to considerable appreciation in RMB in recent years.

14.4.2 Political Stability and National Credit Are a Solid Foundation

Whether the RMB can become an international currency is the result of market selection, based on a strong economic foundation, strong political and military power, a developed financial market, and relatively stable monetary value. An international currency must provide safe storage for foreign capital and only the country with strong political power and political stability can provide such support. China has political stability. Since the reform of the exchange rate system in 1994, the value of the RMB has remained stable. Especially during the Southeast Asian financial crisis of 1997, under the pressure of commodity exports and a slowdown in economic growth, China adhered to the value of the RMB, in order to solve the crisis at an early date. During this period, China acted as a leader and RMB did not depreciate, which played an important role in easing the Asian financial crisis. Thus, the RMB has won a good international reputation. China's monetary authority has amassed quite a rich amount of experience of disinflation, stable currency and a moderate monetary policy to ensure the stable level of the purchasing power of the RMB, which has strengthened people's confidence in the RMB at home and abroad. From 1980 to 2006, China's inflation maintained at a level that was roughly equal to that in the main developed countries. In the future, as China further enriches its experience in macroeconomic regulations with a more mature control concept, methods, and means, domestic inflation is expected to be controlled within a reasonable range.

14.4.3 Close Economic and Trade Exchanges and Currency Swap with Neighboring Countries Are the Premise

The use in the surrounding countries is an important start toward the internationalization of the RMB. The enlargement of the scope of usage overseas improves the credit and acceptance of the RMB, which will eventually become an international core currency accepted generally by people all over the world. In 2000, China and the Asian countries signed the "Chiang Mai Initiative" in Thailand marking an important beginning of the South and East Asian regional financial cooperation. In recent years, China has gradually established its dominance in economic development in South and East Asia. China has political stability, economic prosperity, and the relatively stable value of the RMB. Naturally, the exchange rate risk is negligible. When the surrounding countries are short of foreign exchange reserves and have difficulty in foreign currency settlement, using the RMB in settlement becomes a sub-optimal choice of both parties. Since 2007, the US subprime crisis also gradually led to the depreciation of the USD. Choosing the RMB in settlement, therefore, becomes the first choice of many countries in Asia. Until the end of 2007, among China's border countries, Russia and six other countries opened RMB settlement accounts in border trade with Chinese banks. The RMB has also become one currency of Mongolia. In 2007, the RMB stock in notes within the territory of Vietnam was about 1.8 billion yuan.

14.4.4 The Impact of the International Financial Crisis on the USD is an Important Opportunity to Accelerate the Process of the Internationalization of the RMB

The US financial crisis eventually evolved into a global financial crisis. The decline in the US economy led to a decline in the competitiveness of the USD. When the United States transferred its USD debts, many countries' foreign exchange reserve assets shrank due to the devaluation of the USD. This caused countries to lose faith in the USD and underweight USD reserves. In the post-crisis era, the main developed countries held most of the financial and monetary resources. But the emerging market countries, including China and India, have rapid development. America, Europe, and Japan occupied a big proportion of the world's economy, which gradually began to decline. The pattern of the real economy has changed and there is a significant imbalance in the current international virtual economy too. To rebalance the real and virtual economy, the core problem is to reconstruct the international monetary system. Therefore, China should use the financial crisis as an opportunity to maintain the stability of its economic growth and the RMB value, to enhance the competitiveness of the RMB and lay a solid economic foundation for its internationalization.

14.4.5 Economic Integration and the Reform of the International Monetary System Are the External Conditions

The evolution of the international monetary system over one hundred years is essentially the result of the contest of national economic strength, reflecting the world's thirst for an orderly international monetary order. Collapse of the Bretton Woods System shows that the USD could not be used as a single dominant currency that manipulates the world monetary system. In the G20 financial summit in 2008, the United States, the European Union, and the BRICS put forward the idea of the reconstruction of the international monetary system to realize the "necessary reform of the global financial system." It marks the fact that the world will enter a new period to reconstruct and improve the international monetary and financial system.

The USD is the most powerful international currency today, while the EUR and the JNY are also increasing in importance. After the outbreak of the financial crisis, the international status of the USD changed, and the EUR became the second international currency. Some EU countries, especially France, thought that the impact of the financial crisis on the USD was the

EUR's best opportunity to challenge USD hegemony. Countries seek to raise their currencies, making it necessary to get rid of the dependence on the USD. Changing from the present situation of the dominance of the USD to a basket of currencies is historically inevitable in the development of the international monetary system. Against the background of "competition and conflicts among powers," the choices of paths and strategies of the internationalization of the RMB are particularly important.

14.5 The Way Forward for the Internationalization of the RMB

In the history of the international monetary development, the GBP, the USD, the JNY, and the EUR were once major international currencies. The internationalization of any country's currency has its own historical background and deep political and economic reasons, but the common factor is that the processes of the internationalization of these currencies are on the basis of their countries' powerful economic strength and proactive government policy. At the same time, the processes were not achieved overnight, but experienced over long decades or even a century. Therefore, the internationalization of the RMB should find a path to fit China's national conditions, namely, taking gradual convertibility as the principle, through regional monetary cooperation, and taking a peripheral internationalization-regional internationalization-global internationalization path.

14.5.1 Speed up the Implementation of the Regional Internationalization of the RMB on the Basis of Trade Settlement with the Neighboring Countries with the RMB

The peripheral internationalization of the RMB is the primary form and the recent goal of the internationalization of the RMB, namely, in China's surrounding countries and regions, such as Mongolia and ASEAN's 10 countries to achieve the widespread use and smooth circulation of the RMB, and to make it become the payment and settlement currency, and eventually a reserve currency, thus realizing the functions of international currency within the Asian region.

(1) Present situation of the peripheral internationalization of the RMB

Since December 12, 2008, China has signed bilateral currency swap agreements of a total worth of 803.5 billion yuan with surrounding and closely related trading countries, like R.O. Korea, Indonesia, Malaysia, Belarus, Argentina, Iceland and Singapore.

China has signed bilateral trade currency settlement agreements with eight peripheral countries, including Russia. In April 2009, the State Council took Shanghai, Guangzhou, Shenzhen, Zhuhai, and Dongguan, as pilot cities for cross-border RMB trade settlement, which marks the RMB's extension from the small border trade settlement to the international trade field of a certain scale. In June 2010, the pilot cities for RMB settlement in China's cross-border trade were added by Beijing, Tianjin and 16 other provinces, autonomous regions, and municipalities directly under the central government. By August 2010, the banks had dealt with cross-border RMB trade settlement business with a total of 53.384 billion yuan. In November 2010, China and Russia decided to realize bilateral trade settlement with their domestic currencies. The scope of pilot cities for cross-border RMB trade settlement is expanding gradually and RMB trade settlement in the offshore areas has gradually extended from the ASEAN region to all countries and regions.

(2) The peripheral internationalization of the RMB is to lay a good foundation for the regional internationalization of the RMB

The peripheral internationalization of the RMB strengthened economic and trade exchanges with East Asia, promoted regional convergence in politics, the economy, culture and other aspects, and fostered trust and cooperation among East Asian countries. This provides a good condition for further internationalization of the RMB. After ASEAN, China, Japan, and R.O. Korea, "10+3," have sped up the development of free trade areas, the frequency of the RMB used in neighboring countries is increasing day by day. Meanwhile, due to not involving the capital account opening, this makes China, while fully enjoying the benefits of the regional internationalization of the RMB, reduce the risk of exchange rate, stabilize the RMB exchange rate, and improve the credibility. This can also help the monetary authority to accumulate RMB management experience overseas, and lay the foundation for realizing regional internationalization in East Asia and even Asia.

14.5.2 Promote Monetary Cooperation in East Asia and Realize the Regional Internationalization of the RMB

The regional internationalization of the RMB means close economic exchanges and cooperation with East Asian countries, prompting the influence of the RMB in the whole East Asian region. This would let the RMB gradually become the main payment and settlement currency, eventually becoming an important part of foreign exchange reserves of East Asian countries.

(1) International experience of the currency's regional internationalization

Apart from the EUR, all other single currencies used a certain special historical opportunity to become an international currency. The birth of the EUR, the German mark being at the core, provides a new reference model for currency internationalization, which is based on the theory of "optimum currency area." This theory refers to the efficiency of the use of money in an optimal area. The general payment way is a single common currency, or several currencies with unlimited convertibility. The exchange rates for current and capital transactions are pegged to each other and unchanged, but they use floating exchange rates with other countries outside the region.

(2) The regional internationalization of the RMB is the inevitable stage of its internationalization

First of all, since the breakdown of the Bretton Woods System in the 1970s, the world's monetary system is developing toward a multipolar world monetary system. Although the dominance of the USD in a short period of time doesn't seem to be shaken, the EUR plays a more and more important role in international economic intercourse, and the JNY is still one of the major international currencies. The rapid development of emerging economies makes the status of their currencies in the world show an unprecedented increase. At present, however, no single international currency can challenge the dominance of the USD. Regional internationalization is the only way to gradually realize the internationalization of the RMB. Second, the process of peripheral internationalization of the RMB is accelerated. Economic and trade connections with East Asian countries increase the influence of the RMB. This provides a solid foundation for the evolution of regional internationalization. Finally, currently China is a big economy rather than a strong economy. The path toward internationalization in one step is not realistic. "Strong in trade but weak in finance" is the realistic status, requiring China to abide by the progressive principle in the process of the internationalization of the RMB.

(3) Monetary cooperation in East Asia is the key to regional internationalization of the RMB

Through regional monetary cooperation, the Eurozone was created, driven by "dual-core" Germany and France, while it is difficult for a country to become the core of the Eurozone as a whole. In the path of the internationalization of the RMB, only by implementing regional internationalization with strong regional coverage, can the RMB compete with the strong USD and the EUR.

In recent years, economic and trade ties between China and other Asian countries, particularly the East Asian countries, play a more and more important role in Asian affairs. As the world's third largest economy, Japan relied only on its trade advantages and lacked regional monetary cooperation, leading to a greatly discounted process of internationalization of the JNY. In the region of East Asia, neither the RMB nor the JNY will become the core currency alone. Therefore, the two should complement each other, strengthen cooperation, and jointly promote the development of regional currency internationalization in East Asia and even the whole of Asia.

(4) Regional internationalization of the RMB has a long way to go

The international experience of the EUR shows that regional cooperation regarding currencies has a high similarity and alignment requirements of members with respect to economic, cultural, and political structures. Due to a similar pattern of economic development and an excessive reliance on the

USD, East Asian economies in fact have been sinking into the predicament of the exchange rate, leading to financial fragility. Although the political and economic base for developing the "Asian RMB" in the region does not possess the advantage of the EUR, with the development of ASEAN and ASEAN "10+3," Asia is also working in the direction of regional economic integration. Implementing RMB-based regional cooperation in East Asia not only needs cooperation with the JNY, but also requires countries to work together to reduce political, economic, and cultural differences in realizing common development in the region.

14.5.3 Take Regional Internationalization of the RMB as the Basis for Gradually Promoting the Internationalization of the RMB

The highest form of the internationalization of the RMB is becoming the world's reserve currency, and become a dominant currency after the USD and the EUR. When the RMB becomes an important part of the reserve assets of Asian governments and a major Asian currency, there will be a sharp increase in the payment ability. The financial market and the reflux system will be more mature, opening up to the outside world in a greater degree. The pricing mechanism will be basically completed. China's economic and financial cooperation in Asia will play a leading role, and this will lay the foundation for the RMB to be a major international currency.

In the implementation of the internationalization of the RMB, the most important step is to carry out the process gradually, rather than undergoing the "shock therapy". By absorbing the experience of currency internationalization of other countries and accurately positioning the status of China in the world's economy, China could quicken the coordinated reform of the internationalization of the RMB, while ensuring continuous healthy and stable economic growth at the same time.

14.6 Choices of Strategies for the Internationalization of the RMB

That a country's currency becomes an international currency is an inevitable result of its economic development to a certain degree. The government must take some measures to achieve its objective of becoming an international reserve currency. China has not fully opened the capital account, while the financial system and relevant laws and regulations are not perfect. To become an international currency, the impact and risks faced by the financial system will greatly increase; therefore, it is necessary to take a series of reform measures for the internationalization of the RMB to take place.

14.6.1 Further Improve the Financial System

The process of the internationalization of the RMB depends on the perfection of the financial system in China and on the extent of deepening of its openness. With the deepening of the process, the contact with the international financial market will be closer. The independence of the controlled exchange rate will be weaker. Strong economic strength and a sound financial system will be the important guarantees for financial security and a smooth internationalization of the RMB in China.

(1) Promote the reform of the financial system

Any mature financial market is based on a strong economy, which requires China to realize the transformation of the economic growth pattern and economic restructuring. The global financial crisis shows that the mature financial markets and strict financial supervisory systems are vital for the development of the financial sector. China should establish a sound financial risk control mechanism, conduct and regulate capital operations strictly to promote sustainable and healthy development of the capital market, and encourage appropriate financial innovation.

First, we must realize the transition of the government's function and really set up a modern banking system. Speed up the modern bank governance structure, realize independence and self-financing, and establish a market-based incentive mechanism and supervisory system for reasonable risk-aversion. Second, we must actively encourage financial innovation. We need to build a micro basis for the development of financial innovation, and effectively combine financial innovation and system. Coupled with the national conditions, we can refer to the international experience to guide enterprises' financial innovation and establish an appropriate risk-prevention mechanism.

(2) Establish and perfect laws and regulations on financial supervision

First is to strengthen the construction of the mechanism for internal self-discipline in financial institutions, improve self-oversight systems, and reduce the government's regulation and control of financial institutions, and improve their own regulating ability and the ability in resisting risks. Second is to strengthen the construction of the financial legal system and promote the country's financial legislation in sync with international rules. Active participation in formulating international financial rules would strengthen the voice of the RMB. It also needs, as soon as possible, to introduce laws and regulations on the mechanism for the financial institutions' market withdrawal, futures operations, and administration management, separate operations, and supervision of foreign exchange, policy banks, and trust. To speed up the establishment of a mixed management model in the financial industry is to realize the unified regulation of banking, insurance, securities, trust, and other financial sectors. Third, based on the principle of "fair, just, and open", continue strict law enforcement. Supervise financial institutions in accordance with relevant laws and regulations to ensure fair operations and competition in the financial sector, maintain its vigor and vitality, and provide a good external environment for it. In addition, to improve the management efficiency and the sustained healthy and rapid development of the financial sector, financial regulators and government should keep the independence of the law enforcement, and the transparency and authenticity of information.

14.6.2 Realize Convertibility of the Capital Account

With the deepening of global economic integration, developed countries and many developing countries have opened the capital account to realize convertibility. It is thought that the internationalization of the RMB has five stages, namely, the outflows from the mainland, offshore circulation from Hong Kong, the flow back to the mainland, expanding global currency circulation, and the opening of the capital account. The process of the internationalization of the RMB follows the principle of gradual and systematic measures under the reasonable equilibrium exchange rate to promote its convertibility.

(1) Increase the scale and level of offshore circulation

First is to further expand the swap scale with bilateral trade partners. A bilateral currency swap guarantee in a certain time evades the risk of exchange rate shocks and strengthens financial cooperation. The "Chiang Mai Initiative" signed in 2000 expanded the quantity and amount for ASEAN currency swap agreements, and built bilateral currency swap agreements between China, Japan, R.O. Korea, and ASEAN countries. Based on the existing condition, China should expand the scale of currency swap and the scope of RMB circulation with ASEAN countries and other economies.

Second is to promote the development of cross-border RMB trade settlements. This will reduce the dependence of the surrounding countries and regions on other major currencies, and can also lay the foundation for the regional cooperation on currency in East Asia. Considering the different acceptance of and trust in the RMB in countries and regions, the internationalization of the RMB must advance step by step, and first an area must be selected that is most likely to accept the RMB, like Hong Kong, Macao, and Taiwan of China. Next is ASEAN. Due to close economic and trade exchanges, within the range of ASEAN, China can promote cross-border RMB settlement. Finally, China can select two important trading partners, R.O. Korea and Japan, which also belong to the "10 + 3."

The demand for using RMB to settle trade on the international market is very strong. Once the RMB begins cross-border trade settlement, its proportion of the currency used in global trade settlement will continuously increase. The RMB's international status will be improved and the process of the internationalization of the RMB is expected to deepen further.

(2) A stable domestic macroeconomic environment

The premise under which other countries are willing to hold RMB is currency stability, which in turn is based on the stability of the domestic macroeconomic environment and a prudent monetary policy. A stable macroeconomic environment can reduce the probability of financial crisis during the process of the reform of currency convertibility. The main content of the macroeconomic stability includes fast and steady economic growth, fiscal balance of payments, a reasonable rate of inflation, a reasonable economic structure, and the balance of international payments. A slow or even negative economic growth would lead to a lack of confidence in the market, and it would be difficult to form good expectations. Fiscal imbalances mainly show the large fiscal deficit. Issuing bonds to maintain fiscal balance can cause a rise in the interest rate, lead to short-term speculative capital inflows, and result in the actual currency appreciation, a decline of international competitiveness, and a deterioration of the current account. Increasing the money supply to balance revenue and expenditures can cause capital flight, inflation, and currency devaluation. Inflation can lead to a large number of short-term speculative capital flows. An unreasonable economic structure would lead to the lack of competitiveness of exports, and a decrease in the competitiveness of the current account. Imbalance of international payments can cause the floating of RMB exchange rates and interest rates on the international market, resulting in a lot of capital flows and finally a negative impact on macroeconomy.

(3) Plenty of foreign exchange reserves and strong international liquidity

Plenty of foreign exchange reserves and a good balance of international payments are the premise for a country to realize the opening of the capital account. According to the theory of international reserve demand management and the experience of other countries with freely convertible currencies, there is a need to keep the foreign currency for importation equivalent to a quarter, and enough foreign exchange reserves account for more than 20% of the importations. The proportion of foreign exchange reserves and foreign debts can be used to measure a country's solvency, which should be no less than 30% generally.

Before opening the capital account, a country's foreign exchange is obtained mainly through the current account. Adequate foreign exchange reserves can solve various shocks that exist on the capital market caused by large-scale speculative capital flows and at the same time it can guarantee the stability of a country's currency. The financial crisis in the late 1990s proved that in the country in crisis, a shortage of foreign exchange reserves, too much dependence on foreign capital and opening the capital account without a sound financial system would lead to debt crisis.

(4) A perfect mechanism of exchange rate adjustment

The independent and effective monetary policy is an important means to ensure reducing risks in the process of internationalization of the RMB. A floating and elastic exchange rate system can guarantee true reflection of the value of the RMB on the international market, being better at taking the responsibility of the international monetary system. Therefore, as the internationalization of the RMB gradually expands, adopting a floating and elastic exchange rate system is an inevitable choice.

According to the general policy of the Third Plenary Session of the 16th Party Central Committee, in the case that China's financial power is still relatively weak, the independence and effectiveness of the monetary policy should be ensured, in order to better regulate domestic financial markets. The opportunity that the current macroeconomic basis in China is still relatively well-formed needs to be seized to keep enough foreign exchange reserves. The volatility measured at the level of equilibrium of the exchange rate can be used to gradually relax control over RMB exchange rates, increase the elasticity and flexibility of the exchange rate system, and improve the adjustment mechanism of RMB exchange rates.

14.6.3 Establish RMB Offshore Financial Markets

When the internationalization of the RMB develops to a certain stage, it will inevitably become overseas lending assets, and needs to run an RMB overseas loan business. At this point, the RMB's foreign trade, settlement, and loans will need to establish offshore financial markets. The offshore financial market is also called overseas financial markets. Its characteristics can be simply summarized as that market trading is mainly conducted by non-residents and not restricted by local laws, regulations, and tax systems. The rise of offshore financial markets not only promotes the development of economic globalization and the internationalization of the financial sector, but also provides abundant capital for the economic development of all countries, which is conducive to regulating the balance of international payments.

(1) Give full play to the core position of Shanghai in the process of the internationalization of the RMB

As China's financial center, Shanghai has the most perfect financial system, and has the most developed financial market on the mainland. In 2009, the yearly value-added of Shanghai's financial industry accounted for 12% of its total output value. The core position of the financial industry in Shanghai in economic growth and industrial structure optimization got further ascension. Throughout 2009, the amount of dealing on the Shanghai Stock Exchange was just behind that of NASDAQ and the New York Stock Exchange, ranked first in the Asia-Pacific region and third in the world. The amount of Shanghai's futures market is ranked second among global commodity futures and options. Therefore, Shanghai can provide the RMB offshore financial market with good institutional support and infrastructure support.

To implement the proposal of building Shanghai into an international financial center, which adapts to China's economic strength and the international status of the RMB by 2020, the main tasks are to build, in line with international standards, a multi-functional, multi-level financial market system, which is relatively developed throughout the world; to strengthen the construction of international financial institutions and business systems, and steadily push forward the financial services industry opening-up to the outside world; to improve the international financial service facilities and the layout plans, and enhance the level of international and domestic financial services; to improve the financial legal system, strengthen financial regulations, and maintain financial stability and security. Under the support of the central policy, coupled with the large size of the financial market itself, Shanghai has the potential of playing the core role in the process of the internationalization of the RMB. At the beginning of the "12th Five-Year Plan," the cross-border RMB trade settlement experimentation will expand to the whole nation, and Shanghai can use its locational advantages to build itself into a cross-border RMB settlement and an offshore RMB settlement center. In addition, during the "Twelfth Five-Year Plan", Shanghai will build itself into an offshore RMB forward exchange rate market, through which foreign investors can hedge the exchange risks from RMB assets or liabilities.

(2) Make use of Hong Kong's locational advantage to accelerate the internationalization of the RMB

As China's most important international financial center, Hong Kong has superior conditions unmatched by other cities for building an RMB offshore financial market.

First of all, Hong Kong is the main destination for current overseas RMB circulation. After becoming one of the first pilot cities for cross-border RMB trade settlement, Hong Kong is using its geographical advantages as an international financial center located in the Asia-Pacific region. By 2009, the total amount of RMB bonds issued in Hong Kong had reached 38 billion yuan, including national bonds of 6 billion yuan issued by the Ministry of Finance in October. That was the first time that national bonds had been issued outside the mainland. Issuing national bonds is one of the important measures for formulating the RMB benchmark interest rate and is conducive to improving the financial efficiency of other RMB financial products.

Second, as a regional financial center, Hong Kong's financial market is relatively perfect. In 2009, including the fiscal strength and overseas assets, Hong Kong's performance was beyond the median level of the AAA economic system. Analysis results show that after the global financial crisis, Hong Kong's economy remained robust. Coupled with strong economic fundamentals, solid banking, the mainland's strong economic growth and its supporting measures on Hong Kong, the part beyond the range of the AAA economic system will be further expanded. Research shows that the market has potential demand for RMB as a trade settlement currency. As one of the East Asian financial centers, Hong Kong has a relatively perfect financial system and strong risk control ability, and its vitality and influence in the financial sector are enough to make it an ideal city for establishing an RMB offshore financial market. The construction of the market will promote the process of the internationalization of the RMB.

(3) The offshore RMB market risks and regulations

The RMB offshore market is mainly provided by the central bank on money supply and imports in RMB, while the demand includes overseas investment demand for RMB, exports in RMB, and speculative demand. Supply and demand directly determine the exchange rate and interest rate in the RMB offshore market. If the official exchange rate does not match the real exchange rate decided by the market, a mass flow of international capital will appear, which will cause an exchange rate risk. Also, if the interest rate changes in line with the international conditions, it will lead to arbitrage of the speculative capital by using interest rate differences between the mainland and offshore markets, resulting in an interest rate risk. Considering both supply and demand, if mass speculative capital flows frequently in RMB offshore markets, this will lead to changes in exchange rates and interest rates, and failure of the domestic monetary policy. Therefore, controlling speculative capital from the aspect of demand and correctly guiding fund flows will become the important measures to take to prevent and control risks in the RMB offshore markets.

To prevent interest rate risks and exchange rate risks in the RMB offshore markets, short-term debts can be issued to adjust interest rates and RMB reserve schemes can be established to adjust the exchange rates. First of all, before the establishment of the offshore financial markets, the central bank may consider the issuance of RMB short-term bonds, as reference of interest rates in RMB offshore markets. When interest rates in RMB offshore markets are low, through the issuance of short-term bonds, the bond yield is set higher than interest rates in the offshore markets, in order to attract offshore RMB flow back to the markets. This is to raise interest rates and promote the demand for RMB in the offshore markets. At the same time, the short-term bonds can effectively adjust the interest rate gap between the mainland and offshore RMB markets to guide the flow of speculative capital and finally control the RMB interest rate risk. Second, the formation of the reserves can maintain the stability of the RMB exchange rate. The central bank can use offshore banks to establish RMB reserves schemes and utilize the reserve schemes to adjust the supply of

RMB, ensuring that the supply of RMB in the offshore markets meets the demand for investment and trade.

Issuance of short-term bonds is to adjust the demand for RMB, while the RMB reserve schemes are to adjust the supply. From the aspects of supply and demand, the two may be jointly preventing RMB offshore market risks. By influencing the RMB interest rates, short-term bonds are used to adjust supply and demand. This is an indirect method. RMB reserve schemes are to directly adjust the supply, which is a direct way. At the beginning of setting up of the RMB offshore markets, direct means can be used to reduce supply to achieve a balance. After RMB offshore markets develop to a certain period, to avoid producing large amounts of speculative demand, more indirect means should be used to adjust both the supply and demand and achieve the goal of risk avoidance.

To sum up, the cost-benefit analysis of the internationalization of the RMB can come to the conclusion that the internationalization of the RMB would get more benefits than losses. In view of the current macroeconomic fundamentals in China, the international status of the RMB, and the development of the world monetary system, it shows that the internationalization of the RMB is in line with the general rule of the development of the world currency. Because of China's political stability, developing economy with enough foreign exchange reserves, and other internal factors, combined with the impact of the United States financial crisis on the USD, increasing calls for reforming the international monetary system, the expectation of RMB appreciation, and other external factors, the internationalization of the RMB has possessed good internal and external conditions. But when the current financial market in China is not perfect and the mechanism for financial supervision and the capacity for risk resistance need to be strengthened, the principle that the internationalization of the RMB should advance gradually in due order should be followed, using the successful experience of the Euro, namely, adopting the path from peripheral internationalization, regional internationalization, to global internationalization.

The internationalization of the RMB cannot be built in a day, and is a long and an arduous process. To realize the change of China from "a big economy" to "a strong economy" and from "a trading power" to "a financial power," it needs to transform the huge economic aggregate into real international competitiveness. This also requires the government to make every endeavor to provide supporting policies and intensify economic structural adjustment and reform of the financial system. At the same time, it should be objective, prudent, and pragmatic to motivate the internationalization of the RMB. When the RMB becomes the international currency, there will be proof that China has indeed become an unshakeable economic and financial power.

References

Amiti, Wakelin. Investment liberalization and international trade. Journal of International Economics, 2003, 61 (1): 101-126.

AQSIQ. Annual report of China's technical measures to trade (2006).

Axelrod. The Evolution of Cooperation. Shanghai: Shanghai People's Publishing House, 1996.

Bao Qun, Xu Helian, Lai Mingyong. How does export trade promote economic growth?. Shanghai Journal of Economics, 2003 (3): 3-10.

Buchanan. Liberty, Market and State. Beijing: Beijing Economics College Press, 1988.

Cao Mingfu, Li Shumin.The gain and loss of absolute advantage and comparative advantage. China Industrial Economy, 2006 (6): 68-74.

Cohen. The Future of Sterling as an International Currency. London: Macmillan; New York: St. Martin's Press, 1971.

Du Jiang. Empirical analysis of foreign direct investment and China's economic development. World Economy, 2002 (8): 27-40.

Feng Zongxian, Ke Dagang. International Trade Barrier on the Condition of an Open Economy: Variation Effect, Impact Analysis and Policy Research. Beijing: Economic Science Press, 2001.

Hartmann. Currency Competition and Foreign Exchange Markets: The Dollar, the Yen and the Euro. Cambridge: Cambridge University Press, 1998.

He Xuhong. China's export trade coping with technical barriers to trade. On Economic Problem, 2007 (1): 49-51.

Hu Angang. China's rise and opening-up: From an open great economy to an open strong economy//China Study: 10. Beijing: Social Sciences Academic Press, 2012: 238-255.

Hu Angang, Men Honghua. Revaluation of China's entrance to the WTO: How China can open up, participate, cooperate and improve roundly// China Study: 9. Beijing: Social Sciences Academic Press, 2012: 310-332.

Hu Yi, Chen Jiyong. On the road for mutually beneficial and win-win opening-up. Asia-Pacific Economic Review, 2008 (6): 3-8.

Jiang Boke. International Finance. Beijing: Higher Education Press, 1999.

Jiang Xiaojuan. China's growth in export and change of the formation of exporting merchandise: Contribution of FDI firms. Nankai Economic Studies, 2002 (2): 30-34.

Jiang Xiaojuan. Openness and inclusiveness make a strong country. People's Daily, 2008-04-16.

Kerr. International harmonization and the gains from trade. The Estey Centre of International Law and Trade Policy, 2006, 7 (2): 116-125.

Kojima. Foreign Trade Theory. Tianjin: Nankai University Press, 1987.

Krugman. Does Third World growth hurt First World prosperity?. Harvard Business Review, 1994, 72: 113-121.

Krugman. Strategic Trade Policy and New International Economics. Beijing: China Renmin University Press, 2000.

Li Anfang. Research on the innovation of China's economic opening-up strategy: The background and theoretical foundation of new thinking for the opening-up policy. World Economy Study, 2007 (3): 13-18.

Li Anfang. On the innovation of China's strategy for economic opening-up for a mutually beneficial and win-win nature. Social sciences, 2007 (11): 26-33.

Li Daokui, Liu Linlin. Promote the internationalization of the RMB through a double-track approach. China Finance, 2008 (10): 42-43.

Li Kunwang, Liu Zhongli. Economic Globalization: Process, Tendency and Measures. Beijing: Economic Science Press, 2000.

Li Yining. New Thinking on Regional Development. Beijing: The Economic Daily Press, 2000.

Liszt. The National System of Political Economy. Beijing: The Commercial Press, 1997.

Liu Qun. World currency: The inevitable choice for the RMB to became a strong currency. World Economics and Politics, 2005 (6): 73-78.

Lu Feng. Intra-product distribution of labor. China Economic Quarterly, 2004, 4 (1): 55-82.

Lu Hao. Investigation and reflection on RMB circulation around the boundaries between China and Myanmar and China and Laos. Times Finance, 2007 (9): 119-120.

Mazumdar. Do static gains from trade lead to medium-run growth. Journal of Political Economy, 1996, 104 (6): 1328-1337.

Melitz. The impact of trade on intra-industry reallocations and aggregate industry productivity. Econometrica, 2003, 71 (6): 1695-1725.

Melvin. Intermediate goods, the production possibility curve and gains from trade. Quarterly Journal of Economics, 1969, 83 (1): 141-151.

Mill. Principles of Political Economy with Some of Their Applications to Social Philosophy. Beijing: The Commercial Press, 1991.

Motta, Norman. Does economic integration cause foreign direct investment?. International Economic Review, 1996, 37 (4): 757-783.

Mu Haiping. Looking for the Supporting Point of Competitiveness. Beijing: China Economy Publishing House, 2005.

Pei Changhong. The evolvement of the construction and development of an opening-oriented economy and feature evaluation. Reform, 2008 (9): 15-25.

Porter. Competitive Advantage. Beijing: Huaxia Publishing House, 1997.

Qiang Yongchang. Policy and System Research of Japan's Postwar Trade Development. Shanghai: Fudan University Press, 2001.

Qu Ruxiao, Pan Ailing. Discussion of the protection of foreign trade policy. Journal of International Trade, 2001 (12): 21-25.

Salvatore. International Economics. 5th ed. Beijing: Tsinghua University Press, 1998.

Scherer. Competition policy convergence: Where next?. Empirica, 1997, 24 (1): 5-19.

Shen Lisheng, Wu Zhenyu. Analysis on the rationality of product composition in foreign trade. The Journal of Quantitative & Technical

Economics, 2003 (8): 66-72.

Shi Cailiang. Trade liberalization, industrial protection and selection of China's tariff policy. Contemporary Finance & Economics, 2003 (7): 127-128.

Smith. An Inquiry into the Nature and Causes of the Wealth of Nations. Beijing: The Commercial Press, 1979.

Sun Benzhi, Zhao Shiwei. On the countermeasures against technical barriers to China's foreign trade. International Economics and Trade Research, 2003 (5): 67-70.

Sun Huiyuan. Standard information and trade barrier. Enterprise Standardization, 2004 (7): 48-50.

Tang Renwu, Ma Ji. Looking back on and dispute resolution of Chinese 30-year opening-up. Reform, 2008 (10): 19-35.

Tavlas. Chicago, Harvard, and the doctrinal foundations of monetary economics. Journal of Political Economy, 1997, 105 (1): 153-177.

Tian Wen. Research on the decision of the inra-product trading pattern and benefit distribution. International Business, 2005 (5): 9-13.

Tong Jiadong. Trade Liberalization, Trade Protection and Economic Benefits. Beijing: Economic Science Press, 2002.

Wang Fujun. Theoretical integration of international trade and international direct investment: General theory review of international production. International Economics and Trade Research, 1999 (1): 7-9, 33.

Wang Xiaoxi. On the development and changes of the relationship between international trade and foreign direct investment. Commercial Research, 2003, 10 (270): 22-25.

Wang Xinkui. Benefit Distribution in International Trade and Investment. Shanghai: SDX Joint Publishing House, 1989.

Wang Yong, Jiang Yaosheng. Discussion about trade freedom and trade protection under economic globalization. Economist, 2003 (1): 98-99.

Wang Yongqi. Trade composition and the growth of China: A granger causality test. The Journal of World Economy, 2004 (11): 31-39.

Wang Yuanlong. Convertibility of RMB capital account and strategy and progress on the internationalization of the RMB. China Finance, 2008

(10): 36-39.

Wang Yungui. Continuous deterioration of trade conditions: Chinese extensive import and export trade mode must be changed. Intertrade, 2004 (6): 14-16.

Wang Zhile. 2002/2003 Report on Translational Corporations' Investment in China. Beijing: China Economy Publishing House, 2003.

Wang Zixian, Yang Zhengwei, Song Gang. Developmental direction of the transformation and upgrading of the Chinese processing trade. Intertrade, 2004 (2): 10-13.

Wu Nianlu, Chen Quangeng. Research on the RMB Exchange Rate. Beijing: China Financial Publishing House, 2002.

Xia Youfu. Generation and developmental trend of technical barriers to trade. China's Quality and Brand, 2004 (3): 74-77.

Xie Bing. Trade effect and empirical analysis of foreign direct investment. Economic Review, 2000 (4): 30-35.

Xiong Xingmei, Dai Jinping, et al. The Contemporary Mainstream of International Economics in Practice and Theory. Dalian: Dongbei University of Finance & Economics Press, 2004.

Xu Guangyao. Analysis of China's import trade structure and economic growth correlation. Journal of Intertrade, 2007 (2): 3-7.

Xue Rongjiu. International Trade. Beijing: University of International Business and Economics Press, 2003.

Yu Hui. Associations' strategy under the WTO system. China Industrial Economy, 2002 (3): 39-46.

Yu Lixin, Yang Jing. Coordination of the RMB exchange rate and market-oriented reform of the price of resource products. Intertrade, 2006 (8): 54-57.

Yu Lixin, Yang Jing. Regional coordination and positioning of introducing technology in foreign capital utilization during the 11th Five-Year Plan. Zhongzhi Dangjian, 2006 (6): 38-41.

Zhang Erzhen. Developmental benefit of international trade and its mechanism for implementation. Journal of Nanjing University (Philosophy, Humanities and Social Sciences), 1995 (4): 24-32.

Zhang Erzhen, Ma Yeqing, Fang Yong. Trade and Investment Integration and China's Strategy. Beijing: People's Publishing House, 2004.

Zhang Yunling. Opening-up, Competition and Development. Beijing: Economy & Management Publishing House, 1998.

Zhao Haikuan. RMB should be promoted into one of the world curriencies. Chinese & Foreign Entrepreneurs, 2001 (5): 20-24.

Zhong Wei. The Path of RMB Internationalization. The Journal of World Economy, 2002 (3): 56-59.

Zhu Mengnan. International Finance. Xiamen: Xiamen University Press, 1999.

Index

A

Asia-Pacific   128, 299, 357, 365, 372, 385, 395, 399, 518, 523, 589, 590

E

economic globalization   4, 7, 16, 21, 28, 32, 34, 114, 126, 129, 136, 146, 176, 216, 237, 239, 240, 241, 246, 287, 296, 298, 332, 367, 374, 375, 377, 391, 394, 398, 406, 411, 412, 449, 450, 462, 464, 470, 527, 588

economic regionalization   391, 430

export processing zone   25, 118

F

Five-Year Plan   7, 8, 14, 179, 377, 413, 449, 559, 589

foreign direct investment   15, 25, 82, 106, 108, 109, 110, 112, 113, 114, 118, 119, 120, 121, 124, 125, 126, 130, 134, 138, 140, 143, 144, 145, 177, 178, 179, 180, 181, 182, 183, 184, 185, 186, 187, 188, 189, 191, 196, 200, 201, 202, 205, 213, 214, 215, 216, 217, 218, 220, 221, 222, 223, 224, 225, 226, 227, 228, 229, 230, 231, 232, 236, 239, 243, 244, 245, 261, 262, 363, 378, 408, 409, 410, 427, 439, 440, 441, 446, 456, 457, 466, 467, 468, 469, 472, 473, 475, 476, 477, 478, 480, 481, 482, 489, 490, 574 foreign-invested enterprise   122, 123, 124, 125, 132, 133, 142, 183, 189, 190, 192, 193, 196, 197, 198, 201, 207, 208, 219, 232, 238, 258, 260, 261, 262, 469, 474

G
global value chain   64, 65, 101
globalization   4, 6, 7, 8, 16, 19, 21, 28, 29, 31, 32, 33, 34, 35, 39, 46, 52, 114, 126, 128, 129, 136, 146, 147, 148, 176, 216, 237, 239, 240, 241, 246, 287, 296, 298, 301, 332, 356, 367, 368, 369, 374, 375, 377, 385, 391, 394, 398, 406, 411, 412, 449, 450, 462, 464, 470, 515, 527, 588

H
high-tech industry   85, 163, 191, 192, 193, 520, 566

I
industrial cluster   16, 95, 282, 293, 333, 510, 512
innovation system   202

M
mutual benefit and win-win   3, 4, 5, 6, 7, 9, 10, 11, 16, 19, 21, 27, 28, 29, 30, 31, 32, 33, 34, 35, 40, 41, 42, 43, 45, 48, 69, 81, 95, 177, 211, 246, 247, 493, 494

N
neoclassical   56, 57, 105

P
Pearl River Delta   23, 48, 50, 125, 142, 259, 260, 501, 509, 510, 511, 512, 523, 524, 525, 526
production factor   7, 15, 32, 48, 56, 57, 60, 61, 107, 108, 217, 223, 255, 256, 346, 347, 355, 369, 377, 390,

400, 406, 409, 428, 498

R

reform and opening-up 2, 3, 4, 8, 21, 23, 28, 30, 43, 67, 93, 125, 130, 133, 146, 178, 198, 223, 247, 250, 251, 258, 259, 314, 315, 319, 375, 412, 424, 426, 430, 456, 457, 458, 499, 511, 517, 562, 570, 575

S

special economic zone 22, 23, 367, 443
state-owned enterprise 17, 44, 83, 84, 92, 100, 126, 127, 190, 193, 208, 210, 280, 329, 460, 461

T

technological level 12, 16, 41, 44, 76, 78, 81, 84, 88, 89, 100, 101, 124, 130, 131, 132, 133, 135, 142, 144, 148, 154, 157, 158, 168, 174, 176, 185, 193, 198, 199, 204, 207, 227, 232, 263, 281, 284, 300, 308, 313, 427, 446, 451, 452, 468, 477, 566

technology spillover 84, 94, 177, 178, 179, 180, 181, 182, 183, 184, 185, 186, 187, 188, 189, 191, 194, 196, 197, 199, 200, 202, 203, 205, 207, 210, 211, 281, 513

Y

Yangtze River Delta 23, 24, 48, 50, 125, 142, 446, 501, 509, 510, 523, 524, 525

Postscript

It has taken years to finish this book, which has contained years of my academic thought and collective scientific research achievements, from generating the outline to further polishing. China has made remarkable achievements in the development of export-oriented economy through 30 years of reform and opening-up. Such a historical accomplishment should be attributed to both the great practical experience of Deng Xiaoping, the the Chief Designer of the reform and opening-up, and practice of hundreds of millions of people as well as the theoretical contributions of academics. By serving as a guide, this book aims to explore some of China's current frontier issues of mutual benefit and win-win strategy, and hopes to try groundbreaking theoretical research in this field. The authors hope it would draw more insightful and academic colleagues to write far-sighted and insightful academic works in the relevant field.

The main authors of this book are Yu Lixin and Chen Wanling, while Chen Zhao, Wang Jiajia, Park Young Kyi, Yu Ling, Huang Jing, Yao Wen, Yang Jing, Li Xiaoyuan, Li Chunguang, Dong Ping and Jiang Jiao have participated in the writing of the book. Besides them, Luo Dan, Cheng Jiao, Nie Xinwei, Zhou Ling, Zhao Xin and Wang Dong have also made constructive contributions to the book in managing data and searching relevant documents.

We are especially grateful to the leaders of the Institute for Fiscal and Trade Economics of the Chinese Academy of Social Sciences for their guidance, especially former Director Pei Changhong, Director Gao Peiyong, Deputy Director Jing Linbo for their strong support. We also extend gratitude to Kong Fanlai, Director of the Department of Research, and Zhu Xiaohui, Deputy Director, for their help.

The authors thank Xia Youfu, professor of the University of International Business and Economics, and Professor Yang Changju of Renmin University of China for their book review and appraisal. We made supplements and improvements according to their suggestions.

The authors also thank Feng Yuan, associate researcher, Tang Jing, assistant researcher, Feng Yongsheng, assistant researcher, and Dr. Gao Weikai of the Department of Trade in Services and WTO for their help.

In the process of finalizing and publishing of this book, we have also received support from leaders of the Bureau of Scientific Research, the Chinese Academy of Social Sciences and Zhou Li, Wang Yushui and Cai Shasha of the Social Sciences Academic Press. Any comment or suggestion to improve this book further will be welcome. The relevant literature at home and abroad being referred to in this book has been listed. We are grateful to the authors of the literature both listed and, if there's any, omitted in the book.

The authors